CW01064863

44210
sea

COSENS OF WEYMOUTH

1848 TO 1918

HELPER, her decks crowded with sailors, leaves Weymouth on a liberty boat sailing to the Fleet in Portland Harbour, 1914. AUTHOR'S COLLECTION/SEWARD

COSENS
OF WEYMOUTH
1848 TO 1918

A HISTORY OF THE BOURNEMOUTH, SWANAGE
AND WEYMOUTH PADDLE STEAMERS

RICHARD CLAMMER

BLACK DWARF PUBLICATIONS

VICTORIA *and* EMPRESS *landing passengers at Lulworth Cove during 1906.*

CONTENTS

Units of measurement and money used in this book are those which were concurrent with events described. With regards to money, pre-decimal currency of pounds, shillings (s) and pence (d) can be converted to new pence (p) as follows: £1 = 20s = 100p   1s = 12d = 5p
This of course is a straight conversion and takes no account of inflation

© Black Dwarf Publications and Richard Clammer 2005
Designed by Neil Parkhouse & Alan Kittridge

British Library Cataloguing-in-Publication Data. A catalogue
record for this book is available from the British Library

ISBN 1 903599 14 8

BLACK DWARF PUBLICATIONS

Black Dwarf Lightmoor, 120 Farmers Close Witney, Oxfordshire OX28 1NR
Unit 144B Lydney Trading Estate, Harbour Road, Lydney, Gloucestershire GL15 5EJ
www.lightmoor.co.uk

Printed by The Cromwell Press, Trowbridge

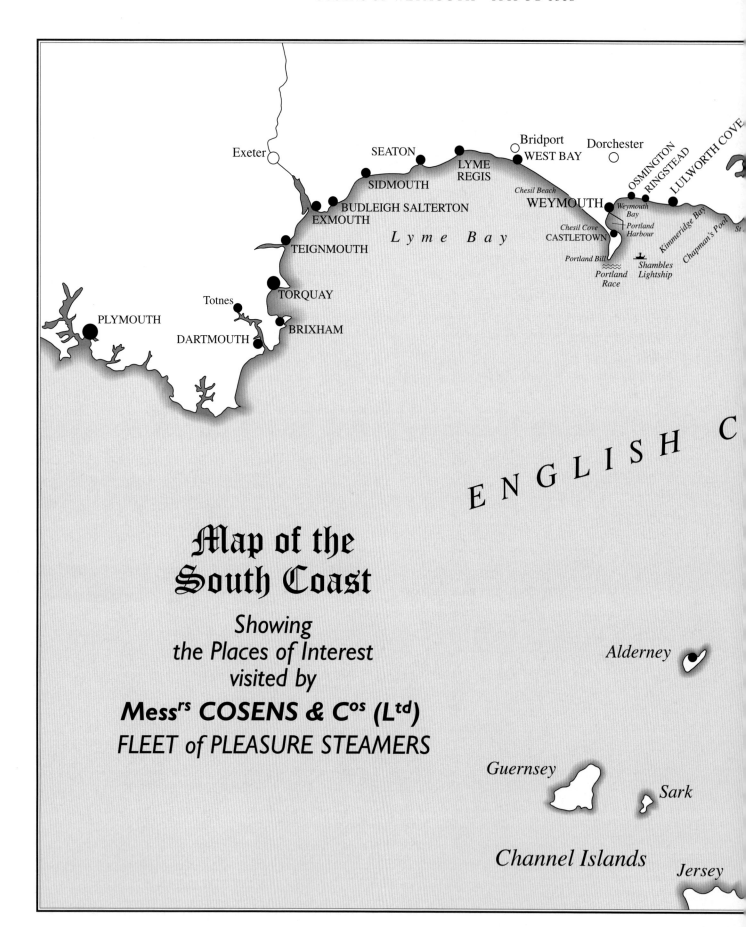

Exeter

SEATON

SIDMOUTH

BUDLEIGH SALTERTON
EXMOUTH

LYME
REGIS

Bridport   Dorchester
WEST BAY

OSMINGTON
RINGSTEAD

LULWORTH COVE

Chesil Beach

WEYMOUTH

*Weymouth
Bay*

L y m e   B a y

TEIGNMOUTH

Chesil Cove
CASTLETOWN

*Portland
Harbour*

Kimmeridge Bay

Chapman's Pool

St

Portland Bill

*Portland
Race*

*Shambles
Lightship*

Totnes

TORQUAY

PLYMOUTH

DARTMOUTH   BRIXHAM

E N G L I S H   C

Map of the South Coast

Showing the Places of Interest visited by

Messrs COSENS & C^os (L^td)

FLEET of PLEASURE STEAMERS

Alderney

Guernsey

Sark

Channel Islands

Jersey

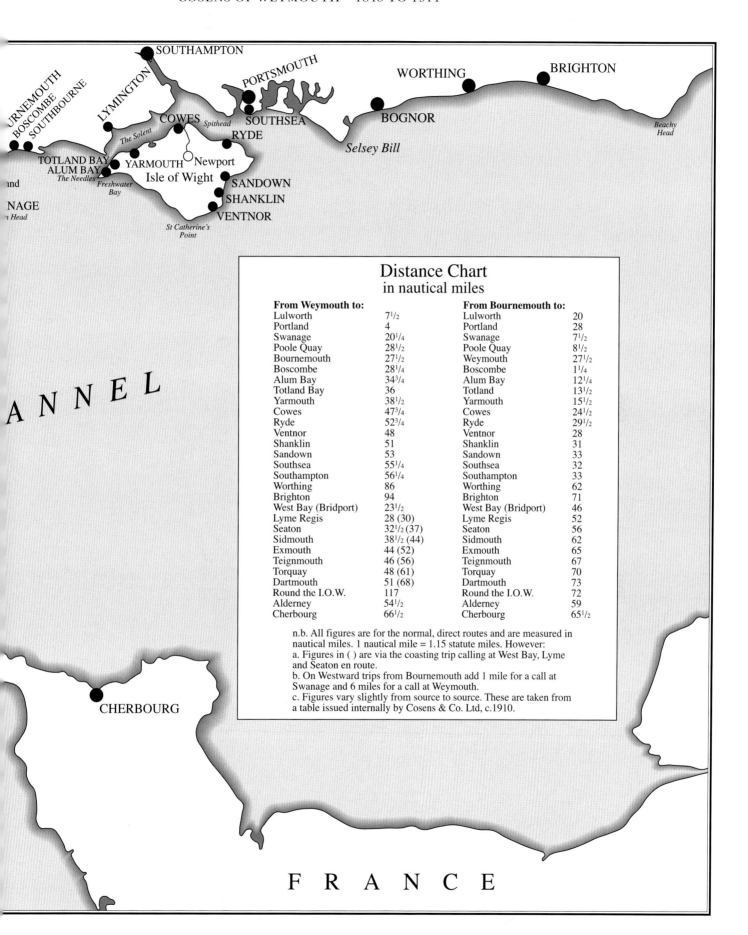

Distance Chart
in nautical miles

From Weymouth to:		From Bournemouth to:	
Lulworth	7^1/$_2$	Lulworth	20
Portland	4	Portland	28
Swanage	20^1/$_4$	Swanage	7^1/$_2$
Poole Quay	28^1/$_2$	Poole Quay	8^1/$_2$
Bournemouth	27^1/$_2$	Weymouth	27^1/$_2$
Boscombe	28^1/$_4$	Boscombe	1^1/$_4$
Alum Bay	34^3/$_4$	Alum Bay	12^1/$_4$
Totland Bay	36	Totland	13^1/$_2$
Yarmouth	38^1/$_2$	Yarmouth	15^1/$_2$
Cowes	47^3/$_4$	Cowes	24^1/$_2$
Ryde	52^3/$_4$	Ryde	29^1/$_2$
Ventnor	48	Ventnor	28
Shanklin	51	Shanklin	31
Sandown	53	Sandown	33
Southsea	55^1/$_4$	Southsea	32
Southampton	56^1/$_4$	Southampton	33
Worthing	86	Worthing	62
Brighton	94	Brighton	71
West Bay (Bridport)	23^1/$_2$	West Bay (Bridport)	46
Lyme Regis	28 (30)	Lyme Regis	52
Seaton	32^1/$_2$ (37)	Seaton	56
Sidmouth	38^1/$_2$ (44)	Sidmouth	62
Exmouth	44 (52)	Exmouth	65
Teignmouth	46 (56)	Teignmouth	67
Torquay	48 (61)	Torquay	70
Dartmouth	51 (68)	Dartmouth	73
Round the I.O.W.	117	Round the I.O.W.	72
Alderney	54^1/$_2$	Alderney	59
Cherbourg	66^1/$_2$	Cherbourg	65^1/$_2$

n.b. All figures are for the normal, direct routes and are measured in nautical miles. 1 nautical mile = 1.15 statute miles. However:
a. Figures in ( ) are via the coasting trip calling at West Bay, Lyme and Seaton en route.
b. On Westward trips from Bournemouth add 1 mile for a call at Swanage and 6 miles for a call at Weymouth.
c. Figures vary slightly from source to source. These are taken from a table issued internally by Cosens & Co. Ltd, c.1910.

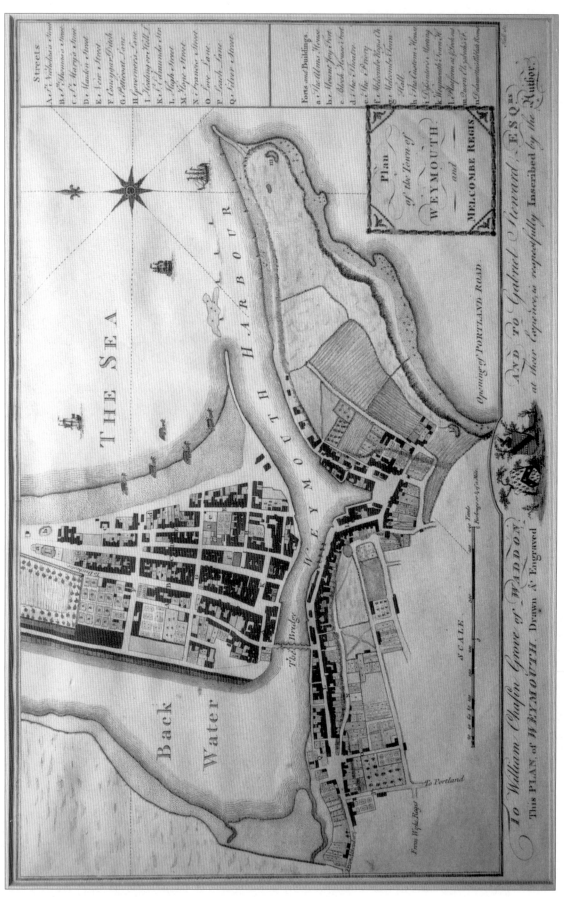

A map of Weymouth in 1774, published in John Hutchins' History of Dorset.

INTRODUCTION

For a period of 119 years, between 1848 and 1967, the name 'Cosens of Weymouth' was synonymous with the fleet of excursion paddle steamers which were a familiar and much-loved part of the summer scene along the coasts of Devon, Dorset and Hampshire. From their home port of Weymouth and their seasonal bases at Swanage and Bournemouth, these fascinating ships offered excursions westwards as far as Torquay and Dartmouth, eastwards to the Solent, Isle of Wight and Brighton, and even across the English Channel to Cherbourg and the Channel Islands.

The history of the company and its passenger steam ship services along the Wessex coast is, of course, inextricably linked to the development of the coastal towns which they served. In the case of the holiday resorts of Weymouth, Swanage and Bournemouth, the relationship was truly symbiotic; in the days before the railways, the steamers provided the main means of transport for the visitors on which the resorts' wealth and growth were based, while in later years the resorts provided the day excursionists who produced the bulk of the ticket revenue upon which the steamer company depended. With Cosens & Co, however, the relationship was even more complex, for with its diverse interests in engineering, ship repairing, ice importing and manufacture, the coal and bunkering trades, salvage, diving and Admiralty contracting, the fortunes of the company were also closely tied to other aspects of the economic and social development of South Dorset.

In order to fully understand the impact and significance of the company's history, it is perhaps helpful to be able to picture the Dorset coast during the middle years of the 19th century when steam ships first appeared on the scene. Although its beautiful and dramatic physical features would be immediately recognisable to the modern eye, the coast was socially and economically a very different place to the one we know today.

The twin towns of Weymouth and Melcombe Regis, which lie at the narrative and physical centre of this history, had gradually established themselves as a fashionable health and sea bathing resort from 1748 onwards but rose to public prominence between 1780 and 1805, when first the Duke of Gloucester and then King George III chose to spend their summers there. Royal patronage, of course, guaranteed the popularity of the resort amongst the rich and fashionable and led to the rapid growth of the town. Tradesmen thrived and the demand for accommodation and entertainment led to the construction of many public buildings and the elegant Georgian terraces which grace the seafront and harbourside to this day.

The harbour itself, which had always been somewhat overshadowed in importance by its larger neighbour Poole and had suffered a long period of decline following the Civil War, also enjoyed a revival in its fortunes. Trade gradually increased, assisted in 1794 by the selection of the port by the Post Office as the mainland base for a regular sailing Packet Service to Jersey and Guernsey, and a number of improvements were made to the harbour quays and warehouses. The construction of the first stone-built Town Bridge in 1824 was followed in 1840 by extensive dredging to provide a greater depth of water, the construction of a new ballast wharf under the yet-unfortified grassy headland of the Nothe and the provision of new slipways on the Weymouth side of the harbour. On the northern side, the short pier known as New Quay End, which had hitherto stretched only a few yards beyond Devonshire and Pultney Buildings, was extended seawards providing, at a stroke, both a fashionable 'marine walk' extension to the promenade and a practical means of increasing the scouring effect of the tidal flow within the harbour. Between the turn of the century and the 1841 census, the population of Weymouth & Melcombe Regis more than doubled from 3,617 to 7,708.

To the south of Weymouth, joined to the mainland by the imposing shingle ridge of Chesil Beach, lay the brooding, limestone bulk of the 'Isle' of Portland. Jutting some four and a half miles into the English Channel, Portland had long been regarded as one of the greatest navigational hazards on the south coast, its inhospitable cliffs made even more threatening by the presence of a fearsome tidal race off its southern tip, caused by the channel tides being forced round the headland. Slightly to

Cosens' ornate letter head illustrates the wide range of the company's activities at the beginning of the 20th century.
AUTHOR'S COLLECTION

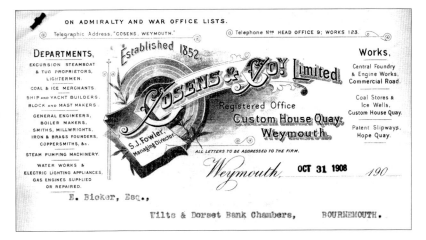

9

A view dated July 1790, showing the ferry which, until the advent of the Cosens steamers, provided the only link between Portland and the mainland. Wyke Regis Church is in the top left and Weymouth Bay on the right.
WEYMOUTH MUSEUM

Lulworth Cove from seawards.
PHILIP BRANNON
ENGRAVING/DAVID HAYSOM
COLLECTION

the hand-operated ferry at Smallmouth near Wyke Regis and thence by foot or horse along the exposed Chesil Beach. In that year, however, the ancient ferry was finally replaced by the wooden Ferry Bridge across Smallmouth and increased contact with the outside world began to change the island forever. By 1841, the population was still fairly stable at 2,853, with the majority still being engaged in the traditional occupations of quarrying the famous Portland stone, farming and fishing with, no doubt, a little salvage work and smuggling thrown in when the opportunity presented itself. The building of the Portland Breakwaters, Naval Dockyard, Verne Citadel and the other major works were still in the unimagined future.

To the west of Portland, the small but vibrant Bridport Harbour (now more commonly referred to as West Bay) was at its peak, with as many as fifteen or twenty vessels loading or discharging in its newly-extended dock basin at any one time and upwards of 500 ships using the port per year. On the western side of the basin, the slipways of the local shipyards were a hive of activity, producing a steady stream of coastal and ocean going sailing ships, the largest of which was the 1,002 ton *Speedy*, launched in 1853. The rigging of these newly-built vessels provided a ready outlet for Bridport's other major industry, rope making, while a thriving net industry found many customers among the local fishermen.

Further west still, the little harbour of Lyme Regis, sheltered by its famous Cobb, had suffered a steady decline in trade since its Elizabethan heyday but, after the building of the Charmouth to Exeter turnpike road, had developed into the secluded and fashionable resort later made famous by Jane Austen's novel *Persuasion*. The only major export from the harbour was blue lias quarried from the surrounding cliffs into barges and transshipped into seagoing vessels for onward carriage.

Ten miles eastwards from Weymouth and entered through a narrow gap in the limestone cliffs, lay the spectacular, almost circular Lulworth Cove, with its tiny fishing village tucked into a sheltered valley just above the beach. The unique geology and scenery of the cove had made it a popular destination for marine excursions from Weymouth since the very earliest days of the resort. As no dedicated passenger vessels yet existed, fashionable parties would employ a local boatman to convey them under sail to Lulworth, where the local fisherfolk no doubt took every opportunity to supplement their incomes by providing a simple catering service.

Further east again, around St. Aldhelm's Head and past the Purbeck stone-loading ledges at Winspit, Dancing Ledge and Tilly Whim, the little town of Swanage lay tucked in the corner of its beautiful bay. During the 1840s, the roads leading to Swanage were still in poor condition and the town was still extremely isolated, most contact with the outside world being by sea. No hint of the modern

the south east of Portland Bill, the shallows of the treacherous Shambles Bank lay in wait for the unwary mariner, while to the west Lyme Bay, created by the curve of the coast towards Torquay, was so feared by sailors that it had earned itself the ominous but accurate soubriquet of 'Dead Man's Bay'. With the prevailing south-westerly winds blowing directly into the bay, any sailing ship caught there in stormy weather risked being blown relentlessly ashore on the unforgiving lee shore of Chesil Beach.

For centuries Portland had been an isolated and distinctive community, marked by its many ancient customs and suspicion of mainlanders or 'Kimberlins'. Until 1839, access to the island had been difficult, the sole alternative to a sea trip being a crossing in

Swanage Bay from Peveril Point

LEFT: *Swanage Bay viewed from Peveril Point. This engraving by Philip Brannon first appeared in 1856 but the plate was later altered to include the pier of 1859. Several of the canon at the battery were salvaged from the warship* HALSEWELL, *wrecked west of Swanage in 1786. The locomotive-hauled train of stone wagons just visible heading out onto the pier is pure artistic licence – mechanical traction was never used on the short Swanage Pier Tramway.*

BOTTOM LEFT: *A huge block of stone is hauled along a horse-drawn tramway from one of the quarries on the Isle of Portland.*

BELOW: *A depiction of the dressing sheds at one of the quarries near Swanage. The horse-operated capstan is hauling stone to the surface, many of the workings in this area being underground. In the shed on the right, a quarryman can be seen dressing paving stones.*
ALL PHILIP BRANNON ENGRAVINGS/COURTESY SWANAGE MUSEUM

resort yet existed, the town being completely given over to the export of Purbeck stone, principally to London, which was quarried from the hills to the south and further west around the neighbouring village of Langton Matravers. All day long, lumbering waggons laden with stone bumped their way down the narrow, rutted High Street to the stone merchants' yards on the foreshore, which were known as 'bankers'. Most of this stone had already been dressed at the quarries and consisted mainly of paving stones, kerb-stones, and stone troughs or sinks. Although a small quay existed nearby, shipment usually involved loading the dressed stone into special high-wheeled carts, which were driven down the Parish Slipway and into the sea up to their axles. It was then transferred by hand to rowing boats or lighters and taken out to ketches rolling at anchor in the bay, where yet again the stone had to be manhandled on board. All this work was carried out in a careful manner to avoid the corners of dressed stones being knocked off or other damage caused by rough treatment. At any time, some thousands of tons of stone could be stacked on the merchants' bankers awaiting shipment and hundreds of local men would be engaged in the trade.

Quarry of the Purbeck paving stone Swanage Dorset

PARKSTONE & POOLE HARBOR, FROM CONSTITUTION HILL.

A lovely panoramic engraved view, showing the extent of Poole Harbour, with the rapidly developing village of Parkstone in the foreground, as seen from Constitution Hill circa 1860. Branksea Island is prominent in the middle distance and Swanage is also shown in the far left distance.
PHILIP BRANNON ENGRAVING/DAVID HAYSOM COLLECTION

Poole, with its huge natural harbour, had long been Dorset's premier port, much of its early wealth generated by the lucrative Newfoundland trade. Following the discovery of the cod-rich banks off the Newfoundland coast by John Cabot in 1497, a large fleet of ships would leave Poole each spring and cross the Atlantic to spend the summer season long-lining for cod on the banks. The cod would be pressed for oil and then dried or salted, a single ship handling as many as a quarter of a million fish in a season. With the approach of autumn, the fleet would set sail for southern Europe where the salt fish found a ready market, returning thence to Poole laden with wine, fruit and other Mediterranean produce, together with a quota of the original fish, train oil and seal pelts. Throughout the winter, Poole shipyards were kept busy refitting the fleet, while other ship owners profited from specialised associated trades such as the supply of salt to the fishing fleet at sea, the express carriage of fish direct from the banks to Europe and an incredibly lucrative contract to supply the complete needs of the shore-based Newfoundland fishing community.

The Newfoundland trade declined sharply from 1815 onwards, when disbanding of the European armies at the end of the Napoleonic war led to a sudden fall in the demand for salt fish. Fortunately for Poole, this dramatic fall in trade was partially offset by a rise in demand for local clay, which was mined from the rich beds on the Corfe and Wareham side of the harbour. By 1840, almost a third of the pottery produced in England was made from Poole materials and a steady stream of clay barges were being towed from the loading points to Poole Quay, for transshipment into seagoing vessels or use in the local pottery works. In addition to the decorative and distinctive Poole pottery, there were several local works producing mundane but essential tiles, bricks and terra-cotta drain pipes.

In extreme contrast to the bustling port of Poole, the present resort of Bournemouth hardly existed at all in 1840. As its name suggests, the town was founded at the point where the River Bourne flowed down from the sandy, inland heaths through a gentle valley to the sea. Following the Inclosure Awards of 1805, the ancient heathlands passed into the hands of private owners, several of whom set about planting vast swathes of pine trees. Their picturesque appearance and health-promoting aroma did much to promote Bournemouth's reputation as a health resort in later years. In 1809, one of the landowners erected a wayside inn called the Tapps Arms at the point where the Christchurch road crossed the Bourne and it was here that a visiting Dorset squire, Mr Lewis Tregonwell and his wife, stopped on 14th July 1810. Tregonwell had been the officer in charge of coast defences in the area during the period 1796-1802 and was now taking advantage of a holiday in Mudeford to show his wife the beauties of the area. So impressed was Mrs Tregonwell that she begged her husband to build them a house which, when they first occupied it in 1812, was the first domestic building in the area. 'The Mansion', as it was known, was soon joined by a number of cottages, some of which were occupied by estate staff and some let to fashionable visitors who wished to indulge in sea bathing. Tregonwell can thus claim to be the true founder of modern Bournemouth.

When Sir George Tapps died in 1835, his son, observing the success of Tregonwell's venture, immediately set about preparing plans to develop his own estate on the east side of the Bourne into a fashionable watering place. An architect was engaged and work began immediately. In 1838, another landowner published plans to develop the area now known as Richmond Hill and by 1840, the embryonic resort had grown sufficiently to persuade Poole bookseller John Sydenham to publish a small guidebook, which gave the following description:

THE SANDS, BOURNEMOUTH

'Thus on spots where, before, the foot of man rarely pressed, but the lowly heath flower blossomed and faded in unnoticed solitude ... a number of detached villas, each marked by distinct and peculiar architectural features, have sprung into existence, affording accommodations of varying extent, so as to be suited to the convenience of either large or small families and adapted, some for extended, others for confined, establishments. To all of these are attached ample gardens, whilst in front are shrubberies tastefully laid out and walks arranged with due regard for convenience and effect. At one end of this range stands a spacious and commodious hotel, erected for the accommodation of more temporary visitants, and fitted up in the most complete style.'

These, together with Tregonwell's previous buildings, the seafront baths and Mr Sydenhams 'Marine Library & Bazaar', formed the basis of a settlement which was to grow rapidly in the years to come and play a very significant part in the subsequent history of the local pleasure steamers.

If the pattern and nature of settlement along the Dorset coast was fundamentally different from today, the transport system was even more so. Although the first boom in railway building had taken place during the 1830s and by 1840 there were 1,497 miles of railway in Britain compared with only 97 in 1830, railway mania had yet to touch Dorset. The London to Southampton line opened in May 1840 but it was to be another seven years before the first train steamed into Dorchester.

It followed, therefore, that all overland transport within the county was by road. Although the turnpike movement of the late 18th century had

greatly improved the main roads and it was possible, for example, to travel from Weymouth to Southampton by the 'Emerald' coach and thence by train to London in eleven hours, many lesser roads were still completely inadequate. In these circumstances, it was not surprising that it was often found to be cheaper and more convenient to move heavy and bulky goods by sea.

In the 1840s, therefore, the harbours, quays and

The coast at Bournemouth from the east, ABOVE, *with steamers and sailing vessels crowding the pier, and west,* BELOW, *from the coastguard's look out.*
BOTH PHILIP BRANNON ENGRAVINGS/DAVID HAYSOM COLLECTION

View from the Coast Guard look out. Bournemouth

creeks of the Dorset coast were crowded with a huge variety of coastal sailing ships carrying every conceivable cargo. In addition to the specific cargoes such as stone and clay referred to above, household coal was an important import and agricultural produce a key export. Small local trading vessels were joined by continental traders, vessels on regular coastal 'packet' services and ocean going ships bearing more exotic cargoes from further afield. It would have been almost impossible to glance to seawards without glimpsing numerous sailing vessels making their way up or down Channel and, in times of strong south west winds, the sheltered anchorages of Portland Roads, Weymouth Bay and Studland Bay would be crowded with wind-bound vessels waiting for the opportunity to weigh anchor and make their westing around Portland Bill.

Amongst these numerous sailing ships, steam vessels were very much a rarity. Following the successful introduction of the pioneering paddle steamer *Comet* on the River Clyde in 1812, the use of steam vessels had spread rapidly and by 1820, a steamer called *Prince Coburg* was operating between Southampton and Cowes. Three years later, the first cross-channel steamer was introduced between Southampton and the Channel Islands, and by 1825 at least one steamer was running a coastal service between the Solent and Plymouth. It seems likely, therefore, that Dorset's first glimpse of a steamship would have been of one of these novel vessels,

belching smoke and sparks as it passed well off-shore on its way to or from the west country.

The first steamers to have been actually based at a Dorset port were the Post Office packets *Watersprite* and *Ivanhoe*, which carried the Channel Islands mail to and from Weymouth, commencing on the night of 7th July 1827. The steamers replaced the sailing packets which had been operating the service since 1794 and, in 1828, they were joined by an additional vessel, *Meteor*. The three paddle steamers ranged from 103 feet to 111 feet in length and were representative of the earliest sea going steamships, with wooden hulls, clipper bows, full sailing rig and tremendously tall funnels. *Meteor* was wrecked in Church Ope Cove, Portland, in 1830 and was replaced by *Flamer* in 1831. By 1837, responsibility for the service had passed from the Post Office to the Admiralty and the end of the decade saw the older vessels replaced and the crossing maintained by *Dasher*, *Cuckoo* and *Wildfire* (ex-*Watersprite*). Also in 1839, a major operator of early coasting steamers, the Commercial Steam Packet Company, who had for some time been operating their paddle steamers *Calpe* and *City of Glasgow* on a coasting service from London to Weymouth calling off Margate, Broadstairs, Ramsgate, Deal, Brighton, Portsmouth, Ryde, Cowes and Yarmouth, announced that the service would be extended on alternate Tuesdays to Cherbourg, providing Weymouth's first steam connection with France.

The Channel Islands steam packet FLAMER entering Weymouth Harbour during the 1830s.   WEYMOUTH MUSEUM

CHAPTER 1
ROSE & THE RAILWAY
1839-1847

The first steam vessel to have actually been owned and registered at a Dorset port would appear to be the paddle steamer *Rose*, which was built in 1832 at Blackwall on the River Thames by B. Wallis & Co. Owned by John Law Jones, a merchant of Fenchurch Street, together with a long list of other subscribing owners including the son of the famous James Watt, she operated on the Thames for five years, until sold to Francis Stavers of Peckham in Surrey on 6th February 1839. Contrary to all previously published accounts, *Rose* was never actually owned by Cosens & Co but she did provide the foundations upon which the company was later to build and it is therefore important to discuss her history in some detail.

Stavers, described in the ship's registration documents as 'Gentleman', was actually a qualified ship's master and it was under his command that *Rose* arrived at Poole on 18th March 1839 to establish a new packet service to Portsmouth. The service had been planned to commence on the first Tuesday in March but due to 'unavoidable circumstances' did not begin until Saturday 23rd March, when *Rose* sailed for Portsmouth at 'half-past eight o'clock in the morning'. Thereafter, she departed from Poole at the same time every Tuesday, Thursday and Saturday, returning from Portsmouth on Monday, Wednesday and Friday. Fares were 5s in the chief cabin or 3s in the fore cabin and bookings could be made through G. Penny Esq. at Poole Quay or Mr W. Marks at the Kings Arms, Portsmouth. It was also anticipated that useful revenue would be generated by towing sailing ships in and out of Poole Harbour.

Unfortunately for Stavers, the Commercial Steam Navigation Company of London also chose 1839 to introduce their larger steamers *Kent* and *Cornubia* on a regular service between Poole, Southampton, Portsmouth and London. Faced with competition from such a large and established operator, *Rose* stood little chance of survival and, by the end of the summer, had been driven out of business and was advertised for sale. A handbill published by Thomas and J.M. Wanhill of Poole in January 1845, at a time when the establishment of another new steam packet company at the port was being discussed, throws some interesting light on the situation. Addressed to 'Our friends and the public', the bill asserted that claims that either *Rose* or the Commercial company's vessels had made a profit were false and quoted a letter from the latter's Southampton agent, Mr Priaulx, to demonstrate *'that the loss of running a boat was considerable, something like £60 per week'*. The handbill continued:

'We think it also right to inform our friends of the number of vessels towed in and out of the port by the steamers while they were here. One only was towed in, viz. the Flora; *and one attempt was made to tow the* Rainbow *to Brownsea; this was the total number that availed of the steamers to perform this so-called essential service. After deducting the expense for getting the steam up, the profit will not give much trouble to calculate.'*

While *Rose* had been struggling to pay her way at Poole, the London & Southampton Railway Company's new line from the capital was steadily creeping its way towards Southampton. Several sections were opened during 1839 and on 11th May 1840, the completed line was officially declared open to Southampton. Aware of this development, a group of businessmen consisting of Weymouth innkeeper George Peace Scott, Henry Drew Esq. of Southampton, William McNeill Esq. of Chipstead, Surrey, and Richard Danvers Ward of Chancery Lane, London, purchased *Rose* and formed the

Steam between *Weymouth and Southampton*, in conjunction with the Railway to London.
ON MONDAY, the 4th MAY NEXT, a very fast and superior STEAM BOAT, (fitted expressly for the Station,) under the command of Lieut. SCRIVEN, R.N., is appointed to leave WEYMOUTH for SOUTHAMPTON with Goods and Passengers and continue running daily.
The hours of leaving the respective Ports will be duly advertized after the time is announced for the departure and arrival of the Trains; and any further particulars may be obtained of Mr. C. B. FOOKS, Weymouth.
WEYMOUTH STEAM PACKET WHARF,
11th February, 1840.

STEAM.
WEYMOUTH AND SOUTHAMPTON,
And by RAILWAY to LONDON.
THE WEYMOUTH and SOUTH-AMPTON COMPANY'S remarkably fast and commodious Steam Yacht, "ROSE," commanded by Lieut. SCRIVEN, R.N., will leave the Steam Packet Wharf, Weymouth, on Mondays, Wednesdays, and Fridays, at 9 o'clock, A.M. precisely, for Swanage, Yarmouth, Cowes, and Southampton; and returning from Southampton to Weymouth, calling off Cowes, Yarmouth, and Swanage, the alternate days, immediately after the arrival of the first Train from London.

FARES:

	Saloon.	Fore Cabin.
From Weymouth to Swanage	7s.	5s.
to Yarmouth	10s.	7s.
to Cowes	10s.	7s.
to Southampton	10s.	
From Southampton to Cowes	2s. 6d.	4s. 6d.
to Yarmouth	5s.	3s.
to Swanage	7s.	5s.
to Weymouth	10s.	7s.

☞ For freight or passage apply to Mr. C. B. FOOKS, Weymouth; Mr. BURT, Swanage; and Mr. PRIAULX, Southampton.
By order of the Directors,
P. T. HARBIN, Secretary,
12, Clement's Inn, London.
N.B.—The Company will not be accountable for any Passenger's Baggage, or any Property whatever, (unless Booked and Paid for at the Office of the Company) or for any damage or loss occasioned by unavoidable delays, accidents, or sea risks whatever; and to prevent mistakes and loss, it is recommended that all Passengers have their Baggage distinctly marked with name and residence in case any should be left on board, which might enable its being forwarded to the owner.

FAR LEFT: A newspaper advertisement from the Dorset County Chronicle of 9th April 1840, announcing the start of ROSE's *service between Weymouth and Southampton.*

LEFT: This newspaper advertisement from the Dorset County Chronicle of 11th June 1840 carried additional information detailing the fares.
BOTH
AUTHOR'S COLLECTION

Weymouth & Southampton Steam Packet Company. On 28th May 1840, when she was officially transferred from London, *Rose* became the first steam ship to be registered at Weymouth. Measuring 108 feet in length between perpendiculars, 14 feet 1 inch in the beam and 9 feet in depth, her wooden hull had a clipper bow adorned with a woman's bust head and a square stern with sham quarter galleries. She was schooner-rigged with two masts and a standing bowsprit and had a tonnage of 86 (57.4 burthen). Her Boulton & Watt steam engines delivered 50hp and were housed in an engine room 33 feet in length. With her open upper deck and complete lack of deck cabins, she was typical of her period and had the appearance of a coastal sailing vessel fitted with huge paddle boxes and an immensely tall funnel.

The new company's plan was to operate *Rose* on a regular service between Weymouth and Southampton, where she would connect with the trains to and from London, providing a more comfortable and convenient alternative to the overland journey by coach. The coaches were surprisingly speedy, the 'Emerald' for example, leaving Luce's Hotel in Weymouth each morning at 8am, travelling via Wareham, Poole, Christchurch and Lymington to Southampton, whence a train would whisk the passengers onwards to London, arriving at 9pm. *Rose*, although she departed one hour later, could not hope to offer a great saving in time but, on a calm day at least, should provide a less bone-shaking travelling experience together with the ability to carry heavy goods.

In view of Stavers' problems at Poole, the new company must also have been painfully aware of the risks posed by the Commercial Co, who were operating their steamers *City of Glasgow* and *William the Fourth* on a regular London-Southampton-Weymouth-Torquay-Dartmouth service and *Grand Turk* on the London-Weymouth-Cherbourg run.

However, as these services only touched at Weymouth every five and seven days respectively, they reasoned that their proposed daily service should attract sufficient local support to justify their risk.

It would appear that trains were running between London and Southampton prior to the official opening of the line on 11th May, as *Rose*, '*commanded by our much-respected townsman Lieut Scriven RN*', made her first departure from Weymouth's Steam Packet Wharf at 9am on Monday 4th May '*with a fashionable and numerous party*'. The local press described her as '*one of the finest and most elegant steamboats that has yet entered this port*' and went on to comment that '*the accommodations and facilities rendered at the wharf for the landing and embarking of passengers and the facilities afforded for the discharge of cargoes reflect great credit on (the company's) active agent, Mr C.B. Fooks*'. The ship then settled into a regular pattern of sailings, leaving Weymouth at 9.00am every Monday, Wednesday and Friday, calling off Swanage, Yarmouth and Cowes *en route* for Southampton, where she connected with the Up train to London. On alternate days, the ship sailed immediately after the arrival of the first train from London and retraced her route to Weymouth. The service proved an immediate success and following a brief reduction in the frequency of sailings during the winter months, returned to its usual pattern in the spring of 1841.

Rose's success had not gone un-noticed by the Commercial company, who decided to try to obtain a slice of the market by introducing their steamer *Edinboro' Castle* on the Weymouth-Southampton service in February 1841. The new ship sailed on alternate days to *Rose*, charged identical fares and was advertised to make the passage in six hours. In addition, the Commercial Co's *Eclipse* left Weymouth every Wednesday for London, calling at Portsmouth *en route*.

In response to this competition, *Rose*'s owners advertised their intention of re-forming themselves into the Weymouth, Southampton & London Steam Packet Company, with an increased capital of £30,000 in 1,500 shares of £20 each. The stated aims of the new company were to introduce new direct services from Weymouth to London and Cherbourg, and to increase the frequency of sailing to Southampton. The number of directors was doubled to eight and now included James Flower, a Weymouth brewer who was to play a significant part in *Rose*'s later history. At least two new ships would have been required to meet these ambitious aims and members of the public were invited to invest in the venture. As nothing more was heard of the proposals, it would appear that the necessary capital was not subscribed and *Rose*, now under the command of Capt Geary RN, continued on her regular route until withdrawn for the winter in December 1841.

In January 1842, Fooks ceased to act as Weymouth agent for *Rose* and transferred his allegiance to an un-named company which advertised its intention

A newspaper advertisement from the Dorset County Chronicle *of 21st May 1840, detailing the services operated by the Commercial Co's ships* CITY OF GLASGOW *and* WILLIAM THE FOURTH.
AUTHOR'S COLLECTION

A superbly detailed lithograph by Day & Son, dated 1840, showing a small paddle steamer leaving Weymouth Harbour. In the foreground, elegant visitors mingle with local mariners on the newly-completed ballast quay under the Nothe. Above the steamer's stern is New Quay End, which was extended during 1840 to create a stone promenade following the line of the timber training wall seen here. From Devonshire and Pulteney Buildings on the far left, Weymouth's elegant Georgian seafront curves around the bay, where a large number of bathing machines are in use. The sailing vessels are cutters of similar design to NANCY, which maintained the winter connection with the Southampton railhead between 1842 and 1846. The identity of the paddle steamer remains a mystery, for while she lacks ROSE's full sailing rig and quarter galleries, no other steamer of this size was known to have visited Weymouth in 1840. Artistic licence perhaps?

WEYMOUTH MUSEUM

An unusual view of the town from the end of the 1840 extension to the quay, thereafter known as New Quay End. The harbour is to the left and Weymouth Bay is to the right. The extended quay provided a fashionable 'marine walk' but appears to have been extremely rough under foot. A steamer, possibly ROSE, *is moored at the steamboat wharf beside the tall bulk of Bank House, today known as the Edward Hotel.*
WEYMOUTH MUSEUM

to introduce a *'new and commodious steam packet fitted with engines of 100hp'* on the Southampton service in the spring. In the event, this ship failed to materialise but *Rose*'s agency passed to Mr Scott of the Golden Lion at Weymouth. Robert Burt, a local stone merchant, acted for the ship at Swanage and a Mr Boucher at Southampton.

In February, it was announced that the sailing cutter *Nancy* would offer two sailings each week during the winter to and from Southampton in place of *Rose*. *Nancy* had been launched in May 1830 from the Weymouth shipyard of William & Thomas Ayles, who also owned 34 of her 64 shares. A 37 ton vessel, measuring 42 feet 6 inches by 15 feet by 7 feet 3 inches, she was a typical local trading vessel of her day and maintained a reliable service throughout the winter. This established a pattern which was to survive for the rest of *Rose*'s time at Weymouth, with the steamer operating through the summer and *Nancy* during the winter.

Rose, having undergone a thorough refit, recommenced for the season on 15th June under the command of Capt Harding. The local press noted that refreshments were now to be had on board at moderate prices and that female stewards had been appointed. It was also stated that:

'… by taking the morning train at Vauxhall, at seven o'clock, the Rose *steamer awaiting the arrival of the train at Southampton, the journey from the metropolis is achieved in the unprecedented short time of seven hours, and as there are many London families waiting for the running of the* Rose *we feel assured that by this safe and expeditious conveyance we shall find considerable augmentation in our list of arrivals.'*

Clearly the vessel was regarded as an essential aid to Weymouth's continued growth as a fashionable holiday resort.

The winter of 1842-3 was marked by a succession of severe gales one of which, on 12th November, drove an unprecedented five steamers to run for shelter in the recently-dredged Weymouth Harbour. These were *Brunswick* (Southampton-Plymouth), *Edinboro' Castle* (Southampton-Torquay), *Zephyr* (London-Dartmouth), *Dasher* (Weymouth-Guernsey) and *Lady De Saumarez* (Southampton-Guernsey), the last of which did not finally reach Guernsey until the following Tuesday! In February, *Nancy* lost her mainsail and bowsprit in a squall off the Needles but succeeded in bringing her bedraggled passengers safely into Weymouth.

Rose began her 1843 season on 6th June but enlivened her routine by providing occasional sailings to Guernsey. At Weymouth, familiarity was obviously beginning to breed contempt, for the facilities at the steamboat wharf, which had earned such plaudits in 1840, now attracted considerable criticism. In September the local press commented:

'We cannot forebear noticing the too common and careless practice, on the arrival of the Rose *steamer, which was again repeated on her reaching this place on Wednesday night last, namely the instant discharge of steam whilst the passengers are landing on the quay, there being no accommodation on the darkest night than a narrow plank without either side rails or ropes.'*

It appears that a local gentleman *'while in the act of conducting his sister on shore, missed his footing owing to being completely enveloped in steam, and fell overboard'*. On rising to the surface he struck himself violently against the paddle wheel and was almost drowned.

The year 1844 followed the established pattern except that another cutter, *Liberty*, introduced a year round service to Southampton and a large coastal paddle steamer, *The Queen*, soon replaced by *Zephyr*, appeared on a weekly London to Torquay service calling at Weymouth. Both of these represented

A steamer, possibly ROSE, approaching the entrance to Weymouth Harbour. The 1840 extension to New Quay End can be seen on the left but, on the right, the Nothe Headland is as yet undeveloped. Between 1860 and 1872, a major fortification was constructed and a new quay, known as the Ballast Wharf, was created where the mooring posts and sailing vessels can be seen on the right.
WEYMOUTH LIBRARY

additional competition for *Rose* but even more concern was raised by the publication, during November, of formal applications to build railways from Southampton to Dorchester and from the Salisbury branch of the London & South Western Railway to Weymouth. Either of these, if completed, would remove the whole reason for *Rose*'s existence. Her owner's gloom at this prospect cannot have been helped by the general atmosphere of dejection at Weymouth, occasioned by the decision to withdraw the Admiralty Channel Islands packets from the port in April 1845 and transfer the service to Southampton.

One of the company's directors, James Flower, the Weymouth brewer, took a more optimistic view than his colleagues and determined to purchase the ship on his own account. The formal transfer of ownership took place on 2nd July 1845, with Flower, most unusually for the time, taking all 64 shares in the vessel. *Rose* was immediately placed on Besant's slip for a full refit of hull, boilers and machinery under the supervision of Capt Robert White who had, until the demise of the packet service, been the respected commander of the Channel Islands packet *Dasher*. Before committing himself to such heavy personal expenditure, Flower had obtained the firm support of *'a large portion of the local tradesmen of Weymouth and its neighbourhood, as well as a number of the most influential agriculturalists and cattle dealers'*. The local press gave enthusiastic coverage of the re-launch of *Rose* on 19th July and heaped praise on Flower for *'his spirited enterprise … which will afford great accommodation to trade as well as to visitors and inhabitants who, we hope, will give the Rose that patronage and support her claims so justly merit.'*

Flower planned to use the ship in a slightly different manner to his predecessors. The regular service to Southampton would continue as before but with only two return trips each week, the other days being occupied with *'trips of pleasure'*. The first

of these took place on 30th and 31st August, when *Rose* *'cruized in the bay'* to witness the gaities of the grand Weymouth regatta. The Southampton service commenced on Monday 4th August, with departures from Weymouth at 9.00am each Monday and Friday, and from Southampton on Tuesdays and Saturdays at 11.00am immediately after the arrival of the train from London. Significantly perhaps, advertisements now placed a greater emphasis on freight, with rates quoted for two and four wheeled carriages, horses and goods at 1s 8d per cwt inclusive of rail travel.

The quality of *Rose*'s refit was put to the test on 9th August when she left Southampton with twenty passengers. It was:

'blowing a strong gale from the SSW with a tremendous sea in the bay and a strong head tide against her. The Brunswick Southampton steamer bound to Plymouth being compelled to bring up for shelter in Portland Roads, it was not expected that this steamer, being of so much less power, would even attempt to pass the Needles; but, nothing daunted and with a determination to try the test of her power and machinery after the general repairs she has undergone, she was kept to sea and arrived in our bay at half past twelve o'clock the same evening, without the slightest injury being done to anything on board. We learn, from several on board, and especially Capt Robert White, late commander of H.M. Mail Packets, that her capabilities as a sea boat, with the general efficiency of her machinery and boilers, enables her to make speed beyond his most sanguine expectations.'

Rose continued to call off Swanage on both her outward and return trips, and the diary of John Mowlem, who became the town's most prominent citizen, gives an interesting glimpse into conditions at the time in this hard-working industrial community. Mowlem was born in Swanage in 1788 and made his fortune paving the streets of London. He founded the internationally known construction company which still carries his name today. Upon his retirement to Swanage in 1845, he determined to improve his birthplace and the lot of the working man:

'*21 November 1845. The* Rose *steamer from Southampton called in the bay with packages but no passengers.*

24 November 1845. Wind N by W, very fine with strong hoar frost. Nine vessels in the bay, all for stone, there are large demands for stone from this place at the present time. One vessel laden in Durlston Bay, one ditto at the cliff. This is very remarkable at this time of year and shows what a demand for stone there is. But I see no improvements in the inhabitants. There is nothing like want with those who can work but not one thinks of old age … Public houses are in great request, the manners are more rude than they were fifty years ago, both men and women. This is to be much regretted by all who wish them well.

25 November 1845. … the roads are a disgrace to any man. Opposite the church men sit in the high road breaking stones promiscuously brought from some quarry, soft and hard, thick and thin, some as big as a child's head. At another place there were pebbles brought promiscuously from the seaside and shot into the street.'

Despite the obvious failings of Swanage as a

destination for excursionists, *Rose* took a large party of them via Lulworth Cove on 11th September, and a week later rounded Portland Bill for a cruise to Bridport and Lyme Regis to view the famous landslip. These pioneering excursions were the first ever recorded by a Weymouth steamer to those destinations and, quite unknowingly, laid a pattern on which Cosens & Co were to build for many years to come. September closed with a flurry of excitement, when five exhausted men were discovered drifting in an open boat off Portland and brought ashore at Weymouth. They turned out to be the crew of the Dutch galliot *Maria*, which had been run down and sunk by an unknown barque. After a night's rest ashore, they were given passage in *Rose* to Portsmouth, where they were delivered into the care of the Dutch Consul.

Rose stopped running for the winter at the end of December and was replaced, as usual, by the cutter *Nancy*. Although *Rose* had survived and at least broken even, she cannot have been too profitable, for in February, Flower advertised her for sale. The advertisement described her as being of 57 tons NM, 87 OM, with two engines of 20hp each by Boulton & Watt and, following her refit, in a fit state to be sent to sea immediately. A postscript added that:

'*Should the* Rose *not be sold, she will resume her running from this port to Southampton in April next, making occasional excursions to Cherbourg, St. Malo, the Channel Islands and various parts of the*

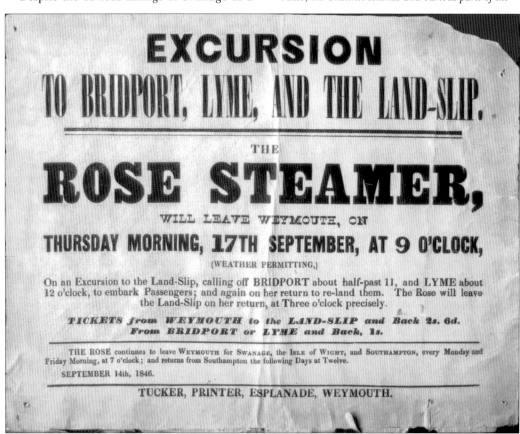

A poster advertising an 1846 excursion sailing by ROSE. WEYMOUTH MUSEUM

coast, of which due notice will be given.'

Rose was not sold and duly re-entered service on 25th May 1846 under the command of Charles Garland, the bi-weekly sailings now being timed to leave Weymouth at 7am and Southampton at 10.00am. The excursion season opened at Whitsuntide with one trip to Southampton and the Isle of Wight, and a second, which was described in marvellous detail by the local press:

'As announced, the Rose *steamer started on the day appointed for a trip round the bay to land passengers at Portland and Lulworth, as well as Chapman's Pool. The company embarked at ten in the morning. The signal gun for sailing being followed by the bell, off she shot from the harbour in gallant style with drums beating and colours flying bound for Portland Roads. The weather continued propitious with a refreshing breeze from the N.E. She went next to Lulworth, passing near the line of the intended breakwater. Several passengers landing at Lulworth proceeded to view Bindon Abbey; others viewed Chapman's Pool, a small bay of deep water and an excellent harbour still capable of improvement, near St. Alban's Head. Leaving Encombe to the left, more of the voyagers proceeded to view Corfe Castle. Thence returning at dusky eve, the lovers of romance were greatly delighted with the moonlight sparkling on the bright blue waters; it required but slight extension of the imagination to fancy themselves in the far-famed Bay of Naples, while the* Rose's *chimney might have been imagined a miniature Vesuvius, but harmless and safely propelling the vessel back to harbour. The creature comforts of the trip were selected with care and in abundance.'*

Further excursions were offered during June to Osmington Mills, Lulworth and around the bay, and on 2nd July, having been delayed for a day by gales, *Rose* left Weymouth at 7.00am for an eight hour daylight crossing to Cherbourg, departing for home during the following afternoon. Passengers were offered the choice of spending a single night in France, or remaining there for a full week to be collected by *Rose* on her next return sailing on 8/9th July. The fare for this remarkable trip was one sovereign. Thereafter, Lulworth became the most frequent destination for local trips. When the Weymouth Royal Regatta was held on 30th and 31st July, the committee proudly announced that it had engaged *Rose*:

'... which will leave the harbour at 8am. precisely and make a circuit of the bay, slipping the mark boats in her course, and return to her moorings in the Roads in time to start the first, second and third class yachts. She will repeat the circuit in the afternoon, as soon as the last yacht rounds the first mark boat. Tickets for admission on board, for either trip or for the whole day, may be had of the committee, or at the Libraries, at 2s.6d. each or for a family party of six persons at

10s. Refreshments may be taken on board or had of the Steward.

The final excursion of the season was a two-day trip to Exmouth on 3rd and 4th September.

Rose completed her season on 22nd October 1846 and was laid up in Weymouth Harbour. The cutter *Nancy*, having been sold to new owners during December, did not take up her customary winter service and so, apart from the weekly visit by *Zephyr* on her coasting service between London and the West Country, Weymouth was left without a regular connection with Southampton for the first time in six years. Neither did *Rose* stir from her moorings when spring arrived, for by that time the official opening of the Southampton & Dorchester Railway on 1st June 1847 was only a few weeks away. Flower must have realised that, despite the popularity of her excursion sailings, his ship could not possibly pay her way once her Southampton and London trade was lost to the faster and more convenient route via Dorchester and the railway.

Bowing to the inevitable, he placed the ship on the market and awaited a buyer. No-one was forthcoming for over a year and it was not until 6th January 1848 that she was sold to George Flower of Stafford. On 24th February she sailed for Plymouth under the command of a Captain Collins and was re-registered at that port on 21st April 1849. During her time at Plymouth, she was re-sold to James Peake of Prince Edward Island, Canada, who planned to use her on a mail and passenger service between Pictou, Nova Scotia and Charlottetown, Prince Edward Island. *Rose* was given a complete refit and, after a trial trip to Falmouth, departed for Canada on or about 3rd July. With her paddlewheels dismantled and lashed on deck, she proceeded under sail, arriving safely at Charlottetown after a passage of 35 days. Following four years on her intended service, she was then sold to the famous shipping company Samuel Cunard & Co and her registration transferred to Halifax, Nova Scotia on 18th June, 1853. Under Cunard's ownership, *Rose* was used to patrol the Atlantic waters around Nova Scotia, New Brunswick and Prince Edward Island to enforce fishing restrictions on US fishermen within the three mile limit. While carrying out a patrol in the Gulf of St. Lawrence on 29th September, she was caught in a severe gale and driven ashore on Rustico Bar, Prince Edward Island and became a total loss.

In her pioneering eight years as Weymouth's first locally-owned paddle steamer, *Rose* played a vital part in increasing the town's accessibility as a holiday resort and also in establishing the taste among locals and visitors alike for steamer excursions along the coast. Her demise left a definite gap in the market and the remainder of this history is the story of how one local entrepreneur stepped in to form a company which was to successfully meet the demand and serve Weymouth and the south coast resorts for the next 119 years.

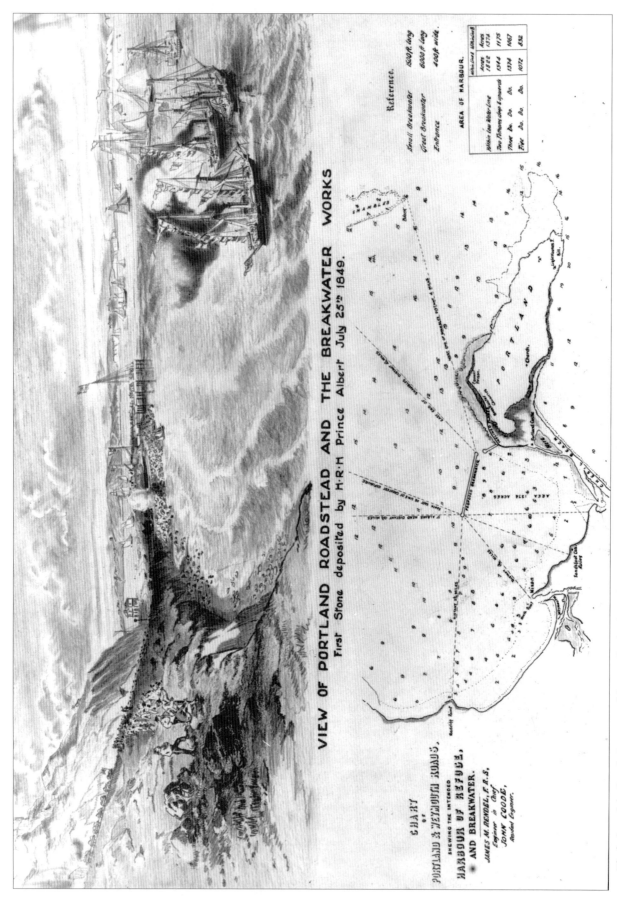

VIEW OF PORTLAND ROADSTEAD AND THE BREAKWATER WORKS
First Stone deposited by H.R.H Prince Albert July 25th 1849.

The laying of the foundation stone of the new Portland Breakwater by HRH Prince Albert on 25th July 1849. This pencil drawing by D.W. Dore shows the view from the east side of Portland, looking north over the new breakwater works and Portland roadstead, towards Weymouth Bay in the distance. Note the inclined railway, which was built to bring stone from the quarries on the top of the island to the base of the breakwater. The chart, which has been rotated through 90 degrees so that north is to the left, is based on Messrs Rendell & Coode's original survey and clearly shows the position of the planned harbour of refuge.

G. CARTER COLLECTION

CHAPTER 2
JOSEPH COSENS' 'SPIRITED UNDERTAKING'
1848-1850

Resident in Weymouth throughout *Rose*'s years on the Southampton service was a seafaring family by the name of Cosens, headed by a master mariner named Joseph and his wife Grace. Cosens is a very old Dorset name which, with its various spellings (including Cozens and Cousens), can be traced back to at least the 16th century. Joseph and Grace had three sons, the eldest of whom, Thomas, was born in 1810 at Lyme Regis where the family was then living. At some time during the next six years, the Cosens moved to Weymouth where their second son, Joseph, was born on 30th May 1816, being christened on 16th August at St. Nicholas Street Chapel. A third boy, named William, was born on 15th March 1827, also at Weymouth.

All three sons followed their father's example and went to sea as a profession, rising steadily to become master mariners in their own right. As each boy in turn reached the age of eleven or twelve, he left home to begin a four year apprenticeship under sail in one of the schooners owned by R. Wilson of London, employed in regular trade between the Thames and Waterford in Southern Ireland or across the North Sea to Rotterdam. Apprenticeship was followed by three or four years serving 'before the mast' as a seaman, before promotion to mate and eventually, after about ten years at sea, elevation to the command of one of Wilson's ships.

The age gap between the brothers meant that each in turn served under his older brother in the same ship. Thus Joseph, who first went to sea in May 1827 in the 110 ton schooner *Wharfinger* (built 1823 on the Isle of Wight), was serving as second mate on the London-Rotterdam route in 1834 under the command of his brother Thomas. In June 1835, Joseph transferred to the 177 ton schooner *Commodore* (built 1833 at Hastings) on the London-Waterford service and served just over two years as mate, before being promoted to command in September 1837. William, the youngest brother, began his apprenticeship on board *Commodore* in September 1839 and remained in the ship until he in turn became master, when Joseph left in 1848 to begin his career in steamboats.

In 1840, Thomas married 32-year old Eliza from Chichester and Joseph married 22-year old Lydia from London. Thomas and Eliza produced two daughters, Eliza in 1841 and Josephine in 1845 but, sadly, Joseph and his wife were not blessed with offspring. Ten years later, in 1850, the youngest brother William was married to a Weymouth girl also called Eliza and the couple had two daughters, Emily Louise in 1855 and Annie in 1857, both of

Capt Joseph Cosens, 1816-1873, the founder of the company.
BRIAN JACKSON COLLECTION

whom grew up to become governesses. As the brothers produced no sons, the family name disappeared from their direct line of succession upon the death of Annie Cosens on 28th October 1939 but lived on for many years in the title of the company which is the subject of this book.

The three brothers, as skilled professional seaman with many year's intimate knowledge of trading under sail in south coast, Irish and near-Continental waters, must have watched the development of the steamboat and railway services with a keen interest. Should they be regarded as a threat to their traditional coasting trade or as a golden opportunity? It was Joseph, the middle brother, who took a particular interest in the Weymouth steamer trade. Thomas remained in sail and took little active part in subsequent developments, while William, still only aged 21, needed to gain some years of experience as a master in sail. Joseph, having commanded the schooner *Commodore* for eleven years, had presumably been able to amass some savings and in all probability had access to additional capital through his wife Lydia and his London shipping contacts. He was also, as subsequent events proved beyond doubt, a natural entrepreneur, with a keen eye for a promising business venture.

It is, of course, reasonable to enquire why Joseph Cosens believed he could succeed where James Flower had so recently concluded that *Rose* could not. The answer appears to be two-fold. Firstly, he would have been acutely aware both of the increasing number of fashionable visitors to Weymouth following the opening of the railway to Dorchester and of the considerable demand for the revival of steamboat excursions following the withdrawal of *Rose*. It is doubtful whether the seasonal excursion trade alone would have tempted him into steamer ownership, had it not been for a second major development – the decision to build a harbour of refuge at Portland.

Portland Roads, sheltered from the south and west by the Isle of Portland and Chesil Beach respectively, had, since time immemorial, provided a safe haven for shipping sheltering from the prevailing south-westerly gales. Unfortunately, however, the Roads were dangerously exposed to winds from the east. As early as 1803, it had been suggested that the construction of a large breakwater would have the dual effect of creating a safe anchorage irrespective of wind direction and a refuge from French attack for English coastal shipping, being placed strategically mid-way between the naval ports of Portsmouth and Plymouth. Although nothing came of these original proposals, in 1843 a Royal commission was appointed to look into the matter again and, by 1844, a complete hydrographic survey had been carried out and the Commissioners for Harbours of Refuge had given their enthusiastic support to the construction of a breakwater.

James Rendell of Plymouth was quickly appointed Engineer in Chief for the project and by 1846, his team, which included Cornish engineer John Coode, was busy with surveying and preliminary works. In January 1847, the government also announced a decision to '*make Portland in Dorsetshire a penal settlement, and to employ the convicts on the Breakwater and her public works in contemplation, such as constructing a citadel and running fortifications entirely around the island.*' Clearly, the proposed works were to be on a vast scale involving the construction not only of the breakwater itself but also a series of inclined railways designed to move stone from the government quarries to the construction site, as well as a convict prison at The Grove and associated roads. There was also to be a huge military citadel on Verne Hill, together with gun emplacements at East Weares, a fort on the end of the Breakwater and another at Nothe Point, Weymouth, plus numerous offices, stores and quays.

Joseph Cosens was, of course, well aware of these developments and realised that the commencement of the works would be accompanied by a vast influx of civilian workmen, convicts and soldiers onto Portland. Realising that the only alternative to a twenty-minute steamer crossing from Weymouth Harbour to Castletown Quay at Portland was a slow and tedious journey by horse drawn carriage or carrier's waggon across the inhospitable Chesil Beach, he reasoned that there was a substantial profit to be made by whoever established the first efficient sea link from the mainland.

The Act of Parliament enabling the works to commence was passed on 11th May 1847. Joseph Cosens bided his time, watching carefully as work on the inclined railway, quays and temporary prison proceeded, and judging the right moment to introduce his steamer service. By the early summer of 1848, the railway was almost operational, the first 350 convict cells and the barracks for the soldiers who were to guard them were complete, and almost 1,000 civilian workmen had arrived on the island. Judging the demand to have reached a level which would justify his venture, Cosens passed his command of the schooner *Commodore* to his younger brother William and used his London contacts to charter a small wooden paddle steamer called *Highland Maid*, which he immediately steamed round to Weymouth.

A poster announcing the times of HIGHLAND MAID's first sailings between Weymouth and Portland, July 1848
WEYMOUTH MUSEUM

Highland Maid entered service between Weymouth and Portland on Monday 15th July 1848 and offered four return sailings for goods and passengers each day. A relatively new ship, she had been built in 1846 at North Shields by P. Legg and fitted with one 22hp engine, giving her a service speed of 8 knots with a consumption of 1½ tons of coal per day. Measuring 66 feet 2 inches in length, 13 feet beam and 8 feet draft, she was used as a tug on the River Tyne until sold to D. Barker and J. Spicer for similar use on the Thames in July 1847. Although a tiny vessel by modern standards, she was an immediate success on the Portland service and, as predicted, generated a considerable demand for pleasure trips. Within days of entering service she was *'affording frequent opportunities for delightful marine excursions to places of interest in the neighbourhood'* and on 18th July took 200 passengers to Portland, where they enjoyed ten hours ashore giving *'ample time to visit the Grove works, prison, Rufus Castle, Cave's Hole, the lighthouse and other interesting features'*. She arrived back at Weymouth at 9pm after *'a day's tour not to be equalled in the West of England'*. Trips to Osmington Mills and evening cruises in the Bay with a band on board apparently proved *'highly gratifying'* and, as the summer progressed, it quickly became apparent from the income generated that Cosens would be justified in purchasing a larger steamer of his own.

As early as August 1848 he had encouraged rumours to circulate that another steamer would shortly be placed on the service but it was not until 26th December that arrangements were completed and the *'fine iron steamboat* Princess' replaced *Highland Maid* on the service between Weymouth and Portland. *Princess* had been launched in April 1847 from Ditchburn & Mare's famous Orchard Yard at Blackwall on the River Thames and engined by the well-known John Penn of Greenwich who, as her first owner, had probably had her completed as a speculation. Measuring 112 feet 5 inches by 13 feet 5 inches by 7 feet 7 inches, she had a round stern, bows decorated with a 'scroll head' but no bowsprit or masts. Almost twice the length of her predecessor, the ship met with immediate approval at Weymouth and the local press was soon singing her praises:

'The great accommodation afforded by this splendid boat, which plies between this port and Portland, induces us to lay before our readers a description of her capabilities and merits. The Princess *is an iron-built boat of great strength and beauty and was not surpassed on the Thames in symmetry, where she was classed A1, being built by Ditchburn & Mare. She is 112 ft long with a good breadth of beam, and almost a new boat. Her oscillating engines are of 40 h.p. with new boilers by the celebrated Woolwich engineers John Penn & Sons, and she is upwards of 60 tons burthen and capable of carrying 500 passengers above decks and below. Her fore cabin measures 37 feet long and her saloon 38, being fitted up with a stove and horse-hair cushioned sofas. She has also the desired advantage of a ladies cabin. Captain Cosens will be in command of the* Princess *whose steaming qualities have surpassed even the expectations of her builders. As a proof she came from the Thames to this port in 26 hours, blowing a gale and a heavy sea on. She occupies but 14 minutes between her departure from our harbour and her arrival at Portland. She is in fact an excellent sea boat and perfectly easy in her steering. Early in the*

PRINCESS attending a regatta in Plymouth Sound during 1868. Although taken eleven years after she had left Weymouth, the ship is little altered from her days in Cosens' ownership, apart from the fitting of a mast which was absent during her early days in Dorset.
PLYMOUTH MUSEUM

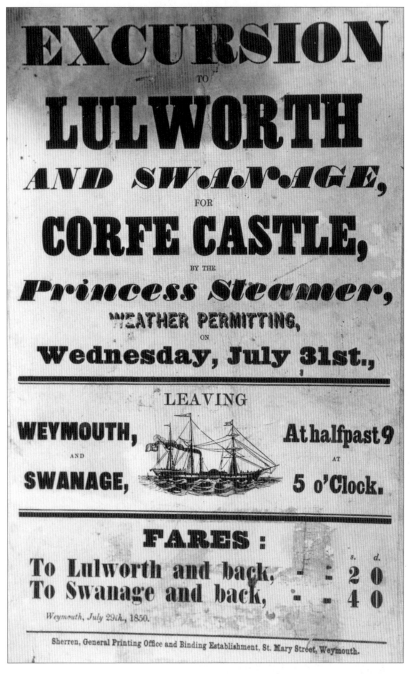

EXCURSION

TO

LULWORTH

AND SWANAGE,

FOR

CORFE CASTLE,

BY THE

Princess Steamer,

WEATHER PERMITTING,

ON

Wednesday, July 31st.,

LEAVING

WEYMOUTH,
AND
SWANAGE,

At half past 9
AT
5 o'Clock.

FARES :

	s.	d.
To Lulworth and back, - -	2	0
To Swanage and back, - -	4	0

Weymouth, July 29th, 1850.

Sherren, General Printing Office and Binding Establishment, St. Mary Street, Weymouth.

Handbill for an excursion by
PRINCESS, *31st July 1850.*
WEYMOUTH MUSEUM

spring she will undergo a thorough cleaning and painting and will be fitted up on deck and below with every accommodation for all classes of passengers. The Highland Maid's *old steward (Mr George Rolls) has been re-engaged for the* Princess *and a licence has been obtained so that passengers can be furnished with every kind of refreshment. We heartily wish this spirited undertaking every success.'*

The ship was registered at Weymouth on 10th January 1849, under the ownership of Joseph Cosens who held 56 of the 64 shares and Frederick Palmer of St. Pancras who held the remaining 8. He was presumably another of the captain's London

contacts, who was prepared to sink capital into the venture. On 23rd January, Cosens mortgaged his shares back to John Penn and did not finally discharge the mortgage until September 1852. This financial link with Penn is of great interest, since he was subsequently to build the engines for five of the company's major passenger ships and to become a significant shareholder after the formation of the limited company.

The first 300 convicts having arrived on the Island during the previous November, the work at Portland gathered pace and *Princess* was kept busy throughout the winter running her regular service for the benefit '*of the inhabitants of Weymouth and Portland and the numerous workmen of all classes connected with the increasing government convict establishment and breakwater.*' Her routine was enlivened by a number of small incidents. In February 1849, Joseph Cosens was in trouble with the town council for attempting to evade harbour dues by landing his passengers at the entrance to the harbour instead of within. Lively debate ensued, culminating in the council offering him a choice of either paying a fixed fee of 25s per week or the same daily rate as other trading vessels. In March, a ship's boy who had been discharged from *Princess* for misconduct, sought his revenge by pouring a jar of vitriol over the steward's dog. He then disappeared and a warrant for his arrest was issued.

Also during March 1849, the Dorset coast was lashed by severe gales and a number of ships found themselves in difficulty. The brig *Prince Regent*, on passage from Newcastle to Teignmouth, was seriously damaged by the furious seas in West Bay and had two of her crew swept overboard and another seriously injured. She was in imminent danger of being driven ashore on Chesil Beach when *Princess* put to sea, battled her way around Portland Bill and towed her safely into Weymouth. Such an act must have required enormous skill and courage on the part of Capt Cosens and was the first of many recorded salvage jobs by his company's steamers. During the same series of March gales, the schooners *Jane* and *Primrose* and an un-named billy-boy laden with wheat were also towed badly damaged into Weymouth, although it is unclear precisely which rescues were carried out by *Princess*.

As spring approached and *Princess's* promised refit was completed, it was announced that, in addition to the Portland service, the ship would be devoted to pleasure trips on at least one day per week. Eastward excursions would include sailing past '*the proud and lofty white cliffs of Albion*' before calling at Lulworth, Chapman's Pool, Swanage, Bournemouth or sailing onwards past the Needles Rocks and up '*the Solent Sea*' to the Isle of Wight. Westward trips would pass round the Bill of Portland and follow the curve of the mighty Chesil Beach to view or land at Bridport, Lyme, the famous landslip, Bere, Seaton, Sidmouth, Budleigh Salterton, Exmouth (with views of Starcross and Powderham Castle), Dawlish to view the coast railway line,

Teignmouth, Babbacombe and onwards to Torquay. It was claimed that *Princess*'s speed of *'14 miles per hour'* would allow her to complete a return trip to any of these destinations in a single day.

Despite this claim, *Princess*'s first excursion to Cowes took place over no less than three days. She left Weymouth at 10.30am on Saturday 12th May 1849, called at Swanage to land and embark passengers and arrived at Cowes at 5pm. Passengers spent the night ashore and on the Sunday morning were offered a cruise to Southampton with time ashore, returning to Cowes during the afternoon. Nobody can have got much sleep that night, for *Princess* sailed again at 2am on the Monday morning, called again at Swanage and arrived in Weymouth at 7.30am in time to take up her regular schedule on the Portland service. Sullivan's Band accompanied the steamer and *'added to the pleasures of the voyage by frequent and successful exercises of their tuneful art.'* The 40 or so passengers who took advantage of the trip paid 10s return (7s 6d single) in the saloon and 7s 6d return (5s single) in the fore cabin, tickets being obtained from Joseph Cosens' office at 1 Belle View.

On 6th June, *Princess* offered her first recorded cross channel excursion to Guernsey. The passage took 6 hours at a cost of 25s or 17s 6d return for the saloon and fore-cabin respectively. Passengers were offered the option of returning from Guernsey at 3pm the following day or remaining in the Channel Islands until the ship's next return trip on Wednesday and Thursday 13-14th June. Connections to Jersey and France were said to be possible and, once again, Sullivan's Band provided the entertainment. Other shorter excursions took place throughout the season and, on at least one occasion, passengers landed at Lulworth were afforded the opportunity to view the inside of Lulworth Castle.

In stark contrast to these cheerful excursions, *Princess* went to Southampton on Wednesday 20th June, to embark a large number of convicts who were destined for the growing convict establishment on Portland. What this heavily-guarded group made of their sea trip is not recorded but it is certain that Capt Cosens was delighted at obtaining this new business, which had hitherto been carried out by government steamers.

A general holiday was declared in Weymouth and Portland on 25th July 1849, to mark the official laying of the breakwater foundation stone by Prince Albert. The sea in the Channel was so rough that the Prince was forced to travel from Osborne House on the Isle of Wight by boat to Southampton, then by train to Dorchester and by carriage to Weymouth, whence a steamer carried him to Portland. Needless to say, the ceremony proved a great attraction and *Princess*, together with every other available boat, was packed to capacity with sightseers anxious to see the foundation stone dropped onto the sea bed and the subsequent progress of the Royal party up the inclined railway, in three gaily decorated wagons, to visit the prison.

During March 1850, *Princess* went to London for a refit but was back on station by the middle of April. Her season followed the pattern of the previous year, with four sailings each day between Weymouth and Portland, plus occasional excursions. On 22nd May, she was hired to carry the Secretary of State for the Colonies, Earl Grey, to the island to view the convict establishment and, in June, went to Portsmouth to collect another group of prisoners. During July, the Royal Agricultural Society of England's Show was held at Exeter and *Princess* offered a special two-day excursion. Leaving Weymouth at 9am on 17th July, she called at Bridport at mid-day, Lyme at 12.30pm, Sidmouth at 2.30pm and Budleigh Salterton at 3.00pm. Passengers spent the night ashore and the ship returned from Exeter on the Thursday evening.

The other development of note was the steady increase in the number of excursionists wishing to view the breakwater works and see the sights on Portland. Although an omnibus ran twice daily across Chesil Beach, *Princess* was by far the fastest and most comfortable way of reaching the island and was regularly filled to capacity. Once ashore, visitors could hire carriages to tour the island or to convey them to the breakwater works. The main contractor for the breakwater, John Towlerton Leather, was constructing a vast timber staging which already stretched over a quarter of a mile from shore. The 100 foot piles were lifted by a gigantic crane, guided into place by divers and then screwed into the seabed. Over 1,000 tons of stone a day were quarried on the top of the island, and sent by way of the inclined railway and lines laid along the staging to be tipped into the sea below. The combination of civil engineering works on such a vast scale and the presence of a convict labour force proved irresistible to Victorian curiosity, and the steamer service flourished. It appeared that Joseph Cosens' faith in his *'spirited undertaking'* had been fully justified.

John Towlerton Leather, 1804-1885, the main contractor for the construction of the Portland Breakwaters, had an extremely distinguished career in civil engineering. Having learned his trade under his uncle, George Leather, during the construction of the Aire & Calder Canal and Goole docks, John went on to become Chief Engineer of the Sheffield Waterworks and was responsible for the construction of most of that city's major reservoirs. In 1839, he branched out into contracting work and became involved in a number of major railway, river-improvement and bridge schemes. His name and reputation are, however, chiefly associated with the major national undertakings of the Portland Breakwaters, the construction of the Spithead forts and the extensions to Portsmouth dockyard. In 1877, he retired from active work to reside at his magnificent home, Levensthorpe Hall near Leeds, from where he devoted himself to the improvement of his extensive estates in Yorkshire and Northumberland and his duties as High Sheriff and Deputy-Lieutenant of the latter county.
MICHAEL CONYNGHAM GREENE

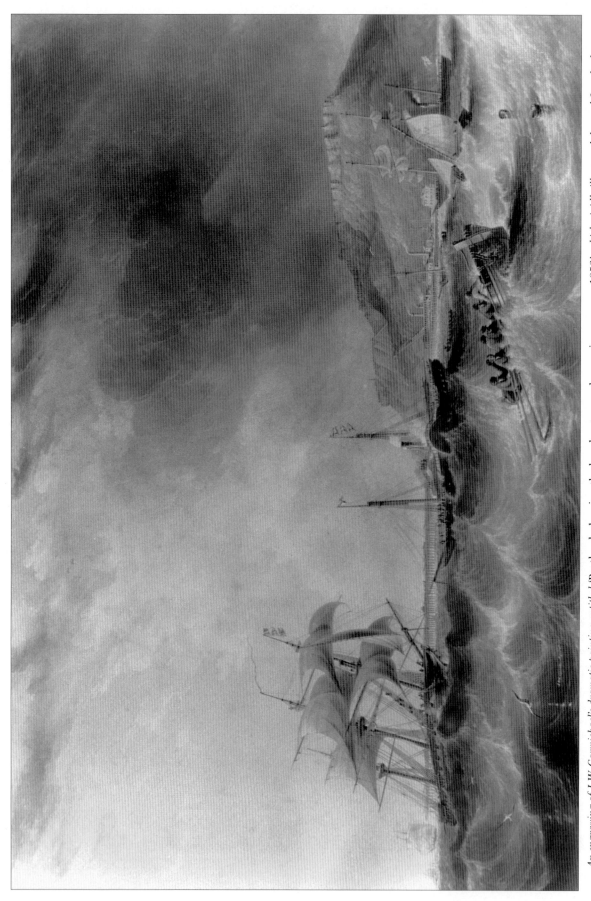

An engraving of J.W. Carmichael's dramatic painting entitled 'Portland, showing the breakwater works now in progress, 1853', which vividly illustrated the need for a harbour of refuge at Portland. A north-easterly gale is blowing, a heavy sea is running in Portland Roads and a number of sailing ships are somewhat foolishly running for shelter on a lee shore. In the background, the breakwater works, the inclined railway down the side of Portland and the massive timber staging from which stone was tipped into the sea, can all clearly be seen. The vessel plunging along in the centre of the picture is J.T. Leather's private steamer. In the foreground, one of Portland's famously seaworthy 'Lerrets' is seen under oars while, to the right, a large coastal paddle steamer is partially hidden behind the mainsail of a Weymouth pilot cutter. In such conditions, it was not surprising that the breakwater staging suffered occasional damage.

MICHAEL CONYNGHAM GREENE

CHAPTER 3
COMPETITION & PARTNERSHIP
1851-1857

Throughout the winter of 1850-51, *Princess* continued her regular Portland sailings. She had just commenced her summer excursion season when news reached Weymouth, on the evening of 17th May, that the 600 ton sailing ship *Seringapatam* had gone ashore in thick fog on the west side of Portland, near a spot known as Mutton Cove. The ship, which had been 143 days homeward bound from Sydney, was laden with a valuable cargo of oil, tallow, copper ore, cotton, wool, skins and mail valued at £30,000. While the local coastguard rendered all possible assistance on the spot, *Princess* put to sea and, '*after great exertions and several hours of unceasing toil*', succeeded in towing her off the rocks and into the safety of Portland Roads, for which Capt Cosens received a salvage award of £500. The *Princess*'s crew very naturally expected to receive a fair share and were dismayed when it was announced that he would give them only £5. They refused his offer and were promptly discharged from the ship, as a result of which they commenced legal proceedings against him in the Court of Admiralty. Although the outcome was not recorded, it is clear that generosity to his employees was not one of the good captain's traits!

Given the immediate success of *Princess*'s operation and the steadily-increasing popularity of the breakwater works as a tourist attraction, it was hardly surprising that others should cast covetous glances at the trade. Joseph Cosens' dispute with his crew must have paled into insignificance when, in June 1851, he discovered that a rival organisation intended placing its own steamer on the Portland service and entering into direct competition. Posters appeared around Weymouth and Portland inviting all interested parties to attend a public meeting at the Portland Arms Inn (now the Royal Portland Arms) at Fortuneswell on Tuesday 1st July, to discuss the formation of the Weymouth & Portland Steam Packet Company.

The new company was to have capital of £2,000 in £5 shares, the majority of which were allegedly already taken, but the precise ownership of their first ship, *Contractor*, is somewhat difficult to analyse. The ship's registration documents show all 64 shares owned by Philip Dodson, a Weymouth builder who had interests in the stone and coal trades, and in later years was described as a railway contractor responsible, amongst other jobs, for constructing Weymouth railway station. Contemporary newspaper sources claim that the ship was owned by William Longman and the sale of shares suggests that others were involved as well. It seems probable a number of local businessmen contributed capital but that

Dodson was the majority shareholder and named as managing owner. The company solicitor was Richard Hare who, ironically, was later appointed joint solicitor for the Weymouth & Portland Railway Company, to which the steamer company was so bitterly opposed.

Contractor arrived in Weymouth on Saturday 16th August 1851 under the command of Capt Beale, having sailed down from Middlesbrough. She had been constructed there in 1849 by J. Jackson and was a wooden, clinker-built paddle steamer, measuring 84 feet 4 inches by 15 feet 8 inches by 8 feet 9 inches. She had a single mast, clipper bow with standing bowsprit and figurehead of a man, and a round, counter stern. Her engine room was 36 feet 4 inches long, with an engine by J. Almond which drove her at between 10 and 12 knots and consumed 5 cwt of coal per hour. Her previous owners were J. Smart and J. Morrell, who had used her as a tug and passenger steamer.

Contractor had no sooner entered service between Weymouth and Portland than, on 1st September, she ran onto an anchor belonging to the schooner *Dorset* near the landing place at Castletown, stove a

A poster announcing a public meeting to discuss the formation of the Weymouth & Portland Steam Packet Co on 1st July 1851.
WEYMOUTH MUSEUM

29

A model of Contractor, *which was donated by Cosens & Co Ltd to Weymouth Museum in 1969, when their old offices and workshops on Weymouth Backwater were demolished for redevelopment. At some stage, the ship's funnel has been repainted in Cosens' post-1901 livery but otherwise the model gives a very accurate impression of* Contractor's *layout. The background is painted with a naive representation of the Nothe headland at the entrance to Weymouth Harbour.*
WEYMOUTH MUSEUM

large hole in her bottom and promptly sank. As the tide rose the vessel was completely submerged, ruining her furniture and fittings and causing serious damage to her machinery. This costly accident must have been a severe blow to her owners and insult was added to injury when Capt Cosens 'kindly rendered much assistance in recovering his rival' and offered to take over *Contractor*'s commitments. It was common practice for sailing ships to lay an anchor well offshore to assist them in warping out of their berth after loading and *Princess* had also

run over one some months before but, being an iron vessel, was less seriously damaged. *Contractor* was eventually raised and was sent to Poole for permanent repairs during October.

Philip Dodson suffered a further blow during September, when one of his laden stone boats foundered off Church Ope Cove whilst returning from a quarry near Portland Bill. Fortunately, the incident was spotted by the crew of *Princess*, who managed to rescue those on board. In December, a barge, laden with convicts bound for transportation, got into difficulties off Portland and was towed in to Weymouth by *Contractor* which was, by then, fully repaired and back in service.

Stiff competition between the rival steamers ensued throughout the winter and into the summer excursion season of 1852. Fares on the Portland service were reduced and, from April onwards, a wide variety of local and long-distance excursions advertised.

Contractor, now under the command of Capt Tizard, offered at least four crossings to Guernsey and Jersey in April, May, June and September, each of which took three days, with two days on passage and one ashore. Both ships visited Southampton, the Isle of Wight, Lulworth, Lyme and all the usual local destinations on a regular basis. Weymouth Harbour must have presented an animated scene at this time for, since August 1850, the steamers of the London & South Western Railway Company had been offering a regular service to the Channel Islands and excursion steamers such as *Medina* from Southampton and *Her Majesty* from Portsmouth had begun to bring parties to view the breakwater works and spend time ashore at Weymouth.

The season was enlivened on 22nd July by a royal visit. Queen Victoria, Prince Albert and the Prince of Wales were returning from a pleasure cruise to the West Country on board the Royal Yacht *Victoria & Albert*, accompanied by the Royal steam tender *Fairy* and the government steamers *Vivid* and *Black Eagle*, when they put into Portland Roads in order that the gentlemen of the party might go ashore to view the progress on the breakwater works. Salutes were fired from the Nothe and the local revenue cutter as the Royal Squadron made its way into the roads and every available vantage point was bedecked with flags. Both *Princess* and *Contractor* set off 'freighted with crowded excess of all grades of society who had ample opportunity of seeing her Majesty and other branches of the Royal Family.' The Queen, who had remained on board the Royal Yacht, 'appeared much pleased and made gracious acknowledgement to the hearty and animated cheers from the numerous parties who were so anxiously engaged in paying their respectful devoirs.' When the Royal Squadron weighed anchor again at 3pm, both the local steamers followed it out to sea, where further ships of the Royal Navy were waiting to escort it back to the Isle of Wight.

A few days after the Royal visit, the simmering tension between the crews of *Contractor* and *Princess* erupted into a serious fight. On the evening of 26th

WHITSUNTIDE HOLIDAYS.

Excursion to the **Channel Islands.**

THE FAST AND POWERFUL STEAM BOAT

CONTRACTOR,
WILL MAKE HER SECOND EXCURSION
[WEATHER PERMITTING,] TO THE ISLANDS OF
GUERNSEY
AND
JERSEY,
ON WHITMONDAY,
Leaving Weymouth at 8 o'clock in the Morning, landing her Passengers at Guernsey at about 4 o'clock in the Afternoon, proceeding immediately to and arriving at Jersey at about 7 o'clock the same Evening.

The "CONTRACTOR" will return from JERSEY on the following Wednesday at 8 o'clock in the morning, calling at GUERNSEY at about 11 o'clock, and arriving at WEYMOUTH about 7 o'clock in the evening.

FARES TO GUERNSEY AND BACK.
Main Cabin, - - - 12s.   Fore Cabin, - - - 8s.
Single Fare, - - - 8s.   Single Fare, - - - 6s.
FARES TO JERSEY AND BACK.
Main Cabin, - - - 15s.   Fore Cabin, - - - 12s.
Single Fare, - - - 10s.   Single Fare, - - - 8s.
STEWARD'S FEE.
MAIN CABIN Passengers, 1s.—FORE CABIN Passengers, 6d. each.
REFRESHMENTS MAY BE HAD ON BOARD.
For further particulars apply to Mr. POTHECARY, Golden Lion Hotel, Weymouth
Dated Weymouth, May 20th, 1852.

SHERREN, General Printing Office, No. 79. St. Mary Street. WEYMOUTH

A sailing bill for Contractor's *excursion to the Channel Islands in May 1852.*
WEYMOUTH MUSEUM

July, *Contractor* was already lying alongside the pier at Portland and loading passengers for her return trip to Weymouth, when *Princess* came alongside and disembarked her passengers over her rival's decks. One of *Princess*'s crew, a Mr Lankester, then went to stand by *Contractor*'s gangway in order to direct passengers who intended to return by the Cosens steamer to the correct vessel. It was here that the dispute broke out. Lankester and his supporters maintained that George Rolls, one of *Contractor*'s crew, blocked the passengers' way and directed them to the stern of his own vessel, while Rolls insisted that Lankester was trying to entice his passengers to board the Cosens boat. Whatever the truth of the matter, a fight broke out and the two men were soon rolling about the deck attempting to strangle and throw each other overboard. Capt Tizard separated them and immediately gave the order to cast off. Lankester had just enough time to scramble on board his own ship before *Contractor* steamed away, carrying away *Princess*'s ropes as she went. Each man accused the other of assault but, when the case came before the magistrates during August, it was dismissed out of hand and each was ordered to pay his own costs!

Early on the morning of 11th August, the most severe gale since the Great Storm of November 1824 struck the Dorset coast. The wind being from the east, there were great fears for the safety of the breakwater staging and, at 10am, Capt Cosens received a message requesting the urgent assistance of *Princess*. On her arrival, it was discovered that the damage was not as severe as was feared, only one or two temporary piles and cross-bracings having broken free. At 3pm, another message having been received, *Princess* put to sea again to the aid of a large vessel, which was reported to be dismasted and in distress off Portland. Sadly, no trace of her could be found and it was presumed that she had foundered in the vicinity of the Shambles Bank.

Contractor had more success when she went to the assistance of the schooner *Eclipse*, which, with her sails blown to ribbons and her tiller broken, was drifting in a disabled state to the east of Portland. With her captain injured and her crew exhausted, great trouble was experienced in passing a tow rope which, owing to the heavy sea then running, subsequently parted five times before the schooner was eventually towed safely into Weymouth Harbour. Several yachts and another trading vessel were also driven ashore and, from the quantity of wreckage found floating in West Bay on the following day, it was assumed that '*many melancholy catastrophes*' had occurred.

Although the constantly-expanding Portland trade appeared to offer more than sufficient employment for the two rival steamers, the competition clearly rankled with Joseph Cosens, who determined to gain the upper hand by obtaining a new and vastly superior vessel in time for the season of 1853. In order to obtain the capital for this scheme, he entered into a partnership with Mr Joseph Drew JP,

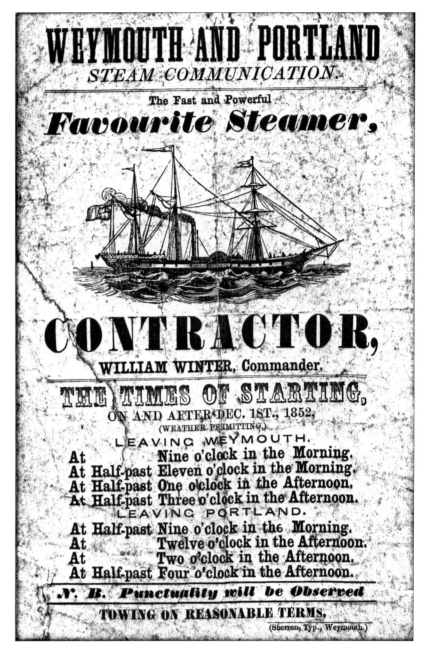

a local confectioner who had recently established himself as proprietor of the *Southern Times* newspaper. Drew had the necessary money and, equally importantly, his paper would be able to provide their ships with the maximum of complimentary publicity while excluding all mention of the opposition! Although a half share in *Princess* was not formally transferred to Drew until 28th September (Frederick Palmer having sold his 8 shares to Cosens some time before), a formal partnership agreement must have been in place early in 1852 in order to allow the order for the new ship to be placed. The business continued to operate from the Steam Packet Office at 1 Belle View, Weymouth but correspondence was now carried out under the letterhead of 'Cosens & Drew'.

Contractor's timetable for December 1852.
AUTHOR'S COLLECTION

Weymouth seafront and pier in 1853, with two steamers in the bay.
NEWMAN

For the design and building of their new ship, Cosens & Drew went to one of the most eminent marine architects and shipbuilders of his day, John Scott Russell. Russell was already celebrated as the inventor of the wave-line principal of hull design and builder of several beautiful and revolutionary ocean-going vessels, and was to receive a great deal of public attention in years to come as the builder of Brunel's troubled leviathan ship *Great Eastern*. Construction of the new ship, which was to be named *Prince*, began during the spring at Russell's Millwall shipyard on the Isle of Dogs in London, which was subsequently to become famous as the building site of *Great Eastern*. It has been stated in every published history and even in Cosens' own

Joseph Drew, JP, LLD, the co-founder of Cosens & Co.
AUTHOR'S COLLECTION

guidebooks, that *Prince* was built on the shoreward side of *Great Eastern* and, in order to reach the Thames, had to be launched through the middle of the great ship. Sadly, as *Prince* was launched in the autumn of 1852 and construction of *Great Eastern* did not commence until February 1854, this delightful story must finally be consigned to the realms of local folklore.

Unfortunately, the completion of *Prince* was delayed by a shortage of iron plate, caused by an unexpected national surge in demand which the ironworks were unable to meet. Since it was apparent that she would not be ready in time for the summer season, it was arranged that Cosens & Drew should undertake a brief charter of a brand new steamer named *Wave Queen*. Built by Russell in 1852 for cross channel service from Belgium, the ship's novel and modern design attracted the attention of the *Illustrated London News*, which commented:

'This beautiful steamer … is an object of much curiosity as she lies at her moorings near Greenwich. She has already made the passage to Denmark; and the result of this and other trials has proved her admirable qualities as a sea boat. She is remarkably dry and easy, and fully instances how much may yet be accomplished by the efforts of science in conjunction with steam and iron. The length of the Wave Queen exceeds 200ft, while her breadth is little more than 13ft. She is fitted with engines of 80 horse power. Her wheels, which are on the feathering principal, are remarkably small and, to the casual observer, appear totally inadequate to the propulsion of a boat of such great size: this however, we are assured, is not the case. The fittings of her cabins, etc. are of the most costly description. Altogether, the Wave Queen, by her novel and beautiful appearance, cannot fail to call forth admiration from*

all who see her, differing as she does from anything hitherto seen upon this river.'

It would appear that the ship was a little too novel for her new owners, who promptly rejected her. Having completed a trial trip from Newhaven to Dieppe, a distance of 72 miles, in four and a half hours, she was subsequently taken by Mr H.P. Maples for the cross channel service which he operated between the two ports on behalf of the London, Brighton & South Coast Railway Co but, in the meanwhile, it suited both Russell and the Weymouth partners to see her gainfully employed in Dorset.

Wave Queen's stay at Weymouth lasted just over a week but in that time she was worked hard, spending two days following the yachts competing in the local regatta and three more running long-distance excursions to Cowes, Torquay and Cherbourg. The latter trip departed from Weymouth at 9.30am on Friday 27th August and left France the following day at noon, all for the sum of 12s 6d. Advertisements for the ship emphasised her speed and comfort, the existence of her innovative plate glass deck saloon and the fact that she was commanded by Joseph Cosens.

During October, Cosens attempted to gain another advantage over his competitor by offering to erect, at his own cost, a new landing stage in the lower part of the harbour for use by *Princess* and *Prince*. The town council agreed by a narrow majority but, having received vigorous objections from Philip Dodson and his supporters, reversed their decision and resolved instead to look into obtaining an Act of Parliament to allow the construction of a new pile pier, together with other facilities required by the Borough.

The new *Prince* arrived at Weymouth on 31st October and was immediately judged to be a great beauty. Although smaller than *Wave Queen*, she shared a certain family resemblance, with small, neat paddle boxes, a long slender hull, and a clipper bow adorned with a small bowsprit and figurehead of a sailor wearing a round cap. She measured 120 feet 5 inches by 13 feet 3 inches by 7 feet 6 inches

and had an oscillating engine provided by John Penn of Greenwich who, it will be recalled, had held a mortgage on *Princess* until only two months previously. It has always been claimed that she was rigged with three masts, a practice normally reserved for the Royal steam yachts and tenders, which allowed her owners to steal an advantage over their competitors by styling her as 'the steam yacht *Prince*' rather than a mere excursion steamer. However, since the earliest photographs and a surviving model of the ship both show her as schooner rigged with two masts, this is another assertion which must be called into doubt.

Only one salvage job was recorded during the winter months. On 3rd February 1853, the barque *Naiad* was towed off the Chesil Beach and, since no-one in Weymouth would undertake her repairs, was taken onwards to Cowes by *Contractor*. Her refit completed, she was towed back to Weymouth by the same steamer and resumed her voyage.

Prince shared the winter service with *Princess* and, after a thorough refit on Besant's slip during April 1853, took over as Cosens' principal excursion steamer. *Princess* was still used on occasional local

This illustration, from the Illustrated London News *of 14th August 1852, clearly shows how sleek and novel* WAVE QUEEN *must have appeared in comparison to the other steamers then in service at Weymouth.*
AUTHOR'S COLLECTION

A handbill advertising WAVE QUEEN's *sailings during August 1852.*
WEYMOUTH MUSEUM

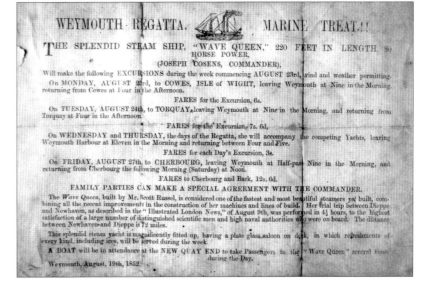

PRINCE at Weymouth. This remarkably early photograph emphasises her slender hull form and small paddle boxes, which showed a far stronger resemblance to WAVE QUEEN than to the earlier Weymouth paddle steamers. The fact that she is shown with the same two-masted schooner rig which is described in her registration documents, must throw doubt on the oft-repeated claim that she was originally fitted with three masts.

AUTHOR'S COLLECTION

A Southern Times advertisement for Cosens service between Weymouth and Portland, 20th November 1852.

AUTHOR'S COLLECTION

excursions and the Portland service but spent more and more time undertaking towage and construction work for John Towlerton Leather, contractor for the breakwater, with whom Cosens had built up a harmonious and profitable relationship. We know that the Cosens vessels sometimes even lay overnight at the breakwater works as, in June, three of *Princess*'s crew were prosecuted for attempting to evade paying the toll by climbing over the toll gate at Ferrybridge in the early hours of the morning. In their defence, they claimed that they had been ordered to walk to Portland to get steam up! It is believed that at this time Joseph's younger brother William took command of *Princess*. He had left the schooner *Commodore* in March 1850 and very probably returned to Weymouth to become mate of the steamer. Now, with Joseph elevated to command of the new flagship, he began a long career as a master with the company which, with one break, was to last for many years.

Competition between *Contractor* and *Prince* was fierce throughout the summer of 1853. In addition to their local trips, both ships went to Cowes and Torquay on several occasions. *Prince* visited Dartmouth and *Contractor*, as in previous seasons, offered a number of two-day excursions to Guernsey. Placed a week apart, these allowed passengers the choice of spending either a day or a week on the island. A slight variation was a call at Alderney on the homeward voyage, to view the breakwater and extensive government works then under construction. A trip scheduled for Wednesday 29th July had to be postponed due to bad weather and excursionists who had crossed the previous week found their stay on Guernsey extended until the following Monday, when *Contractor* was eventually able to battle her way across the Channel. Her typical passage time was 8 hours.

It was common practice to cancel advertised Portland sailings at short notice, in order to respond to unexpected events in the area. In July, for example, both steamers took large parties out to view the Royal Yacht, which had touched into Portland Roads on her way to Holyhead, and on another evening, *Contractor* went to view a shoal of unusually large porpoises which had appeared in the bay. On 23rd July, *Contractor* was engaged on an evening cruise when she came upon the wreck of a ship, completely waterlogged and nearly keel-upwards 2 miles east of Portland Bill. She immediately took the wreck in tow but succeeded in bringing only the masts and spars into Weymouth, the hull having parted company and sunk near the breakwater.

Both sides used all possible means to steal an advantage and there were frequent complaints in those parts of the local press not owned by Joseph Drew, of the steamers racing and other unacceptable practices. On 7th July, for example, a large party was induced to sail in *Prince* to Spithead where, Cosens' placards had announced, the Queen would be reviewing the British Fleet. On arrival it was discovered that no such review had ever been arranged and the Queen was certainly not present. Needless to say, the passengers were not impressed and *'grumbling was the order of the day'*! Back in Weymouth, there was considerable debate as to whether the incident had been due to genuine error, intentional deception or even a hoax on the part of Dodson to blacken Cosens' reputation.

NOTICE.

THE VISITORS and INHABITANTS of WEYMOUTH and PORTLAND are respectfully informed that during the Winter Season, the

"PRINCE" OR "PRINCESS" STEAMER,

(J. COSENS, COMMANDER), will leave Weymouth and Portland at the following hours—

WEYMOUTH.		PORTLAND.
h. m.		h. m.
8—30 A.M.		9—0 A.M.
10—30 A.M.		1—0 P.M.
2—30 P.M.		4—0 P.M.

WEATHER PERMITTING.

Parties availing themselves of the "Prince" or "Princess," will have the advantage of viewing the works of the Portland Breakwater.

A dispute then broke out regarding the landing of passengers at Weymouth. There were complaints in the town council, where both sides had their supporters, that *Contractor* was regularly passing the steamboat wharf and landing her passengers higher up the harbour. A counter claim was then made that this was due to *Prince* and *Princess* monopolising the wharf to the exclusion of *Contractor* and a heated argument ensued. Eventually the harbour master was sent for and, having insisted that *Contractor* regularly passed the wharf even when it was vacant, was instructed to ensure that neither company's vessels should berth anywhere else in the future.

Matters came to a dramatic head on 17th August 1853 when *Prince* ran onto the rocks in Lulworth Cove and was holed. An article in the *Dorset County Chronicle* stated that *Contractor* was already in the Cove taking on passengers for Weymouth when the *Prince* arrived and suggested that the accident was caused by the Cosens ship '*making too eager a grasp*

for those who might otherwise board the Contractor.' This provoked a furious denial from Cosens, whose version of events stated that *Prince* had taken up her position on the beach to the north-east of *Contractor* and had landed about half her passengers when Dodson's ship, in attempting to leave, found herself aground. A rope was passed to *Prince* to assist in hauling her off but, due to a sudden ground swell, *Contractor* was thrown against *Prince*, causing considerable damage to her bulwarks and forcing her onto the rocks. *Contractor* ran out a kedge anchor, got herself afloat and then towed her rival off the rocks but, as *Prince* had her after compartment flooded, she was beached again until the next tide. *Princess* was sent to her assistance and, a temporary patch having been fitted, *Prince* steamed back to Weymouth where permanent repairs were undertaken. A week later, Capt Winter placed an advertisement in the local newspaper denying that *Prince*'s damage was the result of assisting *Contractor*

PRINCESS towing a barge past the timber staging from which stone was tipped directly into the sea to form the first Portland Breakwater. Following the arrival of PRINCE in 1852, PRINCESS spent more and more of her time working for J.T. Leather, the main contractor for the construction of the breakwater.
AUTHOR'S COLLECTION

PRINCESS towing a three masted barque out of Weymouth Harbour in 1854. The presence of Cosens' steamers transformed the commerce of the port by

allowing shipmasters to enter or leave harbour whenever they pleased, irrespective of the wind direction. PRINCESS (enlarged inset above) is rigged with a single mast, which it is believed may have been fitted during her 1850 refit.
WEYMOUTH MUSEUM

Portland from the Nothe, c1855. The steamer from Weymouth has just commenced her twenty-minute crossing and is heading towards the new pier at Castletown, Portland, which can be seen on the right of the picture behind the rigging of the flagstaff. The breakwater staging is clearly visible in the left background, and Portland Roadstead is crowded with anchored shipping.
NEWMAN

and asserting that it was due entirely to '*the situation in which she had placed herself under the voluntary act of Capt Cosens.*'

These exchanges, incidentally, confirm that both steamers were now visiting Lulworth on a very regular basis and provide the first firm evidence of passengers being landed over the ships' bows directly onto the beach. *Rose* had always anchored in the cove and landed her compliment by boat but Joseph Cosens developed a more convenient technique of dropping a kedge anchor or picking up a mooring from the steamer's stern and running her bows gently onto the shingle. A small door in the bulwarks forward gave passengers access to a wheeled landing stage down which they made their way onto the beach. The same method, which was unique to the Dorset and Devon coast, was also used on the open beaches between Bridport and Torquay and was probably introduced by *Princess* in 1849.

By 1853, the fledgling resort of Bournemouth was growing rapidly in size and popularity, with regular omnibus services linking the town to the nearest railway stations at Poole and Christchurch Road. The development of private villas, hotels and other amenities was proceeding apace and the resort had achieved a secure position alongside the other sea-bathing places of the south coast. It did, however, lack the fashionable and practical amenity of a pier and when *Princess* made her occasional visits, she was forced to land passengers in boats. While efforts were made locally to raise the necessary capital through public subscription for a pier, Joseph Cosens suggested that a cheaper alternative might be to provide a moveable jetty mounted on wheels, in much the same style as that used at Lulworth.

Although there was considerable enthusiasm for his suggestion, nothing actually came of the plan and it was not until 1856 that a jetty was eventually constructed.

On 26th October 1853, an interesting transaction took place when *Princess*, without any public announcement, was quietly sold to John Towlerton Leather, the breakwater contractor. As already stated, the ship had spent much of her time over the past few years working on hire to Leather and the transfer of ownership does not seem to have brought about any outward change in her employment. Still commanded by William Cosens, she continued to appear as a Cosens ship on the Portland service and excursions until sold to new owners in Plymouth during 1857. It may have been that Leather found it cheaper to purchase than to hire her but, since he was an extremely wealthy man and a close friend of the Cosens family, it seems more probable the transaction was a means of injecting some capital into the steamboat company.

The first massive stones of the inner breakwater pier head having appeared above the water during July, Prince Albert arrived to make another inspection on 24th August 1854. The visit had not been publicly revealed but, as soon as the Royal Standard was seen fluttering over *Victoria & Albert*, the news was announced by the bellman in Weymouth. *Prince* and *Contractor* both sailed at midday and rounded the yacht at the very moment the Prince Consort was returning on board.

Contractor, which was commanded during 1854 by Capt Richard Cox, increased her number of sailings to Poole but otherwise the season followed the accepted pattern. On 10th August, Chideock regatta was held at Seaton beach and it had been arranged that *Prince* should come round from Weymouth and collect passengers from Bridport and Lyme to witness the festivities. Capt Cosens, however, caused general offence by forgetting his promise and by leaving disappointed passengers waiting at both harbours. On 2nd October, two bottle-nosed whales appeared in Weymouth Bay and were promptly captured and landed at Portland, where they were exhibited for '*the trifling charge of 2d.*' The bellman at Weymouth announced the news and throughout the afternoon and evening the steamers did a brisk trade.

The winter of 1854-55 was particularly severe, with heavy snow, freezing weather and a succession of gales. The breakwater works came to a complete halt, the Portland service was severely disrupted and the brig *Ino* was driven ashore on Weymouth beach and broke up, her cargo of coal being distributed to the poor. At the end of November, *Prince* and *Princess* towed the Dutch galliot *Betty* into Weymouth. The ship had been bound from South America to Bremen with tobacco when she was run down by the warship *Dauntless* and had both her masts carried away. A pilot cutter found her drifting off Portland and put into Weymouth to seek the assistance of the steamers, a salvage award of £500

eventually being shared between the three. In February, *Prince* went to the rescue of the cutter *Edward*, which was bound from Jersey to Plymouth with potatoes when she carried away her rudder.

As early as 1848, the occupant of Portland Castle, Captain Charles Augustus Manning, had proposed the construction of a wooden steamboat pier beside the Castletown stone-loading jetty at Portland but it was not until the winter of 1854-55 that any progress was made with the scheme. In the event, the straight pier of Manning's original plan was replaced with an angled structure constructed on the western side of the stone jetty and extending well out to sea.

The new pier was opened to traffic in the week beginning 25th March 1855, when *Princess* was the first steamer to call. When the excursion season commenced at the end of April, the advantages of the structure became immediately apparent and the *Dorset County Chronicle* waxed eloquent:

'Most of our readers are doubtless aware, from painful experience, of the inconvenient and scrambling process by which landing at and egress from Portland was accomplished. Those who have never performed this perilous feat, when they hear how visitors were formerly ushered into Portland, will better appreciate the means by which this unpleasantry has been obviated. A passage over the encumbered decks of at least one vessel was the first difficulty usually to be encountered, and before the visitor could

consider himself on terra firma and beyond the chances of a broken limb or serious bruise, he was compelled to take the rugged path between sundry tons of stone. All this inconvenience has now been happily remedied. An excellent and commodious pier has been erected by the Crown chiefly for the accommodation of passengers by the steamers, the approach to which is by a road, walled on both sides, so that the public cannot now be incommoded by the immense blocks of stone which used to beset the path of the tourist or visitor to Portland. The advantages resulting from this structure are so obvious that they need no comment and we apprehend that anyone who contrasts the present landing place with the same spot as it existed last summer, will agree with us that, the fee of one halfpenny charged to passengers is an extraordinarily low price for so great a benefit.'

During the 1855 season, *Contractor*, now commanded by Capt Jorgen Nelson Block, began to spend more of her time at Poole and frequently operated day excursions from there to Weymouth. On 16th July, she sailed from Bridport on a day trip to Portland but was prevented from making her return sailing by strong winds and heavy seas which sprang up during the day. Some of her 300 passengers returned home overland but the majority were still stranded in Weymouth two days later. In August, she undertook a number of charter sailings and also operated a special trip to Cowes

A detail from an engraving, showing the Weymouth steamer at Castletown Pier. To the right can be seen Portland Castle and, beyond the shingle causeway of Chesil Beach, the dangerous lee shore of Chesil Cove, where many vessels came to grief. At the shoreward end of the pier is the Castletown stone jetty, with the tall bulk of the Castle Inn.
WEYMOUTH MUSEUM

to view the famous Royal Yacht Squadron regatta, and the race for Her Majesty's 100 Guinea Cup.

Captain Cosens, meanwhile, sought to enhance his reputation in Weymouth by offering a series of free excursions to local organisations, such as the Literary & Scientific Institution and Melcombe Regis National School. Coronation Day was celebrated in Weymouth '*with the usual demonstrations of loyalty and enjoyment*' and *Prince* was kept busy with frequent trips to Lulworth and Portland, while *Medina* and *Contractor* brought large parties from Southampton and Poole respectively. *Prince*'s summer routine was later enlivened by a special two-day sailing to Portsmouth in August, to witness the launch of *HMS Duke of Marlborough* and a day trip on 5th September

to attend a bazaar being held on Brownsea Island, in Poole Harbour, in aid of the Bournemouth Sanatorium. The season ended on 17th October, when the weather finally became too unattractive to tempt either visitors or residents to undertake a trip across the bay. The only recorded salvage job of 1855 was the yacht *Mischief* which, having been towed to sea by *Prince*, was promptly dismasted in the bay and had to be assisted back to the harbour for repairs.

On the night of 26th January 1856, a messenger arrived '*fiery red with haste*' from Portland to report that a large ship was ablaze in the channel. William Cosens immediately took *Princess* to sea but, on arriving alongside the vessel, discovered that she was in fact a steamer bound down-channel, shrouded in her own smoke and funnel sparks. On 22nd February, *Contractor* had more success when she earned herself a £30 salvage award by towing the smack *Ranger* off Hook Sands, at the entrance to Poole Harbour.

A Royal occasion opened the excursion season on Wednesday 23rd April, when a grand Naval Review was held at Spithead. The event was the largest exhibition of Britain's naval might which had ever been attempted and the fleet which Queen Victoria reviewed was genuinely unparalleled in the history of the nation. Unprecedented numbers of visitors flocked to Portsmouth by railway to witness the spectacle and the steamers took full advantage of the demand.

Prince sailed from Weymouth at noon on Tuesday 22nd April and remained at Cowes overnight, before proceeding to Spithead to watch the Royal Yacht steam slowly up and down the lines of anchored warships, returning to Weymouth later the same evening. The fare was 1 guinea and passenger numbers were limited to a maximum of eighty.

During August, *Prince*'s earnings benefited from another visit of the Royal Yacht, bringing Prince Albert on one of his increasingly frequent visits to the breakwater works and, in September, great excitement was caused by the arrival of the large new, first-rate man-of-war *HMS Wellington*. This huge ship created a sensation amongst the sightseeing public, who flocked on board the steamers in order to view her at close quarters. On one afternoon alone, *Prince* and *Princess* carried more than 500 passengers on board to view the warship and, since she remained in the Roads for almost a fortnight, the receipts of the steamers soared.

At Bournemouth, the proposed jetty was finally completed in time for the 1856 season. The eventual design was a wooden structure fitted with tramway rails on its deck, along which a retractable landing stage about 100 feet in length could be drawn out to sea. Although damaged by a gale on 20th August, the jetty was quickly repaired and remained in use until a replacement pier was constructed in 1861. Whilst *Prince* must have visited the jetty occasionally from Weymouth, it would appear that *Contractor*, which was already spending a greater portion of each week at Poole, sought to establish a more regular service between Poole, Bournemouth and Swanage alongside her regular sailings from Poole to Weymouth. Since *Contractor* could clearly not be in two places at once, Philip Dodson decided to seek a second vessel to maintain his presence on the

PRINTED AT ARCHER'S ROYAL LIBRARY, WEYMOUTH.

Portland ferry service and excursions out of Weymouth.

The ship he settled upon was a small, 72 foot by 12 feet 6 inches by 5 feet 8 inches wooden paddle steamer named *Ocean Bride*, which had been built at East Jarrow during 1844. A typical tug of her day she had a single mast, no figurehead or bowsprit,

PRINCE's timetable for Coronation Day, 30th June 1856. The anniversary of Queen Victoria's coronation in 1838 was marked as a public holiday throughout her reign.
WEYMOUTH MUSEUM

A panorama of Bournemouth in 1855, dominated by the Belle Vue Hotel in the centre and showing the still unfinished wooden jetty, which was finally completed and opened to steamers in the following year.
BOURNEMOUTH LIBRARY

weighed 29.25 tons gross (18.43 registered) and was powered by a single 18hp engine. There is some confusion about her exact description, as her various registration documents differ slightly, her previous Newcastle and Stockton details giving her marginally smaller dimensions and the name of *Ocean Pride*. Since all subsequent references to her at Weymouth clearly refer to her as *Ocean Bride*, it seems probable that the discrepancy was the result of a slip of a registrar's pen at some time during her early life. She was registered at Weymouth on 2nd October 1856 and entered service soon afterwards.

1857 was to prove a pivotal year in the history of both Weymouth and its steamer services. On 20th January, with remarkably little ceremony or celebration, the first train left the newly-completed Weymouth railway station and ran to Yeovil and back. The town suddenly became accessible by the Great Western Railway's line via Yeovil from Bristol and London Paddington, and by way of the junction at Dorchester from Poole, Southampton and the capital. This meant, of course, that the resort was no longer the preserve of the wealthy alone but was available to day excursionists from a wide radius. Whit Saturday saw the arrival of over 500 passengers in a train from London but this was completely eclipsed two days later, when a train of nineteen carriages drawn by two locomotives came from Bristol and Bath with twelve hundred passengers, many of whom flocked on board *Prince* and *Ocean Bride* for a cruise in the bay or a visit to Portland. When the train, which was the largest to have visited Weymouth so far, departed in the evening, an extra engine had been added to assist it up the incline towards Dorchester and hundreds of local people

thronged the terminus and the line to witness this novel sight.

Other excursion trains followed on a regular basis and on Coronation Day, 29nd June, the local press commented that '*the influx of strangers was enormous and unless Weymouth had the capability attributed to a carpet-bag – that of never being full – elbow room might have been a scarce commodity.*' At a stroke, the resort had been democratised and the pleasure steamers' potential market had expanded beyond all recognition. In the circumstances, it is hardly surprising that the Channel Islands steamers *Aquila*, *Cygnus* and *Express* quickly began to issue excursion tickets to the islands and also to trespass into Cosens' and Dodson's traditional territory, by offering coastal cruises whenever the opportunity arose.

Competition was fierce and Cosens must have felt some small satisfaction when, on 15th July, *Cygnus* suffered a boiler failure whilst en route from Jersey and had to be rescued by *Prince*. On 13th June, *Prince* had visited Brownsea Island again, this time to allow passengers to visit the castle and the 'paradise' created on the island by its owner Colonel Waugh, prior to its sale. Unfortunately, a brisk easterly wind and rough sea made the passage uncomfortable but the 50 or so passengers who were brave enough to set sail were amply compensated for '*the up and down experiences of life on the ocean wave which had first to be encountered*'. While her passengers were enjoying the island, *Prince* did a good stoke of business conveying local passengers out from Poole Quay, where her elegant proportions presented a considerable contrast to the appearance and demeanour of the two steamers then doing temporary service at the port. Back at Weymouth, Cosens' situation had been rendered more difficult by J.T. Leather's decision to dispose of *Princess* at the beginning of the 1857 season. On 10th April, she was sold to the Devon & Cornwall Tamar Steam Packet Co, who put her to work on river and sea cruises from Plymouth, where she remained until 1882 when she was finally broken up. With *Princess* unavailable to bolster the Portland service and *Contractor* away at Poole, *Prince* and *Ocean Bride* were left to battle it out with their familiar mix of local cruises to Lulworth, Portland and elsewhere, together with longer day trips to points eastwards and westwards.

On 2nd July, the *Dorset County Chronicle* carried the enigmatic statement that '*The* Contractor *steamer, Capt Block, late of this port, the boilers of which vessel burst while at Portsmouth a short while ago, has been purchased by a fresh company and will soon be put in complete repair.*' During the following week, a Poole report added that '*Another steamer, the* Ursa Major, *has been put on to this station to take the place of the* Contractor *and plies between the same ports as the* Contractor *did last season.*' We know that on 22nd September, *Ursa Major*, with Case's Corporation Band on board, made an excursion from Poole to Bournemouth and Swanage, and on a number of other occasions came to Weymouth, thus confirming the nature of *Contractor*'s previous employment at Poole.

No further mention is made of the ship either at Weymouth or Poole until October 1857, when the Weymouth press announced that '*our local steam squadron has recently received an addition in the* Contractor, *which has been thoroughly refitted and is now making the passage to and from Portland, besides daily excursions to various interesting localities in the*

neighbourhood.' It remains obscure whether the 'fresh company' referred to was an error and Dodson refitted the ship at his own expense or whether, more probably, she had been sold directly or indirectly to Cosens & Drew. What is certain is that, by October, she was running again at Weymouth and on 24th April 1858, the ownership of both *Contractor* and *Ocean Bride* was formally transferred to Joseph Cosens. Philip Dodson withdrew from steamer ownership to concentrate on his contracting work and, with seven years of competition at an end, Cosens & Drew found themselves in possession of three vessels and with complete control of the local trade.

Cosens' harmonious relationship with John Towlerton Leather brought one further advantage at the end of the 1857 season, when it was decided to fit a new boiler to *Prince*. Having been ordered from Penn's works, it duly arrived at Weymouth via the GWR in late September and was moved onwards to Portland ready to be lifted into the steamer. The boiler's size and unfamiliar construction excited some curiosity on the Island, where various guesses were hazarded as to its use and possible destination. According to the local press, '*one wiseacre set down the phenomenon as a musical instrument, probably mistaking its tubes for organ pipes. Another, with more practical ideas, considered his friend wide of the mark and with an air of triumph and conviction pronounced it to be an incubator for hatching chickens, imported with a view to increase the supply of poultry for the Weymouth market!*' Once the boiler arrived at the breakwater works, Leather's heavy lifting equipment made such light work of the operation that *Prince*'s old boiler was removed, the new one dropped in and steam raised within the remarkably short time of ten hours.

Brownsea Island in Poole Harbour, which was the destination for occasional excursions by the Weymouth steamers. The castle itself began as a Henry VIII blockhouse, designed to protect the entrance to Poole Harbour, but was repeatedly added to over the years. On her visits, PRINCE would have berthed at the Family Pier of 1852, which can be seen on the extreme left, and from which a covered walk led between two octagonal towers to the castle beyond.
NEWMAN

An historic photograph, showing Brunel's GREAT EASTERN at anchor in Portland Roads. The foremost of her five funnels is clearly missing, so the photograph must have been taken during September 1859, while the damage caused by the tragic explosion on board during her maiden journey from the River Thames was being repaired. GREAT EASTERN's visit and enforced length of stay proved a highly lucrative few weeks for the local steamer trade. The paddle steamer in the centre of the picture has not yet been identified, this task made more difficult because of the number of different vessels which were in use carrying trippers on the highly popular excursions out to see the great Leviathan. All three of Cosens' vessels, PRINCE, CONTRACTOR and OCEAN BRIDE, and both of John Tizard's, BANNOCKBURN and PREMIER, were frequent visitors. In addition, a London & South Western Railway steamer chartered by the Mayor of Weymouth made the trip out once a week and vessels belonging to the Weymouth & Channel Islands Steam Packet Co also made regular excursions. However, it is certainly not one of the Cosens' ships and may well in fact be an Admiralty vessel. JOHN WILLOWS COLLECTION

CHAPTER 4
THE PARTNERSHIP EXPANDED
1858-1860

March 1858 provided two diversions from the humdrum routine of the winter service between Weymouth and Portland. On 3rd March, *Prince* was hired to convey 122 convicts from Portland Prison on board the transport ship *Lord Raglan*, which lay at anchor in the Roads. Sentenced to transportation, most of the convicts would never see England again and their short passage on board the pleasure steamer must have been a melancholy affair indeed.

On 13th March, the brig *Jane & Esther*, bound from London to Constantinople, went ashore near Bat's Head to the west of Lulworth, after her yards had become entangled whilst tacking ship. The local coastguard and fishermen lent immediate assistance and *Prince*, together with a steamer named *Don*, which was employed on the breakwater works, hurried to the scene. Arriving at midday, they made a strenuous but unsuccessful attempt to tow the brig off and, when it became apparent that there was no possibility of saving the vessel, *Prince* turned her attention to salvaging the cargo, which was valued at £20,000 and included large quantities of rice and sugar. In a race against time, *Prince* managed to save about 40 tons before the rising tide flooded the ship and rendered the rest of the cargo unusable.

For some years, a Royal Naval steam warship, *HMS Meander*, had acted as guard ship for the stretch of coast between Torquay and Bournemouth and, when not at sea, spent much of her time anchored in Portland Roads. In 1858, she was replaced by *HMS Blenheim*, which proved a great attraction when she anchored in Weymouth Bay for a week during May, before returning to Portland. On 24th May, a fete was held on board but the weather was so atrocious that the passage to and from the anchored vessel in open ship's boats was considered impractical and *Prince* was pressed into service instead. In torrential rain, only 40 passengers braved the trip but were well rewarded for their efforts by excellent refreshments and dancing to Beale's Quadrille Band in the ship's decorated tweendecks. *Prince* collected the party at midnight and the fete concluded with a fine display of blue lights and rockets.

The main excursion season started at the beginning of June, with the usual selection of local trips in addition to the regular Portland ferry service. Lulworth was visited regularly each Wednesday and occasionally on other days as well, and *HMS Blenheim*, which was frequently thrown open to the public, provided a popular new destination. Long distance trips were generally taken by *Prince* and included, on Thursday 24th

June, an unusual sailing from Weymouth to Totnes on the River Dart. In later years, it became common for steamers to visit Dartmouth, where the passengers transferred to one of the small river paddle steamers for the beautiful trip upstream but there are no other accounts of a Cosens' steamer undertaking the river trip all the way to Totnes itself. On the right tide, it would have been entirely possible for *Prince* to reach Totnes and swing in the river but it is equally likely that the newspaper account of the trip simply neglected to mention the transfer arrangements at Dartmouth.

On 26th July, the large paddle steamer *Brighton* arrived in Weymouth to open the Weymouth & Channel Island SP Co's new service to Cherbourg and *Contractor* was chartered to convey a party of shareholders and guests to meet the new ship at the harbour mouth, where they were put on board to enjoy a champagne reception and complimentary trip round the bay. Although relationships between the two companies appear to have been generally harmonious, with Capt Cosens occasionally advising on the choice of new ships and other technical matters, slight tensions must have arisen when the Channel Island company began to offer periodic coastal excursions in addition to their more frequent trips to Cherbourg and the islands.

Salvage work continued to provide an unpredictable but useful income. On 15th August, the sailing vessel *Eric Baker* was run down by the Prussian ship *Juno* twenty miles south west of Portland and was so badly damaged that her crew abandoned ship and were brought into Weymouth the following morning. Unbeknown to them, however, the buoyancy of their ship's cargo of

A charming model of PRINCE which was, for many years, on display in Cosens' head office in Weymouth. In 1969, during the demolition of the company's old workshops on Weymouth Backwater, the model was discovered in a badly damaged state and restored by Mr Alf Pover, Chief Engineer of the company's last paddle steamer EMBASSY. ALF POVER

Weymouth's new Pile Pier, completed in 1859. The steamer entering the harbour bears no resemblance to any known vessel of the period. NEWMAN

PRINCE, well-laden with passengers, about to depart on an excursion from Weymouth. An odd feature is the ship's funnel, which appears to be painted in a light colour with a black top. Since Cosens' standard funnel colour until 1901 was an austere black, it must be assumed that this picture was taken when the company was undertaking an unrecorded experiment with alternative liveries. Note the bathing machines in the background. AUTHOR'S COLLECTION

timber had prevented her from sinking. Discovered drifting in a waterlogged state by a Cowes pilot boat, she was towed into Weymouth by *Contractor*, resulting in a handsome salvage award to both Cosens and the pilots. Three months later, on 2nd November, the brig *Eliza Robson*, bound from Sunderland to El Ferrol, was beating to and fro in Weymouth Bay while her master had gone ashore by boat to purchase provisions, when she missed stays and was driven onto the beach directly in front of the Royal Hotel. Fortunately, she sustained little damage and *Prince*, which happened to be nearby, quickly succeeded in towing her off.

Behind the scenes, there were also some very significant developments in the ownership of the company. Whether to ease the financial pressures caused by the purchase of Dodson's ships, or with an eye to future expansion, Cosens & Drew decided to extend their partnership. In September 1858, nine shares in each of the ships were sold to Francis Williams of Weymouth and three in each ship to William Cosens. At the same time, Joseph Cosens sold twenty shares in both *Contractor* and *Ocean Bride* to Joseph Drew. Four months later, in January 1859, a Weymouth master mariner named John Gibbs

purchased five shares in each of the vessels from Joseph Cosens, bringing the total number of partners to five. Although Joseph's overall shareholding was significantly reduced, he and Drew were still the majority shareholders and the distribution of the 64 shares in each of the three ships stood as follows: Joseph Cosens 27, Joseph Drew 20, William Cosens 3, Francis Williams 9 and John Gibbs 5.

Although this redistribution of shares had no outward effect whatsoever on the operation of the Weymouth steamers during the season ahead, 1859 was to prove a highly significant year in a number of other ways. New construction seemed to be the order of the day, for at Bournemouth the first piles of a new 1,000 foot wooden pier were driven during July; at Swanage the laying of the foundation stone of a pier was marked by great festivities on 5th September; and at Weymouth the new Pile Pier was completed. This wooden structure was an extension of the 1840 'marine walk' on the northern side of the harbour, its seaward end curving elegantly towards the seafront and terminating in a circular pier head, which bore a small pavilion. Several steamer berths were provided and, from the date of its completion, the new Pile Pier became the principal departure point for Cosens' steamers. On the opposite side of the harbour, work commenced on constructing a major fortification on the Nothe Headland and, early in the spring, the laying of a marine telegraph cable between Weymouth and the Channel Islands was completed. In London, Brunel's leviathan steamship *Great Eastern*, whose launch and completion had been delayed by a disastrous series of technical and financial problems, was finally nearing completion and it was announced that her maiden voyage to the USA would depart from Portland, which would then become her British base. In the event, the fact that Portland Breakwater was still incomplete led to Holyhead being chosen instead but the announcement that the great ship's trial trip from the Thames would terminate at Portland led to a mounting sense of anticipation

amongst the populace of South Dorset and some interesting developments in the steamboat trade.

Communications with the Channel Islands via the new submarine cable were suddenly broken at the end of April and electrical testing indicated that this was due to a break in the cable about four miles from Portland Bill. Unfavourable weather conditions prevented anything being done about the problem until the middle of May, when Joseph Cosens in *Prince* successfully lifted the shore end of the cable and brought it into Weymouth, where a team of men were set to work on the Ballast Wharf replacing the damaged section. Using a grappling iron on the end of a long rope, *Prince* was also extremely fortunate to locate and buoy the other end of the broken cable at the first attempt and, within a few days, had re-laid the shore end and carried a team of cable engineers out to sea to splice the two portions together once again. This was not the end of the cable's troubles for, in November 1859, it broke for a second time and was repaired by a custom-built cable ship, *Monarch*. In March 1860, it fractured again, this time about three miles from Jersey, and *Contractor* was chartered from the morning of 9th March to search for the lost ends. The shore end was duly grappled and lifted, the damaged portion cut out and the sound end buoyed. The seaward end was located several miles towards Guernsey and, after a sufficient length of new cable had been spliced in, *Contractor* set off to relocate the buoy and effect a connection. Unfortunately, as darkness and deteriorating sea conditions made it impossible to do so, the seaward end too was buoyed and *Contractor* put into Jersey late that evening to seek shelter. It was some days before sea conditions moderated enough for her to resume her work and it was not until the following week that she arrived back in Weymouth. When one considers that each mile of

submarine cable weighed 54 tons and that neither *Prince* nor *Contractor* were fitted with any specialised lifting gear, their brief interludes as cable ships seem quite remarkable, and must have called for consummate seamanship and navigation on the part of their masters and crew.

The smallest member of the fleet, *Ocean Bride*, was frequently used, as *Princess* had been before her, for towage and contracting work in connection with the works on the breakwater and Nothe Fort. On 16th May, she was towing a barge heavily laden with concrete from Portland to Weymouth when it quickly became apparent that the seas were too heavy for safety. As the steamer turned to return to the shelter of Portland, the barge shipped a sea and went down stern first drawing her elderly helmsman, John Vile, with her. His son, who happened to be in the bows of the barge, was saved by a boat launched from *Ocean Bride* but the father was drowned.

The summer season followed its usual pattern. On Whit Monday, numerous excursion trains arrived at Weymouth station and all of the steamers were filled to capacity. The annual Coronation Day festivities during June were spoiled by torrential rain but, during July, a period of excessive heat more than made up for the lost trade. Passengers flocked on board the steamers to escape the oppressive atmosphere ashore and it was reported that '*sea breezes and ices are the only luxuries worth living for in the superlatively hot weather.*' The steamers were given an additional boost on 25th July, when Prince Albert, accompanied by Prince Alfred and Prince Arthur arrived on board the Royal Yacht to inspect progress on the breakwater works.

The Channel Fleet which, as the breakwater progressed, had been using Portland more and more regularly as an anchorage, was at anchor in Weymouth Bay throughout the heat wave. The

The hub of the breakwater works during the late 1850s. The inner breakwater has been completed and a temporary railway viaduct built across the entrance to the harbour to enable work on the detached, outer breakwater to continue. On the extreme right is the office of the Engineer in Chief, while the large building with tipping facilities was a coal store known to this day as 'Monkey Island'. Two warships lie at anchor, while one of the small steamers used in connection with the works, possibly OCEAN BRIDE or PRINCESS, makes its way towards Portland.
WEYMOUTH LIBRARY

crews of the thirteen warships, anchored so near the shore in such weather, became increasingly discontented and 300 matelots on board *HMS Hero* declared that if they were not granted shore leave they would take it without permission. Half of the fleet, including *Hero*, was promptly dispatched to Spithead and the crews of the remaining vessels were diplomatically granted shore leave.

It was almost inevitable that with so many sailors ashore enjoying the pleasures of Weymouth's public houses, one or two unfortunate incidents would occur. On the evening of Saturday 30th July, a party of sailors who had broken leave from *HMS Aboukir* were being conveyed back to their ship on board *Contractor* when one of them '*inspired by the spirit of fun, or beer, or bravado, or fear of punishment, or the whole combined*' sprang overboard into the harbour and struck out for the other side. Having landed safely and made his way along the Ballast Wharf to the end of the pier, he realised that he was likely to be captured by those in pursuit, so threw himself back into the water and made for 'Jack in the Basket', the light beacon at the mouth of the harbour. Finally exhausted, he clung to the framework of the beacon until taken off by a coastguard boat which returned him to his ship. A large crowd gathered to enjoy his aquatic exploits but the reaction of his commanding officer must be left to the imagination!

As August drew to a close, excitement began to mount at the prospect of the arrival of *Great Eastern* in early September. The Admiralty moved the large coal hulk *Pitt* from Portsmouth to Portland, chiefly to coal the Channel Fleet but also with an eye to supplying the capacious bunkers of Brunel's enormous ship. *Pitt* was the first hulk to be moored in the Roads and was the precursor of a thriving bunkering trade in which Cosens, amongst others, were to become closely involved. The news that *Great Eastern* would be thrown open to the public led to a flurry of activity, with the announcement of GWR marine excursions from the Channel Islands and the provision of numerous excursion trains to cope with the expected influx of visitors.

Almost certainly, it was the prospect of the potential profits to be made during *Great Eastern*'s visit which persuaded a Weymouth solicitor, John Tizard, to enter into direct competition with the Cosens' steamers. This cannot have been the sole reason, for such a fleeting event would have been an unsound basis upon which to build a business, and he must have been confident that the Portland and excursion trades offered sufficient work for two companies. It may have been that Tizard had personal reasons for wishing to oppose Joseph Cosens and his partners, or even that the reverse was true and that his entry into the trade was the result of some unofficial agreement between the two camps.

For the present, his precise reasoning remains obscure but whatever his motives the fact remains that Tizard set about purchasing two steamers for service at Weymouth. The first, which was registered at the port on 24th August 1859, was *Bannockburn*, a small wooden steamer which had been built by E. Oliver of South Shields in 1847, for a local owner named T. Brewis. She underwent some alterations during 1851 and, by the time she arrived in Weymouth, measured 69 feet 6 inches by 16 feet by 8 feet 4 inches, with a tonnage of 53.21 gross, 10.55 registered. She was sloop rigged, had a round stern without galleries, a 'billet head' bow and was clench or clinker built on wooden frames. Her engine room was 31 feet in length and her single engine had an estimated horse power of 28.

The second vessel, which was likely to prove a far more serious threat to Cosens, was an ex-Clyde steamer named *Premier*. Built in 1846 at William Denny & Co's famous Dumbarton shipyard at a cost of £3,600, she spent the first six years of her life on the Dumbarton Steam Boat Company's regular service between that town and Glasgow. In 1847, she was one of a flotilla of steamers which escorted the Royal Squadron up the Clyde on the occasion of Queen Victoria's visit to Greenock. She had an iron hull, measured 140 feet 2 inches by 17 feet by 6 feet 5 inches and had a tonnage of 98.4 gross, 62 registered. Her vertical boiler powered a 65 horse power steeple engine, which gave her a service speed of about 11 knots.

Bannockburn entered service immediately after her arrival at Weymouth and appears to have been chiefly employed on the Portland service and short trips in the bay. *Premier*'s delivery was delayed and she did not arrive from Glasgow until 24th September, twelve days after the arrival of *Great Eastern*. This must have been a source of great frustration to Tizard, who was forced to look on helplessly while the other local steamers made considerable profits from the great ship's presence in the Roads.

After repeated delays occasioned by assorted difficulties in completing the complex task of fitting out and provisioning the vast ship, *Great Eastern* finally made her departure from London on Wednesday 7th September 1859. On the first day, she was towed down the Thames as far as Purfleet, where she lay for the night before proceeding during the following morning to anchor near the Nore Light. Each successive edition of the Weymouth newspapers carried detailed accounts of her latest movements and when it was announced that she would leave the Nore for Weymouth at 7am on Friday 9th September, the *Southern Times* declared '*Let us then be agape and staring for the advent of our gigantic visitor.*'

The morning of Saturday 10th September dawned bright and clear, with '*more than the usual transparency of the atmosphere*', affording the groups of sightseers who had gathered with their telescopes a clear view of the distant St. Albans Head, round which *Great Eastern* appeared at 8am. A large number of vessels, including *Edgar*, *Neptune*, *Blenheim*, *Imperieuse* and *Biter* of the Channel Fleet, the Admiralty Yacht *Osborne*, with the Duke of Somerset and the Lords of the Admiralty on board, and *Vivid* bearing the Coast Defence Commissioners, were assembled in the Roads, their rigging crowded with seamen anxious to catch a glimpse of the '*floating monster*'. The local steamers, of course, advertised trips to view the arrival and *Prince* sailed from Weymouth at 9.30am. Steaming eastwards, she met *Great Eastern* sailing '*gracefully and easily like the embodiment of some gigantic supernatural ideal*' down the '*radiant pathway*' of the rising sun and quickly turned to steam '*like a diminutive minnow*' alongside. Her passengers, in a frenzy of excitement, cheered and waved but were puzzled when their hearty greetings were not returned by those on board.

As soon as the great ship came to anchor in Portland Roads, the reason for this apparent lack of courtesy became clear. The observant amongst the onlookers had already spotted that the foremost of the ship's five funnels was missing from its rightful place and was, instead, lying lashed to the deck. News quickly spread that while *Great Eastern* was passing down Channel off Hastings on the previous day, an enormous explosion had taken place which tore up the deck, threw the funnel into the air and did tremendous damage to the gilt and mirrored splendour of the ship's grand saloon. A number of firemen and stokers had been killed by the explosion or scalded to death, and another crew member was so badly burned that he jumped overboard and was crushed by the revolving paddle wheel. Several others were severely injured and were immediately put ashore to undergo treatment in Weymouth Infirmary. Needless to say, a pall of gloom was cast over what should have been a happy and auspicious occasion.

A coroner's inquest was convened at Weymouth Town Hall on the following Monday to look into the causes of the disaster. Numerous witnesses were examined, the jury visited the ship to see for themselves the extent of the damage and the combination of circumstances leading to the accident rapidly became clear. Each of *Great Eastern*'s funnels was surrounded by a water jacket casing, which served the dual purpose of pre-heating feed water before it entered the boilers and keeping the funnels cool at the point where they passed through the saloons. Each jacket was fitted with a stand pipe which rose to the top of the funnel and, being open at the top, acted as a safety valve for the water heater. When the machinery was being tested, each jacket had been subjected to a hydraulic pressure test and, in order for this to take place, temporary stopcocks had been fitted to the standpipes. Unfortunately, clear instructions to remove the cocks after testing had been overlooked and, worse still, in the case of the two forward funnels, someone had closed them. The chain of events came to its fatal conclusion when, off Hastings, the engineer on watch experienced some difficulties with the boiler feed water and decided to bypass the water heaters altogether. Sealed off at both ends and subjected to the heat of the funnels, the pressure quickly built up until the forward jacket exploded. Fortunately the engineer immediately realised the cause and

sent a man to open the remaining stop-cock. Had he not done so a second explosion would have followed, decimating the crowds of passengers and crew who had gathered around the site of the blast.

Even while the inquest was proceeding, work on repairs got under way. John Scott Russell, the vessel's builder, sent men and materials from London, and a large number of carpenters and general labourers were employed locally to assist with the work. Because the ship was lying at anchor, all the labourers and materials had to be ferried to and from the shore and it would appear that both Cosens and Tizard were quick to make their steamers available and made a tidy profit from the great ship's misfortunes. The damaged funnel was brought ashore and an intact section, having been acquired by the Weymouth Waterworks Company, was taken by horse-drawn cart to Sutton Poyntz, where it was installed as an overflow spillway in the waterworks intake pond. It survives to this day in remarkably good condition, on display in Bristol. New plates were rolled in London and hoisted on board, where riveters fashioned them into a replacement funnel. A number of plates, tubes and stays in the forward boiler had to be replaced, and numerous deck beams and bulkheads repaired. Carpenters, fitters and decorators swarmed through the interior of the ship and gradually the damaged areas began to take on something of their former glory.

Within a day of her arrival, and notwithstanding the complex and noisy nature of the repairs required, *Great Eastern* was thrown open to the public. The ship's directors, desperate at another expensive delay, realised that charging members of the public to visit the ship would provide a small but useful income and embraced the scheme with enthusiasm. The entry charge on the first day was 5s but this was found to be too high and was reduced to 2s 6d on all subsequent days. Excursion trains converged on Weymouth from all parts of the county and there

PREMIER seen amongst the fleet of vessels greeting Queen Victoria on her visit to the Clyde in 1847. Left to right, the vessels are, the Royal Yacht FAIRY, THETIS, SOVEREIGN, PREMIER and CRAIGNISH CASTLE. AUTHOR'S COLLECTION

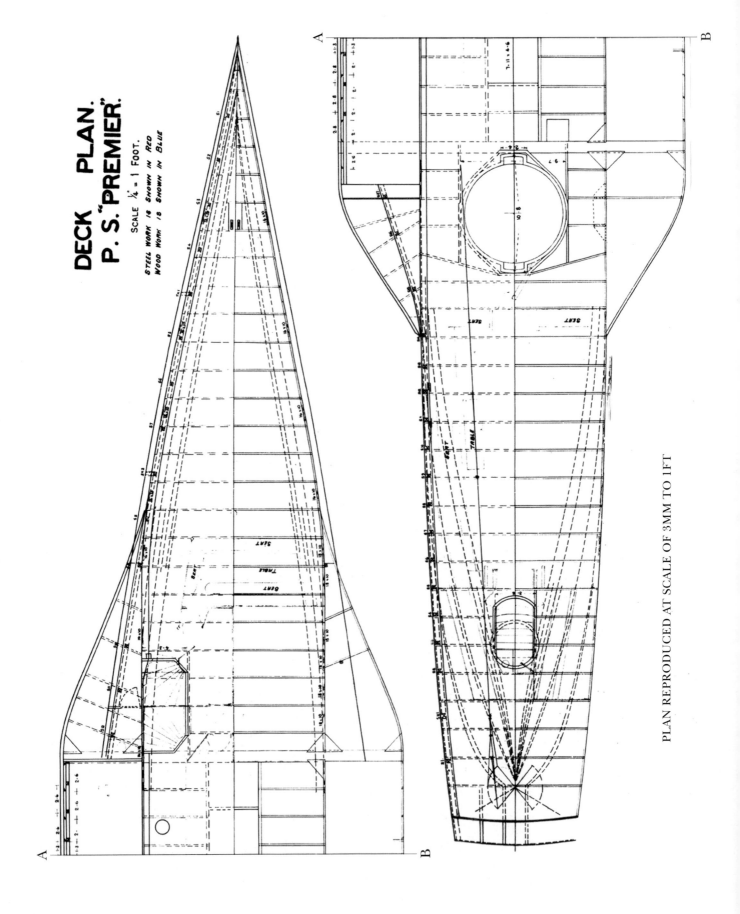

DECK PLAN.
P. S. "PREMIER."

SCALE ¼ = 1 FOOT.

STEEL WORK IS SHOWN IN RED
WOOD WORK IS SHOWN IN BLUE

PLAN REPRODUCED AT SCALE OF 3MM TO 1FT

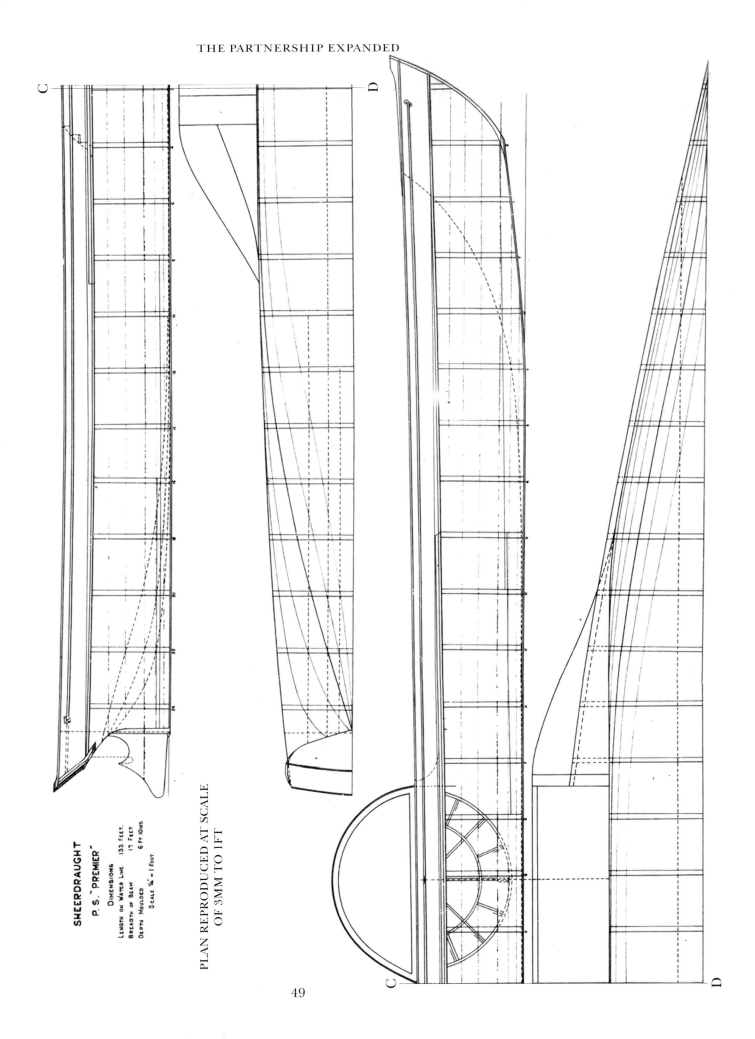

SHEERDRAUGHT
P. S. "PREMIER"

DIMENSIONS

LENGTH ON WATER LINE   133 FEET.
BREADTH OF BEAM   17 FEET
DEPTH MOULDED   6 FT IONS

SCALE ¼ = 1 FOOT

PLAN REPRODUCED AT SCALE
OF 3MM TO 1FT

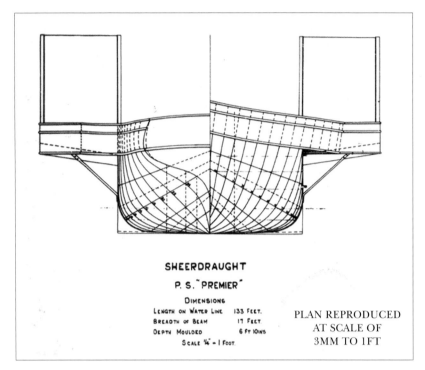

SHEERDRAUGHT

P. S. "PREMIER"

DIMENSIONS

LENGTH ON WATER LINE 133 FEET.
BREADTH OF BEAM 17 FEET.
DEPTH MOULDED 6 FT 10INS

SCALE ¼" = 1 FOOT.

PLAN REPRODUCED
AT SCALE OF
3MM TO 1FT

ABOVE & PREVIOUS TWO PAGES: Linen tracings, dated 1925, of Denny Brothers' original plans for PREMIER. Building commenced on 21st February 1846 and the yard made a profit of £223 19s 9d on the contract price of £3,600.
NATIONAL MARITIME MUSEUM

were reports of hundreds of prospective passengers being left behind at stations along the line. During the first ten days of opening, 18,568 paying members of the public visited the ship. A huge proportion were carried to and fro on board Cosens' *Prince*, *Contractor* and *Ocean Bride*, Tizard's *Bannockburn* and presumably, following her arrival on 24th September, by the newcomer *Premier*. The local press reported that all the steamers were '*inconveniently crowded … but reaping a rich harvest.*' They did not have the trade completely to themselves however, for Philip Dodson, the former Weymouth steamboat proprietor and by now the Mayor of Weymouth and a director of *Great Eastern*, chartered one of the London & South Western Railway's steamers for a day each week. The local Weymouth & Channel Islands SP Co's steamers also advertised excursions from Guernsey and Jersey, and the Poole steamer *Ursa Major* came along to Weymouth on a number of occasions. On Friday 30th September, a public concert was held on board the great ship with soloists accompanied by the Great Eastern Band.

The scene in Portland Roads during the few weeks of *Great Eastern*'s stay must have been animated indeed. In addition to the comings and goings of thousands of visitors on board the local and visiting steamers, there was a constant procession of contractor's barges and workmen. On top of the din of riveting and other construction work, there would have been the spectacle and filth of some 8,000 tons of coal being hoisted out of the hulk *Pitt* and the other colliers alongside, and tipped into the ship's cavernous bunkers. In the confusion, occasional accidents did happen, and towards the end of the month, the L&SWR steamer, on one of her charter sailings from Weymouth, collided with a hulk whilst

coming alongside and tore off one of her paddle boxes. One wonders what a modern health and safety inspector would have had to say about the situation!

With repairs nearing completion, it was announced that *Great Eastern* would depart from Portland on 8th October, on a trial trip to Holyhead without passengers. On the day before she sailed, a presentation was made to Capt R. Fowler of the *Bannockburn* of a handsome rosewood writing-desk richly ornamented with brass. It bore the inscription '*Presented to Capt Fowler by the officers of the Great Eastern Steamship, for his kindness and attention to them whilst lying in Portland Harbour, Oct 7th, 1859*', indicating perhaps that Tizard had been more successful than Cosens at creating a close and profitable relationship between his steamers and the needs of the great ship. With the departure of *Great Eastern* at 4pm the following day, a momentous and lucrative interlude in the history of Weymouth drew to a close and the town and its steamers returned to their normal rhythm of trade.

The autumn of 1859 was characterised by a series of gales and shipping casualties. On 13th October, the collier brig *Templar* of Hartlepool went ashore on the Kimmeridge Ledges and, although she was fortunate enough to float off on the rising tide, was discovered to be making water at an alarming rate. Her master ran for Portland, where he put her aground and sailors from *HMS Blenheim* were sent to assist with pumping. On the next tide, she was taken in tow by *Contractor*, which intentionally grounded her at high water on the sand bar at the entrance to Weymouth Harbour. Here she was lightened of some of her cargo, before moving up harbour to complete discharge and undergo repairs.

On 26th October, a large steamship named *James Dixon* was spotted at anchor and flying distress signals about half a mile south west of Portland Bill. Her cargo had shifted, she had a heavy list to starboard and, with the wind blowing strongly from the WNW, it was clear that she was in imminent danger of foundering or driving ashore. News was sent to Weymouth, where both the Channel Islands steamer *Cygnus* and the *Contractor* were lying. *Cygnus* was in the middle of loading cargo but immediately put to sea and reached the casualty at about 3pm. *Contractor* had insufficient coal on board to sail at once but, as soon as she had bunkered, followed *Cygnus* to sea, arriving off the Bill at about the same time. Both ships manoeuvred close to *James Dixon*, which was rolling very heavily and had dragged her anchors about a mile closer to the treacherous Portland Race, and put heaving lines on board. In the event, the casualty's crew chose to haul in the tow rope from *Cygnus*, which successfully towed her into the safety of Portland Roads. Both rescue ships had placed themselves at considerable risk but, in the nature of all salvage work, on this occasion the Cosens' vessel returned empty-handed while *Cygnus* received a large salvage award.

At the beginning of November, Dorset was struck by a particularly violent gale, and heavy seas tore a 200 foot gap in the breakwater staging and caused other serious damage to the works. A barque narrowly avoided being driven onto the breakwater, numerous boats were torn from their moorings and the Channel Fleet was forced to ride out the storm at sea. Great concerns were expressed for the safety of the newly-established Shambles lightship, which had only been on station off the east coast of Portland since September. In the event, she rode the gale well and, on 3rd November, *Prince* was able get alongside to relieve her crew after their month's duty.

A few days later, the large American sailing ship *St. Nicholas*, which had been in distress in the Channel, was towed into Portland and detained by the Admiralty pending settlement of a £7,000 salvage claim. While negotiations proceeded, her passengers were released and on 15th November, *American Eagle* arrived to convey them onwards to their destination. *Prince* was engaged to transfer the passengers and their baggage from one ship to the other.

As the year 1859 drew to a close, two significant developments took place. Firstly, Weymouth Corporation decided that, rather than collect the harbour and wharfage dues themselves, they would put them up for public auction. Joseph Cosens made a successful bid, obtaining the year's rights for £1,210, a mere £10 above the reserve price. The venture represented a large investment but Capt Cosens must have calculated that the combination of income from vessels using the harbour, combined with the amount he would save on dues for his own fleet, would leave him with a useful profit.

The second development was of a far more profound nature. Behind the scenes, discussions had been underway with John Tizard, owner of the rival vessels *Bannockburn* and *Premier*, regarding the amalgamation of the two fleets. It remains obscure whether Tizard's brief venture into steamer ownership represented a genuine attempt to compete with Cosens or whether, from the very beginning, there was an understanding between the two parties. Tizard was a solicitor, with no personal or practical knowledge of steamer operation, so it is conceivable that his two purchases were a covert way of injecting additional capital into the Cosens partnership.

Whatever the true circumstances, on 3rd January 1860, it was announced that '*a fusion has been effected between the two steam companies running between Weymouth and Portland … and that the whole of the steamers will be retained so that the public will be accommodated equally as well as heretofore.*' Two additional gentlemen – Edward Mace and John Piers Reynolds, both of whom were Weymouth master mariners and the latter master of *Premier* – were brought into the partnership and the overall ownership of shares adjusted by a series of transfers to give the eight partners the same stake in four of the five steamers. The new distribution was: Joseph

Cosens 16, Joseph Drew 14, John Tizard 10, Francis Williams 10, Edward Mace 5, John Gibbs 4, John Reynolds 3 and William Cosens 2. The only exception was in the ownership of *Contractor* where, for some reason, Joseph Cosens held 21 shares and Drew only 9.

Thus, when the annual dinner for employees took place in one of the company's quayside stores on the evening before the share transfers were announced, the proprietors knew that they had more than usual to celebrate. The new partnership included six experienced master mariners, a solicitor and a gentleman confectioner-cum-newspaper proprietor. All were keenly entrepreneurial, relatively wealthy and now had a combined fleet of five paddle steamers at their disposal, ready to develop the ferry, excursion, salvage and contracting trade from Weymouth. The room had been gaily decorated with Christmas evergreens, flowers and '*devices in gas*' and, after the '*good old-fashioned cheer of roast beef and plum pudding had gladdened the hearts of all*' and the usual loyal toasts had been given, Joseph Cosens addressed his men, thanking them for their loyalty and co-operation during the challenging year that had passed. With the formalities over, the men were joined by their wives and '*dancing to the enlivening strains of Jones' Band was kept up for many hours.*'

An engraving of GREAT EASTERN *with her fifth funnel restored, presumably after repairs had been completed. The local steamers are hard at work carrying thousands of visitors to and from the ship, as well as assisting with the transport of men and materials required for the repairs.*
STEWART MORRIS
COLLECTION

The section of GREAT EASTERN's *funnel in use as a strainer at Sutton Poyntz pumping station during the 1970s. The reservoir was filled in during the autumn of 2003 and the funnel removed from the outlet chamber for conservation. In 2005, it was moved to Bristol for display alongside Brunel's surviving ocean liner, SS* GREAT BRITAIN.
R. BRUCE GEORGE

Contractor departing from Castletown Pier, Portland, sometime prior to 1863. The wooden passenger pier extended at an angle from the western side of Castletown Quay, which was used for transshipping stone brought from the quarries on the top of Portland by way of the steeply-inclined Merchants' Railway. Huge blocks of stone are to be seen stacked on the quay. The small pier-head passenger shelter can be glimpsed mid way between the masts of the two sailing ships. The wash from Contractor's paddle wheels indicates that her engines were designed to be disconnecting and could be run independently. Having first gone astern from the pier, her master has rung 'Full ahead' on his port engine to assist his turn to seawards, before engaging his starboard engine for the passage to Weymouth.

Dorset County Museum

CHAPTER 5

THE PORTLAND RAILWAY &
FLEET RATIONALISATION
1860-1865

The summer season of 1860 began on an inauspicious note for the expanded fleet, as a severe north westerly gale prevented any sailing from taking place over the Whitsun holiday period at the end of May and poor weather continued well into June, leading to a number of dramas at sea.

At the beginning of June, a boat from the coal hulk *Pitt* had her masts carried away as she was heading for Weymouth and was about to be driven into the surf on the north shore of the bay, when William Cosens took *Contractor* to sea and was able to tow her safely into port. Towards the end of the month, another small boat was rescued by Joseph Cosens in *Prince*, which was returning from an excursion to Portland Bill. While a party from a small private sailing vessel were enjoying a ramble ashore at Church Ope Cove, some small boys had taken their dinghy and gone for a row. The tide, however, was far too strong for them and the boat drifted rapidly towards The Race where she would undoubtedly have foundered but for the timely arrival of the paddle steamer.

By the end of the month, the excursion season had settled into its usual pattern, with *Prince* and *Premier* undertaking all of the long distance excursions and some of the Portland ferry crossings, while the smaller, older units of the fleet, *Ocean Bride*, *Contractor* and *Bannockburn*, were occupied on a mixture of local trips, towage and contracting work. The familiar mixture of sailings was enlivened by occasional special events, such as the annual Royal Regatta or the

departure of the Channel Fleet on a cruise to Bantry Bay during August, when *Premier* took out a large party to '*witness the noble spectacle of eleven men-of-war proceeding down channel in full sail*'. During August, the frequent moonlight excursions were regarded as particularly fashionable affairs, the romantic atmosphere being heightened by the presence of a band which '*discoursed sweet music*' as the steamer made her circuit of the bay.

On 10th July, Philip Dodson, Cosens' former rival in the steamboat trade, was discovered dead in his bed. The shock felt in the town at the untimely demise of one so prominent in both local business and politics was magnified when the inquest jury announced that the cause of death was suicide. Close friends had testified that Dodson had been unusually depressed and complaining of feeling ill for several months and, although there was no evidence that his wide-ranging business interests were in difficulty, he had chosen to end his life with a dose of prussic acid. Sentiment, however, had little place in the world of commerce; by 9th November, Joseph Cosens had placed a notice in the local press informing the public that he had taken over the Burdon Coal Stores and other premises on Custom House Quay which were formerly occupied by Dodson, and that he would be carrying on the coal business as before. This appears to be Cosens first venture into the coal trade which, it should be remembered, was of vital importance in the 19th century. Coal was an almost universal fuel and came in many varieties – steam coal, kitcheners', bakers',

Weymouth Harbour from the Nothe. The large building to the left of the Town Bridge is Trinity Church, with Trinity Quay below it. To the right, Custom House Quay extends from the bridge past the tall bulk of Bank House (now the Edward Hotel) to the elegant terraces of Pultney and Devonshire buildings. Cosens' coal stores and later their Head Office and ice stores were located on Custom House Quay, just behind the most distant paddle steamer.
NEWMAN

first and second quality household, and many others. All of these arrived at Weymouth Quay in collier brigs from the north east coast or South Wales and were either auctioned straight from the hold, or sold to one of the many local coal merchants for resale around the district. Cosens' involvement in the trade was to develop steadily as the century progressed.

The winter of 1860-61 provided the usual crop of salvage jobs for the steamers. In December, a minor but serious incident took place when *Prince* was towing a Norwegian brig out of the harbour. A man called Richard Attwooll had been engaged to bring the pilot ashore in his boat, which was towing astern of the brig when it took a sheer, capsized and threw him into the water. At the cry of "*Man overboard!*", boats were immediately launched from *Contractor*, *Prince* and the Nothe, and the man was rescued, rushed ashore to a doctor and successfully resuscitated.

During January and February, a far more typical and lucrative sequence of incidents occurred, commencing on Sunday 20th January when the barque *Hardy* of Glasgow was found abandoned about half a mile from shore on the Kimmeridge Ledges. The local coastguard boarded the ship and, finding her deserted, sent word to Weymouth for tugs. *Prince*, a small steamer from Portland called *Hellan* and the Admiralty vessel *Rattler* set off with a number of lighters in tow and spent Monday recovering a good portion of the cargo and bringing it into Weymouth, where it was handed over to the receiver of wrecks. Work commenced again on the Tuesday morning but came to a halt when a

gentleman from Lloyds, the ship's insurers, arrived on the scene and claimed control. Unable to reach an agreement for the recovery of further cargo, the steamers and lighters returned to Weymouth until the Lloyds agent capitulated and work began again. A great deal of valuable cargo was recovered but *Hardy* herself became a total loss. It was later discovered that she had gone ashore in fog and her crew, having no idea of their whereabouts, immediately took to their boat and were later picked up in the Channel and landed at Southampton. Three weeks later, on 14th February, the schooner *Dorothy*, loaded with coal, ran ashore close to the wreck of *Hardy* but rescue attempts were unsuccessful and she too became a total loss.

A second rescue took place during a severe south westerly gale in mid February, when the Spanish brig *Thomas* was seen to be flying a flag of distress and dragging her anchors rapidly across Weymouth Bay towards the Ringstead Ledges. *Contractor* and *Hellan* immediately put to sea and their offer of a tow into Weymouth was readily accepted. The vessel was in a bad way, having carried away her main yard and several sails in West Bay and having sought the assistance of the skipper of the local fishing smack *Charlotte* to pilot her into the bay. *Thomas* was carrying a valuable cargo and as soon as she was moored in Weymouth, a writ was fixed to her mainmast on behalf of the salvors seeking a large salvage payment. In the event an out-of-court settlement was reached with *Contractor* receiving £620, *Hellan* £620 and the *Charlotte* £310. While such windfalls must have made

Construction of a wooden pier at Swanage commenced in September 1859 and two years later, in September 1861, it was officially opened to passenger trade. Although used principally for cargo-handling, the pier added greatly to the attraction of Swanage as a destination for excursion steamers. A 1d toll was charged for each passenger or item of luggage landed at the pier.
PHILIP BRANNON
ENGRAVING/COURTESY
SWANAGE MUSEUM

a welcome addition to the company's coffers, there were personal losses too. Amongst his other financial interests, John Tizard also owned a number of local trading vessels and during a terrific gale on the night of 8th February, one of these, the brig *Sprite*, struck the Longscar Rock near Hartlepool and foundered with the loss of all hands.

At the end of the month, a series of exceptional spring tides meant that, for several days at low water, the Weymouth to Portland steamers were unable to berth at either the Pile Pier or the jetty at Portland and were forced to land their passengers in boats, or berth at the Portland Breakwater.

During the winter months, all the steamers underwent their customary refits. *Premier* had her original vertical 'haystack' type boiler replaced with a new one of a more modern box design, constructed by John Penn & Sons of Greenwich. Together with *Prince*, she ran trials in the bay on the morning of 18th May and everything was found so satisfactory that, by midday, both ships were at anchor and dressed overall to await the arrival of the Queen's Own Yeomanry Cavalry, who were visiting the town for an eight day training exercise. This appears to have been as much a social as a military affair and their arrival was greeted by large crowds and by the flag-bedecked steamers '*blazing away their powder in a liberal manner.*' During the Whitsun holiday which followed, the steamers were well-patronised, with regular trips to Portland, Wednesday sailings to Lulworth and moonlight excursions all attracting large numbers of passengers, many of whom came by train from Bristol and Bath. As the highlight of their visit, the yeomanry put on a military review, which attracted particularly large crowds. The steamer *Sir Walter Raleigh* brought a party of excursionists from Torquay but unfortunately arrived after the spectacle was over.

The spring of 1861 was also marked by an acrimonious dispute with Weymouth Corporation over harbour and pier dues. Perhaps Joseph Cosens had made too great a profit for the Corporation's taste, for at the end of his year as leasee, the harbour dues were taken back into municipal hands and immediately increased. It was proposed that Cosens should pay £30 per annum each for the two steamers which worked all year round, and £2 10s per month for additional vessels. At the same time, it was decided that the Pile Pier tolls for passengers using the steamers should be doubled to 1d each way, forcing the return fare to Portland up from 7d to 9d and that charges should be made for passengers' personal baggage. Both Drew and Tizard used their position as members of the council to question why the Corporation seemed so set against the steamers which brought great benefits to the town while, at the same time, failing to collect any harbour dues at all from the local stone boats which happened to be owned by another member of the council. Little attempt was made to disguise vested interests and lively debate ensued! Cosens resisted all attempts to collect his dues and only agreed to abide by the

Bournemouth's new 1,000 foot pier was officially opened on 17th September 1861, when PRINCE *from Weymouth and* URSA MAJOR *from Poole were the first steamers to call. There was a tendency amongst Victorian artists producing engravings and illustrative work such as this to emphasise the vertical for dramatic effect, which in this view has lent Bournemouth a distinctly 'alpine' air!*
PHILIP BRANNON ENGRAVING/COURTESY SWANAGE MUSEUM

Weymouth Harbour in the mid-1860s, showing the Nothe Fort under construction and the Pile Pier of 1859.
WEYMOUTH MUSEUM

Corporation's ruling after legal action was threatened during May. Things were not improved when the Pile Pier toll collector, carrying out his allotted task a little too vigorously, insisted on charging an entry and exit toll on all the members of a military band who had been engaged to perform a concert on the pier. Outcry in the *Southern Times* (fuelled, no doubt, by Dr Drew, the proprietor) was joined in high season by the vociferous complaints of many of the thousands of visitors who arrived by excursion train and were furious to find the cost of their trip to Portland so steeply increased.

A source of confusion for later maritime historians arose on 25th March 1861, when a second vessel named *Contractor* was registered at Weymouth. This was a small 90 feet 3 inches by 17 feet 2 inches by 9 feet 4 inches, 86 ton wooden paddle steamer (ON 12596), purchased by John Towlerton Leather for use in connection with the breakwater works. Her 40hp engine was housed in an engine room 35 feet 4 inches in length, giving her a registered tonnage of 23. She had been built in 1857 at South Shields, where she had subsequently worked as a tug under the ownership of G. & J. Heads, W. Dodds and others. It is most unusual, if not unique, for two steamers of the same name to be registered simultaneously at the same port and one wonders why Leather was not required to change her name. She remained at Portland for some years, until transferred to Leather's next major contract for the construction of the Spithead Forts, during which she was stranded and broken up in Stokes Bay in January 1866.

The most significant event of the summer of 1861 was the opening of the new wooden pier at Bournemouth. The first pile had been driven on 25th July 1859 but construction had been delayed by storm damage, a series of disagreements between the designer, John Rennie, and the contractor, David Thornbury, and finally by the failure of the bank in which the Bournemouth Commissioners' funds were deposited. Eventually, however, the pier was completed and was opened with great ceremony by Sir George Gervis on Tuesday 17th September 1861. A '*public festival and general holiday*' was declared at Bournemouth, where the celebrations included a fair on the beach, a procession, gun salutes, a firework display, free teas in the Cranborne Gardens and, of course, the arrival of the first pleasure steamers. *Ursa Major* came from Poole and *Prince*, with 100 passengers on board, sailed from Weymouth at 10am.

The completion of the pier, which was 1,000 feet long, 15 feet wide and had a T-shaped head, made Bournemouth a far easier and more attractive destination for the Weymouth steamers and the frequency of their visits increased steadily thereafter. At Swanage, too, a timber pier had been constructed during 1859, chiefly with the export of stone in mind but which also provided a useful calling place for the steamers on their occasional visits. *Prince* and *Premier* continued to provide long-distance excursions as far as the Isle of Wight to the east and Torquay to the west. *Premier* visited the latter on 19th September, departing at 8.30am, arriving at 2pm and sailing again at 4pm. The day was not altogether calm and a newspaper reporter who was travelling on board noted that although '*the moon shone out in all her splendour and heightened the pleasure of the return voyage … the selfish aspiration that there is no place like home was indulged in by several as they neared the landing place at the Pile Pier at about half-past nine'*!

Ever since the railway had first reached Weymouth in January 1857, a number of proposals had been made for the construction of a branch to Portland, together with a tramway along the quayside from the station to the toll house at the Pile Pier. An enthusiastic proponent of the latter was Alderman J.A. Devenish, a member of the well-known local brewing family and a director of the Weymouth & Channel Islands Steam Packet Company. Realising that the future development of the company's trade to the islands would be largely dependent on the establishment of a direct link between ship and railway, he persuaded the promoters of the tramway to join forces with those of the Weymouth & Portland Railway to develop a joint scheme to their mutual benefit. The plans were announced at a meeting at the Royal Hotel, Weymouth, on 7th October 1861 and a deputation was sent to seek the assistance and co-operation of the Great Western Railway in carrying out the scheme.

The proposed railway was, of course, a complete anathema to the steamboat company, whose virtual monopoly of the Weymouth-Portland trade provided the bulk of their income. During November, a letter appeared in one of the local newspapers complaining bitterly about the interest shown by certain members of the Council in the railway scheme and reminding readers of the debt of £18,000 still owing on the harbour, the £12,700 recently spent on the Pile Pier and the £5,000 debt on the bridge. The anonymous writer expressed the view that the steamers were capable of carrying all the required traffic to and from the island and worried that they would suffer badly if the railway was built.

Councillor Joseph Drew, as a major shareholder in the steamboat company, had a very clear self-interest in the subject and found himself in a difficult position when the scheme was debated at a meeting of the Town Council on 30th December. Although Drew gave his wholehearted support to the construction of a harbour tramway, he argued that a railway to Portland would be *'a decided injury to the town'* which *'would greatly tend to injure the interests of the Pile Pier by taking passengers away from it.'* He feared that Portland might become a competitive commercial port to the detriment of Weymouth and very much regretted that both railways had been embodied in the same scheme. He proposed an amendment that *'the Council, as trustees of the harbour and Pile Pier, do take the necessary steps to oppose in Parliament any bill having for its object a railway from Weymouth to Portland'* but, pitted against four prominent councillors who were also directors of the Weymouth & Channel Islands Steam Packet Company, he was defeated by six votes to four.

With the support of Weymouth Council behind it and despite a lone, desperate petition on behalf of the steamboat company against the Bill, the Weymouth & Portland Railway Act received Royal Assent on 30th June, 1862. Although construction work was slow and the railway did not finally open to traffic until 16th October, 1865, Cosens and his partners must have realised that it was the end of an era. With the end of their monopoly of the Portland trade in sight, serious thought would have to be given to the survival of the company.

As if to rub salt into the wounds, 1862 opened with a number of events which emphasised the growing importance of Portland. Firstly, to mark the completion of the breakwater staging, J.T. Leather gave a grand dinner to 310 of his workmen and staff. Nearly six million tons of stone had already been tipped from the staging and the breakwater itself was now almost a mile and a half long. High above it, fortification of the Verne Citadel was proceeding apace and the foundation stone for the second phase was laid during January. Secondly, during February, the boys training ship *HMS Britannia* arrived in Portland Harbour but, following complaints that the boys were suffering from seasickness, the old 'wooden wall' was transferred to Dartmouth, where her name survives to this day as the famous Royal Naval College. Her brief presence, however, was an indication of the Admiralty's interest in the anchorage and a hint of developments to come. On the night of 17th February, the mail steamer *Ceylon* hit Portland Bill in fog which was so thick that the lighthouse keepers could hear voices on board but never glimpsed the ship. Miraculously, the ship did not touch bottom and suffered only the loss of her bowsprit before continuing on her voyage to Southampton. Capt Cosens, no doubt, bemoaned the loss of a potential salvage job!

At Weymouth, the Town Council, chastened perhaps by the criticism it had received the previous season, changed its mind again and decided to put collection of the Pile Pier tolls out to tender. Joseph Cosens and John Tizard (who were presumably acting in their own right and not on behalf of the steamboat company) competed against each other at the auction on 11th March, with Joseph obtaining the rights for three years at £790 per annum. Determined to make a success of the venture, he engaged the Pile Pier Band to perform a concert at the end of the pier every evening from June onwards and provided refreshments and *'choice wines'* in the pavilion on the pier head. Season tickets were made available, dancing was frequent and the pier quickly established itself as a fashionable place to spend the evening, remaining well patronised until mid-October.

The season got off to a good start in May with the annual Weymouth regatta, which was marked by half-day closing throughout the town. Races for coastguard punts, jolly boats, gigs, galleys, skiffs and canoes were all keenly contested. The band from *HMS Emerald* played on the pier and the steamers offered afternoon cruises and moonlight excursions round the anchored Channel Fleet. Thereafter, they settled into their normal pattern, with Lulworth being visited regularly on both Wednesdays and Saturdays, and periodic trips advertised to Torquay, Bournemouth and Swanage.

At 3 o'clock on the morning of 16th June, the routine was interrupted when *Bannockburn* set off on an unexpected and unwelcome excursion. A party of blue jackets belonging to one of the men-of-war at Portland, having '*indulged in too copious a libation to Bacchus*' during a run ashore, were considering how they could get back to their ships long after the last liberty boat had gone, when their gaze fell on *Bannockburn*. Climbing aboard, they cast off, set her jib and sailed her out of the harbour. Realising that they would be unable to set a course for Portland, they descended into the ship's boat and rowed back to their ship where, hoping to destroy the evidence of their adventure, they pulled out the bung in the bottom of the boat and let her sink. *Bannockburn* drifted unattended until she was spotted near White Nothe later that morning and brought, undamaged, back to port.

The fourteenth anniversary of the inauguration of Cosens' steamer service from Weymouth fell on 15th July 1862 but the *Southern Times* noted gloomily that a major exhibition in London had led to the cancellation of almost all the excursion trains to the town and had diverted so much of the traditional seaside trade that, during June and July, the steamers had carried 10,000 less passengers to and from the harbour than in the corresponding period during the previous year. Timed as it was to follow closely on the news of the Portland Railway Act, these statistics must have seemed a cruel indication of things to come.

Towards the end of August, matters took a temporary turn for the better when the revolutionary *HMS Warrior* arrived in the Roads and was thrown open to visitors. She remained in the area until 8th October, when she sailed, in company with a squadron of other warships, to mark the King of Portugal's marriage at Lisbon. Throughout this six week period, *Premier* did a brisk trade ferrying large numbers of sightseers out to the ship, where they were able to wonder at her immense size, powerful armament and novel construction.

The season closed with news of the death, on 13th October, of Capt Francis Williams, who had been a part owner of the company since 1858. His shares in the ships passed into the joint ownership of his executors, John Gibbs (an existing shareholder) and Frederick Steggall of Wyke Regis. Over the next three years, all of these shares were redistributed to Martha Williams and Francis Williams of Wyke Regis, Francis Williams of Brighton (all of whom

were presumably relatives of the deceased) and Capt J.P. Reynolds of Weymouth, another existing shareholder.

Conscious of the pending contraction of the Portland trade and aware of the potential income to be made from towage and salvage work, Cosens decided, during the winter of 1862-63, to dispose of the ageing *Contractor* and replace her with a more powerful, custom built tug. *Contractor* carried out her last salvage job on Saturday 10th January 1863, when it was discovered at daybreak that the 138 ton brig *Challenger* was hard ashore, completely upright and with all sails set, in Newton's Cove near the Nothe Fort. A Weymouth coastguard boarded her but, finding her deserted, sent for the steamer to relieve her of her cargo of railway iron and materials before she went to pieces. Work continued non-stop into the Sunday, when large crowds gathered on the Nothe to watch the drama and it was noted that '*the congregations at the various places of worship have diminished in consequence.*'

The crew of the brig had meanwhile come ashore in their boat, having abandoned ship near the Shambles the previous evening when their vessel sprang a serious leak and appeared to be in danger of foundering. In fact she had remained afloat and gently sailed herself ashore onto a conveniently sandy bottom and into the hands of the waiting salvage company. Having been emptied of her cargo, the brig was finally towed into Weymouth Harbour during the first week in February. Cosens, of course, received a handsome salvage award.

Having served Weymouth well for twelve years, *Contractor* was sold on 27th February to Henry Lee and Henry Lee senior, contractors of Nine Elms, London, who promptly resold her to Plymouth where she was registered in January 1864 and joined her former fleet-mate *Princess* under the ownership of the Devon & Cornwall Tamar Steam Packet Company Ltd.

Contractor was not the only departure from the company for, shortly afterwards, William Cosens accepted an offer from J.T. Leather to become his marine superintendent on the construction of the Spithead Forts. In addition to a number of shore batteries, it was planned to build six circular armoured forts on the sands of Spithead, to defend the approaches to Portsmouth naval base. The forts were designed by Capt E.H. Steward, RE; the noted civil engineer Sir John Hawkeshaw advised on the method to be adopted for constructing firm foundations on tidal sandbanks; and Leather was appointed as the contractor who would actually undertake the work. His experience with the Portland Breakwater was of great relevance, as a wooden staging on screw piles was built over each site, from which the prepared stone and concrete blocks were lowered by crane and guided into position by divers. All of the materials were prepared at a work yard at Stokes Bay and carried to the sites by barges from a specially constructed pier. Work on the forts at Sturbridge Shoal and Ryde

A surviving ticket for BANNOCKBURN's *Weymouth-Portland sailings.*
WEYMOUTH MUSEUM

A poor quality but extremely rare photograph showing Commodore *moored at Trinity Quay, Weymouth.* AUTHOR'S COLLECTION

Sands had to be abandoned, as no satisfactory foundation could be found, but four more at Spit Bank, Horse Sand, No Man's Land and St. Helens were eventually completed. William Cosens was placed in charge of the pier and all waterborne transport and remained at Stokes Bay until 1869 when he returned to Weymouth to resume command of one of the pleasure steamers.

Contractor's replacement arrived in Weymouth on the evening of Saturday 25th April 1863. Named *Commodore*, she was a wooden, clinker-built tug from the yard of Mr A. Woodhouse at South Shields. She was 93 feet long, 18 feet 6 inches in the beam and drew 9 feet 6 inches of water, with a tonnage of 96.3 gross, 26.1 registered. In the style of other contemporary tugs, she was of plain design with a single mast, round counter stern and an undecorated straight stem, and was significantly shorter and beamier than the long and slender *Prince* and *Premier*. Although her strong construction and 60hp engine, which is believed to have been of a side lever or grasshopper design, were designed to make her capable of undertaking any towage or salvage job which might present itself, she was also intended for use in the passenger trade. She was fitted with small passenger saloons below decks and, after her arrival at Weymouth, Cosens spent some time *'attending to those details which promote passenger comfort.'* It was announced that during June she would make an excursion to Cherbourg.

A fascinating view of Weymouth Harbour, thought to have been taken during the winter of 1865. Two pairs of goods wagons can be seen standing on the tramway which had been opened in October of that year, connecting Weymouth station with the quay. COMMODORE *is moored at the quay while, in the foreground, another steamer is hauled up on the slipway. Although it is not possible to be absolutely certain as to her identity, the vessel is likely to be either* OCEAN BRIDE, *which had been sold to J.T. Leather in February 1865 but continued to work in the area, or* BANNOCKBURN, *which was converted into a coal barge sometime after August of the same year. The slipway itself passed into Cosens' hands in 1876 and became their No.1 slipway. The building behind the steamer's foremast became the Slip Master's house and was occupied by a succession of Cosens' employees until it was demolished during the 1970s.* WEYMOUTH LIBRARY

Commodore did not have to wait long to undertake her first rescues. On the evening of 18th May, after a period of unnatural calm, a light south easterly breeze veered suddenly into the north-east and increased to a violent gale which, accompanied by blinding rain, continued to rage throughout the following day. At Portland, the ketch *Woodside* was driven onto the outside of the breakwater and had gone to pieces before *Commodore* could reach her. *Louisa Pitt*, loading at Portland, parted her cables and was driven ashore in front of Portland Castle and two more vessels, *Liberty* and *Dorset*, were wrecked. On her way back from the breakwater, *Commodore* was able to take a lady and gentleman off a yacht which, plunging about at anchor in the roadstead, was in imminent danger of driving ashore. Her next recorded salvage job was on 2nd November, when she towed in the brigantine *Norman* which, having lost her fore yard and blown out all her sails, had been forced to anchor in a dangerous position two miles from the Shambles lightship and hoist a signal of distress.

The summer seasons of 1863 and 1864 followed their usual pattern, except that both Bournemouth and Swanage were visited on average twice a week. The management had noted that the Poole steamer *Ursa Major*, while sailing *to* Swanage several times a week, rarely offered an excursion *from* the town and sought to take advantage by touching there *en route* for Bournemouth. The regular Lulworth, local and moonlight excursions continued alongside the Portland ferry and trips to Torquay were offered

SATURDAY, JULY 16, 1864.

VOLUNTEER CAMP, LULWORTH.

THE most pleasant and convenient ROUTE to the CAMP will be by RAIL to WEYMOUTH, thence per STEAMER to LULWORTH COVE. Passengers Landed within a few minutes walk of the Camp. Steamers will run as follows:—

	Leave Weymouth.	Leave Lulworth.
Monday, July 25	11.30 A.M.	12.30 P.M.
	4. 0 P.M.	7. 0 P.M.
Tuesday, July 26, and following days.	7. 0 A.M.	8. 0 A.M.
	11.30 A.M.	12.30 P.M.
	4. 0 P.M.	7. 0 P.M.

☞ The usual Fares only charged. Volunteers of the Dorset Battalion in Uniform, Sixpence.

WEYMOUTH AND CHANNEL ISLANDS STEAM PACKET COMPANY LIMITED.

GUERNSEY REGATTA,

ALLOWING ELEVEN DAYS.

ON MONDAY, JULY 25, 1864, one of the FAST Paddle Wheel STEAMERS belonging to the above Company will make an EXCURSION to GUERNSEY direct, at 11.30 A.M., after the arrival of the Bristol Excursion Train.

FARES THERE AND BACK!
Saloon 18s.   Fore Cabin 12s.
Steward's Fee included.
Children under 12 years Half-price.
Passengers holding these Tickets will have the privilege of going on to Jersey on the following or any other Wednesday, Friday, or Monday, at noon; the Return Journey to be completed on or before Thursday the 4th of August.
July, 1864.   J. MAUNDERS, Manager.

A newspaper advertisement for sailings to Lulworth in connection with the annual Volunteer Camp.

on two occasions. *Prince* and *Premier* appear to have been completely interchangeable on the long distance sailings.

April 1864 was enlivened by rumours that Garibaldi (the famous Italian patriot and soldier, whose campaigns are credited with unifying Italy) was about to visit the Channel Fleet at Weymouth. Excitement ran high in the town and every likely vessel in the offing was closely inspected in case the great man was on board. This provided an early-season boost to passenger numbers and when he did finally arrive by train, the opportunity was taken to run a trip to watch him inspecting the fleet. The main season began, as usual, at Whitsun and during June loadings were increased by the presence of the Dorset Battalion summer camp at Lulworth. Cosens' adverts proclaimed that the most pleasant route to the camp was by rail to Weymouth and thence by steamer to Lulworth Cove, from which it was then only a few minutes walk. The frequency of sailings was increased to three times daily for the duration of the camp and a special reduced fare of 6d was offered to volunteers in uniform.

One long distance excursion which was worthy of mention in the local press took place on 16th July, when *Premier* left Weymouth with 50 passengers at 7.30am bound for her annual trip to the River Dart. The report mentioned that on this occasion the steamer arrived in the Dart at low tide and was therefore unable to proceed very far up the river, lending weight to the theory that, since *Prince*'s visit in 1858, Cosens' steamers had indeed penetrated all the way to Totnes on those years when the tide was suitable. *Premier* landed her passengers at Weymouth at 11pm, their fifteen and a half hours at sea being sweetened by the best efforts of Jones' Quadrille Band. She ran a number of special trips to Cowes during August and it is interesting to note that Weymouth also became the destination of more excursions from the Solent. The Portsmouth steamer *Prince Consort* and *Courier* from Southampton both visited during July, with the latter's trip ending in tragedy when one of her passengers drowned whilst bathing at Weymouth.

The autumn saw *Commodore* involved in two salvage jobs, the first of which was of a most unusual nature. On the evening of 26th October, news reached Weymouth that a vessel had been spotted floating bottom-upwards off Portland and that, although a small fishing boat had attempted to take her in tow, the services of a tug were required. *Commodore* picked up the derelict early next morning some 6 miles SSW of the Shambles and succeeded in bringing her slowly into Portland. It took numerous attempts and the services of a diver before the vessel was successfully righted three days later. She turned out to be the chasse-marée *Hortense* of Fecamp, which had been on passage from Bordeaux to Brussels with a cargo of wines, brandy and confectionery. Vessels of her class were noted for their vast sail area and it was assumed that she had been caught by a sudden squall, carrying away her masts and capsizing at the same instant. The body of her captain was found in the cabin but the rest of the crew, of whom no trace was found, were presumed to have been lost overboard at the moment of disaster. A large crowd gathered to watch her being towed, with a temporary ensign flying at half mast, up through Weymouth Town Bridge to be handed into the care of the receiver of wrecks. The second service was of a more mundane nature when, on 18th November, *Commodore* towed in the schooner *Bathurst* which, having had several sails blown out and been forced to run for shelter in Weymouth Bay, was dragging her anchors and required immediate assistance.

The year closed with an exciting incident in early December, when a rumour began to circulate on Portland that a mass break-out by convicts had taken place. A signal was sent from the prison for troops at Weymouth to proceed with all haste to restore order and Capt Cosens was asked to delay the 11.30am boat in order to carry them to the island. Within half an hour, soldiers from the Nothe had been assembled, joined by members of the 85th regiment and just after midday, 200 troops set sail in *Prince*. Anticlimax greeted their arrival, however, when it was discovered that a mistake had been made in hoisting the signal and that only one convict, who had since been recaptured, had actually escaped!

The first three months of 1865 brought the usual winter storms and with them some useful income from salvage. On the night of 13-14th January, the wind was so strong that the Channel Islands steamer was prevented from sailing and several vessels which were sheltering in Portland Harbour ran foul of each other and were damaged. The French schooner *Nicholas Joseph* received so much punishment that she had to be towed into Weymouth by *Commodore*, which immediately sailed again on a fruitless errand to find a vessel which was rumoured to be ashore at Abbotsbury. Cosens claimed £350 for their

services to the schooner but, since her owners were unwilling to pay and the ship was sold by auction for only £200, they were forced to settle for a smaller sum. The cargo of the chasse-maree *Hortense* had meanwhile been sold by auction and the hull purchased by a Frenchman. Cosens benefited twice from the arrangement, receiving a salvage payment of £180 and then obtaining the contract for *Commodore* to tow the vessel to Fecamp. Finally, on 22nd March, the full rigged ship *Anna* was attempting to beat out of the anchorage when she missed stays and drifted onto the breakwater. The captain engaged the services of two local boats to run out anchors in the hope of heaving her off but each time the anchors came home and he was forced to send for a tug. After a good deal of parleying over terms, *Commodore* was engaged and had no difficulty in towing her to a safe anchorage for the sum of £50.

1865 was undoubtedly another pivotal year in the history of the steamboat company. Work on both the Portland Railway and Harbour Tramway had been completed during 1864 and their opening depended only on the receipt of final safety approval from the Board of Trade and the settlement of some disputes over joint running arrangements between the two railway companies involved. Cosens realised that stiff opposition for the Portland trade was imminent and that, especially during the winter months, many of their regular passengers were likely to prefer the comfort of a railway carriage to the rigours of a sea trip. To add to their worries, the company was aware that J.T. Leather's contract for the construction of the breakwater was due to end in December 1866 and that they could not rely on as close and profitable a relationship with his successor, John Coode, who intended to complete the works using government direct labour. With their income from both the Portland service and contracting work under threat, some new thinking was required.

A rare photograph of the first Bournemouth Pier sometime prior to the T-shaped head and 300 feet of its length being swept away in a storm on 5th January 1867. The steamer has not been positively identified but might well be Ursa Major.
BOURNEMOUTH LIBRARY

Chesil Beach, with a train heading for the mainland along the newly-opened railway, viewed from the top of Portland, circa 1865.
NEWMAN

Cosens responded by rationalising their fleet still further and by expanding their involvement in the coal trade. Firstly, the opportunity was grasped to sell the little *Ocean Bride* to Leather on 13th February. She was now too small and elderly to be of much use in the passenger trade and had spent much of the previous two years laid up but was ideally suited as a tug and general workboat for Leather's contracting work. She had already served him well for several years on hire from Cosens and was well known to William Cosens who was now acting as Leather's

marine superintendent at Stokes Bay. Whether or not she was transferred there to be used on the Spithead Forts contract or remained at Portland is unclear but she was sold to the Crown in April 1867 and was certainly still working at Portland during 1876.

The second vessel to go was *Bannockburn* which, also deprived of contracting work, had her engines and boilers removed and was converted into a barge. Her register was closed on 24th August 1865. Thereafter, she was used as an additional coal barge, partly to store coal for Cosens' own steamers but also, when the opportunity arose, to take bunkers out to the increasing number of steamships which were calling at Portland Roads. With the breakwater nearing completion and steam power becoming more common, Cosens reasoned that bunkering was bound to be a growing trade.

With the fleet reduced to the three relatively powerful and modern vessels, *Prince*, *Premier* and *Commodore*, the opportunity was also taken to publish a new timetable for the regular Weymouth to Portland service. From the beginning of February 1865, steamers left Weymouth at 9.30am, 11.30am, 2.00pm and 4.30pm, returning from Portland at 10.00am, 12 noon, 2.30pm and 5.00pm. The company reasoned that the 20 minute sea crossing would still attract large numbers of summer visitors and that, combined with an expansion of other excursion sailings, good luck in the salvage trade and the new venture in bunkering, everything possible had been done to meet the challenge of the Portland Railway when it eventually opened to traffic on 16th October 1865.

The rival to the steamboats. A painting of Portland, showing a train bound for Weymouth crossing Ferrybridge Viaduct, which carried the line from Chesil Beach onto the mainland. The railway, which opened to passenger traffic in October 1865, had a serious impact on Cosens' passenger figures, especially during the winter months.
STEWART MORRIS

CHAPTER 6
THE OLD ORDER PASSES
1866-1875

Cosens' survival strategy appears to have proved satisfactory, for over the next few years the established pattern of trade continued with only minor alterations. Although no precise figures have survived, it is clear that the winter trade to Portland suffered so badly from railway competition that, from the autumn of 1865, it was decided to withdraw the service altogether. When the summer service recommenced at the beginning of May, prices had been reduced by the abolition of pier tolls at Portland and the local press reflected that '*the opportunity of enjoying healthful sea breezes will doubtless render this route as heretofore a favourite with those whom business or pleasure may call to Portland.*' Certainly the sea trip was as cheap as and faster than the railway journey and, for visitors at least, offered the added attraction of viewing the breakwater works and anchored warships at close quarters. The seasonal service proved profitable and, henceforth, *Prince* and *Premier* spent their winters laid up in Weymouth Harbour, while *Commodore* was kept constantly in steam and available for whatever work might present itself.

The mainstay of *Commodore*'s employment was towing sailing vessels in and out of Weymouth Harbour, taking the coal barge out to bunker steamers in the Roads and occasional longer coastal or cross-channel towage contracts. Salvage work was, by its nature, highly unpredictable but offered generous returns if successfully accomplished. Although records for only a small proportion of the tug's service have survived, those for the period 1866-69 provide us with a useful insight into a fairly typical selection of tasks.

In February 1866, the 400 ton French barque *Georgiana* was wrecked near St. Alban's Head and Cosens, hoping to make a good profit from salvaged cargo and fittings even if they failed to tow her off, purchased the hull at public auction. The gamble more than paid off, as the final account showed an enormous income of £2,000. In September, *Sarah Anne*, which had been damaged by heavy seas off Bere Head, was rescued, whilst in January 1867, a series of severe SE gales, which destroyed the 'Jack in the basket' beacon and part of the breakwater staging, kept the tug busy in recovering floating timber and other wreckage. On the night of 19th January, the schooner *Isabella*, mistaking the temporary 'Jack in the basket' for Portland lighthouse, steered straight onto Weymouth beach and her crew were forced to take to the rigging and cling there until the following morning when they were rescued. The schooner broke her back and began sinking into the sand but *Commodore* succeeded in stripping the

wreck of her masts and fittings. In July, a brigantine named *Jane Innes*, which had been discovered deserted and derelict off the Eddystone light by a passing steamer, was towed into Portland for a charge of £5, and on 1st December *Commodore* went to the aid of the barque *Alice Graham* which was in danger of driving ashore near Worbarrow. Disabled in a gale during the previous day, she was a large ship heavily laden with pig iron and *Commodore* struggled all night to tow her off the lee shore and bring her into Portland Roads the following morning. During the same night, the small steamer *Don* from the breakwater works had also been driven ashore and flooded, so *Commodore* immediately proceeded to tow her into Weymouth where she was pumped out and repaired.

Rescues during 1868 included the schooners *Scotia*, which sprang a leak off Portland Bill on 14th July and *Emma & Mary*, which, laden with a cargo of coal for Cosens' coal stores, had her sails blown out in Weymouth Bay on 24th October. Both were rescued by *Commodore*. During December, the 2,400 ton passenger steamer *Barossa*, bound from New York to Bremen, broke her propeller shaft near Ushant and drifted helplessly until discovered by the small steamer *Great Yarmouth*, which towed her slowly up the Channel until the tow broke in heavy weather off Portland. While *Great Yarmouth* landed the passengers safely at Portland, *Commodore* put to sea and remained with the derelict until a new tow rope could be passed. On 5th February 1869, the crew of the brigantine *Henry & Dora* was rescued by local boats after she struck the breakwater. *Commodore* rushed to the scene and, finding her too badly-damaged to be saved, set about stripping her of her masts and fittings, before she finally went to pieces the following day.

COMMODORE at Weymouth. Note the lifeboat in davits on the starboard side aft of the funnel. This boat was carried while she was on passenger service but left ashore when she was engaged in winter towage and salvage work.
AUTHOR'S COLLECTION

GRAND NAVAL REVIEW AT SPITHEAD.
In the presence of Her Majesty the Queen, H.R.H. the Prince of Wales, and the Sultan,
ON WEDNESDAY, JULY 17, 1867.

THE fast and powerful Steamer COMMODORE will leave WEYMOUTH on WEDNESDAY, the 17th, at 4 o'clock in the morning, returning the same night after the Review and Illumination of the Fleet.

Tickets for the day, 15s. each.
REFRESHMENTS TO BE HAD ON BOARD.

WEYMOUTH AND CHANNEL ISLANDS STEAM PACKET COMPANY (LIMITED).
REVIEW AT SPITHEAD.

This Grand Naval Review is arranged to take place in the presence of H.M. the Queen, H.R.H. the Prince of Wales, the Sultan, the Members of the Houses of Lords and Commons, the Foreign Ambassadors, &c., &c.

TWO of the magnificent Mail Steam Ships belonging to the above Company are appointed to leave WEYMOUTH HARBOUR for PORTSMOUTH to attend this REVIEW, viz.:—The "Brighton," on SATURDAY, the 13th inst., at 3 P.M., and the "Aquila," on TUESDAY, the 16th inst., at 8 A.M.

Fare to Portsmouth by either Steamer, 5s.
Excursions on Monday and Tuesday from the Portsmouth Piers to view the Fleet, 2s.
Tickets to cruise about the scene of the Review on the 17th, and to remain to witness the Illuminations, £1 1s.
Return Fare to Weymouth late on Wednesday night, or, as circumstances may dictate, early on Thursday morning, 5s.
These tickets should be taken on or before Saturday, the 13th inst., to enable the Company to make the necessary catering arrangements, which will be at the usual moderate rates.
Sleeping accommodation will be provided for a limited number at 5s. per head per night.
JOSEPH MAUNDERS, Manager.
Weymouth, July 11, 1867.

GRAND NAVAL REVIEW AT SPITHEAD.

THE Solent Steam Packet Company will despatch a Commodious STEAMER from Lymington on WEDNESDAY, the 17th, which will proceed direct to the FLEET, and attend all its Evolutions.
The Boat will leave Lymington Pier as soon as the Train arrives that is due at Lymington at 8.25, and will return to Lymington after the Anchorage of the Fleet.
Times of Starting:—From Lymington, 6.30; from Yarmouth, 9.0; from Cowes, 10.0; from Ryde, 10.30.
Tickets, 10s. 6d. each.

The same Company have also arranged for a SELECT PARTY in another commodious Steamer, with an efficient captain and crew, at 20s. each.
This Boat will attend the Evolutions of the Fleet, and wait for the Grand Illumination of the Fleet at Night.
Many Tickets are already taken, and an early application is necessary. Passages guaranteed in the 20s. Boat only to those who have Tickets, as the number is limited. This latter Boat will leave Lymington Pier at a quarter to nine, calling at Yarmouth, Cowes, and Ryde (if required).
N.B.—The Steamer between Lymington and Portsmouth will not make her usual Passage on the day of the Review.

March 1869 witnessed a rather unusual event, when an attempt was made to re-launch the hull of the German brig *Amalie*, which had been driven ashore in Chesil Cove, Portland, on 1st February. The crew had been rescued through the bravery of a local fisherman, Thomas Flann, and the ship thrown above the high water mark without suffering any serious damage. Her hull was sold by auction to a local firm, who constructed a large wood cradle under the ship, cleared away the shingle and laid heavy baulks of timber to form an incline down which to push her back into the water. A period of light north-easterly winds provided the perfect conditions and, by the application of screw-jacks

and windlasses, *Amalie* was successfully moved down the beach to the low water mark. At this point, the wind swung back to the south west and a rising tide and surf quickly scoured away the temporary slipway and threatened to destroy the brig. A telegram was immediately sent to Cosens who, having anticipated that their services would be required, despatched *Commodore* immediately. Arriving on the scene at 5pm on 13th March, she made three attempts to tow the hull off using *Amalie*'s own ropes but these broke each time. Realising that it would result in a far larger salvage payment to Cosens, the contractors were reluctant to allow *Commodore* to use her own tow rope but, with *Amalie* bumping more violently against the beach as every moment passed, they had little option but to agree. The next attempt was crowned with success but unfortunately *Amalie*'s rudder was torn off in the process, making the tow back around Portland Bill a slow and difficult business. The casualty sheered about wildly at the end of the tow rope and it took many hours before she was brought inside the breakwater where, with part of the tug's crew on board, she was anchored for the night. At daybreak next morning, *Commodore* moved her into Weymouth Harbour where, to the delight of owner and salvor alike, she was found to have suffered remarkably little damage.

An important event in Weymouth's maritime history occurred on 26th January 1869, with the formal inauguration of the town's first RNLI lifeboat, the ten-oared, self-righting *Agnes Harriet*. Accompanied by a colourful procession of local dignitaries, the vessel was drawn through the streets on a carriage pulled by six grey horses, before taking up her permanent station on a new slipway on the south side of the harbour. The new boat provided a useful complement to the services provided by *Commodore* and was heartily welcomed on a stretch of coast where, hitherto, the only means of life-saving had been either the steamers or local fishing boats.

The planned expansion of long-distance excursion sailings also became apparent from 1866 onwards. As *Prince* was now the principal steamer on the Portland service and local excursions, it fell to *Premier* to provide an increased number of sailings to Swanage, Bournemouth, Ryde, Cowes, Portsmouth, Torquay and Lyme Regis. Competition was experienced from the Weymouth & Channel Island SP Co who, in addition to their regular excursions to the Islands, took the opportunity to offer occasional day trips to the Isle of Wight on board one of their large cross channel steamers. On Wednesday 17th July 1867, when a Grand Naval Review was held at Spithead in the presence of the Queen, both companies offered excursions from Weymouth. The Channel Island company sent *Brighton* five days in advance, to operate daily trips from the Portsmouth piers around the assembling fleet, with *Aquila* following on the day before the review. The fare was 5s each way from Weymouth, plus £1 1s for the review day cruise itself, and limited sleeping accommodation was offered on board the steamers. Oddly, Cosens appear to have sent only the little *Commodore*, which left Weymouth at 4am and returned late the same night after watching the review and the subsequent illumination of the fleet, for a fare of 15s. From 1868 onwards, the popularity of the occasional visits to Lyme Regis prompted the company to advertise a regular weekly trip in high season, although the exposed nature of the route meant that there were many cancellations due to bad weather.

Excursion trains continued to provide huge numbers of passengers for the steamers. During August 1868, 700 employees of a cloth manufacturer in Trowbridge arrived by rail and, preceded by a brass band, paraded along the esplanade to the pier where they embarked on *Premier* and *Commodore* for a day trip to Lulworth Cove. So important were these rail excursionists to the economy of both the town and the steamer company that, periodically throughout the 1860s and 70s, proposals were made to construct a new steamer pier on Weymouth seafront close to the railway station. Such an arrangement, it was claimed, would boost income by saving potential passengers the trouble of walking round the bay to the Pile Pier. In the event, the proposals came to nothing, probably because the gently shelving nature of Weymouth beach would have demanded a very long and therefore expensive pier if the steamers were to be able to call at all states of the tide.

Cosens must also have kept an interested eye on developments at Poole, where there were several attempts to establish new steamer services. *Ursa Major* had been replaced in 1865 by *Royal Albert*, which continued to offer regular trips from Poole to Swanage and less frequently to Bournemouth, together with occasional excursions to Lulworth and elsewhere until 1871. In May 1870, a small steamer called *Pearl* was chartered to compete with *Royal Albert* but lasted for less than a season. Two unsuccessful attempts were made to establish cross channel services from Poole to Cherbourg and the successive vessels employed – *Albion*, *Queen of the Isles* and *Spicy* – all supplemented their incomes by running local excursions. Trips to Portsmouth and the Isle of Wight were reasonably commonplace and on 21st July 1868, *Spicy* made history by offering the first excursion to Cherbourg from Bournemouth Pier. Although they were not in direct competition with Cosens, the success or otherwise of these vessels must have provided the Weymouth company with a useful indication of the potential demand for excursions from Swanage and Bournemouth. Their interest must have been heightened further when, in June 1868, they were approached by a Mr Crickmay who wished to either purchase or hire a steamer to operate from Swanage. Although nothing came of the negotiations, subsequent developments at Swanage may have caused Cosens to regret that they had not grasped the opportunity.

In July 1869, almost ten years after her first visit

East Cliff Bournemouth

to Portland, news was received that *Great Eastern* was bound once again for Dorset. Following her disastrous maiden voyage, nothing seemed to have gone well for the ship or her directors, who struggled constantly with insolvency. Unable to finance a voyage on her intended route to Australia, they had instead employed her on a number of unprofitable transatlantic trips, had chartered her briefly to the government as a troop ship and had then laid her up at Milford Haven. Reactivated in 1865 and stripped of her sumptuous interior, she was

Despite the loss of the pier head and 300 feet of its length in a storm early in 1867, as these two engravings show, the remaining portion of Bournemouth Pier was in good enough condition to still be used regularly by steamers from both Poole and Weymouth. NEWMAN

Cranbourne Gardens, Bournemouth

converted into a cable layer, her cavernous interior making her the only ship in the world capable of carrying sufficient submarine cable to cross oceans. In this guise she earned herself a place in history, by completing the first commercially successful transatlantic cable on 27th July 1866. After another brief and unsuccessful interlude as a passenger ship, *Great Eastern* had again been converted into a cable ship and was now under charter to the French Telegraphic Company, for whom she was intending to lay a cable between France and America.

At about noon on 14th July, Capt Cosens received a telegram informing him that the great ship was off the Isle of Wight and due to arrive in Weymouth Bay at about 5pm. He immediately organised an excursion and at 2.30pm, *Premier* set off with a '*numerous party*' on board and met *Great Eastern* just to the east off St. Alban's Head. As *Premier* turned to steer a parallel course, Jones' Quadrille Band struck up '*Auld Lang Syne*', the two ships dipped their ensigns to one another and numerous cheers were exchanged. Loaded with 3,300 miles of cable and drawing 34 feet of water, the huge ship must have presented an unforgettable sight from the decks of the little pleasure steamer, which remained '*within a biscuit's toss*' all the way back to Portland. *Great Eastern* remained at Portland taking on coal until the following Saturday, when she sailed for Brest, from where she successfully laid a cable to Newfoundland.

By 25th October, she was back at Portland again, this time painted white in preparation for laying the Anglo-Indian cable from Suez to Bombay, and *Prince* ran an excursion to witness her arrival. Perhaps because of the time of year, or more probably because the novelty of the great ship was said to have '*worn pretty well threadbare*' in the locality, the demand for tickets was only moderate. Those who did sail enjoyed the customary exchange of greetings as *Prince* '*dodged about her bulky companion like a water sprite, sometimes heading her, sometimes steaming up close to her and sometimes allowing her to go ahead.*' As before, *Great Eastern* remained at Portland for about a week taking on coal. She was opened to the public on a number of days, providing the steamers with some welcome late-season income.

During the late 1860s, Joseph Cosens had begun to experience difficulties with his eyesight and, by the end of the 1868 season, was forced to relinquish command of *Prince* to Capt George Haill, confining himself to managing the company's affairs ashore. As his eyesight continued to deteriorate, this too became a struggle and, by mid-1869, he was practically blind and dependent on a Mr Humphrey who would lead him around the town on his business errands. Realising his brother's plight, William Cosens resigned from his post with J.T. Leather at Spithead, returning to Weymouth to take command of *Premier* on 20th May and to involve

By 1872, the construction of the Nothe Fort at the entrance to Weymouth Harbour had been completed and the garrison was installed. This view emphasises the popularity of the Nothe and the Ballast Wharf beneath as a fashionable promenade, from where visitors to the town could observe activity in the bay and harbour.

WEYMOUTH MUSEUM

John Butcher, Cosens' longest-serving engineer, came to Weymouth with PRINCE *when she was first delivered by John Scott Russell in 1852. He is believed to have been born in 1827 and remained with the ship throughout her time at Weymouth and even after she was sold to Ellett & Matthews for service at Exmouth. He was living on board while she was laid up at Weymouth when he died of* 'general debility' *on 10th May 1890.*
AUTHOR'S COLLECTION

suggests that for the period 1862-1875 the trade grew steadily as follows:

YEAR	TONNAGE	PROFIT
1862	62.5	
1863	224	
1864	70	
1865	147	
1866	764	
1867	336	
1868	428	
1869	576	
1870	737	
1871	811	£ 471
1872	1,074	£ 878
1873	1,423	£ 1,131
1874	1,530	£ 838
1875	1,431	£ 750

Evidently, the trade was not without its dangers, however, for on 28th September 1870, a coal porter named Henry Hawkins fell off a gangway and drowned while carrying coal across two other vessels to *Prince*.

Having lost the lease of the Pile Pier and wharfage dues for a number of years to Messrs Gibbons and Ayling respectively, Cosens successfully regained control of both in 1871. The sum of £1,420 was paid for the harbour dues in 1871, increasing to £1,500 in 1872 and a profit of £200 declared for the year ending April 1872. The pier had earned the council £550 in 1868-69, £542 in 1869-70, and £620 in 1870-71. Cosens paid £600 in 1871-72, reducing to £500 in the two subsequent years and clearly needed to work hard to make any useful profit. Every effort was made to attract promenaders to the pier, where weekly, monthly and annual tickets were made available. The company continued to rent the pier until 1880 and leased the harbour dues until 1875.

It is also apparent that, during the 1860s, the company had developed the ability to maintain its own steamers. We know that in 1870 they had a blacksmith's shop and by 1874 were renting workshops and yards somewhere on Weymouth Quay from a Mr Hopkins. A Mr William Hinde was in charge of the workshops and a small team of men and, as the company's superintendent engineer, worked closely with the masters and seagoing engineers on the maintenance of the steamers. It is worth observing that early ships' engineers frequently came from a metal working or ship building background and learned marine engineering as they went along. John Butcher, the company's senior engineer, had come from London with *Prince* when she was first delivered and several others, including Thomas Ruddock and James Jackson, who had charge of *Premier*'s engines during the 1860s, came from the tug-building towns of the north-east coast such as South Shields. Only gradually did locally-born engineers emerge, the first Weymouthian in charge of a Cosens' engine room being Henry Vye,

himself once again in the affairs of the company. It is also interesting to note that the earliest surviving '*Accounts of Voyages and Crews*' for the company reveal that the older Cosens brother, Thomas, served as mate of *Commodore* from 1863 until 1872.

By 1870, Joseph's health was so bad that, at the monthly meeting on 29th November, he expressed a wish to leave the company and asked if the remaining shareholders would purchase his shares for £2,000. This dramatic announcement provoked a series of emergency shareholders' meetings to consider the future management of the company. It was initially proposed that William Cosens and Simon Jenkin Fowler (who had joined the company as clerk in 1863) should be appointed managers of the steamboat and coal businesses respectively but, since both declined, it was finally resolved that Capt Mace be appointed overall manager, whilst William would retain day-to-day control of the steamers. A board of directors consisting of Messrs Drew, Mace and Gibbs was appointed but there was unanimous insistence that Joseph should retain his shareholding. The steamers continued to trade under the title of The Weymouth & Portland Steam Packet Co and the coal business as J. Cosens & Co, although Joseph was required to sign a declaration that he held the lease of both the coal stores and the blacksmith's shop in trust for the company. The new arrangements came into effect on 1st January 1871.

The coal business seems to have been a success. Regular cargoes arrived in small sailing ships and, as word of the facility spread, an increasing number of steamers, such as *May Queen* on 9th May 1870, put into the bay for bunkers. Although the company records are somewhat contradictory, one abstract

who took over *Commodore* from Jackson in 1866 at the age of 27 and was promoted to *Premier* in 1871. William Hinde junior, the 22 year old son of the superintendent engineer, having learned his trade for two years as fireman on board *Prince*, was promoted in 1871 to take Vye's place as engineer of *Commodore*.

The month of December 1870 saw a small but extremely significant development in the company's trade. The Channel Fleet, consisting of Her Majesty's ships *Minotaur*, *Agincourt*, *Northumberland*, *Monarch*, *Warrior* and *Inconstant*, was at anchor in Portland Roads when a heavy gale blew up, preventing all communication between ship and shore in small boats. *Commodore* was hired to run to and fro four times per day and proved so popular with the officers and men that the Admiral decided to continue the arrangement until the fleet sailed for Christmas leave on 20th December. When *Commodore* took a party to witness the departure of the fleet, her owners probably did not realise that henceforth, whenever the fleet was at Portland, one of their steamers would be hired as a liberty boat and that, by 1914, the trade would represent a large portion of their income.

The following year saw a major change of pace at Swanage. On 1st May 1871, prominent Swanage-born London contractor and local landowner George Burt, introduced the 135 foot steamer *Heather Bell* on a regular service between Swanage, Poole and Bournemouth, and with frequent excursions to Cowes, Alum Bay, Lulworth and Weymouth.

Extensive advertising and the judicious provision of complimentary trips for local worthies and school children created a great deal of support for the ship and over 1,000 passengers were carried during her first three days in service. The pier head and 300 feet of the new Bournemouth pier had been swept away by a memorable gale on 5th January 1867 but the remaining length was now used at least twice a day by *Heather Bell*, whose popularity seemed to increase as the season progressed. *Royal Albert* remained on her Poole-Swanage service and continued to compete with *Heather Bell* until at least the end of the 1876 season. Clearly, there *was* a large demand for passenger sailings in the locality and Cosens must have regretted allowing such a large and well-found steamer to penetrate a market which they had declined to enter only three years earlier. To add to their gloom, the weather throughout the season was unusually bad and passenger figures were severely depressed.

Possibly as a response to the arrival of *Heather Bell*, a decision was made to modernise *Prince* during the winter of 1871-72, by removing her clipper bow and replacing it with a straight stem of a less ornamental design. The work was carried out at Weymouth by Mr Hinde and his team, and had the effect of fractionally reducing the ship's length without in any way interfering with her carrying capacity. *Premier* had another new boiler fitted at the end of the season, built by John Penn who had also supplied a replacement tubular steel boiler for *Commodore* in 1870.

George Burt's HEATHER BELL, *which was built in 1858, posed a considerable challenge to Cosens' interests when she entered service between Swanage, Bournemouth and Poole on 1st May 1871.*
BERNARD COX

PRINCE (nearest the camera) and PREMIER moored together in Weymouth Harbour sometime between 1872 and 1878. PRINCE has had her main mast removed and her clipper bow replaced by a straighter stem but PREMIER is still in her original condition, with enormous paddle boxes and a spoon bow. Her foresail, which has been hoisted to dry, was frequently set at sea to steady the ship and add speed if the wind was favourable. The bathing machines are again prominent on the beach in the background.
AUTHOR'S COLLECTION

During this period, Thomas Hardy, the famous Wessex novelist and poet, travelled on board the steamers on a number of occasions. One excursion from his fictional Budmouth (Weymouth) to Lulstead Cove (Lulworth) inspired a brief section entitled '*July the Twenty First*' in his early novel '*Desperate Remedies*', which was first published in 1871.

An evening excursion to Lulstead having been '*announced through the streets of Budmouth one Thursday morning by the weak-voiced Town Crier*', the heroine Cytherea and her brother Owen embark at 6pm and, having reached the Cove, walk inland to admire the scenery. Owen, anxious to view a medieval ruin further inland, strikes off on his own and, inevitably, fails to return in time for the homeward sailing. The anxious Cytherea, hearing '*the distant bell from the boat … followed by a lively air from the harps and violins on board*', returns to the beach where the other passengers are embarking '*by the primitive plan of a narrow plank on two wheels – the women being assisted by a rope.*' As sailing time comes and goes, her delay provokes a remark from the fictional Capt Jacobs (based, presumably, on either Capt Cosens, Mace or Haill), '*a thick set man of hybrid stains, resulting from the mixed effects of fire and water, peculiar to sailors where engines are the propelling power.*'

A decision having been made to leave Owen to return by train, '*off went the plank; the paddles started, stopped, backed, pattered in confusion, then revolved decisively, and the boat passed out into deep water.*' Cytherea meets and feels an immediate romantic attachment to an acquaintance of her brother, the handsome, young Mr Springrove:

'*A conversation began, which was none the less interesting to the parties engaged because it consisted only of the most trivial and commonplace remarks. Then the band of harps and violins struck up a lively melody, and the deck was cleared for dancing; the sun dipping beneath the horizon during the proceedings and the moon showing herself at their stern. The sea was so calm, that the soft hiss produced*

Arishmel Gap, Calver Cliff & Caves & Lulworth Castle, Dorset

by the bursting of the innumerable bubbles of foam behind the paddles could be distinctly heard. The passengers who did not dance, including Cytherea and Springrove, lapsed into silence, leaning against the paddle-boxes, or standing aloof – noticing the trembling of the deck to the steps of the dance – watching the waves from the paddles as they slid thinly and easily under each other's edges.

Night had quite closed in by the time they had reached Budmouth Harbour, sparkling with its red, white and green lights in opposition to the shimmering path of the moon's reflection on the other side, which reached away to the horizon till the flecked ripples reduced themselves to sparkles as fine as gold dust.'

Hardy's closely-observed description captures, quite beautifully, the experience of countless thousands of passengers over the long history of the Lulworth service.

On this part of the south coast, 1872 is chiefly

Lulworth Castle could be glimpsed by steamer passengers through the Arishmel Gap, on the approach to Lulworth Cove. PHILIP BANNON ENGRAVING/ COURTESY SWANAGE MUSEUM

The Combined Channel and Reserve Squadron
AT ANCHOR IN PORTLAND ROADS,
On the occasion of the visit of H. R. H. the Prince of Wales to lay the last Stone of the Portland Breakwater, August 10th, 1872.

On 10th August 1872, the Royal Navy's Channel and Reserve Squadrons assembled in Portland Harbour to salute the Prince of Wales, who had arrived on board the Royal Yacht VICTORIA & ALBERT to lay the final stone and declare the works completed. The twin 1.6 mile long breakwaters now sheltered the largest man-made harbour in the world, of some 2,130 acres. S. MORRIS COLLECTION

The Channel Fleet at anchor in the shelter of the newly-completed Portland Breakwaters, circa 1873.
NEWMAN

remembered as the year in which the completed Portland Breakwaters were officially opened by Prince Albert, Prince of Wales. The vast structures, the construction of which had consumed over five million tons of stone and the lives of 22 workers, now stretched for over three miles and enclosed an area of 2,130 acres, forming the largest man-made harbour in the world. The appointed day, 10th August, was declared a public holiday in Weymouth and Portland, and sightseers crowded every vantage point to watch for the arrival of the Prince on board the Royal Yacht *Victoria & Albert*. *Premier* was engaged to carry the mayor, corporation and other official guests from Weymouth to the ceremony, and duly put to sea into the teeth of '*a perfect gale and blinding rain*'. The official party sought what little shelter was available on board and were greatly relieved, '*after the shipping of seas and the boisterousness of the wind*', to see the squall pass and the weather improve. *Premier* landed her passengers at Portland's Admiralty Pier, while *Commodore* and the cross channel steamer *Brighton* followed, crowded with members of the public who were anxious to witness the unfolding spectacle. The Channel and Reserve Fleets headed by fifteen major ironclads had assembled in the harbour and fired a thunderous Royal salute as the Prince of Wales arrived to lay the final stone, which bore the inscription '*THESE ARE IMPERIAL WORKS AND WORTHY OF KINGS.*'

If the main excursion season of 1872 passed uneventfully, the same could not be said for the company's salvage work. In early January, *Commodore* put to sea one night under the command of William Cosens and battled her way round Portland Bill, in the face of tremendous seas, to rescue the French brig *Leopold Augusta*, which was in danger of driving ashore in Chesil Cove. A few days later, she was called to *Ravensworth*, ashore at Osmington, and towards the end of the month brought in the dismasted

ketch *Mary Stevens* and assisted the large steam ship *Filey*, whose anchor winch had failed off Whitenothe. February saw the American barque *Energy* assisted off the lee shore of Chesil Beach, while in October, the German schooner *Rewertdina* was towed into Weymouth after losing some of her crew overboard in a gale. Also during October, a Mr Stone was drowned after his yacht *Agnes* sank in the bay and *Prince* was sent out with a diver on board to attempt to recover his body. As soon as the task had been successfully accomplished, *Prince* hoisted a pre-arranged signal and steamed slowly into the pier, where hundreds of people had gathered to witness the sad spectacle of the flag-covered corpse being carried ashore on a grating. A week later, the hull of the yacht was raised by Cosens and brought into Weymouth Harbour.

The completed harbour of refuge at Portland proved its worth in January 1873, when over 200 ships, including ten or more screw steamers, were wind-bound there for several weeks. Several of the steamers ran short of coal and took in bunkers from Cosens' hulks before proceeding on their voyages. On 20th January, *Commodore* was cruising about at sea, hoping to pick up a towage job, when she recovered a fine but anonymous ship's boat, drifting empty, a mute testament to the human cost of the recent storms.

Preparations for the season ahead were almost complete when the shareholders were stunned by the news of the sudden death, on 4th April, of John Tizard. A prominent townsman, he was well-known as mayor, alderman, solicitor, officer in the local volunteer rifle corps and ship-owner, as well as a major shareholder in the steamboat company, and was widely mourned. His funeral was an impressive affair, with a long procession of members of the town council, the steamer owners and crews wending their way slowly to the cemetery. When Tizard's shares were offered for sale by his executors, they were quickly purchased by Joseph Drew for £125 each. Drew retained three for himself and distributed two to Capt Mace, one each to William Cosens and Capt Reynolds and three to the company clerk, S.J. Fowler. It is interesting to note that dividends were calculated on the basis of pounds per 64th share and were declared as many times per year as the board judged fit. In 1873, five dividends of £5 each were distributed, giving a total of £25 per 64th to each shareholder.

The 1873 season began on 21st May, when *Prince* ran the first excursion to Lulworth and then settled into its familiar pattern. Matters were enlivened on 5th May when *Great Eastern* arrived with yet another submarine cable on board and *Prince* advertised an excursion to meet her. As it was blowing hard from the east and the bay was unpleasantly rough, it was decided to offer the passengers a few hours on board *HMS Devastation*, which was anchored in Portland Harbour, before setting off to meet *Great Eastern* a mile or so out to sea. As she rounded the head of the breakwater, she was greeted with the usual sentimental tunes from Jones' band and the passengers returned ashore well satisfied with having seen two famous ships for the price of one. *Devastation* spent much of the summer at Portland and, being regularly open to the public, proved a very popular destination for the steamers.

Premier went more frequently to Swanage where, from April, George Burt had introduced a small screw steamer named *Lothair* to run alongside *Heather Bell* and to maintain a winter service for which the larger vessel had proved uneconomical. Unfortunately for Burt, the crown of *Heather Bell*'s furnace collapsed off Cowes on 13th June due to the incompetence of her engineer, who had allowed her boiler to run almost dry of water. The ship was towed to Day & Summer's shipyard at Southampton for repairs and was out of service until mid-August, during which time Burt appears to have chartered the steamer *May Flower* to fill her place.

September was marked by a spell of very poor weather, which caused the cancellation of many trips but did bring in some unusually early income from salvage. A derelict sloop, *HM&R* of Goole, was towed in on 3rd September and a few weeks later, *Commodore* experienced one of her rare failures when the brig *Vivid*, having been caught alongside Castletown Pier at Portland in a sudden onshore gale, sank in her berth after the tug had struggled unsuccessfully to tow her off.

With *Premier* and *Prince* laid up for the winter, the company's employees were just emerging from their short but well-deserved Christmas festivities when news reached Weymouth that Joseph Cosens, the founder of the company, had died suddenly while on a visit to London. Together with his wife Lydia, he had spent Christmas at the house of a Mrs Reynolds in Edmonton, where he died suddenly, aged 57, of 'bronchus cordus', a lung-related illness. Numerous local shop-keepers immediately put up their shutters and flags were flown at half-mast by shipping in the harbour, as a mark of respect for a man who, through his commercial activities, had contributed an enormous amount to the success of Weymouth as a watering-place. In reporting his death, the *Dorset County Chronicle* commented:

'During the season thousands of visitors came here solely for the purpose of enjoying the excursions which were daily carried out to some of the charming spots in the locality by means of these steamboats. Apart from these, however, the deceased was a man who deeply had the interests of the town at heart ... and his advice and counsel were listened to with attention and respect. He was one of those persons whom the town could ill afford to lose, and we are sure that his death will be lamented by a large number of inhabitants.'

The report of the funeral, which took place on Friday 2nd January 1874, gives an interesting insight into the composition of the company at the time and of Cosens' other connections in the town. The procession, which left his house at 3 Pultney Buildings

at noon, was arranged as follows:

Mr W. Hallett (the undertaker)

The Hearse

The first carriage, containing:
Capt W. Cosens, Mr Thomas Cosens,
Mr T. Lanning, Mr R. Damon

The second carriage containing:
Mr Fowler (company clerk), Capt Robens,
Capt Bartlett, Rev W. Lewis

The third carriage containing
the owners of The Steam Packet Company:
Dr Drew, Capt Mace, Capt Gibbs, Mr J. Reynolds

The fourth carriage containing:
Mr W. Roberts, Mr Smith (brokers),
Mr Mace (harbourmaster)

Behind these walked Mr Humphrey who used to
lead the deceased about

Then came the employees and a friend or two
connected with the company
walking two by two as follows:
Mr Skinner (carpenter) & Mr Carter (fitter)
Capt R. Fowler &
Mr W. Jeffery (the company's printer)
Mr W. Hinde junr & Mr H. Vye (engineers)
Mr F. White & Mr J Oldridge (mates)
Mr Chick (foreman) & Mr Cole (bargeman)
Mr Talbot & Mr Norster (seamen)
Mr W. Cox (toll collector) &
Mr Furmidge (pierman)
And four others connected with the steamers.

The bearers were:
Mr W. Hinde (superintendent engineer),
Mr J. Butcher (engineer)
Capt Ayles, Capt Haill, Mr G. Bowering (mate)
and M. W. Bowering (steward)

In accordance with the custom at the period, neither Lydia, his widow, nor any other females were present at the funeral. As a freechurchman, Joseph had expressed a wish to be laid beside his mother in the 'dissenters' side' of Melcombe Regis cemetery.

Although he had latterly played little part in the affairs of the company, the death of the founder caused further reorganisation to take place. From January 1874, William Cosens was appointed Commodore on a weekly wage of £3 and Mr S. J. Fowler was promoted from clerk to Company Secretary on an annual salary of £150. Both men, together with Mr Hinde the superintendent engineer, were given full powers over their own departments, Mr Fowler being given specific control of the wharfage, pier and coal stores, which henceforth

The grave of Joseph Cosens and his wife Lydia in Melcombe Regis cemetery. Joseph died on 28th December 1873 and Lydia on 12th April 1877. Several other members of the Cosens family, Joseph Drew and numerous of the company's captains, engineers and staff are buried in the same cemetery. AUTHOR

traded as Cosens & Co. With Dr Drew in the chair, Messrs Mace and Gibbs acted as directors and the leases on the workshops and coal stores were transferred to Dr Drew and Capt Mace respectively. It was resolved that more permanent arrangements for the future management of the company would be discussed and decided upon in due course.

While these new arrangements were under consideration, the 1874 and 1875 seasons proceeded very much as normal and no outward changes were visible to passengers. Since the beginning of the decade, influenced by the national 'early closing' movement, all of the businesses in Weymouth had agreed to close at 5pm, in order that the evening could be devoted to recreation and pleasure. The steamboat company had responded by providing a regular 6pm sailing to Lulworth Cove, offering passengers an hour on shore before arriving home at 9pm. When a letter appeared in the *Southern Times* during July 1874 urging Dorchester shopkeepers to imitate their Weymouth counterparts, Mr Fowler immediately responded that:

> *'If two or three gentlemen would form themselves into a committee with the purpose of ensuring a general closing on Wednesday evenings at five, I have no doubt that the railway companies would arrange to bring passengers down to Weymouth at a reduced fare and our company would then put on a special Dorchester boat so as to ensure that the passengers return in time for the up mail train.'*

August Bank Holiday Monday 1874 was blessed by fine weather and over 4,000 excursionists arrived in Weymouth by train, many of them flocking on board the steamers for either a day trip to Swanage and Bournemouth, a shorter voyage to Lulworth, or a visit on board *Great Eastern*, which had arrived on the previous evening to coal before laying another cable to Newfoundland. She was thrown open to the public for two days and large numbers took advantage of an hourly shuttle service provided by the steamers to and from the ship. Later in the week, when *Premier* was making a moonlight cruise round the great ship, a gentleman was standing on the paddle box when he lost his balance and fell overboard. Lifebelts were thrown, a lifeboat launched and, although it was too dark to see the man, his lusty shouts acted as a guide and within three minutes he had been recovered. The speed with which the rescue was effected greatly impressed the passengers and William Cosens was declared the hero of the hour. After laying her cable, *Great Eastern* called briefly at Portland again on 8th September and *'sent a boat ashore to Messrs Cosens & Co., the steamship's agents here, for letters and telegrams.'* From this note, it would seem likely that Cosens had been acting as her agents since her first visit to Portland and were almost certainly acting in a similar capacity for a number of other visiting ships. It was a role which would have dovetailed very well with their bunkering trade, which was now widely advertised in the shipping press.

A period of windy weather in mid-August made the narrow entrance to Lulworth Cove impassable for some days and led to the diversion or cancellation of a number of sailings. By the end of the month, a period of calm prevailed and when an excursion to meet the yachts competing in the Southsea to Weymouth passage race was undertaken, *Premier* had to steam as far as St. Alban's Head before encountering the magnificent craft, with every stitch of canvas set, becalmed on a glassy sea. The yachts, which included the 192 ton schooner *Gwendolin* and the 136 ton yawl *Florinda*, were owned by the ultra-wealthy of the day and spent the summer sailing from port to port along the south coast competing in local regattas. The racing became a popular spectator sport and added a cosmopolitan new dimension to the seaside scene. For the final evening of the Weymouth regatta, the esplanade was *'lighted up by various coloured fires'* and there was a small firework display but the most attractive feature was the Pile Pier, which *'was charmingly illuminated with diverse coloured lanterns and fires and from where a large number of rockets were discharged'*, all at the expense of the steamboat company. The sailing lists also indicate that Lyme Regis was visited more frequently than in previous years and that Alum Bay on the Isle of Wight, where a wooden pier had been constructed during 1869, was now a fairly regular destination. From 1875, Bridport, Seaton and Sidmouth also appeared with increasing regularity.

The 1875 season opened at the beginning of May, when the Weymouth-Portland service re-opened, to

be followed two weeks later by the Whitsun Holiday sailings. Although the weather was a little too windy for many tastes, a fair number of passengers enjoyed trips to Bournemouth, Lulworth and to visit *HMS Warrior*. At the beginning of June, the boy's training ship *HMS Boscawen*, which had replaced another wooden wall at Portland in 1873, was opened to the public and many took advantage of the opportunity to view this former first rate ship of the line, which had seen action in the Black Sea, Mediterranean and the English Channel. Needless to say, the only means of access was by Cosens' steamer!

August Bank Holiday was especially busy, providing a 'golden day' for the steamers, which sailed full all day and had to turn away numerous excursionists who, it was noted, '*mostly consisted of the working classes*'. On 16th August, *Premier* was returning from a day trip to Bournemouth with 200 passengers on board, when she was enveloped in a thick fog off Swanage and land was not seen again until Weymouth pier head was sighted. With her engine at slow ahead, her whistle sounding regularly and the lead being heaved continuously, *Premier* felt her way carefully along, guided only by the soundings, her compass and William Cosens' intimate knowledge of the coast. The non-arrival of the ship had caused considerable alarm amongst visitors who had friends on board and, when she finally emerged from the fog, several hundred who had gathered on the pier to watch for her arrival gave vent to their joy with rounds of hearty cheers. The bell on the pier had been rung all evening to try to guide her in and *Commodore*, with Dr Drew, Mr Fowler and Capt Gibbs on board, had set off during the evening to try to locate *Premier*. Neither ship had seen the other and, with *Premier* safely alongside, it was now *Commodore*'s turn to lose her bearings. Capt Cosens set off in an open boat which he moored to a buoy off the harbour mouth.

Although he could not see the missing steamer, he could hear her paddle beats and, by dint of shouting, was eventually able to guide her safely in to port. The incident is a vivid reminder that the steamers carried no navigational instruments other than a compass and lead line, and that their safety record, when operating in all weathers along a busy and treacherous coast, was little short of miraculous.

A few days later, the annual regatta was enlivened by the opportunity to visit the new fort at the end of the breakwater. Cosens took the opportunity to engage the services of a Capt Parker and his sister who were well known in the swimming world and provided additional entertainment by '*performing a number of surprising gymnastics*' in the small mooring basin at the fort.

The season had been a profitable one and closed with the declaration of an additional £7 dividend, giving a total for the year of £32 per 64th share. Behind the scenes, however, the deliberations about the future structure of the company were nearing a conclusion and 1876 was to prove a year of profound changes.

The truncated Bournemouth Pier in 1875, a year before a further 100 foot length was swept away in a storm. The steamer could be ROYAL ALBERT, *which maintained a service from Poole to Swanage and Bournemouth until at least 1876.*
BOURNEMOUTH LIBRARY

Bournemouth in 1868. The fledgling resort is beginning to spread over the surrounding hillsides, and Sydenham's new Marine Library & Bazaar can be seen in its prominent position at the shoreward end of the pier.
BOURNEMOUTH LIBRARY

An unidentified steamer at Bournemouth Pier, circa 1875.

AUTHOR'S COLLECTION, COURTESY THE LATE ERIC PAYNE

CHAPTER 7

THE LIMITED COMPANY &
DEVELOPMENTS TO EAST & WEST
1876-1881

The year of 1876 opened with the acquisition of the lease of the Weymouth slipway formerly occupied by Mr C. Besant. In its existing state, the slip was about 80 feet in length but Cosens immediately set about extending and improving it so that, by the middle of 1877, it had been fitted with a 3hp vertical steam engine for hauling up the cradle and was capable of accommodating any of the company's steamers. In addition to undertaking their own maintenance, Cosens were now able to offer a repair facility to other vessels and this, combined with a rapid expansion in their engineering department, provided a steady source of income, which helped to compensate for the unpredictability of the excursion and salvage trade in some of the difficult years ahead.

Income from salvage during the spring was almost non-existent. On the morning of 9th April, following a particularly tempestuous night, two ship's boats were spotted near the Portland Race and both the lifeboat *Agnes Harriet* and *Commodore* put to sea to render assistance. Off Church Ope Cove, they encountered a Weymouth pilot cutter with one of the boats in tow and noted that the Shambles lightship was flying an unusual signal. *Commodore* arrived alongside a few minutes ahead of the lifeboat, to discover that the remaining boat had managed to reach the lightship and her crew had taken refuge on board. The men were transferred to the tug and their boat taken in tow but hopes of a salvage job were dashed by the fact that none of them spoke English and it was impossible to discover what had become of their ship. Only when *Commodore* reached Weymouth again was it discovered that they were from the French barque *Ondine*, which they had abandoned in a waterlogged and unmanageable state off Lyme Regis the previous evening. Frustratingly for Cosens, the valuable barque had remained afloat and was brought safely into Exmouth by the Budleigh Salterton coastguards.

The following evening, a vessel was reported under jury rig off Portland Bill and *Commodore* again set off in hot pursuit. The vessel was the schooner *St. Olaf*, which had been dismasted some days earlier but was sailing so fast under her temporary rig that no help was required and *Commodore* returned empty-handed to her moorings.

The coal trade continued to generate a healthy income but another dispute broke out when the Weymouth council announced their intention to enforce the collection of wharfage dues on all bunkering coal taken from the harbour to ships in the Roads. Cosens, using the feeble argument that they had never charged themselves when they were lessees of the harbour dues, initially refused to pay but, having received legal advice, eventually gave in with a bad grace and conceded to the Council's demands.

The Portland service commenced for the season during April, followed by the excursion sailings in mid-May. In an attempt to boost passenger numbers, the company reduced excursion fares by 25 per cent, issued one guinea season tickets to cover all sailings from Weymouth and abolished Pile Pier tolls for steamer passengers. Improved standards of catering were introduced with the stewarding contract for all three steamers being let to Capt Bowering of *Prince*, who provided staff, stock and utensils at his own expense. Hoping to benefit from the extra trade generated by *Heather Bell*, regular sailings to Swanage and Bournemouth were increased to twice weekly, while westward trips from Weymouth to Seaton, Sidmouth, Beer or Lyme Regis were advertised at least once a week during the high season. Portsmouth, Alum Bay and other Isle of Wight piers featured regularly as long distance destinations and every opportunity was grasped to offer occasional sailings to special events. One of these took place on 16th May, when *Premier* offered a 4s excursion to Portsmouth where the steamship *Seraphis*, on board which the Prince of Wales had recently travelled to India and back, was thrown open to public inspection. Open days on board the boy's training ship *HMS Boscawen*, *HMS Warrior* and other warships in Portland Harbour regularly produced long queues for the steamers and the innovation of offering occasional free trips to the pupils of various local schools generated a great deal of goodwill in the town. A reporter travelling with a party from Mr Thurman's Academy on 17th August felt moved to '*draw to the attention of the public the energetic way in which the company is now managed and the great liberality often displayed by them.*'

Much of this energy was, of course, due to the chairman Dr Drew and company secretary S.J. Fowler who, behind the scenes, were steering the business steadily towards incorporation as a limited company. During March, Joseph Cosens' widow Lydia, who had developed cancer and was fast declining, sold her shares to Dr Drew, who held them on behalf of the company until 10th June 1876, when Cosens & Company Ltd formally came into being. The memorandum of association stated that '*the objects for which the company is established are the conveyance of passengers, merchandise and goods in ships, barges and boats between such places as the company shall from time to time determine, to be coal and general*

Cosens' steam launch PRINCESS, *pictured in Weymouth Backwater.* AUTHOR'S COLLECTION

merchants and to do all other such things as are incidental or conducive to the attainment of the above objects.'

The new company's capital of £12,800 in 128 fully paid up shares of £100 each was distributed as follows:

Joseph Drew, JP 66
John Gibbs, Master Mariner 24
John Piers Reynolds, Brewer 12
Edward Mace, Master Mariner 10
William Cosens, Master Mariner 6
Simon Jenkin Fowler, Accountant 6
Edward Beale Mace, Builder 4

J.W. Williams was the only shareholder in the private company not to continue into the limited company and E.B. Mace was the only addition. All of the shareholders were residents of Weymouth and brought with them many years of experience in the steamboat business.

At the first meeting of the new company, held at the registered offices on Custom House Quay on 1st July 1876, Dr Drew, Capt Mace and Capt Gibbs were appointed directors and S.J. Fowler company secretary. The private company was formally wound up on 7th July, the closing minutes reflecting that the dividend drawn over the five years of its existence had amounted to £16,320 on a capital of £12,800, representing an average of £11 11s 9d per cent per annum.

The new regime did not allow grass to grow under its feet and, on 11th September, an extraordinary general meeting was held at Dr Drew's house at 6 Devonshire Buildings, to propose raising an additional £5,000 capital to finance the purchase of a steam launch and an additional steamer. Mr Fowler was dispatched to various ports around Britain to inspect possible vessels and, by the time the increase in capital was formally approved on 29th September, had settled on a 55 feet by 9 feet 4 inches by 4 feet 6 inches wooden steam launch called *Lady Bird*, which was offered for sale by John William Shepherd, a merchant of Royal Chambers, Hull. A price of £550 was agreed and the transfer of ownership took place

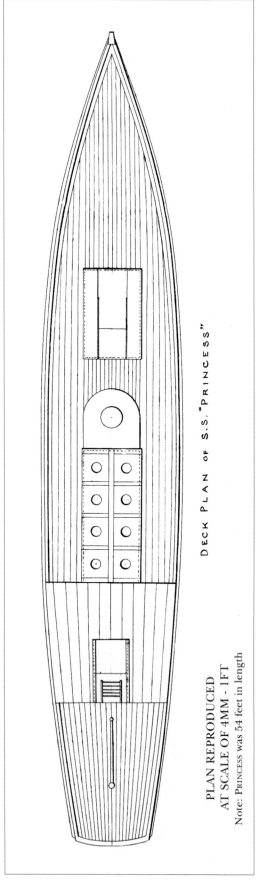

DECK PLAN OF S.S. "PRINCESS"

PLAN REPRODUCED AT SCALE OF 4MM - 1FT
Note: PRINCESS was 54 feet in length

on 16th October 1876. Capt Bowering was sent to Hull to steam her round to Weymouth, a considerable challenge in such a small and unfamiliar craft at the period of autumn gales. She had a square stern, small cabins fore and aft, two lug-rigged masts and was powered by a compound condensing steam engine (cylinders 13 inches and $8^1/_2$ inches diameter by 9 inches stroke) by C.D. Holmes of Hull. On arrival at Weymouth the launch was renamed *Princess* and appears to have been used in connection with the company's bunkering trade, diving operations and in carrying supplies and personnel to and from the new Chequered Fort at the end of the Portland Breakwater.

The proposal to add an additional passenger steamer to the fleet was closely connected with developments at Bournemouth and Swanage. It appears to have been an open secret that George Burt's *Heather Bell* was experiencing boiler and other structural problems, so it came as no surprise when, after she finished her season on 7th October, the *Bournemouth Observer* announced:

'The Heather Bell *excursions are over for this year and for ever and we are looking rather anxiously at what Bournemouth is going to do as regards the next boat to run between the two places. The spirited owner of the* Heather Bell *has clearly shown that neither place can any longer be without one.*'

A key figure in subsequent developments was David Sydenham, proprietor of the Marine Library & Bazaar near Bournemouth Pier and one of the town's earliest and most influential inhabitants. Sydenham had been Burt's agent since 1871 and, as well as being privy to *Heather Bell*'s impending demise, was keenly aware of the potential of steamer excursions and the importance to the town of a continued service. For several months, therefore, he and a group of other local gentlemen had been quietly investigating possibilities and, by the time a public meeting was held at Town Hall Buildings on 12th October, their thinking was already well developed.

Sydenham announced that he had been in discussion with Cosens, who had offered to let the *Prince* on charter for £45 per week or to sell her for £3,000. This, of course, explains why Cosens were considering the acquisition of a new steamer. A Mr McWilliam, a Bournemouth Commissioner and developer had been in contact with the shipbuilder John Inglis of Glasgow who, with his eye on obtaining an order to build a new ship, had replied that he would '*be glad to go shares*' if a new company was formed. Another gentleman, Mr Robinson, had received a communication from Hardcastle & Co of Sunderland, offering the Clyde steamer *Largs* for sale at £3,800, while George Burt had intimated that if anyone at Bournemouth wished to purchase *Heather Bell* at a fair valuation, he would be willing to take a large proportion in shares or, alternatively, that he would purchase 20 shares and work the company to mutual advantage. With these alternatives

before it, the meeting decided to appoint a committee consisting of Messrs D. Sydenham, J. McWilliam, W.B. Rogers, E. Haytor and J. Robinson to '*confer further with the Weymouth or any other company*' and report back as early as convenient. Significantly, an editorial in the *Bournemouth Observer* expressed strong support for the formation of a local company and voiced concern that '*if we now invite a Weymouth Company to come to our assistance we might at a future time have some difficulties in getting rid of them.*'

Opinion in Swanage favoured the retention and repair of *Heather Bell*, which Burt was willing to sell for £800 but Southampton shipbuilders Day & Summers estimated that it would cost at least £2,000 to replace her boiler, re-plate her bottom and carry out other essential work. The committee felt that this was a large sum for such an elderly ship, especially in view of doubts about her service speed even after repairs. The offer of the 195 foot steamer *Vale of Clyde*, which was claimed to steam at 18 knots, for the sum of £4,500 was also considered but the committee's deliberations were thrown into disarray when, on 11th November, a further 100 foot length of Bournemouth Pier was destroyed in a gale. It will be recalled that the pier head had already been swept away in 1867 and it was feared that this latest disaster would render the pier unfit for further steamer traffic. All discussions of the formation of a local company were therefore put on hold, pending an investigation by the Bournemouth Commissioners into the future of the pier and Cosens, deprived of a potential buyer for *Prince*, postponed the question of a new steamer for Weymouth for the time being.

The winter of 1876-77 saw only a moderate amount of salvage work. During November, the barque *Roberto* of Halifax, having recently sailed from Portland, found herself becalmed and was driven broadside onto the outside of the breakwater by a heavy SE swell. The little *Ocean Bride*, which was still employed by the Admiralty at Portland, attempted to refloat her but had insufficient power to do so. *Commodore* was then sent for and, after considerable

Sydenham's Marine Library & Bazaar, which stood in a prominent position near the entrance to Bournemouth Pier was, for many years, the hub of the resort's steamer activity. Its proprietor, David Sydenham, started his career as a book seller and went on to publish many of the town's early guide books. He acted as agent for HEATHER BELL *from 1871 until her demise in 1876 and for the next five years served as secretary to the companies which chartered a variety of steamers to serve the resort. From 1881 until his death in 1911, he served as Cosens' local manager and conducted his energetic marketing campaigns from the Marine Library. Notices on the building advertise the Reading room and the availability of pianofortes.*
BOURNEMOUTH LIBRARY

exertion, successfully towed the casualty off. *Roberto* lost part of her keel and rudder in the process but was otherwise undamaged and Cosens received an award of £750 for their services.

During a severe gale on 4th and 5th December, a large number of ships were taking refuge in the shelter of Portland Harbour when the smack *Liberty* began to drag her anchors towards the breakwater. *Commodore* was quickly alongside but, finding that there was nobody on board, had great difficulty passing a tow. It was far too rough to launch a boat, so Capt Cosens took *Commodore* as close to the smack as he dared and several of his crew, timing their jump to the roll of the casualty, leapt into her rigging. *Liberty* was no sooner safe and snug in Weymouth Harbour than *Commodore* put to sea again to rescue the French brigantine *Hippolite*, which had been dragging her anchors across the bay so rapidly that her master had ordered both masts to be cut away to reduce windage. *Commodore* came across her just off Osmington and having agreed terms, brought her into harbour at 2.30pm.

On 19th February, a similar gale caused the yacht *Dart*, which was anchored in the bay, to drag her anchors and collide with the brigantine *Vulcan*. The yacht was so severely damaged that it was feared she might founder and, as daylight broke, a signal was hoisted for *Commodore* to bring her into safety. A sum of £5 was agreed for the tow but when the owner failed to pay, the yacht was arrested and subsequently sold to pay Cosens' bill and the crew's wages.

Back at Bournemouth, it had rapidly become apparent that the pier was beyond repair and a temporary landing stage was constructed to allow the resumption of steamer services from July 1877, while the local Commissioners drew up plans to finance a more permanent replacement. The committee, having finally formed itself into the Bournemouth Steam Packet Company with Mr Sydenham as secretary, chartered a steamer named *Criterion* from Sunderland and opened their excursion season on 16th July, as soon as the temporary landing stage became available. As well as trips to Swanage, Poole and the Isle of Wight, *Criterion* made a three day cross-channel excursion to Cherbourg between 19th and 21st August, taking about eight hours on the outward passage and rather longer, in poor weather, on the return. Burt's *Lothair* and the Poole-based *Royal Albert* continued in service, offering occasional excursions in addition to their regular trade between Poole and Swanage.

Cosens, of course, sought to keep their vessels firmly in the public eye by sending *Premier* or *Prince* down from Weymouth on at least two days each week. In order to ensure their continued superiority over any other vessel at Bournemouth, plans were laid to rebuild and modernise *Premier* during the coming winter and John Penn, the London engineer and shipbuilder, was asked to quote for a new engine and paddle wheels for the ship, together with '*a sister boat complete with all modern improvements*'.

In the event, the improvements to *Premier* went ahead but the matter of an additional steamer was once again deferred.

Part of the reason for Cosens' caution may have been that 1877 was an exceptionally short and stormy season, and that so many sailings had to be abandoned that passenger revenue fell considerably. At Weymouth, a small steamer from Portland named *Mistletoe* had the temerity to attempt to undercut Cosens by advertising cheap Thursday evening trips in the bay but does not seem to have survived for many weeks. Rather more seriously, a Capt Elliott and Mr Northover set up in opposition in the bunkering trade, and Cosens were forced to purchase their coal hulk and buy them off with a royalty of 2s 9d per ton on all coal sold to steamers in the Roads.

On the plus side, however, the list of shareholders expanded steadily as the new share capital flowed in, the engineering department's earnings increased dramatically and, most significantly of all, a considerable profit was made from providing a liberty boat service to the Channel Fleet in Portland Harbour. As luck would have it, the fleet was present for rather longer than was normal and the income generated neatly offset the shortfall on excursions. The company was successful in obtaining the lease of the Pile Pier for another three years and an article in the *Southern Times* pointed out that, after the drop in passenger figures following the opening of the Portland railway, the excursion trade had developed to such an extent that, for the past three years, more people had embarked at the pier than ever before. A reserve and sinking fund was created by investing £640 and the end of year dividend, although 5 per cent down on the exceptional 1876 figure, was a very healthy 10 per cent.

One of the worst shipping disasters ever to occur off the coast of Dorset unfolded during the night of 11th September, 1877. A south westerly gale was howling up the English Channel and a heavy sea was running, whilst torrential rain and the total lack of moonlight made visibility particularly poor. Bound down Channel from London were two large sailing ships, the iron, three-masted clipper *Avalanche*, bound for New Zealand with 34 crew and 63 passengers on board, and the wooden ship *Forest*, for New York with a crew of 21 hands. Just after 8pm, both ships were approximately twelve miles SW of Portland Bill, close hauled on opposite tacks, when they suddenly became aware of each other's flickering navigation lights. *Avalanche* should have given way immediately but delayed doing so until the very moment that the master of *Forest* decided on evasive action and the two ships came into violent collision.

Within five minutes, *Avalanche* had disappeared beneath the waves, taking all but three of her company with her and *Forest* was so badly damaged that the order was given to abandon ship. Three boats were launched but by morning two had been overwhelmed and only twelve men were left alive to be rescued and brought ashore at Chesil Cove, through the heroic actions of some Portland fishermen in their seaworthy local beach boats known as lerrets.

Forest had not, as supposed, sunk after the collision but was spotted drifting capsized and waterlogged with her stern high in the air off Portland, where she posed a serious threat to other shipping. Therefore, while the grim business of recovering the numerous bodies which had begun to wash ashore on Portland continued and the official inquiry got underway, *Commodore* put to sea on Thursday 13th September to tow her in. The rough sea and unusual position of the hulk made it impossible to connect a tow and on the following day two further attempts, one with the assistance of the channel island steamer *Cygnus*, also failed. It was assumed that *Forest*'s bowsprit was dragging on the seabed and that her anchors and cables had fallen out and were tethering her, with her bows under water, in a position six miles SSE of the Shambles lightship. On Saturday, *Commodore* went out again bearing the company's most experienced staff and the captains of *Aquila* and *Cygnus* to see what could be done but, finding it impossible in the heavy swell to put men onto the keel or find anywhere to attach a tow rope, returned to harbour once again.

From Monday onwards, *Premier* began running a series of rather macabre excursions to view the wreck and tremendous excitement was generated when it was announced that *HMS Defence* of the Channel Fleet would be sent to destroy the wreck by gunfire on Tuesday. An excursion to view the operation was immediately announced but the patience of the spectators was sorely tried when the ironclad's shells simply passed through the hull and subsequent attempts to sink her with explosive charges and mines only resulted in her floating higher in the water. Attempts continued over the next few days when *'gunpowder was exploded by hundredweights'* but with equally little success. The daily excursions to watch the fun proved immensely popular and the navy became the target of a good deal of barbed humour. One excursionist, writing to the *Southern Times* explained:

'If the combined powers of H.M. ironclad Defence *with four steam launches and pinnaces, a real live admiral CB, officers innumerable, with men unaccountable, were unable to provide us with amusement, Jones' Band were, as always, equal to the occasion. We, steaming alongside the* Defence, *played 'Rule Britannia' with great effect; no living satirist could have outdone this … Pieces of the wreck picked up are sawn and sold freely to passengers and a wag enquires the price per ounce of sawdust … "Why has the* Defence *taken up her station over a mile away from the scene of operations?" enquires another … "Why, 'tisn't likely he wants his men to see what a mess they are making of it." is the prompt reply. "Is that really the Trinity House* Galetea?" *says a visitor … "Yes, she is likely come down with Pate de Fois Gras and a special consignment of dry champagne for the Admiral and officers engaged on this arduous duty" is the answer.'*

In fairness, it should be acknowledged that *Forest*, being a wooden ship and without cargo, would have had natural buoyancy and a great deal of air trapped within her upturned hull. Each attack by the navy probably shook more ballast out of her and caused her to float even higher in the water. Eventually, on 22nd September, *HMS Defence* succeeded in towing her off the Shambles Bank and took her further down Channel where, with an enormous explosive charge, she was finally blown to pieces. The remains were brought into Portland and sold to be broken up for firewood. Relatives of those lost in the disaster

COMMODORE, in the middle background, lying at her mooring on Trinity Quay, Weymouth, sometime between 1877 and 1886. The large paddle steamer on the right is BRIGHTON, *which ran from Weymouth to the Channel Islands and Cherbourg until 1887, when she was wrecked off Guernsey. To the right of her forward funnel can be seen the bay window of Cosens & Co Ltd's Head Office at 10 Custom House Quay. The building to the right of the office was the company's sail loft, coal store and, from 1884 onwards, ice house.*
WEYMOUTH LIBRARY

PREMIER as she appeared after her major refit during the winter of 1877-78. The photograph is dated 26th June 1880.
AUTHOR'S COLLECTION

requested that a memorial be erected on Portland and two years later, St. Andrew's Church – known locally as 'Avalanche Church' – was consecrated at Southwell, where it may be visited to this day.

After the horrors of *Forest* and *Avalanche*, subsequent salvage jobs that autumn must have seemed insignificant but one in particular stood out, due to the acrimony of the court case which followed

St Andrew's or 'Avalanche' Church, Portland, consecrated in 1879, overlooks the site of the tragic collision between the sailing ships FOREST and AVALANCHE, and was erected by public subscription in memory of all who lost their lives.
AUTHOR

the rescue. On the morning of 15th October, following hurricane force winds during the previous night, a schooner was reported in distress and *Commodore*, under the command of Capt Ayles and with five extra men plus Capt Cosens and Capt Gibbs on board, put to sea to lend assistance. The vessel was *Helena*, with her yards and main boom carried away and most of her sails in tatters. *Commodore* was manoeuvred alongside and, after some discussion, a tow passed. Back in the safety of Weymouth Harbour, the master of the schooner insisted that he had agreed the sum of 30s for a tow, while William Cosens countered that he had refused to discuss prices at all but now claimed £30 for salvage services. The schooner's master refused to pay, so his vessel was arrested and the matter went to court, where Cosens argued that it was ludicrous to suppose that their tug would have put to sea in such conditions and with so many extra hands on board, simply to agree a standard towage job for 30s when the printed rate for the task was £7. They challenged the assertion that the schooner was under command and could have made Portland unassisted and were eventually awarded £20 and costs.

Three days after the rescue of *Helena*, there were fears that history had repeated itself when the steamer *Knapton Hall* and the sailing ship *Loch Fyne* were in collision. The sailing vessel had been thrown onto her beam ends in the recent hurricane and, in

attempting to go to her assistance, the steamer had collided with her and sunk. A lifeboat had foundered drowning nine men but *Loch Fyne* had remained afloat and made for Portland. *Prince* went out to offer a tow but, being offered only £5, declined the job and left the casualty to make port by her own devices. Agreeing towage and salvage rates was evidently a very hard-nosed business indeed.

During the winter of 1877-78, the extensive rebuilding of *Premier* went ahead as planned on the company's slipway at Weymouth. The ship was cut in half and lengthened by 8 feet by the insertion of a completely new 65 foot midships section. A new keel was fitted, floors and frames renewed, two new stringers added, and the topside plating shifted or replaced as required. The paddle deck, angle beams, rudder and masts were replaced, and the sponsons lengthened to 75 feet. Her original, large paddle boxes were replaced by much smaller ones, which reached just above the level of the bridge deck, and new paddle wheels, supplied by J. Penn & Son of Greenwich, were fitted. The upper deck was replanked and fitted with new scuppers and a new 45 foot bridge deck bearing the ship's wheel and passenger seating was added and surrounded by galvanised wire netting stretched over the rails and stanchions. The old spoon bow was removed and replaced with a straight stem, and below decks the passenger accommodation was remodelled. Provision was made for a separate ladies cabin and WC aft, and a bar and counter were fitted to the forward saloon. The boiler was fitted with new stays.

The whole of the work was carried out by the company's own staff under the supervision of superintendent engineer Mr Hinde. *Premier* was launched on Tuesday 2nd April and towed to Castletown Quay, Portland, where her new engine was lifted in by a large crane belonging to Messrs Scriven. Built by J. Penn & Son, it was of an oscillating design, with two cylinders 25 inches in diameter and 33 inch stroke and a combined horse power of 50 (200ihp).

On 30th May, an invited party joined the ship on a trial trip to St. Alban's Head. Under the close supervision of a commissioning engineer from Penns, she attained an average speed of 12.75 knots at 44 revs per minute on a steam pressure of 23lbs per square inch. Everyone present expressed themselves delighted with the outcome and congratulated the company on creating what was effectively a new ship for £4,400, approximately half the cost of building from scratch. Certainly, the company now had a vessel which would be the equal of anything likely to present itself at Bournemouth during the season ahead. A slight problem occurred later in the season, when the helmsmen on board *Premier* complained that excessive heat from the funnel was making their job unbearable and it was suggested that the wheel be moved to the forward end of the bridge deck. As a temporary measure, the bottom of the funnel was fitted with an insulating felt casing.

Premier ran her first public cruise from Weymouth to Alum Bay on Whit Monday 10th June 1878, rejoining her fleet mates which had been in service since Good Friday.

Prince, too, had received an unusually thorough

The British Reserve Squadron at anchor in Portland Harbour during June 1878. This magnificent fleet provided Cosens with a double source of income – by carrying visitors to view or visit the ships and by providing liberty boats to carry the sailors to Weymouth for shore leave. Among the many notable ships in this picture are, top right, the boy's training ship BOSCAWEN, which remained permanently moored at Portland for many years and, below her to the left, the famous HMS WARRIOR, which is now preserved at Portsmouth.
WEYMOUTH MUSEUM

overhaul during the winter and was reported to be running faster than ever before. The season then followed its accustomed pattern, apart from an experimental extension of operations in south Devon. The management realised that if a new steamer was built, *Prince* would become surplus to requirements unless a new trade could be found for her and therefore seems to have been testing the water with an eye to the future. The number of Devon towns visited on westward trips from Weymouth was extended to include Dawlish, Seaton, Sidmouth, Beer, Lyme, Torquay and Plymouth. On a number of occasions, trips were advertised *from* those towns to Weymouth. On 11th July, for example, *Premier* left Weymouth at 5am, steamed light to Sidmouth where she collected passengers at breakfast time and, after touching at Seaton and Lyme, rounded Portland Bill to give her complement half an hour on board the ironclad *Gorgon* and one and a half hours in Weymouth, before returning westward once again. It is also known that *Prince* spent some time actually based in south Devon, offering cruises between the various locals towns. At Weymouth from 1877 onwards, regular trips to Ringstead were offered and, in 1878, special cheap late afternoon trips were provided to connect with the 5pm train from Dorchester. Ringstead, which is just across the bay from Weymouth, is protected by an extensive reef and is not the easiest of places to approach by sea. We know that passengers went ashore to enjoy a lobster tea but it is not recorded whether the steamer made a beach landing or if her compliment were ferried ashore in boats.

At Bournemouth, the local company, which had changed its name to The Bournemouth & South Coast Steam Packet Company Ltd, opened their 1878 season on Easter Monday 22nd March with another chartered steamer named *Lord Collingwood*. She remained on station until mid September when, her charter having presumably expired, she was replaced for the remainder of the season by *Transit*. Both Cosens and the local company appear to have done well at Bournemouth as, by the beginning of September, the Board of Trade was issuing warnings about the habitual overcrowding of the steamers. Then, on 3rd September, everything changed when the Thames excursion steamer *Princess Alice* was in collision with a cargo vessel near Woolwich and sank with the loss of over 650 lives. The nation was stunned by the scale of the catastrophe and, fearing that a similar incident could occur elsewhere, the travelling public deserted the steamers in droves. Passenger traffic throughout the kingdom was effectively paralysed and income for the latter end of the season took a severe fall.

In addition, 1878 was a year of general economic depression in Britain and a large number of cargo steamers had been forced to withdraw from trade. Far fewer called for coal at Portland and Cosens' receipts from bunkering fell by £800. Once again, the situation was saved by the healthy income generated by the liberty boat trade to the Channel Fleet and by a further expansion of the engineering department, one of whose major jobs was to repair ironwork on board the steamer *Greatham Hall,* which had put into Portland after suffering serious gale damage. Cosens had already announced a 12 per cent dividend and the transfer of a further £1,204 to the sinking fund when the unexpected downturn in the passenger and coaling trades took place, and the company found itself with a serious lack of cash in hand. In order to avoid drawing on reserves, instructions were issued to keep maintenance costs to an absolute minimum during the winter ahead.

Notwithstanding the difficulties of the season, a special meeting was called on 23rd September to consider the advisability of building or buying a new steamer, and of financing her by raising a further £5,000 in share capital over and above the £5,000 already allowed through the special resolutions of 1876, making a total capital of £22,800. The motion was passed unanimously at an EGM on 1st October and the directors given permission to raise an additional £10,000 by issuing loan or debenture bonds. They were also empowered to '*sell, exchange or charter the* Prince *steamer*' should they consider it in the company's interests to do so.

Within four days of the official notices being issued, all of the bonds had been taken up and 36 new shares issued. An order was immediately placed for the new steamer, which was to be named *Empress*. She was to be built by Samuda Brothers of Poplar and engined by John Penn & Son, at a cost of £8,710. Significantly, both these influential gentlemen agreed to become shareholders in the company, the price of their shares doubtless being offset against the cost of the ship. Samuda purchased 4 shares but Penn took a block of 16, making him the second largest shareholder in the company after Joseph Drew. Needless to say, the association of such an eminent engineer with the company was widely publicised and used to imply the technical superiority of Cosens' vessels over all other south coast pleasure steamers. A first instalment was immediately paid and a delivery date of 1st May 1879 agreed. There was some discussion of adding a deck saloon to the new vessel but, when it was realised that this would take her over 100 registered tons, it was decided not to proceed. Samudas were, however, asked to build a bow landing stage of a new and improved design and Cosens announced that, in addition to introducing a service from Weymouth to the Isle of Wight, *Empress* would be making regular trips to Torquay, calling at the open beaches of the Devon towns en route.

Construction proceeded rapidly and *Empress* was launched from Samuda's yard on 7th April 1879 by Miss Reynolds, the daughter of Cosens' deputy chairman, J.P. Reynolds. In design, she was an enlarged and improved version of *Premier*, measuring 160 feet 1 inch by 18 feet 5 inches by 8 feet 3 inches, with a tonnage of 163.5 gross, 98 registered.

An elderly gentleman old 'salt' on Bournemouth Pier sits and admires the brand new EMPRESS. As built, the ship had a small square saloon on her foredeck and frames to support an awning over her bridge deck. Both of these features quickly disappeared. The vents in her paddle boxes radiated from a point just above her sponsons but the design was later altered so that they fanned out from the junction of the white and the black paintwork instead. The tiny deckhouse in front of her mainmast covered the stairs to the saloon below but otherwise the only shelter for passengers on deck was provided by the canvas dodgers, which could be rolled up from the bulwarks to provide a degree of protection from the wind and spray. The view also provides good detail of some of the decorative ironwork on the rebuilt pier.

WEYMOUTH LIBRARY

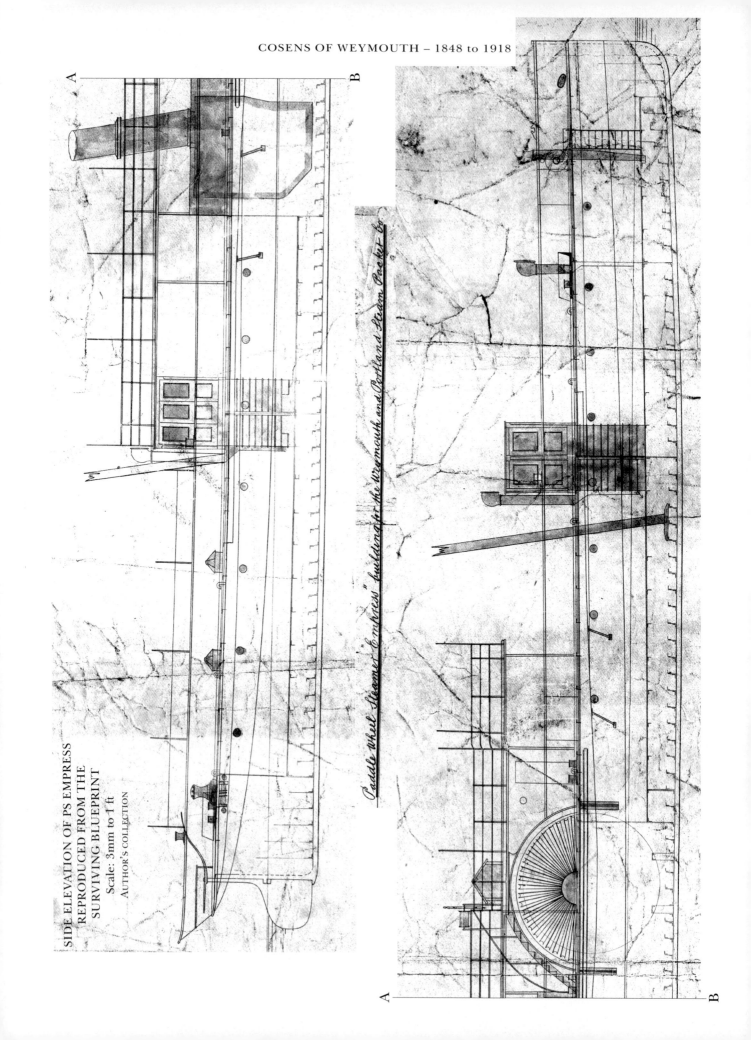

SIDE ELEVATION OF PS EMPRESS
REPRODUCED FROM THE
SURVIVING BLUEPRINT

Scale: 3mm to 1 ft

AUTHOR'S COLLECTION

Paddle Wheel Steamer Empress" building for the Weymouth and Portland Steam Packet Co.

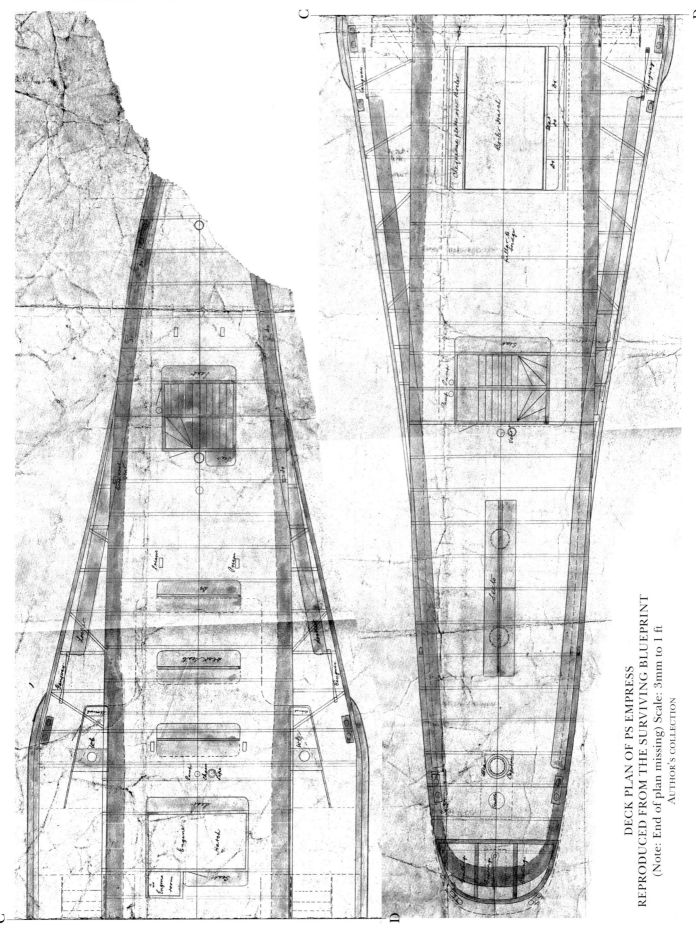

DECK PLAN OF PS EMPRESS
REPRODUCED FROM THE SURVIVING BLUEPRINT
(Note: End of plan missing) Scale: 3mm to 1 ft
AUTHOR'S COLLECTION

*A passenger's view of
EMPRESS's compact
oscillating engine.*
AUTHOR'S COLLECTION

A passenger's view of EMPRESS's compact oscillating engine. AUTHOR'S COLLECTION

With fitting out completed, *Empress* ran her trials on the Thames under the personal supervision of Messrs Penn, Samuda and Fowler, attaining a mean speed of 13.2 knots during four runs over the measured mile, her engines exceeding their contract horse power by 15 per cent. A celebration luncheon was held on board and, at 10am on Monday 12th May, she left the shipyard to have her compasses adjusted off Greenhythe. At 2pm, William Cosens formally assumed command at Gravesend and the ship sailed for Weymouth. The South Foreland was passed at 7.30pm, Dungeness at 9.20pm and Beachy Head at just after midnight, at which point a thick fog descended, requiring a very sharp look out to be kept on board. With innumerable fog horns and steam whistles being heard from vessels making their way up and down channel, *Empress* proceeded at 5 knots until 6.50am, when the fog became even thicker and, believing that the ship had run her distance to the Isle of Wight, Capt Cosens ordered soundings to be taken at regular intervals. Finding that she was drawing into shallow water, he let go the anchor at 7.40am in 5 fathoms. When the fog cleared, Horse Sand Fort at Spithead was sighted close by and *Empress* made for Ryde Pier, from where a telegram was sent to Weymouth informing the directors of the ship's progress.

As soon as the news was received, *Premier* was made ready and, at 11am, left Weymouth Harbour in a heavy downpour of rain on a public excursion to greet her new fleet mate. The two steamers met off the entrance to Lulworth Cove. Bunting was run up on board *Empress*, *Premier* dipped her ensign and Jones' Band struck up the National Anthem.

As soon as the two ships were running side by side towards Weymouth, *Premier*'s engineer, Henry Vye (who had recently been promoted from *Commodore* to allow Robert Hinde jnr to take over the *Empress*), expressed his scepticism about the new ship's rumoured speed and announced loudly that "*It will take a good boat to pass this one Sir!*" Both ships immediately worked up to full speed and, within a few minutes, he was forced to concede defeat as *Empress* drew effortlessly ahead and arrived in Weymouth well ahead of her companion.

A local trial trip for directors, shareholders and port officials was held on Thursday morning, 15th May. With Jones' Band playing on deck, *Empress* left harbour at 11.20am, steamed round the bay to show herself off to the public ashore and then headed for Lulworth Cove, where the new landing apparatus was tested for the first time. *Empress* then headed for Portland and much comment was made on her speed, lack of vibration and steadiness in a seaway, as well as her superior passenger accommodation. On the lower deck aft was an elegant main saloon and a ladies saloon fitted with WCs, while forward was a large refreshment saloon with bar, tables and reversible seats, and a separate saloon '*for the accommodation of dinner parties*'. The hull was divided into seven compartments by six watertight bulkheads. On deck, the 75 foot promenade or bridge deck was fitted with an awning for use on hot days (the more likely possibility of rain not being mentioned!) and, in light of the *Princess Alice* disaster, all deck cushions were filled with cork and all other lifesaving equipment was fully approved by the BoT. The neat oscillating engines which drove *Empress* were of 52hp, had cylinders of 30 inches diameter and 33 inches stroke, and used steam at a pressure of 29lbs per square inch. As the piston rods connected directly to the cranks on the paddle shaft and the cylinders themselves rocked to and fro to create the necessary movement, the engine was extremely compact and was tucked away below the level of the main deck. The engineer controlled the engine from the bottom plates and passengers passing along the engine room alleyways could obtain only a partial view of the revolving machinery. The paddle wheels were relatively small and the paddle boxes did not extend above the level of the bridge deck. The ship had a passenger certificate for 323 on long day trips, 373 on short trips and 650 in smooth waters.

Whilst the steamer cruised off Portland, luncheon was served by the stewardess, Mrs Bowering and once the meal was over '*an abundant supply of champagne was served out and ... advantage was taken to have a little speech making*'. After a great deal of mutual congratulation had taken place, the breeze began to pick up and, as spray started to blow over the bow, *Empress* was turned homeward, arriving back at Weymouth at 2pm.

Within her first month in public service, *Empress* visited Swanage, Bournemouth, Ryde, Alum Bay, Portsmouth, Cowes and Seaton in addition to the usual local destinations, and had introduced the promised day trips from Weymouth to both the Isle of Wight and Torquay. Torquay sailings took a little over four hours in each direction and, on arrival, *Empress* was advertised to offer cruises to view the Mewstone or landing trips to Slapton or Dartmouth. Unfortunately, May and June were blighted by wet and windy weather and, although *Empress* usually managed to battle her way round from Weymouth, four of the first five local excursions had to be abandoned.

At Bournemouth, a new operator appeared on the scene when Messrs Sharpe Brothers announced the introduction of their *'new, powerful, swift and yacht-like paddle steam packet Royal Saxon'* from 12th April onwards. In fact, her arrival from Sunderland was delayed for a few days by bad weather but thereafter she commenced a full programme of excursions in direct competition to the established Bournemouth & South Coast Steam Packet Company, who continued to operate their smaller, chartered *Transit*. With *Lothair* and the Poole tug *Telegraph* also offering regular sailings from Poole to Swanage, competition quickly became intense and, by the end of April, a fare-cutting war had begun. *Royal Saxon* issued season tickets and cut the price of a first class ticket to Alum Bay from 3s to 1s. *Transit* responded by cutting her fares by an average of 25 per cent. The *Bournemouth Observer*, with which *Royal Saxon's* manager Mr H. Nash was closely associated, stopped carrying advertisements for the Bournemouth Company who, on 26 May replaced *Transit* with the larger *Florence* which carried fifty more passengers than her rival. The two companies remained locked in battle until the end of August, when Sharpe Brothers conceded defeat and withdrew *Royal Saxon* ostensibly *'in consequence of the disadvantages at present attending the passenger traffic by steamboats from Bournemouth pier, owing to its dilapidated and unfinished condition'* but, in reality, because the price-cutting war had bankrupted them. In an attempt to recoup some of her losses, the victorious *Florence* extended her season until 18th October and ran a special trip to Portsmouth to view a *'Grand Torpedo Attack & Naval Review'* at Portsmouth but her end of year accounts revealed that the brief and disastrous competition with *Royal Saxon* had absorbed practically all of her owners' retained profit from the two previous seasons.

Cosens watched these developments with interest but, beyond sending a Weymouth steamer to Swanage and Bournemouth at least twice a week, were content to bide their time. With the arrival of *Empress*, *Prince* had become surplus to need and, with any thought that she might be employed at Bournemouth dashed by the developments there, an alternative use had to be found for her. During June, she was chartered to someone in Plymouth but non-payment of the hire fee led to her being repossessed and transferred to Torquay. The previous season's experiment of operating between the South Devon towns had persuaded Cosens that it would be

An advertisement from the Torquay Times & South Devon Advertiser announcing the beginning of Cosens' service from Torquay, under the 'local' title of the Torquay & Weymouth Steam Packet Co. AUTHOR'S COLLECTION

worthwhile basing the ship at Torquay for the whole season and attempting to develop a profitable new trade along the coast.

Accordingly, Mr Renwick of 1 Cary Place, Fleet Street, was appointed local agent and *Prince*, under the command of Capt Bowering, made her first excursion from Torquay to Weymouth on Monday 7th July. The following day saw her make two return sailings to Slapton, with the option of a day ashore or morning and afternoon non-landing trips. On Wednesday, she went twice to Dartmouth, where arrangements were made for her full-day passengers to join the Dartmouth SP Co's river steamer *Newcomin* for the beautiful return trip on the Dart to Totnes, before catching the afternoon sailing back to Torquay. Thursday took her to Sidmouth via Budleigh Salterton, where she landed her passengers straight

The framed original of this photograph was inscribed 'The steamer PRINCE on Budleigh Salterton beach, inaugurating the steamboat service from Torquay along the coast, 1879.' Her first recorded call there took place on Thursday 10th July en route from Torquay to Sidmouth. Note that the ship is not yet fitted with Cosens' patented hinging landing gear but is landing passengers over her bows by way of an enormous, straight gangplank.
AUTHOR'S COLLECTION

onto the beach via her patent bow landing stage. Friday and Saturday saw her back at Slapton and Dartmouth respectively. The Sabbath was, of course, an off-service day. *Prince* was also offered for hire to private picnic and chapel parties, and her towing ability was widely advertised. *Empress* continued to come from Weymouth, usually on a Thursday and while her passengers were enjoying time ashore at Torquay, she offered an onward sailing to Slapton. Suddenly, Cosens were extremely well-represented at the Devon resort.

As the season continued, a number of variations and additions were made to this basic programme of sailings. Seaton became a more common destination than Sidmouth and in addition to beaching at Budleigh Salterton *en route*, the steamer also called off Dawlish, where the shore being too flat to allow the use of the bow landing stage, passengers were landed in boats. The weather was somewhat poor until mid-July, after which matters improved and passenger numbers rose steadily, only to fall again when a major storm stuck the area, causing extensive damage.

The next important event in the calendar was the laying of the foundation stone for the new Eddystone Lighthouse. Postponed from earlier in the year by bad weather, 19th August 1879 was the new scheduled date and arrangements were made for special excursions from both Weymouth and Torquay. They were so vividly described by a reporter from the *Torquay Times*, that his account is worth quoting extensively:

'The Weymouth Steamboat Company is an enterprising body and it has justified the compliment in nothing more than the elaborate arrangements it made for scouring the coast from Weymouth to Berry Head for intending visitors to the Eddystone, on Tuesday, when the Duke of Edinburgh laid the foundation stone and the Prince of Wales assisted. The Empress, *an elaborately and well-appointed boat left Weymouth in the morning at three o'clock, the 150 passengers by which having probably sacrificed a night's rest*

for the prospective enjoyment. When the first watch of chanticleer had been sounded, the Prince, *a less pretentious but scarcely less useful boat, stood outside Budleigh Salterton and Sidmouth to fulfil an advertised engagement and in the pride of the morning holiday makers damped their umbrellas in a prompt journey to a few boats by whose aid they got safe aboard. Dawlish and Teignmouth were ports of call on the way to Torquay, and a fair contribution to the expectant and happy number were made with less appearance of nocturnal arousements. The two boats kept their time well and the human shipments took place with steady alacrity under a weeping sky. The early train brought many who had been induced to disregard the calls of daily toil by the invitations, effective in their enticements, of the Company's posters to come and see the Royal ceremony; and at 9 o'clock the cabs and omnibuses had deposited these at the pier's entrance to find their way, though the imposition of a penny gate, to the deck of the* Empress. *In a quarter of an hour the boat had moved away, on a journey of 40 miles, to give 250 loyal Englishmen and women, fresh and weary, wet and dry, the opportunity of witnessing a sight in a century.'*

The author then waxed eloquent about the key features of the passing coastal scenery, Paignton, Brixham, Berry Head, the mouth of the Dart, Slapton Sands, Start Point, Prawl Point and Bolt Head, before the steamer turned her bow offshore and headed for the position of the Eddystone Light. Peering through the driving rain, her company eventually made out a group of ships clustered around a scaffolding tower but, as *Empress* approached the position, the Royal Standard was hauled down and the vessels steamed away. A hailed enquiry from a nearby vessel quickly established that the foundation stone had been laid minutes before the Weymouth steamers arrived on the scene and the great event had been missed. Covered, no doubt, in embarrassment, Capt Cosens immediately turned *Empress* about to begin her long journey homeward. The newspaper reporter concluded the sorry tale:

'And then the Eddystone was behind us, and then there was a steady downpour, and then we passed the Start with the saloon deck empty, and then the Berry was rounded and passengers were provoking steam by pressing streaming garments against the funnel; and then we were comparing our anticipations of the morning with our realizations of the day, and telling friends how we didn't see the Princes lay the foundation stone of the New Eddystone.'

The Royal Regatta in Torbay in 1879 was a fashionable affair, the glamour of the occasion being enhanced by the presence in the bay of the Prince of Wales on board his magnificent schooner yacht *Hildegard*. *Prince* abandoned many of her regular trips in favour of short cruises to watch the yacht races or spot the wealthy and aristocratic owners on their anchored vessels. Unfortunately, on 2nd

September she got rather too close to the action and collided with the schooner *Dawn*, snapping off her jib-boom and then running into and damaging a gig towing astern of Lord Hasting's yacht *Aline*. The season ended on 14th September with a well-patronised trip to Seaton, after which *Prince* returned to Weymouth to lay up for the winter.

The Torquay experiment, although not returning a tremendous profit, had proved sufficiently successful that the directors, hoping for more favourable weather during 1880, decided to commit *Prince* to a further season on the station. Indeed, the company's 1880 sailing programme followed that of 1879 almost exactly, with *Empress* and *Premier* operating the main Weymouth excursions, *Prince* at Torquay and *Commodore* engaged on the Portland ferry, towage, liberty boat work and short trips from Weymouth. At Weymouth, the collection of the Pile Pier tolls reverted to the corporation at a very timely moment, for the whole structure was becoming increasingly cranky and a continuation of Cosens' lease could have involved them in expensive repair work. The Bank Holidays saw the customary influx of excursion trains and many thousands of day visitors took advantage of the steamers, which remained the resort's principal attraction. On Whit Monday, a strong easterly wind enlivened proceedings and it was noted that those passengers who had joined *Empress* for her trip to Bournemouth and Alum Bay '*had a thorough dusting and will long remember the trip*'! Both the Channel and Reserve Squadrons were now using Portland Harbour on a regular basis and trips to view or visit ironclads such as *Minotaur*, *Warrior*, *Northumberland*, *Belle Isle* and *Agincourt*, together with the associated liberty boat work, remained an important feature of the Weymouth programme. A surviving record gives the following intriguing snapshot of the season and is contained in the table below.

In order to add to her summer income, it was decided at the end of the season, that *Prince*, together with the steam launch *Princess*, should be fitted out for trawling. Although no precise records survive, it may be assumed that *Prince* was fitted with a beam trawl of the type which had been pioneered on board the South Shields tug *Messenger* in 1877. A heavy wooden beam was used to keep open the mouth of the net, which was shot and hauled over the port side aft of the paddle box. *Prince* must have been fitted with some sort of temporary Sampson post for hauling and handling the heavy gear but sadly no photographic evidence survives. While *Princess* was limited to working inside Weymouth Bay, *Prince* appears to have ventured further afield in search of fish, her range limited solely by the necessity of returning to port frequently enough to land her catch in good condition. In the event, the severe winter weather curtailed her voyages so badly that it was impossible to judge the potential profitability of the venture. In the spring, her nets and gear were placed in store and the directors resolved to try again the following year.

Towing and salvage also made an important contribution to income, with *Commodore* generating £202 on towing and £151 in salvage awards and *Prince* £62 and £60, while *Empress* and *Premier* earned £9 and £40 respectively on towage alone. In January 1880, *Commodore* had brought the schooner *General Brailmont* into Portland after she had suffered severe collision damage and on 15th November, *Prince* towed the full-rigged ship *Glenavon* off the breakwater. The most profitable salvage job of the year occurred later in the same month when the 222 foot screw steamer *Arklow*, bound from Glasgow to Southampton, went aground in thick fog on the Kimmeridge Ledges. Her crew were landed safely in a coastguard boat on the evening of 19th November but it was not until the following afternoon that the news reached Weymouth. *Commodore* immediately proceeded to the scene, where she discovered *Arklow* firmly ashore with a large hole ripped in her

	EMPRESS	*PREMIER*	*PRINCE*	*COMMODORE*	*TOTAL*
Coal Burnt	329tons 12cwt	203tons 11cwt	238tons 16cwt	183tons 12cwt	955tons 11cwt
Miles Run	6,547	3,666	63,681	6,581	
Weight of coal/mile	112.77lbs	124.3lbs	84lbs		
Passengers carried	18,977	37,650	10,926	11,986	79,539

Passengers Carried on excursions from Weymouth, Bridport, etc	35,600
Passengers Carried at Torquay	10,786
Passengers Carried to Portland	33,153
Total	79,539
Cash taken at Torquay by *Prince* (gross)	£ 749 9s 0d
Cash taken from Bridport	£ 535 17s 8d
Cash taken trading to HM fleet	£ 161 11s 9d
Total number of long excursions from Weymouth	56
Total number of short excursions from Weymouth	188
Trips advertised westwards	20
Trips performed westwards	15

PREMIER landing passengers on one of the Devon beaches on a flat calm day during the late 1870s. Close examination of the photograph reveals that she is using Cosens original system of a single, heavy gangway, supported on a large roller near the ship's bow. A little further aft, a metal bracket has been fixed to the bulwark and it would appear that, as soon as the ship left the beach, the gangway would be hauled up with the aid of blocks and tackles set up on the foredeck and stowed outboard of the bulwarks on the roller and bracket. Although this arrangement must have been quite secure in calm weather, the gangway must have been prone to damage when the steamer was digging her bows into a heavy sea. Note that everyone in the photograph is wearing a hat. Although bowlers appear to be the favoured style amongst most of the male passengers, a fair number of top hats are also on display.
BRIAN JACKSON COLLECTION

bottom. It soon became evident that there was no realistic chance of towing her off, so arrangements were made through the receiver of wrecks for Cosens to salvage the cargo. Operations commenced the next following morning with *Commodore*, assisted by *Prince*, shuttling to and fro with barges in tow, while a large work force, engaged by Cosens, laboured to get the cargo out of the flooded ship before she went to pieces. *Arklow*'s wreck was sold by auction on 9th December to a Mr Brice of Glasgow, on strict conditions that no attempt be made to move or dismantle her for fourteen days, in order to allow Cosens adequate time to complete their work. For some weeks, Brice employed a tug named *Admiral* on removing machinery and fittings from the wreck, which subsequently disintegrated during the winter gales. Although the salvage claim was not finally settled for over a year, the work on *Arklow* eventually yielded an income of over £1,500. Useful income was also generated by the rescue of the barque *August*, which was one of several ships driven ashore between Ferrybridge and Castletown during a severe easterly gale on 18th January 1881.

The most significant developments of 1880, however, occurred at Bournemouth, where the local Bournemouth & South Coast Steam Packet Company who, it will be recalled, had exhausted most of their reserves during the costly price-cutting war of 1879, repeated their charter of *Florence* and opened their season in early April. Unfortunately, however, a dispute which rapidly developed into a law suit arose with her owner, Mr Havelock, who promptly cancelled the charter and announced that he would

run the ship on his own account from 17th April onwards. Finding itself without a ship, the company was forced to eat humble pie and approach Cosens to plead for the use of *Prince* but the Weymouth directors, having committed her to operate out of Torquay, declined to assist. Enquiries were then made at London, Liverpool, Hull and Glasgow for a suitable ship and eventually *Carham* was located on the Clyde. Built in 1864 for the North British Railway, the 141 foot ship had latterly been operating between Strome Ferry and Portree. Her delivery from Scotland drew another £141 from the company's depleted funds and their depression was compounded by the arrival of another competitor for the Bournemouth trade, *Sunshine*, owned by a Mr W. Powell, a few days before *Carham* entered service on 31st May 1880. *Florence*'s owner seems to have experimented with a few Sunday sailings during late April but called down such a storm of protest against *'such iniquitous and abominable proceedings'* that his Sabbath-breaking was very short-lived. Thus, from May onwards, *Carham*, *Florence* and *Sunshine*, together with *Lothair* and *Telegraph* from Poole, and a 15 ton yacht named *Frederick William*, competed for the Bournemouth trade, and Cosens must have felt themselves well out of the fray. The situation could not last and, by 19th June, *Sunshine* had been withdrawn. *Carham* and *Florence* offered similar trips to Alum Bay, Ryde, Yarmouth, Portsmouth, Cowes, Swanage and Weymouth, and were frequently scheduled to undertake identical sailings on the same day. In July, the first sign of co-operation between the Bournemouth company and Cosens appeared

PRINCE landing passengers at Budleigh Salterton, probably circa 1885.

AUTHOR'S COLLECTION

EMPRESS embarking passengers at Lulworth Cove in the summer of 1880. Although her paddle box slats remain unaltered, her forward deck saloon and awning frames have been removed and the white paint on her sponson houses replaced by scumbled varnish. Also, although she is still steered from the deck, a light navigation bridge has been constructed forward of her funnel.

DORSET COUNTY MUSEUM

when *Carham* was advertised to undertake a three day excursion to Cherbourg between 24th and 26th July, with *Empress* covering her local excursions while she was abroad. In the event, *Carham* damaged her paddle box while berthing at Cowes Pier on 23rd July and the intended cross channel trip had to be abandoned. *Carham*'s repairs took a week and during this period *Empress* was again advertised to cover one of her main sailings each day.

Fortunately, *Carham* was back in service by the beginning of August, and all of the local steamers were present on 11th August when, amid great public celebration, the new Bournemouth Pier was officially opened by the Lord Mayor of London, Sir Francis Truscott. Designed by the famous Eugenius Birch, the new pier was built of iron and measured 838 feet in length. The neck of the pier was 35 feet wide, while the pier head itself was 110 feet in width with landing stages on each side, providing sufficient space for four steamers to berth simultaneously. Throughout the day the local steamers offered short cruises in the bay and evening trips to view the celebratory firework display, and thereafter settled into their usual pattern of stiff competition. The pier attracted large numbers of visitors and undoubtedly boosted the receipts of the local fleet, while Cosens steadily increased the frequency of their visits from Weymouth.

By September, the owners of *Carham* and *Florence* had come to their senses and reached an agreement not to compete on the same routes on the same days but the damage was already done and the season drew to an unhappy end for all concerned. On 4th September, *Florence* was going astern from Bournemouth Pier when she ran down a pleasure boat operating from the beach, drowning four of the nine occupants. The ship finished her season soon afterwards, never to appear at Bournemouth again and her master, Joseph Robertson, was subsequently found guilty of manslaughter. *Carham*'s season finished on 8th October and, her charter having expired, she departed two days later for Glasgow, carrying a limited number of passengers who paid 10s each for this long and unusual single trip. The little *Lothair*, which they had been operating between Swanage and Poole for several seasons, had also been withdrawn on 1st October and later in the month departed for the Mediterranean, where she was to undertake a packet service in Greek waters.

During the winter of 1880-81, the struggling Bournemouth Company, which was now without either a ship or funds, learned that it had lost its law suit against the owner of *Florence* and, faced with a sizeable bill for legal costs and expenses, was forced to consider its future. While private attempts were made to obtain a fresh injection of capital, Mr Sydenham also opened negotiations with Cosens, who expressed an immediate willingness to work the station for the following season. A final meeting of shareholders and potential new investors was held on 18th February 1881, at which, with little new capital promised, it was decided to bow to the

inevitable, wind up the affairs of the Bournemouth Company, abandon any attempt to form a replacement company and accept Cosens' offer. Mr Sydenham immediately forwarded a copy of the resolution to Cosens and, on the following Tuesday, travelled to Weymouth to meet with the board and finalise arrangements. It was agreed that, from Easter Monday 18th April 1881 onwards, Cosens would maintain at least one steamer on the Bournemouth station. Mr Sydenham would become the company's local agent and, in return for 10 per cent of the Bournemouth income, would undertake all advertising, printing and other agency costs at his own expense. The steamer would lay overnight and bunker at Swanage where, for 5 per cent of local ticket revenue, Mr Henry Hixson (who had acted as steamer agent for Burt and others since 1875) was appointed agent and placed in charge of coal storage. Public notices announcing the new arrangements appeared in the local press on 23rd March.

On that very evening, however, a public meeting was called by a group of local businessmen at Bournemouth Town Hall, to '*consider whether it would be more conducive to the interests of Bournemouth to have a boat under more immediate local supervision.*' Their aim was to launch a company which would command widespread local support through the issue of a large number of reasonably cheap shares. Mr Sydenham introduced a note of caution by pointing out that the old company, despite its best endeavours, had only ever succeeded in attracting a total of 43 shareholders and that very few local gentlemen had accepted his invitation to attend the final meeting on 18th February, at which the formation of a new company had been discussed. It was because of this apparent lack of local support that he had reached his agreement with Cosens and he wished it to be known that he would not have done so had he been aware of any realistic proposal to form a new local concern.

Nevertheless, the meeting voted in favour of a new company, a committee was elected to drive matters forward and, by 2nd March, the prospectus

The Bournemouth, Swanage & Poole Steam Packet Co's LORD ELGIN, *which entered service at Bournemouth in opposition to Cosens'* EMPRESS *on 16th May 1881.* AUTHOR'S COLLECTION

Lord Elgin turning in Swanage Bay while, in the background, Empress heads for Bournemouth. SWANAGE MUSEUM

for the Bournemouth, Swanage & Poole Steam Packet Company Ltd had been issued. The authorised capital was to be £10,000 in 2,000 shares of £5 each and the hunt was immediately begun for a suitable steamer. The directors of the new company had significant financial interests in the growth of Bournemouth, several were prominent in local politics and at least one, James McWilliam, was a builder and developer. Sydenham's earlier remarks and his acceptance of Cosens' agency had evidently ruffled some feathers within the new camp, and an acrimonious exchange of accusation and counter-accusation soon began to appear in the local press. Sydenham was accused of encouraging Cosens '*to take away some three thousand pounds per annum which justly belongs to Bournemouth*', of making his agreement with Cosens *after* he was aware that a new local company was proposed and of timing his public announcement to do the maximum amount of damage to the attendance at the public meeting. It was said that he was '*unmistakably ... the enemy of Bournemouth*' and would soon find himself in a very isolated position. Sydenham replied that his arrangement with Cosens had been confirmed in writing on 18th February, well *before* the public meeting, that the new company had acted in an underhand way by sending its secretary, Mr C. Waters, to Weymouth to try to persuade Cosens to renege on the agreement and added a few barbed comments about the high pressure tactics which the new company was having to adopt in order to sell sufficient shares in the town.

The battle lines were thus drawn up. On the one hand was the new Bournemouth Company, which believed passionately that Cosens, in following the interests of their Weymouth shareholders, would draw wealth out of Bournemouth to the detriment

of the town, whereas a local company would, in addition to keeping any profits within the community, have the wider interests of the town at heart and endeavour to offer the best possible facilities at the lowest fares compatible with making a fair return. Mr Sydenham, on the other hand, was aware that none of the directors of the new concern had any experience of practical ship owning or operation and preferred to throw in his lot with an established company run by experienced master mariners, who could guarantee a reliable service.

It appears that while Cosens sent *Premier* round to Swanage and Bournemouth on Easter Monday, and *Telegraph* and her running mate *Stella* commenced their Poole to Swanage sailings from 2nd May, with a steamer called *May* operating from Bournemouth for two weeks early in the month, neither of the main protagonists began their main excursion season at Bournemouth until later in May. The Bournemouth Company purchased a five-year-old steamer named *Lord Elgin* from John Kidd of Leith, for whom she had been operating excursions on the Firth of Forth. Although her 160 foot length was identical to that of *Empress*, her greater tonnage, compound diagonal engine, raised quarterdeck, forward deck saloon and extensive bridge deck arguably made her the superior vessel, and the new company must have been well-pleased with their purchase.

As if to emphasise this fact, *Lord Elgin*'s first scheduled trip was advertised, rather pointedly, to Swanage and Weymouth on 16th May 1881. In the event, bad weather prevented her from sailing further than Swanage but the gauntlet was thrown down and her weekly timetable regularly included trips to Weymouth, Portland and Lulworth Cove. Cosens' first Bournemouth advertisement appeared on 28th May, announcing that from Monday 30th May, either *Premier* or *Empress* would offer trips to Alum Bay via Yarmouth, Weymouth via Swanage, Cowes via Yarmouth, and to Swanage, Ryde and Portsmouth. *Lord Elgin* offered a very similar programme at almost identical fares, the lessons of previous price-cutting wars evidently having been noted by both companies. From the beginning of June, Cosens' adverts mentioned both *Premier* and *Empress*, indicating a distinct increase in the tempo of the competition and attempting to establish the superiority of their ships by stating '*These vessels are engined by the eminent engineers John Penn & Son, are the fastest on the station by several miles an hour, and therefore afford time to passengers for visiting at the several towns to which they ply, and in addition ensure getting home early in the evening.*'

Mr Sydenham must have had his tongue firmly in his cheek as he wrote these adverts for, unbeknown to the public, *Empress* had suffered some serious mechanical problems at the end of the previous season, resulting in John Penn supplying and fitting a new paddle shaft completely at his own expense. *Lord Elgin* also experienced some teething problems and, on the evening of 11th June, made a single trip to Southampton where she spent the next twelve days undergoing repairs. During her absence, her trips were undertaken by either *Carisbrooke* or *Southampton*, on hire from the Southampton, Isle of Wight & South of England Royal Mail Steam Packet Company Ltd (hereafter referred to as the Southampton Company). This was an indication of things to come, for some years later that company decided to base its own steamers at Bournemouth and eventually became owners of *Lord Elgin* herself.

Empress initially undertook the majority of the Bournemouth sailings but, after complaints from Capt Cosens about the massive increase in working hours for him and his crew, the board experimented with alternating her roster with *Premier*'s on a weekly basis, one ship serving Bournemouth and eastwards, while the other covered Weymouth and westward. This arrangement commenced in mid-June and appears to have lasted well into the summer.

Meanwhile, supporters of the Bournemouth Company kept up their barrage of complaints against Cosens in the local press. On 20th July, Joseph Cutler, one of their directors, published a vitriolic letter in the *Bournemouth Observer*, accusing Cosens of circulating '*scandalous reports about the Lord Elgin*', of tempting would-be winter residents away from Bournemouth with untrue statements about the superiority of Weymouth's climate and of implying local credentials which did not exist by adopting the title 'The Bournemouth, Swanage & Weymouth Steam Packet Company' on their adverts. Cosens had indeed been somewhat cheeky in reversing the order of the title habitually used by the Weymouth steamers and had doubtless done so with the full intention of confusing the travelling public with a name extremely similar to that of their

rivals! Cutler went on to state that he was '*utterly ashamed of those inhabitants, rich or poor, who either patronise the Weymouth boats or exhibit their bills*' and, having heard rumours that Cosens were considering building an additional steamer for the 1882 season, threw down the gauntlet by announcing his own company's intention to do likewise during the coming winter. Further newspaper articles eulogised *Lord Elgin*, promoting that fact that '*she is by far the largest and most powerful vessel on the station*' but neatly sidestepping the question of speed by stating that '*the directors have given instructions to their captain on no occasion whatever to attempt racing*'. A letter from an anonymous '*frequent passenger*' continued the attack, by accusing Cosens of a '*flagrant breach of faith*' by leaving passengers waiting '*on the miserable erection which is dignified by the name of a pier at Swanage*' for over an hour for their return sailing to Bournemouth by *Empress* or *Premier* and then crowding them instead into '*a miserable little boat called* Prince, *which barely contained standing room for them.*'

As the season progressed, Cosens' sailings settled into a fairly regular pattern. On Mondays and Fridays, a steamer usually went to Weymouth calling at Lulworth Cove in both directions, Cowes was a favoured Wednesday destination and long distance excursions took place on Tuesdays. On 2nd August, *Empress* was advertised to run the only trip of the season to Brighton and, on 16th August, operated Cosens' first day trip from Bournemouth to Cherbourg. Although the weather was less than ideal, about seventy passengers parted with 10s 6d each to reserve a ticket and *Empress* duly set off from Bournemouth at 7am, leaving Swanage half an hour later to cross the Channel. The passengers cannot have enjoyed very long on French soil, for the ship departed again at 3pm for an eight hour passage back to Bournemouth. Torquay featured several times as a Tuesday destination and Isle of Wight calls now included the extraordinary, newly-opened, five-span suspension pier at Seaview. Curiously, Totland Bay Pier, which had been completed in March 1880, did not appear regularly in either company's advertisements and one excursion to a musical concert there required passengers to land at Alum Bay Pier and walk overland to their destination!

Both companies attempted to enhance their reputations by offering free excursions to local hospitals and schools, and by employing bands to play on board. Cosens favoured '*grand marine concerts*' by the Royal Italian Band, while the Bournemouth Company emphasised its local roots by employing the Bournemouth Town Band and advertising the fact that the panelling in *Lord Elgin*'s saloons was newly-embellished with paintings by local artists.

The regular overnight berthing and bunkering of a steamer at Swanage and the consequent need to keep the local coal-store well-supplied, prompted Cosens to expend £550 on the purchase of their only sailing ship in May 1881. This was the 64 feet

EMPRESS berthed at the original Swanage Pier, circa 1881. As well as landing and embarking passengers at the pier, the steamer lay there overnight and took on coal under the supervision of the company's local agent, Henry Hixson. The pier was shared with commercial vessels and was fitted with a standard-gauge tramway and two cranes, to assist in the handling of cargo and its transport between the ships and Swanage town. One of the cranes toppled into the sea in 1884 and its operator was drowned.
DORCHESTER LIBRARY

5 inches-long, 53 ton ketch *Mermaid* of Jersey, which was put to work carrying cargoes of coal direct from South Wales to Swanage. *Mermaid* also contributed to the supplies held in the company's hulks in Portland Harbour and its coal store on Weymouth Quay but her limited capacity meant that additional cargoes continued to be purchased from commercial colliers. During the summer of 1881, the company's engineering workshops at Weymouth were also enlarged and improved by Cosens' staff, in order to keep pace with the rapidly increasing demand for their services.

With the competition between Cosens and the Bournemouth Company firmly established, the season drew to a windy end during mid October. Both had announced that their last excursions would be on 15th October but a series of gales made landing at Bournemouth impossible and many of the final week's sailings had to be abandoned. Taking advantage of a lull in the weather, *Empress* left Swanage for her winter berth at Weymouth on 15th October '*with the hearty good wishes of all and amid hurrahs and adieux.*'

At Weymouth, *Commodore* had been kept extremely busy by the period of bad weather. On the night of 13th-14th October, the wind was so strong that even Portland Harbour was not a place of safety for smaller craft and the tug lay with steam up awaiting the inevitable calls for assistance. The first came on the morning of 14th October, when the smack *Esther* of Plymouth was driven right out of the roadstead by the force of the wind but, after having a considerable portion of her bulwarks carried away by the heavy seas, was brought safely into Weymouth. A few hours later, another smack, *Union* of Fowey, was spotted in apparent distress close to the breakwater and *Commodore*, commanded by Capt Thomas Bowering and carrying several extra hands, put to sea again. *Union* had originally anchored in the commercial area close under the lee of Chesil Beach but had steadily dragged her anchors until she was perilously close to the breakwater. Her crew put out extra

anchors but, fearing for their lives, were taken off by a local boat. By the time the tug arrived, the ship was deserted and considerable skill was required to put some hands on board and secure a tow. Capt Bowering later stated that the wind had been gusting to Force 12 and, even in the shelter of Portland Harbour, the seas were so large that '*he had rarely seen bigger ones twenty miles off land.*' *Union* was successfully brought into Weymouth but when the salvage case came to court, her master attempted to avoid payment by claiming that he and his crew had merely gone ashore to dry out, change their clothes and enjoy a meal in a public house. He attempted to sue Cosens for unlawful seizure of his ship but the assessor was not impressed by this ruse and Cosens duly received an award of £35.

Two weeks later, the Dorset coast was visited by yet another severe gale and at daybreak on 28th November, the lookout man Cosens kept posted on the Nothe during periods of bad weather, reported that the French schooner *Jane Elise* was on her beam-ends and dragging her anchors rapidly towards Osmington. Capt Cosens immediately took *Commodore* to sea and, finding no trace of the schooner's crew, decided to put two men – Hardy and White – on board. A tow rope was passed and the schooner's cables slipped but, at that moment, a heavy squall passed over and the ship was thrown further onto her side. With the schooner's ballast shifted, her stern high out of the water making steering impossible and a tattered topsail acting as a brake, the tug found it impossible to make any headway and it was feared that the casualty might founder at any moment. A flag was hoisted to summon the Weymouth lifeboat to rescue the two men but, when no response came, Capt Cosens realised that he would have to undertake the task himself. He therefore slipped the tow and ran *Commodore* straight for the schooner, which was now only just outside the line of jagged rocks. Lines and lifebuoys were thrown and, after two attempts, both men leaped to safety. With no room to turn and the rocks close under her bows, *Commodore* had no choice but to steam full astern through the enormous waves, several of which broke on board, carrying away most of the deck fittings and smashing both paddle boxes. As she attempted to turn into the seas, another wave swept her from stem to stern, demolished the forward bulkhead of the engine room and swept the recently-rescued Hardy into the machinery. The engine was stopped and the man pulled clear, by which time the water in the boiler room had reached to within a foot of the stokehold and it was feared that another large sea would put the fires out altogether. *Commodore* eventually limped alongside Weymouth Pier, where injured members of the crew were put ashore and the full extent of the damage to the ship became apparent. Although the little tug had failed in her salvage mission and *Jane Elise* became a total loss on Osmington beach, both *Commodore*'s seaworthiness and Capt Cosens' fine seamanship attracted widespread praise.

CHAPTER 8

INTENSIFIED COMPETITION
& FLEET EXPANSION

1882-1887

An exceptionally busy December, during which *Commodore* salvaged a number of vessels including the schooner *Jane Eliza* and the barque *Paher*, combined with the general increase in the size of vessels she was called upon to assist, persuaded Cosens that the time had come to replace her with a larger tug. Accordingly, in March 1882, *Commodore* was offered to the Government for £1,650 and Mr Fowler was sent to Dundee to inspect another vessel whose owners were asked to accept *Commodore* in part exchange. Evidently this arrangement was not to their liking for negotiations broke down and, with no alternative second-hand replacement available, it was decided to retain *Commodore* for a further season.

Cosens then turned their mind to the construction of a brand new vessel and approached their favoured engineers and shipbuilders, Messrs Penn and Green, for a quotation. Both yards, however, had full order books and were unable to help. Enquiries to other shipbuilders throughout the United Kingdom proved equally fruitless, as the industry was enjoying a huge boom at the time and work was so plentiful

that nobody was able to meet the specified delivery date. Cosens were then introduced to Mr James Watkins of Fenchurch Street, nephew of William Watkins the well-known London tug owner, who offered to arrange the construction of a suitable vessel in time for the 1883 season at a cost of £5,365. Watkins, drawing on his family's tremendous experience, prepared a specification for a modern tug, which would be equally suited to salvage work, long-distance towage and the summer excursion trade, and by June 1882 a contract had been signed. In order to circumvent the difficulties in the British shipyards, Watkins sub-contracted building of the iron hull to a Dutch firm, Messrs Smit & Zoon of Kinderdik near Rotterdam, while the engines were constructed by the Vulcan Iron Works of Hull. Funds for building the new tug were quickly raised from existing shareholders by issuing further unallotted shares from the Cosens' authorised capital.

Having discovered that Cosens' rumoured new vessel was to be a tug and not an additional passenger steamer, the Bournemouth Company's threat to build a new vessel for the 1882 season evaporated,

EMPRESS at Swanage Pier in the 1880s. In the centre of the picture can be seen the famous clock tower, which was originally erected in 1854 on the southern approach to London Bridge as a memorial to the Duke of Wellington but within a few years it was found to impede traffic flow. During 1866-67, it was dismantled and each stone was carefully numbered and packed before being brought by sea to Swanage. George Burt presented it to Thomas Docwra, who re-erected it in the grounds of his house, The Grove.

DAVID HAYSOM COLLECTION

for the moment, into thin air. The Bournemouth season was opened by *Lord Elgin* on Saturday 8th April, followed two days later by *Empress* which, unlike her rival, was welcomed back to Swanage by flags and cannon salutes.

The season quickly settled into its accustomed pattern, with the usual mix of excursions on offer and *Premier* joining *Empress* on the Bournemouth sailing lists from the week before Whitsun. Between 8th and 10th July, *Empress* offered a special three day excursion to Cherbourg for a fare of 10s 6d, while the Bournemouth Company, who never sent *Lord Elgin* across the Channel, responded by advertising a three day trip to Torquay between 15th and 17th July. In order to demonstrate the superiority of their ship over Cosens' *Prince*, which was again based at Torquay for part of her time, *Lord Elgin* was thrown open to the public on the Sunday and several thousand visitors were reported to have thronged on board. On the Monday, before returning to Bournemouth, the ship caused further irritation to Cosens by offering a short non-landing cruise from Torquay to Exmouth for the benefit of local residents. *Empress*'s final long trip of the season was from Bournemouth to Seaton for the regatta on 1st August.

Prince spent much of her time at Torquay but sometimes returned to help out at Weymouth for several days a week. On 6th September, while the ship was *en route* from Torquay to Exmouth, a tragedy occurred when a fireman named Bishop was jerked overboard while attempting to fill a bucket with water from the sponson. A boat was immediately launched and lifebelts thrown but, before help could reach him, Bishop disappeared. *Prince* immediately returned to Torquay and subscription books were subsequently placed on board the company's ships to raise money for Bishop's widow and three children. It was the company's first loss of life at sea and was particularly distressing since, during her winter refit, *Prince* had been fitted with a seawater tap in the engine room, with the express purpose of avoiding any member of the crew having to collect water by the dangerous bucket and rope method.

It is interesting to note that, during 1882, Cosens' Bournemouth newspaper advertisements omitted the paragraph referring to the superiority of their vessels' speed but that every opportunity was seized to use editorial comment to make the same point! On 18th April, for example, it was trumpeted in the *Southern Times* that *Empress* had taken a party from Bournemouth to *HMS Agincourt* at Portland in 2 hours 7 minutes including a stop at Swanage and, on the return leg, had steamed from Swanage to Bournemouth in 33 minutes. On 13th May, she followed the same route to take a party to a ball on board *HMS Northumberland* and completed the passage '*at unsurpassed speed*' in under two hours.

The weather during the first half of the season was particularly dismal, with a succession of rainy days and gales leading to an alarming fall in passenger numbers. During the first week in June, strong easterly winds caused all sailings from Bournemouth and Weymouth to be abandoned for seven days and it was not until the beginning of August that the weather settled into anything resembling a normal summer pattern. Thereafter, passengers returned in droves and in one seven day period, more passengers were carried from Bournemouth alone than had ever been recorded in the history of the company. To everyone's relief, the overall figures for the season grew to 95,323 passengers carried, an increase of 11,414, over 1881.

The wild weather inevitably saw a number of sailing ships in difficulty along the Dorset coast. On 29th April, the 1,250 ton *Alexandrovna* was driven ashore near Tilly Whim Caves with the loss of her entire crew, her destruction being so complete that all Cosens could do was to offer a series of rather ghoulish excursions to view the wreckage-strewn coast during the following week. On 9th May, *Commodore* responded to a report of a vessel floating bottom-upwards in West Bay and succeeded in towing her as far as the Shambles Bank before the tide turned and the tow-line parted. The fact that the wreck's masts and sails were still standing under water made her impossible for the little tug to handle alone and it was not until the next morning, when *Empress* arrived from Bournemouth to assist, that the derelict was brought slowly into Portland Harbour. On 24th May, the vessel, which was discovered to be the Norwegian barque *Skulda*, was finally righted and brought into Weymouth where, on 13th July, her cargo of 30,000 floorboards was sold by auction. For salvage of *Skulda*, together with the yachts *Freda* and *Amathea*, Cosens received £1,122 in awards. Added to the £365 earned from towage and £287 trading to the Fleet at Portland, this went some way to offsetting the poor early season passenger figures and left the company with a trading profit of £1,704, only £389 down on the previous twelve months.

If 1882 had been a year of mixed fortunes, 1883 was to prove one of overall prosperity and of significant developments in the company's operations. The most eagerly-awaited event was, of course, the arrival of the new tug *Queen*, which was due to be delivered early in April. Unfortunately, floods in Rotterdam during the winter severely delayed the completion of the hull and Smit & Zoon found themselves liable for a £300 penalty, as well as for a substantial insurance premium to enable the ship to be towed across the North Sea during a period of winter gales. At Hull, the Vulcan Iron Works also failed to meet its delivery date and, having worked its employees day and night to complete the job, suffered an unwelcome overtime bill and penalty totalling £500. Cosens must have been somewhat ambivalent about the delays, as a saving of £800 from a total building cost of about £6,000 must have been seen as handsome compensation for the loss of a few weeks early season availability. Throughout the construction period, Cosens' manager and secretary, S.J. Fowler, had paid regular visits to both Rotterdam and Hull to inspect progress and in mid April, Mr Hinde jnr was sent to Hull to oversee the installation of the engines and boilers, and attend the sea trials.

Queen finally arrived at Weymouth early on the morning of Whit Monday, 21st May, after a very rough trip from Hull and was immediately pressed into service to help cope with the heavy demand on the Weymouth to Portland service. She was then withdrawn for two days to *'undergo redecoration'* before her official trial trip on Thursday 24th May. Although Smit & Zoon had completed her fitting out before she left Rotterdam, they had not reckoned with the coal dust and smoke of Hull docks, nor the minor damages caused during the fitting of the machinery and the whole job had to be repeated at their expense.

By 24th May, however, all was spick and span and the new tug sailed at 11am to show off her paces to an invited party of 60 shareholders and guests. The day chosen was, by happy coincidence, Queen Victoria's birthday, which allowed the toasts to *'Her Majesty'* and the inclusion of the *My Queen* waltz among the selection of popular music provided by Jones' Band, to enjoy a double significance. On the bridge for the first trip was Capt George Haill, who had been mate of *Lord Elgin* until poached from the opposition in March 1882 to take command of *Commodore*. Together with his Mate John Lowe, AB John Martin, engineer Joseph Carter and fireman Albert Clark, he had transferred to the new tug on 18th May, passing command of the old *Commodore* to Henry Parsons, who moved from Cosens' coal ketch *Mermaid*.

The assembled party expressed themselves well pleased with the new iron tug, which measured 110 feet 2 inches long, 19 feet 7 inches wide and had a depth in the hold from the tonnage deck of 8 feet 9 inches, which equated to a draft of about 5 feet when loaded with ten tons of coal and an equal weight of passengers. With a gross tonnage of 146.19 (77.07 registered), she was considerably larger than her predecessor and far better fitted for passenger service. Below decks were two large saloons, the after one measuring 21 feet by 17 feet, with an adjoining 13 feet by 6 feet ladies cabin, both panelled in birds-eye maple and mahogany, and with seating upholstered in crimson velvet. The forward cabin was *'a pretty and comfortable compartment'* of somewhat plainer appearance, measuring 21 feet 6 inches by 6 feet 6 inches, off which the steward's pantry and the captain's and chief engineer's cabins opened. The companionways to both saloons were fitted with portable 'porches' or deckhouses, which could be removed during the winter months when the vessel was engaged in towing. The panelling and fittings of the saloons were also designed to be easily removed, partly to allow access to the hull plating for painting and inspection but also so the vessel could be stripped out when employed on salvage duties.

On the main deck, the sponson side houses contained a galley, seaman's mess, lamp room, steward's pantry and what were delicately described as the *'requisite offices'*. The engine house was entirely enclosed in stout walls of teak to ensure that, even in the roughest weather, there was no possibility of the engines or boilers being flooded by seas breaking onto the decks. The engines themselves were a pair of surface condensing, disconnecting side-levers or 'grasshoppers', whose simple, rugged design and low centre of gravity made them the almost universal choice for use in tugs of the period. The cylinders, which were encased in cedar wood secured with brass bands, had a diameter of 26 inches and a stroke of 48 inches and, driving feathering paddle wheels, were variously described as having a combined horse power of 70, or 300 Indicated horse power. Steam was provided by a single, cylindrical boiler with a working pressure of 40psi. With a service speed of 11 knots, great play was made of the fact that her disconnecting engines would make her far more manoeuvrable when on salvage duties while, in passenger service, she would be able to save valuable time by swinging in the harbour without the use of ropes. It was also noted that she was fitted with two wide staircases up to the bridge deck, in order to accelerate the movement of matelots when engaged on liberty boat duties for HM Fleet.

It is interesting to note that, due to her unusual building arrangements, *Queen* was originally registered in Hull under the ownership of James Watkins and transferred to Cosens and the Weymouth register on 18th May. Watkins agreed to accept *Commodore* in part payment for her replacement and she was officially sold to him on the same day, departing for London on 22nd May. At the same time, Cosens board were discussing the fact that the steam launch *Princess* was now a little too small for her work in connection with the coal hulks and breakwater forts, and approached James Watkins to see whether he had anything suitable on his books. Watkins offered to take *Princess* and the ketch *Mermaid* in part exchange for a vessel he had available but, after several week's heart searching, Cosens decided that the ideal ship for their purposes would be *Commodore*! She was therefore re-purchased from Watkins at her original sale price plus costs and an amount to cover the repairs carried out while she was in London. By 6th July 1883, she was back on the Weymouth register.

The excursion season, which had opened at Easter with short trips from both Weymouth and Bournemouth, proved to be a profitable one. Long distance excursions were added to the timetables from the first week in April. A period of north easterly winds during June rendered a number of trips uncomfortable and led to the cancellation of a planned trip by *Empress* from Bournemouth to Worthing. However, all of her monthly sailings from Bournemouth and Swanage to Torquay were completed without interruption. The usual mix of excursions to and round the Isle of Wight,

The new tug QUEEN *towing a sailing ship out of Weymouth Harbour.*

Lulworth, Portsmouth and Weymouth provided the backbone of the Bournemouth schedules and Cosens took every opportunity to emphasise their numerical superiority over the Bournemouth Company by heading their local sailing bills 'Empress, Premier, Queen or Prince', and sending Queen to show the flag whenever the opportunity arose. That trade was buoyant at Bournemouth is illustrated by the fact that both Cosens and the master of Telegraph were prosecuted by the local magistrates for overcrowding their vessels. Premier, despite having a certificate for only 278, had sailed for Swanage and Weymouth on 24th August with no less than 410 on board and was duly fined £10 plus costs for her transgression. Cosens argued fruitlessly that only the Board of Trade had the right to take such action, and paid up with an ill will and a strong suspicion that the Bournemouth Company may not have been unconnected with the magistrates' actions! 35,855 passengers were carried on the Bournemouth station during the season, whilst at Weymouth, 46,305 undertook excursions and 33,585 used the Portland ferry. Ten out of the scheduled eighteen westward coasting trips were carried out, whilst during her periods at Torquay, Prince carried a rather modest 3,433 passengers. Since she had carried a total of 18,070 during the season, it is apparent that her time at the Devon resort was now limited to a few days per week in high season and that for the rest of the time she was a key member of the Weymouth fleet. It is often assumed that the company's tugs contributed little to the passenger trade but a glance at the figures

gives an emphatic lie to this notion. In her first season, Queen carried 27,443 compared with Empress's 31,004 and Premier's 26,844 while even the little Commodore had carried a useful 15,817 passengers, chiefly on the Portland service.

Between them, the steamers had run 7,490 more miles than in 1882, carried 23,855 more passengers and had increased the company's revenue by £1,000. Despite the fact that the season had been a pleasing one and that the Bournemouth market was expanding steadily, Cosens were keenly aware of the risks posed by competition from both Lord Elgin and Telegraph, which had now been joined by another tug named Comet, to offer an increased frequency on the Swanage to Poole service. In order to boost their popular support at Bournemouth and Swanage, Cosens held a special meeting on 31st July and decided to replace the company's existing £100 shares with 1,140 of £20 each and to offer unallotted shares to residents of Bournemouth and Swanage at a discount of £3 each.

Tension was increased yet further during August, when the Bournemouth Company announced that it had placed an order with Ramage & Ferguson of Leith for a new 232 ton steamer named Bournemouth. Measuring 190 feet by 21 feet 1 inch by 8 feet, she would be 30 feet longer than either Lord Elgin or Empress and, fitted with powerful compound diagonal engines, would provide a serious threat to Cosens' interests. The board was aware that competition had already led to the wasteful situation of the rival steamers duplicating each other's routes and departure times but realised that, unless a truce

A glimpse of the Poole tug TELEGRAPH, on one of her occasional excursions to Weymouth during the early 1880s. The ship has just cast off from the landing stage and is using her 'backed' foresail to swing herself round in the harbour before departing. In addition to local towage, TELEGRAPH offered excursions and a regular service between Poole and Swanage for many years.
AUTHOR'S COLLECTION

could be agreed with the Bournemouth Company, they would have no option but to raise additional capital and build another steamer to meet the threat of *Bournemouth*. Accordingly, Cosens wrote to the Bournemouth Company suggesting that instead of going to the expense of building a new vessel each, the two companies should amalgamate to create a single concern, which would be so strong that it could keep any other competitors at arm's length for years to come.

This radical proposal was immediately rejected but evidently caused some rifts within the Bournemouth Company boardroom, for both the chairman and two of the directors promptly resigned. Cosens expressed their regret at the decision but made it clear that while *'we do not want to enter into a war of competition but to work as harmoniously as we possibly can with that company if they will allow us'*, if faced with a direct challenge *'we do intend to compete … to the utmost of our powers.'* In predicting the outcome, they referred sarcastically to a popular travelling circus of the time and stated *'we think that Barnum's will not be the only white elephant seen in this country.'*

With the gauntlet thrown down, Cosens turned to planning their new steamer. During early September 1883, James Watkins was summoned to a meeting at Weymouth to consult over the options. Initially, and rather surprisingly, it was suggested that Watkins should accept *Empress* plus £1,000 in exchange for building a new vessel of superior size and speed, from which it can be inferred that not

everyone on the Cosens board was satisfied with the ship's performance. Memories of her mechanical difficulties during 1881 must have combined with worries that her boiler was insufficiently powerful to get the best out of her engines to convince some directors that she would be seriously outclassed by the new *Bournemouth*.

By 24th September, the feeling had shifted to retaining *Empress* and raising capital to build a new vessel either wholly within or outside the UK but not split as had been the case with *Queen*. Three days later, it was being suggested that *Empress* be sold in part exchange for *two* new sister ships and then that immediate permission be sought to construct one new vessel and that a second be ordered only if *Empress* could be sold on suitable terms. A special meeting was held on 17th October at Weymouth Guildhall to discuss the matter and seek the opinions of shareholders. It was reported that an offer had already been received for *Empress* from potential buyers in Le Havre but a spirited defence of the ship by Capt William Cosens resulted in approval being given to raise £10,000 additional capital in £20 shares on the strict condition that she was retained and that the new ship's engines be constructed by John Penn & Co.

A contract was quickly drawn up with Watkins who, unable to find a British shipyard which could meet the required delivery date, was again forced to sub-contract the construction of the hull to Messrs Smit of Rotterdam. At the same time, it was decided to try to increase *Empress*'s speed by ordering a new boiler from Penns and transferring her part-worn one into *Commodore*.

At Weymouth, the company's bunkering trade from the coal hulks in Portland Harbour had been suffering mixed fortunes over the past few years. The profit during 1882 had been negligible and there was increasing competition from large, specialist, outside firms, such as Collins & Co of Dartmouth and the Powell Dyffryn Company, both of whom placed hulks in the harbour. Roberts & Co, another small Weymouth coal firm who found themselves in a similar position, had managed to obtain the agency for Powell Duffryn and Cosens decided that their best tactic for survival was to imitate Roberts by seeking the agency for the Cwmaman Coal Company who, in January 1883, announced their intention of setting up a major coaling station at Portland. On 17th May, the *Southern Times* announced that negotiations had been completed and that Cosens had accepted the agency. The Cwmaman Company was already engaged in bunkering at Dartmouth, Plymouth and Falmouth, and stated that they would be placing the hulks *George Canning* and *Skulda* (which Cosens had salvaged in May 1882) in the Roads immediately and adding a third after a few weeks. These, together with the hulks already owned by Cosens and a fourth hulk placed on station by Collins & Co, were predicted to bring a great deal of trade into Portland Harbour and generate a welcome demand for labour in Weymouth and Portland.

As agents to the Cwmaman Company, Cosens could now purchase coal direct from the hulks at greatly reduced prices and no longer had any need for their own ketch to bring coal round from South Wales. *Mermaid* was therefore placed on the market and sold during May to a Mr Hebley for £380. It must be presumed that the topping up of the Swanage coal store was either put out to contract or carried out by Cosens themselves, using one of the tugs and their own coal barges from Weymouth.

For reasons which still remain obscure, the arrangement with the Cwmaman Company did not prove a success and, after a six month trial period, the agency was abandoned in November 1883. Thereafter, the supply of coal for the company's steamers was put out to competitive tender and Cosens withdrew from the bunkering trade. At the same time, it was decided to convert the coal stores on Custom House Quay into ice wells and commence an alternative trade importing Norwegian block ice. A lease was obtained on a sail loft above the coal store and adjoining the company offices, and a decision was made to extend and modernise the offices during the coming winter. An unlooked-for benefit of the arrival of the coaling giants in Portland Harbour was a steep upturn in demand for the services of the workshop department in undertaking running repairs to vessels calling for bunkers.

During 1883, Cosens' long-standing chairman,

Dr Joseph Drew, had been suffering from declining health and was increasingly unable to take his accustomed place on the local magistrate's bench or attend board meetings. In September, the directors had rejected his offer of resignation and he continued to play an active part in the affairs of the company until 1st December, when he held his last meeting with the manager. The following day, he took to his bed complaining of severe pain and early on the morning of 3rd December, he died of compressed gout. 'The Doctor' had been a prominent local figure for many years and was in many ways the quintessential Victorian businessman. Confectioner, newspaper proprietor, steamboat owner, magistrate and mayor, he had served on the Town Council for over a quarter of a century and was known throughout the South West for his learned historical lectures. His knowledge of the steamer trade was unrivalled and his successor, Mr George E. Eliot, must have taken on his mantle with considerable misgivings. To assist him in his task, the company secretary, Simon Jenkin Fowler, was promoted to the joint post of manager and secretary, whilst his younger brother, Robert Fowler, was appointed as office assistant.

The winter of 1883 and spring of 1884 proved a particularly busy and profitable period for Cosens' salvage department. *Queen*'s first call-out took place on the evening of 22nd September, after the steamer *Ferncliffe* and the barque *Fratteli Giggino* collided south of Durlston Head. As soon as the flares were sighted, *Empress* put to sea from her overnight berth at Swanage and succeeded in locating one lifeboat full of the steamer's crew. *Ferncliffe* sank immediately and settled on an even keel some distance off Old Harry Rocks, where her masts became something of an attraction for passengers on the Bournemouth-Swanage service. The barque disappeared into the night and *Queen* spent many hours searching for her further down Channel, only to discover that she too had foundered shortly after the collision.

QUEEN, with COMMODORE behind, moored at Custom House Quay, probably in the later 1880s. The photograph reveals interesting details of the coaling arrangements at Weymouth. Following the opening of the Harbour Tramway in 1865, coal could be brought in by rail and hauled straight to the quay in wagons like the one on the right. From there it could be transferred to one of Cosens' coal stores (out of shot to the right) or tipped into barges like the one in the foreground. The steamer would either berth alongside the barge, or the barge would be towed to the steamer by the launch PRINCESS, before the filthy and back-breaking task of shovelling the coal into the ship's bunkers began.

George E. Eliot, who succeeded Joseph Drew as Chairman of Cosens & Co Ltd from 1883 to 1897. AUTHOR'S COLLECTION

Simon Jenkin Fowler, who had served as Company Clerk since 1863 and Secretary since 1874, was promoted to the post of Manager and Secretary upon the death of Joseph Drew. AUTHOR'S COLLECTION

On Christmas Eve 1883, the Great Western Railway's cross-channel packet *South of Ireland* departed from Cherbourg on a routine crossing to Weymouth but encountered dense fog patches *en route*. She drifted off course and, at 1.35am on Christmas morning, ran hard ashore in a small rocky cove known as Pondfield, just to the east of Worbarrow Bay. Fortunately, the sea was flat calm and the crew of five, together with the only passenger on board, were able to launch a lifeboat and row for four hours along the coast to Weymouth, where they raised the alarm at 6am. For some reason, neither of Cosens' tugs was available, so steam was raised on *Prince* which was laid up above the Town Bridge and, within a few hours, she was on her way to the casualty with two barges in tow. When she finally located *South of Ireland* in the thick fog, it immediately became apparent that there was little chance of saving her. With the engine and boiler rooms already flooded and water beginning to seep into the cargo holds, there was a danger that her bulkheads might collapse, trapping the salvage crew below decks. It was therefore decided to strip the saloon of its furniture and fittings, and remove all deck gear and moveable fittings before returning to Weymouth for the night. Next morning, the steamers and barges returned with workmen and timber to shore up the bulkheads, before salvaging about two thirds of the cargo. With the rise and fall of the tide, the bow section, which was trapped on the rocks, had more or less separated from the remainder of the vessel and some hopes were entertained of saving at least the engines and boilers. Large salvage pumps were sent for from Glasgow but, by the time they had arrived and were loaded into barges at Portland, the weather had become unsuitable for their use. Instead, *Commodore* and a barge spent the next two days recovering a further portion of the remaining cargo before, on 2nd January 1884, the weather settled down enough for *Queen* and *Commodore* to get the pumps to the scene. Within half an hour, the engine room, boiler room and aft saloon had been pumped dry and at high tide the two tugs made a combined effort to tow the wreckage clear of the rocks. Sadly, their success was short-lived for the remains of *South of Ireland* quickly sank into deep water and all further thoughts of salvage were abandoned.

At 4am on 31st January, the 908 ton steamship *Devonia* was at anchor in a south-westerly gale about a mile off the end of Portland Breakwater, when she was run into by the 1,298 ton *Darlington*, which was making her way towards the anchorage for shelter. *Devonia* immediately began to fill with water and, with her pumps unable to cope, a distress signal was fired. *Queen*, together with Collins & Co's diminutive 16 ton tug *Alert* and the Admiralty tug *Fairy*, all made for the scene and succeeded in beaching *Devonia* in shallow water under the lee of Chesil Beach. After standing by for some time to ensure that she did not drift back amongst the anchored shipping, *Queen* returned to Weymouth to collect the salvage pumps, timber, cement and

workmen needed to effect a temporary repair and, by 6am on 1st February, she had pumped the casualty dry enough for her boiler fires to be re-lit. At a subsequent hearing in the Admiralty Court, the judge estimated *Devonia* and her cargo to be worth £17,500 and awarded *Queen* £650 for her efforts. At about the same time, the court awarded Cosens £819 for the rescue of the *SS Thales* and this, together with the income from the *South of Ireland* incident and a number of smaller services, boosted salvage income to a new high. These awards were of direct interest to a wide range of people involved. The tug's master and crew naturally received a share but so too did all of the directors and the manager Mr Fowler who, on this occasion, received an additional 5 per cent commission in view of the exceptional character of the rescues. Commission was also paid to the local Lloyd's agent and gratuities to the chief officers of the local coastguard stations, presumably to thank them for ensuring that Cosens were always the first to know when a potential salvage case was developing!

The spring of 1884 saw major developments at the company's premises on Custom House Quay, Weymouth. The conversion of the old coal stores into ice wells by lining them with a thick insulating layer of deal and cork progressed steadily and, by February, detailed plans were being laid for managing the new trade. In addition to advertising in the *Dorset County Chronicle* and *Western Gazette*, it was decided to seek agents in Weymouth, Dorchester, Blandford and Yeovil to sell ice on behalf of the company and to appoint a Weymouth ice store manager. To get the trade under way, an initial supply of 70 tons of ice was purchased from a supplier in Southampton but, thereafter, the bulk of supplies were obtained direct from the Baltic. Each spring, usually in April, one or more cargoes of Norwegian block ice would arrive by sailing ship to be unloaded onto Custom House Quay, where Cosens' staff would use large metal tongs to drag the blocks along specially-laid planks into the ice rooms. Here they would be stacked four or five high to maximise storage capacity and minimise melting. Experiments were undertaken with a Tangye hydraulic lift but, after this proved unworkable, the only aids to handling the heavy ice blocks were a small jib crane and a series of chain tackles. In the days before domestic refrigeration, ice was in great demand by both businesses and wealthier households, and a brisk trade soon developed. There must have been a great deal of loss by melting, since the ice was distributed around the locality by horse and cart but it seems that a full ice room in April was sufficient to maintain a reliable supply to customers throughout the year. The trade continued until the outbreak of the First World War, when the company moved instead towards the manufacture of ice and into cold storage, both of which trades are described in detail in the companion volume to this book.

Above the ice store, which occupied the ground floor of a large warehouse, were two further spacious

floors known as the store and the sail loft. Each was fitted with loading doors and a hand hoist, which allowed materials to be lifted from the quayside below. The loft in the second-floor roof space was the preserve of the riggers and sailmakers, who made and repaired all of the steamers' sails and canvas work, looked after standing and running rigging, and made up the various hawsers and tackles required in the barge and salvage departments. The first floor was used for storing all manner of ships' gear and supplies and, during the winter months, was the base for repairing and varnishing deck seats and other moveable gear.

In the angle between this building and the warehouse next door was a narrow and slightly tapering strip of land, into which had been squeezed a ground floor yard and a small, first floor office building. These offices had become inadequate for the company's expanding business and, by March 1884, had been extended and completely remodelled to the design of local architect J.T. Whettam. The first floor had been extended almost to the depth of the adjoining warehouse and a range of new rooms created, one behind the other in a line and accessed from a common corridor. At the front of the building was the secretary and clerk's office, whose projecting bay window enjoyed an uninterrupted view of the harbour from the pier head to the Town Bridge and allowed the management to observe the movements

of every employee working on the quayside, slipways or moored steamers. Behind this were the lavatories, then the manager's office and finally the boardroom, which was illuminated by a rear-facing bay window and an ornate skylight. To increase the lighting levels, the rear offices were also fitted with panels of glass prisms in their floors to diffuse light from the yard below and all were match-boarded up to the level of a dado rail. A door from the linking corridor led into the adjoining stores and a new flight of stairs led down to the main entrance on the quayside. This was flanked on the right by the entrance to the ice house and on the left by a new storekeeper's office, which formed a secure front entrance to the yard beneath the offices.

The 1884 season opened on 31st March, when *Premier* and *Lord Elgin* commenced sailings from Swanage and Bournemouth. Bad weather kept both ships confined in Poole Harbour for most of the first week and, following a brief lull, the high winds soon returned and led to the cancellation of many trips until 24th April, when calm seas finally returned. At about the same time, *Queen* emerged from her refit with an extension to her funnel, which had been fitted to improve her steaming qualities.

In Rotterdam, work was progressing swiftly on the hull of the new steamer, which Cosens announced would be named *Victoria*. Determined to avoid the

A three-masted barque of the type which brought ice cargoes to Weymouth, moored at Custom House Quay. Cosens' sign-written Head Office, which also housed their stores, sailmakers' and riggers' lofts, and ice store, can be seen between the vessel's two forward masts. WEYMOUTH MUSEUM

PREMIER with a coal barge alongside, berthed at Custom House Quay in 1884. She displays her original square counter stern, which was replaced by a more elegant, curved design during the following winter. To her left, the twin bow windows belong to Weymouth's Georgian Custom House. The ground floor of the massive brick warehouse was in use as Dyer's Coal Stores while, beyond that, the projecting first floor bay window of Cosens' Head Office can be clearly seen. The vessel swinging in the harbour is GAEL, while VULTURE is laid up in 'The Cove' to the right. Both ships were used on the cross-channel service to Cherbourg.
AUTHOR'S COLLECTION

problems they had encountered with *Queen*, Messrs Smit were working overtime to ensure that they earned the £3 per day bonus for early delivery. Cosens had appointed a local agent to visit the yard daily and report on progress, whilst Robert Fowler travelled to Holland regularly to inspect the work. By May, she was ready to be towed to the Thames to receive her machinery at Penn's yard and additional crew members were being recruited.

The impending arrival of two new rival steamers – *Bournemouth* and *Victoria* – quite naturally led to an increasing air of anticipation in Swanage and Bournemouth, and the same questions hung on everyone's lips. Which ship would prove the faster? Would the larger *Bournemouth* finally break Cosens' grip on the station and allow the local company to gain the ascendancy?

News from Leith that *Bournemouth* had achieved 16 knots on trials added fuel to the debate and it was generally agreed that *Empress*'s days as the fastest steamer on the South Coast must be numbered. When *Bournemouth* arrived alongside her namesake pier for the first time at 8am on Sunday 18th May, her twin funnels and greater length only served to emphasise her apparent superiority and the local populace were agog to learn the outcome of her first contest with *Empress*. Patience had to be exercised for, on Monday, *Bournemouth* ran a private trip for shareholders and, on Tuesday, operated her first public sailing round the Isle of Wight, so it was not until Wednesday 21st May that the rival steamers came head to head on an evening cruise from Bournemouth to Yarmouth. To the Bournemouth Company's consternation and Cosens' delight,

Bournemouth arrived at Yarmouth Pier only three minutes ahead of *Empress*, despite the fact that the latter had not been slipped for three months and therefore had a significantly dirtier bottom than her rival. Cosens were quick to publish the following comparison in the local press:

BOURNEMOUTH	*EMPRESS*
Length, 190ft	Length , 160ft
Breadth, 21ft	Breadth, 18ft.
Engines, 1000ihp	Engines, 345ihp
2 boilers, 80lbs pressure	1 boiler, 30lbs pressure
3 engineers, 6 firemen	1 engineer, 1 fireman
Cost about £14,000	Cost about £9,000

Despite *Bournemouth* being sent to Southampton for scrubbing and anti-fouling, subsequent races between the two ships produced similar results. Although *Bournemouth* was undoubtedly the faster of the two, the difference was marginal and certainly not what her owners had anticipated when they opted for a vessel with powerful, modern and costly compound diagonal engines. Cosens smugly suggested that their prediction about white elephants was about to be proved correct and took every opportunity to praise *Empress* as a '*wonder for speed*' and a craft which, given her smaller dimensions and power, '*surpassed the most sanguine expectations of her best friends.*'

Determined to compete with Cosens on every front, the Bournemouth Company applied for and obtained a cross-channel certificate for their new flagship and announced that her first sailing to Cherbourg would take place on 4th July. They added

proudly that she carried '*a number 2 Board of Trade certificate, entitling her to ply on any part of the coast of the United Kingdom and from the river Elbe in Germany to Brest at the entrance to the Bay of Biscay; and is the only vessel on station authorised to do so.*'

Realising that *Bournemouth*'s superior size would make her a serious competitor on the Cherbourg excursions, Cosens cast about for an alternative attraction and pre-empted the opposition by advertising a day trip from Bournemouth and Swanage to Alderney on 13th June for a fare of 7s 6d.

The day dawned sunny and windless. *Empress* departed from Bournemouth at 8am and, after calling at Swanage, set off across the Channel with one hundred passengers on board. The sea was so glassy that most of the passengers were able to enjoy the substantial luncheon provided by the stewardess Mrs Bowering and the passage was enlivened by a large school of porpoises, which disported themselves around the ship for much of the journey.

By 1.35pm, *Empress* was safely berthed inside the massive Alderney breakwater and many of her passengers headed for a nearby hotel recommended in their guide books, hoping that their creature comforts would be adequately provided for. Alas, it rapidly became apparent that no arrangements had been made for an invasion of hungry foreigners and '*patience had to be exercised*' before their wants could be supplied. Other more adventurous passengers climbed aboard a '*country van which had been extemporised to do duty as a char-a-banc*' and set off on a tour of the island, which included a stop for refreshments at the country house of the van's owner. A third group accepted the offer of the local magistrate to accompany them on a brief walking tour, which concluded with afternoon tea in his delightful garden and gifts of flowers and vegetables to all who would accept them.

Shortly after 4pm, as the passengers began to

assemble on the landing stage ready for a 4.30pm departure, it became apparent that all was not well. It quickly emerged that one of the passengers, '*less wise and prudent than he should have been*', had contravened the local laws by '*attempting to surreptitiously convey on board rather a large quantity of the narcotic weed*' and had been handed over to the local customs officers to be dealt with on the following day. With the drama resolved, *Empress* cast off at 4.55pm and reached Swanage four hours and forty minutes later. Here, she was subject to a further routine search by customs officers from Poole but was alongside Bournemouth Pier five hours and 25 minutes after leaving Alderney.

The trip, which was believed to the first ever steam excursion to the island from England, was hailed as a great success and was repeated on 27th June and 22nd July. Thereafter, until the First World War, Alderney appeared as a regular high-season destination on Cosens' Bournemouth sailing bills. On 24th June, *Empress* offered an unusual sailing from Bournemouth and Swanage direct to Seaton in Devon, where passengers were landed onto the open beach using the ship's patent landing gear.

With *Empress* and *Bournemouth* competing for the long distance excursion trade, *Lord Elgin* was freed to concentrate on the Swanage service and local excursions. In order to equal her frequency of three return sailings per day and maintain their full programme of sailings from Weymouth, Cosens were forced to deploy their fleet with considerable ingenuity while they awaited the arrival of their new vessel *Victoria*. At Weymouth, every Monday saw a steamer – usually *Premier* – depart at 10.30am for a day trip to Swanage and Bournemouth, where she would be employed on the 'ferry' before returning to Weymouth at 4pm. On Tuesdays and Fridays, long distance sailings were offered to either Cowes, Yarmouth or Totland Bay on the Isle of Wight, or

The new, iron Bournemouth Pier of 1880. Designed by the famous Eugenius Birch, it cost £21,600 to build and was 838 feet in length. Covered shelters and a bandstand were added to the 110 feet wide pier head in 1885, as shown in this photograph. EMPRESS and two other steamers are moored on the far side of the pier.
DORCHESTER LIBRARY

to one of the Devon resorts such as Seaton. On 4th July, a day trip to Alderney was advertised. Thursday was the traditional day for the Grand Westward Coasting Cruise, calling at Bridport, Seaton, Sidmouth, Budleigh Salterton and Torquay, and, although both *Prince* and *Premier* were equipped for beach landing, *Empress* with her greater size and speed was usually recalled from Bournemouth to carry it out. Wednesdays and Saturdays were reserved for local sailings and on the former, additional evening trips to Lulworth were provided in connection with the early closing movement. On several occasions during June and early July, *Prince* offered a Monday afternoon single sailing to Torquay, where she ran local excursions until Thursday afternoon before returning again to Weymouth. This enabled a presence to be maintained at Torquay, while ensuring that enough ships were available for the Weymouth local services when *Premier* was away on her long distance Monday and Friday jaunts. Conversely, one of the Weymouth steamers was often sent along to Bournemouth to maintain the local sailings and Swanage ferry, while *Empress* was away on long day trips. Cosens' management must have longed for the arrival of *Victoria*!

The new steamer arrived at Weymouth from the Thames on Saturday 5th July and was immediately

thrown open to the press and public, who expressed themselves well pleased with what they saw. Although only six feet longer than *Empress* and of a basically similar design, she gave the impression of being a far larger and more spacious ship. Cosens had specified that, in order for her to pass through the narrow arch of Weymouth Town Bridge, her extreme breadth over the paddle boxes must not exceed *Empress*'s 31 feet 6 inches and her designers had achieved the apparently impossible by increasing the beam of her hull by 1 foot 2 inches to 19 feet 3 inches, while at the same time reducing the width of her paddle wheels by a similar amount. The following table provides an interesting comparison between the two ships:

	VICTORIA	*EMPRESS*
Length	166ft	160ft 1in
Beam of hull	19ft 3ins	18ft 1in
Extreme breadth	31ft 6ins	31ft 6ins
Depth fr main deck	8ft 7ins	8ft 3ins
Hull	Steel	Iron
Gross tonnage	192	163
Engine	2-cyl osc	2-cyl osc
Cyl diameter/stroke	35ins/36ins	30ins/33ins
NHP	75	52

A builder's half-model of VICTORIA, showing her proposed design.
AUTHOR'S COLLECTION

Victoria was the first steel vessel to join the fleet, all of her predecessors having been constructed from iron or timber. Her hull was fitted with six watertight bulkheads, whilst her frames and floors were much more closely-spaced than was the norm, to give her the necessary strength for regular beaching along the Devon coast. Large bilge keels were fitted to help reduce rolling in a seaway. Her twin cylinder, simple, oscillating engine was of the classic John Penn design and fundamentally the same as *Empress*'s, except that both the stroke and bore of the cylinders were larger. Like her fleetmates, she was fitted with a jet condensing system for cooling used steam but, unusually, her boiler, which operated at a pressure of 30lbs psi, was of a rectangular or 'tank' design.

Below decks her accommodation followed the usual pattern. Aft, on the lower deck, was the 38 foot by 18 foot main saloon and a 15 foot by 11 foot ladies cabin, both panelled in inlaid birds-eye maple, upholstered in green Utrecht velvet, and fitted with elegantly framed mirrors and hand painted deck-heads. The main saloon was fitted with tip-back seats and tables, and a handsome sofa occupied the centre of the floor. Access from the main deck to the saloons was by way of a spiral staircase, at the foot of which were situated the stewardess's pantry and sleeping cabin. At the forward end of the ship was the all important, 36 foot by 18 foot refreshment saloon, with its long tables, hanging trays suspended from the deck-head and a large refreshment bar right across the forward end. The steward and stewardess were enabled to communicate with each other from their respective ends of the ship by means of a brass speaking tube. Opening off this compartment were the captain's cabin and the second class lavatories. Forward again and accessed by a traditional curved companionway was the crew's fo'c'sle, with small, separate berths for the mate and chief engineer, scrubbed wood table and benches, and space for the crew to sling their hammocks.

The open main deck was punctuated by the central engine house and sponson side houses, which contained the usual crew galley, lamp rooms, mess room and toilet. Ahead of the engine and facing the large, hooded companionway to the forward saloon, stood the quartermaster steam steering engine with its large wheel. Forward, there was a combined steam windlass and capstan, while aft, was a second capstan whose steam engine was concealed beneath the deck in the tiller flat. This neat arrangement, much favoured by Cosens, meant that only the barrel of the capstan was visible on deck and steam was exhausted directly through the ship's side, where it caused less inconvenience to passengers. *Victoria*'s most innovative feature was probably the saloon, which was fitted in the centre of the upper deck aft, just behind the mast. This small cabin which was fitted with seating, comfortably upholstered and curtained, was to prove an extremely popular concession to passengers who required shelter from the elements on rough days but who could not face the thought of going below!

Victoria made her first public sailing on Monday 7th July, when she took the regular day trip from Weymouth to Swanage and Bournemouth, before making several crossings on the ferry while her passengers were enjoying time ashore. This, of course, was the ideal way both to show her off to the public and to rattle a sabre in the face of the enemy. The following day, she went to Torquay, where she met *Empress* which had come down from Bournemouth and on the return sailing the opportunity was taken to test the relative speed of the two ships on a race from Ore Rock, Torquay to Portland Bill. *Victoria* passed the Bill after 2 hours 39 minutes, twenty minutes ahead of *Empress*, thereby establishing a superiority over her fleetmate and, by implication, over the rival *Bournemouth*, of one and a half knots.

On Wednesday 9th July *Victoria* departed for Bournemouth, where she took on board the local shareholders and directors, together with a large party of invited guests, for an official trial cruise to the Needles. Although the Bournemouth press reported the event in detail, it is significant that the same edition carried a long and florid letter from 'a visitor', extolling the virtues of *Bournemouth* and the delights of one of her trips to Cherbourg. During the afternoon, *Victoria* returned to Weymouth and, at 5pm, set off on a second trial trip, this time for the benefit of the Weymouth shareholders. With the Brunswick Band dispensing suitably patriotic tunes, she steamed along the line of the breakwater and then around *HMS Minotaur* which was at anchor in the bay, before the assembled worthies retired to the saloon to indulge in the customary speechmaking and toasts.

Behind the scenes, however, a bitter dispute had been raging between Cosens and Watkins & Co regarding *Victoria*'s speed. The contract had required Watkins to produce a vessel with a trial speed the same as *Empress*'s but with a service speed of a half a knot more. Watkins maintained that the recent race from Torquay to Portland had demonstrated conclusively that *Victoria* was one and half knots faster than *Empress*, even after the latter's recent reboilering and that the terms of the contract were therefore fulfilled. Cosens countered by claiming that *Empress*'s original service speed had been 13 knots and not 12 as Watkins asserted, and therefore demanded the payment of £100 penalty because *Victoria* had not achieved her contract speed. The whole issue hinged on the imprecise wording of the contract and a lack of agreement over data relating to *Empress*.

Watkins clearly felt very hard done by and were moved to state their side of the argument in an open letter to the *Southern Times*. After rehearsing the difference of opinion over the contract, the letter went on to state:

'We have spent fully £500 more on her than our contract required us to do, so as to assist the company

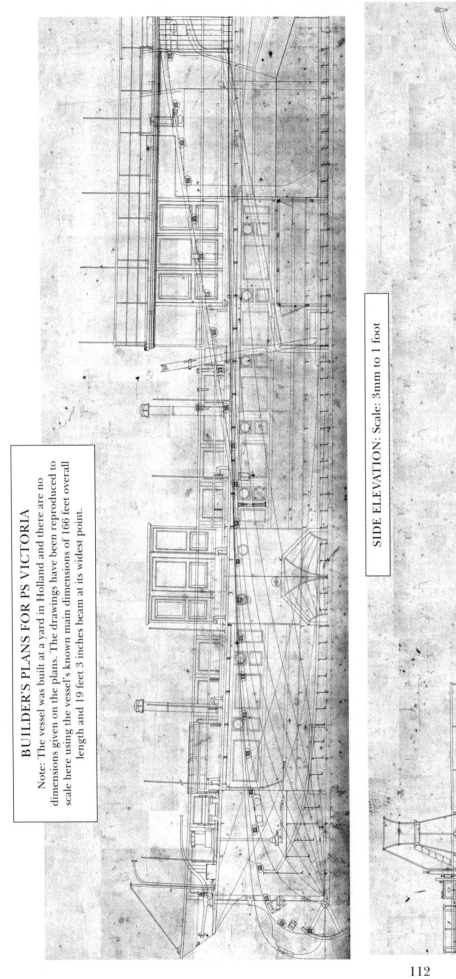

BUILDER'S PLANS FOR PS VICTORIA

Note: The vessel was built at a yard in Holland and there are no dimensions given on the plans. The drawings have been reproduced to scale here using the vessel's known main dimensions of 166 feet overall length and 19 feet 3 inches beam at its widest point.

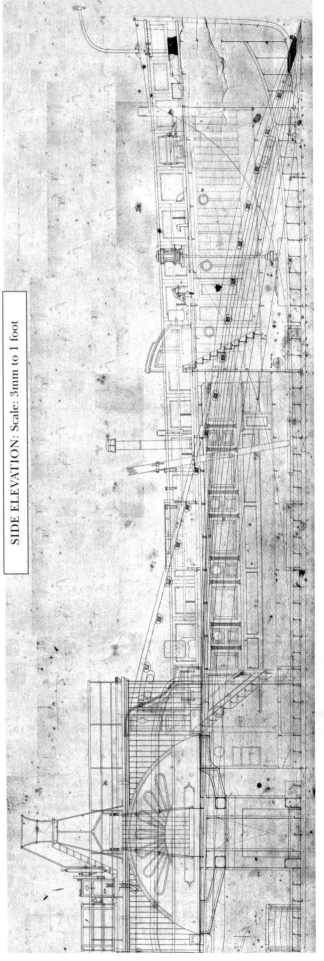

SIDE ELEVATION: Scale: 3mm to 1 foot

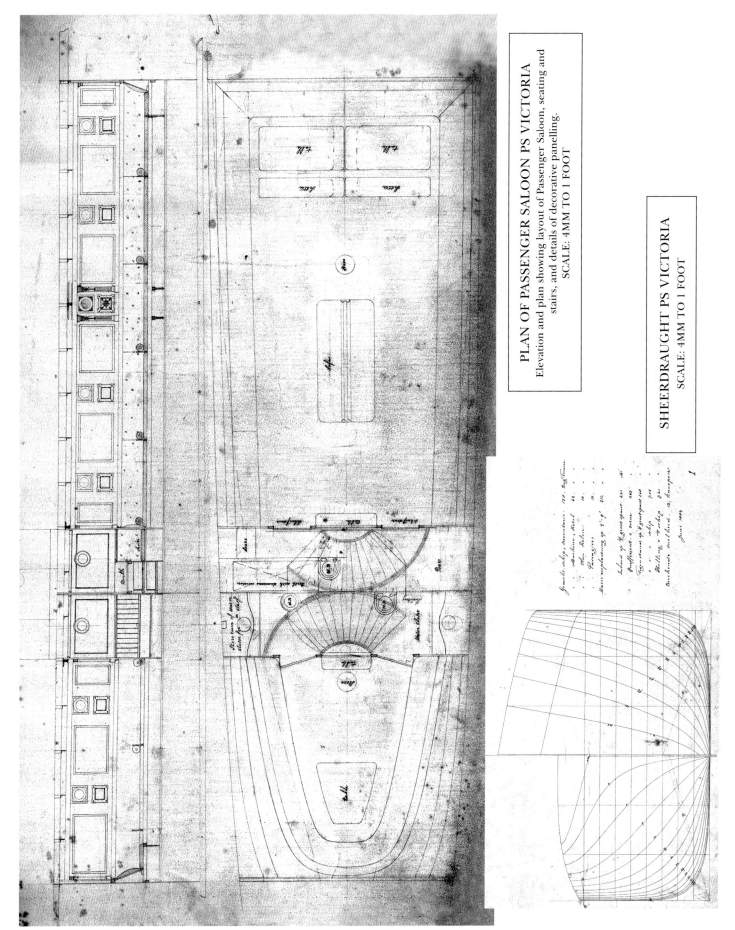

PLAN OF PASSENGER SALOON PS VICTORIA
Elevation and plan showing layout of Passenger Saloon, seating and
stairs, and details of decorative panelling.
SCALE: 4MM TO 1 FOOT

SHEERDRAUGHT PS VICTORIA
SCALE: 4MM TO 1 FOOT

A truly astonishing photograph of three steamers berthed together at Lulworth Cove during the summer of 1884. In the centre, the new VICTORIA has a bow rope out to a bollard at the top of the beach and her stern secured to a permanent mooring. A wheeled landing stage has been drawn out from the beach and passengers embarked through the small doorway in her bulwarks, where a member of the crew is standing. EMPRESS (nearest the camera) and LORD ELGIN are moored alongside and have embarked their passengers over VICTORIA's decks. The occasion must have been a very special one, for it was extremely unusual for two Cosens' steamers to be in the cove at the same time and the rival LORD ELGIN would normally have been refused all landing rights.
WEYMOUTH LIBRARY

in their oppositions. We have shown the company how, by the scientific reduction in the size of the wheels, the vessel could be a foot wider and yet go through the bridge. We have produced for £1,500 less than the Empress cost a more handsome vessel, bolder and better fitted in every way and with one and a half knots more speed, and the result is not one single word of praise or thanks but a reduction made of £100 from our price for speed penalty and attempt to get another £100 from us for delays which we might say were due to the company and not by us … We were directly instrumental in saving the company £1,000 on the engines also, and when they were hard up for a boat let them have the Commodore back at £100 less than others had offered us. We have done other work for the company besides teaching them what they wanted and building the Queen, for which vessel after she had been at work a year and earned £1,000, we offered the company £1,000 over the cost price, and verily we have our reward.'

Having registered their disgust at Cosens' penny pinching attitude, Watkins gave way but must have derived some satisfaction that their open letter had been printed in the adjacent newspaper column to a self-congratulatory description of *Victoria*'s trial trip. The two companies never worked together again.

Victoria held Board of Trade passenger certificates to cross the English Channel with 194 passengers, to trade anywhere between the Lizard and Brighton with 350 and to carry up to 470 on shorter cruises from Bournemouth or Weymouth. It was widely assumed that she would replace *Empress* at Bournemouth but, in the event, Cosens decided to retain her at Weymouth in order to boost long distance sailings from that port. She immediately took over the westward coasting trips to the Devon beaches and Torquay, and was to remain closely associated with the service until its eventual demise in 1932. As the season progressed, the frequency of long trips between Dartmouth to the west and Brighton to the east increased steadily. Her presence allowed *Prince* to be released to spend more time at Torquay during July and August, and for *Premier* to shadow *Lord Elgin* on the Bournemouth to Swanage service and short trips to the Isle of Wight. A steamer was also sent regularly to Bridport, from where trips were offered to Weymouth, Exmouth, Torquay and elsewhere.

An additional steamer naturally demanded additional crew and the arrival of *Victoria* led to a major reshuffle of the company's seagoing personnel. At the beginning of the season, Capt Bowering was promoted from *Premier* to *Empress*, freeing William Cosens to stand by the new ship in the builders yard and assume command as soon as she was ready.

114

Capt George Haill moved to *Premier* from *Queen*, where he was replaced by James Beale, who had recently joined the company. Capt Masters retained command of *Prince* and Henry Parsons of the little *Commodore*.

It was important to Cosens that the new ship was seen often at Bournemouth so, in addition to her scheduled excursions from Weymouth, it became the practice to exchange her rosters with *Empress* on a fairly regular basis. *Victoria*'s first public excursions from Bournemouth were on 14th July, when she went to Weymouth in 2 hours 34 minutes against a strong tide, headwind and heavy sea and, after returning to Bournemouth, sailed again on an evening cruise round the anchored ironclads in Portland Harbour. Thereafter she took her share of long trips to east and west, enabling passengers from Bournemouth and Swanage to visit the Devon beaches and resorts more frequently than hitherto, although it remains unclear whether she ever crossed the Channel.

The Channel Fleet, under the command of HRH The Duke of Edinburgh, spent much of the summer in Portland Harbour and Weymouth Bay, and proved a great attraction to visitors from both Weymouth and Bournemouth. Six ironclads and a flotilla of torpedo boats were present and on most days at least one major warship was thrown open to public inspection. On several evenings, torpedo attacks were staged and the ships demonstrated their novel

electric searchlights, which amazed onlookers by lighting up objects for miles around. All this provided a rich source of income for the competing Bournemouth steamer companies while, at Weymouth, the smaller steamers ran an almost continuous service to view the Fleet and Cosens made a handsome profit from providing their usual liberty boat service for the hundreds of sailors on shore leave.

As August progressed, the competition at Bournemouth became more and more intense. In addition to visiting Torquay, Dartmouth, Weymouth, Portland, Brighton, Cowes, Totland and sailing round the Isle of Wight, *Bournemouth* trespassed on Cosens' new territory by running a day trip to Alderney on 1st August. On Bank Holiday Monday, 4th August, the Southampton steamer *Princess Beatrice* landed a party at Bournemouth and was promptly chartered by the local company to boost their fleet for the day. Cosens responded by

Victoria's ornate paddle box crest.
COURTESY GERARD COX

It is thought that the bell-top to EMPRESS'S *funnel was removed and the design of her paddle box vents altered during the winter of 1884, following the renewal of her paddle wheels. These alterations, as well as the mooring arrangements at Lulworth, are clearly visible in this post 1885 photograph.*
DORSET COUNTY MUSEUM

QUEEN at Weymouth Pile Pier. In the foreground, a selection of splendid private yachts lie at their moorings under the Nothe.
WEYMOUTH LIBRARY

ensuring that *Empress*, *Victoria* and *Premier* were in the area for most of the day and Swanage residents must have felt themselves in a second heaven as, boosted by the regular service to Poole by *Telegraph* and *Comet*, excursions from their pier exceeded all previous records.

A tragedy occurred on board *Bournemouth* during an evening cruise on Regatta Day, 20th August. A number of fireworks, which were to have formed part of the regatta celebrations, had been set up on her foredeck but, while they were being set off, one particularly powerful rocket misfired and ran amok among the passengers, one of whom was killed.

During early September, a period of poor weather disrupted sailings and, on 6th September, became so bad that steamers returning from the Isle of Wight were forced to land their passengers at Poole. *Empress* suffered some damage to her paddle floats and the following day suffered further mechanical problems and was forced to return to Swanage for repairs.

Prince finished her Torquay season on 27th September and the final Bournemouth and Swanage sailings of 1884 took place on 11th October, leaving both companies to take stock of their positions. The Bournemouth Company leaked a report indicating their shareholders' intention to place a third steamer on the station for 1885 but, in view of *Bournemouth*'s

higher than expected running costs and the price-cutting caused by the stiff competition with Cosens, this appears to have been more bravura than reality. The last Thursday trips from Bridport to Torquay and Exmouth took place on 4th and 11th September respectively, and the Weymouth vessels were withdrawn a few days later.

At Swanage, which was still without a railway connection, the residents felt the isolation caused by the withdrawal of the steamers very keenly, and canvassed the owner of *Telegraph* and *Comet* to provide a winter service. It was agreed that *Telegraph* would leave Poole at 8am and 3pm, and Swanage at 9.15am and 4pm each Thursday and Saturday to connect with the trains at Poole, and the service commenced on 30th October.

Over the winter, *Premier* was subject to an intensive programme of maintenance and improvement. During October, she had been slightly damaged in a collision with a barge she was towing (for which her master was suspended and chief engineer sacked) and had to be withdrawn for repairs. At the same time, it was decided to replace her original, rather square counter stern with a new one of more elegant, elliptical design. Her 1872 boiler was worn out and it was decided to break it up *in situ*, before replacing it with a new one designed by a Mr Edwards of London. The boiler was constructed

Victoria arriving at the open beach at Bridport (also referred to as West Bay) during one of her westward coasting voyages from Weymouth. The crew in the stern have dropped a kedge anchor and are about to haul it tight to keep the ship at 90 degrees to the shore, while those in the bows are preparing to lower the patent landing gear and disembark the small group of passengers. Even in the slight swell which is running in this picture, the operation required great skill and judgement. The ship would sometimes berth in the harbour entrance but, whenever conditions were suitable, Cosens preferred to save harbour dues by calling at the beach. After Bridport, the ship would call at some combination of Lyme Regis, Seaton and Sidmouth before arriving at Torquay.

AUTHOR'S COLLECTION

The crew of VICTORIA sometime between 1884 and 1888. A large proportion of the crew transferred together from EMPRESS and moved again to the new flagship MONARCH when she was commissioned in 1888. Seated on the front row are, from left to right, Chief Engineer William Hinde jnr, Capt William Cosens and the Mate, Harbin John Hardy. Other long-standing crew members included Able Seamen George Anthony Whitby, John Smith and Thomas Cole, and Firemen Henry Rice and Albert Leighton. Stewards, cooks, ordinary seamen and ship's boys came and went with greater frequency.
WEYMOUTH MUSEUM

and fitted by Day, Summers & Co at Southampton but all other work was carried out by the company's own engineering department at Weymouth.

It was a source of increasing frustration to Cosens that their No. 1 slipway at Weymouth was too small to accommodate either *Queen*, *Empress* or *Victoria*, all of which had to be sent to Southampton or Portsmouth for their annual docking. The management reasoned that they could avoid this annual outlay, generate more work for their own workforce and create a valuable, revenue-earning asset for the company, if the slipway was enlarged. As soon as Mr Ayles, the owner of the slipway, agreed to a long extension of the lease and the refit of the smaller steamers was completed, Cosens' engineering staff began the reconstruction. New rails were laid, a larger cradle constructed, a more powerful steam winding engine was fitted and, by early the following year, the slipway was complete.

The work on *Premier* and the slipway, together with

some expensive repairs to Portland Pier, the renewal of *Empress*'s paddle wheels and thorough refits to the other steamers, added to the cost of re-boilering *Empress* during 1883, meant that a considerable debt was accumulating in the repair and renewal fund, which it was hoped to pay off in the season ahead.

The opening months of 1885 proved a busy and profitable period for the salvage department. The first drama unfolded on the morning of 14th January, when a telegram reached Cosens stating that a large ship was aground on the Kimmeridge Ledges. At the time, the Great Western Railway steamer *Gael* was seriously overdue on a passage from Cherbourg to Weymouth and fears were entertained that, in a repeat of the *South of Ireland* disaster four years earlier, it was she who had gone aground. *Queen*, followed by *Commodore* with a barge, were immediately dispatched to Kimmeridge, where they discovered the French steamer *Guyenne*, loaded with 2,000 tons of iron ore, firmly aground on the ledges. *Gael*, it later transpired, had suffered a serious breakdown in mid-Channel and finally limped into port nine hours later.

A conference on board *Guyenne* concluded that the most effective way of saving the ship would be to jettison as much of her cargo as possible, before the high tide returned during the evening. The French crew and all the available men from the two tugs immediately set to work under the direction of Capt Bowering, whilst *Queen* was sent back to Weymouth to collect 40 more labourers and the necessary gear for discharging the cargo using steam winches. By high tide that evening, over 200 tons had been thrown overboard and the tugs made a strenuous but unsuccessful effort to refloat the casualty. During the night, much anxiety was caused by the deteriorating weather conditions, which caused *Guyenne* to roll and thump alarmingly on the rocks but work went ahead steadily and on the morning tide she was towed into deep water. Although her hull had been punctured by the rocks,

During a major refit in the winter of 1884-85, PREMIER was re-boilered, fitted with a fatter funnel and given a new, elliptical counter stern. These alterations are visible in this photograph of her departing from Weymouth on yet another excursion.
AUTHOR'S COLLECTION

she was fitted with double bottoms, which enabled her to survive the short voyage back to Portland, where temporary repairs were carried out.

An even more dramatic rescue took place during a gale on 2nd February, when the 1,020 ton steamer *Cheerful* lost her propeller in the vicinity of the Shambles light ship. A passing German ship made repeated attempts to take her in tow but, after breaking several hawsers, eventually collided with *Cheerful* and caused such serious damage to both ships that she was forced to give up. By this time, *Cheerful*'s predicament had been spotted by the Portland coastguard and *Queen*, with a picked crew under the command of Capt Haill, was on her way

to the scene. *Queen* passed a line and ordered *Cheerful* to slip her cable but the shackles jammed and it took fully two hours before the heavy anchor chain could be cut through by hand. By this time, the tide had begun to ebb, *Queen*'s tow rope had parted and *Cheerful* was driving rapidly towards the rocks near Portland Bill. The coastguards, who reported the seas as '*running mountains high*', stated that she was aground and were in the process of rigging their rocket line-throwing apparatus to rescue the crew, when Capt Haill made one last, desperate attempt to save the ship. In an act of great skill and gallantry, he took *Queen* through a gap no greater than her own length between *Cheerful* and the rocks,

PREMIER, nearest the camera, with her new, larger funnel and counter stern, lying alongside VICTORIA in Weymouth Harbour. The small screw tug has not been identified.
AUTHOR'S COLLECTION

VICTORIA at Lulworth Cove.
AUTHOR'S COLLECTION

119

A rather grainy but rare view of PRINCE and VICTORIA landing passengers together on Seaton Beach during 1886.
AUTHOR'S COLLECTION

succeeded in passing his last remaining line and towed her seaward, where *Commodore* was waiting to assist.

Cosens were awarded £1,400 for the rescue of *Cheerful*, of which 9.5 per cent was distributed among the crews of the tugs. The income from *Guyenne* is not recorded but £500 was received later in the year for a service to SS *Parana*, plus additional awards for the salvage of *Cortesia* and rescue of the yacht *Vendetta*.

Painfully aware of the high and wasteful cost of the previous season's competition, Cosens arranged a conference with the Bournemouth Company during March 1885 to explore the possibility of some limited co-operation. It was grudgingly agreed that, until Whitsun, each company would operate only one vessel at Bournemouth and that, except on bank holidays and long distance excursions, each company's season tickets would be valid on the other's steamers.

It was perhaps symptomatic of the half-hearted nature of the agreement that when *Victoria* and *Bournemouth* opened the season on 4th April, Cosens' advertisements made no mention at all of the new arrangements. It was left to Edward Bicker, secretary of the Bournemouth Company, to announce that *'when only one steamer is worked by this company and one by the Weymouth company, season tickets will be available by either company's steamers; also on wet or stormy days, when only one steamer shall ply from Bournemouth to Swanage and back.'*

The delicate truce was, however, short-lived. When, on 24th April, the Bournemouth Company announced their intention of bringing a second steamer into service from 4th May, Cosens insisted that the agreement had been breached and immediately withdrew themselves. *Empress* was sent from Weymouth to balance *Lord Elgin* and, by early May, the competition was back to its previous sorry state. The stakes were raised considerably during June, when a meeting of the Bournemouth Company shareholders was called to consider the advisability of carrying the war into the enemy camp by placing

a boat on the Weymouth station. The meeting was an odd affair, since very few of the fifty shareholders who had signed the motion were present and the company directors were opposed to the suggestion. A representative of the group of shareholders who were prepared to guarantee the cost of hiring such a vessel mischievously explained that *'the Weymouth people would no doubt be very glad of a better boat than they at present obtained, the* Victoria *and* Empress *being engaged at Bournemouth.'* If a Weymouth company could operate ships from Bournemouth, why should not the reverse apply in equal measure? The company agreed to co-operate with any syndicate of shareholders which was formed but, as no more was heard of the matter, it can be assumed that the main aim of the meeting had been to enrage the Cosens' management.

By a cruel twist of fate, both the Easter and Whitsun holiday and the peak month of August were dogged by exceptionally bad weather, which hit both companies' revenue extremely hard. As each sought to gain an advantage over the other, a number of new destinations appeared on the sailing bills, and Bournemouth and Swanage passengers found themselves provided with more variety than ever before.

From the beginning of May, Cosens introduced a regular thrice weekly service to Yarmouth, Cowes, Ryde and Portsmouth on Mondays, Thursdays and Saturdays, together with early closing day excursions each Wednesday evening to Totland or Swanage. The Bournemouth Company responded by adopting identical fares and departure times on several of the key routes and, before long, the local newspaper was full of letters complaining about the dangers of racing. Both companies took some heed of their critics and, on 13th June, the following announcement, signed by Edward Bicker, appeared in the *Bournemouth Observer*:

'Sir, Permit me to inform the public through the medium of your columns that my directors have determined in order to avoid any appearance of racing with the Weymouth company's boats, to alter the time of starting when making the regular trip to Yarmouth, Cowes, Ryde and Portsmouth. The Bournemouth *will therefore leave the pier at 10.30 a.m. next week and at 10.15 a.m. the following week.; Cosens and Co having also agreed to leave at 10.15 a.m. next week and 10.30 a.m. the following week and so on, alternately, until further notice.'*

Evidence suggests that this letter was very much a sop to the public and that intense competition continued on many sailings. On Wednesday 24th June, for example, when Cosens advertised the first ever cheap evening trip to Lymington for a fare of 1s, the Bournemouth Company responded by advertising *Lord Elgin* for an identical sailing. Although the two ships left the pier together and entered the narrow and winding Lymington river at almost the same moment, the Bournemouth press concentrated on praising the local boat and added, almost as a postscript, 'on entering the channel the steamer Victoria was seen following closely in the wake of Lord Elgin.' How the residents of sleepy Lymington reacted to the arrival of two large excursion vessels on the same evening tide has, sadly, gone unrecorded! On 28th July, Cosens advertised a 'Special Excursion to the New Forest', which involved Victoria in sailing from Bournemouth at 10.00am and landing her passengers at Lymington on the morning tide. The excursionists could then choose to spend the day at Lymington or to travel onwards by train to Brockenhurst in the heart of the New Forest, before rejoining their steamer for the evening trip homewards.

Bournemouth innovated by offering special three day excursions to both Torquay and Jersey, repeated her crossings to Cherbourg and went eastwards to Brighton on a number of occasions. She imitated Cosens' 7th August trip to Alderney with a similar excursion a week later and made certain that she shadowed Victoria on her annual trip to Dartmouth regatta.

With intense competition and racing an almost normal feature of daily life, it was not surprising that some errors were made. On 23rd July and again on 20th August, Empress was prosecuted for being overcrowded at Torquay on her arrival from Weymouth and Sidmouth but Capt Bowering was let off with a reprimand in view of the 'difficulties in the Westward system of ascertaining the exact numbers on board'. More seriously, Premier narrowly avoided a serious collision with Lord Elgin and Capt Haill, whose responses at the board's official enquiry were regarded as 'most unsatisfactory', was dismissed from the company's employ. He must have been a somewhat unpredictable man for, although he could demonstrate extraordinary nerve and seamanship as in the rescue of Cheerful, he had also been suspended on a previous occasion for endangering Premier and there were a number of other charges relating to his conduct!

During September, Premier had suffered a fracture in one of the cylinders of her main engine, resulting in a lengthy period off service while the expensive repairs were undertaken. The Torquay season closed on 12th September and the last Bournemouth steamers, Empress and Lord Elgin, were cheered away from the pier on 17th October. Despite breakdowns, stiff competition and the worst of weather, Cosens had managed to increase their revenue by £628 and derived great satisfaction from declaring a dividend of 5 per cent. In stark contrast, the Bournemouth Company were unable to pay their shareholders anything at all.

Cosens had already been relatively successful in attracting new shareholders from Swanage and Bournemouth, and now sought to extend their base of local support at all their ports of call by reducing the nominal value of their shares. At a special meeting held in November 1885, it was decided to replace the existing 1,640 £20 shares with 6,560 valued at £5 each, in the hope that the lower price would encourage more tradesmen and 'ordinary' people to purchase a stake in the company.

The year had also seen significant developments at Swanage. The long awaited railway had finally opened to passenger traffic on 20th May and, with its infamous isolation gone forever, all barriers to the town's development as a fashionable resort were removed at a stroke. After the commencement of the goods service on 1st June, more and more of the stone trade transferred from sea to the railway, the untidy 'bankers' or stone yards around the bay were steadily replaced by promenades and seaside architecture, and the pace of development in the town accelerated. Although the need for Telegraph's winter service had disappeared, the effect on the other steamer companies was overwhelmingly positive in the years ahead. As more and more summer visitors poured into the resort, the demand for excursions from the pier grew steadily and, as the town developed, it became an increasingly attractive destination from both Weymouth and Bournemouth. Crucially, the regular summer service between Swanage and Bournemouth remained both faster and more attractive than the circuitous rail journey, and was heavily used by visitors and residents alike.

The following years, 1886 and 1887, will chiefly be remembered as years of fog and strandings, which saw Cosens engaged in more major salvage jobs than ever before. On the evening of 15th May 1886, the liner Palala on passage from London to Natal via Portland for orders, ran hard aground on the Kimmeridge Ledges in clear but windy weather. Queen, commanded by Capt Beale, arrived on the scene at 9pm but, with a heavy swell breaking over the ledges and the tide falling fast, it was impossible to approach the casualty. The tug and a coastguard boat stood by all night and on the morning tide an unsuccessful attempt was made to tow Palala free but, when it became apparent that she was in imminent danger of breaking up, all attention was turned to rescuing the eight passengers and their baggage. The sea was now so heavy and both vessels rolling so violently that it was impossible for Queen to come alongside Palala, so an alternative means of rescue had to be devised. A heavy line was passed between the two vessels and tensioned by a steam winch, whilst the terrified passengers – most of whom were women and children – were drawn across in a large basket. Despite the tremendous risks involved, the task was successfully accomplished and Queen landed her human cargo at Weymouth, whilst the ship's crew got safely ashore in their own boats. Continuing bad weather over the next few days frustrated Cosens' attempts to recover either her cargo or the two oxen which were stranded on board but, on 19th May, Victoria was able to offer an excursion from Weymouth to view the wreck. The following day, the sea conditions had abated sufficiently to allow Queen and her barges to commence work at the site and over the next few days a considerable amount of cargo and the two oxen were recovered. *Palala* proved a popular destination for excursions from both Weymouth and Bournemouth until, as unsettled weather returned, she quickly went to pieces.

The month of October 1886 proved to be a particularly busy one for the tugs, with no less than three major incidents occurring in rapid succession. On the night of 14th-15th October, *Commodore* found the barque *Zaima* of Gothenburg floating bottom-upwards in the Channel, with her masts still standing and some of her sails set. She was towed into Portland, where Cosens' divers cut away her top hamper and the hull was righted, before being taken into Weymouth for repairs and re-rigging.

The next major casualty occurred on the night of 27th October, when the 3,000 ton steamer *Sumatra*, with a valuable cargo and 90 passengers on board, went ashore in fog on Chesil Beach. Cosens' manager, Mr Fowler, was summoned from his bed by a coastguard who had run the four miles from Fleet, and both *Queen* and *Commodore* were promptly dispatched to the scene. Due to the dense fog and heavy ground swell, it took great skill to locate *Sumatra* and get the tow ropes on board but, by 3am, the task was accomplished. The tugs succeeded in keeping her stern off the beach until the rising tide enabled them to tow her clear. £1,500 plus costs was awarded for the rescue.

Two days later, while making for Portland Harbour in thick fog and drizzle to pick up a Channel pilot, the 3,923 ton liner *Persian Monarch* went aground on the outside of the Breakwater. *En route* from New York to London, she had already landed the majority of her passengers at Plymouth but still had on board a large general cargo, 340 oxen and 12

horses. Unfortunately, the grounding took place at the very top of a spring tide, which made subsequent attempts to refloat the vessel doubly difficult.

With the tide falling fast, *Queen* and *Commodore* had no possibility of refloating *Persian Monarch* that night, so laid out kedge anchors to prevent her drifting broadside on the Breakwater and then returned to Weymouth to collect lighters with which to remove her cargo. Work went on throughout the night and, after another failed attempt to tow her off next morning, for the whole of the following week. Cosens' staff were joined by a party of soldiers and sailors from Portland, plus a gang of 'lumpers' employed by the ship's owners, and with every available lighter pressed into service, the work of lightening the ship went forward apace. On 1st November, the cattle were ferried ashore and tethered in an enclosure at the Portland coaling depot and several unsuccessful attempts were made by *Lydian Monarch*, one of the casualty's fleetmates, to tow her off. Each attempt strained *Persian Monarch* more severely and, when a storm passed through on 3rd November, there were great fears for her safety. By Friday 5th November, however, she had been lightened sufficiently for another fleetmate, *Grecian Monarch* to finally refloat her.

The litany of disasters continued unabated into 1887. On New Year's Day, the schooner *Aurora* missed stays and ran ashore at Godnor Point near Portland Bill but was towed off by *Queen* and brought into Weymouth for repairs. Then, at 11pm on 12th January, the liner *Pongola* was feeling her way through thick fog to pick up a pilot at Portland, when she mistook the lights on Weymouth seafront for those on the Breakwater and ran aground off Greenhill.

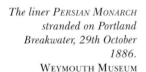

The liner PERSIAN MONARCH *stranded on Portland Breakwater, 29th October 1886.*
WEYMOUTH MUSEUM

Fortunately, the seabed is flat and sandy in that location and at high tide next morning, *Queen* and *Commodore* earned a reasonably easy £500 by towing her off. In the process, the cable of *Pongola*'s own kedge anchor wound itself round her propeller, so *Queen* towed her to an anchorage at Portland, where one of Cosens' divers freed the obstruction. By a curious coincidence, *Pongola* was a sister ship of *Palala*, which had been wrecked at Kimmeridge the previous summer.

In March, a full rigged ship named *Westland* went ashore, again in dense fog, close to the remains of *Palala* at Kimmeridge. *Queen* and *Commodore* groped their way to the scene but, after several hours searching, found no sign of the casualty. They were about to anchor for the night and re-commence their search at daybreak, when some fishermen came off from the shore and reported that *Westland* had been floated off with the aid of the coastguards and had proceeded on her voyage.

On 1st April, *Queen* towed in the schooner *Peggy*, which had been dragging her anchors in a gale, and, on 3rd June, was called to the aid of yet another ship, the schooner *Sagterland*, aground in fog on the notorious Kimmeridge Ledges. Her cargo was removed and taken to Weymouth in lighters and the following day, with loss of 20 feet of her keel, she was pulled off and placed on Cosens' slipway for repairs. Once again, the company had benefited twice from a single rescue!

Those rescues which were reported in the newspapers or recorded by name in the company records were, of course, the most dramatic and noteworthy. However, the minute books contain frequent other references to '*salvage reports received*'

or '*income from various salvages*' and it is evident that the tugs undertook numerous dangerous tasks which have, frustratingly, gone unrecorded. On other occasions, such as the total loss of the steamer *Nor* on Chesil Beach in January 1887, the tugs were unable to assist. In addition, of course, they were engaged on an almost daily basis in towing sailing vessels in and out of Weymouth Harbour, moving coal barges and lighters, assisting the diving teams, and transporting workmen from the engineering department to and from vessels requiring repairs in Portland Harbour. Their contribution to the company's overall revenue should not be underestimated.

Reverting to 1886, *Victoria* and *Lord Elgin* made their first sailings from Bournemouth on 4th April and the season ahead looked set to follow its accustomed pattern. At Swanage, a Mr Lose was appointed as Cosens' agent at a salary of 15s per week plus 5 per cent of the local takings and a new, larger coal store was rented near the pier. Mr Sydenham continued as the company's highly-valued local manager at Bournemouth in return for 10 per cent of the takings. A new master, Capt George Hurdle, was employed to replace the sacked Capt Haill on board *Premier*, while her engineer Henry Vye was demoted to *Queen* for insobriety and replaced by George Besant. Perhaps there was something about *Premier* for, by October, Besant too had been dismissed for insobriety! William Cosens had been ill during the winter but, despite fears to the contrary, was in his usual place on *Victoria*'s bridge when the season commenced.

Relationships with the Bournemouth company got off to another bad start when, without consultation, they reduced the price of their season

The steamer NOR, *wrecked on Chesil Beach in January 1887. Unlike* PERSIAN MONARCH, *which in the view on the previous page looks in a far worse predicament, neither Cosens' tugs nor any other vessels were able to assist her and the steamer became a total loss.*
AUTHOR'S COLLECTION

Wreck on the Chesil Beach

QUEEN rounding the old Bar Buoy at the entrance to Weymouth Harbour, on her way home from another towage job.
AUTHOR'S COLLECTION

tickets and Cosens were forced, by '*popular local feeling*' to do the same. A ticket for either company could now be purchased for 1 guinea. So incensed were Cosens by the '*vacillating policy*' of their rivals, that they refused to enter into any further negotiations on any subject. Once tempers had cooled, however, Cosens realised that co-operation would be very much in their interests and attempted, unsuccessfully, to discuss timetables and the dangers of racing. The following extract from the Chairman's annual report summarises the situation very neatly:

'*There is a source of loss – I will not call it loss, but an absence of gain – to which I should like to refer, and that is the practice to which we have been obliged to submit when running side by side with the local company at Bournemouth ... It is a very obvious thing that if two steamers run side by side they must share the traffic between them, whereas if the traffic could be so arranged that they could run to different places on the same day, the probability is that instead of the steamers running with half their cargo they would take their full complement, and thus materially add to the general revenue. We have done everything in our power to try and arrange with our friends at Bournemouth to carry out some agreement of this kind. We have offered to submit our programmes to them in order that they may not run to the same places on the same days and hours, and we have asked them to make up their programmes and show us when we would avoid clashing with them ... but I am afraid our Bournemouth friends seem to enjoy the satisfaction of cutting off their noses to spite their faces ... for they still insist on carrying on this unprofitable game. We do not ask them to be liberal with us and we do not care to be liberal to them, but we do ask them as business men to do what will be mutually advantageous to the two companies in such a simple way. Such an arrangement would also prevent ... any appearance of the steamers racing. We caution our captains and officers to avoid anything approaching to racing and have even gone as far as to order our captains to alter their times of sailing five or ten minutes when*

another boat is announced to leave for the same place at the same hour, but ... however willing the captain and crew may be not to race, yet it is more than can be expected of human beings if they do not put on an extra shovel of coal to creep up on their neighbours.'

These exhortations clearly had little practical effect, for competition at Bournemouth soon reached its usual frantic pitch. With *Victoria* and *Empress* spending the bulk of their time there and *Premier* going along on a very regular basis, it was decided to retain *Prince* at Weymouth to bolster the local service. This meant a virtual abandonment of regular sailings from Torquay, which had to content itself with whatever short trips could be fitted in by *Victoria* or *Empress* while their long distance westward passengers were enjoying time ashore. Both company's sailings followed a very similar pattern to 1885, although *Victoria* did make one crossing to Cherbourg from Bournemouth on 24th August and two ships from each company ran special excursions to view a Naval Review at Spithead on 23rd July. In addition to Cosens' frequent sailings from Weymouth, it was possible to visit Lulworth Cove less regularly from Bournemouth and Swanage as well. *Lord Elgin* was not equipped for beach landing and presumably lay at anchor while her passengers were ferried ashore in small boats, or occasionally lay alongside whichever Cosens' steamer was already at the beach.

The 1886 season did not prove a happy one for the Bournemouth Company. Following her Easter debut, *Lord Elgin* appears to have experienced some mechanical problems, for she was withdrawn from service and did not reappear again until 27th May. Although *Bournemouth* had begun her excursions on 10th May, this meant that the local company was unrepresented on the Swanage service for several weeks. Then, on Whit Monday, *Bournemouth* was *en route* to Torquay with a full complement of passengers when the tubes in one of her boilers failed. By the time she limped into Torquay several hours late, a sea fog had descended and the majority of her passengers elected to return home by rail. Steaming on one boiler only, *Bournemouth* left on her homeward voyage at 8.20pm and finally landed her remaining passengers at Bournemouth Pier at 4.40am next morning. She then departed to Southampton for repairs and survey, and was away until 12th July, during which time the Southampton steamer *Princess Helena* was chartered to cover her programme. These misfortunes, however, were but small ones compared with the disaster which was to follow a few weeks later.

On Friday 27th August, both *Empress* and *Bournemouth* were scheduled to make day trips from Bournemouth and Swanage to Torquay, and *Victoria* to Dartmouth from Weymouth. All three vessels made a good passage westwards but at 4.30pm, shortly after departing on their homeward journeys, ran into a dense fog bank. Capt Perrin of *Bournemouth* posted additional lookouts in the bows but continued at full speed until 6pm, when his

BOURNEMOUTH, her back broken forward of the boiler room, lying wrecked on the rocks of Portland Bill.
BRIAN JACKSON COLLECTION

dead reckoning told him that he should be in the vicinity of Portland Bill. The ship's sails were taken in, speed reduced to about 9 knots and her course altered slightly to the south but, just as the order to take soundings was about to be given, cliffs were spotted right ahead.

Travelling too fast to stop, *Bournemouth* drove violently aground on the west side of Portland at a spot just below the old higher lighthouse. Her forward compartment was instantly stoved in, her foremast lifted from its step and bent like a bow, and the foredeck planking began to open up. The firing of distress signals and continuous sounding of her whistle quickly brought the coastguards to the cliff top and a rocket line was used to rig a breeches buoy between the ship's aft funnel and the shore, while a telegram was sent to Cosens at Weymouth for help. *Bournemouth*'s lifeboats were quickly launched and a full load of women and children landed in Chesil Cove where bonfires had been lighted to guide the boats through the fog. Large numbers of Portland fishermen also put off to the rescue and spent the next few hours ferrying passengers ashore to Chesil Cove or Portland Bill, while a few more were landed by breeches buoy. The last person to leave the stricken ship was Capt Perrin at 11.30pm.

The initial telegram requesting Cosens' assistance had failed to identify the steamer concerned, so there was considerable anxiety that either *Empress*

or *Victoria* had come to grief. As *Queen* put to sea to grope her way slowly to the scene and Mr Fowler travelled overland to take control of the rescue efforts on Portland, a large crowd gathered on Weymouth Pier to await news of their friends and relatives at sea.

In point of fact, due to the skill and care of their masters, both ships were safe. Capt Bowering in *Empress* had decided that the only way to be certain of his position was to make visual contact with Portland Bill. As soon as he had run his prescribed distance by dead reckoning, he stopped and reversed the engines to reassure his passengers that the ship was well under control. Having explained his plan, he then put the ship dead slow ahead and crept onwards through the fog until the cliffs were sighted about 50 yards ahead. *Empress*'s course was then set parallel to the coastline, and she successfully felt her way around the island and into the safety of Weymouth, where she arrived at 8pm. Capt Bowering would not take the risk of continuing to Bournemouth until the fog had lifted and eventually set off at 6am the following morning in bright sunshine. On board *Victoria*, Capt Cosens had adopted different tactics, by standing much further offshore and making for the sound of the fog horn on the Shambles lightship, from where he set course for Weymouth.

With all of her passengers and crew safely ashore, attention turned to the wreck of *Bournemouth* itself. Delayed by the fog, *Queen* had arrived on the

scene too late to be of any assistance but the following day, *Victoria* combined an excursion to the scene with putting the ship's manager and Lloyd's agent on board to carry out a thorough survey. It quickly emerged that *Bournemouth*'s back was broken, her engine room and saloons half full of water and her bulkheads in danger of giving way. There were fears that her after section, which was rising and falling with the ebb and flow of the tides, would break off and sink into deep water. The vessel was abandoned as a total loss and the Independent Salvage Company of Liverpool engaged by the underwriters to recover the machinery and other fittings. Large cranes were rigged on the cliffs and sections of the dismantled engines lifted ashore but a plan to float the boilers out of the ship and tow them round to Portland failed. An initial auction of her lifeboats, anchors, chains, seats and other recovered fittings was held at the Victoria Hotel, Portland on 11th September and, on 4th October, her hull and remaining fittings were purchased by Cosens for a nominal sum of £7 10s. They had greater success in recovering the boilers, along with *Bournemouth*'s forward steam windlass which, once repaired, was fitted to *Queen* for handling her heavy, winter tow ropes. This arduous task had hitherto been carried out manually and, in a gale, could occupy several hours. However, with the aid of the new winch, the crew could pass a tow in as little as a quarter of an hour. It must have been a bitter pill for the Bournemouth Company to swallow, that the remains of their shattered flagship should pass into the hands of the very company she had been built to oppose.

At the subsequent Board of Trade inquiry into the loss of *Bournemouth*, Capt Perrin was severely criticised for the grave errors of judgement which

had endangered both his ship and passengers, and had his certificate suspended for one year. Everyone was painfully aware that the passengers had had a remarkably lucky escape and that, had there been any sea running when the steamer struck the rocks, a massive loss of life would certainly have ensued.

Three days after the *Bournemouth* drama, on 30th August, it was *Queen*'s turn to find herself in trouble. She was *en route* from Portland to Weymouth with a full load of passengers when another sudden sea fog rolled in and she grounded on the ledges of rock beneath the Nothe Fort, at the entrance to Weymouth Harbour. Since she was only 20 yards from land, the passengers were put ashore in boats, while *Queen* refloated undamaged on the rising tide and resumed her trips to Portland. *Premier* and *Empress* also found themselves fog bound at their destinations and their passengers had to be returned to their respective starting points by railway.

One result of the foggy season was to increase the number of boat drills carried out on board the company's steamers. Up to this time, the Board of Trade had been content if the crews practised launching the boats once or twice at the beginning of the season but it was now felt that this should be done every week or two in harbour. On one occasion, Cosens experimented with a lifeboat drill at sea but, when '*ladies began to faint and other people became alarmed*', the idea was discontinued!

The Southampton Company's steamer *Princess Helena* was immediately chartered to cover *Bournemouth*'s programme for the rest of the season, while her owners considered the matter of her permanent replacement. Although she had cost over £14,000 to build, *Bournemouth* had only been insured for £7,000 and this somewhat limited their room for manoeuvre. In the event, a suitably-priced

Patroness: Her Majesty The Queen

ROYAL NATIONAL LIFE BOAT INSTITUTION

FOR THE

Preservation of Life from Shipwreck.

(INCORPORATED BY ROYAL CHARTER.)

ESTABLISHED 1824.

SUPPORTED BY VOLUNTARY CONTRIBUTIONS.

Vice Patron.

His Royal Highness the Prince of Wales, K.G.

President.

His Grace Algernon George, Duke of Northumberland, P.C.

Chairman.   Dep.y Chairman.

Sir Edward Birkbeck, Bart. M.P. V.P.   Colonel Fitz-Roy Clayton.

Northumberland
President.

At a Meeting of the Committee of the Royal National Life Boat Institution for the Preservation of Life from Shipwreck held at their Offices, London, on the 2nd day of December 1886 the following Minute was ordered to be recorded on the Books of the Society, and to be communicated to Henry Fooks. Esqre

Resolved, That the best thanks of the Royal National Life Boat Institution be presented to **Captain William Cosens** Master of Steamer "Victoria" of Weymouth in acknowledgment of his valuable co-operation in collecting contributions on board that vessel, in aid of the Funds of the Weymouth Branch of the Institution.

Edward Birkbeck
Chairman.

Charles Dibdin
Secretary.

A certificate presented to Capt William Cosens by the Royal National Lifeboat Institution, in thanks for collections made on board VICTORIA *in 1886.* AUTHOR'S COLLECTION

candidate was located on the Clyde, where Capt William Buchanan was offering his nine-year-old steamer *Brodick Castle* for sale. Intended for service between Ardrossan and the Isle of Arran, she was a robust, heavily-built ship, designed to operate all year round in every kind of weather, and boasted some excellent and spacious internal accommodation. Measuring 207 feet 6 inches by 21 feet 7 inches by 7 feet 5 inches and of 283 gross tons, she was larger than any other excursion steamer operating on the South Coast and seemed to fit the Bournemouth Company's requirements ideally.

Her purchase completed, *Brodick Castle* left the Clyde on 29th March 1887 and arrived at Weymouth on the morning of 2nd April, to embark a large party of directors and shareholders for an inaugural cruise to Bournemouth. The choice of Weymouth, as a departure point as well as the destination for her first public cruise on 7th April, was no doubt intended to demonstrate the vast superiority of the new vessel over anything which the Cosens' fleet had to offer. Her appearance, with two closely-spaced funnels forward of her enormous paddle boxes, a long, raised fo'c'sle, a spacious promenade deck

127

BRODICK CASTLE, seen here backing away from Bournemouth Pier, presented a formidable challenge to Cosens' interests when she appeared in the area in the spring of 1887.

covering a short deck saloon aft and an extensive, raised quarter deck, was certainly unlike anything seem at Bournemouth before and the public flocked to see her. On Easter Monday, she carried 1,600 passengers between Bournemouth and Swanage compared with *Victoria* and *Empress*'s combined total of 1,300. On the same day, a 14 year old boy was summoned to appear before the local magistrates for leaving his horse and cart unattended at the Pier Approach. Pleading guilty, the boy explained that *"he had heard people talk so much about the* Brodick Castle *that he went to see it, and when he came back the policeman had hold of his horse."* His mother added that the horse was a quiet one and that her son, *"like all other boys, was anxious to see the ship"*. The bench inflicted a fine of 1s plus costs!

With a passenger certificate for 456, the new ship had a greater potential earning capacity than her Cosens rivals and was also significantly faster. Set against these advantages, however, was the coal consumption of her enormous, simple diagonal engine, whose two cylinders measured $38\frac{1}{4}$ inches in diameter with a stroke of 66 inches. Originally built in 1864 for the Clyde steamer *Eagle*, it had proved too powerful for that vessel and was removed and built into the hull of the new *Brodick Castle* in 1878. To provide the steam for such an engine required a prodigious amount of coal and her extravagant appetite, which had no doubt accounted for Buchanan's desire to dispose of such a relatively new ship, soon became apparent to her new owners. Even when operating at 14 knots, her fuel costs soon proved to be 20 per cent higher than *Bournemouth*'s had been and far in excess of the economical Cosens' ships.

Brodick Castle was withdrawn from service for a few days at the beginning of May and sent to Southampton *'in order to effect some improvements which will further increase her already unequalled popularity'* but was back on station, alongside *Lord Elgin*, by 16th May. As in the previous season, her owners adopted a policy of duplicating Cosens' sailing times and destinations, which led the Weymouth Company to place the following notice in the *Bournemouth Observer* on 21st May:

Special Notice

The Local Company having adopted the regular days worked year by year by this company for plying between Swanage, Bournemouth, Yarmouth, Ryde and Portsmouth, the directors resolve to avoid running steamers side by side to the same place on the same days, and to give increased variety of excursions to visitors, they will until further notice use Mondays and Saturdays for other long excursions, selecting Tuesdays and Fridays for their services to Yarmouth, Ryde and Portsmouth.

Railway Facilities

Messrs Cosens & Co have made arrangements that throughout the season their steamers will be timed as far as practicable to meet the requirements of excursionists visiting Swanage, Bournemouth and Weymouth by the London & South Western Railway and the Midland Company's trains.

This pronouncement was repeated several times during the months ahead but, although matters were somewhat improved, some sailings were still duplicated and competition between the rival

STEAMBOAT EXCURSIONS.

BOURNEMOUTH, SWANAGE, & POOLE STEAM PACKET COMPANY, LIMITED

THE LOCAL CO. THE LOCAL CO.

STEAMERS:
PRINCESS HELENA AND LORD ELGIN.

EXCURSIONS DURING THE WEEK ENDING SEPTEMBER 18, 1886.

REGULAR DAILY SERVICE TO SWANAGE
By Steamship
LORD· ELGIN.

Special Notice !! THE SPLENDID SALOON STEAMER
PRINCESS HELENA
WILL, weather and other circumstances permitting, carry out the Excursions named below (and during the remainder of the season).

MONDAY, September 13th.—COWES, RYDE, and PORTSMOUTH, at 10.15.
TUESDAY, Sept. 14th.—WEYMOUTH, calling at Swanage, at 10.15.
WEDNESDAY, September 15th.—TOTLAND BAY, Isle of Wight. Leaving Bournemouth at 10.15; returning from Totland Bay at 2.30. EVENING EXCURSION by steamship *Princess Helena* to TOTLAND BAY, at 4.30; returning at 6.30. Fare, 1s. Steamship *Lord Elgin* to POOLE, at 5.30 (via Swanage). Fare, 6d only.
THURSDAY, September 16th.—TOTLAND BAY, COWES, and SOUTHAMPTON, at 10.15.
FRIDAY, September 17th.—ROUND the ISLE OF WIGHT, at 10.15.
SATURDAY, Sept. 18th.—COWES, RYDE, and PORTSMOUTH, at 10.15.
First-class Refreshments on board at Moderate Charges by Messrs. Styring and Co., Poole.
LAVATORIES, LADIES' CABINS, AND STEWARDESSES.
The Directors reserve to themselves the right of making any alterations in the above programme, which the exigencies of the weather or other circumstances may require.
For further particulars see the Weekly Sailing Bills, or apply to the Company's agent, Mr. H. HIXSON, Swanage ; or of EDWARD BICKER, Secretary and Manager, Richmond Chambers, Bournemouth.

Bournemouth sailing times for September 1886.

BOURNEMOUTH EXPRESS STEAM PACKET SERVICE.

BOURNEMOUTH SWANAGE, WEYMOUTH & TORQUAY  STEAM PACKET Co. (Cosens & Co., Limited)

STEAMERS :
VICTORIA, EMPRESS, PREMIER, QUEEN, PRINCE, COMMODORE
The Vessels with Black Funnels.

THE above Company's Fast and Splendidly-equipped Passenger Steamships
VICTORIA, EMPRESS & PREMIER
Are appointed to carry out the Excursions named below, unless prevented by unforeseen circumstances, during the
WEEK ENDING SEPT. 18TH, 1886.
SWANAGE AND BOURNEMOUTH DAILY.
NOTICE.—Alteration of time.

Bournemouth to Swanage.	Swanage to Bournemouth.
Monday, 10.30,1,3.30,& 6.30	Monday 9,9.15,11.45,2&5.30
Tuesday, 10.45, 2.50, & 6	Tuesday,9, 9.15, 12.15, 4.50
Wednesday, 10.15, 5, & 8	Wednesday, 9, 3.15, & 7
Thursday, 10.45, 2.50, & 6	Thursday,9,9.15, 12.15, 4.5
Friday, 10.45, 2.50, & 6	Friday, 9, 9.15, 12.15, & 4.50
Saturday, 6.30 p.m.	Saturday, 9 & 9.15 a.m.

And at the close of the long Excursions.
MONDAY, THURSDAY, & SATURDAY —Regular Service. Tickets for this service issued to return any day within one week of issue. YARMOUTH, RYDE, & PORTSMOUTH. Leaving at 10.15.
MONDAY, September 13th.—Regular Service.—WEYMOUTH, calling at SWANAGE. Leaving at 10.30. Circular Tickets, returnable by Railway or Steamer, are issued in connection with this service from Bournemouth to Weymouth, or Swanage, and vice versa. Fares—Weymouth 4s 8d, Swanage 3s 8d.
TUESDAY, September 14th.—COWES & SOUTHAMPTON, calling at YARMOUTH. Leaving at 10 15.
WEDNESDAY, September 15th.—ROUND THE ISLE OF WIGHT. Leaving at 10.15. LULWORTH, calling at SWANAGE. Leaving at 10.15.
THURSDAY, September 16th. — YARMOUTH, RYDE, & PORTSMOUTH, at 10.30.
FRIDAY, September 17th.—ROUND THE ISLE OF WIGHT, at 10.15.
SATURDAY, September 18th. — YARMOUTH, RYDE, & PORTSMOUTH, at 10.15. TOTLAND BAY, at 10.30 and 2.45.
Further particulars can be obtained of the Local Manager, Royal Marine Library, Bournemouth; J. LOSE, the Company's Agent, Swanage; S. NICHOLLS, The Pier, Yarmouth; or of S. J. FOWLER, General Manager, Head Office, Custom House Quay, Weymouth.
The Directors reserve to themselves the right of making any alterations in the above Programme which the exigencies of the weather, traffic, or other circumstances may require.
By Order,
D. SYDENHAM,
Local Manager.

steamers remained keen. On Whit Monday, the Southampton Company's *Princess Beatrice* landed a large party at Bournemouth and spent the rest of the day on charter to the local company, who used her to increase their capacity on the Swanage service while *Brodick Castle* ran a long day trip to Brighton. This was an arrangement which was to be repeated on most bank holidays in the years ahead. The Bournemouth Company moved many of their own long sailings to Mondays in imitation of Cosens and would frequently run to Dartmouth at the same time as a Cosens' steamer was departing for Torquay. Both companies deployed so many ticket touts at the pier gates that they were eventually prosecuted for obstruction.

On 23rd July, a Grand Naval Review was held at Spithead in celebration of Queen Victoria's Golden Jubilee and both companies advertised excursions to witness Her Majesty passing up and down the long lines of assembled warships on board the Royal Yacht *Victoria & Albert*. Cosens sent *Victoria* and *Premier* and their rivals *Brodick Castle* and *Lord Elgin*, all four steamers being sold out well in advance of the event. In the two days before the actual review, all scheduled excursions which passed through Spithead were fully booked and the demand remained so great that both companies abandoned their other advertised sailings, reduced the frequency of the Swanage service, and sent all available steamers, fully-laden, to view the assembled fleet.

On 25th August, *Empress* advertised an excursion from Bournemouth to Ventnor, where the new Royal Victoria Pier had recently been completed. Two previous attempts to provide the balmy Isle of Wight resort with a satisfactory pier had ended in disaster. The original Ventnor Pier & Harbour Project was swept away by heavy seas in 1867 and a second, iron pier was wrecked in a similar circumstances during 1881, only months after its landing stage had been opened to shipping. The new 110 foot pier, which was equipped with a horseshoe shaped landing stage, had received a single isolated call during July to mark the official hand over by the contractors but regular services did not begin until August. The demand for *Empress*'s first trip was so great that *Premier* abandoned a planned sailing to Lulworth Cove and followed her fleet mate with the overflow, which had been left waiting on Bournemouth Pier. Thereafter, Ventnor appeared quite regularly among Cosens' destinations although, curiously, the Bournemouth Company showed no interest whatsoever in following suit. In the years ahead, the relatively exposed location of the Royal Victoria Pier earned it a reputation as the hardest South Wight pier to berth alongside and the first to have calls abandoned in periods of strong wind.

August 1887 also saw the opening of a substantial new 370 foot pier at Alum Bay and a consequent increase in calls by Cosens' steamers. Passengers would steam ashore at this delightful and isolated spot to admire the famous coloured strata in the cliffs, purchase glass phials filled with layers of the coloured sands, or enjoy refreshments at the tiny restaurant on the shore. All of the facilities at Alum Bay were owned and operated by members of a local fishing family, the Isaacs, who also offered boat

Passengers stream ashore from a steamer berthed at Alum Bay Pier, Isle of Wight. This view, published as a postcard by the French company Leon & Levy (LL), was probably taken around 1905.
ROY BRINTON COLLECTION

trips to the nearby Needles rocks. The story is often told that the pier master, Alfred Isaacs, sold glasses of water for the apparently exorbitant fee of 1d but, when it is realised that all goods including drinking water had to be carried down the slippery cliff by donkey, the charge seems a little less unreasonable!

Along at Weymouth, the season followed its accustomed pattern with few incidents of note until the end of August when, on two weeks in succession, *Victoria* found herself fog bound. On 25th August, she had come from Weymouth to Lyme Regis and Sidmouth and was half way between the two places on her homeward voyage when a thick fog descended. The anchor was dropped off Golden Cap and it was not until 5am the following morning that conditions improved sufficiently for her to feel her way into Lyme and land her passengers. By this time, '*not a drop of water or beer remained on board*' and it was reported that '*many of the ladies were in a pitiful state*', though whether as a result of thirst or intoxication was not made clear.

A week later, on 1st September, history repeated itself. *Victoria* had been to Dartmouth, calling at Lyme and Sidmouth *en route*, and left at 4pm on her return journey. Thirty of her capacity crowd were landed at Sidmouth but once again, just off Lyme, a dense fog set in. Lyme is far too dangerous a harbour to approach in such conditions, so the ship came to anchor and her passengers settled in for the long night ahead. The ladies made themselves comfortable in the cabins, while the gentlemen smoked and chatted on deck and *Victoria*'s steam whistle and bell sounded their regular fog signals. The memory of *Bournemouth*'s stranding in similar weather exactly a year previously led to a high degree of anxiety ashore but those who knew Capt Cosens assured strangers that he was far too careful and experienced an officer to run any risks and was sure to be anchored in safety waiting for the fog to lift, which it eventually did at 5am next morning. As the tide was low, the Lyme passengers were put

ashore in boats and *Victoria* proceeded to Weymouth, where she made her appearance through the lingering mist at just after 8am. Despite their unplanned night at sea, her company were in high spirits and responded to cheers from the relieved crowd on the pier with a chorus of '*We won't go home till morning.*'

For the first time since 1879, *Prince* did not spend any of her time based at Torquay but was retained for the whole of the season at Weymouth, where her presence allowed *Victoria* to spend more time at Bournemouth. The abandonment of Torquay, which had always been marginal in terms of income, lead to welcome savings in agency fees, berthing charges and other expenses but caused an outcry amongst the local residents, who found themselves without an excursion service for the first time in eight years and led to interesting developments during the spring of 1888.

As the season drew to a close in October, it became apparent that 1887 had been a year of mixed fortunes for Cosens. On the debit side, income had not yet covered the heavy expenditure on two additional diving suits and pumps, a second powerful steam salvage pump and new rocket line equipment for the salvage department. The absence of the Channel Fleet for most of the summer had meant that earnings from liberty boat work were negligible. Although the Fleet Review at Spithead had generated useful income, the Jubilee celebrations themselves had kept people at home and Cosens, in common with the railways and other steamer companies, had experienced a serious drop in passengers during the early season. On the credit side, however, a steadily growing demand for repairs to vessels visiting the Portland coal hulks had led to increasing trade for the workshop department and, despite the stiff competition, passenger numbers at Bournemouth had increased. A 5 per cent dividend was declared and a substantial amount added to the reserve and depreciation funds, which allowed the company's policy of constant repair and renewal to its steamers to be continued.

Nonetheless, the appearance of the vastly superior *Brodick Castle* at Bournemouth had proved a considerable shock to Cosens and represented a serious threat to their long-term future on the station. It was painfully apparent that they must either concede defeat or provide a larger and faster steamer of their own. David Sydenham, the Bournemouth manager, strongly urged the latter course and during the autumn of 1887, tenders were sought from several major shipbuilders for a new steamer, while Mr Fowler, the company manager, combed the shipbrokers' advertisements for details of second hand tonnage. One ship was viewed at Plymouth but proved unsuitable and, by December, the shareholders had granted their permission to raise additional capital, sell *Prince* to pay part of the cost and order a brand new vessel.

CHAPTER 9
MONARCH & WINDSOR CASTLE
1888 – 1895

At an extraordinary general meeting held on 5th January 1888, the shareholders formally gave their permission for the raising of £15,000 capital through mortgages or debenture bonds and confirmed the board's decision to accept John Penn & Son's tender for the construction of the new steamer. Although Penn's quote of £14,000 was not the lowest received, the decision to accept it was influenced by a number of powerful factors. Firstly, Penn had constructed highly satisfactory and economical machinery for four previous Cosens' vessels; secondly he was one of the company's largest and most influential shareholders; and finally and most importantly, he was willing to agree to incredibly tight deadlines and deliver the new ship by the end of June 1888. This remarkable feat would be achieved by sub-contracting the construction of the hull to R. & H. Green Ltd of Blackwall, while Penn concentrated on the engine and boilers. Penn did Cosens a further favour by agreeing to accept any unallotted debenture bonds as a temporary deposit against the last two payments for the new ship. Cosens agreed to redeem half of the bonds after six months, the remainder after eighteen and pay 5 per cent interest.

The name *Monarch* was chosen for the new steamer, which was carefully designed to equal or outclass *Brodick Castle* in every particular. With dimensions of 210 feet by 22 feet 2 inches by 9 feet, she would be slightly longer and broader than her rival and weigh 32 tons more. Her simple diagonal engine with twin cylinders of 41 inches diameter and 48 inch stroke was designed to give her a contract speed of 15 knots and Cosens were allowed the right of refusal if 14³/₄ knots were not obtained during the trials. A penalty of £100 would be payable for every tenth of a knot below 15 knots and a bonus for every tenth above. A detailed specification was quickly agreed, the contract signed and construction commenced immediately.

At the same time, the board decided to make substantial improvements to *Victoria* by lengthening her by 9 feet amidships and fitting a surface condenser. Hitherto, *Victoria*, like all of her fleet-mates, had been fitted with a jet condenser, whose purpose was to condense exhaust steam from the engine to create hot feed water, which could then be passed back into the boiler for reuse. This was achieved by spraying a fine jet of cold sea water onto the steam within a condenser chamber. Although admirably simple, the system resulted in the contamination of the feed water with salt, which caused severe pitting and corrosion, and accounted for the short life of many early boilers. Salt water contamination in the boilers also led to priming problems, which caused rapid and unpredictable fluctuations in water level within the boiler and could lead to serious trouble unless monitored very carefully by the engineer. By contrast, in the more complex and expensive surface condenser, the exhaust steam passed through a nest of sealed tubes around which sea water was constantly pumped inside the condenser chamber, ensuring that the condensate remained free of all impurities and the boiler immune from corrosion. It was argued that the expenditure on a surface condenser would quickly be justified by savings in fuel costs, maintenance and the greatly extended life-span of the boiler, while the resulting lengthening of *Victoria*'s hull would increase her speed substantially and make her an even better sea-boat than hitherto. During February, she was despatched to Southampton where Day, Summers & Co carried out the alterations for a fee of £850.

With *Monarch* on order and the Torquay station abandoned, the old *Prince* was now surplus to the company's requirements and was advertised for sale. For some months, Cosens had been in discussion with two Exmouth gentlemen, Messrs George Ellett and George Matthew. They were interested in filling the vacuum left by Cosens' departure by establishing their own excursion steamer service along the Devon coast and, by March, the company had agreed to sell them *Prince* for £1,050. This sum, although disappointingly low, more than paid for the costs of the alterations to *Victoria* and was

VICTORIA's engine room, showing her twin oscillating cylinders, which were lagged with mahogany strips held in place by brass straps. The oblong objects bolted to the cylinders are two of the four valve chests. The original jet condenser was positioned in a chamber beneath the oval bolted cover in the foreground between the two cylinders, whilst the air pump, which was driven from the centre crank above, was fitted where the large circular plate can be seen. At normal operating speed, the engine rotated at 28rpm.
BERNARD COX

131

This delightful poster, in full colour and designed to advertise the imminent arrival of MONARCH, hung for many years in Cosens' Swanage steamer office.
COURTESY GERARD COX

THE
WEYMOUTH, BOURNEMOUTH & SWANAGE STEAM PACKET COMPANY.

COSENS & CO., LIMITED.

NEW STEEL CLIPPER SALOON STEAMSHIP,
"MONARCH,"
NEARLY 900 HORSE POWER.

Engines and Boilers made by the world-famed Engineers, Messrs. JNO. PENN & SONS, Greenwich : and the Hull and Equipment by Messrs. R. & H. GREEN. Ship Builders (Established more than a Century), Blackwall, London.

This Magnificent Vessel will be amongst the largest and fastest Excursion Steamers on the South Coast of England, is specially designed, equipped and certified by the Board of Trade to cross the Channel, fitted with the Electric Light, Life-saving Rafts, Spacious Kitchen for Refreshment Department, and every convenience for the comfort of Passengers, and forms the latest addition to the above Company's Popular Excursion Steamers, universally known to Tourists for their high character and punctuality on Excursions at the English Channel Watering Places from Brighton to the Start Point, for nearly half a century.

Steamers: "MONARCH" (new), "VICTORIA," "EMPRESS," "PREMIER," "QUEEN," "COMMODORE."

General Manager ... Mr. S. J. FOWLER, Head Office, Custom House Quay, Weymouth.
Branch Offices ... { Mr. D. SYDENHAM, Marine Library, Bournemouth, (close to the Pier.)
Mr. J. LOSE, Swanage.
Mr. S. NICHOLLS, The Pier, Yarmouth, Isle of Wight.

Also Agents at Portland, Bridport, Lyme Regis, Seaton, Sidmouth, Torquay and Dartmouth.

MONARCH moored to buoys in the River Thames during her trials, June 1888. As built, she had a very short fo'c'sle head and the steps from her promenade deck down to her forward well deck were extremely steep.
AUTHOR'S COLLECTION

accompanied by an agreement that *Prince* would return each winter to Weymouth, where her refits and repairs would be carried out by Cosens. Indeed, there is evidence that Cosens' interests in the new Devon concern ran somewhat deeper and that co-operation was seen as preferable to maintaining a Torquay station independently. John Cox, formerly the mate of *Premier*, was released to become *Prince*'s new master and in later years, when Ellett and Matthew's partnership was reformed as the Devon Steamship Co, Cosens' manager S.J. Fowler appeared as one of the company directors.

The coming of spring was marked at the end of April by the arrival, on board the sailing vessel *Forsete*, of a somewhat unusual 230 ton cargo of ice for Cosens' ice store at Weymouth. The winter in the Baltic had been particularly severe and, as a result, the individual blocks of ice weighed between 5 and 6 cwt each instead of the usual 3 cwt. Crowds of interested onlookers gathered on the quay to watch the slippery cargo being manhandled ashore. The ice ships themselves were also of some interest, as most were fitted with large windmill pumps on deck to help clear their bilges of the constant

The battle lines drawn up! Rival steamer offices face each other across the Lower High Street in Swanage in 1890. Cosens' office was the flat-roofed building on the left, with the house flag flying from a mast. This was formerly a stone office and weighbridge belonging to Charles Burt but, from 1871, housed James Thomas Hillier, who acted as agent for George Burt's HEATHER BELL. In about 1874, Hillier was replaced by Henry Hixson who, in 1881, became joint agent for both Cosens and the Bournemouth Company. In 1886, John Lose took over as Cosens' agent and Hixson moved across the road to his own shop (adorned with the bold signwriting in this photograph), where he continued to act for the Bournemouth Company. William Cosens replaced John Lose in 1889 and, when Hixson died in January 1890, the Bournemouth Company moved next door, into part of the stone-roofed cottage nearest the camera. Following the death of William Cosens in 1898, Alfred Ward was appointed joint agent, taking up year-round occupation of the flat-roofed building in December 1900. On the left, stone awaiting shipment can be seen stacked in one of the stone yards, referred to locally as 'Bankers'.
SWANAGE MUSEUM

accumulation of water from their slowly-melting ice cargoes. The rhythmic, creaking sound of their wind-pumps while the ships were at sea led to them being universally known as 'Onkers'.

When the excursion season opened at Easter, *Victoria* was sent to Bournemouth to run alongside *Empress*, while *Premier* was kept at Weymouth to partner *Queen* and *Commodore*. With her increased length and speed, it was no doubt felt that *Victoria* would provide more effective competition for *Brodick Castle* on the long distance excursions, until the arrival of *Monarch* later in the year. The Bournemouth Company was clearly in a less sound financial position than Cosens, for in March they appealed for an additional £5,000 in capital '*for the purpose of supplying new boilers and additions to the steamship* Brodick Castle *and for reducing the Company's overdraft at their bankers incurred to purchase the above steamship.*'

By the middle of June, *Monarch* had been completed and was running trials on the Thames. The press reported that, on a six hours trial over the Maplin measured mile, she had averaged just under 17 knots but a note in the minute book contradicted this, stating '*that the* Monarch *having only attained 14¼ knots and drawing 3 inches too much water, the right of refusal should be exercised unless sufficient compensation be secured from the contractors.*' Clearly there was a problem, for Penn immediately offered £1,000 and the board, '*having in view the difficulty of obtaining a suitable vessel on charter and the serious loss attendant on giving up the* Monarch *on the verge of the season*', decided that it was '*in the best interests of the company that litigation should be avoided and the vessel delivered without delay.*' Needless to say, the public knew nothing of these boardroom deliberations but was encouraged to believe that the new ship would be a 'flier' and more than a match for *Brodick Castle*.

Monarch arrived at Weymouth for the first time on Sunday 24th June and was immediately thrown open to public inspection. Although far larger and fitted with twin funnels, a raised fo'c'sle deck and a

MONARCH running speed trials in June 1888.
AUTHOR'S COLLECTION

narrow deck saloon aft, she bore a strong family resemblance to *Empress*, with small, neat paddle boxes which projected only just above the level of her upper deck. Her well-raked funnels retained the rather antiquated bell-tops which were a hall mark of the Cosens' fleet at that time and, combined with her two masts surmounting a long, narrow hull, gave her a well balanced profile. Hull and funnels were finished in black enamel, sponson side-houses were 'scumbled' or wood-grained to give the appearance of panelled timber and deckhouses were of varnished teak. The bows, counter stern and paddle boxes were adorned with elaborate carved decorative scrolls painted in gold leaf and the overall appearance of the ship was truly striking.

The elaborately furnished accommodation was set out in the traditional manner, with a dining saloon aft and bar forward on the lower deck, while the galley, lavatories and crew mess were located in the sponson houses. The main innovation was the narrow, full length deck saloon on the main deck aft, which was a logical development from *Victoria*'s smaller, isolated deck saloon. An open alleyway allowed passengers to walk right around the saloon at main deck level, whilst the roof provided a narrow but welcome promenade deck above. The accommodation was illuminated throughout by electric light.

Down below, the 900ihp simple diagonal engine was a considerable advance on anything which had been seen in Weymouth before. It was unusually steeply inclined in an attempt to save space and, in the style of the previous oscillating engines, the crankshaft was supported on a top plate with apertures to allow for the swing of the crank. This, combined with the fact that the engineer controlled the engines from a position on the ship's bottom plates between the two cylinders, meant that passengers did not get the intriguing view of the machinery which became so familiar in later vessels. The engine was fitted with a surface condenser driven by a centrifugal pump, and steam starting and reversing gear. Steam was provided at 30psi by two triple-furnace return tube boilers, one forward and the other aft of the engine.

At the request of the Board of Trade, the forward bulwark of the upper deck accommodation was substantially built and fitted with sliding access doors. The aim of this, together with the raised fo'c'sle deck, was to reduce the possibility of the engine or boiler rooms being flooded by heavy seas during cross channel excursions. *Monarch* was certificated to carry 309 passengers across to France, 511 between Beachy Head and Start Point, 588 inside a line between the Isle of Wight and Portland Breakwater, and 1,082 within Southampton Water.

Rather than entering service immediately, *Monarch* lay in Weymouth Harbour for a number of weeks while engineers from Cosens and Penns made final adjustments to her engines and fittings, and the electric lighting plant was fitted. A steam dynamo and boiler provided by a Mr E.S. Hindley

was mounted on the upper deck amidships, whilst the wiring was carried out by Mr Petter, a Yeovil ironmonger. It seems that in the rush to meet the completion date, a number of jobs had not been finished to Cosens' satisfaction and also that strenuous efforts were being made to maximise the steamer's speed before she appeared on the public stage. Under the command of William Cosens, *Monarch* finally set off on her official trial trip at 8.15am on Saturday 7th July, carrying an invited party of directors, shareholders and builders' representatives. Off Lulworth, the welcome sound of the steward's bell summoned the passengers to breakfast in the main saloon, where '*eggs poached to perfection … coupled with ham, bacon and corned beef, together with tea and coffee, laid a substantial foundation for the morning's trip.*' At Anvil Point, a crowd had gathered to see the new steamer pass and the lighthouse keepers hoisted a flag signal wishing her a pleasant voyage. By 9.50am, *Monarch* was alongside Swanage pier, where she collected a further party of invited guests. The new steamer then turned her bows towards Bournemouth, where she lay off the pier while *Empress* and *Victoria*, both dressed overall for the occasion, and the two opposition steamers, embarked passengers for their morning trips. The guests who came on board included Mr Fisher, chairman of the Bournemouth Commissioners, with several of his board. One of these was a Mr Hankinson, who was a major Cosens shareholder and a vocal supporter of their interests in the town. As the ship headed for the Isle of Wight, the 250 passengers now on board were provided with '*champagne and other beverages ad lib*'. Between Totland Bay and Yarmouth, *Monarch* fell in with *Empress*, demonstrating her superior speed by drawing quickly ahead, before easing off to allow the older vessel to take the pier first and land her passengers. *Monarch* was then cheered alongside Yarmouth Pier, where, the usual penny toll having been waived in honour of the occasion, many of the guests took the opportunity to stretch their legs ashore. The steamer then departed once again for the 18 mile passage to Bournemouth. After one hour and one minute, *Monarch* was alongside the pier and the official party made its way ashore to a luncheon at the new Town Hall. The significance of holding this prestigious event – complete with the usual, widely-reported speeches and toasts – in Bournemouth rather than Weymouth was not of course lost on the management of the opposition company!

The travelling public was naturally agog to discover whether *Monarch* would prove faster than *Brodick Castle* and did not have very long to wait before the first head-to-head contest took place. On Thursday 12th July, Cosens advertised a trip to Brighton, which was immediately imitated by the Bournemouth Company and, as news of the impending race spread, more than 500 passengers rushed to book tickets aboard their favoured steamer. *Brodick Castle* was timed to leave Bournemouth at 8.00am and *Monarch* at 8.15am, the former calling at Ryde and the latter at Yarmouth and arrangements were made for pier masters along the route to report their progress by telegram. At Yarmouth, *Monarch* had gained one minute on her rival but by Ryde the advantage had been lost. The two steamers arrived at Brighton at 1.00pm and 1.15pm respectively, showing that they were precisely matched on a run of 75 miles. Both departed on their homeward sailings at 4.00pm and arrived alongside Bournemouth Pier within two minutes of each other, having taken 5 hours 40 minutes on passage against an unfavourable tide. The Weymouth press claimed a dead heat but the Bournemouth newspapers, pointing out that *Monarch*'s departure point from West Pier Brighton was three minutes closer to Bournemouth than *Brodick Castle*'s from Palace Pier, insisted that the latter was the victor.

A few days later, *Monarch* was the victor by a narrow margin on a trip around the Isle of Wight but, during the numerous contests which took place throughout the rest of the season, the two steamers proved to be very evenly matched. The Bournemouth Company's advertisements described *Brodick Castle* as '*The fastest and only steamer on the station ever granted an unlimited home trade certificate*', while Cosens insisted that *Monarch* was '*the fastest and most commodious steamer on the South Coast*', subtly altering the company title on their local adverts to 'The Bournemouth Express Steam Packet Company (Cosens & Co Ltd). In an attempt to use safety as well as speed as a selling-point, a note was added that:

'*The magnificent steamers* Monarch, Victoria *and* Empress *are among the fastest in the district, specially designed for the English Channel, are constructed in no less than seven watertight compartments to minimise the risk to their passengers from accidents at sea, and their sea-going qualities are of the highest character.*'

A surviving account, allegedly written by 'A Cockney' but more probably by a Cosens' stooge, gives a wonderful impression of the excitement generated in Bournemouth by the 'Battle of the Boats' which ensued:

'*I cried out for the youngest and was rewarded by the* Monarch, *an infant of this year's growth, with admirable parents and as yet too young to sin or even play tricks. So to the* Monarch – *bound for Ventnor and round the Isle of Wight – I started. From the moment of boarding the vessel a certain tremor of excitement was apparent, not caused by the engines, for they were of course quiet; not by the sight of a Cockney voyager; I dare not take the credit of the suppressed emotion. After a few chance words the secret oozed out. It seemed a rumour had gained ground that the* Brodick Castle, *the fine boat of the local company, was to be pitted against the* Monarch *the new boat of the original company who, some years ago came to the rescue and practically created the present traffic. This report had been solemnly denied,*

DEATHS.

August 2nd, at Bournemouth, "the superiority in speed, as in other respects," of the " BRODICK CASTLE," over all other Modern Steamships, Aged 3 weeks. Deeply regretted.

A scurrilous handbill, circulated by Cosens in August 1888, to celebrate MONARCH's *victory over* BRODICK CASTLE *in one of their many races.* AUTHOR'S COLLECTION

for the posters of the local company bore slips across them disclaiming any intention of racing yet, alas for human nature, nobody believed the protestation. And when the Brodick Castle *suddenly slipped away, the rush of sailors to the sides of the* Monarch, *the way her fine old Captain ran to his bridge and, heedless of the stream of would-be passengers, gave the word to start, confirmed people in their theory. Now, when a man or a crowd embrace a theory, no amount of contrary facts will disillusion them. Speaking candidly, the facts were not so very contrary. The boats did not race of course, that was quite understood, but each boat was determined to do its best, utterly ignoring the presence of the other. Now, a Briton loves a race and all her male passengers straightway forsook all hopes and aims except the one of seeing the* Monarch *beat the* Brodick Castle. *In spite of the latter having such a good start the* Monarch *soon passed her and headed her rival, reaching Ventnor some five minutes in advance. After we all landed up came the* Brodick. *We cheered her and a few exchanged some chaff with her passengers and crew, but nobody was spiteful and in spite of the contest no fights darkened the pier, but the two streams of tourists blended in a procession up the pier while the boats nestled side by side like a pair of sleepy ducks. So harmonious were they that the passengers from the other boat passed over ours to gain their own deck; not a single infernal machine was deposited in an engine room and, in spite of the temptations, we did not blow up the* Brodick Castle *even in metaphor. At five o'clock, as the moment for starting drew near, everyone strained to the utmost pitch. How those two boats started, close as they were together, is a mystery. We were off in a second; like two impatient greyhounds from a leash, away they sprang. The coaling of the* Brodick *showed she was putting forth all her legitimate power, while the stokers of the* Monarch *saw that their engines did their duty well. In the sense of employing extraordinary means to gain speed at the cost of safety or comfort it was no race. But in a fair way each boat did its level best, and the honour is shared by both. Certainly the* Monarch *gained and kept her distance, but she had a splendid second, and when at length Bournemouth Pier was sighted, the crowds waiting welcomed them with royal cheers. Her crew had mounted flowers. Her fine old salt who, on his bridge, commands the admiration not only of his male passengers, but in a special degree of his lady voyagers, had a floral tribute that would not have disgraced a prima donna. Even we, who only acted as ballast to the boat, felt we had done something to be proud of. It was a splendid finish to a splendid day and when landed we all rushed to greet our rival, and there was honest pride that Bournemouth should own two such boats.'*

This spirited account prompted an immediate response from Henry Newlyn, the chairman of the Bournemouth Company who, having *'unhesitatingly denied'* that his steamer had indulged in racing, went on to add:

'The alarming discharge of steam from the Monarch *on her arrival at Bournemouth Pier spoke volumes, and to any person qualified to judge proved simply that the* Monarch, *after having been docked, her bottom repainted for the purpose, and carrying only 264 passengers was forced to the utmost and performed the remarkable feat of arriving at Bournemouth Pier, after a run of 30 miles, only seven minutes in advance of the* Brodick Castle *which has been out of dock more than four months, was carrying 420 passengers and was not forced; thereby demonstrating to all competent judges the* Brodick Castle's *unquestionable superiority.'*

Unable to remain silent in the face of such a public slur, Mr S.J. Fowler penned an immediate retort on behalf of Cosens:

'Sir, We are glad to see, by our friend Mr Newlyn's letter, that we are likely to get his support in helping us to do what we have long wished to do – viz, arrange the programmes of the two steamboat companies so that the very appearance of racing may be avoided, and further gather that all that has been done during his absence in the north and since his return by the more ardent spirits on the local company's directorate, does not receive his sanction. On our part we have from the first day of the Monarch's *arrival simply acted on the defensive. On our earliest appearance with our new vessel at Bournemouth we learned that the* Brodick Castle *had been cleaned a few days before, and found her waiting our sailing for the inaugural race to Swanage and, although the* Monarch *proved slightly the fastest, we were content to describe her as being among the fastest in the district. Then came the advertised race to Brighton on 12 July ... The programmes were headed with a jubilant line and newspapers in Scotland brought into request to give publicity to the report that* Brodick Castle *had beaten the* Monarch *by 2 minutes in a run of 70 miles; but in No. 3 race, when our turn came, silence reigned!; and because the* Monarch *proved the best by 16 minutes on the full run round the Isle of Wight (about 70 miles), the whole scene has changed ... The jubilant betting of 10 to 2 by many prominent supporters of the local company prior to the start demonstrated too plainly that, notwithstanding the printed slip issued to the public about 'No racing allowed!!' it was known what was meant. We venture to affirm that some person or persons connected with the local company caused her to be moored 'head out'*

at the pier that morning to get a start, and otherwise did all they could throughout the day to hold their self-named title of being the crack ship and the fastest on the station. We have shown that upon equal terms, with the Monarch *properly trimmed and as clean as the* Brodick Castle, *we have the right to the title of the fastest boat, although we may lack the 'impartial' help of some of the local newspapers. We only wish to add that the* Monarch *can only work low pressure at 30lbs to the square inch, as compared with* Brodick Castle *when being driven at 60lbs per square inch; and we have no doubt that John Penn & Son will be able to answer for our machinery and boilers, without the slightest cause for anxiety on our part, and, being also the only excursion steamer on the station allowed by the Board of Trade to cross the Channel, we have said quite enough to demonstrate the unquestionable superiority of the* Monarch.'

Monarch made her first Cross Channel excursion to Cherbourg on Thursday 19th July, with 250 passengers on board. She sailed from Bournemouth at 8.17am and arrived in France at 1.38pm, after a passage of 5 hours 21 minutes. She sailed again at 4.20pm and arrived at Swanage, where customs officers were waiting to examine passengers' baggage, at 9.00pm. From there she proceeded to Bournemouth, where a crowd of over 1,000 spectators was waiting to welcome her home at 10pm. Further crossings were advertised for Thursdays 16th and 30th August, while on alternate weeks she went from Bournemouth to Torquay in direct opposition to *Brodick Castle*. On Friday 20th July, in order to satisfy the demands of the locals for a chance to sail on board their new flagship, she made her first long distance sailing from Weymouth to Torquay, though foggy weather caused many of her intending passengers to go ashore before she sailed.

The summer of 1888 was, unfortunately, marked by extremely poor weather. Temperatures were unseasonably low and frequent heavy rain was punctuated by periods of dense fog, as on 22nd June, which proved to be one of the foggiest days ever remembered in Swanage, leading to great disruption of the steamer services. In the morning, both *Empress* and *Lord Elgin* had left Bournemouth for Swanage at the same time and *Brodick Castle* had set off for Weymouth when the fog descended. Capt Hurdle brought *Empress* alongside at Swanage on time but the two rival ships lost their bearings and were eventually guided into the pier – *Brodick Castle* one and a half hours late – by *Empress's* steam whistle. In a highly partisan reference to the loss of *Bournemouth*, the *Dorset County Chronicle* noted *'surely if a captain of a steamship is awarded a gold watch by the grateful public for running his ship onto the rocks, the conduct of Capt Hurdle who saved the lives of the* Brodick Castle's *passengers by his superior knowledge of the difficult art of navigation, ought to receive a commensurate reward.'* In the next edition, the managers of the Bournemouth Company responded by insisting,

The crew of EMPRESS at Lulworth Cove on 1st July 1888, the day on which Capt William Bowering (seated right) left the ship to transfer to VICTORIA and the mate, Lewis St Barbe Rawle (leaning on the chair) joined her from PREMIER. The engineer (seated left) is Joseph Carter, while the seamen in ship's jumpers are Dan Purkins (2nd from left), John Bowering, Matthew Kenway and Robert White. On the left is Mrs Penny, the stewardess, while the ship's boy, Bill Buxey, is on the right. The cook/steward is John Burt and the man with the pipe is Frederick Richards, the fireman.
BERNARD COX

with some justification, that there had been no danger to their ships or passengers and that their ships had proceeded slowly simply in the interests of safety! On August Bank Holiday, a fine morning gave way to an afternoon of torrential rain and, when *Monarch* and *Brodick Castle* took almost 1,000 passengers to view the Royal Yacht Squadron regatta at Cowes on 14th August, both ships became fog-bound and had to lay overnight at Yarmouth.

In addition to the competition between *Monarch* and *Brodick Castle*, there were two other interesting developments at Bournemouth during the season. Firstly, on 2nd August 1888 a new 300 foot pier was opened at Southbourne. This hitherto remote settlement some $3^1/2$ miles to the east of Bournemouth, had been rendered more accessible and attractive by the construction of a direct road and toll bridge in 1883 and by the completion of an esplanade and sea wall in 1885. *Lord Elgin* joined in the opening celebrations and four days later a regular daily service between Bournemouth and Southbourne was introduced. It remains unclear just how frequently Cosens or the local company called but a reluctance on their part may have led to the second notable development.

At the beginning of September, it was announced that a further steamer named *Nelson*, '... *one of the steadiest boats on the coast, having a BoT certificate to cross the channel ... (with) ... sufficient saloon space to accommodate all her passengers under cover in wet weather.*' would shortly be making an appearance at Bournemouth. Her timetable indicated that, with the exception of a single excursion to the Isle of Wight, it was intended to employ her on a regular shuttle service between Southbourne, Bournemouth

and Swanage, and it seems probable that she was backed by Southbourne interests anxious to promote the growth of their resort. In the event, *Nelson* did not appear on station until 12th September – nine days after her advertised starting date – and she survived for only two days. On Friday 14th September, she was seen to depart from Southbourne in the direction of the Isle of Wight and shortly afterwards the Bournemouth pier master received a telegram informing him that *Nelson* '*would not again call at Bournemouth Pier.*'

On the evening of 12th September, *Victoria* had sailed on an excursion to view Bournemouth's 'illuminations' or firework display and, armed with a good supply of blue-lights and flares to add to the celebration, had anchored in the bay. Capt Bowering was personally setting off the rockets from a tube on the ship's rail, when one failed to ignite. As he approached to replace it, it exploded causing severe burns to his hands and face, and he was rushed ashore to receive medical attention. Initially there were fears that he would lose his sight but, happily, he made a full recovery during the winter and was able to resume his employment at the start of the 1889 season.

At Weymouth, the season followed its accustomed pattern, the slight discontent of the local population at being forced to accept the company's older, smaller boats being ameliorated to some extent by *Victoria* being sent along regularly to undertake the westward coasting trips, with *Monarch* running occasional long distance excursions. One unusual trip took place on 2nd August, when an excursion was advertised from Weymouth around Portland Bill to Abbotsbury, where passengers were landed

directly onto the massive shingle ridge of the Chesil Beach. Although other landings had occurred many years before, Abbotsbury was a particularly difficult and exposed place to beach a steamer, and both tidal and sea conditions had to be perfect for an attempt to be made. Fortunately, the chosen day was a flat calm and passengers were able to spend two hours ashore exploring the delights of this exceptionally beautiful and historic Dorset village.

Monarch retreated to winter lay up at the end of September and it fell to *Empress* to close the season with a cruise from Bournemouth to Swanage, Brownsea Island and Poole Harbour, during which the Royal Italian Band provided a 'Grand Marine Concert'. Although filled with excitement, the 1888 season had not proved an easy one for Cosens. The poor weather during the peak months of July and August had depressed the passenger figures and although the 108,000 carried represented an increase of 28,000 on 1887 and had yielded a £1,200 increase in income, costs had increased even faster. Insurance premiums to provide the security required by the increased number of bondholders had cost far more, the cost of advertising and commission to agents had increased and the supply of stores to *Monarch* had added £800 to the bills. The competition to win favour in Bournemouth had led both companies to issue more complimentary tickets than was economically sensible and meant that, although the steamers often sailed with large numbers on board, a fair proportion of these were contributing nothing to the company's income. To add to the troubles, the winter of 1887-88 had been a quiet one for the salvage department, with only the steamer *Envoy*, which was towed in from Lyme Bay on 4th December, and the schooner *Thetis*, which

got into trouble on 1st May, yielding any significant income. The Channel Fleet had visited Portland very little during the summer, causing a drop of £400 in liberty boat income and the raw summer temperatures had led to a fall in demand for ice. All this meant that the company's overall income was down by £2,500 and a dividend of only $2\frac{1}{2}$ per cent could be declared, causing disappointment among some shareholders who had looked to the advent of *Monarch* as the beginning of a financial bonanza.

The directors took a more sanguine attitude to the situation and pressed ahead with further modifications to *Victoria* during the winter of 1888-89. The starting and reversing of her engine had hitherto been achieved by the engineer manipulating a set of long manual levers, an operation which required considerable skill and strength. It had been discovered, however, that this system could not be relied upon to deliver the speed and reliability required when manoeuvring alongside piers and in crowded anchorages, so it was decided to fit steam starting and reversing gear instead.

Monarch also underwent slight modification when her fo'c'sle head was extended aft by several feet, to improve her seaworthiness on exposed cross-channel sailings. Not only did this improve her profile but it significantly reduced the chance of passengers in her forward well deck receiving an unexpected soaking when she dug her bows into a steep sea. At the same time, her promenade deck was extended forwards and the steep steps down to the well deck replaced with an elegant new stairway, which followed the curve of her forward saloon companionway.

The winter and spring also saw a welcome crop

of salvage jobs for the company. On 25th November, the schooner *Mary Davies* left Weymouth in the face of a heavy gale to load stone at Portland but was quickly forced to drop anchor. During the night, she dragged towards Osmington and the lifeboat *Friern Watch* was launched to take off her crew. The following morning, *Queen* brought her safely into Weymouth, where she was reunited with her crew before sailing again for Portland and London. Tragically, *en route* she went ashore near Seaford and became a total wreck.

During January, in weather too bad for even *Queen* to put to sea, Cosens were forced to sit helplessly by while the ketch *Ada* was lost with all hands in Lyme Bay and, a few days later, were cheated of a lucrative job when a barque which had gone ashore on Portland Breakwater floated off just as the tug approached her. During February, the tug *Storm Cock* carried away her towing gear during a Channel gale and put into Weymouth for repairs. At this time, Cosens seem to have been working in close conjunction with one of their minor shareholders, Mr Ayles, who owned a slipway and shipbuilding yard on Nothe Parade, roughly opposite Cosens' Head Office. With their own slipway in almost constant use, it made sense for Cosens to co-operate with Ayles in order to accommodate all the repair work which presented itself.

During February, work had been begun to increase the depth of water in Weymouth Harbour and its approaches but the whole operation seemed dogged by bad luck. Firstly, the dredger *Witham*, which was carrying out the work, sprang a leak and sank off the harbour mouth, where several attempts to raise her failed. Then, on 2nd March, Cosens attached four barges to her at low water, by means of some huge baulks of elm timber which had been fetched from Cardiff specifically for the purpose, and succeeded in lifting her on the rising tide. Floated further inshore, she was beached again and divers sent down to locate the leak. Salvage pumps

were placed on board and, on the next tide, *Witham* was towed into harbour, where Cosens were contracted to give her a thorough overhaul. At the beginning of May, *Witham* broke some of her machinery and Cosens were again engaged to repair it. Finally, an additional mud hopper, which had been sent for from Southampton, foundered off the Isle of Wight *en route* to Weymouth. Due to the Town Council's failure to meet its agreement with the Great Western Railway to complete the dredging in time for the summer season, Channel Island mail steamers ran aground in the harbour entrance on several occasions and great difficulty was experienced in swinging them safely within the harbour. As a result, Cosens benefited from a payment of £2 per day for towing the GWR ships stern first out of the harbour, swinging them in the bay and then towing them back to their berths. This unwelcome expense concentrated the Council's mind and the dredging was finally completed during the following winter.

The most notable wreck of 1889 took place on 8th March, when the 2,019 ton steamer *Vera* stranded broadside on to the Chesil Beach near Langton Herring. As soon as news was received, Mr Fowler, together with the Receiver of Wrecks and the local Lloyd's agent, set off overland, while *Queen*, commanded by Capt Beale, was ordered to sea. Unfortunately, the tremendous sea that was running made it impossible for her to even approach the wreck, let alone attempt any rescue operation, and Mr Fowler signalled from the beach that she was to put about and return to Weymouth. The following day, however, the wind veered to the north east and, with Chesil Beach providing a useful lee, work began on recovering *Vera's* cargo. Some was unloaded into tugs and barges alongside, some directly onto the beach and Cosens received 40 per cent of its substantial sale value in recognition of their services. Sadly, attempts to refloat the ship herself failed and the wreck was subsequently sold

The ill-fated dredger WITHAM *and attendant mud hoppers working in Weymouth Harbour. To their left,* COMMODORE *is moored to the new GWR landing stage and baggage shed, which was completed during 1889.*
AUTHOR'S COLLECTION

* E.S. VERA WRECK ON THE CHESIL BEACH - APR.1889. W.W.T*

The wreck of VERA on Chesil Beach in April 1889, after Cosens had completed the recovery of her cargo.
AUTHOR'S COLLECTION

for £20 but the income generated by the sale of the cargo allowed Cosens to declare a windfall dividend of 2¹⁄₂ per cent and to distribute welcome bonus payments to all the managers, directors and staff involved.

In May 1889, following the death of its owner Mr Collett, Cosens were able to purchase the lease of the long-established Weymouth Foundry on Lower Bond Street. The site appears to have consisted of three separately rated but adjoining premises, comprising the foundry itself, a house, a shed and '*machinery, plant and appurtenances*', sited conveniently close to the quayside in Weymouth Backwater. The foundry made an extremely useful addition to the company's other engineering facilities, which appear to have been located on nearby West Street. Additional staff were employed, a number of improvements carried out and the amount of new work generated quickly justified the investment.

Victoria opened the Bournemouth season for Cosens on 6th April 1889 and was joined by *Empress* in time for the Easter Bank Holiday weekend. The weather was exceptionally fine and a large number of visitors went afloat, both at Bournemouth and on the Weymouth to Portland ferry service. Unfortunately, the start of the full Weymouth excursion season on 1st May was greeted by less favourable weather and *Queen* had only a few brave souls on board when she ventured out into a blustery and uninviting bay.

Monarch, being too large for the Weymouth slipway, had been to Southampton for dry-docking and was reported to have achieved 16.5 knots over

the measured mile at Stokes Bay on 17th May. As she was about to enter service at the beginning of June, it was announced that her master, Capt William Cosens, had decided to retire from the sea and would instead be taking up a position as the company's representative at Swanage. Apart from a short period working for J.T. Leather on the construction of the Spithead forts during the late 1860s, William Cosens had an unbroken record of service with the company since 1850 and from 1852 had commanded each of its new ships in turn. However, the long hours of standing on exposed, open bridges and the responsibilities of navigation assisted only by compass, lead line and local knowledge, had begun to take their toll, and for some years his health had been starting to fail. He was paid £2 per week plus 8s for lodgings for his new post, which involved running the local booking office, arranging advertising and ensuring that the coaling of the steamers at Swanage Pier was carried out efficiently. His predecessor, Mr Lose, was appointed money collector on board *Monarch*.

Needless to say, the retirement of such a popular and important figure, noted for his '*cheerful face and genial manners*', attracted a great deal of attention and comment. A number of farewell ceremonies took place, including a presentation at the Royal Marine Library, Bournemouth, of a purse containing £65 and an address inscribed on vellum. This beautiful illuminated document included a painting of Bournemouth Bay with *Monarch* arriving at the pier, and an illustration entitled '*The Man at the*

Wheel', which represented John Hardy, the mate who had served alongside Capt Cosens on *Empress*, *Victoria* and *Monarch* for many years past. The inscription read:

'To Captain William Cosens. We have the pleasure on behalf of the subscribers to present you with the accompanying purse of £65. The actual value of the gift is but a slight index of the respect and esteem you have won from a large number of your friends. Your services, extending over 35 years in connection with the passenger steam pleasure on this coast, have not only been efficiently and faithfully rendered, but the tact, urbanity and consideration displayed towards some hundreds of thousands of passengers have called forth a widespread and spontaneous utterance which seemed to demand this permanent record. To your comparative retirement you will carry the best wishes of all who have known you for your health and happiness.'

A few months later, the officers and crew of the fleet presented him with a large, framed photographic portrait of himself.

The departure of William Cosens prompted a major reshuffle of masters. Capt Bowering, who had recovered from his injuries *'with only minor disfigurement'*, was promoted to *Monarch*, while Capt Beale of *Queen* took his place on board *Victoria*. Capt Beale was replaced by Alfred Cox, who was new to the company but the arrangement did not prove satisfactory and Cox was dismissed in September and his place taken by Capt Haill. Capts Hurdle, Masters and Fowler retained command of *Empress*, *Premier* and *Commodore* respectively.

During August, the company suffered another significant loss when Mr William Hinde snr, their superintendent engineer for the last forty years, died in a London hospital. Special arrangements were made for the funeral, to be held on a Sunday, 20th August, in order that the entire staff of the company could attend and, on the previous evening, all the steamers were called home to Weymouth. The hearse and the six coaches bearing the chief mourners (including the deceased's son, William Hinde jnr, the chief engineer of *Monarch*) was followed by a long procession, consisting of : The Captain and 12 crew of *Monarch*, Captain and 7 crew of *Victoria*, Captain and 8 crew of *Empress*, Captain and 6 crew of *Premier*, Captain and 8 crew of *Queen* and the Captain and engineer of *Commodore*. Following them were two steam launch crew; five men and an apprentice from the carpenters' department; three men and three apprentices from the engineering department; Mr Drake, six men and four apprentices from the foundry; Mr Pover from the ice store; four men from the coal department and a messenger boy. The coffin bearers were the six longest-serving men from the company's shore staff.

The season of 1889 followed very much the same pattern as 1888, with the competition at Bournemouth

remaining as keen as ever. *Monarch*'s first long trip was to Brighton and thereafter she settled into her regular pattern of sailings to Torquay, Dartmouth, Brighton, round the Isle of Wight and the five-hour Channel crossing to Cherbourg. On Saturday 13th July, she sailed with 130 passengers on a special three day excursion to Jersey, departing from St. Helier at 11am on Monday and arriving back at Bournemouth at 8pm. During September, she made at least one excursion to Alderney, whilst another Royal review of the fleet at Spithead provided a welcome boost to income at the end of July and beginning of August. Better weather during the season meant that overall passenger figures were up again to a record 128,000 and, after their disappointment in 1888, shareholders were able to look forward to a far healthier dividend of $5\frac{1}{2}$ per cent.

A further development of significance was the opening of another new pier, on 29th July 1889, at Boscombe, roughly half way between Bournemouth and Southbourne. *Premier* made several special excursions from Bournemouth as part of the opening celebrations and thereafter both Cosens and the Bournemouth Company began to make regular calls. The morning steamer from Swanage would normally call at Boscombe, in order to transfer intending passengers to the long distance steamers at Bournemouth pier and an evening sailing would retrace the route in reverse. Whichever Cosens

Capt William Bowering (centre), who commanded MONARCH *from 1889 until 1896. He is seen here with the helmsman and Mate, Mr Anderson, standing beside the ship's extraordinary decorative binnacle.*
JOHN HAYSOM

At the start of her first trip of the 1889 season, MONARCH pauses in Weymouth Bay to show off her extended fo'c'sle and modified steps to the official photographer. AUTHOR'S COLLECTION

steamers had undertaken excursions to the Isle of Wight or further eastwards would also call at Boscombe to disembark passengers on the homeward journey. With slight variations in timings, this was an arrangement which was to endure until the outbreak of the First World War in 1914.

The high season routine at Weymouth was interrupted in a most unusual manner, when a large vessel went ashore on the Shambles Bank off Portland at daybreak on 4th July and began to fire signals of distress. *Queen* immediately rushed to the scene, where she found the steamer *Metabele* of Aberdeen hard and fast on the outer edge of the shingle bank, on a swiftly ebbing tide. By the time the tide had turned, *Queen* had been joined by *Commodore* and Messrs Collins' Portland tug *Alert*. Together, they succeeded in refloating the casualty and towing her into Portland, where Cosens divers examined her for damage before she proceeded on her voyage to South Africa.

For the past two years or so, *Queen* had been kept in steam day and night, summer and winter, in anticipation of lucrative salvage jobs. This intensive use had left little time for major maintenance and, by the summer of 1889, she was showing serious signs of wear and tear. It was therefore judged essential that her boiler, engine and hull all receive a major overhaul early in the winter, before the company's staff became absorbed in the refits of the excursion vessels. The problem, however, was that she would be out of service for several weeks and the little *Commodore* was no longer powerful enough to handle the bigger casualties which were

now being encountered. Rather than leave the Dorset coast without salvage cover, it was therefore decided to obtain an additional tug and Mr Fowler travelled to Dundee, where *Lass O' Gowrie* was purchased for £3,125.

This steel tug, which had been built in 1883 by Eltringham & Co of South Shields, was extremely similar in appearance and dimensions to *Queen*, weighing 128 gross tons and measuring 106 feet by 19 feet 8 inches by 9 feet 7 inches. She was powered by a 70hp jet condensing, side lever engine constructed by J.P. Renoldson & Sons, with 37 inch diameter cylinders and a stroke of 54 inches. As soon as the sale was completed on 5th November, the tug set off for Weymouth, where she was renamed *Albert Victor* on 6th December. *Queen* was immediately withdrawn to begin her refit.

With the company now in possession of a pair of well-matched, powerful salvage tugs, it was evident that *Commodore*'s days were numbered. She was sold by auction on 25th April 1890 for £300 to Joseph Campbell, a forage dealer of Holyhead and sailed from Weymouth for the last time on 28th April on her four day passage to Anglesey. The little ship, whose daring salvage exploits had led every harbour-side urchin in Weymouth to believe '*she was made of cork and couldn't sink*', had served Cosens well for 27 years and her departure must have left an emotional gap in the harbourside scene. *Commodore* only remained in Campbell's ownership for eight months, before passing briefly to William Bustard and then, in January 1891, to John Johnston, a Liverpool tug owner. In June 1893, she was sold

Boscombe Pier, opened in 1889, was included in a triangular service from Swanage and Bournemouth and became a regular calling point for steamers on eastward excursions. In this 1890s Francis Frith photograph, MONARCH is seen departing the pier, with LORD ELGIN approaching and BRODICK CASTLE manoeuvring offshore. AUTHOR'S COLLECTION

COMMODORE moored at Cosens' higher landing stage in Weymouth Harbour during 1889. Astern of her is the new GWR landing stage and baggage shed, opened earlier that year.
WEYMOUTH LIBRARY

to William Leonard of Middlesbrough and was finally broken up during 1894.

Albert Victor did not have long to wait before her first call-out. On 11th January 1890, she went to the assistance of the schooner *Minnie*, which had gone ashore between Worbarrow and Kimmeridge but, in the conditions prevailing, could do little more than bring her master back to Weymouth to negotiate with the Lloyd's agent. A plan was laid to return to the wreck the following morning and jettison the cargo but continuing rough weather made any work impossible for several days. Eventually, the seas died down and Cosens were successful in landing the cargo and refloating *Minnie*.

Thereafter, *Albert Victor* settled into a routine of regular local and channel towage work, combined with summer employment on the Portland ferry service and local excursions from Weymouth. Ironically, the next two years proved to be exceptionally lean ones for the salvage department and the management must have wondered whether their investment in the new tug was a wise one. In October 1890, *Albert Victor* went to the aid of the schooner *Fannie C*, whose master, discovering that she was on fire, had deliberately beached her on the Chesil Beach near Portland. The tug and a barge went round from Weymouth in the hope of saving her cargo but fear of an explosion made it too dangerous to leave men on board. Her sails were

ALBERT VICTOR being launched, bows first, from Cosens' No. 1 slipway.
AUTHOR'S COLLECTION.

MONARCH on a visit to Southampton's Royal Pier.
AUTHOR'S COLLECTION

A poster for the weekly westward coasting trip from Weymouth to Torquay, June 1890.
WEYMOUTH MUSEUM

taken in and sent ashore but shortly afterwards the flames took hold and the vessel was burnt to the waterline. Cosens were also involved with the wrecks of the French barque *Ehen*, which drifted ashore in light winds near Portland Bill on 21st April 1890, and the steamer *Thames*, which became a total loss in Chesil Cove on 2nd January 1891. However, neither generated any significant income and winter receipts during 1890 fell by £2,100.

Despite some very poor weather during July, passenger figures for 1890 rose by another 28,000 to 156,323, with most of the increase being at Bournemouth. This was scarcely surprising, when one takes into account the phenomenal growth of the resort, whose population had increased from 695 in 1851 to 16,859 in 1881 and doubled again in the next decade to 37,650 in 1891. The boundaries had constantly expanded to absorb Boscombe, Southbourne, Winton and other outlying areas and, on 23rd July 1890, Bournemouth formally became a Municipal Borough. This burgeoning resident population, together with the ever-expanding number of seasonal visitors who arrived by rail, provided a large and growing market for both steamer companies and augured well for the future. Cosens' passenger receipts increased by £2,000 and season ticket sales by £400, while back at Weymouth, the regular trading of the engineering department, foundry and slipway were all generating a steadily increasing profit.

The sailing programme for 1890 was almost identical to previous years. *Monarch* managed to reduce her passage time to and from Cherbourg to 4½ hours each way during a trip at the end of June,

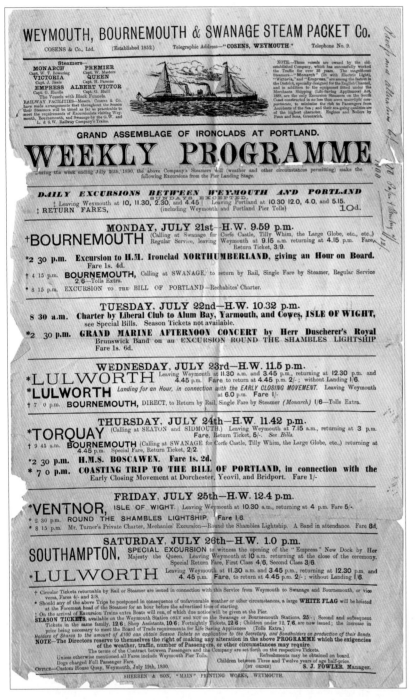

A Weymouth weekly sailing bill for July 1890.
WEYMOUTH MUSEUM

whilst *Victoria* provided an unusual three-day excursion from Weymouth to Plymouth on Saturday 21st June, to visit the Royal Agricultural Show there. The steamer sailed at 6am, calling at Torquay *en route* and offered passengers the choice of returning from Torquay or Plymouth by rail on the Monday or Tuesday, or on board *Victoria*, either on Monday 24th June or a week later on 30th June. This amazingly flexible package was offered for the grand price of 6s return, with half price for season ticket holders.

The most dramatic event of the season unfolded

on 14th August, when *Victoria*, during a return leg of a coasting trip to Torquay, found herself in serious difficulties in Lyme Bay. The day had dawned fair and both *Victoria* and *Monarch* had gone westwards but, a little after midday, a gale accompanied by heavy seas blew up, giving rise to considerable anxiety as to how the two ships, or the other steamers which had set off on long cruises from Southampton, Bournemouth, Weymouth and Torquay, would get back to their starting points. As the evening drew on, an anxious crowd gathered on Weymouth Pier, where they were kept informed of developments. Reports were received that *Empress* had reached Bournemouth safely, whilst *Monarch* had been seen passing Portland Bill, homeward bound from Dartmouth. A battered *Premier* finally drew alongside after encountering fearful conditions on her passage home from Swanage. Nothing, however, had been heard of *Victoria*. A few minutes later, word came from the Abbotsbury Coastguard that a steamer had been sighted offshore flying signals of distress and this was followed by the alarming news that she had begun firing flares and that rocket apparatus had been set up on the beach to render assistance in the event of her coming ashore. For some reason, it was assumed that the vessel must be the small excursion steamer *Lady of the Isles*, which had left Weymouth for Torquay some time earlier and nobody seemed to consider the possibility that *Victoria* herself might be in trouble. *Queen* was immediately dispatched to the scene but it was not until half past ten at night, when she escorted *Victoria* into Weymouth Harbour that the full story unfolded.

Victoria had enjoyed a safe passage from Weymouth to Torquay in the morning, although during the exposed leg between Portland Bill and Lyme Regis heavy seas were encountered and one passenger described her decks as '*resembling a cottage hospital*'. After allowing her passengers time ashore, *Victoria* left Torquay at 3pm and, with the wind and sea astern, enjoyed a reasonably comfortable passage homewards until, off Abbotsbury, a loud noise was heard emanating from the engine room. The engine was immediately stopped and it was soon discovered that the port crank pin had fractured, bending the crank arms and disabling the engine. After an hour of desperate work, the engineer succeeded in disconnecting the damaged crank and, with canvas set on both masts, *Victoria* began to work her way out of Lyme Bay under sail, assisted by the starboard paddle wheel. With the sea increasing and his ship rolling violently, Capt Beale feared that he might be unable to weather Portland Bill and would be driven ashore on Chesil Beach to leeward so, at 7.45pm, began to fire rockets and signal guns to attract the attention of lookouts ashore. With his signals acknowledged, he continued to work *Victoria* offshore in conditions which '*may be easier imagined than described*' and, in a remarkable act of seamanship, managed to round the Bill just as *Queen*'s lights hove into view. Once in the lee of Portland and with the wind on her beam, *Victoria* made better progress and, with the tug standing by, *'came round like a puffin'* and reached the safety of Weymouth harbour. Whether the passengers realised the extreme danger of finding themselves disabled and embayed on the most feared lee shore on the south coast went unrecorded but, before they made their weary way ashore, they had managed to raise a collection for the crew and give three cheers for their *'brave captain'*. *Victoria* was subsequently towed to Southampton for repairs to her engine and, during her absence, *Empress* was recalled from Bournemouth to maintain the long distance sailings from Weymouth.

On 6th October, *Victoria* was the first steamer from Bournemouth and Swanage to call at the new pier which was still under construction at Shanklin, Isle of Wight. Work on this elegant, 1,200 foot iron structure had begun in August 1888 and, although it had officially opened to steamer traffic during August 1890, there was still a good deal of work to be done. Capt Beale expressed himself well pleased with the berthing arrangements and it was noted that, once the pier was fully completed, Shanklin would be included regularly in Cosens' itineraries.

As the season drew to a windy end on 25th October and *Empress* was forced to cancel her last call at Swanage, it emerged that residents there were lobbying Cosens to provide a winter service. The railway, although regular and reliable, was a slow and circuitous means of reaching Bournemouth and Poole, and it was felt that the more direct steamer service might well prove a popular alternative. Messrs Fowler and Sydenham gave the proposal their careful consideration but decided that, on balance, the idea did not make economic or practical sense. Although no more was heard of the matter for the moment, the idea was revived during the winter of 1902-3, when a new winter service was introduced by *Victoria*.

Emboldened by the ever-expanding local market and frustrated by their inability to gain the upper hand over Cosens, the Bournemouth Company chose the winter of 1890-91 to announce the building of yet another steamer, to be named *Windsor Castle*. Their plan was to produce a ship which would be so much larger and faster than *Monarch*, that passengers would desert Cosens in droves and the long distance and cross channel trade would become their own preserve. An order was duly placed with the Southampton Naval Works for one of the largest excursion ships ever to sail in British waters, a 796 ton paddle steamer measuring 244 feet 6 inches by 27 feet 6 inches by 10 feet 3 inches and driven by powerful, 337hp triple expansion engines. The news that this formidable vessel would be delivered in time for the summer season sent shivers of apprehension through the Cosens' boardroom but a decision was made not to respond for the time being.

Meanwhile, down in Devon, Messrs Ellett and Matthew's steamer service from Exmouth, using Cosens' former *Prince*, had proved sufficiently successful for a new steamer to be ordered. A

WEYMOUTH, BOURNEMOUTH & SWANAGE STEAM PACKET Co

COSENS AND COMPANY, LIMITED. (*Established* 1852.)
Telegraphic Address—"COSENS, WEYMOUTH." Telephone No. 9.

STEAMERS { MONARCH-Capt. W.T. Bowering VICTORIA-Capt. J. Cox EMPRESS-Capt. G. Hurdle } The Vessels with
{ PREMIER-Capt. W. Masters QUEEN-Capt. G. Haill ALBERT VICTOR-Capt. H. Parsons } Black Funnels

NOTE—These vessels are owned by the old-established Company which has successfully worked the Traffic for 40 years. The magnificent Steamers—MONARCH (lit with Electric Light), VICTORIA, and EMPRESS—are among the fastest in the District, specially designed for the English Channel, and in addition to the equipment fitted under the Merchant Shipping (Life-Saving Appliances) Act, 1888, are with but one exception the only Excursion Steamers on the South Coast constructed in no less than seven *watertight compartments* to minimise the risk to Passengers from Accidents of the Sea ; and their sea-going qualities are of the highest character. Engines and Boilers by Penn and Sons, Greenwich.

Railway Facilities—Messrs. Cosens & Co. have made arrangements that throughout the Season their Steamers will be timed as far as practicable to meet the requirements of Excursionists visiting Weymouth, Bournemouth, and Swanage by the G.W. and L. & S.W. Railway Companies' Trains.

THE IRONCLADS AT PORTLAND.

WEEKLY PROGRAMME

During the week ending Aug. 27th, 1892, the above Company's Steamers will (weather and other circumstances permitting) make the following Excursions from the PIER LANDING STAGE.

DAILY EXCURSIONS between WEYMOUTH & PORTLAND
(SUNDAYS EXCEPTED)

Leaving Weymouth at 10, 11.30, 2.30, & 4.45 | Leaving Portland at 10.30, 12, 4, & 5.15.
RETURN FARES (including Weymouth and Portland Pier Tolls) 10d.
Special Single Fare by last Boat to or from Portland 6d.

MONDAY, August 22nd—H.W. 7.23 P.M.

Note Altered Time. Fares—Return Ticket s. d.
‡9 15 a.m. BOURNEMOUTH direct, thence to SWANAGE, for Corfe Castle, Anvil Lighthouse, etc., returning at 4.30 p.m. Special Return Fare 3/2
2 30 p.m. H.M. IRONCLAD "ANSON," giving, with kind permission, an hour on board ... 1 2
‡3 30 p.m. BOURNEMOUTH, calling at Swanage for Corfe Castle, Anvil Lighthouse, etc., to return by Rail, Special Single Fare 2/-
8 30 p.m. Excursion in the Bay, round the Ironclads ... 8

TUESDAY, August 23rd—H.W. 8.2 P.M.

10 30 a.m. SEATON, Devon, returning at 3.30 p.m. Special Return Fare ... 2 8
2 30 p.m. Round the SHAMBLES LIGHTSHIP, passing the Ironclads ... 1 6

WEDNESDAY, August 24th—H.W. 8.34 P.M. Weymouth Regatta.

11 30 a.m. and 3 45 p.m. LULWORTH COVE, returning at 12.30 and 4.45 p.m. Fares—for the day 2/- ; Single Fare, or the Morning Trip without landing 1/6 ; 3.45 Trip to return without landing 1/- or at 8 p.m. 1/6
3 0 p.m. WEST BAY, Bridport (*Victoria*), returning at 7 p.m. in connection with the Early Closing Movement, subject to confirmation in the morning of the 24th. See Special Bills ... Special Fare 1 8
Privilege and Complimentary Tickets and Free Passes not available.
4 30 p.m. H.M. IRONCLAD "ANSON," giving, with kind permission, an hour on board ... 1 0
6 0 p.m. EARLY CLOSING TRIP TO LULWORTH, landing for an hour, returning at 8 p.m. ... 1 0
Shop Assistants are allowed the privilege of leaving for Lulworth by the 3.45 Trip, to return without landing or at 8 p.m., at the Evening Fare 1/-

THURSDAY, August 25th—H.W. 9.6 P.M.

6 15 a.m. DARTMOUTH, DEVON (calling at Seaton and Sidmouth), returning at 3 p.m. (*Victoria*). (See Bills) ... Special Fare 5 0
Circular Tickets, returnable by Rail from Torquay to Weymouth. Fare, including Steamer and 3rd class Rail, 10/- : Season Ticket Holders, 7/- ; Excess 1st class Rail, 6/- ; 2nd class, 3/- Trains leave Torquay 1.7 and 4.28 p.m., due at Weymouth 8.30 and 10.47 p.m., or EXPRESS from Torquay at 2.48, due at 8.30 p.m. Fares from Dartmouth to Torquay, 1st Class 2/3, 3rd Class 1/3.
2 30 p.m. H.M. IRONCLAD "ROYAL SOVEREIGN," giving, with kind permission, an hour on board ... 1 2

FRIDAY, August 26th—H.W. 9.38 P.M.

9 30 a.m. RYDE, Isle of Wight, returning at 3.30 p.m. (*Victoria*) ... 4 2
2 30 p.m. Round the SHAMBLES LIGHTSHIP, passing the Ironclads ... 1 6
8 30 p.m. Excursion in the Bay, round the Ironclads ... 8

SATURDAY, August 27th—H.W. 10.8 P.M.

11 30 a.m. and 3 45 p.m. LULWORTH COVE, returning at 12.30 and 4.45 p.m. Fares—for the day 2/- ; Single Fare, or the Morning Trip without landing 1/6 ; Afternoon Fare 1/-
4 0 p.m. H.M. IRONCLAD "HOWE," giving, with kind permission, an our on board ... 1 2

Should any Trip be postponed in consequence of unfavourable weather or other circumstances, an Ensign will be hoisted at the Foremast head of the Steamer for an hour before the advertised time of starting.
‡ Circular Tickets returnable by Rail or Steamer are issued in connection with this Service from Weymouth to Swanage and Bournemouth, or vice versa. Fares 4/- and 5/-. (See Special Bills.)
On the arrival of Excursion Trains extra Boats will run, of which due notice will be given at the Pier.
SEASON TICKETS, available on the Weymouth Station ONLY and NOT on the Swanage or Bournemouth Stations, 25/-; Second and Subsequent Tickets in the same family, 12/6 ; Local Shop Assistants, 10/6 ; Fortnightly Tickets, 12/6 ; Children under 12, 7/6, are now issued. Pier Tolls extra.
Holders of Shares to the amount of £100 can obtain Season Tickets on application to the Secretary, and Bondholders on production of their Bonds.
NOTE—The Directors reserve to themselves the right of making any alteration in the above PROGRAMME which the exigencies of the weather, traffic, number of Passengers or other circumstances may require. The terms of the Contract between Passengers and the Company are set forth on the respective Tickets.
Dogs charged Full Passenger Fare. Children between Three and twelve years of age half-Price.
Unless otherwise mentioned all Fares include Weymouth Pier Tolls. Refreshments may be obtained on Board.
(BY ORDER) S. J. FOWLER, General Manager.
OFFICE—Custom House Quay, Weymouth, Aug. 20th, 1892.

SHERREN & SON, WEYMOUTH.

(left margin) From Ships 8.30, 10.30, 12, 1, 4, 5.15, 6.30, all inclusive of Tolls. See Bills.

(left margin) SPECIAL STEAMERS TO & FROM H.M. IRONCLAD FLEET AT PORTLAND :—From Weymouth 7.15, 10, 11.30, 4.45, 6. Men, Single, 6d. ; Officers, Single, 6d. ; Men, Return Tickets, 10d. ; Officers, Single, 6d. Sunday Times :—From Weymouth 7.15, 11.30, 5.15. From Ships 8.15, 1, 6.15. Visitors' Fare, Return Tickets, 10d.

(right margin) COSENS & COMPANY, Limited, Steamboat Proprietors, Iron and Brass Founders, Engineers and Lightermen, Coal, Ice and General Merchants, &c., Custom House Quay, Weymouth. Two Steam Pumps. Submarine Divers, and Salving Appliances always ready. Agency for the Boiler Insurance and Steam Power Co., Limited, and Orient Line to Australia, and Castle Line to Cape Colony. Parcels forwarded to all parts of the World per Messrs. PITT & SCOTT'S Agency.

An August 1892 Bournemouth sailing bill. BRIAN JACKSON COLLECTION

MONARCH *at Ventnor Pier on the Isle of Wight. She is moored 'head out' to allow her to make a faster departure from the pier, a practice sometimes adopted when a race with* BRODICK CASTLE *seemed imminent.*
AUTHOR'S COLLECTION

prospectus had been issued for the formation of The Devon Steamship Company Ltd, with capital of £12,000 and Cosens' manager, Mr S.J. Fowler, was named as one of the provisional directors. His role was to negotiate a contract for the construction of the new vessel with the same two yards which had built *Monarch* – J. Penn & Son and R. & H. Green – and to agree the detailed specification and to oversee the construction. Cosens themselves invested in the new concern by purchasing a block of preference shares and were contracted to supply the ship with beach landing gear.

His task completed, Fowler resigned as a director at the first general meeting of the new company in March 1891 but was accorded the honour of naming the new steamer *Duchess of Devonshire* at her launching ceremony during April. The completed ship, under the command of ex-Cosens master J. Cox, put into Weymouth on 17th May during her delivery voyage, to collect her landing gear, boats

and other items which had been constructed locally. Considerable interest was shown in her family resemblance to the Penn-built ships in Cosens' own fleet.

With the arrival of *Duchess of Devonshire* at Exmouth, the old *Prince* was sold to a Mr C.E. Newton-Robinson of London, who operated her on a service from Lee-on-the-Solent. *En route* from Exmouth to her new base, she put into Weymouth for the last time while Cosens spent a week carrying out some maintenance work on board. The old ship's register was finally closed in September 1897, when she was converted into a lighter.

On 9th March, *Monarch* sailed from Weymouth to drydock in Southampton and arrived safely shortly before a tremendous storm, accompanied by hurricane force winds and heavy snow, struck the south coast. At Weymouth, *Premier* had just been launched from the slipway and *Victoria* was being towed down harbour when the storm arrived,

Filled to capacity, VICTORIA *hurries out of Weymouth towards Portland. In line with Cosens' standard practice, her house flag and name pennant are being lowered to save wear and tear at sea. They would be hoisted again as the ship approached her next pier.*
AUTHOR'S COLLECTION

Weymouth Harbour, with QUEEN *moored at Custom House Quay while* ALBERT VICTOR *prepares to tow a pair of laden mud hoppers to sea to dump their spoil. The bucket dredger* WITHAM *is on the right.*
AUTHOR'S COLLECTION

causing all further work to be abandoned. By teatime, the tide, boosted by low pressure and strong easterly winds, had overtopped the quays, flooded part of the town and washed away the foundations of the quay at Ferry's Corner near Cosens' engineering works. At the top of the tide, a barque moored in the Backwater broke loose from her moorings and hit the dredger *Witham*, which in turn fell heavily against *Empress* and *Premier* in their lay-up berths. Both paddle steamers were in danger of being swept broadside on to the Backwater dam, when *Empress*'s remaining stern mooring parted and they drifted clear to be recovered and re-moored later in the day. The unfortunate dredger, which had sunk and been salvaged by Cosens on a previous occasion, capsized and sank again. In the bay, two schooners managed to reach safety but another was smashed to pieces near Preston, whilst a large steamer that had grounded on Chesil Beach managed to get off unaided. For several hours, Weymouth was effectively cut off from the outside world. The Preston beach road was buried under tons of shingle and the Channel Islands boat train became stuck in a snowdrift. Headed by a snow plough and hauled by four engines, the train finally battled through to Weymouth at 6pm the following evening.

Before the season began, Cosens entered into a lively discussion with Weymouth Council, who proposed to maximise their revenue by installing two turnstiles at the pier entrance. Cosens, who collected the tolls on behalf of the council, fiercely opposed this suggestion, arguing that the imposition of a standard toll would be grossly unfair to the 10,000 blue-jackets who used the liberty boats in an average year, as well as to passengers patronising the 15 minute crossing to Portland. They added that a penny toll added to a long distance excursion fare might be acceptable but 1d on top of a 4d single ticket to Portland was disproportionately high and

would result in a massive loss of trade. Fortunately, the Council saw sense and left the collection of tolls in Cosens' hands.

By this time, Mr Ayles' slipway had been sold to the Great Western Railway and was no longer available for use by Cosens who had, in consequence, to turn away work due to lack of space. Frustrated by this turn of events, the company resurrected a proposal that either a drydock or two large new slipways should be constructed in Weymouth Backwater at the foot of Boot Hill. The new facility would be large enough to accommodate the Channel Islands mail steamers, *Monarch*, or any visiting ships and each slipway would have space to haul two vessels ashore at a time using steam hauling gear. As the town's only ship repairers, Cosens could see the obvious benefits to their own trade but a public meeting in July 1891 failed to persuade the Corporation to finance the scheme and no more was heard of it.

The season of 1891 again followed its accustomed pattern, enlivened by only a few notable incidents.

VICTORIA steams away from Swanage Pier, bound for Bournemouth, circa 1890.
DAVID HAYSOM COLLECTION

A busy day at Swanage Pier in 1891 or 1892. LORD ELGIN is backing away from the inner berth, with VICTORIA just astern. On the outer end of the pier, PREMIER is moored nearest the camera, while two of the Southampton Company's steamers, on a visit from the Solent, lie on the opposite side.

AUTHOR'S COLLECTION

Taken a little later on the same day, MONARCH has now replaced LORD ELGIN on the inner berth. Both views are the work of the locally well known photographer Walter Pouncy, whose main premises were at 38 High West Street, Dorchester. His subsidiary studio in Swanage opened in January 1888 and was managed by Thomas Powell, who set up his own photographic studio in 1898, on the corner of Station Road and Shore Road.

AUTHOR'S COLLECTION

At 4.45pm on 13th April, *Victoria* left Swanage Pier followed moments later by *Lord Elgin*. Both steamers were going full astern with about half a ship's length between them, when *Lord Elgin* suddenly veered towards the Weymouth ship and struck her heavily on the starboard side. The case went to court and the adjudicators found that, while *Victoria* had no room to manoeuvre, *Lord Elgin*, being the outside ship, had the whole of Swanage Bay at her disposal and should have swung to seaward before heading for Bournemouth. *Lord Elgin* was held totally to blame for the collision and the Bournemouth Company was ordered to pay the full cost of repairs plus costs.

During July, *Victoria* again found herself fogbound off Sidmouth during one of her westward 'omnibus' trips from Weymouth to Torquay and was forced to spend the night at anchor. On the evening of 15th August, a rare and serious accident occurred onboard *Albert Victor* whilst the tug was off the Shambles, towing the brig *Primrose* from Weymouth to the Channel Islands. The ship's fireman, Henry Vye, was hanging lanterns in the engine room when he caught his foot in the crank and crushed his heel in a frightful manner. The tug immediately returned to Portland, where Vye was landed by boat and rushed to Weymouth hospital. The report of the incident revealed the interesting fact that, by this time, all of Cosens' employees were covered by a mutual assurance plan, so Vye's wife and family were adequately provided for while he was unable to work.

The year 1891 was notable for its very poor weather, especially during August when many trips had to be cancelled and again in early October, when heavy gales disrupted the closing weeks of the season. The weather was so bad that, on 6th October, the large coal hulk *J.M. Reed*, operated by Messrs Collins & Co on behalf of the Powell Duffryn Company, foundered at her moorings in Portland Harbour. Later during the same morning, another smaller coal hulk broke from her moorings and went ashore at Bincleaves, from where she was recovered by *Queen*. During the following June, Cosens succeeded in raising the hulk of *J.M. Reed*. A steam grab was used to recover the 2,000 tons of steam coal on board, after which lifting barges were employed to gradually move the wreck into shallow water. Cosens' divers plugged her leaks and salvage pumps finally cleared her of water. The job was a long and difficult one, which resulted in much favourable publicity for the company.

In view of the poor weather, Cosens must have derived much satisfaction from the fact that their own passenger receipts remained steady, while the Bournemouth Company's experienced a significant drop. Furthermore, the anticipated threat from the new *Windsor Castle* had failed to materialise. Although the Bournemouth Company had advertised her widely in their local guidebooks and press, the new ship had run into serious trouble even before she was launched during June. Possibly due to the fact that her designer, Sir Henry Biles, had never worked on a paddle steamer before, a

number of serious problems arose at the design stage and then, while construction was under way, the Southampton Naval Works went into liquidation. Valuable time and money were lost while lawyers worked out a solution and the unfinished hull was eventually handed over to Day, Summers & Company for completion. Cosens, by contrast, remained on an even keel, declared another 5 per cent dividend and even discussed adding a third tug to their fleet.

Further delays on *Windsor Castle* meant that it was not until the middle of the next excursion season, on 29th July 1892, that she finally ran her trials and was handed over to her owners. The following day, with 360 guests on board including representatives from both the Southampton Company and Cosens, she set out on her inaugural cruise from Southampton to Bournemouth, with a formal lunch being served on board. During the speeches which followed, Mr Day alluded to the difficulties which had been encountered and stated that *'the vessel could not succeed as she was designed and he had formed the opinion some months ago that she would have to have new paddle boxes, wheels and the centre of gravity of the engine would have to be raised'*. As the ship came alongside Bournemouth Pier, she was greeted by the applause of a large crowd of well-wishers and was thrown open to public inspection for an hour, before departing on her first public sailing to Poole with 600 passengers.

The ship had cost her owners a massive £32,000, which compared most unfavourably with the £14,000 which Cosens had paid for *Monarch* in 1888. Many argued that a better and cheaper vessel could have been obtained from one of the Clyde yards where, for example, the comparable *Duchess of Hamilton* had been built in 1890 for £24,400. With her full width promenade deck, raised fo'c'sle, fiddle bow and large oval funnel, *Windsor Castle* was an impressive if not beautiful ship, and her 17 knot speed and large passenger capacity promised to make her both an efficient earner and a serious threat to *Monarch*.

The two ships came head to head on Bank Holiday Monday, 1st August, when both were scheduled to go round the Isle of Wight. *Monarch* completed her trip in 5 hours 4 minutes, while *Windsor Castle* confirmed her superior speed by doing the same journey in 4 hours 47 minutes but then broke down and had to be withdrawn for four days while repairs were carried out. Mechanical unreliability became something of a hallmark for the new ship and her tendency to take up a permanent list to one side or the other frequently prevented her from attaining full speed while carrying passengers. The fact that she had missed the bulk of the lucrative high season, combined with her high building costs and subsequent repairs meant that 1892 had been a disappointment but shareholders of the Bournemouth Company confidently looked forward to a bonanza in the following year.

Cosens noted these developments with some concern and decided that it would be prudent to seek the shareholders' permission to raise an additional £10,000 in capital, in case they were forced to respond with a new steamer of their own. The motion was approved during July 1892 and the shares allocated but, sensing that *Windsor Castle* might prove more of a hindrance than a help to their rivals, any decision to order a new vessel was deferred.

The 1893 season opened on Easter Monday, when both the Weymouth-Portland ferry and the Bournemouth-Swanage service attracted considerable numbers. The first trip to Lulworth followed on 26th April, when *Empress* operated a special afternoon excursion in connection with the early closing movement. At about this time, her master, Capt Hurdle, fell ill with typhoid and, although he made a good recovery, the illness left him feeling so depressed that, on 11th June, he cut his own throat with a razor. His place on board *Empress* was taken by Capt William Stone. The early season was exceptionally fine and the number of passengers gave rise to hopes of a record year but, sadly, very poor weather during August, plus the expense of the wasteful competition with the Bournemouth Company, almost exactly cancelled out the gains.

A curious accident occurred during May, when one of Cosens' coal drays collided with another cart on Trinity Quay. It its fright, the dray-horse became unmanageable and the dray toppled over the quay wall, drawing the unfortunate animal with it. The horse became jammed under *Premier*'s paddle wheel and, despite the efforts of various crew and onlookers to pass a rope around its neck and tow it to safety on the nearby GWR slipway, was dead before it could be got ashore. A few days later, on 1st June, *Premier* undertook an unusual trip when she was chartered by the landlord of the Royal Breakwater Hotel at Castletown and went direct from Portland to Bournemouth. From time to time, *Premier* also went round to Bridport, to offer a cruise in Lyme Bay to the local populace whilst her Weymouth passengers enjoyed time ashore.

Much to Cosens' relief, the Channel Fleet under the command of Admiral Fairfax spent much more time at Portland during 1893 and the Weymouth steamers were kept busy ferrying officers and men ashore from the various warships, such as *Royal Sovereign*, *Rodney*, *Narcissus*, *Immortalite*, *Bellona* and *Speedwell*. When Weymouth Council attempted to levy a 2d toll on each sailor, Fairfax complained bitterly and Cosens withdrew the service. After two days, the Council capitulated and agreed to abolish the toll. The service resumed at the reduced single fare of 4d for bluejackets and 5d for officers. To induce officers to take lodgings ashore, a special return fare of 9d was also offered! Fairfax was evidently not the easiest man to work with for, in early 1894, it was again reported that '*unfortunate differences*', which had arisen between him and Cosens, had resulted in the service being withdrawn. It was not reinstated until June 1894 when his replacement,

MONARCH at Alum Bay Pier, with the famous Needles rocks visible in the background.
PSPS ARCHIVE

Admiral Fitzroy, won the immediate gratitude of both Cosens and the men of the fleet by quickly re-establishing a harmonious relationship, restoring the liberty boat service and throwing many of his ships open to regular public inspection.

On August Bank Holiday 1893, the excursion traffic at Bournemouth broke all previous records. *Monarch* took 480 passengers round the Isle of Wight, while *Empress* and *Victoria* between them carried

3,000 to and from Swanage. The Bournemouth Company had, in their usual manner, chartered one of the Southampton Company's boats – this time *Solent Queen* – for the day, and with three vessels on the Swanage run carried 3,440. *Windsor Castle* took 800 to Portsmouth. Two days later, a severe gale swept in after all the steamers had departed on their day trips and their respective masters had to exercise great skill and judgement to ensure their

QUEEN (left) and ALBERT VICTOR (right) manoeuvre the racing cutter ECLIPSE into Weymouth Harbour after she was dismasted in the Portland Race.
AUTHOR'S COLLECTION

passengers were got safely ashore. *Victoria*, on her way to Torquay, was 20 miles west of Portland Bill when heavy seas forced her to turn back. *Monarch*, in mid Channel *en route* to Cherbourg with the wind and sea on her beam, gave her passengers an exciting ride before running for shelter in Weymouth, from where her trippers had to return by rail to Bournemouth. *Empress* abandoned a sailing to Cowes and *Premier*, having come from Weymouth to Bournemouth, was forced to divert to Swanage, from where her passengers too were sent home by train. Happily, no passengers were injured and all the ships escaped without damage.

Although the season had been altogether more favourable than 1892 and Cosens had made a comfortable profit, it soon became apparent that things had gone very badly for the Bournemouth Company. At a packed and ill-tempered annual general meeting, the *'very disappointing season'* was blamed on a number of factors. Abuse was heaped on Gladstone's government for causing a general depression in the land, catering costs had increased while a 'leakage' in the department had led to a fall in receipts, and shareholders accused the management of inflating the balance sheet by *'putting down visionary amounts'* and of *'blundering'* in their choice of the flagship's designer. Most seriously, however, both *Brodick Castle* and *Windsor Castle* were proving very expensive to run. A chart of running figures, compared to the Clyde steamer *Duchess of Hamilton*, nicely demonstrated the problem:

following morning *Queen* had been despatched to search for her. She proceeded 15 miles into the Channel but found nothing and, by 9.30am had limped back to Weymouth with her paddle box and side houses demolished by a tremendous sea which had swept on board off Portland. A telegram was then received from Swanage, stating that *Antelope* was anchored there and short of fuel. *Albert Victor* set off loaded with 10 tons of coal, which was quickly transferred to the stranded mail steamer and both vessels returned safely to Weymouth. At the end of January, Cosens successfully raised one of the Channel Coaling Company's water tankers, which had foundered during a blizzard, and placed her on their slipway for repair.

During the winter of 1893-94, major developments regarding Cosens' engineering and workshop premises also took place. With the lease of the Weymouth Foundry in Lower Bond Street due to expire, the company decided that, rather than apply for an extension, it would make more sense to move the entire business to a new site on West Street, close to the site of their original workshops. At the heart of the new development was the disused Theatre Royal, which Cosens planned to convert into a new foundry.

The building had a long and fascinating history, having originally been built as a Dissenters' Chapel in 1804 and serving in that capacity until 1864, when the congregation transferred to a newly-built church on Gloucester Street. The old building was

	Days scheduled to run	Days lost to weather	Days lost to repairs	Miles run	Expenses per mile	Income per mile
Windsor Castle	159	16	14	18,249	8/1	7/11
Brodick Castle	172	25	-	13,032	5/9	4/9
Lord Elgin	166	5	-	11,119	3/2	4/5
Duchess of Hamilton	134	-	-	16,550	5/11	4/10

With their two largest ships losing money at an alarming rate and only *Lord Elgin* making any profit at all, the company's finances were evidently in a serious state. To make matters worse, *Windsor Castle* had cracked a cylinder in her main engine, repairs to which had cost £1,944, bringing the total capital cost of the ship to an astronomical £39,000. This had partly been raised through a bank loan, which was steadily gathering interest. Something had to be done. Since *Brodick Castle*, with her coal-hungry single-cylinder engine, was losing the company one shilling for every mile she steamed, the radical decision was made to seek a charterer for her and to operate only two ships from Bournemouth during 1894.

While Cosens awaited developments, the winter months were filled with the usual refits to the steamers and one or two notable salvage jobs. During a severe gale on 18th November, the GWR steamer *Antelope* failed to arrive on her regular sailing from the Channel Islands, and by 3am the

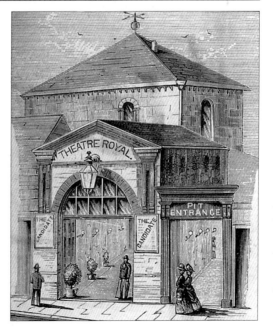

The main entrance to Weymouth's Theatre Royal. Originally a Dissenters' Chapel, it spent many years as a music hall and theatre before being converted into Cosens' foundry in 1893-94. Later used as Cosens' ice factory, the building was finally demolished during 1968, while the grand entrance arch to the old theatre lingered on for some years more as an isolated feature in the shoppers' car park which occupied the site.
WEYMOUTH LIBRARY

During 1894, Bournemouth Pier was extended to 1000 feet by the addition of another 162 feet to the pier head and landing stages. In this view, work is still underway; a crane can be seen on the pier head and the new pavilion has yet to be constructed. For the steamers it was still business as usual, however, with EMPRESS lying alongside while, in the distance, MONARCH and BRODICK CASTLE can be seen racing towards Boscombe Pier, just visible top left.
AUTHOR'S COLLECTION

purchased by Joseph Cosens, who converted it into the Weymouth Music Hall. A report of the opening night in 1865 praised the interior decoration but criticised the exterior appearance of the building, while a review of the performance was less than flattering. When Madame Ruderdorff rendered 'God Save the Queen', she apparently 'surprised the audience with a very discordant shake' and 'the piano-forte was awfully flat.' The writer went on to comment that he had hoped 'that Capt Cosens' speculation would have been more successful from a pecuniary point of view, but we regret to say that the audience was not near so large as we desired or expected.' Capt Cosens quickly realised that he was better suited to running steamboats than music halls and promptly let the lease to a Mr Belton, of the Theatre Royal, Drury Lane. Belton adopted a more up-market approach, renamed the premises 'The Theatre Royal and Concert Hall' and engaged a number of well-known acts and performers from London. In 1870, the lease passed to George Haill and, following the death of Capt Cosens, his executors sold the freehold to Joseph Drew during the winter of 1875-76. After

Drew died, his executors retained the building, which continued in use as a theatre under the management of a Mr Harry Wheeler until the end of 1893, when it was sold to Cosens & Co Ltd.

At the same time, Cosens purchased the leasehold of several plots of land adjoining the old theatre and set about constructing and equipping a completely new range of machine, fitting and engine shops. Most of these lay to the west of West Street, on a strip of undeveloped land facing directly onto the steamers' winter lay up berths in Weymouth Backwater. Thus, by the spring of 1894, the whole of the company's foundry and workshop facilities were located in close proximity to one another on a highly convenient quayside site. Development continued over the next few years, numerous small acquisitions and alterations took place, and a timber yard to the north of the foundry was acquired and converted into a boiler-makers' shop. Most importantly, modern machinery and equipment was fitted, enabling Cosens to undertake whatever marine or general engineering jobs came their way. Consideration was also given to opening a branch

EMPRESS at Bournemouth Pier, showing interesting detail of her bridge deck and fittings. The photograph formed one half of a 19th century stereo card.
BOURNEMOUTH LIBRARY

of the engineering works at Castletown, Portland, but the scheme was not proceeded with.

As the 1894 season dawned, it was announced that *Brodick Castle* had indeed found a charterer and was to spend the summer running excursions in the Bristol Channel. She had been hired by a syndicate of Bristol businessmen styling themselves 'The Bristol & Ilfracombe Pleasure Steamers Co Ltd' who, rather ambitiously, intended to enter into competition with the large and established local fleets operated by P. & A. Campbell Ltd and Edwards & Robinson Ltd. *Brodick Castle* sailed from Poole on 8th May 1894 and entered service two days later. By 14th July, she had been absorbed into the Edwards & Robinson fleet and spent the rest of the season operating their Cardiff to Weston ferry service and on occasional excursions to Newport, Chepstow and Clevedon.

With one of their major ships absent and their finances in dire straits, the Bournemouth Company were at last persuaded to enter into a sensible working agreement with Cosens for the 1894 season. The excessive number of 800 complimentary tickets, which had caused such a leakage of revenue during

1893, was reduced to a more reasonable 150 and the practice of sending rival long-distance steamers to the same destinations on the same days ceased immediately. A joint Swanage service was introduced, with alternate departures provided by each company and full inter-changeability of tickets. This allowed the frequency to be increased to hourly throughout

157

VICTORIA embarking passengers at Lulworth Cove.
AUTHOR'S COLLECTION

the day, reduced running costs significantly and was far more convenient for the public, who also benefited from a far better distribution of long excursions throughout the week.

Despite these sensible measures, another poor summer ensured that things did not improve for the Bournemouth Company. Whether rumours of their financial difficulties and of *Windsor Castle*'s unreliability played a part is unclear but, as the season drew to a close, it became apparent that passengers had deserted them in droves and receipts were down by £2,500, yielding their lowest income since 1891. The board announced '*the complete failure of long excursions*' and, weighed down by the millstone of their flagship's excessive capital and running costs and the knowledge that *Brodick Castle*'s charter would not be renewed in 1895, came to the bitter conclusion that *Windsor Castle* would have to go.

She was advertised for sale at the end of the season and was eventually sold to the Glasgow, Ayrshire & Campbeltown Steamboat Company, for whom she entered service on 1st June 1895 under the new name *Culzean Castle*. Although over the years many second-hand Clyde-built steamers, such as *Brodick Castle*, came south to operate, she was one of the very few English-built steamers ever to do the reverse. Sadly, however, she proved no more reliable in Scottish waters than she had on the South Coast and after various changes of name and

ownership, ended up in Japan, where she was eventually wrecked in 1931.

The co-operative running arrangements were continued into 1895 and, with its debts reduced by the sale of *Windsor Castle*, the Bournemouth Company began, very slowly, to recover. *Monarch* was once again the only local steamer with a cross channel passenger certificate, making the most of her monopoly by running an increased number of sailings. A surviving account of one such trip to Cherbourg, on 17th September, gives a flavour of why these excursions to a foreign shore were always regarded as a special adventure. On this particular day, Cosens had arranged for Weymouth and Dorchester passengers to be conveyed by special train to Swanage, where they joined the steamer on her outward run from Bournemouth. Thick, patchy fog was encountered within the first half hour of the voyage and a collision with a sailing ship narrowly averted but, once clear of land, the rest of the crossing was completed in brilliant sunshine and a perfect calm. The correspondent continued:

'About a mile from the famous breakwater, bristling with its guns and surrounded by powerful fortifications, we could see the pilot cutter lying in placid water, like the proverbial painted ship upon a painted ocean. A small boat put off and shortly afterwards we were hailed with the query "Pilot,

Messieurs?" But we didn't want one. Capt Bowering has passed through the breakwater too many times to require any assistance in navigation in that vicinity and we steamed on, full ahead, until we reached the beginning of the Napoleon Basin, where the usual salutations from a crowd of urchins reached our ears, the burden of which was "vun penny", "o'ny vun penny", a bit of English they seem to have learned by heart. We were soon alongside, and the vessel having been boarded by several French customs officers, we were allowed to go ashore, having made the passage across in about five hours. The various places of interest in the old town were visited, a few of the party having availed themselves of a char-a-banc drive into the open country beyond. The return journey was commenced at about ten minutes past four and quite a crowd of spectators assembled on the quay to witness our departure. We steamed slowly out of the basin, accompanied along the sea walls by the street arabs, of which Cherbourg seems to have a goodly company. They were all clamouring for "vun penny" and the scrimmages for the shower of coppers which were thrown ashore were amusing. A few minutes later we were full steam ahead and in an hour's time the hazy French coast had faded from sight.'

During the evening, a Mr Jackson entertained a party of friends, including Mr Fowler and Mr Sydenham, to a special meal in the dining saloon and, by the time the numerous toasts were given and acknowledged, *Monarch* was safely back alongside Swanage Pier.

This opportunity for Weymouthians to cross the Channel in *Monarch* was very much the exception to the rule and, for some time, Cosens had been under increasing local pressure to provide the occasional direct sailing from Weymouth to Cherbourg. Unable to do so without withdrawing *Monarch* from the lucrative Bournemouth station, they decided to charter an additional vessel for the summer of 1895.

The vessel selected was *India*, a large sea-going paddle tug, originally built for William Watkins in 1876 and employed by him during the summer months of 1890-93 on excursions from Margate. A striking vessel with a clipper bow and twin funnels set athwartships, she had been sold in 1894 to the Tees Tug & Lighter Company of Middlesbrough. Although at only 139 feet 8 inches in length she was far smaller than *Monarch*, she had a fine reputation as a seaboat and possessed the appropriate certificate to enable her to carry 196 passengers on cross-channel excursions. Her charter commenced on 19th July 1895 and would have lasted until 10th October had not her owners requested her early return to Sunderland, where she was urgently required to run passenger and liberty boat trips in connection with an unexpected visit by the Channel Fleet. Released by Cosens, she departed from Weymouth on 7th September, by which time she had completed six trips to Cherbourg and had provided welcome high-season capacity on several of the company's other routes.

In stark contrast to their rival's precarious state of survival, Cosens enjoyed a sound and broadly

INDIA arriving at Weymouth during the summer of 1895. The initials of her owners, The Tees Tug & Lighter Co, can be seen above her wheelhouse windows.

INDIA entering Weymouth Harbour. Behind, PREMIER can be seen moored to the Pile Pier.
AUTHOR'S COLLECTION/
SEWARD

pleasing year in 1895. Not only had they succeeded in forcing the subdued Bournemouth Company into a running agreement which had been desired for many years but their own passenger figures had increased by 12,000 to 221,580. Bournemouth passenger income alone had amounted to £10,500, compared with £2,500 only four years earlier, whilst during the season, *Monarch* had carried 59,175 passengers, berthed 1,345 times alongside various piers and steamed a total of 12,665 nautical miles.

It was true that there had been some heavy expenses during the year. *Victoria*, *Queen*, *Premier* and the steam launch *Princess* all required major

restoration of their boilers at the end of the season. *Premier* had had her entire after end re-plated and Castletown Pier at Portland had undergone extensive repairs. All this amounted to £4,308 in expenditure but the company's healthy financial state allowed this to be absorbed without difficulty. Indeed, it was also planned to fit a patent ventilator to *Monarch*'s dining saloon and electric light to *Empress*, while further capital was invested in the Devon Steamship Co who had placed an order for a second steamer, *Duke of Devonshire*. As with her sister, Cosens acted as consultants during her construction and were given the contract to fit her with electric lighting

PRINCESS in Weymouth Backwater
AUTHOR'S COLLECTION

and provide their patent beach landing gangway and other equipment.

Great satisfaction was derived from the increasingly broad basis of the company's other sources of income. Since the advent of Admiral Fitzroy, the trade with the Channel Fleet had become far more regular and profitable, whilst *Princess* and the company's other smaller steam launches were regularly engaged in servicing the breakwater forts and carrying members of the Royal Artillery garrison to and fro. Work had also just commenced on constructing two further breakwaters to fully enclose Portland Harbour, whilst employment on existing Government works at Portland was reported to be increasing. There were hopes expressed too that the company might obtain a contract to repair the torpedo boats based at the new depot in Portland Harbour. The engineering works and foundry beside Weymouth Backwater had, as planned, been redeveloped on a single site and fitted out with a variety of modern equipment, some of which had been designed and patented by the works manager, Mr Drake. Finally, the opportunity had been taken to purchase the remaining twenty years of the lease on the old-established ship-building yard, formerly operated by a Mr Carter, adjoining Cosens' main slipway. Work had immediately begun on installing a modern cradle and steam

hauling gear, and a large sheerlegs crane was under construction. Although somewhat smaller than the main slipway, this facility would enable Cosens to haul out and repair a wide range of yachts and smaller vessels and add considerably to their income.

As the year drew to a close, the *Southern Times* was moved to comment:

> *'It is not our custom to go out of our way to congratulate prosperous commercial concerns, but we look upon Cosens & Co. as a public institution of the highest importance to Weymouth, and as we should regard anything that would interfere with its continued development as a disaster to the town, we can with equal sincerity express gratification at the fact that such a large measure of success has attended the company's operations during the past year.'*

At the AGM, hopes were expressed that '*the comfortable and economical working arrangement*' between Cosens and the Bournemouth Company would '*never again be disturbed*' and Mr Sydenham, the Bournemouth agent, who had previously been eulogised '*as a man of war, defending their castle against all who might assail it*', was now praised for the '*judicious, careful and peaceable*' qualities which made him '*eminently fitted for making the most of the piping days of peace.*'

A snow-covered EMPRESS *slumbers in winter lay-up alongside Commercial Road in Weymouth Backwater. The land, which had been reclaimed from the sea, remained undeveloped until the mid 1880s, when a variety of quayside buildings began to be constructed. Cosens had held leases on five lots of 'Backwater land' as far back as 1868 but did not carry out major development of the site until 1893-4, when a wide range of workshops were built, backing onto their new foundry on West Street. Cosens' property extends from the third tall building with the flagstaff, to the point where the quay curves out of site.*

AUTHOR'S COLLECTION

MONARCH at the new Swanage Pier in 1897 or 1898. Designed by R. St. George Moore and built by Alfred Thorne, it was an unusual and elegant structure. The old pier, to the right, continued to be used as an overnight and coaling berth for the steamers and for landing fish and general cargo. The tramway was reduced from standard gauge (4 feet 8½ inches) to a narrow gauge of 2 feet 6 inches.
AUTHOR'S COLLECTION

CHAPTER 10

'RAPACIOUS STEAMERS FROM THE WEST'
1896-1902

As the winter proceeded it became apparent that, despite a relatively successful 1895 season, the Bournemouth Company's finances were still in a dire condition. In March 1896, it was announced that the company had gone into liquidation and been reconstituted as Bournemouth & South Coast Steam Packets Ltd. The liquidator, Mr J.T. Hamilton of Southampton, was invited to become a fresh member of the new board but the other two directors, Henry Newlyn (Mayor of Bournemouth) and James McWilliam, had long associations with the old company. Edward Bicker continued as secretary and manager.

Bicker enjoyed a cordial personal and professional relationship with Mr David Sydenham, Cosens' long-standing Bournemouth manager, and the two men ensured that the boardroom changes had no outward effect on the co-operative operating arrangements between the two companies. The 1896 season therefore got off to a relatively serene start on 30th March, when *Monarch* was the first steamer of the year to touch at Yarmouth Pier, with a large party from Swanage and Bournemouth. She continued in service all week, to be joined on Easter Weekend by *Empress* and the two ships of the Bournemouth Company.

At Weymouth, the early season activity was boosted by the presence of the Channel Fleet in the anchorage. On 2nd April, the steamers brought 2,000 men ashore to be dispatched on leave by special trains, returning them to their ships five days later. On 10th April, *Queen* was kept busy ferrying men of the Dorset Volunteer Artillery and the 1st Volunteer Brigade of the Dorset Regiment from both Weymouth and Portland, to visit the warships *Majestic*, *Magnificent* and *Royal Sovereign*. On Easter Monday, the men of the Channel Fleet staged a successful regatta in the bay with races for pinnaces, launches and cutters. Cosens provided barges to mark the start and finish lines, ran short trips to view the racing and generated unseasonably healthy income from Pile Pier tolls, as the public flocked to witness the festivities.

The main season opened, as usual, at Whitsun and the programme quickly settled into its accustomed pattern. *Victoria* remained the principal long distance steamer from Weymouth, offering sailings to Swanage and Bournemouth on Mondays and Saturdays; Lulworth on Wednesdays; and the long coasting trip either to Torquay or Dartmouth calling at West Bay, Lyme Regis, Seaton and Sidmouth on Thursdays. On Tuesdays and Fridays in high season she usually offered a long eastward excursion to either Yarmouth, Totland, Cowes,

Ventnor, Shanklin or Southsea but deviated from this pattern whenever an interesting alternative presented itself. During August, she went several times to view the Cowes Week regatta and the inspection of the Channel Fleet by Lui Hung Chang off Southsea, whilst from the middle of the month Teignmouth in Devon was adopted as her main Friday destination. In September, as the hours of daylight grew shorter, the westward trips were shortened to terminate at Exmouth and on Tuesday 8th, a special trip was offered to Torcross in Devon, departing at 9.00am and returning at 4pm, for a fare of 4s 2d.

On the days she went to Bournemouth, *Victoria* offered sailings from the pier while her Weymouth passengers were ashore and, conversely, *Monarch* frequently appeared at Weymouth and was able to offer Weymouthians a single late afternoon trip to Swanage or Bournemouth with an evening return by rail. Interestingly, no cross channel trips operated direct from Weymouth but intending passengers were conveyed instead by the 7.20am train to Swanage, where they joined *Monarch* for the crossing to either Alderney or Cherbourg for a fare of 8s.

Premier, *Queen* and *Albert Victor* maintained the ferry service to Portland at 10am, 11.30am, 2.30pm and 4.45pm, returning half an hour later, offered regular trips to view the Shambles Lightship and Portland Bill, and supplemented the Wednesday and Saturday sailings to Lulworth Cove. Whenever the fleet was in Portland, at least one major warship was thrown open to the public and full advantage was taken of this opportunity by offering a shuttle service for visitors, cruises round the warships and an increased frequency on the Portland service. The regular liberty boat service to the Channel Fleet also kept the smaller units of the fleet occupied at set intervals throughout the day.

At Bournemouth, the previous season's arrangements continued with *Empress* and *Lord Elgin* offering a joint Swanage service, while *Monarch* and *Brodick Castle* distributed the long distance sailings between them. On 15th August, *Monarch* went from Bournemouth, via Yarmouth and Ryde, to Worthing and Brighton but was seriously delayed in berthing at the latter when the pier staff initially refused to take her ropes. After a reduced period ashore, her passengers re-embarked for a 4pm departure, arriving back at Bournemouth at 8.30pm.

The main event of the season at Swanage was the opening of an elegant new pier. Constructed of greenheart timber, the 642 foot structure curved in a crescent shape slightly to the north of the original 1859 pier. The head of the new pier was higher than the main structure and was approached by two sets of stairs. A full length landing stage was constructed on either side and an additional berth was provided further towards the shore, on a small stage extending from the western side of the pier neck. Although *Lord Elgin* made the first steamer call on 1st May, construction continued throughout the season and it was not until 29th March 1897 that the completed structure was finally opened to all traffic. Although deprived of its passenger traffic, the original pier continued to be used as the overnight berth and coaling station for Cosens' Bournemouth steamers, as well as for the handling of commercial cargoes.

The closing weeks of the 1896 season were marked by a succession of severe gales, which seriously disrupted the steamer programme and led to a significant fall in passenger numbers. On Monday 21st September, for example, Cosens advertised a cheap excursion direct from Weymouth to Torquay and *Victoria* set out with 160 passengers on board in almost perfect weather. By midday, however, an ominous swell began to develop and shortly afterwards a strong southerly wind accompanied by torrential rain sprang up, causing the steamer to roll heavily in a beam sea. On arrival at Torquay, many of the bedraggled passengers opted for an immediate return by train. Anxious to be safely round Portland Bill before darkness fell, Capt Cox informed the remaining passengers that the ship would depart half an hour early, at 3.30pm. *Victoria* was less than an hour into her homeward passage, however, when the wind and sea increased so dramatically that Capt Cox decided the only prudent measure was to put the ship about and return to Torquay, from where the passengers were sent home by rail. *Victoria* remained gale bound at Torquay until Wednesday morning when, taking advantage of a slight improvement in the weather, she put to sea again. Conditions in Lyme Bay proved to be

atrocious and, as she approached Portland Bill, it became apparent that the combination of a southerly gale and ebb tide had whipped the notorious Portland Race into such a fury that it was far too dangerous to attempt the inshore passage between the Bill and the breakers. *Victoria*'s bow was therefore turned out into the Channel and, after battling with heavy head seas, she was eventually able to pass to the south of the Race and shape a course for the Shambles lightship and Weymouth, where she eventually arrived at 12.30pm.

The same fine weather on 21st September had also persuaded the master of the schooner *Glean* to sail from Bridport Harbour, only to find himself embayed and driven relentlessly towards the lee shore of Chesil Beach a few hours later by the rising gale. By good fortune and seamanship, the schooner managed to claw her way off shore and around Portland Bill. Unfortunately, by the time she was off Portland Breakwater her ballast had shifted and there was so much water in the hold that her master began burning flares. As the schooner drove rapidly to leeward across Weymouth Bay, *Albert Victor* put to sea and, after two attempts, was able to take the casualty in tow about half a mile off Osmington and bring her safely into harbour.

The fall in September revenue was offset to some extent by the increasing success of the works departments ashore. The excellent facilities offered by the two slipways and the newly-equipped engineering works were attracting trade from all around the locality and, to provide stock work for the employees in slacker moments, the company had begun building steam pinnaces. The boats measured 22 feet by 5 feet by 2 feet 6 inches, were designed to carry both passengers and up to a ton of cargo, and were built of elm with teak top strakes and decks. The engines were 5ihp tandem, surface condensing compound, powered by a vertical boiler with a working pressure of 125psi. Hulls, engines and boilers were all designed and constructed by Cosens' own staff. The first boat was launched on 12th October, achieved 8 knots on trials and was described as being '*nicely cushioned, with an air of comfort and respectability throughout.*' The intention was to advertise the new boats for sale and, if buyers were not forthcoming, to let them on hire for private fishing and excursion parties during the summer months. Cosens' boat building department must have been very busy at this time for, in addition to the new pinnace, October also saw the completion of ten lerrets for the Admiralty and a number of square-sterned boats for use on the breakwater works.

Another interesting piece of work for the shore staff was the provision of fittings and equipment for the Devon Steamship Co's new paddle steamer *Duke of Devonshire*, which had been built by R. & H. Green and engined by John Penn & Sons of Greenwich under the supervision of Cosens' manager Mr S.J. Fowler. Cosens invested in the new ship by purchasing a block of preference shares and received

The building of the Devon Steamship Co's DUKE OF DEVONSHIRE and her near sister DUCHESS OF DEVONSHIRE was supervised by Cosens, who also fitted the patent beach landing gear, searchlight and other equipment. In 1938, the DUKE, seen here backing away from a south Devon beach, joined Cosens' fleet as CONSUL.

AUTHOR'S COLLECTION

THE BOURNEMOUTH, BOSCOMBE, SWANAGE, AND WEYMOUTH STEAM PACKET COMPANY
(Cosens & Co., Limited.) Estd. 1852.

The above Company's fast and splendidly equipped Passenger Steamships

MONARCH AND EMPRESS

Are appointed to carry out the Excursions named below, weather and circumstances permitting.

N.B. Arrangements have been made whereby the Season Tickets of this Company are available on the Steamers of the Bournemouth Local Company between Bournemouth and Swanage as last year, and until further notice at Half First-class Fare, on the "Brodick Castle" on excursions to Teignmouth, Torquay, Dartmouth, Brighton or Worthing.

RAILWAY, PIER, &c., ARRANGEMENTS.

Passengers by this Company's Boats may, on production of Steamer Ticket to the ISLE OF WIGHT Central Railway Co. travel by rail from Yarmouth to Cowes, Sandown or Ryde (St. John's Road), or vice versa, rejoining the boats at Ryde or Yarmouth, at Special low Single Fares—First Class 1s. 6d., Third 1s. 3d. between Cowes and Ryde (St. John's Road); 1s. 3d., and 1s. between Cowes and Yarmouth; 6d. and 4d. Yarmouth and Freshwater.

At VENTNOR or SHANKLIN Station passengers, on production of their Steamer Ticket, travel by Rail from thence to Ryde Pier Head, First Class 2s, 3d., Second Class 1s. 6d., SANDOWN 1s. 9d. First Class, 1s 3d. Second, rejoining the Steamer at Ryde.

For the convenience of Residents in the Island CIRCULAR TICKETS available by Steamer from Ventnor to Ryde, returning by Railway, are issued on board in connection with the excursion ; Fare, First Class 4s., Second Class 2s.

Passengers having travelled by the Steamer to WEYMOUTH or PORTSMOUTH, but desiring to return by rail, can do so at special reduced fares upon production to the Booking Clerk at the respective Railway Stations of a Steamboat Voucher to be had on application to the Captain of the steamer.

LAMBERT'S COACH runs in connection with the "Monarch" between YARMOUTH and FRESHWATER BAY.

SATURDAY, JULY 11TH, SPECIAL CHEAP LONG DAY EXCURSION

ROUND the ISLE of WIGHT, SHANKLIN, RYDE & PORTSMOUTH
GIVING OVER 5 HOURS ON SHORE AT EITHER PLACE.
Leaving Swanage at 7, Bournemouth at 8, Boscombe 8.15 ; returning from Southsea at 5.30, Ryde 5.50, on arrival of train leaving Shanklin 5.15, due at Ryde 5.35.
Fare Three Shillings. Season Ticket Holders' 2s.

BOURNEMOUTH AND SWANAGE DAILY SERVICE.
The EMPRESS, in conjunction with the LORD ELGIN, will leave
BOURNEMOUTH for Swanage at 10.15, 10.45, 12, 2.30, 3, 4.30, 5.15 and 6.15
SWANAGE for Bournemouth at 9.15, 11, 12.15, 1, 3.30, 4.30 and 5.30
BOSCOMBE for Bournemouth and Swanage at 10, and 2.30.
The Steamer leaving Swanage at 12.15, 1, 4.30 and 5.30, proceeds to Bournemouth and Boscombe.
On WEDNESDAY the Morning times will be the same. The Afternoon times Bournemouth to Swanage at 3, 3.30 and 5.30, returning at 4, 5 and 7.

MONDAY, JULY 13TH.

WEYMOUTH, giving about Three hours on shore
PASSING THROUGH THE POWERFUL CHANNEL FLEET
In Portland Roads, about to depart for the summer evolutions.
Leaving Boscombe at 9.45, Bournemouth 10.30, Swanage at 11 o'clock ; returning from Weymouth at 4 o'clock to Swanage, Bournemouth and Boscombe.

TUESDAY, JULY 14TH.

ROUND THE ISLE OF WIGHT, & SOUTHSEA
CALLING AT VENTNOR & RYDE.
Leaving Swanage at 9.15, Bournemouth 10.30, Boscombe 10.40, Ventnor 12.45 ; returning from Southsea Pier at 3.30, Ryde at 4 o'clock, on arrival of the train leaving Ventnor at 3.10. Note Railway arrangements above.

WEDNESDAY, JULY 15TH,

A RUN UP POOLE HARBOUR and the Wareham Channel
Passing Branksea Island and Castle, giving views of the beautiful scenery of Parkstone, the upper reaches of Poole Harbour, northern side of the Isle of Purbeck, &c.
Leaving Boscombe at 10, Bournemouth at 10.30 ; arriving back by 1 o'clock.
FARE—2/- FIRST-CLASS, 1/6 SECOND

Early Closing Excursion to WEYMOUTH
Leaving Boscombe at 2.30 (by Empress), Bournemouth at 3 o'clock, Swanage at 3.30 ; returning at 7 o'clock. Fare 2/-
And to SWANAGE at 3 o'clock, Fare 2/- & 1/-, and at 3.30 & 5.30, Fare 1/-, returning at 4, 5 and 7.

THURSDAY, JULY 16TH,

WORTHING AND BRIGHTON
CALLING AT RYDE.
Giving 2 hours on shore at Brighton, nearly 4 at Worthing.
Leaving Swanage at 7.30, Bournemouth at 8.30, Boscombe at 8.40, Ryde 10.45 ; returning from Brighton at 4, Worthing at 4.45, Ryde 6.45.
Fare—First Class 6s., Second 5s. Season and Short Term Ticket Holders of both Bournemouth Steampacket Companies 3s.

FRIDAY, JULY 17TH,

YARMOUTH (FOR FRESHWATER AND CARISBROOKE), COWES AND PORTSMOUTH
Leaving Swanage at 9.15, Bournemouth 10.30, Boscombe 10.40, Yarmouth 11.45 ; returning from Southsea Pier at 3.15, Cowes at 4 o'clock, Yarmouth at 4.45.

SATURDAY, JULY 18TH,

Totland Bay and Southampton
FOR THE DOCKS, ATLANTIC STEAMSHIPS, &c.
Leaving Swanage at 9.15, Bournemouth 10.30, Boscombe 10.40, Totland 11.45, returning from Southampton at 3.30, Totland at 4.45.

The Directors reserve to themselves the right of making any alteration in the above Programme which the exigencies of the weather, traffic, or other circumstances may require.

RETURN FARES. BOURNEMOUTH TO	1ST CLASS s. d.	2ND CLASS s. d.	RETURN FARES. SWANAGE TO	1ST CLASS s. d.	2ND CLASS s. d.
Swanage	2 0		Bournemouth		1 6
Lulworth	3 6	2 6	Lulworth	3 0	2 0
Weymouth	4 0	3 0	Weymouth	3 6	2 6
Totland Bay	4 6	3 0	Totland Bay	3 0	2 6
Yarmouth	5 0	2 6	Yarmouth	3 6	3 0
Cowes	4 6	2 6	Cowes	4 0	3 0
Ryde or Portsmouth	4 6	3 6	Ryde or Portsmouth	4 0	3 0
Southampton	4 6	3 6	Southampton	5 0	4 0
Ventnor, Shanklin or Sandown	4 0	3 0	Ventnor, Shanklin or Sandown	4 6	5 6
Round the Isle of Wight	5 0	4 0	Round the Isle of Wight	5 6	4 6
Between Yarmouth and Ryde or Portsmouth				3 0	2 6
Between Yarmouth and Cowes				2 0	1 6

The Terms of the Contract between Passengers and the Company are set forth on the respective Tickets.
Children between 3 and 12 years of age Half-price. Dogs charged full passenger fare.

REFRESHMENTS ON BOARD AT MODERATE CHARGES.

All information may be obtained of the Local Manager, D. SYDENHAM, Bournemouth ; Captain W. COSENS, the Company's Office, Swanage ; or of the Managing Director, S. J. FOWLER, at the Head Office of the Company, Custom House Quay, Weymouth.

BY ORDER, D. SYDENHAM, LOCAL MANAGER.

Office—Royal Marine Library, Bournemouth.

SYDENHAM, PRINTER, BOURNEMOUTH.

STEAMER EXCURSION SEASON, 1896.
THE BOURNEMOUTH, BOSCOMBE, SWANAGE, AND WEYMOUTH STEAM PACKET COMPANY,
(Cosens & Co., Limited.) Estd. 1852. Season 1896.

The above Company's fast and splendidly equipped Passenger Steamship

MONARCH

Is appointed to carry out the Excursions named below, weather and circumstances permitting.

NOTE.—During the remainder of the season arrangements are made by which the Season Tickets of both Bournemouth Companies are available on either steamer that may be running.

RAILWAY, PIER, &c. ARRANGEMENTS.

At VENTNOR or SHANKLIN Station passengers, on production of their Steamer Ticket, travel by Rail from thence to Ryde Pier Head, First Class 2s, 3d., Second Class 1s. 6d., SANDOWN 1s. 9d. First Class, 1s. 3d. Second, rejoining the Steamer at Ryde.

Passengers having travelled by the Steamer to WEYMOUTH or PORTSMOUTH, but desiring to return by rail, can do so at special reduced fares upon production of a Steamboat Voucher to be had on application to the Captain of the Steamer.

LAMBERT'S COACH runs in connection with the "Monarch" between YARMOUTH and FRESHWATER BAY.

SATURDAY, SEPTEMBER 26TH,

TOTLAND BAY (ISLE OF WIGHT) AND SOUTHAMPTON
FOR THE DOCKS, ATLANTIC STEAMSHIPS, &c.
Leaving Swanage at 9.15, Bournemouth 10.30, Boscombe 10.40, Totland 11.45 ; returning from Southampton at 3, Totland at 4.15.
Giving Four hours at Totland Bay and Two hours at Southampton, time for a visit to the Docks and splendid ocean passenger steamers.

The MONARCH will leave Swanage daily at 9.15.

MONDAY, SEPTEMBER 28TH,

ROUND THE ISLE OF WIGHT
CALLING AT VENTNOR & RYDE.
Leaving Swanage at 9.15, Bournemouth at 10.30, Boscombe 10.40, Ventnor 12.45 ; leaving Ryde on the return at 3 o'clock on arrival of the train leaving Ventnor at 2.10.
Note Railway arrangements above. Bournemouth to Swanage at 5.30.

TUESDAY, SEPTEMBER 29TH.

SWANAGE for CORFE CASTLE
The Great Globe, Tilly Whim Caves, Anvil Lighthouse, &c.
Leaving Bournemouth at 10.45 and 3 o'clock (Boscombe at 10 and 2.30), returning from Swanage for Bournemouth and Boscombe at 12.15 and 4.45.
Bournemouth to Boscombe and Swanage at 5.30.

WEDNESDAY, SEPTEMBER 30TH,

Morning Cruise to TOTLAND BAY (Isle of Wight)
Leaving Bournemouth at 10.30, Boscombe 10.40, returning from Totland at 1 o'clock. Giving about One hour on shore. FARE 2/-

THE LAST EARLY CLOSING EXCURSION OF THE SEASON.

A 3 hours cruise UP POOLE HARBOUR
the WAREHAM CHANNEL, thence by OLD HARRY ROCKS to DURLSTONE HEAD, ANVIL POINT, &c.
Leaving Bournemouth at 3, Boscombe at 3.15, returning to Boscombe & Bournemouth about 6 o'clock. FARE 1/6. Bournemouth to Swanage at 6 o'clock.

THURSDAY, OCTOBER 1ST,

SWANAGE for CORFE CASTLE
The Great Globe, Tilly Whim Caves, Anvil Lighthouse, &c.
Leaving Bournemouth at 10.45 and 3 o'clock (Boscombe at 10 and 2.30), returning from Swanage for Bournemouth and Boscombe at 12.15 and 4.45.
Bournemouth to Boscombe and Swanage at 5.30.

FRIDAY, OCTOBER 2ND,
THE CHANNEL FLEET AGAIN IN PORTLAND ROADS.

WEYMOUTH, giving about 2 hours on shore
And by permission of the Commanding Officer One hour on board

H.M. Battleship RESOLUTION in Portland Roads
Leaving Boscombe at 10, Bournemouth at 10.30, Swanage at 11 o'clock ; returning from Weymouth at 3.30 to Swanage, Bournemouth and Boscombe.

SATURDAY, OCTOBER 3RD,

SWANAGE for CORFE CASTLE
The Great Globe, Tilly Whim Caves, Anvil Lighthouse, &c.
Leaving Bournemouth at 10.45 and 3 o'clock (Boscombe at 10 and 2.30), returning from Swanage for Bournemouth and Boscombe at 12.15 and 4.45.
Bournemouth to Boscombe at Swanage at 5.30.

The Directors reserve to themselves the right of making any alteration in the above Programme which the exigencies of the weather, traffic, or other circumstances may require.

RETURN FARES. BOURNEMOUTH TO	1ST CLASS s. d.	2ND CLASS s. d.	RETURN FARES. SWANAGE TO	1ST CLASS s. d.	2ND CLASS s. d.
Swanage	2 0	1 6	Bournemouth	2 0	1 6
Weymouth	4 0	3 0	Weymouth	3 6	2 6
Totland Bay	4 6	3 0	Totland Bay	3 0	2 6
Southampton	4 6	3 6	Southampton	5 0	4 0
Round the Isle of Wight	5 0	4 0	Round the Isle of Wight	5 6	4 6

The Terms of the Contract between Passengers and the Company are set forth on the respective Tickets.
Children between 3 and 12 years of age Half-price. Dogs charged full passenger fare.

REFRESHMENTS ON BOARD AT MODERATE CHARGES.

All information may be obtained of the Local Manager, D. SYDENHAM, Bournemouth ; Captain W. COSENS, the Company's Office, Swanage ; or of the Managing Director, S. J. FOWLER, at the Head Office of the Company, Custom House Quay, Weymouth.

BY ORDER, D. SYDENHAM, LOCAL MANAGER.

Office—Royal Marine Library, Bournemouth.

SYDENHAM, PRINTER, BOURNEMOUTH.

Two Cosens' Bournemouth bills for 1896, showing fascinating details of the high-season, two-ship operation in July, compared with MONARCH's lone service in the closing days of the season. Note also the comprehensive arrangements for connecting railway and coach services. AUTHOR'S COLLECTION

a sub-contract to provide the ship's capstans, steering gear, lifeboats, beach landing gear and deck seats. They also installed electric lighting, including a powerful searchlight mounted just ahead of her funnel. Having run trials on the Thames, the new steamer called at Weymouth on 5th July, where she was thrown open to public inspection before proceeding to her new home port of Exmouth. Many years later, in 1938, *Duke of Devonshire* was purchased by Cosens and, renamed *Consul*, served the firm until 1962.

The winter of 1896-7 passed without any major salvage jobs but *Albert Victor* did sustain considerable damage whilst engaged in a piece of routine towage. On the night of 8th December, whilst bringing a three-masted schooner into Weymouth, she had just slipped the tow rope and manoeuvred to one side of the harbour to allow the schooner to slip past into her berth, when disaster struck. The schooner '*smelled the ground*' and sheered suddenly towards the tug. Rather than have his funnel carried away by the schooner's bowsprit, Capt Hardy elected to collide intentionally with the mooring chains of *Monarch*, which was laid up for the winter in a berth under the Nothe Fort. Sadly, however, this was not enough to take him out of danger. The advancing bowsprit swept the tug's lifeboat, davits, chocks and bridge rails overboard and pressed her so heavily against *Monarch* that her anchor was forced in through her bow plating and the decorative scroll work destroyed. A number of seats on the foredeck were also badly damaged and *Monarch*'s moorings

were severed. The bill for repairs came to £32, a substantial sum for the time.

The year 1897 is chiefly remembered for the tremendous naval review held at Spithead on 26th June, as a climax to the nation's celebration of Queen Victoria's Diamond Jubilee year. Cosens quite naturally looked forward to the substantial additional trade which would be generated by this event but never for one moment anticipated the profound effect it was to have on the future pattern of trade at Bournemouth and on the development of their own fleet.

The Jubilee celebrations aside, the season was unremarkable. The programme of sailings and the running arrangements with the Bournemouth Company continued unaltered, although poor weather during the high season led to a fall of 16,000 passengers compared with the previous year, whilst the absence of the Fleet from Portland for most of the summer meant that 55,000 less sailors were carried by the liberty boats. Weymouth was rocked by the collapse of the local bank, an event which caused financial disaster to many individuals and businesses in the area, and had an inevitable effect on Cosens' order books. Fortunately, the company itself banked with the Capital & Counties Bank of London and therefore escaped any direct loss. The only unusual trip recorded took place on 10th July, when *Monarch* landed passengers at Freshwater Bay on the south-western tip of the Isle of Wight. Fortunately, weather conditions were perfect, allowing the steamer to anchor whilst her passengers were ferried ashore in small boats.

Taking advantage of the temporary fall in demand for liberty boats, Cosens were able to withdraw *Albert Victor* for a major refit. A steep increase in demand for cross-channel towage had dictated that both reliability and improved fuel economy were essential, so it was decided to replace her boilers and convert her engine to surface condensing. The new components were supplied by J.P. Reynoldson of South Shields, the original builders of the ship's engine, but all other work was carried out by Cosens' staff. The new 10-ton sheerlegs crane beside the No. 2 slipway was used to lift out the old machinery and the engine was transported to the Backwater engineering works for a complete overhaul, re-erection and the fitting of the new condenser. Meanwhile, the tug was placed on the No. 1 slipway for restoration of her hull. When all was finished, the engine and new boilers were lifted on board, new decks were laid and the ship was back in service in time for the Whitsun Bank Holiday, 1897.

The high spot of the season was, of course, the Diamond Jubilee Review itself, the largest display of naval might ever assembled anywhere in the world. As the great day approached, 173 British warships, including 21 battleships and 39 cruisers, together with numerous foreign men-of-war, formed themselves into several lines each five miles long. Excursion steamers from all over Britain

In Celebration of the Queen's Diamond Jubilee, 1837-1897.

flocked to Spithead to witness the spectacle. Some had been sent by their owners, other chartered by local syndicates or travel agents such as Thomas Cook and most were based at either Southampton or Portsmouth. In addition to the numerous steamers deployed by the various local companies, visiting ships included *Britannia*, *Cambria*, *Westward Ho* and *Lorna Doone* from the Bristol Channel; *La Marguerite*, *Koh-I-Noor*, *Oriole*, *Philomel* and *Halcyon* from the Thames; *Duke of Devonshire* from Exmouth; *Solway* from Grimsby; *India*, *Cynthia*, *Brighton Queen*, *Warrior*, *Bonnie Princess*, the French *Jupiter* and the White Star tender *Magentic*. In the days leading up to the review, these ships offered a staggering array of sailings and there were reports of steamers laying four abreast at Ryde Pier to embark passengers.

On the great day itself, both *Monarch* and *Brodick Castle* sailed from Swanage and Bournemouth, via Boscombe and Yarmouth, to view the assembled fleet, before coming to anchor while the review itself took place. In the evening, they set off again to view the fireworks and illuminations, returning to Bournemouth at 1am and 4am respectively the following morning. Demand for tickets, even at the premium prices charged, was unprecedented and it is recorded that it '*vexed the heart*' of David Sydenham to turn away so many potential passengers. Since the numerous visiting steamers which were reported to be present at Bournemouth that morning were also full to capacity, it remains a mystery why Cosens did not allocate more ships to the review. Although no conclusive records survive,

it appears that *Empress* and *Lord Elgin* remained on the Swanage service and that neither *Victoria* nor *Premier* were sent along from Weymouth.

Monarch left Swanage at 8am, Bournemouth at 9.00am, collected a party of pre-booked passengers at Yarmouth and arrived in Spithead at noon. She steamed slowly between C and D lines of the fleet, before turning and retracing her course between A and B lines. *Monarch* happened to have the Italian ensign in place of honour amongst her bunting and,

An overall impression of the 1897 Golden Jubilee Review, showing how the fleet was positioned and with the Royal review flotilla passing through from right to left.
AUTHOR'S COLLECTION

John Geach Rowe, JP, had been a director of Cosens & Co Ltd since 1883 and succeeded G.E. Eliott as chairman in 1897. He held the post for twenty four years until his death in 1921, when he was replaced by Thomas Lynes (1921-38).
AUTHOR'S COLLECTION

on passing the Italian cruiser *Lepanto*, was cheered by her crew. Shortly after 1pm, she came to anchor in her allocated spot amongst the other pleasure steamers and her passengers took full advantage of the excellent catering laid on by Mr Graham and his staff in the dining saloon.

At 2pm precisely, a signal gun was fired and the Trinity House yacht *Irene* led the Royal review flotilla out of Portsmouth Harbour. The Royal party embarked on *Victoria & Albert*, followed by *Elfin* and the P&O liner *Carthage* carrying distinguished foreign visitors. Next came *Enchantress* with the Lords of the Admiralty, *Wildfire* with Mr Chamberlain and the colonial Premiers, *Eldorado* with ambassadors, the liners *Danube* and *Campania* with members of the Houses of Lords and Commons respectively, *Fire Queen* with the C-in-C Portsmouth and finally *Escort* with the Mayor and corporation of Portsmouth on board.

This remarkable convoy steamed regally up and down the lines of warships and, as it passed the spot where *Monarch* was anchored, Capt Bowering quietly weighed anchor and, ignoring the shouted instructions of several irate naval patrol officers, proceeded to steam the whole length of the outside line precisely parallel with the Royal Yacht. Thousands of passengers on board the other pleasure steamers looked on with mingled chagrin and amazement at Capt Bowering's daring, while those on board *Monarch* experienced unsurpassed views of the proceedings all the way to Cowes. From there she headed straight for Bournemouth, arriving during a tremendous thunder storm to embark passengers for the evening illuminations cruise. On the homeward voyage, the passengers raised an eight guinea subscription for distribution amongst the officers and crew as a mark of appreciation for their memorable day afloat. Capt Bowering's exploits

were exceeded only by those of Sir Charles Parsons who, in a determined attempt to show off the potential of the world's first steam turbine vessel *Turbinia*, famously sped through the lines of the fleet at 32 knots, shaking off all attempts by naval patrol vessels to catch him.

The evening cruise to the illuminations was conducted in steady rain. *Monarch* and *Brodick Castle* anchored near the liner *Campania*, which had an excellent band on board and were thus able to benefit from a free concert, while their passengers marvelled at the spectacle of hundreds of illuminated ships whose displays of rockets, fireworks and searchlights appeared to turn night into day. The fleet remained in Spithead for a number of days after the review and the illuminations were repeated on the evening of Monday 28th June, with sailings continuing until the warships began to disperse.

With the excitement over, the visiting excursion steamers returned to their home ports and everyone expected the pattern of sailings on the south coast to return to its familiar rhythm. This, however, was not to be. P. & A. Campbell Ltd, the Bristol Channel steamer operators who had sent their magnificent new steamers *Britannia*, *Cambria* and *Westward Ho* round for the review, had quickly realised their superiority over all the existing local vessels and decided that a good profit was to be made from basing *Cambria* at Southampton for the rest of the season.

Cambria was 225 feet long and boasted a full length promenade deck, superior passenger accommodation and a speed of some 20 knots. From her Southampton base, she made her first sailing around the Isle of Wight, calling at Ryde and Southsea, on 7th August and the following day paid her first visit to Bournemouth. Her weekly

P. & A. Campbell Ltd's
CAMBRIA, whose arrival on
the South Coast sparked a
period of fierce competition at
Bournemouth.

timetables included sailings to Brighton, the Isle of Wight piers, round the Island, a cross-channel trip to Boulogne and, most significantly from Cosens' point of view, regular trips to Boscombe, Bournemouth and Weymouth. The Weymouth sailings touched at Bournemouth and Swanage *en route* and *Cambria*'s glamorous appearance and cheap fares quickly began to tempt passengers away from the local vessels. The interloper's effect was felt chiefly by the Southampton Company and other Solent operators in whose territory she was based but her impact at Bournemouth was sufficient for Cosens to announce '*a defensive and offensive alliance*' with the Bournemouth Company and the cutting of fares on the Bournemouth to Swanage and Weymouth routes. The Isle of Wight press was loud in its praises of the Campbell steamer and when she ended her season on 29th September, departing for winter lay up in Bristol, Cosens' relief must have been tempered by the announcement that she would be returning far earlier in 1898 to begin a second season on the south coast. After four years of relative calm, a new era of competition had begun.

On 2nd September, a serious, if somewhat amusing, incident occurred in Weymouth Harbour. *Brodick Castle*, which had just landed 300 passengers from Bournemouth, was laying alongside the pier when she was run into by the incoming Channel Islands mail steamer *Reindeer*, whose bows wrecked her port lifeboat and completely demolished one of the sponson side houses where the gentlemen's lavatories were situated. A passenger who was using the facilities at the time was extricated from the debris with some difficulty, badly bruised and with his dignity severely compromised! Cosens' shore staff undertook emergency repairs to *Brodick Castle*, which returned to Poole later that evening while her passengers were sent home by rail.

At the end of the season it was announced that Capt Bowering of *Monarch* would be retiring due to ill health and would be replaced for the 1898 season by Capt Cox from *Victoria*. Capt St. Barbe Rawle was promoted from *Empress* to *Victoria*. At Swanage, Capt William Cosens came to the end of his last season as the company's agent. Since he retired from active command in 1889, Cosens had been looking after the company's seasonal interests from an office on the south side of the High Street near the pier but, with his health failing fast, now retired permanently to his home in Weymouth. In February 1898, he was formally replaced by Mr Alfred Ward, who acted as joint agent for both Cosens and the Bournemouth Company.

Cosens' concerns about the competition, although serious, were as nothing compared with those of the Southampton Company, whose interests had been directly and successfully threatened by *Cambria*'s predatory presence in their home waters. In order to meet her challenge, they commissioned a design for a comparable paddle steamer but unrest in the shipbuilding industry made it impossible to have her built in time for the 1898 season. Instead, they sought to charter a suitable vessel for the interim period and their choice fell on *Lorna Doone*, a steamer which had received very complimentary notices during her brief visit to the Spithead Review during the previous season.

Lorna Doone had been built for Edwards, Robertson & Co of Cardiff to compete with the P. & A. Campbell fleet in the Bristol Channel trade. At the end of 1895 she had passed to John Gunn of Cardiff, who chartered her to a Brighton company during 1896 before rejoining the fray on the Bristol Channel for the 1897 season, at the end of which he too succumbed to Campbell's superiority. Gunn was only interested in selling the ship and, unable to locate any other suitable candidate for charter, the Southampton Company purchased her in April 1898. Although a little slower than *Cambria* and designed with an open foredeck, she was of a very similar size and boasted extensive and comfortable passenger accommodation.

Lorna Doone's first public excursion took her to Bournemouth and Swanage on Easter Monday, 11th April 1898 and it quickly became apparent that the Southampton Company intended to use her on very similar routes to *Cambria*. Campbells, who must have been very irritated that they had permitted such a suitable ship to fall into the hands of their opponents, returned to the fray on Whit Saturday, 28th May and a few weeks later upped the stakes by sending a second steamer, *Glen Rosa*, to join *Cambria* on the South Coast.

Both companies ran regularly to Bournemouth and, more seriously from Cosens' point of view, to Swanage or Weymouth, touching at Bournemouth to collect passengers *en route*. To make matters worse, a price-cutting war ensued. In 1897, *Cambria*'s passengers had been able to travel from the Solent to Bournemouth for 2s 6d or 3s 6d first class. By May 1898 this had fallen to 2s and by early July to 1s. The Southampton Company was forced to follow suit and by mid July it was possible to sail to Weymouth, Bournemouth, Brighton or round the

Lorna Doone, purchased by the Southampton Company in 1898 to counter the threat posed by CAMBRIA, *added considerably to the pressure felt by Cosens at Bournemouth.*
AUTHOR'S COLLECTION

Seen here in Swanage Bay, the Poole-based screw steamer ALERT *ran in opposition to Cosens between 1898 and 1900. In August 1899, however, she seems either to have been chartered by or to have run in co-operation with Cosens for, together with their regular steamers and the chartered* CYNTHIA, *she appeared on the company's sailing bills.*
DORSET COUNTY MUSEUM

MONARCH *departs from Weymouth, with the Pile Pier and seafront in the background.*
AUTHOR'S COLLECTION

Island for a flat fare of 1s by either company's ships.

Cosens watched these developments with dismay. On most days of the week, Bournemouth Pier was now being visited by steamers far superior to anything the local fleet could offer and which, with their high speed and low fares, were tempting away an increasing proportion of Cosens' traditional passengers. Early in the season, as soon as the opposition began to bite, a decision was reached in consultation with the Bournemouth Company to reduce fares on the Bournemouth to Swanage service by 30 per cent. Unfortunately, the resulting loss in revenue was compounded by the unseasonably cold and windy weather which kept visitors away from the seaside until mid July, by which time earnings were some £2,500 below expectations.

As if competition from Campbells and the Southampton Company was not enough, the Poole Towing & Passenger Steamers Ltd decided in 1898 to place a small, twin screw steamer named *Alert* on

service from Bournemouth. As well as regular trips to Poole and a three cornered Bournemouth –Swanage –Poole service, her programme included excursions to Lulworth, round the Shambles lightship, Alum Bay, Totland Bay and Lymington. In subsequent seasons, calls were also made at Warsash and possibly at Studland, and she continued in service until the end of 1900, when she was sold to new owners at Newhaven.

Matters were made even worse by a steep rise in the price of bunker coal, although some comfort was derived from the fact that Cosens' relatively economical ships were less seriously effected than coal-hungry flyers owned by the rival companies. Economies were made by using cheaper coal on board the tugs but, in order to avoid passenger complaints about excessive smoke and damage to clothing from soot and hot embers falling on deck, there was no option but to continue to use the best Welsh steam coal on board the passenger ships.

Fortunately, the weather improved dramatically from the beginning of August and September proved to be something of an Indian summer, with visitors flocking back to the coast and patronising the steamers in large numbers, reducing the shortfall on Cosens' passenger revenue to just over £1,000 by the end of the season.

On 12th August, *Monarch* was about three hours into the return voyage from Cherbourg on one of her regular cross-channel trips when the officers picked out a lighthouse on the English coast. Assuming it to be on Anvil Point near Swanage, neither Capt John Cox nor the mate Mr Anderson bothered to confirm its identity and it was not until two hours later that it was discovered to be St. Catherine's on the Isle of Wight. By now the ship was seriously off course and was very late in arriving

back at Bournemouth Pier. The directors took an extremely serious view of the officers' failure '*to use the ordinary means adopted by mariners to test the character of every light they saw before using it for their guidance*' and demoted both men with immediate effect. Capt Cox was moved to *Premier* and replaced by Capt Rawle from *Victoria*. Albert Masters moved from *Empress* to *Victoria* and was in turn replaced by Capt Alfred Cox from *Premier*. Despite a petition from his many friends and supporters in Bournemouth, mate Anderson was required to swap places with Mr Pearce from *Empress*. Cosens' management was extremely proud of its unbroken record of passenger safety and had no intention of allowing standards to fall. Capt Alfred Cox's promotion did not last very long since, at the end of the season, he was given one month's notice, as was Capt Pearce of *Queen*. It was stated that '*while both were excellent seamen, and may be well suited to large, ocean-going steamers, they had proved themselves incapable of handling our much smaller craft, leading to great risk and consequent damage.*' Their dismissal is a reminder of the tremendous skills required by pleasure steamer skippers, who navigated close inshore along a busy coast in all weathers, without the aid of any modern navigational aids, and berthed their ships many times each day at a wide variety of piers and jetties.

On 12th September, *Lorna Doone*, on passage from Bournemouth to Weymouth, broke down off St. Albans Head with feed pump trouble. At the request of the coastguard, Cosens immediately dispatched one of their paddle tugs from Weymouth and must have been very frustrated when, just as the tug drew alongside, successful repairs to *Lorna Doone* allowed her to get under way again. There would have been great satisfaction and propaganda value in towing the rival flagship into port but, in the end, they had to be content with enjoying the critical press reports of her passengers' long delay at Weymouth and their subsequent difficulties in returning to the Isle of Wight by train and ferry.

As the season drew to a close it became apparent that the severe competition and rising fuel costs had hit the delicate finances of the Bournemouth Company very badly. A loss of £800 was declared and, as had become almost the norm, no dividend was issued to shareholders. Cosens, once again, was assisted by the broad and diverse nature of its other trading departments and was able to declare a 5 per cent dividend. In order to ensure that this remained the case the company's memorandum of association was altered in June 1898 to broaden its aims and allow the development of whatever electrical, mechanical or contracting work might present itself in the future.

During 1898, the salvage and diving departments were presented with a number of jobs which generated a useful income for the company. In April, the coal hulk *Patrick Henry* sank at her moorings in Portland Harbour with 800 tons of coal on board. After an Irish firm failed in their efforts to salvage

the vessel, being forced to abandon their contract, the hulk and her cargo were sold at public auction for £10 to Cosens. They immediately set to work using barges, mechanical grabs and divers to remove 600 tons of her cargo. With that accomplished, lifting barges and tugs were used to raise her off the seabed. At each low tide the lifting cables were winched tight and at each high water the wreck was pulled a little closer to the shore. Eventually, she was in sufficiently shallow water for divers to fit collision mats over the various holes in her hull and, with the four large salvage pumps on board *Queen* and *Albert Victor* working hard, she was soon afloat and riding happily at anchor. The remaining coal was discharged and the hulk sold to the highest bidder.

On 17th June, a large liner, *Briton*, homeward bound from Capetown to Southampton, grounded

In a former life, Cosens' diving boat was the original Weymouth Lifeboat AGNES HARRIET, which was donated to the RNLI by the Earl of Strafford in 1868. Following her replacement on station by FRIERN WATCH in 1887, she was looked after by her former coxswain, Francis Carter, until 1891, when he sold her to Cosens for £5 and a ton of coal. She remained in use as their diving boat until the late 1930s. In the first view, ABOVE, the diver is seen climbing back on board while one of the crew is just opening the lid of the large, hand-cranked air pump. The second view, BELOW LEFT, shows the diver preparing to descend, while one of the crew stands ready to crank the air pump. The vessel was eventually sold by Cosens for use as a local fishing boat and is said to have been wrecked on Portland Breakwater in the 1950s.
TOP: AUTHOR'S COLLECTION
BOTTOM: BRIAN JACKSON
COLLECTION

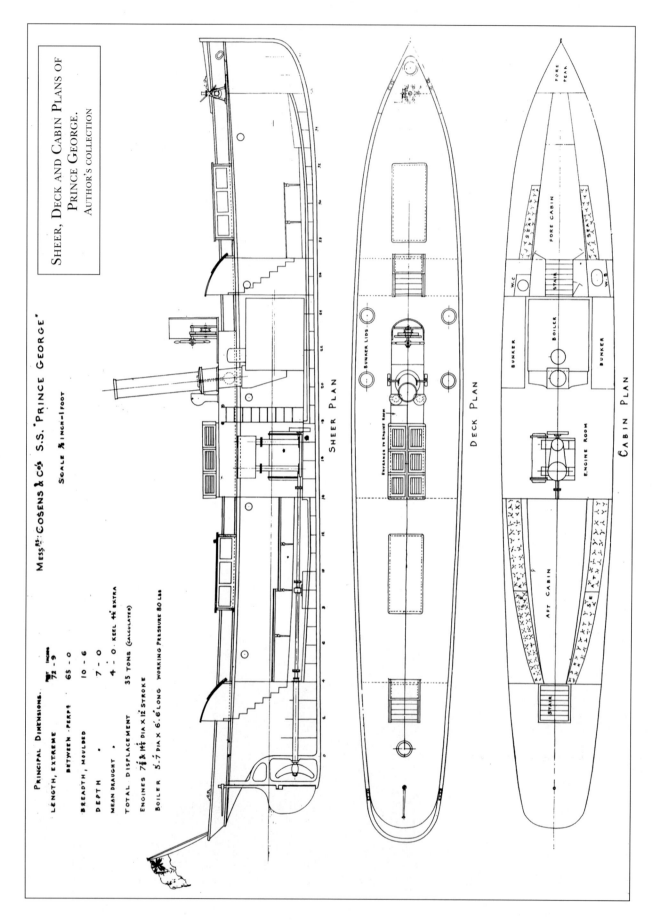

SHEER, DECK AND CABIN PLANS OF PRINCE GEORGE.
AUTHOR'S COLLECTION

MESSRS COSENS & COS S.S. "PRINCE GEORGE"

SCALE 3/8 INCH=1 FOOT

SHEER PLAN

DECK PLAN

CABIN PLAN

PRINCIPAL DIMENSIONS.	Feet	Inches
LENGTH, EXTREME	72	9
BETWEEN PERPs	65	0
BREADTH, MOULDED	10	6
DEPTH	7	0
MEAN DRAUGHT	4	0 KEEL 4½" EXTRA

TOTAL DISPLACEMENT   35 TONS (CALCULATED)

ENGINES 7¼ & 14¼ DIA X 12 STROKE

BOILER 5'-7" DIA X 6'-6" LONG WORKING PRESSURE 80 LBS

on the Shambles Bank in calm but hazy weather and was soon left high and dry by the falling tide. *Queen* and *Albert Victor*, together with G.H. Collins' tug *Verne* and the Channel Coaling Co's *Petrel*, hurried to the scene, as did *Premier* with a large party of sightseers, but nothing could be achieved until evening high water. Further excursions advertised during the afternoon proved extremely popular but Cosens were deprived of a significant salvage claim by the arrival of two large tugs from Southampton to attempt to refloat the ship. *Victoria* was engaged to stand by the liner in case the attempt proved unsuccessful and it was decided to land her passengers before night set in.

A service was also recorded to the steamer *Eugene Rouxhall* and on 29th September the brigantine *Eleanor* stranded on the submerged rocks of the new breakwater but was successfully towed off by *Albert Victor* for a fee of £60. In connection with the salvage work, it is recorded that a fee of £5 per annum was paid between 1898 and 1900 to a Mr Bothwell, the tenant of 4 Trinity Road, Weymouth. The house, which had recently been vacated by Mr S.J. Fowler, the company's managing director, was known to the coastguard and all other interested parties as Cosens' communications centre during salvage jobs, and the payment was to ensure that the telephone was manned day and night when an emergency was under way.

Another wreck purchased at auction by Cosens was that of the Channel Coaling Co's little steamer *Alert*, which had sunk in a severe storm at Portland during the winter of 1897-98. The wreck was successfully raised and her engine and boilers, which were in excellent condition, taken to the company's works at Weymouth and thoroughly restored. Mr Drake, the works manager at that time, then set about designing a small steam tug around the machinery and construction began beside the No. 2 slipway in the early spring. On 6th June, the completed hull was transferred to the slipway cradle and at evening high water a large crowd gathered to watch the managing director's daughter, Miss Daisy Fowler, name the little ship *Prince George* and send her down the ways in the traditional manner. The hull was then towed to the Backwater where her machinery was lifted in and fitting out completed.

Prince George was constructed of steel, measured 67 feet 7 inches by 10 feet 5 inches by 6 feet 9 inches and had a gross tonnage of 27.2. Her compound, surface condensing engine, which was built by N. Sana of Penryn in 1875, had cylinders of $7^3/_4$ and $14^1/_4$ diameter and 12 inches stroke, and developed 75ihp. The boiler, built by Kincaird & Co of Greenock in 1891 worked at 85psi. The ship achieved a trial speed of 9 knots but this was later improved when a new propeller designed by the new works manager Mr Wise was fitted. Below decks, the little ship had a nicely upholstered and appointed saloon aft and a somewhat simpler second class cabin forward. Her funnel could hinge to allow her to pass under Weymouth Town Bridge at all states of

the tide, and her size and design made her equally suited to passenger carrying, towing, salvage or contracting work.

Cosens were successful in obtaining a new contract with the War Office, commencing on 1st November, to supply water transport to the breakwater forts and other military depots at Portland. *Prince George* immediately superseded *Princess* as the principal craft on these duties. Troops, food, water and many other supplies had to be carried to and fro and, under the command of Capt Painter, a retired GWR Channel Islands packet master, the new steamer quickly proved herself ideal for the unglamorous but essential job. *Princess* and *Prince Edward*, Cosens' third and smallest steam launch, were far from redundant and found themselves very busy both in support of their bigger sister and in connection with the numerous coastal defence works in the district. Indeed, even the larger tugs and excursion steamers were occasionally pressed into service in connection with drills and exercises on the forts, and the temporary defensive dolphins which marked the line of the new, partially completed breakwaters. *Princess* was taken in hand early in 1899 and given new decks

The new PRINCE GEORGE, with Capt Painter at the wheel, poses for an official photograph in Weymouth Backwater, just opposite the company's engineering works.
PETER FERGUSON

Capt Bowering surveys the scene from the bridge as MONARCH manoeuvres alongside Bournemouth Pier. Note the steamer chairs piled on the paddle box.
AUTHOR'S COLLECTION

and a thorough mechanical and structural refit by Cosens' apprentices, emerging fit for many more years service.

As 1898 drew to a close, the sad news was received that Capt William Cosens had died on 13th November, aged 71, at his home in Lennox Street, Weymouth. William had been associated with the company since 1850, a master since 1853, and fleet commodore after the death of his brother Joseph in 1873, until his own retirement in 1889. Since that time until February 1898, he had acted as Cosens' agent at Swanage and his passing marked the severance of the last link with the pioneering days of the early company. Ships in the harbour flew their flags at half mast as a sign of respect and, when he was interred at Melcombe Regis cemetery on 16th November, the pall bearers were six of Cosens' oldest employees.

On 26th January 1899, Capt Bowering, who had taken William Cosens' place as fleet commodore and master of *Monarch* from 1889 until retiring due to ill health at the end of the 1897 season, also died. Bowering had joined Cosens as ship's boy on board *Prince* in 1853, remaining in the post for three years before leaving to become a fireman in the Channel Islands packet steamers. He returned to Cosens as a fireman in 1861 but quickly changed departments and served as an able seaman until being promoted to mate in 1866. In 1876, he obtained his master's certificate and was appointed to the command of *Prince*, thereafter working his way through all of the company's steamers to become senior master and commodore. For many years from 1878 onwards, he had also submitted an annual tender to provide catering on board the Cosens' steamers, a service which was actually organised and supervised by his wife and which earned the couple a steady additional income.

The New Year of 1899 brought some stormy weather and with it a useful crop of salvage jobs. The construction of the two new breakwaters to enclose the anchorage at Portland had reached the stage where the millions of tons of huge rocks which had been tipped into the sea to form the core of the massive structures were now visible at low water. Despite the fact that the line of the breakwaters was clearly marked by a row of wooden dolphins with hawsers stretched between, at high tide the reef of rocks was hidden beneath the surface and proved a navigational hazard to numerous ship masters. On the evening of 4th January, during a gale and heavy rain, a large Greek steamer named *Georgios Michaelinos* hit the rocks with such force that she grounded as far as her foremast. *Queen* and *Albert Victor* were on the scene within 15 minutes and, after manoeuvring with some difficulty amongst the numerous buoys which threatened to foul their paddle wheels, managed to tow the casualty off at high water. After spending the night at anchor in Weymouth Bay, she was towed at first light into Portland Harbour, where Cosens' divers examined her bottom plates and found them badly buckled and scraped but sufficiently intact to allow her to proceed on her voyage.

Between 11th and 13th February, a particularly savage gale, accompanied by the highest tide for twenty years, swept up the Channel and caused widespread flooding and damage in Weymouth. On Monday night, 13th February, the steamship *Stuart* began to drag her anchors and threatened to run amock amongst the numerous merchantmen and the warships which were sheltering in the harbour. In response to *Stuart*'s distress rockets, the tugs put out and *Albert Victor* managed to pass a tow. Just as she was getting the steamer under control, a steam launch from one of the warships collided with the tug, forcing her to stop her engines. The wind immediately took charge and the tow had to be slipped. No sooner had *Albert Victor* established a new connection than *Queen*, coming to lend assistance, fouled the tow rope, which had to be slipped again. At this point *Stuart*'s anchor cables parted, her crew took to the boats and she was blown onto the submerged breakwater, where she stranded. All the while the tide was rising and in a particularly savage gust, the steamer was blown clean over the ledge of rocks and started to drift rapidly to leeward. *Albert Victor* followed in the hope of putting some men on board but, owing to the violent rolling of the steamer, was prevented from doing so and *Stuart* finally drove ashore on rocks between Osmington and Preston. The following morning, under authority from the Lloyd's agent, Cosens put a master and salvage crew aboard the casualty, raised steam and got her pumps, winches and main engines working. *Albert Victor* and *Queen*, having failed to refloat her on the morning tide, were joined by *Premier* for another attempt during the evening but this too failed. As high water approached, the ground swell became so heavy that

By 1899 the new breakwaters had begun to break surface between the temporary dolphins and formed a splendid artificial reef on which several vessels ran aground, providing welcome salvage work for Cosens' tugs.
BRIAN JACKSON COLLECTION

Stuart's bottom plates were stoved in and the pumps were unable to cope with the influx of water. The weather became so bad that it was judged unsafe for the salvage party to be taken off by the Weymouth lifeboat and they were forced to remain until the morning, when they were landed on the beach by

With Cosens' salvage crew on board, STUART *is pictured high and dry on the rocks near Preston.*
WEYMOUTH MUSEUM

175

breeches buoy. *Stuart* remained firmly aground for seven weeks, until a Swedish salvage company finally succeeded in blasting away the rocks under the ship and refloating her on 10th April.

Whilst the *Stuart* drama was being played out, the brigantine *Susannah Thrift* had run for shelter in Portland Roads but then dragged her anchors onto the new breakwater. The lifeboat *Friern Watch* was launched but, unable to make any headway into the gale, returned to harbour for the assistance of a tug. *Albert Victor*, having just left *Stuart*, took the lifeboat in tow but, on arriving at the casualty, discovered that the Portland tug *Petrel* had already succeeded in towing her off. It is of interest that between August 1897 and the arrival of Weymouth's first motor lifeboat in 1924, Cosens held a contract to tow the sailing/pulling lifeboat to the scene of any disaster for a fee of £1 per hour during daylight and £2 at night, with a minimum charge of £3 per call out. Once at the scene, the lifeboat would concentrate on saving life while the paddle tug attempted to salvage the vessel concerned.

During another storm on 8th April, *Queen* rescued a small sailing vessel in Portland Roads and, together with *Albert Victor*, went to the assistance of the steamer *Katherine* and a French steam trawler, both of which had grounded on the submerged breakwater. Unfortunately for the tugs, the former floated off without assistance, while the Frenchman agreed terms with the Channel Coaling Co's rival tug *Verne*. In the event, *Verne* failed to pull her free and the trawler spent all night precariously balanced on top of the breakwater, before coming off at the top of the next high tide under her own power. A few weeks later, services were rendered to the ketch *Ada* and the vessels *Hansa* and *Gemini*, the latter case leading to a legal dispute between

Cosens and the Channel Coaling Company about the apportionment of salvage dues between their respective tugs.

On 4th March, it was the turn of Cosens' own *Victoria* to become a casualty, when the Channel Islands steamer *Ibex*, entering Weymouth Harbour too fast and at the wrong angle, hit her squarely on the port sponson. The main paddle spring beam was broken and the impact was transmitted across the ship with such force that the starboard sponson was pushed outward, breaking off two piles on the pier. Fortunately *Victoria*'s mooring ropes broke and some of the energy was absorbed as she was pushed up harbour by *Ibex*. By a strange coincidence, the steamer was occupying the same berth as *Brodick Castle* had been when she was rammed by *Reindeer* in 1897. Had *Ibex* struck *Victoria* anywhere but on the sponson it is certain that she would have been cut through and sunk but, as it was, she was quickly surveyed and placed on Cosens' slipway, where the engineering staff set about carrying out major repairs. In her absence, *Empress* was rushed into service to cover the early season sailings.

The year 1899 also saw the signing of a new 21-year lease with Mr Ayles for the No. 1 slipway at Weymouth. The construction of two large iron sheds at the adjoining No. 2 slipway, together with the recently-installed electric lighting and steam hammer, allowed a range of ship repairing and boat building operations to be carried on day or night with even greater efficiency. To keep pace with the company's increasing trade, the Head Office at 10 Custom House Quay was enlarged again and a new board room constructed on the first floor at the rear of the premises. The old board room was converted into offices.

At Castletown, Portland, a new steamer jetty had

MONARCH and VICTORIA berthed together at Teignmouth Pier in south Devon. The pier was originally opened in 1867, restored and re-opened in 1876, and enlarged in 1887. The pavilion was completed in 1890. It is probable that MONARCH had come from Bournemouth and VICTORIA from Weymouth to mark some special event.
AUTHOR'S COLLECTION

been under construction since August 1897 and was finally completed in October 1898. It was a long, narrow, wooden structure, built onto the western face of the massive stone jetty, and incorporated a set of naval landing steps at its shoreward end. The old pier, which had extended from the north-western corner of the jetty, was demolished during the winter and Cosens' vessels started using the new facility at the start of the 1899 season. Unfortunately, the depth of water at the new jetty proved inadequate and the steamers repeatedly grounded at low tide, provoking a flurry of correspondence between Cosens and Cluttons, the Crown Receivers who acted on behalf of the pier's owners, the Crown Office for Woods, Forests & Land Revenues. Cluttons, having recently increased the rent for the jetty to £110 per annum, promised to undertake the dredging but, unwilling to accept disruption to their passenger service, Cosens offered to do it themselves for a fee of 7s per cubic yard of spoil shifted. A steam grab dredger and hopper were hired from Weymouth Corporation and by early July, the task had been completed.

Before the main passenger season commenced, *Monarch* was given an extremely thorough £1,100 refit to improve her facilities and ensure that she was in the best possible condition to face the expected competition from *Cambria* and *Lorna Doone* during the year ahead. Her paddle wheels were re-bushed, the paddle box facings renewed, and she was repainted and re-grained internally

and externally. All of her upholstery, curtains and floor coverings were replaced but the most obvious outward sign of the refurbishment was a pair of new funnels, the tops of which now lacked their familiar but somewhat antiquated bell-tops but were instead cut parallel with the waterline.

The rival companies had not, of course, been idle either. *Lorna Doone* emerged on 17th May, having undergone a major refit which included the stiffening of her hull, rebuilding of the engine, fitting of two new water tube boilers and a complete refurbishment of her accommodation. She now sported two funnels in place of her previous single stack and indications were that her speed had improved substantially.

Cambria arrived back in the Solent at the end of May (this time without the support of *Glen Rosa* which was required in the Bristol Channel) and within days the familiar pattern of competition between herself and *Lorna Doone* had been re-established. Both ships continued to visit Bournemouth, Swanage and Weymouth with great regularity and Campbells now sought to challenge Cosens' traditional monopoly of the Cherbourg trade, by offering a number of excursions from Southsea, Southampton and the Isle of Wight piers to the French port via Bournemouth. There was even a suggestion that Campbells considered basing *Cambria* at Bournemouth for several days each week, a move which would have been ruinous for

MONARCH and EMPRESS moored for the night at the old Swanage Pier, circa 1899. The narrow gauge tramway lines along the pier can be seen clearly. On the right, the Wellington clock tower is seen again, which was re-erected here in 1867 following its removal from the Southwark end of London Bridge. The original clock kept very poor time and was consequently never brought to Swanage.
TYTHE BARN MUSEUM

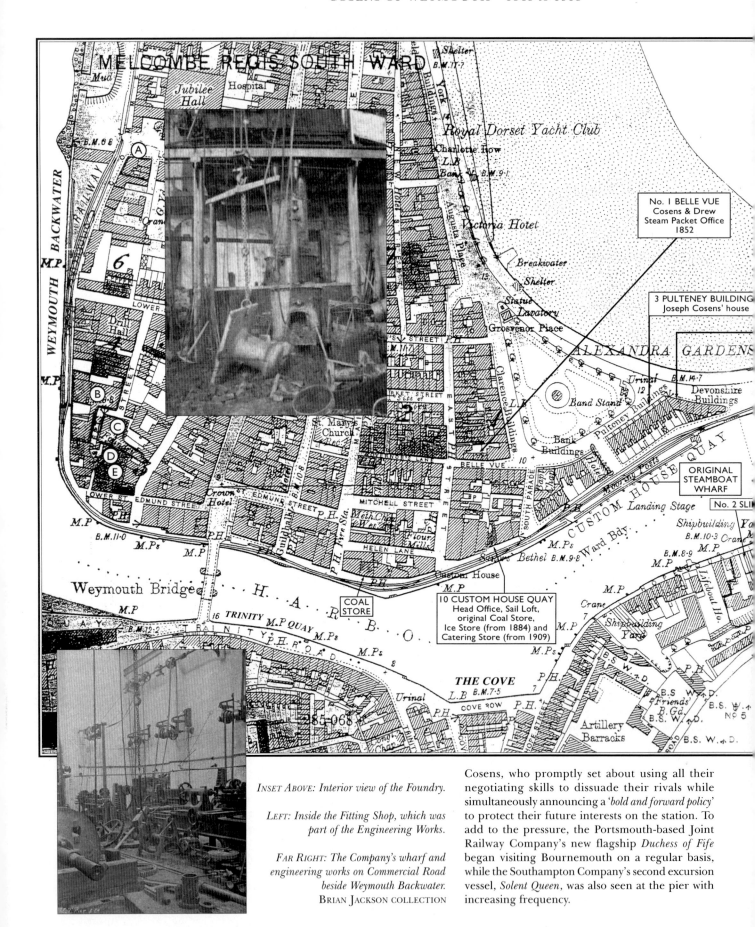

INSET ABOVE: Interior view of the Foundry.

LEFT: Inside the Fitting Shop, which was part of the Engineering Works.

FAR RIGHT: The Company's wharf and engineering works on Commercial Road beside Weymouth Backwater.
BRIAN JACKSON COLLECTION

Cosens, who promptly set about using all their negotiating skills to dissuade their rivals while simultaneously announcing a 'bold and forward policy' to protect their future interests on the station. To add to the pressure, the Portsmouth-based Joint Railway Company's new flagship *Duchess of Fife* began visiting Bournemouth on a regular basis, while the Southampton Company's second excursion vessel, *Solent Queen*, was also seen at the pier with increasing frequency.

WEYMOUTH HARBOUR
1901
SHOWING COSENS' PREMISES and OTHER SIGNIFICANT WEYMOUTH BUILDINGS

KEY TO BUILDINGS MARKED AT FAR LEFT OF MAP
A – FOUNDRY & ADJOINING WORKSHOPS
 Taken over from Mr Collett in 1889 and occupied until 1894
B – COSENS' COMMERCIAL ROAD ENGINEERING WORKS
 Site developed from 1894 onwards
C – COSENS' FOUNDRY
 From 1894. Formerly Congregational chapel 1804-64, Music Hall &
 Theatre Royal 1865-93, Lower Foyer to St. Nicholas St. used as Store
D – ROSE COTTAGE
E – FOUNDRY COTTAGES

WEYMOUTH BAY

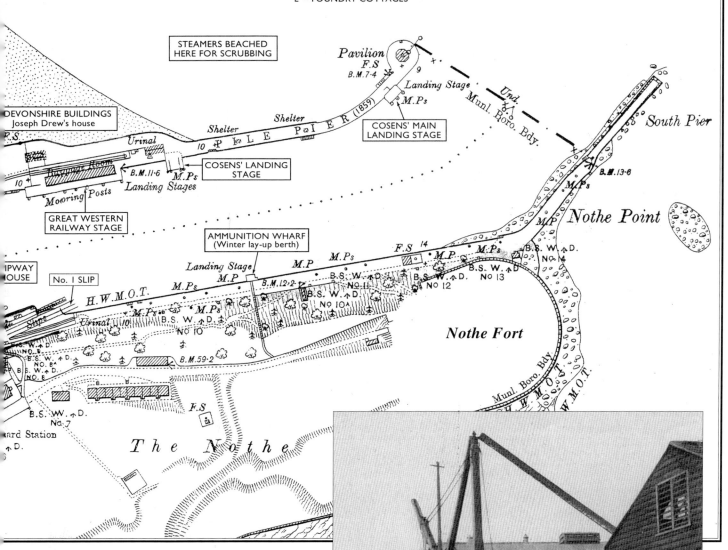

What was to be done? 1899 was proving a *'short, sharp season'* with no lack of prospective passengers and, despite the hot competition, generated a healthy income of £15,271 from fares and stewarding plus a further £1,254 from season tickets. The indications were that the ever-growing resort of Bournemouth was capable of providing more than enough trade to ensure Cosens' survival, provided that they were willing to invest in an additional steamer of sufficient size and quality to maintain customer

loyalty by comparing favourably with *Cambria* and *Lorna Doone*.

It was apparent that there was little possibility of building a new ship in time for 1900 and so shipbrokers were contacted and Mr Fowler began to tour Britain to inspect second-hand vessels which were available for sale or charter. Almost unbelievably, he travelled to Glasgow in June to view *Culzean Castle*, which was none other than the disastrous *Windsor Castle* whose design faults and astronomical running costs had so nearly brought the Bournemouth Company to its knees in 1895. Clearly nothing had changed, for she was quickly rejected on grounds of condition, stability and cost. Two other steamers also failed to meet Mr Fowler's requirements and at this point news broke that the Southampton Company had placed an order for a fast new flagship, of equivalent size and speed to *Cambria*, to be delivered in time for the 1900 season. Cosens now abandoned the idea of buying second hand and issued a press release in late June 1899 stating:

'For some time past it has been freely circulated that this company intended at once to take steps to defend their position in the excursion business at Bournemouth, Swanage, and Weymouth, which they have, successfully and with universal approval, maintained upon a first-class basis for so many years, – as against the opposition of the Bristol steamers. Circumstances, however, are such that no suitable steamer can be obtained on hire, but one or two boats are in the market for absolute sale to bona-fide buyers. The largest of these has been inspected during the present week by Mr Fowler (Managing Director) and Mr Hinde (Superintendent engineer) on behalf of Messrs Cosens & Company. On Thursday a meeting of the directors was convened to receive their reports and consider the present situation, and it was unanimously decided that in the best interests of the shareholders it would not be desirable to buy up any vessel which, although adequate for the immediate

purpose, would not prove permanently equal to the rapidly increasing patronage accorded the company, but rather, as occasion demands, to build a new and fast steamer on the Clyde which, with the company's present fleet, would be capable of carrying on the excursion traffic worked by them on the coast. In the meantime no stone will be left unturned to act on the defensive, in which the Board felt the share and bond holders, as well as the multitude of their patrons, would agree.'

Both the Channel Fleet and the Reserve Squadron were at Portland during July, August and September, and the demand for liberty boats was unprecedented. The terms of the contract between Cosens and the Admirals commanding meant that the needs of the warships had to be given absolute priority and consequently, as high season approached, there were insufficient steamers to maintain the normal programme of excursions. To add to the problem, *Victoria* was spending more time assisting *Empress* and *Monarch* to cope with the demand at Bournemouth, and Weymouth residents were beginning to complain that they were deprived of long trips by the larger units of the fleet.

To resolve the problem, Cosens chartered the exceptionally handsome excursion steamer *Cynthia* from her owners on the Tyne for the months of August and September. *Cynthia* had been built in 1892 for William Watkins and Co, the London tug firm who had been so closely involved with the building of Cosens' *Victoria*, for seasonal excursion work out of Margate. She was a successor on that service to the paddle tug *India*, which Cosens had also chartered during 1895, and was therefore a ship with several tenuous Cosens connections. She measured 153 feet 4 inches by 21 feet 4 inches by 10 feet 3 inches and, most helpfully, held a cross-channel passenger certificate.

As soon as she arrived at Weymouth, *Cynthia* took over a number of the longer excursions. She was

not equipped for beaching and could not therefore visit Lulworth Cove or carry out the westward coasting trip but she proved immensely useful on all the other routes. The smaller steamers were thus cleared to concentrate on the Fleet traffic and the Weymouth programme was saved from any cuts. At the beginning of August 1899, a second ship, the 108 feet 7 inches by 18 feet 6 inches by 9 feet 7 inches iron paddle tug *Forth* was also taken on charter. Built in 1884 as *Flying Owl* for the Clyde Shipping Co of Glasgow, she had moved to the River Forth in 1892 and, at the time of her charter by Cosens, was owned by the Grangemouth & Forth

Towing Co, who used her for towing and summer excursions. *Forth* was limited to the Fleet traffic and short trips from Weymouth but again released some of *Premier*'s time and allowed a slight but welcome expansion in the local sailing programme. The combined cost of the two chartered steamers was £1,100.

Cynthia certainly went to Swanage on several occasions, including to the regatta on 24th August, to Cowes on 25th August and Southampton on 12th September, whilst also offering direct sailings from Weymouth to Alderney on 15th August and to Cherbourg on 26th August. The weather in the days

The Tyne-based excursion steamer CYNTHIA, which was chartered by Cosens during the high season of 1899 to help meet the demands generated by the stiff competition at Bournemouth and the requirements of the Channel Fleet at Portland.
AUTHOR'S COLLECTION

The paddle tug FORTH was also chartered during the summer of 1899 to act as a liberty boat to the Channel Fleet.
PHILIP THOMAS COLLECTION

CAMBRIA, on one of her high speed dashes from the Solent, is seen here resting alongside the new Swanage Pier, left, while CYNTHIA and a topsail schooner are moored to the old goods pier, on the right. The quantity of bunting in evidence suggests that the photograph was taken on Regatta Day, 24th August 1899.

DAVID HAYSOM COLLECTION

leading up to the Alderney trip was somewhat boisterous and discouraged all but the most hardy from advanced booking. However, the day itself dawned bright and calm and 150 visitors and a dozen Weymouthians embarked for a 9.00am departure. The first few hours of the voyage were conducted in bright sunshine but, at 12.40pm, *Cynthia* ran into a thick fog bank. Speed was reduced, regular soundings taken and, for the next few hours the steamer crept onwards through the fog. By 2pm, Capt Smith calculated that he was about two miles from the notorious Casquets Rocks and five miles from Alderney. Unwilling to proceed further in such dangerous waters, he lay to hoping that the fog would clear but when it failed to do so he decided to set course for Weymouth. The disappointed passengers made good use of the catering laid on by Mr Graham and his staff, while the steamer felt her way back through the fog bank but, at 5.30pm, she emerged into bright sunshine once again. At 8.00pm, after eleven hours at sea, *Cynthia* was safely berthed in Weymouth Harbour where the only people to express any discontent were the waiting customs officers when informed that the steamer, having failed to reach Alderney, had nothing on board liable for duty!

As the season drew to a close in October, detailed discussions were opened with the Bournemouth Company regarding plans to defend Bournemouth against the predations of Campbells and the Southampton Company. The Bournemouth Company's somewhat cheeky opening proposal was that *Brodick Castle* should be disposed of and replaced with a new steamer which would remain their property but that Cosens should lend them two thirds of the building or purchase costs. Unsurprisingly, Cosens felt unable to agree to this bizarre demand and suggested instead that a separate joint company be set up to own the new steamer.

During November, the Clyde steamer *Strathmore* was inspected at Glasgow and her sister ship *Britannia* at Rye but neither were deemed suitable and by the end of the month, following a conference with the London shipbroker Mr Constant, the two companies had reached an understanding that:

• *Brodick Castle* would be retained for at least one more season.

• Cosens would be willing to hire an additional boat for two months during 1900 to replace *Empress* on the Swanage service, allowing her to move to Weymouth to support the high season fleet and excursion traffic.

• The two companies would co-operate as closely as possible to defend their position at Bournemouth.

• A new steamer would be ordered for delivery in May or June 1901.

• Finally, and most controversially, that an alliance should be sought with the Southampton Company, who might be persuaded to use one or more of their steamers at Bournemouth to help defeat the Campbell threat. The proposal hinged on the idea that the three south coast companies would have a common interest in defending their waters against the interloper from Bristol but seemed to ignore the obvious dangers of inviting the powerful Southampton Company to take an even closer interest in Bournemouth.

The Devil, as ever, was in the detail and the year ahead was to be marked by increasingly acrimonious discussions about precisely how these general aims were to be achieved and, more importantly, financed.

The 1900 season began quietly over the Easter period and the early-season income was boosted by the presence of the Reserve Squadron at Portland during April. *Cambria* arrived back in the Solent at the end of May in readiness for the Whitsun holiday period and, by the beginning of June, was in fierce competition with *Lorna Doone* once again. *Cambria* was now supported by a second steamer, *Albion*, which Campbells had purchased during the previous season from the Belfast & County Down Railway. A handsome and distinctive ship, she was easily recognisable by the way her short foredeck was raised to bulwark level and surrounded by an open rail. At 200 feet by 25 feet by 8 feet 3 inches, she was smaller and slower than *Cambria* but held a cross-channel passenger certificate and boasted passenger accommodation superior to any in the Cosens' fleet. Both vessels visited Bournemouth on Whit Monday, *Cambria* continuing to Weymouth, whilst *Albion* terminated at Swanage.

The Southampton Company's new flagship *Balmoral*, which had been launched on 14th May and achieved 19.51 knots on her trials on the Clyde, arrived at Southampton on 14th July. She was a large and impressive ship, measuring 236 feet by 27 feet 1 inch by 9 feet 6 inches and with a gross tonnage of 473, which made her 11 feet longer, 1 foot wider and 53 tons heavier than *Cambria*. To the untutored eye, the two ships were almost identical in appearance, each having full-length promenade decks and a single, white funnel.

Significantly, her inaugural trip for directors and shareholders on 17th July took her to Bournemouth and on her homeward leg she came head to head with *Cambria* for the first time. On that occasion, *Balmoral* was the victor but throughout the season ahead, the two flyers proved to be so evenly matched that their regular races became a source of great excitement all along the Wessex coast. Two days later, the rivals raced across the Channel to

P. & A. Campbell Ltd's ALBION, pictured off Southsea, came frequently to Bournemouth and Swanage during 1900 and subsequent seasons.
JOHN PATRICK COLLECTION

The Southampton Company's new 19 knot flagship BALMORAL was almost identical in appearance to her rival, Campbell's CAMBRIA.
JOHN PAGE COLLECTION

ALBERT VICTOR moored alongside a coal hulk at Custom House Quay, Weymouth, circa 1900. The masts and funnels of three of the GWR Channel Island mail ships can be seen in the background.
AUTHOR'S COLLECTION

Cherbourg from the Solent and Shanklin, while *Albion* went direct from Bournemouth and within a few weeks both companies were offering regular Cherbourg sailings via Bournemouth. Cosens' *Monarch* was now seriously outclassed as a cross-channel steamer and with *Cambria*, *Albion*, *Balmoral* and *Lorna Doone* calling in on most days of the week and taking every opportunity to carry passengers between Bournemouth and Swanage, Cosens were forced to admit that their fleet had been *'temporarily eclipsed by their migratory rivals'*. The Southampton Company showed no interest in co-operating with Cosens against P. & A. Campbell Ltd and, unwilling even to agree on a common fare structure for the Swanage service, discussions collapsed, leaving Cosens to complain bitterly about the *'cutting tactics and unfriendly spirit'* of a company which they hitherto *'had regarded as one of themselves'*.

To add to Cosens' woes, the price of steam coal rose very steeply during the 1900 season and the weather during August could not have been more unkind. A succession of wet and windy days came to a peak over the Bank Holiday weekend, when a gale which swept across the south of England led to the abandonment of most sailings and left the few steamers which had ventured out gale-bound at their destinations. Passenger numbers fell by 100,000, representing a loss of £2,500 in revenue in comparison with 1899.

Behind the scenes, negotiations continued between Cosens and the Bournemouth Company regarding the best way forward. During March, detailed discussions were held with A .& J. Inglis,

the Glasgow shipbuilders, regarding the exact price and specification for the new ship and Dr Inglis himself visited Weymouth to meet with Cosens' board. A meeting in June with the Southampton Company to discuss the possibility of them becoming the successor to the Bournemouth Company and entering into a joint running agreement with Cosens having failed to reach any agreement, all attention was turned to financing the new ship.

It was glaringly apparent to all concerned that the precarious finances of the Bournemouth Company would make it impossible for that concern to make any meaningful contribution and so, at the end of August, the directors finally agreed to wind up the business and give Cosens one month's option to purchase. On 4th September, Cosens issued a notice to their shareholders outlining two possible options. The first was to purchase the Bournemouth Company and absorb its vessels into the Cosens' fleet, in which case shareholders' permission would be needed to raise the necessary capital. The second option was to float a completely new and separate company, based in Bournemouth but under Cosens' management and with significant Cosens' funds invested in it. Cosens board felt that either option would be successful and called an extraordinary meeting for 17th September to discuss the matter in detail. After a lengthy debate, the meeting voted unanimously in favour of the resolution

'That provided it is found impracticable to float a new company as referred to in the attached circular, the Directors are hereby empowered to purchase, upon

*the best terms possible, the undertaking known as the
Bournemouth & South Coast Steam Packets, Ltd;
and under the powers contained in Sections 43 and
44 of the articles of association, to increase the capital
of the company to £72,800, by the creation of 4000
new shares of £5 each (£20,000) upon such terms
and conditions, and with such rights and privileges
annexed thereto, as Directors shall determine.'*

On 5th October 1900, an offer was formally
submitted to the Bournemouth Company to pay
off their bondholders by the substitution of £5,000
worth of Cosens' preference shares; and to pay
£3,150 in cash (or 5s in the £) on the ordinary paid
up capital of the company in return for *Brodick
Castle*, *Lord Elgin*, the lease of the Hamworthy Wharf
and all workshops, plant and other assets in their
ownership.

At the same time, on a wave of confidence, the
Board agreed to confirm the contract with Inglis
and go ahead with the building of the new ship.
Shipbuilding prices were somewhat inflated at the
time but, when a price of £24,000 to include the
installation of electric lighting and various other
extras was agreed, the contract was signed and a
first payment of £5,000 made during the last week
in October.

Cosens' offer for the assets of the Bournemouth
Company was, by any standards, a very low one and
based on the assumption that its affairs were in such
a poor state that any figure would be accepted. The
Bournemouth directors, however, had some pride
left and responded that they were unwilling to
entertain any offer of less than £10,000. Cosens
refused to negotiate and in November were outraged
to discover that *Brodick Castle* and *Lord Elgin* had
been advertised for sale on the open market.

— S. S. EMPRESS.

Published at Sydenham's Library, Bournemouth.

To mark the arrival of MAJESTIC *and the adoption of the new buff-funnelled livery in 1901, Sydenham's Library published Cosens' first set of official post cards in 1902. The major units of the fleet were depicted, together with a coloured representation of the company house flag. This particular card showed* EMPRESS *passing Old Harry Rocks and the message was written by someone who had sailed aboard another member of Cosens' fleet the previous day: 'My Dr. Lal, Went across to France yesterday & have got half cooked. We had a magnifique trip …' The rest of the message is partially obscured but seems to indicate that the trip had been to Weymouth to see the Fleet.*

DAVID HAYSOM COLLECTION

An impasse ensued until the Bournemouth Company's annual general meeting on 27th December, when it was revealed that yet again the profits had declined and no dividend could be paid to ordinary shareholders. For some time both the ships had been mortgaged for £5,000 each to Henry Newlyn, who was also trustee for the £5,000 due to the company's debenture bond holders. One shareholder pointed out that "*£40,000 had been lost on running that most unfortunate company*" and urged that instead of accruing further losses it would be far better to re-open negotiations with Cosens and attempt to "*sell up, wind up and get rid of the whole concern*".

It was clearly essential to both parties that a satisfactory working agreement should be re-established before the start of the new season at Easter 1901 and discussions recommenced. By the end of February, matters were well advanced and on 19th March 1901, a formal agreement was drawn up. The key points were:

1. That Cosens would purchase *Brodick Castle*, freed of her mortgage to Henry Newlyn, for £3,000, a sum sufficient to meet the amount apportioned to the ship by the debenture bond holders. The full payment would be made on or before 1st December 1902, and in the meanwhile Cosens would pay interest at the rate of 5 per cent to the bondholders through Newlyn, who was acting as their trustee.

2. *Lord Elgin* would remain the property of the Bournemouth Company, although subject to the £5,000 mortgage to Henry Newlyn. In the event of the company being unable to pay the interest on the £2,000 apportioned to the ship by the debenture bond holders, Cosens guaranteed to do so.

3. In the event of *Brodick Castle* being immediately resold for a sum of more than £3,500, Cosens agreed to share any profit equally with the Bournemouth Company.

4. Cosens would refund the cost of any maintenance work carried out on the ship between 1st November and the purchase date, together with a proportion of insurance premiums, mooring fees and other expenses.

5. Except for exceptional occasions agreed between the two companies, *Lord Elgin* would be limited exclusively to the Bournemouth – Swanage service. Tickets for the service would be interchangeable with Cosens and the fares pooled as previously.

6. The Bournemouth Company's advertising sites would be retained and their handbills would advertise Cosens' long distance excursions. An outward appearance of the two companies being entirely separate undertakings would be maintained.

7. Cosens would be at liberty to share the Bournemouth Company's Hamworthy berth and would contribute appropriately to the rent.

8. The agreement would be for an initial period of three years, renewable annually thereafter. Either company could give six months notice, in October, to withdraw from the agreement.

The surviving copy of the agreement had been signed by the Bournemouth Company but not by Cosens, while clues in the minute books suggest that further manoeuvrings took place and that it was not until later in the season that matters were finalised. On 13th July, Cosens resolved to pay off the bondholders in full, with interest, to the sum of £5,000 and to obtain a fresh valuation on *Brodick Castle* so that she might be '*absolutely purchased*'. Whatever the case, the Weymouth Custom House Registers show that the ship was formally transferred to Cosens' ownership on 26 August 1901.

Although the takeover of *Brodick Castle* after so many years must have given Cosens a certain amount of satisfaction, it also left them with a major financial headache. The unexpected cost of the purchase had to be added to the £24,000 already committed to the new ship, which was now nearing completion in Glasgow. The board abandoned the notion of setting up a new Bournemouth-based operating company and instead exercised its option to seek £20,000 worth of new capital through an ordinary share issue. Although there was plenty of interest in the new shares, insufficient had been allotted in time to cover the costs of the instalments still due to A. & J. Inglis & Co, so Cosens were forced to ask their bank for assistance. Bearing in mind the large amount now committed to their own and the former Bournemouth Company debenture bondholders, who had first charge on the company's assets, the bank would only agree to issue a mortgage on the joint and personal guarantees of the directors.

Once these guarantees had been obtained, a mortgage was arranged through the Capital & Counties Bank for £6,500 at 5 per cent interest and a further two mortgages with a client of the company's London ship broker, Mr Constant, for a total of £3,500 at 6 per cent. Together these allowed the account with the shipbuilder to be settled in full and on 25th April, the new flagship, which had been named *Majestic*, commenced her trials on the Clyde.

On her first set of speed trials over the Skelmorlie measured mile, *Majestic* averaged only 15.3 knots and, since this did not meet her minimum contract speed of 16 knots, she was taken back to the shipyard for alterations. Her 13 feet 9 inch diameter paddle wheels had been fitted with eight paddle floats measuring 10 feet 6 inches in width by 2 feet

9 inches in depth and these were now increased to 3 foot depth. These and other small alterations clearly had their effect, for on a second set of trials on the Gareloch on 11th May, *Majestic* achieved a fully-loaded average speed of 16.1 knots.

In drawing up the specification for *Majestic*, Cosens had decided that there was little point in attempting to outdo *Cambria* and *Balmoral* in size or speed, and decided to go instead for comfort and seaworthiness. At 215 feet 5 inches by 27 feet 1 inch by 8 feet 9 inches she was 9 feet 5 inches shorter but 1 foot wider than *Cambria*, and 27 feet 1 inch shorter than *Balmoral* whose beam was identical. She drew less water than her rivals and, at 408 gross tons, was also considerably lighter. The proportions of her hull made her an exceptionally good sea-boat and the decision to fit portholes rather than large windows to her forward saloon was intended to make her less prone to heavy weather damage during cross-channel excursions. Her passenger certificates allowed her to carry 408 passengers on cross-channel voyages, 794 between Newhaven and Start Point, 935 inside the Isle of Wight and 1,455 in smooth waters.

When running at speed, the powerful compound diagonal engines fitted to *Balmoral* and *Cambria* had a tendency to cause the passengers to sway to and fro with every thrust of the pistons. While communicating a tremendous sense of power, this sensation could become somewhat wearing on long passages and Cosens decided to eliminate the problem by fitting a three-cylinder, triple expansion engine to *Majestic*. The engine, which had cylinders 21, 35 and 54 inches in diameter with a stroke of 60 inches, was exceptionally smooth in operation as well as being highly efficient and relatively economical to run. It also represented an enormous technological jump for the company, whose other ships were powered

This photograph is believed to have been taken on the Clyde, before MAJESTIC set off on her delivery trip to Weymouth. Note that the bridge has not yet been fitted with its protective canvas dodgers. The toe rails all around the ship at promenade deck level and the spirket plate in the bows were only painted all white during her first season in service. AUTHOR'S COLLECTION

BELOW: *In a charming studio photograph taken at the time of* MAJESTIC*'s commissioning, a youthful Capt Lewis St. Barbe Rawle (seated right) poses in his Commodore's dress uniform, with his Chief Engineer Mr Rowlands (seated left), the mate and ticket collector. Born in 1865, Capt Rawle joined Cosens as steersman of* PREMIER *in 1887, moved to* EMPRESS *in 1888 and obtained his mate's ticket in 1889. He seems to have left the company to go 'deep sea' and qualify as a master but returned in 1894 as mate of* QUEEN *and* VICTORIA. *On 6th March 1896, he was appointed master of* QUEEN *and from 1898-1900 commanded* MONARCH. *In 1901, he took command of the new flagship* MAJESTIC *and served as the company's senior master and Commodore until his death by drowning in Newhaven Harbour on 6th May 1916.*
ANDREW GLADWELL/
PSPS ARCHIVE

MAJESTIC steaming out of Weymouth Bay on her inaugural trip, 20th May 1901.   AUTHOR'S COLLECTION

by old fashioned oscillating engines or, in the case of *Monarch*, a two-cylinder, simple diagonal. Steam was provided by two, single-ended boilers with six furnaces, working at a steam pressure of 160psi.

The ship's seaworthiness and smooth running was complemented by excellent accommodation. The spacious, 204 foot promenade deck ran the full length of the vessel, apart from a small rope-handling deck aft, and was broken only by the single, large funnel and a handsome teak deckhouse surmounted by the navigating bridge. Curiously, Cosens continued the rather outdated practice of placing the bridge behind the funnel, an arrangement which severely compromised the helmsman's ability to see what lay ahead. The deckhouse contained a small passenger saloon, toilets and stairs to the main deck below, where the spacious dining saloon, bars, lounges, separate ladies' cabin and tea room were all lavishly panelled, decorated and upholstered by Messrs Wylie & Lockhead of Glasgow. The ship was illuminated throughout by electric light.

Majestic left the Clyde on the morning of 14th May, under the command of Capt Lewis St. Barbe Rawle, who had been promoted from *Monarch*. In order to conserve coal and avoid the necessity of putting into any intermediate port to refuel, Rawle had been ordered not to exceed three-quarters speed on passage and *Majestic* duly arrived in Weymouth at 8.30pm on the evening of Wednesday 15th May. A large crowd cheered her into the harbour and, after the waiting directors had made a brief inspection, was allowed to tour the ship. A military band which had been playing nearby came on board the brilliantly illuminated steamer and played a lively selection including 'Auld Lang Syne' and the National Anthem. The next morning, all the Cosens' ships in harbour, including *Empress* which was undergoing repairs on the slipway, were dressed overall and *Majestic* was opened to inspection by ticket holders only. During the afternoon, *Monarch* brought a large party from Bournemouth and in the evening *Majestic* was opened to the general public.

Dressed overall, *Majestic* departed on her inaugural cruise from Weymouth at 3pm on Monday 20th May with a large party of invited guests. In addition to the directors and shareholders, the Mayor and Corporation, the army and navy, magistrates and

MAJESTIC, on the far right, berthed at Princess Pier Torquay, on a long day trip from Bournemouth to visit the Torquay Royal Regatta. The voyage was 73 nautical miles in each direction.
AUTHOR'S COLLECTION

other prominent townsmen were all represented. The ship cruised around the Shambles lightship and on her homeward leg hove to inside the breakwater, while champagne toasts were drunk and speeches made in the spacious dining saloon. The band of the 1st Dorset Volunteer Artillery provided the musical entertainment and all on board expressed themselves delighted by the impressive new addition to Cosens' fleet.

The following day, *Majestic* proceeded to Swanage and Bournemouth where, once again, prominent local townspeople were embarked for a second inaugural voyage. This time, she sailed out into the Channel before returning to the smooth waters of Poole Harbour, where the speeches and toasts could be enjoyed without any fear of unpleasant motion. Retracing her steps, the ship was cheered in and out of both Bournemouth and Swanage piers, before returning to Weymouth for the evening.

On the following afternoon, *Majestic* made an unexpected and unadvertised appearance at Swanage to carry her first fare-paying passengers on a short early-closing day excursion. The ship's official maiden voyage took place on Whit Monday 27th May, when she departed from Weymouth at 8.30am for Bournemouth and a cruise around the Isle of Wight, returning from Bournemouth at 4pm.

The takeover of *Brodick Castle* and the building of *Majestic* also marked a significant change in the livery of the Cosens' fleet. Hitherto, the ships' archaic bell-topped funnels had been painted black all over. Combined with a black hull and dark, grained woodwork, this gave a rather severe and out-dated appearance which compared unfavourably with the brighter paint schemes of the rival

companies and would certainly not be suited to the new flagship. The opportunity was therefore taken to adopt the buff, black-topped funnel colours of *Brodick Castle* and apply them to the rest of the fleet. Curiously, no documentary evidence has ever been located for the precise date of the change but it can be assumed that it occurred during March or April in time for the opening of the season. At the same time, it would also appear that *Lord Elgin*'s funnel colour was changed from buff to red with a black top, in order to emphasise the continued and separate existence of her owners.

The advent of *Majestic* made it possible for the company to respond to complaints that Weymouth was not receiving its fair share of long distance excursions. When the morning tides were flowing eastwards, the ship was rostered to begin at Weymouth and call at Swanage and Bournemouth before proceeding to the Isle of Wight, Southsea or beyond. On alternate weeks, when the tides made a westward trip more appropriate, she would begin at Bournemouth and call at Swanage and Weymouth, before setting off round Portland Bill on a direct sailing to Dartmouth or Torquay. Her 16 knot speed and comfortable accommodation made such trips perfectly practical and so, once or twice a week henceforth, the residents of both resorts benefited in equal measure.

Majestic immediately replaced *Monarch* on the Cherbourg trips and principal long-distance excursions. Although not as fast as her rivals *Cambria* and *Balmoral*, she quickly built up a loyal following of passengers who appreciated her superior comfort. With *Monarch* and *Brodick Castle* both available for full and half-day excursions to

Towards the middle of the excursion season, it was Cosens' practice to send each ship in turn to Weymouth to have her bottom scrubbed and a new coat of anti-fouling paint applied. There was no need to go to the expense of using a slipway. The ships were simply beached on Weymouth's gently-shelving sands and, as the tide receded, a gang of men from the workshops would complete the work. During the summer of 1901, whilst this work was underway on each of the vessels, an unknown photographer captured a series of images which reveal the steamers in fascinating detail. Here, BRODICK CASTLE displays the white paintwork which was applied above bulwark level when she was absorbed into the Cosens' fleet. Note that her steering wheel was not on the bridge but on the deck between her paddle boxes.

WEYMOUTH LIBRARY

As the tide floods in, men are working from pontoons and stagings to complete MAJESTIC'S *antifouling. The white boot-topping between the black hull and the antifouling lasted only for the 1901 season.*
WEYMOUTH LIBRARY

Surrounded by paddling children, for whom this close-up of the hull of a paddle steamer must have been quite a novelty, MONARCH displays the rather austere varnished and scumbled upperworks which she retained until 1903.

WEYMOUTH LIBRARY

This photograph of EMPRESS clearly illustrates the way in which her keel sloped upwards towards the bow, to facilitate grounding on the West Country beaches and at Lulworth Cove.
WEYMOUTH LIBRARY

VICTORIA showing her sloping forefoot and the small davit right aft, used for handling the kedge anchor. This would be dropped over the stern and hauled tight, to keep the ship at right angles to open beaches while landing passengers.

WEYMOUTH LIBRARY

The final photograph in this sequence shows a group of children, complete with buckets, spades and sailor-suits, paddling past the team of men hard at work applying a coat of paint to the paddle tug QUEEN.
WEYMOUTH LIBRARY

BRODICK CASTLE at Victoria Pier, Cowes, during regatta week. Having arrived from Bournemouth, the steamer has put a bow line ashore and then backed away from the pier to allow the wind and tide to turn her round so that her bows are facing northwards, ready for her homeward departure.
CRAWFORD
ALEXANDER COLLECTION

the Isle of Wight, Solent and Weymouth in direct opposition to *Albion* and *Lorna Doone*, Cosens' flexibility at Bournemouth increased significantly. *Empress* and *Lord Elgin* continued to provide the core Swanage service, occasionally opposed by visiting Southampton Company steamers such as *Solent Queen* and *Prince of Wales*, while *Victoria* offered additional sailings to Lulworth Cove on the days when she came along from Weymouth. Competition was intense and on August Bank Holiday it was reported that no less than ten different steamers called at Bournemouth Pier, embarking between them some 10,000 passengers.

Apart from the arrival of Cosens' new flagship, the 1901 season was punctuated by a number of memorable incidents. On 3rd May, a serious collision occurred between *Empress* and *Albion* off Bournemouth Pier as both ships departed simultaneously at 10.45am. *Albion* had left the western landing stage, swung astern towards Poole and was going ahead towards Boscombe when she hit *Empress*, which had backed away from the eastern stage and was now turning to port to head for Swanage. *Albion*'s bow, which was severely twisted by the force of the collision, cut into *Empress*'s port sponson, cracked several hull plates and caused serious damage to her side houses and paddle box. The impact rolled her violently to starboard and there was momentary alarm among the passengers, several of whom fearing that she might founder, jumped aboard the *Albion*. Coastguards on the West Cliff who saw the collision take place rushed to the pier, launched their boat and were alongside the steamers in a matter of minutes but thankfully were not needed. Both ships were able to limp back to the pier and land their passengers safely, *Monarch* carrying her fleet-mate's shaken complement onwards to Swanage.

Empress was discovered to be making water and a tug was sent for to tow her back to Weymouth, where she was immediately put on the slipway for survey and repair. The damage was sufficiently serious to keep her out of service for several weeks

but the irritation caused was tinged with relief that the results had not been more serious. Had *Albion* been travelling fractionally faster, *Empress*'s hull would undoubtedly have been cut through, with potentially disastrous consequences. An arbitration hearing held in November, found both steamers equally to blame for the incident.

A week after the collision, Cosens' head office on Custom House Quay was broken into and £170 stolen. A few weeks later, police enquiries led them to Capt Symes, who had just been promoted from mate of *Monarch* to command of *Albert Victor*. Some of the money was recovered from his lodgings and the rest from behind the panelling in his cabin on board the tug, and 22 year-old Symes was arrested for the crime and sentenced to six months imprisonment with hard labour. A sad end to a very promising career.

At Torquay, the shopkeepers of Victoria Parade, anxious to maximise their profits, had been petitioning the Town Council to insist that excursion steamers visiting the resort should disembark their passengers at the nearby Haldon Pier rather than the traditional berth at Princess Pier. Both the ships' masters and their passengers, however, preferred Princess Pier and complained bitterly when the Council gave in to the traders' demands. Cosens threatened to withdraw all sailings to Torquay and matters came to a head when *Victoria* arrived there on 23rd July. Her master announced that he intended landing his passengers at Princess Pier or not at all and if he was prevented from doing so Cosens would cease to call with immediate effect and adopt Paignton Pier as their destination instead. When the pier master refused to take his ropes, '*an exceedingly lively passage of words*' ensued but eventually the determined attitude of *Victoria*'s skipper won the day, and his passengers were permitted to land. Six days later, *Majestic* arrived at Princess Pier but, finding no pier staff present to take her ropes and receiving no response from repeated blasts on her steam whistle, backed out into the bay again. Those ashore assumed that Capt Rawle intended to carry out Cosens' threat to make for Paignton instead but were delighted to be proved wrong. *Majestic* came ahead again and this time came so close to the landing stage that several crew members were able to jump ashore and take her ropes. Two or three hundred excursionists then surged ashore and, declining to pay the 1d toll, forced their way past the dumbfounded pier master and a member of the Town Council, and into Torquay. Thereafter the Torquay pier authorities adopted a more conciliatory attitude and Cosens' steamers continued to call.

In September, as the weather broke and the season began to draw to a close, the board were able to look back on a truly momentous year in the company's history. Despite the '*rapacious and merciless tactics*' of the rival steamers which had come '*like Van Tromp, with brooms at their mastheads and threatened to sweep the Channel clean*', the poor late season passenger figures, a fall in trade to the Fleet and the total absence of salvage work, the company had survived. Although some shareholders carped at the disappointing 3 per cent dividend and looked whimsically back to the golden years of the 1870s when the happy band of proprietors had been able to enjoy 15 per cent from their limited capital, they had to admit that the business was now in completely different circumstances. It was now a major employer with a broad and diverse industrial base which, although faced with unprecedented expenses during the past year, had much to be pleased about. A new flagship had been built, the rival *Brodick Castle* had been absorbed into the fleet and the relentless growth of Bournemouth (which reached a population of 59,762 in 1901) had pushed passenger figures up by 45,000 to a new record of almost a quarter of a million.

Passenger figures			
	1900	1901	Change
Bournemouth	81,129	128,684	47,555 +
Weymouth	34,403	39,095	4,692 +
Portland	36,392	44,623	8,231 +
H.M. Fleet	44,390	29,147	15,243 –
Total	196,314	241,549	45,235 +

Receipts at Bournemouth showed such a dramatic increase that, somewhat meanly, Cosens decided to reduce the commission payable to their local manager, David Sydenham. Henceforth, he received 6 per cent on earnings up to £6,000, 4 per cent from £6,000–£12,000 and 3 per cent on any figure above £12,000.

During the winter of 1901-2, a number of alterations were carried out to members of the fleet. A patent smokeless furnace fitted to *Prince George*'s boiler during September proved such an immediate success that *Victoria* was equipped with one in October, and *Empress* and *Monarch* during March 1902. *Victoria* was fitted with a solid bulkhead across the forward end of her engine room to provide better protection in heavy weather, while *Brodick Castle* received a major refit, including the re-decking of her promenade deck.

The addition of two large new steamers, both of which were too wide to pass through Weymouth's Town Bridge, meant that from 1901 onwards there was not always room in Weymouth Harbour for the whole fleet to lay up during the winter. It therefore became the practice for *Majestic* and *Brodick Castle* to spend the winter on moorings in the Wareham Channel at Poole, leaving in rotation for refit at Weymouth and dry docking at Southampton. While one of the ships was at Weymouth, *Monarch* would usually take her place on the buoys. A skeleton crew, often consisting of the master or mate and chief engineer, remained on board each ship to carry out maintenance work and act as watchmen. One of Cosens' steam launches would be sent round to Poole each autumn to provide the crews with a link to the shore and to act as a workboat.

Empress and *Lord Elgin* opened the 1902 season on 17th March with the usual Bournemouth – Swanage service, together with a daily smooth water cruise up Poole Harbour, while at Weymouth the Portland service and short cruises in the Bay provided the equivalent experience. *Monarch* began at Bournemouth on 29th March and three days later had the honour of being the first ship to call at the new Victoria Pier at Cowes on the Isle of Wight. For many years, Cowes had received less visiting steamers than other Island resorts because of difficulties surrounding access to the existing Fountain Pier. This structure was owned by the Southampton Company which, quite understandably, discouraged rival vessels by charging them excessively high pier tolls. Although their own *Lorna Doone* used it fairly regularly, it was also claimed that the depth of water, tidal flow and position of the pier made it unsuitable for larger steamers, with the consequence that the tradesmen of West Cowes were deprived of a considerable amount of potential trade.

Pressure for an alternative became intense and, by the summer of 1900, the Cowes Pier Act had passed through Parliament. Completed in time for the 1902 season, the new pier was only 170 feet long, had a cast iron girder shank approached between two elegant pagoda-like toll-booths and a broad timber pier head which could easily accommodate the largest of pleasure steamers. It immediately became a regular and popular destination for Cosens' cruises from Bournemouth and over 300 calls by various companies' steamers were recorded during the inaugural season.

Queen Victoria having died on 22nd January 1901, the accession of King Edward VII had been somewhat overshadowed by the nation's mourning for a Sovereign who had reigned for a remarkable 64 years. Now, with the dawning of a new year, the public and steamer companies alike were looking forward to a major Fleet Review, which had been announced for 28th June 1902. This was the first time that a review had been held to celebrate a Coronation and demand for tickets was intense. As early as March, Cosens had placed newspaper advertisements for trips by *Majestic* and *Monarch* at 25s and 21s respectively for the review itself and 6s and 5s for the evening illuminations. An announcement that prices would be raised during June stimulated demand to such a degree that both ships quickly sold out and Cosens were forced to add *Victoria* to the sailing list to cope with the overflow.

Cosens, of course, were not alone in responding to the forthcoming event. In addition to all the local steamers, a number of visiting excursion ships were scheduled to operate from Southsea, Southampton and the Isle of Wight piers, while P. & A. Campbell Ltd selected Bournemouth as their starting point and planned to send both *Westward Ho* and *Britannia* round from Bristol to join *Cambria*. *Westward Ho* was committed to passengers arriving by rail from Bristol but the other two sisters were open to local bookings.

197

Sandown Pier, Isle of Wight, with BRIGHTON QUEEN alongside. TERRY CRESSWELL COLLECTION

Excitement was mounting steadily when, on 24th June, news was received that the King had undergone an operation and that the Review would have to be postponed. As the fleet of 130 warships had already assembled, many of the steamer companies, including Cosens, quickly reduced their fares and advertised numerous trips to view them. Pre-booked passengers were offered the option of retaining their tickets pending the announcement of a revised Review date, or receiving a full refund. Many of the visiting steamers received news of the cancellation before leaving their home ports but others had already arrived in the Solent and offered limited trips before returning home. Campbell's *Britannia* ran as advertised from Bournemouth but her passengers were given a 16s refund.

When the Review eventually took place on 16th August, rather less visiting steamers appeared on the scene than had been planned for in June. *Britannia* did re-appear at Bournemouth, however, offering trips to the Review and illuminations, together with a further sailing on 18th August to view a procession of 100 warships passing the Royal Yacht off St. Helens, on their way to sea to stage a sham battle. To Cosens' immense relief, she sailed from Bournemouth at 6pm the same evening, offering a single trip to Cardiff and Bristol with return by rail. *Majestic*, *Monarch* and *Brodick Castle* were all well-filled on their respective trips to the Review and evening illuminations.

The rest of the season was characterised by the usual intense competition at Bournemouth. The Southampton Company had added another new excursion paddle steamer, *Queen*, to their fleet and their vessels came to Bournemouth even more frequently than before. The Joint Railway Company's

Duchess of Fife came down from Portsmouth on most Wednesdays in high season and while her passengers were ashore, operated special cheap trips to Swanage for a fare of 1s return. Cosens struck back by offering long day excursions from Clarence Pier, Southsea, to Bournemouth and Swanage. *Brodick Castle* would leave Bournemouth at 7am on early morning sailings to Southsea, where her passengers were allowed 9 hours ashore. She would then depart from Clarence Pier at 9.45am for Yarmouth, Bournemouth and Swanage, returning during the late afternoon in order to collect her morning passengers.

In March 1902, Capt Alec Campbell, Managing Director of P. & A. Campbell Ltd, not content with his company's inroads at Bournemouth and Southampton, purchased the Brighton, Worthing & South Coast Steamboat Co's two steamers *Princess May* and *Brighton Queen* on his own account. *Princess May* was never used on the South Coast but *Brighton Queen*, which was even newer and larger than *Cambria*, was to prove a formidable addition to Campbell's resources. She was operated as one of their fleet and enabled Campbells to interlink their Southampton and Brighton sailings, and offer an even wider selection of excursions covering the whole coast from Weymouth to Hastings. By changing steamers at Brighton, for example, passengers were occasionally able to sail all the way from Southampton to Boulogne and back in a day. The splendid *Brighton Queen* began to appear regularly at Bournemouth on long day trips from Brighton and always advertised a single trip to Ryde or Brighton on her return leg, with rail return. *Albion* and *Cambria*, of course, were even more frequent visitors on their trips from Southampton and the Isle of Wight. It must have come as something

266 CHERBOURG — Départ du " *Majestic* ", steamer excursionniste anglais

Collection P. B , Cherbourg

of a relief to Cosens when *Brighton Queen* hit a rock off Hastings on a return sailing from Boulogne during August and was off service for the rest of the month. Her place at Brighton had to be taken by one of the Southampton-based steamers, which temporarily reduced Campbell's ability to compete at Bournemouth.

Cross-Channel sailings from Bournemouth reached their numerical peak in 1902. *Cambria*, *Balmoral* and *Majestic* were all crossing to Cherbourg on a regular basis and large crowds continued to gather on the pier to watch them race homewards at the end of the day. The debate over which was the fastest of the opposition ships remained unresolved, while *Majestic*'s reputation for seaworthiness and comfort became more firmly established as each week passed. *Monarch* very occasionally went to Cherbourg on a special charter but her cross-channel forays were otherwise limited to the Alderney trips, which usually took place once a month during July, August and September.

Writing during the 1960s, R.J. Sutton recalled some evocative details of one such crossing to Cherbourg:

'We had a special party on board – the Buffaloes or some similar organisation, essentially male and very robust. Billy Driscoll, a well-known seaside concert-party organiser who had a pitch on Bournemouth Pier and ran a pierrot show, was engaged for the journey and, to provide music, brought a portable

harmonium. He and his party gave entertaining shows on deck and added to the gaiety of the occasion.

On arrival at Cherbourg practically everyone landed after being checked for matches – then contraband, as it was a French Government monopoly I believe – and I remember seeing Billy marching back to the ship with his party, each one of whom shouldered a long bread baton, the loaf of the day in France. It was evident too that each had engaged in drinking several glasses of penny ports and they were smoking penny cigars. Followed by a jeering crowd they arrived at the Quai de Caligny somewhat boisterously and marched on board just as the boat was to sail.

Billy went on to the fo'c'sle head with his portable organ and the crowd were soon singing popular songs of the day, winding up with patriotic airs and 'God Save the King'. As a final, if mistaken, gesture of friendship the organ struck up 'La Marseillaise'. We necessarily had to hum it as few of us could have known the words, but this brought execration upon us from the now very resentful crowd thronging the quay. The French expressed their annoyance by throwing small coins at the musicians and the whole of the passengers soon began to feel these coins, for they really were thrown and it was little consolation to be hit in the face by a franc piece! Even to a small boy who later collected the coins to be used on a later visit!

In the **Daily Mail** next morning appeared an apology from the French authorities who blamed

MAJESTIC departing from Cherbourg en route for Bournemouth, as depicted on a French-published picture postcard. The crossing generally took the ship about 4¹/₂ hours.

BERNARD COX COLLECTION

rowdy elements for the near-riot, but I shall always remember "A bas les Anglais" shouted in unison by the anti-British crowd, and I for one was glad when we cleared the mole and were out of danger from the excited and exasperated French mob.'

R.J. Sutton also recalled that

'... one of the characters of the steamers in the early 1900s was John Driscoll, the 'fruit man'. He had a pitch on the Majestic *in 1902 and used to come striding down Bournemouth Pier just before sailing time with his huge display basket on his head. He was a Cockney-Irishman and dressed in the style of the barrow-boys of the day. A long-skirted coat with voluminous pockets, a scarf round his neck, a disreputable old cap (which concealed a small cushion when he was carrying the basket), his drainpipe or bell-bottomed trousers, his chin whiskers and his clay pipe completed a picture of a rather taciturn, tall old man who will always remain in my memory. His pitch was a locker just forward of the funnel. His basket was a store-room and display stand most ingeniously contrived, and he sold exotic fruits rarely seen in the shops. I even remember mangoes, for once he gave me one that was going off, and I haven't tasted one since!*

He only went on long trips and this sometimes meant a transfer to Monarch, *which then did the Alderney run exclusively for some reason. One day that summer old John did not turn up. Instead, a lithe young fellow came on board jauntily carrying the basket but very gingerly negotiating the gangway with his unusual load. He remained on board each day for about three weeks and became quite popular. He had a pleasant tenor voice and knew all the popular songs of the day. He boasted that he was a boxer and was 'resting', and said that he was Driscoll's nephew.*

One very blustery day, bright with sun but with a high wind and the aftermath of a summer gale overnight, the Monarch *was doing the long trip of the day, 80 miles round the Isle of Wight calling at Ventnor and Ryde, so we transferred to her. We passed the Needles and went outside the island, breasting quite a high sea which, as the bows dipped, tossed fine spray over the fo'c'sle head, upon which appeared the loveliest rainbow that one could wish for. In shimmering colour it hung over our bows, bisected by the sharp stem of the boat, and was so fascinating that all eyes turned towards it admiring the unusual beauty of the sight, and nearly everyone succumbed! I have never seen so many seasick people in my life. For some reason I was immune but even the Chief Steward – North I remember – went down, and the substitute fruit man was lying in the scuppers begging me to put him out of his misery!*

He failed to turn up a few days later and old John was back. He was curiously silent regarding his nephew and baulked all questions.

Fourteen years later I was in the army and a man loaned me some books. Among them was a copy of the life of Dan Leno, with a rather unusual portrait on the cover without make up. Dan Leno, the greatest comedian of them all, as a private citizen. And there, staring me in the face, was the nephew of old John Driscoll, our temporary fruit man. Or could I have been mistaken? I often wonder ..."

Mr Sutton's lively experience on board *Monarch* was, unfortunately, fairly typical of the season's weather and many potential passengers opted to remain ashore. The Coronation fiasco necessitated the return of some £2,000 in advance fares, which were never fully recouped at the alternative August Review and the presence of the Reserve Squadron in place of the Channel Fleet at Portland led to a slight fall in liberty boat earnings. Despite these difficulties, however, the company was able to declare another 3 per cent dividend and to reduce and consolidate the mortgages on *Majestic*.

During the August Bank Holiday, the Bournemouth police had appeared at the pier to check the passenger numbers and summonsed the masters of *Victoria* and *Monarch* for overcrowding. The cases came to court during late September. Capt John Cox of *Victoria* was accused of carrying 18 passengers in excess of his permitted 375 but countered by producing both ticket books and mechanical hand counters or 'clickers' to demonstrate that only 374 had been on board. The police were accused of including stewards who had passed to and fro along the gangways several times and babes-in-arms within their numbers, and the magistrates dismissed the case. Capt Hardy of *Monarch* explained that, having brought his ship from Weymouth he was placed on the Swanage traffic for the remainder of the day. During the afternoon he was sent as relief boat to help clear a backlog of 800 passengers who were waiting on Swanage Pier. He and the mate counted 487 on board and sailed leaving a large number behind. On arrival at Bournemouth the police accused him of having nine more passengers than his permitted 491. The Captain attempted to explain the difference by claiming that children who had been carried on board at Swanage and were therefore not counted, must have walked ashore at Bournemouth and been included in the total. Cosens' solicitor spoke strongly in support of the Captain, complaining that it was vexatious and frivolous of the police to bring charges over nine passengers on a day when thousands had passed through the turnstiles and any master wishing to exceed his load could easily have done so by many hundreds. Given that *Monarch* was certified to carry 982 in smooth water, it would have been an easy matter to embark all of the overflow from Swanage but instead the master had done his best to stick to legal limits. The magistrates were clearly sympathetic to this argument and contented themselves with imposing a nominal fine of £1 plus costs.

As the season drew to a close, an offer was received through a shipbroker for the purchase of both *Majestic* and *Monarch* but was promptly

VICTORIA landing passengers at Seaton, circa 1902.
CRAWFORD ALEXANDER COLLECTION

refused. *Majestic*'s final crossing of the year to Cherbourg on 30th September proved a stormy affair, with the sea getting steadily rougher as the day progressed. *Majestic* arrived in the French port an hour behind schedule and her sea-sick passengers were only able to enjoy three quarters of an hour's respite ashore, before she sailed again at 3.45pm. Having purchased the obligatory postcards and souvenirs and visited the famous vegetable market, the passengers returned reluctantly on

EMPRESS at Swanage Pier, circa 1902.
AUTHOR'S COLLECTION

A group of passengers enjoying the sunshine on MAJESTIC's after deck during 1902. Note that, curiously, the only two women in the photograph seem anxious to conceal their identities and are hiding their faces from the camera!
AUTHOR'S COLLECTION

where, having missed their train, her Weymouth passengers were offered the choice of overnight accommodation in Bournemouth, or a cab to Hamworthy Junction to catch the mail train home.

Cambria had finished her season a few days earlier and departed from Bournemouth at 1pm on Friday 26th September, on a single trip to Bristol where she was due to arrive at 7am next morning. Unbeknown to Cosens, she was never to return and Campbell's competition at Bournemouth was at an end.

Although Campbells never stated their reason for withdrawing from Southampton and Bournemouth, it may be inferred that their new Brighton business offered far better commercial prospects. The opposition on the Sussex Coast was less intense and the magnificent *Brighton Queen* had the long-distance and cross-channel market more or less to herself. Furthermore, the fare-war which had resulted from the competition with Cosens and the Southampton Company must have cut profit margins on the Hampshire and Dorset coasts to the bone and made running such an expensive ship as *Cambria* an extremely marginal undertaking. From 1903 onwards, both *Brighton Queen* and *Glen Rosa* frequently visited the area from their new base at Brighton but never again competed directly for the Bournemouth trade. However, it is no exaggeration to assert that *Cambria*'s six-year sojourn on the South Coast was directly responsible for the complete transformation of the local steamer services, a major step-change in the affairs of Cosens & Co Ltd and, of course, the construction of their new flagship *Majestic*.

board and the vessel departed. Once clear of the breakwater, it became clear that the seas had increased yet further and the rest of the trip was described as 'exhilarating'. The windward side of the deck was constantly drenched with spray and, as darkness began to fall, more solid water began to break on board. The majority of passengers remained below and those few who braved the dangers of the deck were soon soaked through. The ship finally arrived at Bournemouth at 10.00pm

Capt St. Barbe Rawle stands at the telegraph as MAJESTIC prepares to depart from Boscombe Pier.
DORCHESTER LIBRARY

CHAPTER 11

WINTER SERVICES & PRESSURE FROM SOUTHAMPTON

1903-1908

On Boxing Day, 26th December 1902, *Victoria* inaugurated an experimental winter service between Bournemouth and Swanage. From the very beginning it was made clear that this unlikely innovation was intended to generate prestige rather than profit but could be carried out at very little cost to the Company. *Majestic* and *Brodick Castle*, which were laid up for the winter in Poole Harbour, both had caretaker crews on board and it was reasoned that, when the weather was suitable, a selection of these could provide a crew for *Victoria*, while on bad days they could continue with their maintenance work. Thus, for the price of the coal alone, Cosens would be able to generate substantial goodwill among local residents by offering the convenience of a winter ferry service between the two towns.

The Board of Trade issued a special limited winter certificate for 224 passengers and *Victoria* left Bournemouth twice a day at 11.00am and 2.30pm, returning from Swanage at 12.30pm and 3.15pm. At the end of each day, she advertised a one way *'picturesque, smooth water cruise up Poole Harbour'* for a fare of 1s and spent her nights berthed at Hamworthy Wharf. *Monarch* was kept in reserve at Weymouth ready to be brought into service should *Victoria* experience any difficulties.

The weather during the opening months of the new service was extremely unsettled and financial returns were predictably discouraging but, realising the promotional value of keeping their steamers in the public eye all year round, Cosens kept faith with their passengers and maintained the schedule until the commencement of the Easter programme on 23rd March. Indeed, the experiment was judged to be sufficiently successful that it was repeated each winter until 1908. A little known but unique episode in South Coast pleasure steamer history.

The withdrawal of the Campbell steamers meant, of course, a halving of the competition at Bournemouth, and 1903 and 1904 provided a welcome period of relative calm in which Cosens could draw breath and consolidate their position. The hard-worked *Victoria* opened the Easter sailings with *Lord Elgin* and was joined a week or so later by *Monarch*, which offered the first Round the Isle of Wight trip of the season on 3rd April. *Premier* had her boiler re-tubed and her engine fitted with a link starting motion before she entered service in May. On 4th May, *Monarch* offered a special early-season excursion to Cherbourg, to witness the departure of King Edward VII for home following a State Visit to France. Having called at Boscombe *en route* from Swanage, she left Bournemouth Pier

at 9.00am with 150 passengers on board and steamed through dense fog until 11.00am when the weather cleared and she was able to make better speed to Cherbourg. The departure of the King on board the Royal Yacht escorted by a squadron of warships had been advertised for 3pm, so *Monarch*'s passengers were disappointed to discover that it had been postponed to late evening, long after the steamer's 4pm departure for home. Having spent several enjoyable hours ashore, they therefore had to content themselves with cheering the assembled warships. *Monarch*'s bridge, upper deck and bows had been draped with large banners proclaiming 'Long live the King' and other patriotic mottoes, and each warship in turn dipped her ensign to the steamer as she passed through their lines. Fog was again encountered on the homeward journey and although Boscombe was reached at 9.30pm, it was another hour and a half before the steamer was able to grope her way into Bournemouth Pier and land the last of her disappointed passengers.

Monarch went to Cherbourg again on 21st May and offered a day trip to Torquay on 23rd, before *Majestic* appeared on 1st June to take over the long distance excursions. Throughout the high season she offered regular sailings to Cherbourg, Brighton, Dartmouth and Torquay, and Round the Island, while *Monarch* and *Brodick Castle* concentrated on the shorter full and half-day sailings. The Dartmouth trips were normally arranged to connect with one of the small river steamers, which would offer *Majestic*'s passengers the popular option of continuing up the picturesque River Dart to Totnes and back. The only trip of the season visiting Worthing was advertised for 13th July.

A rare survivor from the winter service; another of the 1902 series, this postcard was written on board VICTORIA *on Saturday 16th Feb 1903.*
CRAWFORD ALEXANDER
COLLECTION

203

VICTORIA making her way down Weymouth Harbour from her overnight berth, to commence her day's sailings from the Pile Pier during 1903. MONARCH is moored at Trinity Quay and the hulk PATRUUS of Jersey lays alongside an unidentified brig, while QUEEN, with a coal barge alongside, is moored outside Cosens' Head Office. The masts of the ex-convict ship SUCCESS from Australia, which was moored in Weymouth as a floating attraction, can be seen above the roof tops on the right.

AUTHOR'S COLLECTION

Monarch continued to offer a monthly trip to Alderney and, most unusually, *Majestic* was scheduled to go there on 19th August although, in the event, the trip was abandoned due to bad weather. Unfortunately, the same period of high winds also led to the cancellation of a charter by a syndicate of Bournemouth residents which would have taken *Monarch* to Jersey three days later. The steamer was scheduled to depart from Bournemouth at 10.00am and Swanage at 10.35am on 22nd August, arriving in Jersey during the course of the afternoon. The whole of Sunday and Monday morning would have been spent on the Island before the ship departed for home at midday, all for a fare of 17s 6d.

The Southampton Company's *Balmoral* and *Lorna Doone* continued to visit Bournemouth and offer onward trips to Swanage or Weymouth on about five days each week, while their smaller steamers *Queen*, *Solent Queen* and *Prince of Wales* made regular appearances. The Joint Railway Co's *Duchess of Fife* continued to offer cut-price trips between Bournemouth and Swanage on her day trips from Portsmouth and Cosens were forced to reduce their own fares to 1s on the midday sailing whenever their rival was in the area.

Unfortunately, 1903 was a season of extremely unfavourable weather. Throughout July and August, *'rainy days succeeded rainy days with melancholy iteration, the monotony only broken by cold winds of such unutterable bleakness as to make sea trips a grim irony'* and the passenger figures, which might have been expected to improve following the departure of Campbell's vessels, fell by 15,000. Sailings were cancelled completely on 19 days and on many others the

steamers failed to cover their running costs. On 10th September, the whole of the region was swept by a violent gale, which caught several steamers at sea. *Brodick Castle* had been making an excursion round the Isle of Wight and had got almost as far as Christchurch on her return voyage when she encountered such terrific seas that Capt Tilsed decided to put back to Yarmouth, where the ship spent the night alongside the pier. Some of her 260 passengers returned by ferry to Lymington and thence by rail to Bournemouth, while others opted to find overnight accommodation in the town. *Majestic* was homeward bound from Southsea when she too was forced to turn back and anchor off Yarmouth. Unfortunately, the wind continued to veer and increase to such an extent that Capt Rawle was forced to run eastwards up the Solent in search of a more sheltered anchorage. The gale raged for most of the night and it was not until the following morning that the steamers were able to return to their bases and resume normal sailings. *Majestic* made her last sailing on 7th October and the disappointing season drew to a close on 24th October at both Bournemouth and Weymouth.

If 1903 was a dismal excursion season, it was certainly a very memorable one for Cosens' salvage department, being punctuated by a number of major services and numerous smaller ones. The first incident, which must have caused great frustration in the boardroom, took place during a gale on the evening of 29th January, when the 2,360 ton screw steamer *Woodburn* was attempting to enter Portland Harbour. The ship was in ballast and riding high out of the water so that, as she approached her anchorage, a gust caught her bow and blew her rapidly towards the new breakwater. Her master used the engines to prevent her from going broadside on to the construction works and signalled for urgent assistance. *Albert Victor* was close by embarking officers and men from *HMS Empress of India* for the evening liberty boat run to Weymouth but her master felt unable to respond until he had put his passengers ashore. By the time he had done so and returned to the scene, the Portland tugs *Verne* and *Petrel* had succeeded in towing *Woodburn* off and claiming the salvage fee. The directors' reaction to the *Albert Victor*'s actions can only be imagined!

A second and rather more successful service took place two days later when, with a severe gale still raging, a large steamer was sighted flying signals of distress some twelve miles to the west of Portland Bill. *Queen* was despatched immediately and *Albert Victor*, which was again tendering to warships at Portland, was sent in pursuit as soon as *Premier* arrived to take over her duties to the Fleet. *Petrel*, *Verne* and two large tugs which happened to be laying in Portland Roads also joined in the hue and cry but the Cosens' tugs had a sufficient lead to arrive at the casualty first and pass their tow ropes. The steamer was the 2,208 ton *Elswick Park* of Newcastle, which had broken her propeller shaft, damaged her rudder and was drifting without power broadside on to the heavy seas. No sooner had towing commenced than *Albert Victor* fouled *Queen*'s towrope and suffered serious damage to her paddle box, lifeboat and davits. *Queen* was forced to slip and recover her cable whilst her damaged consort attempted to control the yawing casualty alone. Unfortunately, *Petrel*, *Verne* and one of the visiting tugs, *Dragon*, arrived on the scene at this very moment and were immediately engaged to take over the tow. *Queen* and *Albert Victor* were

relegated to steering duties at the casualty's stern. *Elswick Park* was successfully brought into Portland Roads but early the following morning, as the winds reached hurricane force, began to drag her anchors. As soon as Mr Fowler received news of the incident, the Weymouth lifeboat was launched and *Queen* steamed to the scene, where she discovered that *Elswick Park* had collided with and damaged the Cardiff steamer *Pwentland*. In the prevailing conditions, it was decided that any attempt to disentangle their anchor chains would be hopeless, so the two vessels were lashed securely together and *Queen* stood by all night to render further assistance if required. When the weather finally abated, the two ships were separated and re-anchored, Cosens sharing the final salvage settlement with the rival tugs. At about the same time, Cosens earned £65 for services to the brig *Wilson*.

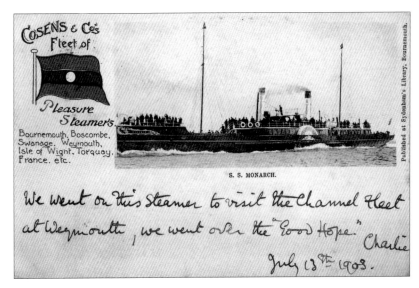

A postcard of MONARCH, *sent on 13th July 1903.*
JOHN PATRICK COLLECTION

S.S. " Majestic " leaving Bournemouth Pier.

By 1905, David Sydenham had published a new series of photographic cards on behalf of the company, each with the houseflag in the top left corner. In this view, MAJESTIC *is seen backing away from Bournemouth Pier. Note the brown toe rails round the deck and the absence of the white boot topping.*
CRAWFORD ALEXANDER COLLECTION

The reality! A dramatic shot of ALBERT VICTOR putting to sea on a salvage job in the teeth of an easterly gale.
AUTHOR'S COLLECTION/
SEWARD

Two views of the stricken SHAMROCK III dismasted in Weymouth Bay.
BELOW: Cosens' diving boat is alongside while one of their smaller steam launches passes by in the foreground.
BOTTOM: This close up view shows the buckled remains of SHAMROCK III's 170 foot metal mast, and the sails and rigging draped over her port side. Cosens' staff and the yacht's crew work together to sort out the chaos.
BOTH AUTHOR'S COLLECTION

During April, a casualty of a very different kind occurred in Weymouth Bay involving Sir Thomas Lipton, who became famous for his repeated and costly attempts between 1899 and 1920 to regain the America's Cup for Great Britain. On 6th April, Lipton's latest yacht, *Shamrock III*, accompanied by her predecessor *Shamrock I* and Sir Thomas's splendid steam yacht *Erin*, had arrived in Weymouth Bay to undertake a series of trial races prior to crossing the Atlantic to challenge the American yacht *Reliance* for the cup. Visitors flocked to Weymouth to watch the fun and Cosens immediately announced two trips each day – at 11am and 3pm – to watch the races. These generally followed a triangular course from Weymouth, round the Shambles Lightship, across to Lulworth Cove and back to Weymouth Bay. All went well until 11th April, when a steam yacht carrying spectators came far too close to the racing yachts and collided with *Shamrock I*, causing severe damage to her enormous, hollow, wooden spinnaker boom. The boom was landed at Weymouth and taken to Cosens' Engineering Works on the Backwater, where the repairs drew a large crowd of onlookers. Working day and night, carpenters completed the work in four days and the spar was duly returned to the yacht.

Designed by the famous William Fife, *Shamrock III* was 134 feet long and spread a breathtaking 14,154 square feet of canvas from her single mast. The tubular metal construction of the mast proved to be a weak link in her design and, when the yacht was caught in a gust off Weymouth on Friday 17th April, it crumpled and collapsed, allowing her entire rig to fall overboard. As it did so, one of her crew was knocked overboard and drowned, whilst two others suffered serious injuries. Cosens were soon on the scene and set to work cutting away the wreckage to salvage the rig, using a combination of tugs, steam launches, the diving boat and men from the workshops. The task was complex and attracted huge crowds, who flocked on board the excursion steamers to visit the scene of the disaster. At noon on Saturday, *Queen* took the yacht's enormous mainsail in tow and dragged it into the harbour, where the crane of the GWR steamer *Lynx* was used to lift it into one of Cosens' barges. By mid

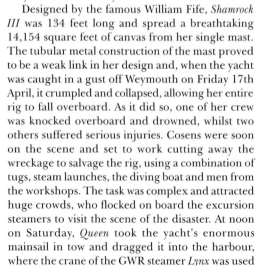

afternoon, the bulk of the running gear had been cut away from the mast which, suspended from two barges, was brought into Weymouth and alongside Cosens' No. 2 slipway at 6 pm. Here, the crane was used to adjust it more carefully and at 8pm, *Queen* took the barges and their 170 foot burden up through the Town Bridge, berthing them outside the company's engineering works. During the night, the barges began to show signs of damage owing to the tremendous weight they were carrying and early on Sunday morning, it became necessary to call out a gang of men to lift the mast onto the quayside using the sheerlegs crane. The next few days were spent stripping the mast of all re-usable fittings and then sawing it into three portions, while Cosens' steam launches dragged the seabed to recover the large quantities of debris which were lying there. *Shamrock III* was eventually towed away to receive a new mast but, before departing, Sir Thomas Lipton expressed his personal gratitude to Cosens for their prompt attention and efficient workmanship.

The same gale which had trapped *Brodick Castle* and *Majestic* in the Solent on the afternoon of 10th September, also caught a tug and lighter belonging to Sir John Jackson at sea off Portland. As the two vessels were making for the safety of Portland Roads, the tow parted and the lighter with nine men on board began to blow rapidly to leeward, passing through the notorious Race and narrowly missing the Shambles Bank. *Albert Victor*, which was laying off the breakwater in the hope of some salvage work, was quickly on the scene and managed to pass a tow. A course was set for Portland but, as the wind increased in force and veered into the north-west, the tug and the lighter were driven relentlessly downwind towards St. Alban's Head. Fearing that they would be driven ashore, Capt King headed out to sea and, when the tide turned and the sea became even more ferocious, made the decision to run eastwards towards the Isle of Wight, through the confused waters of the dangerous St. Alban's Race. Just before daybreak on 11th September, the tow parted and, with seas breaking clean over both vessels, *Albert Victor*'s crew began the arduous task of hauling the heavy, sodden rope on board before reconnecting the tow. The fact that the tug's towing gear had been carried away, her paddle box damaged and a sail blown to ribbons cannot have helped matters, but at 7.10am, the exhausted crew were rewarded for their exertions by bringing their charge safely into the shelter of Swanage Bay. A telegram was sent to Weymouth to reassure the waiting friends and relatives that everyone was safe. The men on board the lighter, who had been convinced that she would founder or capsize as the 400 tons of shingle in her hold continually shifted to and fro, expressed profound gratitude for the bravery of their rescuers.

While *Albert Victor* was engaged in this dramatic service, *Queen* went to the rescue of the large steam dredger *Weser*, whose engine room had become flooded during a stormy passage round Portland Bill. With her fires out and deprived of power, she was swept round the Bill and through the Race before the tug put a line on board and brought her into Weymouth. Sadly, the crew of cutter *Missions to Seamen* were not so lucky and were drowned when their little vessel foundered off Portland during the same gale. On 25th October, the Russian schooner *Emma Maria* defied the best attempts of three tugs to save her and became a total loss on Chesil Beach while, the very next day, the Norwegian barque *Patria* drove ashore right beside her.

The income from these salvage cases helped to offset some of the fall in passenger revenue but, as had been the case for several years, it was the works and engineering departments which provided the steady income upon which the stability of the company relied in years of poor weather. August had witnessed the sudden and unexpected death of Mr William Hinde, who had been the company's superintendent engineer for many years and who had been largely responsible for the success and expansion of the engineering works and foundry, as well as for the regular maintenance of the steamers. His loss was keenly felt and, in acknowledgement of the importance of this side of the company's work, he was replaced by two people. Mr Mark Frowde was appointed Works Manager on a salary of £200 per annum, while a Mr Frederick Jones, a highly experienced marine engineer, was recruited to fill the post of Marine Superintendent. Both men were to give long and loyal service to the company.

Another loss suffered by Cosens' during December 1903 was the death of John Penn, the celebrated London engineer, who had been the single biggest

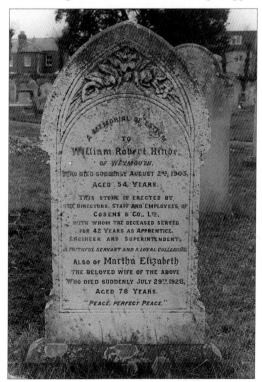

William Hinde's gravestone in Melcombe Regis cemetery.
AUTHOR

shareholder in the company. Penn had been associated with the company since 1848 when he helped Joseph Cosens to finance the *Princess* and had accepted a block of shares in the limited company in 1878 as part payment for the construction of *Empress*. He had built the engines for *Empress*, *Victoria* and *Monarch*, as well as providing a valuable source of engineering and commercial advice right up to the building of *Majestic* in 1901.

In March 1903, a new contract had been signed with the Army Service Corps for the continued employment of *Prince George*, *Princess* and other steam launches in supplying transport to and from the breakwater forts and dolphins. Although the Channel Fleet had not been much in evidence, the Reserve Squadron had used Portland a great deal during the year and had provided the smaller steamers with a reasonably steady source of income. There was also a marked increase in the demand for long-distance towage. Although a dividend of only 3 per cent was declared, diversification had saved the day and hopes were high for a more successful season in 1904.

The winter of 1903-04 saw *Empress* undergo her largest refit for many years. Her engine was fitted with a surface condenser and a link starting motion, both constructed by the Thames Iron Works at a cost of £490 and £59 respectively. A new boiler was ordered from Mordey, Carney & Co of Southampton for £720 and a larger saloon was constructed on the upper deck aft of the funnel. Her small bridge deck had always spanned the space between the boiler casing and the tiny deck house which enclosed the aft companionway but the whole space was now infilled, altering the vessel's profile and providing welcome shelter for passengers.

It would appear that *Victoria* was also fitted with an enlarged deck saloon at this time since, when she commenced the winter service on 1st February 1904, it was noted that passengers were benefiting from her '*increased shelter and comfort*'. The alterations to *Victoria* and *Empress*, together with smaller improvements to some of the other vessels, enabled the overall passenger capacity of the fleet to be increased by 400, which significantly increased earning power when the steamers were filled right up.

The company was involved in another salvage case on 26th February, when the tugs went to the assistance of the full rigged ship *Alauda*, which had come to anchor in a very dangerous position within feet of the rocks near Grove Point on Portland. On arriving alongside, the tugs were told that their services were not required and returned to their duties tendering to the Home Fleet. However, less than an hour later, news was received that *Alauda* had hoisted a signal of distress. Leaving their liberty boat duties for a second time, the tugs returned to the casualty, whose stern was now grounded firmly on the rocks and set about towing her off. The combined efforts of *Queen* and the Portland tugs

ABOVE: EMPRESS in Swanage Bay following her major refit during the winter of 1903-04. The new, cowl-topped funnel and the deck saloon aft of the paddle boxes are clearly visible.
H.A. ALLEN COLLECTION

RIGHT: During the refit, EMPRESS's wheel, which had previously been located on her upper deck, was moved up onto the bridge and a small, V-shaped, varnished shelter erected to protect the helmsman. Directly beneath this, on the upper deck, a curiously shaped deck-house was built to house the steam steering engine. The ship is pictured in Lulworth Cove, circa 1904.
AUTHOR'S COLLECTION

WINTER SERVICES & PRESSURE FROM SOUTHAMPTON

Verne and *Petrel* failed to move her but when *Albert Victor* added her power, the casualty slid off the rocks. *Alauda* was brought in to Portland Harbour and beached in shallow water to prevent her sinking. Since neither her own nor *Verne*'s pumps were sufficient to stem the influx of water, *Albert Victor* brought out a large steam salvage pump and a gang of Cosens' workmen, who quickly had the situation under control. Cosens carried out temporary repairs but both the pump and men remained on board *Alauda* while she was towed to South Shields for permanent repairs.

The 1904 season itself was unremarkable, with the patterns of sailings and competition almost an exact repeat of 1903. Despite the encroachment of the Southampton Company, Cosens refused to adopt similar tactics by basing a steamer in the Solent, instead reiterating their intention of '*defending their own castle to the utmost.*' Fortunately, the weather was far kinder and passenger figures increased again to just over half a million. The only recorded mishap took place on 7th July, during one of *Victoria*'s regular coasting trips from Weymouth to Torquay. She had picked up 80 passengers at West Bay on the outward leg but during the day, a stiff southwesterly wind sprang up and heavy swell developed, making the return call at the open beach very risky indeed. However, with consummate skill, Capt Hardy succeeded in running the steamer onto the beach and 60 passengers had disembarked over the

heaving bow landing gear before a lady slipped and fell into the sea. She was quickly hauled to safety but, with the surf increasing by the moment, Capt Hardy decided to take no further risks and hauled off the beach without further delay. In doing so, part of the gangway was torn off and left to be recovered by the local coastguard. Cosens' West Bay agent, Norman Good, immediately telephoned Weymouth and arranged for the last train to Bridport to wait for *Victoria*'s arrival in order that the twenty local passengers stranded on board could return home later that night.

The season of 1904 was also the first in which Cosens decided to take the catering on board the steamers into their own hands. Hitherto, the catering rights had been let by tender at regular intervals, frequently on a ship-by-ship basis. For twenty one

VICTORIA arriving at Trinity Quay, Weymouth, circa 1904, after backing up the harbour. Her bow ropes are already ashore and her forward capstan working hard, while the heaving line thrown by the crew in the stern is just being hauled ashore.
AUTHOR'S COLLECTION

EMPRESS, MAJESTIC and MONARCH coaling at the old Swanage Pier, circa 1904. The photograph reveals the trucks on the narrow-gauge tramway, fishing nets hanging to dry and even a stone jar of cider standing in the foreground.
SWANAGE MUSEUM

THE CATERING DEPARTMENT
— OF —

COSENS & CO.'S FLEET OF PLEASURE STEAMERS.

In the capacious Dining Saloons, Viands of the Best Quality are served in First-class Style according to the following Popular Tariff.

(Subject to any alterations that may be found necessary.)

BREAKFASTS, LUNCHEONS, TEAS, Etc.

	s.	d.
Breakfasts.—Plain	0	9
,, with Cold Meat	1	6
,, ,, Hot ,,	1	9
Luncheons.—Cold Joints	2	0
,, Fish, Salmon	2	0
,, Lobster	2	0
,, Cold Joints with Fish	3	0
,, Chicken, etc.	2	0
,, ,, ,, with Fish	3	0
,, Ham, Tongue	2	0
(inclusive of Vegetables, Salad, Cheese, etc.)		
,, Hot Joints	2	0
,, Chicken	2	6
(Inclusive of Vegetables, Salad, Cheese, etc.)		
Tea.—Plain, Cake with Bread and Butter	0	9
,, Cold Meat	1	6
,, Fish—Salmon	2	0
,, ,, Lobster	2	0
,, Chicken, etc.	2	0
,, ,, with Fish	3	0
Cup of Tea or Coffee	0	3
,, Cocoa or Chocolate	0	4
Pot of Tea, 1 person	0	6
,, 2 persons	0	10
,, 3 ,,	1	2
,, 4 ,,	1	6
Bovril, per cup	0	4
Bread and Butter, per Slice	0	1
Roll and Butter	0	3
Preserves	0	2
Salad	0	3

Biscuits, Sponge Cakes, Chocolates, etc.

The chief Dining Saloons—situate underneath the Grand Saloon on the Quarter-Deck—are provided with every facility for the comfort of the passengers and the convenience of the Stewards, and a prompt and efficient service is a special feature.

Catering Manager :—
E. HARFORD,
Cosens & Co., Ltd., Swanage.
26

WINE LIST.

	½-Bottle. s. d.	Bottle. s. d.
Champagne.		
Heidseick	6 6	12 6
Perrier Jouët	4 6	9 0
Moët	4 6	9 0
Hock.		
Sparkling	3 0	5 0
Still	2 6	4 0
Burgundy.		
Beaune	2 0	3 6
Claret.		
St. Julien	2 0	3 6
Medoc	1 6	3 0

Port and Sherry, per Glass ... 6d.

LIQUEURS.
Per Glass.
Cherry Brandy, Bénédictine, Green and Yellow Chartreuse, Kummel ... 6d.
All Spirits ... 4d. & 6d.

Peach, Orange and Angostura Bitters.

ALES, STOUT & MINERAL WATERS.

Worthington's Pale Ale	3d.	6d.
Bass's Pale Ale	3d.	6d.
Guinness's Stout	3d.	6d.
Raggett's Stout	3d.	6d.
Allsopp's Lager	—	3d.
Champagne Cider	3d.	6d.
Apollinaris	4d.	8d.
Perrier	4d.	8d.
Schweppe's Soda	3d.	6d.
Dry Royal	—	3d.
Seltzer or Potass	2d.	3d.
Soda	2d.	3d.
Lemonade	2d.	3d.
Ginger Beer and Ginger Ale	—	3d.

Sandwiches—Ham ... 2d. & 3d.
Cigars ... 3d., 4d. & 6d.
Cigarettes and Tobacco. Caps and Hat Guards.
27

This price list, published in Cosens' 1912 Official Guide, illustrates the range of drinks and foodstuffs available on board the larger steamers.
AUTHOR'S COLLECTION

years, from 1878 to 1899, Capt Bowering and his wife had been successful in bidding for the bulk of the fleet, although following the opening of the Bournemouth station in 1881, it became necessary to appoint a local caterer for whichever steamers were based at Swanage. A succession of individuals, including a Mr Ginder in 1885 and Messrs Graham and Brown in 1887, undertook this work, until in 1899, following the death of Capt Bowering, the contract for the entire fleet was let to a Mr Percy Graham for £350. In 1900, *Victoria* was let to a Mr Stribling for £80, *Monarch* and *Empress* to Mr Graham, and the smaller steamers to Mr W. Masters for £5 each. In 1901 and 1902, Mr Graham controlled all of the vessels for £620 per year but in 1903, refused to offer more than £525. In 1904, he declined to tender at all and the company decided to take matters into their own hands.

A Mr Mark Smith from Southampton was appointed catering manager at 50s per week, plus the cost of weekday lodgings ashore and his rail fare home once a week. A catering store was set up at Swanage and Mr Smith set about appointing stewards and cooks to all of the Bournemouth-based ships but things quickly began to go wrong. By May,

a private detective had been appointed to look into 'irregularities' within his department and Mr North, senior steward of *Majestic*, was dismissed in July. During 1904 alone, £1,800 was spent in Weymouth on catering stores and equipment, £1,200 in Bournemouth and £600 in Swanage. In view of the extra work involved in overseeing this new department, an extra director was appointed to the board and a directors' catering sub-committee set up. Mr Smith's tenure was also a short one for, by the beginning of 1905, a Mr Harford had been appointed to take his place. The rights for *Victoria* were let separately to a Mr Lankester for £70, while Mr Masters retained *Premier*, *Queen* and *Albert Victor* for a nominal sum of 5s each in exchange for providing his own licences, staff and equipment. Mr Harford remained with the company for many years and under his skilled supervision the catering department went from strength to strength, contributing a significant amount to the income of the marine department.

Catering on board the larger, long-distance steamers was quite sophisticated, with a wide range of hot and cold meals, together with cold snacks, teas, beers, wines and spirits on offer. The fare on board *Victoria* and *Empress* was of a somewhat simpler nature, while on local trips from Weymouth it was limited to teas, cakes, chocolate and, of course, the essential alcoholic drinks sold from the male preserve of the forward bar.

In May 1904, Cosens had been appointed as official contractors to the War Office and Admiralty, and almost immediately vessels began to arrive from as far afield as Liverpool. With five ships to be refitted during the summer, the engineering works found itself at full stretch and the number of apprentices under training was increased to 26. Pressure was further increased in July, when it was discovered that *Queen* required extensive and urgent repairs to her bottom plating. It was little surprise when the final accounts for the year showed that receipts in the trading departments had reached £19,826, only a little short of the £21,149 earned from passenger fares and stewarding.

On 15th August, the Home Fleet arrived in Portland and demand for liberty boats became so heavy that Cosens attempted to charter an additional steamer to avoid having to cancel scheduled excursions. Mr Constant, the London shipbroker, was approached for help but had no suitable vessels on his books, so Cosens were forced to fall back on creative timetabling to see them through the crisis.

In the early days of the company, it had been the custom to hold an annual '*dinner to employees*' in celebration of the season that had passed. As the company grew – in 1904 it employed over 200 men – this became less practical and the tradition lapsed for some time. In 1898, a small, informal smoking concert had been held in Swanage for the crews of the Bournemouth fleet and by 1904 this had grown into a large, annual event. The concert was held in the billiard room of the Ship Hotel at Swanage, which had been decorated with signal flags and name pennants from each of the local ships and was attended by their masters and crews. Mr David Sydenham, Cosens' revered Bournemouth manager, was in the chair and toasted the unfailing courtesy and capable seamanship of the men who '*made the wheels go round*'. After a number of further speeches and toasts, the assembled company settled in to an entertaining evening of popular songs and recitals from members of the audience.

Sadly, David Sydenham's health had begun to decline during 1903 and he had not been seen on Bournemouth Pier or in the booking office as regularly as before. Having guided the development of Cosens' Bournemouth business since its inception in 1881, he was held in great esteem by all who knew him and was greeted at the concert by tumultuous cheering and applause. Despite his declining mobility, he remained firmly at the helm of the Bournemouth station, advising on policy and strategy and supervising his nephew Reginald 'Rex' Sydenham and his long-standing assistant Mr Frost, who now undertook the bulk of the day-to-day practical tasks on his behalf.

By 1905, the two new breakwaters designed to enclose Portland Harbour were nearing completion and local mariners had noted how significantly their construction had altered the local tidal flows and sea conditions in Weymouth Bay. Their assertions were vividly illustrated on the night of 14th January 1905, when a south-easterly gale drove an unprecedented volume of water into the Bay, creating the most violent, breaking waves on the harbour bar that had been seen in living memory and causing a severe surge inside Weymouth Harbour. Several ships were damaged at their moorings and it was generally agreed that, had the tide been on springs rather than neaps, the lower end of the town would have been flooded.

By Sunday morning, 15th January, the gale had increased in fury and at 10.00am, the 4,000 ton steamer *Torridge*, at anchor off Newton's Cove, hoisted signals of distress. *Queen*, commanded by Capt Read, fought her way through the breaking seas on the bar and quickly passed a tow but no sooner had the weight been taken than one of *Torridge*'s anchor cables parted and she took a wild sheer, breaking the tow rope. Having completed the arduous task of recovering her long, sodden cable, *Queen*, now joined by *Albert Victor* under the command of Capt King, made another attempt to establish a connection with the casualty, which was now yawing erratically to and fro on her single anchor, just clear of the rocky, lee shore. Unfortunately, just as *Queen* ranged close alongside, *Torridge* sheered towards the tug, demolishing her paddle box and causing serious damage to her sponson. Fortunately, the paddle wheel itself could still be turned and *Queen* was able to claw off the lee shore and return to the safety of Weymouth. Shortly afterwards, *Albert Victor* suffered similar but less extensive damage and was also forced to abandon the salvage attempt. Happily, *Torridge*'s anchor held and later in the afternoon when the wind veered slightly, she was able to regain the open sea under her own steam.

The incident was a stark reminder, if any was needed, of the extreme risks which the tug crews took each time they put to sea to attempt a rescue. It was a task in which business and humanity were curiously blended and where the hope of a handsome salvage award was always balanced by the possibility of serious damage or loss of life. Absolute mutual trust

David Sydenham, Cosens' Bournemouth Manager from 1881 until his death in 1911. AUTHOR'S COLLECTION

A rather grainy view of QUEEN, *with a badly-damaged starboard paddle box and sponson, probably after the* TORRIDGE *rescue attempt.* AUTHOR'S COLLECTION

Profits appropriated in Dividends, Debenture Interest, Depreciation and Reserve Accounts, since the Year 1876, when the Company was incorporated.

Year	Rate	Ordinary Share Capital £	Amount £ s. d.	Preference Dividend £ s. d.	Debenture and Loan Interest £ s. d.	Reserve Fund £ s. d.	Depreciation Account £ s. d.	Total Appropriation £ s. d.	Annual Expenditure for Repairs and Maintenance since 1883 £ s. d.	Memo. of Extraordinary Expenses, &c.
1876	15	12800	1920		5 15 0			1925 15 0		Steam Launch purchased and Slipway acquired
1877	10	,,	1280		69 0 5			1989 0 5		
1878	12	,,	1536		248 3 11	1024 0 0		2808 3 11		s.s. *Premier* rebuilt.
1879	2½	16400	410		483 7 6			893 7 6		Wet Season s.s. *Empress* built.
1880	7½	,,	1230		471 12 7	42 2 3		1743 14 10		
1881	7	,,	1148		487 9 0	378 17 1		2014 6 1		
1882	8	,,	1312		488 0 5	51 0 2		1851 0 7		
1883	8	22800	1824		489 11 8	179 14 2		2493 5 10	2075 11 3	s.s. *Queen* built.
1884	6	32800	1968		487 10 0	354 2 8		2809 12 8	3126 4 7	s.s. *Victoria* built. New Boiler to s.s. *Empress*
1885	5	,,	1640		550 15 8	58 18 0		2249 13 8	3325 19 7	New Boiler to s.s. *Premier*.
1886	5	,,	1640		553 11 8	271 5 8		2464 17 4	2075 0 2	New Machinery at Slipway. New Boiler to Steam Launch.
1887	5	,,	1640		553 8 3	415 10 0		2608 18 3	2515 18 10	Jubilee Year.
1888	2½	,,	820		926 0 0	94 17 0		1840 17 0	2247 7 4	s.s *Monarch* built. s.s. *Victoria* lengthened and fitted with Surface Condenser.
1889	5½	,,	1804		1268 8 3	105 6 0		3177 14 3	2833 16 10	Foundry and *Albert Victor* purchased.
1890	5	,,	1640		1218 15 0	109 1 0		2967 16 0	2757 9 9	
1891	5	,,	1640		1218 15 0	112 6 0		2971 1 0	2708 6 8	
1892	6½	35795	2251 16 0		1218 15 0	1700 2 0		5170 13 0	2649 10 3	
1893	5	39170	1949 6 8		1213 10 10	320 17 0		3483 14 6	2723 9 9	
1894	4	40535	1621 8 0		1208 6 8	142 1 0	500 12 4	3472 8 0	3053 16 9	New Works inaugurated and *Premier* partially replated.
1895	5	40535	2026 15 0		1208 6 8		350 0 0	3585 1 8	3608 11 7	The boilers of *Victoria*, *Queen*, and *Princess* restored, and second half of *Premier* plated.
1896	4	42800	1712 0 0		1208 6 8		349 7 8	2269 14 4	4100 2 6	Additional Slipway acquired for Yacht Repairs and Boat Building.
1897	5	42800	2140 0 0		1208 6 8		500 0 0	3848 6 8	4497 3 11	New Tubular Boilers and Condenser fitted to *Albert Victor*.
1898	5	42800	2140 0 0	155 2 6	1208 6 8		500 0 0	4003 9 2	2581 0 5	s.s. *Prince George* built by and taken over by the Company.
1899	6	42800	2568 0 0	291 17 3	1208 6 8		500 0 0	4568 3 11	2691 10 6	General Offices enlarged and New Sheds erected at Slipway.
1900	5	42800	2140 0 0	345 0 0	1192 14 2		369 0 0	4046 14 2	3528 12 9	s.s. *Majestic* in course of building.
1901	3	48645	1459 7 0	719 0 0	1762 11 7		420 7 0	4361 5 7	3673 7 8	s.s. *Majestic* acquired.
1902	3	48695	1460 17 0	594 16 10	1877 5 9		421 7 0	4354 6 7	4653 18 8	New Boiler and Surface Condenser to s.s. *Empress*.
1903	3	48695	1460 17 0	663 15 9	1688 6 11	253 5 0	431 2 0	4497 6 8	4344 5 2	
1904	3	48695	1460 17 0	731 18 6	1642 4 6		431 2 0	4266 2 0	4209 6 8	

166½ = 5.74 per cent. per ann.

*Equal to an Average Appropriation of £2947 per annum for 29 years.

This table, taken from Cosens' Annual Directors' Report and Balance Sheet for 1904, neatly summarises some key features of the company's finances since its incorporation in 1876.
AUTHOR'S COLLECTION

in the skill and seamanship of everyone on board was a pre-requisite for putting to sea and in the case of *Torridge*, Capt King of *Albert Victor* was judged to have fallen short of the required standard. At a special meeting on 26th January, the board reported that the crew had lost faith in their captain and were refusing to sail with him again. Possibly influenced also by his previous failure to salvage *Woodburn* in 1903, they found King guilty of dereliction of duty and poor seamanship. He was dismissed from the ship and, rather than accept a post ashore, resigned from the company. He was replaced by Capt Hardy from *Victoria* until March, when a Mr J. Tucker was appointed on a one month trial. In due course, the directors repented of their rather harsh decision and by August 1905, Capt King was back in the company's employ and commanding his old ship once again.

Early in February 1905, *Queen* received a further £65 worth of damage following a collision with *S.S. Cassell* but a few weeks later was able to redeem herself in a particularly dramatic and profitable rescue. At 10.00am on 26th February, with hurricane force winds blowing in the channel, news was received from the Portland coastguard that a large sailing ship had been sighted on her beam-ends six miles to the west of Portland Bill. Weymouth's new lifeboat, *Friern Watch*, was launched and *Queen* was ordered to sea, being joined by the cruiser *HMS Scylla* as she passed through Portland Harbour. *Albert Victor* followed and took the lifeboat in tow. The casualty proved to be the 1,000 ton iron barque *County of Anglesey* which, by the time *Queen* and *Scylla*

had arrived on the scene, had been carried by the tide and wind to a position about a mile south of the Shambles Lightship. The lifeboat took off two terrified apprentices but the remainder of the crew was persuaded to stay on board and attempt to save the ship. *Queen* succeeded in getting a tow onto her stern and shortly afterwards some of the crew managed to make their way forward along the sloping deck and make fast a line from *Albert Victor*. *Queen* then slipped her tow and put a second hawser onto the barque's bow, before the two tugs commenced the tow to Weymouth. While passing through the tremendous seas in the vicinity of the Shambles Bank, the tugs' decks were repeatedly swept by breaking water and it was anticipated that the barque might founder at any moment. However, with *Scylla* standing by and the lifeboat in close attendance, she was brought safely into the shelter of Portland Harbour after an arduous five-hour tow.

Her problems, however, were far from over. When her anchors were let go it was discovered their chains had become so tangled that only a few fathoms were available. The barque's crew were too exhausted to be of any assistance, so the two tugs held her steady while Capt Masters of *Monarch* and a crew of Cosens' staff were summoned from ashore to sort matters out. Their labours were not assisted by the fact that a barrel of oil had overturned in the paint locker, spilling all over the foredeck and cables, making it practically impossible to gain a foothold on the slippery deck. With the deck sloping at over 45 degrees, the men had to be tied in position and, with the gale increasing again after a brief lull, there were still fears that the barque might capsize. The tugs continued to hold the ship in position until 4am next morning, when Capt Masters and his men succeeded in paying out 60 fathoms of cable and *County of Anglesey* was finally judged to be safely secured. At 8am, the tugs were finally released from their duties and returned to Weymouth. During the following day, men engaged at Portland laboured to trim the barque's 600 ton cargo of sand ballast and by late evening she was upright once again. The following day, accompanied by a tug, she sailed for repairs at Liverpool. Cosens received £400 plus costs for the rescue, together with £70 for raising the hulk of Messrs Miller's *Grand Duchess* which had sunk at Portland.

The winter service commenced on 6th February, when *Victoria* carried 150 passengers between Bournemouth and Swanage. During early March, a conference was held with the Southampton Company in the hope of agreeing mutually beneficial arrangements for the Swanage service but, when they refused to even consider the introduction of a common, slightly increased fare structure, the talks broke down and all other proposals were abandoned.

Far from co-operating with Cosens, the Southampton Company chose 1905 to increase the tempo of their competition at Bournemouth. *Lorna Doone* and *Balmoral* came down from Southampton even more frequently and, from July onwards, *Solent Queen* was based at Poole and introduced a regular Bournemouth to Swanage service in direct opposition to Cosens. The Southampton Company also announced that they had placed an order for a new vessel, to be named *Princess Royal*. She would be delivered in time for the 1906 season and would replace *Lorna Doone* as the company's premier Southampton-based excursion steamer. *Lorna Doone* could then be based at Poole and operate in direct opposition to *Monarch* and *Brodick Castle* on full and half-day trips to Weymouth and the Isle of Wight, while *Balmoral* would continue to challenge *Majestic* for the long-distance and cross-channel trade. Suddenly, after two seasons of relative calm, Cosens were faced with the prospect of another fight for survival.

In the short term, however, there was little to be done. With no additional ships available, there was no option but to meet *Solent Queen*'s challenge with the available resources. *Empress*, in co-operation with *Lord Elgin*, continued to provide the backbone of the Swanage service, with the other steamers providing additional crossings whenever their excursion timetables permitted. Needless to say, further fare-cutting took place. The season got off to a good start on Good Friday, with fair weather bringing out considerable crowds over the Easter weekend. The main season followed its accustomed pattern but was, as always, enlivened by one or two unusual incidents.

On 2nd May at Weymouth, a tragic and extraordinary chain of events took place while

The barque COUNTY OF ANGLESEY *at anchor in Weymouth Bay after her dramatic rescue by* QUEEN *and* ALBERT VICTOR.
AUTHOR'S COLLECTION

several hundred sailors, fuelled no doubt by large quantities of ale consumed in Weymouth's numerous pubs, were being conveyed back to their ships after a period of leave. *Premier* had just passed the breakwater dolphins when three sailors were heard to suggest that a swim would be a good idea. Moments later one of them had disappeared overboard and several more jumped in to effect a rescue. *Victoria* and *Queen* were close astern and almost immediately numerous members of their inebriated complement began to plunge overboard in an ill-judged attempt to assist the men in the water. Within moments chaos reigned. Life belts and heaving lines were thrown and boats were launched from *Premier* and *Victoria*. *Albert Victor*, heeling dangerously as her passengers crowded to one side to witness the excitement, then appeared on the scene. By this time, up to 150 men were in the water and being buffeted by the paddle wash from the four manoeuvring steamers, so it was a remarkable testament to the skill and prompt action of their crews that only one person was drowned.

On 26th May, the Royal Yacht *Victoria & Albert*, with the Queen, the Royal children and Prince and Princess Charles of Denmark on board, came to anchor in Weymouth Bay, escorted by *HMS Aboukir*. The esplanade, pier and ships in the harbour were immediately decked with flags and loyal messages were sent on board by the Mayor and Corporation. Cosens promptly organised a series of short trips to view the anchored ships. As *Victoria*, draped with a large banner declaring 'Welcome Home', drew alongside the yacht, Her Majesty appeared on deck, waved graciously to the excursionists and proceeded to take a photograph. *Victoria* then steamed slowly round *Aboukir* before landing her excited passengers, who streamed ashore boasting that '*not only have we seen the Queen, but she has taken our photograph.*'

The naval anchorage at Portland was exceptionally busy during the summer of 1905. A new torpedo-boat-destroyer base had been established at the beginning of the year and large numbers of these small, fast warships were to be seen moored in their

As the evening shadows lengthen, crowds of sailors stream onto Weymouth quayside to join one of the liberty boats waiting to return them to their ships. Moored at the GWR landing stage are ALBERT VICTOR (nearest the camera), PREMIER outside QUEEN and then MAJESTIC. In the distance at the Pile Pier are EMPRESS and VICTORIA. A Channel Island boat train stands at the platform and, to its left, are the pier turnstiles and steamer booking office.
AUTHOR'S COLLECTION

trots close to Castletown Pier or berthed in the new pens which had been constructed adjoining the massive naval coaling pier in the rapidly-expanding dockyard. During July, the Channel Fleet and the destroyers were joined by three reserve divisions to undertake joint manoeuvres, so not only were the liberty boats kept unusually busy but additional steamers were laid on to take visitors to and from whichever ironclads were open to the public.

Majestic continued to call regularly at Weymouth on her long trips westward from Bournemouth and, when the tide served, began her day at Weymouth and ran eastwards to Bournemouth, the Isle of Wight and beyond. On one such occasion, Monday 24th July, she was timed to depart from Weymouth at 8am for Bournemouth and Brighton. On the return trip, she left Brighton at 4.15pm, called at Bournemouth at 8.30pm and arrived at Weymouth at 11.00pm, where special trains were waiting to take passengers onwards to Dorchester or Portland. The return fare from Weymouth to Brighton was 5s 2d.

Two days before her Brighton trip, *Majestic* had called at Weymouth *en route* for Torquay and collected 150 passengers. Amongst these was a visitor from Wiltshire who, together with his wife and youngest child, had boarded the vessel believing her to be the Portland boat. Three other children had been left on Weymouth beach to enjoy themselves during what had been intended as a very short absence. By the time the parents had realised their mistake, the steamer was well into her passage and nothing could be done until she arrived at Torquay, when Capt Rawle immediately sent a telegram to the Chief of Police at Weymouth. The children were

located and looked after until the steamer arrived home during the evening, when it was reported that *'the family reunion defied description'*.

Weymouth passengers were also offered a very occasional cross channel trip and on Thursday 27th July, *Monarch* was advertised to sail direct from Weymouth to Cherbourg, departing at 9.30am and arriving home at 9.00pm for a fare of 6s 2d.

Also during July, the Cape liner *Johannesburg* put in to Weymouth Bay, after suffering an engine room explosion which had killed six of her crew. Cosens were engaged to remove all of her main steam pipes, bring them ashore for testing, repair or renewal and then return the ship's engines to full working order. While this work was carried out under the supervision of Mr Jones, Cosens' Marine Superintendent, the company offered to reduce the monotony endured by the liner's passengers by giving them free access to the excursion steamers. Each morning, *Victoria* called alongside and collected all those who wished to go on a cruise or spend the day ashore and returned them to the liner at the end of the day.

The first week of August saw a spell of very boisterous weather which kept passengers away but, fortunately, more serene conditions returned in time for a week of unusually interesting trips. On Tuesday 8th August, *Victoria* went to Cowes to observe the King's Cup Yacht Race and cruise around the combined British and French Fleets, which were anchored in Spithead in readiness for a review the next day. At 4pm the same afternoon, *Queen* offered one of her rare passenger excursions beyond Weymouth Bay, when she sailed with a full complement direct to

Spithead to view the evening illuminations. Despite the fact that the little tug boasted neither speed nor the most comfortable of accommodation and that she was at sea for most of the night on her return passage, her passengers disembarked tired but happy, proclaiming that for a fare of 2s 8d they had enjoyed the best value on the coast.

While *Queen* was away from base, news was received that a large yacht named *Cariad* had gone ashore on the Kimmeridge Ledges and *Albert Victor* was sent to render assistance. After towing for some hours, she successfully refloated the yacht at 1am on Wednesday morning.

At 9.00am on Wednesday 9th August, *Victoria* set off for Spithead once again to watch the Review of the combined fleets take place, while on Thursday, an 8.30am coasting trip to Teignmouth regatta via West Bay, Lyme and Seaton was offered, together with a 10.00am sailing via Portland to West Bay regatta. It was also regatta day at Lulworth and the loadings on all trips to the Cove proved unusually heavy.

The six return trips each day between Weymouth and Portland proved as popular as ever, and the steamers were often filled to capacity. For a grand fare of 1s return, passengers could enjoy the sea breezes, view some of the most beautiful coastal scenery in the kingdom, pass close to a staggering selection of major British warships and then go ashore to marvel at the massive stone quarries of the rugged Isle of Portland and, if they were lucky, see convicts at work. Indeed, the morbid taste for viewing the convicts became so strong that, in 1905, the Home Office forbad the taking of photographs and actually kept the convicts inside the prison on August Bank Holiday.

At Bournemouth, great alarm was caused on the morning of Wednesday 12th July, when rumours began to circulate that *Majestic* and *Balmoral* had collided off Boscombe and that the former had foundered with great loss of life. Happily, the truth, though serious, was far less dramatic. The two steamers had left Bournemouth together and as they approached Boscombe Pier, *Balmoral*, which was the seaward vessel, had turned sharply and unexpectedly to port and cut across *Majestic*'s bows. Although Capt Rawle immediately rang 'hard astern', a collision was unavoidable and *Majestic*'s stem was seriously damaged as it cut into *Balmoral*'s stern. Both vessels were able to continue with their day's programme but *Majestic* then proceeded to Weymouth where Cosens' workshop staff worked night and day to make good the repairs and return her to service on 17th July.

On 26th July, a dense fog suddenly descended over the Solent and caught both *Monarch* and *Majestic* at sea. *Monarch* was on a sailing round the Isle of Wight but it was decided to land her passengers at Ventnor for the afternoon. *Majestic* was scheduled for a double run between Bournemouth and Shanklin, and was returning to the Island during the afternoon when she very nearly went ashore near Bonchurch. A gentleman who was fishing in a small boat shouted warnings and the steamer was able to bring up only yards from the rocks. She eventually groped her way into Shanklin Pier at 7pm and both she and *Majestic* crept safely back to Bournemouth later that night.

The Review of the French and English Fleets at Spithead quite naturally proved the greatest money-spinner for the Bournemouth fleet during August, and a wide range of trips were offered to view the assembled fleet and the spectacular illuminations.

QUEEN departing from Weymouth on a passenger sailing. The photograph is the work of well known Weymouth-based photographer E.H. Seward, who took a wide range of views of the town, the harbour and the railway. He photographed many of the ships using the harbour and numerous of the locomotives based at or visiting Weymouth engine shed. He sold much of his work as picture postcards.
AUTHOR'S COLLECTION

Crowds of passengers flock ashore from PREMIER *at Castletown Pier, to enjoy time ashore at Portland while, between the two iron fences, the return passengers wait to embark. In the right foreground, two ladies amuse themselves at the penny-in-the-slot fortune-telling machine, while behind them blocks of cut Portland stone can be seen awaiting transshipment. The metal shed in the foreground was a waiting room for the naval steps. In the distance, a schooner ghosts past the coal hulks anchored in Portland Harbour.*
BRIAN JACKSON COLLECTION

On Tuesdays in high season, it became the norm to send either *Majestic* or *Monarch* from Bournemouth to Worthing via Clarence Pier, Southsea. These trips were advertised heavily in the Portsmouth press as offering '*76 miles for 2s 6d*'. Although timings varied slightly with tidal conditions, they generally left Southsea at about 11.00am, took two and a half hours on passage and returned from Worthing at 4pm after approximately two hours ashore.

August drew to a close with a period of severe gales which seriously disrupted sailings. On the morning of Saturday 26th August, *Monarch* made a safe but rough passage from Bournemouth to Cherbourg arriving at 2.45pm. The decision to sail was probably influenced by the fact that the previous two crossings had been cancelled due to bad weather and the company was anxious not to disappoint its public again. By the time the passengers had re-embarked after an hour and a half ashore, the wind had risen considerably and it was evident that the steamer was in for a 'dusting' on her way home. The beam-seas in the Channel proved so violent that Capt Masters decided to reduce speed and alter course for Weymouth, where *Monarch* eventually arrived at midnight. On 28th August, *Majestic* was forced to terminate her trip from Bournemouth to Torquay at Weymouth and the following day *Victoria* had to abandon a sailing to Torquay regatta.

Fortunately, the weather returned to a more settled state by the end of the week and substantial crowds were carried over the August Bank Holiday

weekend. Indeed, numbers were so healthy on the Weymouth to Portland service that Capt King of *Albert Victor* and Capt Read of *Queen* were both summonsed for allowing overcrowding. Despite pointing out that the company had carried in excess of 10,000 passengers on Bank Holiday Monday alone, had laid on extra boats, employed additional ticket counters and taken every other reasonable precaution to prevent such an eventuality, the case was lost and both Captains were required to pay fines and costs.

Despite the increased competition at Bournemouth and the boisterous weather during parts of August, the 1905 season had proved a refreshing success. The weather had been generally kind, passenger numbers had increased to over half a million (three quarters of a million counting return trips), returns from passenger fares and stewarding had reached a total of £24,090 and profits were up. It was true that the general economic depression had led the trading value of £5 shares to fall to £2 10s and the unsettled state of several government departments had led to a decline in orders for the works department but a dividend of 3 per cent could still be declared.

With the excursion steamers slumbering in their winter lay up berths, the work of the salvage tugs and liberty boats continued unabated. During November, a large pontoon was being towed from the East coast to Liverpool when she began to fill with water and the tug captain decided to put into Portland. Arriving at night, he allowed the pontoon to strike one of the large mooring buoys near

MONARCH *in Swanage Bay on 10th August 1905 and privately printed up as a postcard (photographic paper with 'POSTCARD' printed on the back was freely available). The original card was sent to Capt Masters on 16th August and bore this message:* 'Dear Sir, This is a snap shot taken with my hand camera on Thursday last by my brother from *Lord Elgin* off Swanage. Enjoyed the moonlight trip Friday, got back into camp about 1.30 a.m. Yours, etc. C.W. Nesbitt.' *The ship displays the new funnels fitted in 1904. Her mainmast and the gilt decoration on her paddle box were both removed during 1906.*
JOHN HAYSOM

Bincleaves and she quickly foundered in seven fathoms. Cosens were contracted to raise and repair her and over the next fourteen days successfully completed the difficult task. Tugs and lifting barges were used to raise the pontoon on each tide and drag her slowly into shallow water near Whithead's torpedo pier. A cofferdam was erected but, when this proved ineffective, she was lifted further inshore until her decks were awash and she could be pumped dry. On 23rd November, a tug was summoned to tow her round to Weymouth but it soon became apparent that the leaks were gaining and she might founder again. The situation was saved by throwing a sail over the most serious hole and driving in a wooden plug. The short passage was completed in extremely rough seas but by early evening, the pontoon was high and dry on Cosens' No. 1 slipway.

The liberty boat service continued throughout the winter whenever the Fleet was in the anchorage and, although providing a welcome source of income to Cosens and Weymouth tradesmen and publicans, was far less popular in Portland. Tradesmen there argued that because the steamers always landed sailors at Weymouth they were responsible for drawing trade away from the Island. They also claimed that it was outrageous to charge sailors a 4d steamer fare when they had the *right* to go ashore for nothing in ship's boats. Their complaints, however, fell on deaf ears, as it seems that all concerned regarded the steamer fare as a small price to pay for the relative speed and comfort of the service which Cosens provided.

During the winter of 1905-06, *Monarch* was extensively re-decked, *Brodick Castle* was fitted with a new intermediate shaft and *Victoria* had her boiler

lifted out by one of the large cranes at Portland Dockyard. With *Victoria* out of service, it fell to *Empress* to open the winter service at Bournemouth on 5th January.

In March 1906, a second and far more successful conference was held with the Southampton Company, at which a number of points were agreed regarding the Bournemouth to Swanage service. The first, which considering the new *Princess Royal* was almost ready for launching must have pleased the Southampton Company enormously, stipulated that neither company would purchase or charter any new steamers for the service during the season ahead. A pooling arrangement for fares was introduced but it was agreed that, in the early season before the Southampton Company boat appeared

MONARCH *departing from Bournemouth Pier during 1905. The stern rope has already been let go and is being secured by the seaman beneath the lifeboat. Capt Masters having 'sprung off' by using a forward rope to pivot the ship against the pier, has his hand on the telegraph and is about to ring full astern to take her away from the pier.*
VICTOR GRAY COLLECTION

At Bournemouth Pier

On a still winter's day a spritsail-rigged coasting barges drifts slowly up Weymouth Harbour, while QUEEN awaits her next salvage call.
AUTHOR'S COLLECTION

The crew of VICTORIA pictured on board the steamer at Weymouth on 12th September 1906. Capt Harbin John Hardy is the tall figure in the centre of the group while the mate, Alfred Hope, stands beside him. When Hardy was promoted to MONARCH in 1908, Hope remained in VICTORIA to train her new master, Capt Pearce, in the skills of beaching the steamer during the weekly westward coasting trips. Some time later, he too transferred to MONARCH and, with the exception of brief spells in temporary command of PREMIER, remained with the ship until his retirement, aged 77, in 1930. The seaman holding the RNLI collecting box is Bob Ferguson. Cosens made a regular habit of collecting for the lifeboat on board their steamers.
PETER FERGUSON

on the station, Cosens could charge 6d extra for use of the bridge deck, whilst thereafter fare levels would be fixed by open competition. On Mondays and Thursdays, Cosens would use one steamer on a Bournemouth to Weymouth service calling at Swanage *en route,* and on Wednesdays and Saturdays, *Empress* would be taken off the Swanage service and ply to and from Lulworth instead. On these days, *Brodick Castle* would take her place and receive three-fifths of the pooled earnings.

Whilst indicating some limited co-operation between Cosens and the Southampton Company,

the agreement still left the latter holding a trump card in the form of the new *Princess Royal.* As *Monarch, Brodick Castle* and *Majestic* joined their smaller consorts in service on 2nd April, 14th April and 1st May respectively, Cosens must still have been bracing themselves for the impact of her entry into service.

In the event, they need not have worried. The new ship was launched on 10th April, ran trials on 28th May and entered service on Whit Sunday 2nd June. She remained in passenger service for two or three weeks but was then suddenly and unexpectedly returned to her builders as unsatisfactory. The precise reasons for this remain opaque but it would appear that the ship did not reach her contract speed during the extended trial period and that there may also have been some problems with the design of her accommodation.

Whatever the case, *Princess Royal* was rejected and the Southampton Company found itself unexpectedly short of tonnage. Since *Lorna Doone* was now required to continue as their principal Southampton-based vessel, the plan to base her at Poole was abandoned and *Solent Queen* was recalled from the Swanage service to bolster the fleet on the Solent. The agreement made in March thus became meaningless and Cosens were able to celebrate their good fortune. Not only had the expected competition on the long distance sailings failed to materialise but they could look forward to reaping the lion's share of the trade on the lucrative Swanage service.

As if this turn of good fortune was not enough, the weather decided to co-operate and the 1906 season was marked by record hours of sunshine and

EMPRESS glides into Lulworth Cove during 1906 to berth alongside VICTORIA, which has been at the beach for some time and is re-embarking her passengers before departing. Note VICTORIA's paddle boxes which were painted black from about 1905 until 1908.

AUTHOR'S COLLECTION/SEWARD

smooth seas. Excursionists flocked to the coast and, for the first time in the company's history, passenger figures topped one million. Income from passenger fares and stewarding increased by £3,633 to £27,723 and season ticket sales rose by £100 to £1,718.

During July, it had been discovered that *Albert Victor* needed some urgent repairs to her bottom plating and it was debated whether to charter or purchase another steamer to cover the Fleet Contract while she was under repair. The Southampton Company's elderly *Carisbrooke* and *Southampton* were both for sale but, in the event, it was decided to delay a decision pending definite news as to the movements of the Fleet. As luck would have it, the Fleet was away on exercises during late July and Cosens were able to repair the tug before demand

Weymouth Harbour

for liberty boats increased again later in August. While she was out of service, *Brodick Castle* was used occasionally on the Fleet Contract but was found to be rather large for berthing alongside warships. To overcome the problem, one of the smaller steamers was often used as a pontoon between *Brodick Castle* and the warship. It was also discovered that unexpected repairs were required to the wooden Castletown Pier at Portland and it was agreed that Cosens would contribute 4 per cent, while the government department of Woods & Forests, which owned the pier, would pay the balance.

Apart from a collision between *Brodick Castle* and the yacht *L'Avengro* during late August, no further problems were reported and the established pattern of sailings yielded the most successful season in many years. Not only was the company able to increase its dividend to 5 per cent but also to place a healthy sum into the reserve account, pay off all outstanding repairs and suspended payments, and reduce the amount owed on *Majestic* by a further £1000.

As September turned to October, the dark evenings and gales of autumn presented additional problems for the steamers on the Fleet Contract. For some time it had become the practice for the anchored warships to deploy an anchor buoy in addition to their ordinary watch buoy. These buoys were all unlit and, as each ship swung differently in response to wind and tide, it was impossible for the steamers to predict their whereabouts. As a consequence, the steamers were constantly colliding

with the anchor buoys and, during October alone, *Victoria*, *Premier*, *Queen* and *Albert Victor* all suffered an array of paddle wheel damage, including broken floats, bent radius rods, paddle arms and cross stays. Cosens wrote to Admiral Neville begging that the practice of using anchor buoys be discontinued during the winter months but his reply is not recorded.

Unfortunately for Cosens, it appeared that the good fortune of 1906 could not last and, in stark contrast, the season of 1907 was marked by changeable weather and a resumption of stiff competition at Bournemouth. *Victoria*, having operated the winter service from 1st February until Easter, was moved to Weymouth to cover the Fleet Contract, while *Brodick Castle* and *Monarch* opened the Bournemouth season on Good Friday. As usual, *Lord Elgin* operated as an additional member of the fleet on the Swanage service and was included in Cosens' advertisements. The Southampton Company sent *Solent Queen* to compete over the Easter weekend but then withdrew her to Southampton to await more significant developments.

The season had no sooner got underway when a 3,512 ton Russian cargo steamer went aground on the cliffs about a mile east of St. Alban's Head, on the night of 14th-15th April. The Cyrillic alphabet used on her bows clearly caused great confusion in the local press, for the ship is variously referred to as *Hepapa*, *Ceres* and *Cerara*, the latter appearing to be most favoured.

A circa 1905 commercial postcard view looking down Weymouth Harbour from the Town Bridge. In the foreground, BRODICK CASTLE is seen in winter lay-up at Trinity Quay, while ALBERT VICTOR is moored to Custom House Quay, outside Cosens' Head Office, in the left background.
AUTHOR'S COLLECTION

News reached Cosens at 2.40am and *Queen*, under the command of Capt Read, set off with the utmost haste. Indeed, her crew acted so smartly that, in the bustle and darkness, Capt Hardy, who had intended to sail with her, fell into the harbour and was injured. The tug was alongside *Cerara* at 5.30am, immediately passed her heaviest cable and began towing. At 9.30am, she was joined by *Monarch*, which had sailed from Poole as soon as news reached her and the two ships continued towing until early afternoon, when it became apparent that, with the tide falling, the casualty was not going to come off.

Cerara was now lying with her head towards the east, her bows pinioned on the rocks and her forward compartments badly flooded, while she bumped heavily in the swell. While *Queen* and *Monarch* lay off awaiting the turn of the tide, the Channel Coaling Company's tugs *Petrel* and *Verne*, the salvage steamer *Greencastle* and a tug named *John Bull* all arrived on the scene. Attempts were made to lay out kedge anchors to prevent *Cerara* swinging round as the tide turned but each time the hawsers parted and the attempt had to be abandoned. By 4.30pm, she was facing west and an attempt was made to lighten her forward by jettisoning her anchors and cables. *Queen* made fast and commenced towing at 5.00pm to hold the vessel's stern in deep water and, by 7.00pm, all the vessels present except *Greencastle* had also passed ropes and joined in the struggle. Fifteen minutes later, *Cerara* slid off the rocks and the slow tow to Portland began.

This stage of the operation was actually one of the most dangerous for the tugs. *Cerara* was making water fast and was so severely down by the head that she was virtually unmanageable. As she was towed slowly towards safety, she kept sheering violently off her course and putting the tugs at risk of 'girding'. This meant that if the tow rope was suddenly dragged from its proper position over the tug's stern to a position on the beam, the tug could be pulled sideways through the water and capsized. *Queen* and the other tugs had to slip their tow ropes repeatedly to avoid this fate and several other ropes were broken under the strain. Eventually, however, *Cerara* was manoeuvred into Portland Harbour and grounded in shallow water at 9am on 16th April, *Queen* by then having been in attendance for some 30 hours.

Cosens' divers were sent down to inspect the damage and discovered that the whole of *Cerara*'s forefoot had been ripped off and a good deal of the bottom plating buckled and cracked. Temporary repairs were carried out, before the Russian ship departed for dry docking at Southampton. The ship and her cargo had been worth £72,000 and the

Taken later on the same day, this view shows MONARCH *manoeuvring close to* CERARA, *which has swung round with the tide.*
AUTHOR'S COLLECTION

Admiralty Court, in praising the work of Cosens and the other salvors, had no hesitation in awarding £10,000 for their work. *Queen* was awarded £1,500 and *Monarch*, in view of the risks she had taken in spite of her great value and unsuitable towing gear, a further £2,000.

Following their rejection of *Princess Royal* in 1906, the Southampton Company had immediately set about locating a replacement steamer. The vessel chosen was the Galloway Steam Packet Company's *Stirling Castle*, which entered service on 20th May 1907. Her presence in the Solent allowed her owners to implement their original plan for 1906 and transfer *Lorna Doone*, as well as *Solent Queen*, to the Bournemouth station. From Whitsun onwards, therefore, these two formidable ships posed a direct challenge to Cosens on both the Swanage service and the full and half-day excursion sailings. *Balmoral*

Another superb Seward photograph, entitled 'Through the white foam proudly dashing at Weymouth.' PREMIER *heads out of Weymouth in a brisk easterly wind, most probably on liberty boat service.*
AUTHOR'S COLLECTION/
SEWARD

continued to touch at Bournemouth and Swanage during her long-distance dashes from Southampton.

All pretence of co-operation had now disappeared and open warfare ensued. It would appear that, for the first two or three weeks of the competition, no coaling arrangements had been made at Poole and that either *Lorna Doone* or *Solent Queen* were forced to return to Southampton on alternate nights to coal,

while the other vessel lay over at Swanage Pier. From July onwards, satisfactory arrangements were made locally and the two steamers became resident at Poole.

In order to steal a march over their competitors, Cosens negotiated an arrangement with the Ryde, Sandown, Shanklin and Ventnor Pier companies, whereby passengers would no longer pay pier tolls but Cosens would be billed monthly for the appropriate amount. Fare cutting began again and by August, books of coupons were on sale offering a 25 per cent discount on the normal 1s 0d fare from Bournemouth to Swanage. Since the agents who sold the coupon books also took a $2^{1}/_{2}$ per cent commission, the company only received 8d. Long distance fares were cut in proportion and both companies accused each other of selling tickets at below the advertised rates to attract passengers on board. Cosens took to selling blocks of tickets to a 'steamboat syndicate', who in turn advertised and sold them on to other groups and individuals at reduced rates to tempt them away from the Southampton ships. Free passes were issued in profusion, which allowed the holder to benefit from the same reductions as season-ticket holders and ticket agents began to vary prices almost on whim to ensure that their ships sailed fully-laden. In August, for example, Mr Sydenham was accused of selling 5s 6d Cherbourg tickets for 3s but responded by pointing out that Mr Bouverie, the Southampton Co's agent, had been selling Swanage tickets for 6d! 'Shop Assistant Season Tickets' were also introduced at 15s each, giving the holder unlimited travel on two days per week throughout the season. One friend of the company calculated that this worked out at 7d per day and suggested that '*philanthropy was, to use Mr Churchill's words, a terminological inexactitude and that the word charity would be more applicable.*'

✠ Channel

In (n)ever Loving Memory
OF
A REPUTATION,
The well-beloved child of B a'L MORAL,

Lost in the English Channel on
September 6th, 1907;

Age UN Known.

———

" Though lost to sight to memory dear "
(Even at 3/-).

———

My dearest friends don't grieve for me,
    Though I've lost *one* reputation
I've another gained : " More time at sea
    Than any boat on the station "

Though inducements other boats hold out
    Of passages quick—take warning !
'Tis but with me that you can shout
    " We won't *get* home till morning."

And though a treasur'd memory
    Is the late " Channel Greyhound "
We're much more near to accuracy
    As the " *late Channel Stay*-hound."

COSENS AND Cº S.S. "MAJESTIC" LEAVING CHERBOURG.

F.R.FitzGerald /06

MAJESTIC

In 1906, the artist F.R. Fitzgerald was commissioned to paint a series of pictures of the major vessels of the Cosens' fleet, which were published as official company picture postcards and sold on board the steamers. The images were also used in the company's guidebook. The originals hung in Cosens' Weymouth offices throughout the rest of the company's history and, fortunately, good photographic copies were made of the majority. This delightful, lively set of images are reproduced here and on subsequent pages, although those of VICTORIA and LORD ELGIN have been scanned from copies of the postcards and are therefore of slightly lower quality. MAJESTIC, Cosens' flagship, is depicted here departing from Cherbourg.

MAJESTIC departing from Bournemouth on one of the special 'Steamboat Syndicate' excursions, in this case to Dartmouth on 20th June 1906. Souvenir copies of the postcard were on sale at the pier when the steamer returned in the evening.
AUTHOR'S COLLECTION

BELOW: The Home Fleet's visit to Bournemouth, 26th – 30th July 1907. LORNA DOONE and BALMORAL are moored nearest the shore, with MONARCH and MAJESTIC astern.
BOURNEMOUTH LIBRARY

BOTTOM: BRODICK CASTLE steams through the anchored fleet.
DORCHESTER LIBRARY

Given that the price of coal was at its highest for many years and that dreadful cold and wet weather up until the beginning of July kept passengers away, this rush to cut prices was evidently a recipe for disaster. By mid season, it was apparent that the steamers were failing to cover their costs.

Happily, however, the weather improved during July and passengers flocked on board once again. On 13th July, *Brodick Castle* ran down the yacht *White Swan* in Swanage Bay and damaged her beyond repair. The crew was rescued by the steamer but Capt Tilsed and the lookout, A.B. Parish, were both severely reprimanded. It was suggested at the time that the positioning of the steamer's navigating bridge behind the funnels may have been a contributory factor and it is possibly significant that, during the following winter, *Monarch*'s bridge was moved forward of her funnels.

Between 26th and 30th July 1907, the Home Fleet paid a visit to Bournemouth Bay and for several days Cosens abandoned practically all their other excursions in order to offer cruises round the assembled warships and to land passengers on those which were open to the public. *Majestic*, *Monarch*, *Brodick Castle* and *Lord Elgin* operated from Bournemouth Pier, while *Empress*, *Victoria* and the little *Queen* from Weymouth were based at Boscombe. A tremendous row broke out when the Southampton Company falsely accused Cosens of '*doing the showman business by having a band parading the streets to collect people and march them onto your boats*' and the recriminations rumbled on for many months. Along at Weymouth, it was announced that a local company, Turners, had purchased the paddle tug *Telegraph*, which had been a familiar part of the scenery at Poole and on the passenger service from there to Swanage for many years. It was suggested that *Telegraph* would shortly be entering the passenger trade at Weymouth but, as nothing more was heard of the matter, it can be assumed that Turners repented of their rash idea.

☛ COWES REGATTA WEEK Visit of H.M. KING EDWARD VII. Grand assemblage of Royal and other Yachts in Cowes Roads.

Pleasure Sailings from Bournemouth, Boscombe, Swanage, Poole, etc.
(Weather and circumstances permitting), by Cosens & Co.'s Fleet of Steamers,

Majestic, Monarch,  Brodick Castle

VICTORIA and EMPRESS In conjunction with the LORD ELGIN.

The return times from intermediate Piers, or places of call, are based upon the supposition that the Steamer performs the day trip contemplated, and that no occasion has arisen to necessitate any alteration in respect to the exigencies of the weather, traffic, or otherwise.

Saturday, August 3

Majestic
Monarch.
Victoria
Majestic and Monarch
Brodick Castle
Note Starting Time 9.15 a.m.

Imposing Naval Inspection and Review by H.M. KING EDWARD VII. in the Solent at 3 p.m. this day.
Grand assemblage of nearly 200 British and Swedish Warships. (Lines of the Fleet closed from 1 to 4 p.m.)
To the REVIEW. Giving Passengers a grand Cruise Round the Fleet before taking up position for the Review. Leaving Swanage 8.45. Bournemouth 10. Boscombe 10.10, back about 6. Fare 6/- Season Ticket Holders 3/- No Increase of Price on day of sailing.
To the REVIEW. Giving passengers a grand Cruise Round the Fleet before taking up position for the Review. Leaving Swanage 8.45. Bournemouth 9.50, Boscombe 10 a.m., back about 6.15. Fare 5/- Season Ticket Holders 2/6. No Increase in Price on day of Sailing.
Popular Trip to the REVIEW and after the Review giving passengers a Cruise through the Lines of the Fleet. Leaving Bournemouth 11.15, back about 7.30. Fare 3/6. No Increase of Price on day of Sailing. Season Tickets not available.
Special Trips to view the Illuminations of the Fleet. Leaving Swanage 5.15 (by Empress), Bournemouth 6.30, Boscombe 6.45, returning to Boscombe, Bournemouth & Swanage immediately after the display. Fare 2/6. Season Ticket Holders 1/6.
Cruise to the FLEET fully dressed in Readiness for the Review and giving nearly 8 hours at COWES. Leaving Poole 8, Boscombe 8.45 (by Empress), Bournemouth 9.15, returning from Cowes (Victoria) Pier at 8, back about 10. Fare 3/- Season Tickets not available.

Bank Holiday, August 5
Brodick Castle
Season Tickets not available.
Osborne House (Cowes) open to the Public this day instead of August 6

Long Day at COWES (for Osborne House), and **PORTSMOUTH.** 10 hours at Cowes, 8 hours at Portsmouth. Leaving Poole at 6.15 a.m., Bournemouth 7.15 a.m., returning from Southsea (Clarence Pier) at 7, Cowes 7.40. Fare 3/- Giving passengers a grand view of the Fleet of Warships in the Solent.

NOTE—Grand Farewell Cruises Round the Fleet.
Monarch
Majestic
Majestic
Majestic

Four Grand Farewell Cruises Round the Imposing Fleet of nearly 200 British and Swedish Warships in the Solent, as Reviewed by H.M. The KING, also a close view of the Fleet of Royal and other Yachts in Cowes Roads.
Visitors to Bournemouth, Boscombe and Swanage should not fail to witness this unparalleled Naval Pageant.
☛ NOTE TIMES OF STARTING AND POPULAR FARES.
Leave Swanage 8.15, Bournemouth 9.15, Boscombe 9.25, back to Bournemouth only about 2. Fare 2/- From Swanage 6d. extra
,, ,, 9.15, ,, 10.20, ,, 10.30, ,, B'mouth & Boscombe only ,, 2.30 ,, 2/6 ,, ,,
,, ,, 2.45, ,, 3.0, ,, ,, ,, ,, 6.45 ,, 2/- Note Popular Fare
,, ,, 7.0, ,, 7.10, ,, to Bournemouth only ,, 10.30, ,, 1/6 Note Cheap Fare.
Swanage Passengers must change at Bournemouth on the return to the regular Service Steamer.

Swanage Service this day,
Note alteration of times.

Between Bournemouth and Swanage HOURLY from 8 a.m. to 8 p.m., by 'Majestic,' 'Monarch,' 'Victoria,' 'Empress' and 'Lord Elgin. Fare 1/- Return.
Boscombe for Swanage 8.30 a.m. and 2.30 p.m. returning from Swanage to Bournemouth only every hour. Fare 1/-

Bournemouth, Boscombe and Swanage DAILY SERVICE.

1/- Return Fare Single Fare 9d. any part of Steamer after 1.35 trip.
By BRODICK CASTLE and LORD ELGIN. From August 6th to 10th. RETURN FARE, 1/6 First-Class, 1/- Second.
Return Fare 1/- Single Fare 9d. any part of Steamer after 1.35 trip.

Note Increased Advantages and Extension of Service.
Bournemouth for Swanage at 10, 10.45, 12, 12.45, 2.30, 3, 4.15, 5, 6, 6.45 and 7.45.
Swanage for Bournemouth at 9.30, 11, 11.30, 12.45, 1.35, 3.30, 4.15, 5.15, 6 & 7.
Boscombe for Swanage at 10.15, 12.20, and 3.10
On Wednesday and Saturday later trip Swanage to Bournemouth only at 8 p.m.
The Steamer leaving Swanage at 11.30, 6 & 7 proceeds to Boscombe. Late trips Bournemouth to Swanage daily (weather permitting) about 10 p.m. apply daily at Sydenham's Library, opposite Bournemouth Pier, or Mr. A. J. Ward, Steam Packet Office Swanage

Tuesday, August 6
Brodick Castle
Note Starting time 9.30 a.m.
Majestic
Note Starting time 10.20 a.m.
Monarch
,,
Majestic
Swanage Service this day see above.

R.Y.S. REGATTA AT COWES. GRAND YACHT RACE FOR THE KING'S CUP.
COWES (7 hours on shore), calling at **YARMOUTH.** Fare 2/6. Season Tickets not available. Leaving Boscombe 9, Bournemouth 9.30, returning from Cowes at 6.30, back about 8.30.
TOTLAND, COWES, RYDE, and a Grand Cruise towards the **Nab Lightship,** to view the grand Yacht Race for the King's Cup as far as practicable. Leave Swanage 9.0, Bournemouth 10.20, Boscombe 10.30, returning from Ryde 3.15, Cowes 3.50, Totland 4.45. Special Fare 2/6 including Ryde Pier Tolls. From Swanage 6d. extra.
Morning Cruise to COWES ROADS, giving passengers a close view of the Royal and other Yachts now assembled. Leaving Swanage 9.30, Bournemouth 10.30, Boscombe 10.40, back at 2.45. Fare 2/-. From Swanage 6d. extra. Swanage passengers must change at Bournemouth on the return to the Daily Service Steamer.
Afternoon trip to COWES Over 2 hours on shore. Brilliant Afternoon Social Scenes at Cowes. Leave Swanage 1.35 (by Lord Elgin), Bournemouth 3, Boscombe 3.10, return from Cowes 7.15 Fare 2/- Swanage 6d. extra. Season tickets not available
Tickets only available for the return journey on the respective steamer upon which the outward voyage was made.
Grand Evening Cruise to COWES ROADS, giving passengers a close view of the Royal and other Yachts now assembled. Leaving Bournemouth 6.10. Boscombe 6.25, back to Bournemouth only about 10. Fare 1/6 only.
SINGLE TRIP to POOLE by Brodick Castle. Leaving Boscombe 8.30 Bournemouth 9.0. Fare 6d.

Wednesday, August 7
Brodick Castle
Note Starting Time 9.30 a.m.
Monarch
Note Starting Time 10.20 a.m.
Majestic
,,
Monarch
Swanage Service this day see above.

GRAND YACHT RACE FOR THE EMPEROR'S CUP.
COWES (7 hours on shore), calling at **YARMOUTH.** Fare 2/6. Season tickets not available. Leaving Boscombe 9. Bournemouth 9.30, returning from Cowes at 6.30, back about 8.30.
TOTLAND, COWES and RYDE. Leaving Swanage at 9, Bournemouth 10.20, Boscombe 10.30, return from Ryde 3.0. Cowes 3.35. Totland 4.35. Special Fare 2/6 including Ryde Pier Tolls. From Swanage 6d. extra.
Morning Cruise to COWES ROADS, giving passengers a close view of the Royal and other Yachts now assembled. Leave Swanage 9.30, Bournemouth 10.30. Boscombe 10.40, back at 2.45. Fare 2/- From Swanage 2/6
Swanage passengers must change at Bournemouth on the return to the Daily Service Steamer.
Afternoon trip to COWES, calling at **Yarmouth.** Over 2 hours on shore. Brilliant Afternoon Social Scenes at Cowes. Leaving Swanage 1.35 (by Lord Elgin), Bournemouth 3, Boscombe 3.10, returning from Cowes at 7.15. Fare 2/- Swanage 6d. extra. **Plain Teas** with Cake 9d. with Plate of Meat 1/-, served in the spacious Saloons on this trip.
Tickets only available for the return journey on the respective steamer upon which the outward voyage was made.
Grand Evening Cruise to COWES ROADS, giving passengers a close view of the Royal and other Yachts now assembled. Leaving Bournemouth 6.10, Boscombe 6.25, back about 10 to Bournemouth only. Fare 1/6 only.
SINGLE TRIP to POOLE by Brodick Castle. Leaving Boscombe 8.50. Bournemouth 9.0. Fare 6d.

Thursday, August 8
Majestic
Note Starting Time 9.15 a.m.
Monarch
Note Starting Time 10.15.
Brodick Castle
Swanage Service this day see above.
Monarch

CHERBOURG The French Port and Arsenal. Grand Assemblage of French Warships Nearly 3 hours on shore. Leave Swanage 8.10, Boscombe 8.45 (by Empress), Bournemouth 9.15 return from Cherbourg 4.30 to Swanage & Bournemouth, back about 9.15. Fare 5/6. Season Ticket Holders 3/- including French Landing Tax. To prevent disappointment book at Sydenham's Library, opposite B'mouth Pier.
Totland, Round the Isle of Wight, giving passengers a close view of the Royal and other Yachts in the Solent, and One Hour at SHANKLIN (for the celebrated Chine, &c,). Leaving Swanage at 9.30, Bournemouth 10.30, Boscombe 10.40, return from Shanklin 3.15, Totland 5.15. Fare to Totland only 2/- **For the grand trip of nearly 100 miles 3/-** including Shanklin Pier tolls. From Swanage 6d. extra.
WEYMOUTH Cruise Round the Fleet in Portland Roads, and by kind permission of Officer Commanding, one hour on board H.M.S. ARGYLL or such other of H.M. Ironclads available for visitors. Leaving Bournemouth 10.30, Boscombe 10.40, Swanage 11.20. Leaving Weymouth at 2.30 for the Ship. The 'Brodick Castle' returning from Weymouth 4.10 for Swanage, Bournemouth and Boscombe, back about 6.15. Fare 3/- From Swanage 2/6
EVENING CRUISE TO SWANAGE. Leaving Boscombe 7.45, Bournemouth 8.15, returning at 9.20 to Bournemouth only. Half-hour on shore. Accompanied by the Bournemouth Postmen's Band. Fare 1/- Season Ticket Holders 6d.
SINGLE TRIP to POOLE by Brodick Castle. Leaving Bournemouth 6.30, Boscombe 6.45. Fare 6d.

Friday, August 9
Monarch
Note Starting time 8.45 a.m.
Majestic
Giving passengers time at Cowes for Osborne House. Public admission to State Apartments, Durbar Room, and the Park.
Brodick Castle
Note Starting Time 10.20 a.m.
Majestic
Swanage Service this day see above.
Brodick Castle

TORQUAY Over Two hours on shore. Leaving Boscombe 8.20, Bournemouth 8.45, Swanage 9.20, returning from Torquay at 4.30 for Swanage, Bournemouth and Boscombe. Fare 5/- Single 4/- Season Ticket Holders 2/6.
ROYAL COWES TOWN REGATTA AND SPORTS. OSBORNE HOUSE OPEN THIS DAY.
GRAND YACHT RACES FOR TOWN PRIZES OF £100. R.Y.S. PRIZES OF £65.
TOTLAND, COWES (for Osborne House), **RYDE and a grand Cruise through Portsmouth Harbour** giving passengers a close view of the Swedish Warships, H.M.S. 'Victory,' and British Ships of War. Leaving Swanage 9.30, Bournemouth 10.30, Boscombe 10.40, returning from Ryde 3, Cowes 3.30, Totland 4.20, back at 6.0. Fare 2/6 including Ryde Pier Tolls. To Totland 2/- From Swanage 6d. extra
YARMOUTH AND COWES (for Osborne House). Leaving Swanage at 9.30, Bournemouth at 10.20, Boscombe 10.30, returning from Cowes at 3.20, Yarmouth 4.10, back at 5.30 to Bournemouth and Swanage only. Fare 2/6. To Yarmouth 2/- From Swanage 6d. extra.
EVENING CRUISE TO COWES ROADS for the grand FIREWORKS DISPLAY and ILLUMINATIONS of Royal and other Yachts. Accompanied by the BOURNEMOUTH POSTMEN'S BAND. Leaving Bournemouth at 7, Boscombe 7.10, returning to each Pier immediately after the display. Fare 2/6. Season Ticket Holders 1/6.
EVENING CRUISE TO COWES ROADS for the grand FIREWORKS DISPLAY and ILLUMINATIONS **FROM SWANAGE** Direct. Leaving Swanage at 6.45, returning to Swanage direct immediately after the display. Fare 2/- Season Ticket Holders 1/6.

Saturday, August 10
Majestic
,,
Monarch
,,
,,
Empress
,,
Swanage Service this day see above.

Grand 85 miles cruise ROUND the ISLE of WIGHT Leave Swanage 9.30, Bournemouth 10.30, Boscombe 10.40, back 3.30. Fare 2/6. From Swanage 3/-
Afternoon trip to WEYMOUTH 1 hour on shore. Leave Boscombe 3.15, Bournemouth 3.45, Swanage 4.15, return from Weymouth at 7. Fare 2/- PLAIN TEAS with cake 9d. with plate of Meat 1/- served in the spacious Saloons this trip.
7 hours at VENTNOR (Isle of Wight). Leaving Swanage 9, Boscombe 9.40 (by Empress). Bournemouth 10, return from Ventnor 6.30. Fare 2/6, including Ventnor Pier Tolls From Swanage 6d. extra.
Morning trip to Ventnor Leave Boscombe 9.40 (by Empress). Bournemouth 10 back at 3. Fare 2/- From Swanage 6d. extra Season Tickets available only on the Morning Trip, arriving back at 3, and not the Day or Afternoon Trips.
Afternoon trip to Ventnor 1 hour on shore. Leave Bournemouth 3, Boscombe 3.10, return from Ventnor 6.30. Fare 2/-
LULWORTH. Leaving Bournemouth 10.30, Boscombe 10.40, Swanage 11.40, returning from Lulworth at 3.30 Landing by stage and not by small boats. No landing charges at Lulworth. Two hours on shore. Return Fare to Lulworth 2/6 From Swanage 2/- Lulworth Fishermen act as Guides to the Fossil Forest.
SMOOTH WATER EVENING CRUISE TO STUDLAND BAY AND UP POOLE HARBOUR by Empress. Leaving Swanage at 5, Bournemouth 5.50. Boscombe 6, back about 8. Fare 1/-
SINGLE TRIP to POOLE via Swanage by Brodick Castle. Leaving Bournemouth 7.45, Boscombe 8.0. Fare 6d.

Tickets on Board the Steamer. The Catering Department undertaken by the Owners (Cosens & Co.) is unsurpassed. Mr. E. Harford, Manager.
Children Half-price on all fares exceeding 1/-. Bicycles 1/- each single journey. Swanage traffic 6d. each. Deck Chairs 1d. Dogs charged full passenger fare.
Season Tickets and all information to be obtained at the Offices of the two Companies:—D. SYDENHAM (Cosens & Co. Ltd.), Royal Marine Library, Bournemouth; E. BICKER (Bournemouth and South Coast Steam Packets, Limited), Wilts and Dorset Bank Chambers; of Mr. S. J. FOWLER, Managing Director Cosens & Co., Ltd., Custom House Quay, Weymouth; Mr. A. J. WARD, Steam Packet Office, Swanage; Mr. C. J. HEARSON, Stationer, Yarmouth, or the Local Agents.

By order, D. SYDENHAM, Local Manager.
Telephone No. 130,

Office—Royal Marine Library, Pier Approach, Bournemouth
August 2, 1907.

Sydenham, Printer Bournemouth.

A Bournemouth sailing bill illustrating the wide variety of trips available in August 1907.
AUTHOR'S COLLECTION

MAJESTIC

EMPRESS

COSENS AND Cº S.S. "MONARCH" OFF THE NEEDLES.

F. R. Fitz Gerald. 1906

MONARCH

September and October saw a number of dramas and tragedies unfold at Weymouth. The first occurred on 13th September when, in dense fog, the Blue Funnel liner *Patroclus*, laden with a cargo of wool, wheat, bananas and metal ores from Brisbane, ran hard aground in thick fog at Blacknor Point, Portland. *Queen* and *Albert Victor*, together with their arch-rivals *Verne* and *Petrel*, were quickly on the scene but, with the tide falling quickly, were unable to move the enormous ship. A breeches buoy was rigged between the ship and the cliffs in case it became necessary to evacuate her crew and two battleships arrived to offer their assistance. While a contract for her salvage was being negotiated with the Liverpool Salvage Association, an immediate start was made on lightening the ship of her cargo and, over the next few days, the local tugs were kept busy shuttling to and from Weymouth towing lighters piled high with salvaged goods. Meanwhile, specialist salvage vessels arrived and a special train brought 400 tons of equipment to Portland to assist in the refloating. Large crowds of spectators flocked to the scene and, on the Sunday following the stranding, a Salvation Army band took the opportunity to preach and play hymns on the cliff top, while below them the local fishermen, with more secular matters in mind, concentrated on carrying ashore as much free wheat as their little boats could manage. On 22nd September, with no less than eleven steam pumps working at full capacity, *Patroclus* was successfully refloated.

It was during this period, on 16th September, that a terrible accident occurred on board *Queen*, which was laying at Weymouth Pier having just disembarked a full load of liberty men. The engineer, John Bagg, discovered that her starboard engine had 'stuck' on dead centre and opened the door into the paddle box, with the intention of using a bar to lever the paddle wheel round, prior to disconnecting the two engines in readiness for swinging in the harbour

for the next trip. For some reason, Bagg had actually climbed onto the paddle wheel which, possibly because the steam had not been fully turned off, then started to move. Bagg was crushed between the wheel and the ship's side and died later in hospital of internal injuries. His widow was paid £300 in compensation.

A further tragedy occurred on the evening of 3rd October when *Albert Victor*, *Premier* and *Queen* were steaming in line ahead into Portland Harbour to return liberty men to their ships. Coming the other way was a pinnace from *HMS Talbot*, taking the ship's Captain, his wife and servant ashore. The night was dark and moonless, and after passing *Albert Victor* safely, the pinnace attempted to cross the bows of *Premier*. Seeing that a collision was inevitable, Capt Cox stopped the steamer's engines but her bows cut into the pinnace throwing her crew into the water. The Captains's wife, Mrs Yelverton, was hauled to safety but the pinnace, whose engines had not been stopped, forged ahead into the darkness and sank. Boats were immediately launched from *Premier* and *Queen* and were successful in rescuing all but one of the people in the water. Sadly, the Captain's servant was drowned.

As the season drew to a close, it became apparent that *Brodick Castle*'s elderly boilers were reaching the end of their life and a major discussion ensued about the future of the old ship. She was now 29 years old, somewhat outdated in appearance and her huge, 1864-vintage, single cylinder engine was increasingly uneconomical in an era of rising coal prices. On the other hand, Cosens needed every ship they had to fend off the competition from Southampton, and had nothing to replace her with.

A full survey was carried out and, during November, Mr Jones presented a plan to compound the engine, fit new boilers and thoroughly modernise the old ship. A. & J. Inglis Ltd on the Clyde quoted £7,070 for the work and Day, Summers & Co of

Southampton £8,690 to include an evaporator. The Inglis tender was accepted and Cosens' bankers were approached for a loan to cover the costs but a few days later, when Mr Jones visited Glasgow for discussions, Inglis raised some important technical points, which caused the whole project to be suspended.

By sheer chance, Mr Jones had made his journey to Glasgow via London, where he paid a visit to Mr Constant, the company's shipbroker. Constant informed Jones that he had just discovered that *Princess Royal*, which had previously been rejected by the Southampton Company, was for sale by J.I. Thornycroft & Co and might be obtained for £12,000. A sale had previously been agreed with a Turkish company in Constantinople but the deposit had not been paid and the vessel was therefore back on the market. While she had been in the hands of her builders, they had increased her waterline length to 217 feet 2 inches by the insertion of a 21 foot 7 inch section at a point 4 feet aft of the original centre line. This had increased her buoyancy and lifted her waterline, with the intention of increasing her speed. At the same time, the engines had been moved 6 feet 5 inches forward, her main deck saloon extended to the full width of the ship and a number of other small improvements made, all of which made her a very suitable candidate to replace *Brodick Castle*. Cosens instructed Constant to proceed

with his enquiries in the utmost secrecy and resolved meanwhile to spend as little as possible on *Brodick Castle* and to offer her for sale.

The severe competition and fare cutting at Bournemouth in the face of bad weather and increased coal prices had, it seems, worked to the advantage of neither company. In December 1907, common sense finally prevailed when, at yet another conference, a limited degree of co-operation was finally agreed.

Fare cutting was outlawed and in its place a common scale of charges was agreed for all sailings as follows:

• **From Bournemouth** to Cowes, Ryde, Southsea, Ventnor, Shanklin, Sandown, Southampton, Round the Isle of Wight and vice versa, 3s including tolls at everywhere except Cowes.

After 2pm or morning trip without landing, 2s. From Swanage, 6d extra.
• **From Bournemouth** to Weymouth 2s 6d, from Swanage 2s or including one of HM ships, 3s and 2s 6d respectively.

After 2pm and morning trips without landing, from Bournemouth 2s, from Swanage 1s 6d.
• **From Bournemouth** to Alum Bay, Totland Bay and Yarmouth. Day ticket 2s.

Afternoon or morning trip without landing 1s 6d, exclusive of tolls.

Taken from the upstairs window in the Slip Keeper's house beside Cosens' No. 1 slipway, this 1907 view shows VICTORIA, EMPRESS and MONARCH at the landing stages, while QUEEN, hoping for a short towage job, follows a topsail schooner up the harbour. The building in the right foreground is today used as a mast store for Weymouth Sailing Club and as a boathouse for the RNLI inshore lifeboat.
AUTHOR'S COLLECTION

BRODICK CASTLE

The postcard version of Fitzgerald's painting of VICTORIA at Lulworth Cove. Publication of the postcards is actually credited to Sydenham & Co, Bournemouth; David Sydenham was Cosens' Bournemouth agent and also owned the Marine Library & Bazaar located close by the pier, from where publication of the postcards would have been handled. Some versions of the postcards – such as the one shown here – were printed on textured card simulating art canvas.
AUTHOR'S COLLECTION

Between 1901 and 1908, LORD ELGIN, although owned by the Bournemouth Company, was effectively a member of the Cosens' fleet and was employed exclusively on the Bournemouth to Swanage service, where interchangeability of tickets and a common timetable was the norm. In 1907, Fitzgerald was therefore commissioned to produce this delightful painting of her off Old Harry Rocks, sporting the red and black funnel colours which her owners adopted in 1901 to distinguish her from Cosens' buff-funnelled steamers.
DAVID HAYSOM COLLECTION

C. 41542. LULWORTH COVE: ARRIVAL OF BOAT.

This tinted card showing VICTORIA arriving at Lulworth is the nearest thing to colour photography in the Edwardian era. It was produced by the Photochrom Company Ltd of Tunbridge Wells, who were masters of the art of colour tinting. They produced many of their picturesque views such as this in larger versions, which were supplied to various of the pre-Grouping railway companies for use as carriage prints.
AUTHOR'S COLLECTION

233

A fascinating view of The Nothe and Cosens' slipway facilities at Weymouth, taken from the GWR cargo stage probably circa 1905. ALBERT VICTOR has been drawn up stern first for repairs on the larger or No. 1 slipway. The three-storey building by her stern was the slip-keeper's house, while to the right of that can be seen the fencing across the smaller No. 2 slip, which ran at right angles to the quay wall. When a vessel was being launched, the fencing was removed and a wooden bridge across the gap in the quay wall was lifted clear by the large sheerlegs crane. The No. 2 slip had been acquired from Mr Carter during 1895 and, following the installation of a new cradle, steam winding engine and other facilities, was used for repairing smaller vessels, as well as for building PRINCE GEORGE in 1898. The small building with the first floor bay window was occupied by the Coastguard until 1923, when it became the club house for the Weymouth Sailing Club.

BRIAN JACKSON COLLECTION

A photograph of PRINCESS ROYAL, still in Southampton Company livery but with her new name added in white ink, which was included in Cosens' 1907 Directors' Report and Balance Sheet. The ship is at her moorings in the River Itchen at Southampton.
AUTHOR'S COLLECTION

• **Swanage service** Saloon 1s 6d otherwise 1s. Children half price.

Evening trips after 6pm and single trips 1s.
Wednesdays and Saturdays 1s after 2pm.
Special trips for fireworks, etc. 1s 6d.

With the proviso that, should these mutual arrangements be used in any way offensively by one company against another, the arrangement will be forthwith null and void.

• **Cherbourg Trips** Fares 6s exclusive of English tolls but including French tax. Season tickets not available. Trips to Alderney and the Channel Islands not embraced in this proposal.

The trips to Cherbourg to be run by the respective companies on alternate days, Mondays and Thursdays, and no intermediate trips by either company unless agreed.

Each company maintained its own season ticket system, and there was to be no interchangeability of tickets on the Swanage service.

Behind the scenes, negotiations for the purchase of *Princess Royal* proceeded discreetly. Since J.I. Thornycroft & Co shared a large number of directors and shareholders with the Southampton Company, it was unlikely that they would knowingly have acted against the latter's interests by allowing the ship to fall into Cosens' hands. Constant therefore worked through an agent, who was able to purchase the ship on Cosens' behalf for the sum of £13,000 on the proviso that she would be used neither by a Southampton company nor by the Turks and that the identity of his principals would be revealed as soon as the deposit was paid.

By the time that Thornycrofts discovered Cosens' involvement, the deal had been concluded and the ship passed into her new owners hands on 29th January 1908. The Southampton Company must have been furious at the turn of events, especially since the purchase price was well below the sum which Thornycrofts had originally been asking. Cosens applied to change the ship's name to *King Edward VII* but, when the Board of Trade replied that it was already taken, the decision was made to name her *Emperor of India* instead.

Because there were no berths available in Weymouth Harbour, *Emperor of India* was steamed to Poole, where the board of directors inspected her during early February. They were greatly impressed with what they saw. For £11,000 less than it cost to build *Majestic* in 1901, they had obtained a virtually new steamer of comparable size and power, which would be capable of undertaking any of the company's long-distance or cross-channel sailings. To illustrate their point they published the table of comparison, below:

	MAJESTIC	EMPEROR OF INDIA	MONARCH
Length	215ft	216ft	210ft
Breadth	27ft	25ft	22ft
Gross Tonnage	408	487	314
Passenger Certificate:			
– Cross Channel	408	481	314
– Between Portsmouth & Start Point	794	776	586
– Between Newhaven and Weymouth	794	776	586
– Inside the Isle of Wight	935	915	672
– Between Weymouth and Portland	935	915	672
– Smooth waters	1,455	1,390	739

ABOVE: A charming watercolour depicting the view along Swanage High Street towards the sea in 1909. In the centre of the painting is Cosens' booking office, with the company house flag fluttering proudly overhead, while at the pier the funnels of both a Cosens' and a Southampton Company steamer can be seen. On the horizon lies the tantalising, chalky outline of the Isle of Wight, inviting prospective passengers to step on board a steamer and sail away to explore its rural charms. DAVID HAYSOM COLLECTION

LEFT: This unusual souvenir postcard from Weymouth was posted in 1909 and shows ALBERT VICTOR arriving at the landing stage, while a crowd waits to embark for the next trip. A coal barge is moored in the foreground, and both the Nothe Fort and Stone Pier are clearly visible in the background. BRIAN JACKSON COLLECTION

PAGE RIGHT: Cosens' ephemera; CLOCKWISE FROM TOP LEFT: Front cover of Cosens' Official Guide, circa 1912, which was sold on board for 3d; TOP CENTRE: Inner and outer of 1912 season tickets. Cosens used the same format for a range of other tickets, including short term passes allowing twelve trips within fourteen days and shareholders complimentaries. The covers were bound in a range of colours (maroon and blue are seen here) and embossed with the company name. The tickets were designed to fold in half for convenient storage; TOP RIGHT: An embroidered EMPRESS badge, which deckhands wore stitched across the chests of their seamens' jerseys, and a cerise coloured liberty boat ticket; CENTRE RIGHT: Cosens' cap badge and company label; BOTTOM RIGHT: One of the 1901 series of official cards, showing VICTORIA in Lulworth Cove and an officer's cap badge bearing the company's house flag; BOTTOM CENTRE: MAJESTIC jersey badge; BOTTOM LEFT & CENTRE: Front and reverse of coupon books circa 1907, which gave the purchaser a 25 per cent discount on steamer tickets and also a page which contained two coupons; CENTRE LEFT: Purple coloured liberty boat ticket.

EMPRESS

COSENS & Cᵒ'ˢ, Lᵀᴰ.

OFFICIAL GUIDE

TO PLACES OF INTEREST
VISITED BY THE
COMPANY'S FLEET OF PLEASURE STEAMERS.

3 MAPS AND PLANS.

DESCRIPTIVE TEXT,
47 . COLOURED . AND
OTHER ILLUSTRATIONS,
THE "AUTOCHROME"
PROCESS.

COSENS & CO. LIMITED.
SEASON TICKET FOR 1912.
NOT TRANSFERABLE. No. 1027
Available for any of this Company's Steamers
(weather and circumstances permitting) on advertised trips
only, unless otherwise notified.
Every time it is used it must be produced to the Collector
on board the Steamer, and the Registered Owner must SIGN
HIS or HER NAME in the Company's Check Register, for
verification of ownership on request.
Any person other than the Registered Owner using this
Ticket will be held guilty of fraud and prosecuted accord-
ingly, and the Ticket cancelled.
This Ticket is not available unless signed by the owner.

M. C. FROWDE
F. M. JONES | Joint Managers.

Registered Office, Weymouth.

Registered Owner ...

This Ticket is issued subject to the printed conditions circulated
by the Company one of which is that the Company is not responsible for
any accident or injury to, or death of, life, or loss or damage to the property
of the holder of whatever nature and whether caused by perils of the sea,
accidents incidental to navigation or defects latent or otherwise in Hull
tackle, machinery or staging piers gangways or other property of the
Company, or by any act, neglect, or default of the Company, Pilots,
Master, Engineers, Officers, or Mariner or any other person in the Company's
employ or otherwise howsoever.

Signature of Owner ...

COSENS & CO., Ltd.
FLEET TICKET 9717
SINGLE.
To be given up at the Gangway.

BOURNEMOUTH BOSCOMBE
SWANAGE & WEYMOUTH
STEAM PACKET COMPANY
COSENS & CO. LIMITED.

COSENS & CO., Ltd.
FLEET TICKET 530
SINGLE.
To be given up at the Gangway.

PRICE THREEPENCE

EDWARD J. BURROW, Publisher,

Cosens & Co.'s
Buff Funnel Steamers.

Majestic,
Emperor of India,
Monarch
(Cross Channel Steamers)

Victoria, Empress,
Helper,
Premier, Queen,
Albert Victor.

Cosens & Co.'s
Buff Funnel Steamers.
Majestic, Emperor of India,
Monarch, Empress,
Victoria, &c.

Book No. ...

Containing 20
1/= Coupon Tickets
20/=

Name ...

Address ...

Telegrams :
Cosens,
Weymouth.

Telephones :
Weymouth,
333 & 123
Night 131
Swanage 116
B'mouth 4180

COSENS & CO., LTD.
BUFF FUNNEL
EXCURSION STEAMERS.

COSENS & CO.'s
Fleet of

Pleasure
Steamers.

Bournemouth, Boscombe,
Swanage, Weymouth,
Isle of Wight, Torquay,
France etc.

S. S. VICTORIA IN LULWORTH COVE.

Published at Sydenham's Library, Bournemouth.

Cosens & Co.'s
Buff Funnel
Steamers.
Majestic, Emperor of India,
Monarch, &c.

Coupon Ticket 1/-

No. 2684

This Ticket must be produced to the Purser
on going aboard the Steamer, who will
exchange Coupons for an Ordinary Ticket.
They are issued subject to the conditions
printed on the Company's Time Tables and
Bills.

MAJESTIC

Having been repainted in Cosens' colours, EMPEROR OF INDIA is pictured at her moorings in Poole Harbour, dressed overall for the Directors' inspection in February 1908.
CRAWFORD ALEXANDER COLLECTION

Unlike *Majestic, Emperor of India* had an open foredeck, which deprived her of a forward saloon and decreased her seaworthiness in heavy seas but in all other respects she was a worthy fleet mate. On the main deck aft was a large first class saloon, with seating beautifully upholstered in Utrecht velvet and old gold, arranged in alcoves and tapestry curtains at the windows. The panelled bulkheads and deck head were painted white with gold lining. At the forward end of the saloon was a ladies' cabin to one side and the first class refreshment bar to the other. Forward of the engine and boilers on the main deck was a short second class deck shelter, fitted with large windows and wooden, slatted seats. On the lower deck aft was the first class dining saloon, while in the equivalent position forward was the second class dining saloon, catering stores, and cabins for the master, mate, chief and second engineers, steward and purser. The ship was lit throughout by electric light and the large, uncluttered promenade and foredecks provided ample space for her passengers. On the promenade deck behind the funnel was a timber deckhouse containing a small refreshment bar. Although less smooth and technically advanced than *Majestic*'s triple expansion engine, *Emperor of India*'s compound diagonal was a powerful machine developing 210 nhp through two cylinders of 30 inches and 57 inches diameter and 60 inch stroke.

The finance for the new ship came from two sources. Firstly, it happened that £15,000 worth of debenture bonds issued in 1888 to finance the building of *Monarch* were due for redemption on 1st January 1908. It had been decided to issue new replacement bonds to the increased total of £25,000 well in advance and, to the delight of the board, over £20,000 was taken up immediately. The balance continued to flow in steadily and a mortgage was obtained from the Capital & Counties Bank to cover the difference.

At the Company's AGM on 3rd February 1908, the Chairman looked back on a difficult season with some degree of satisfaction. Despite the appalling early season weather, increased costs and competition, passenger numbers had still increased to almost one and a quarter million and allowed income from fares and stewarding to remain static in the face of swingeing price cuts. The unexpectedly large income from salvage, towage and trading to the Fleet had offset early season losses and it was again possible to declare a dividend of 5 per cent. It had been a year of immense uncertainties and changes in the command structure of the Channel Fleet had put the future profitability of the Fleet Contract in

A poor quality but rare view of EMPEROR OF INDIA's dining saloon, which was situated on the main deck aft, taken from an old Cosens' guidebook.
AUTHOR'S COLLECTION

EMPEROR OF INDIA'S compound diagonal engine, viewed from the engineer's control platform. Note the canvas screens which have been lowered to protect the engine room from coal dust while bunkering was taking place. Coal was carried on board in baskets and tipped down the bunker hatches, which were located in the engine room alleyways on the far side of the screens.
WEYMOUTH LIBRARY

considerable doubt. The company had nevertheless committed itself to a further year's contract from 1st January 1908 and hoped that trade would continue to prove a success.

The Managing Director, Mr S.J. Fowler, then responded to criticisms that Weymouth had been unfairly deprived of large steamers and long-distance trips during the past season by presenting an incisive analysis of the current state of the company's affairs. He pointed out that long experience had shown Weymouth had almost unique requirements and that no ship which was not small and adaptable enough to trade to the Fleet, enter Lulworth Cove, or land passengers on the open beaches of Dorset and Devon, could ever pay her way. *Victoria*, he asserted, was about the ideal size and a larger steamer, unable to beach and engaged solely in long distance excursions from the resort, would never

VICTORIA sweeps in to Bournemouth Pier during 1908. During the previous winter, steps had been constructed down the forward side of the small deckhouse on the foredeck but they were not provided with handrails or access from the upper deck until later in the year.
AUTHOR'S COLLECTION

COSENS & C?. "S.S. EMPEROR OF INDIA". OFF BOURNEMOUTH PIER.

EMPEROR OF INDIA

When EMPEROR OF INDIA joined the fleet in 1908, Fitzgerald produced this final painting, showing the ship steaming away from Bournemouth Pier on an excursion to Swanage or Weymouth.

cover the cost of her own coal. Bournemouth, on the other hand, with its rapidly-expanding population and huge numbers of visitors, had an entirely different pattern of trade. Apart from the occasional trip to Lulworth Cove, the ability to beach was unimportant and what was required was a fleet of large, fast steamers capable of carrying huge numbers of passengers on longer trips. Provided the supply of large steamers at Bournemouth could

keep up with the demand and fend off the competition, then Weymouth would benefit from their visits. Without them, the company could not survive and Weymouth would lose everything. As regards the incursions of the Southampton Company, he reiterated that Cosens' policy remained one of *'defence not defiance'*. While determined to defend their own castle, they still had no intention of carrying the fight into the enemy's home waters

Following hard astern of another member of the fleet, EMPEROR OF INDIA *swings through the northern entrance to Portland Harbour.*
AUTHOR'S COLLECTION/
SEWARD

Another Leon & Levy postcard, showing BRODICK CASTLE *at Swanage Pier. Numerous series of 'LL' postcards were produced covering English towns and cities, mostly in the southern half of the country.*
AUTHOR'S COLLECTION

The waterlogged cargo steamer SANDAL *in Portland Harbour, with* ALBERT VICTOR, PRINCE GEORGE, QUEEN, *the diving boat and one of Messrs Collins' tugs alongside.* AUTHOR'S COLLECTION

by basing steamers in the Solent.

By contrast, the actions of the Southampton Company during the 1908 season made it abundantly clear that not only did they intend to carry the battle into Cosens' camp but that they intended to stay there on a long-term basis. During the winter, they had placed an order with the Ailsa Shipbuilding Co of Troon for a brand new steamer intended specifically for the Bournemouth station and had carried out a major refit to *Stirling Castle*. The latter appeared on the Swanage service on 6th April, replacing the more familiar *Solent Queen* and was joined by *Lorna Doone* a few weeks later. Cosens followed their usual early-season pattern, whilst *Emperor of India* was moved firstly to Weymouth for final fitting out and then to Southampton for dry docking. It was originally intended that she would enter service on 17th April but this was postponed whilst Thornycrofts undertook some additional work, which was required in order for her to obtain a cross-channel passenger certificate.

Emperor of India's inaugural trip from Weymouth took place on the bright but bracing afternoon of 24th April, with the accustomed selection of directors, shareholders and invited guests. The ship steamed round the Shambles Lightship before laying to in the shelter of Portland Breakwater, whilst the Mayor of Weymouth proposed success to the new steamer and the customary responses were made. No luncheon was provided but biscuits and wine were served while the guests, glad to take shelter from the biting northerly wind, took a more than usually close interest in the furnishings of the saloons. On the following day, 25th April, it was intended to repeat the occasion at Bournemouth but a heavy blizzard, which disrupted communications all along the Dorset and Hampshire coast, forced a cancellation. A few days later, a fatal tramway disaster occurred in Bournemouth and all thought of a celebration was immediately abandoned. The inaugural cruise was postponed indefinitely and in fact never took place, the ship quietly entering service at Bournemouth without any further fanfares.

On 20th July 1908, the Southampton Company's new steamer, significantly named *Bournemouth Queen*, entered service at her namesake resort. Beautifully proportioned and with a full-length promenade deck, she bore a strong family resemblance to *Balmoral*, of which she was really a smaller, more economical version. With a speed of 15 knots, she was intended to compete directly with *Monarch*, *Brodick Castle* and *Emperor of India* on the medium distance excursions and immediately proved a great success. She initially replaced *Stirling Castle* on the Swanage service, while *Lorna Doone* and *Balmoral* continued to cover the longer trips. With their white funnels and similar profiles, the three Southampton ships now presented a clear and attractive fleet image and proffered a strong challenge to Cosens' position at Bournemouth.

Emperor of India more or less replaced *Brodick Castle* on full and half day excursions while the latter,

which had been patched up just enough to obtain her passenger certificates, appeared more and more on the Swanage service and the Fleet contract. The comfortable arrangement with the Bournemouth & South Coast Steam Packets continued and *Lord Elgin*, sporting her red funnel, continued to operate as a virtual member of the Cosens' fleet between Bournemouth and Swanage. The advent of *Emperor of India* allowed Cosens to revise their timetable and offer more long distance trips from Bournemouth, with calls at Teignmouth and Exmouth being recorded in addition to the more usual destinations. *Monarch* continued to visit Lyme Regis on a fairly regular basis. As promised by Mr Fowler, the long-distance steamers touched at Weymouth on many of their westward trips or began their eastward trips there whenever the tide served. When Weymouth was their destination, the larger steamers were usually pressed into service on short, local cruises, thereby enabling local residents to sample some of the delights which were commonplace at Bournemouth.

Cosens continued to advertise regular cruises from Clarence Pier, Southsea to Brighton, Worthing, round the Island and to Bournemouth. From 1st August, they also began advertising sailings from the Isle of Wight piers in the island press. Although the bulk of these were return sailings to Bournemouth while the steamer's full-day passengers were enjoying time ashore on the island, there were also some interesting variations, including cruises to the Nab Lightship or Selsey Bill from Ventnor, Shanklin and Sandown. One thing which did not alter, however, was the matter of Sunday sailings. It had been noted that certain excursion steamer operators on the South Coast and Bristol Channel had introduced Sunday sailings and were reaping large rewards as a result but Cosens' management made it clear that they had never yet exploited the Sabbath and intended to follow a policy of '*inflexible adherence*' in the future!

At the beginning of the season, Capt Masters, the long-standing skipper of *Monarch*, had resigned to take up a post as a fisheries officer. His departure led to a major reshuffle of deck officers, and the arrangements for the 1908 season were as follows:

Vessel	Master	Mate
MAJESTIC	Rawle	Miles
EMPEROR OF INDIA	Tilsed	Holyoak
MONARCH	Hardy	Carter
BRODICK CASTLE	Shippick	Reddicliffe
VICTORIA	Pearce	Hope
EMPRESS	Cox	Bowering
PREMIER	Painter	Leddy
QUEEN	Read	Pavey
ALBERT VICTOR	King	Cook

It should be noted that there was a strict order of seniority amongst the company's vessels and that masters could expect to be promoted up the ladder as vacancies occurred. Capt Tilsed, who had been

From the top, Captains Masters, Rawle, Tilsed, Hardy and Pearce.

One of Cosens' longest serving mates, Alfred Hope, pictured here in 1917 with his granddaughter, Doris Dannett.
PAM EBBE

inherited along with *Brodick Castle* from the old Bournemouth Company, was promoted to *Emperor of India* but, bearing in mind his penchant for 'assertive' navigation and his sinking of a yacht during the previous season, was '*urged to give strict caution and care in his new undertaking*'. Shippick was promoted from mate to take his place. With Capt Hardy having moved from *Victoria* to *Monarch*, *Victoria*'s mate Mr Hope was left in post due to '*his long experience in the beaching business westwards*' but was assured that his seniority would not be overlooked once the new master had become used to the trade. Capt Read was also assured that he would not lose seniority by remaining in *Queen*, where his superb seamanship

and specialist knowledge made him invaluable in the salvage trade. Captains Cox and Painter were engaged for one season only.

Despite the fierce competition at Bournemouth and the alternative attractions of the White City Exhibition which diverted many visitors from the seaside, the first half of the 1908 season proved extremely profitable. It seemed that the ever-expanding population of Bournemouth was providing more than enough passengers for both companies and, by mid-August, all previous records had been broken and profits were up by £2,100 compared with 1907. Then, on 17th August, the weather broke and an apparently endless succession of gales and rain brought the steamers to a virtual standstill. All Lulworth and westward beaching trips were cancelled and visitors, instead of flocking on board the steamers, had to content themselves with watching the lifeboat go out and the tugs putting to sea to seek salvage work. As the dreadful weather continued into September, visitors left the coast in droves and never returned. Those who did remain in the resorts were alarmed by lurid reports of the sinking of the pleasure steamer *Rhos Neigr* off North Wales and the near loss of the Southampton Company's *Queen* following her grounding off Selsey Bill, and avoided sea trips. By the end of the season, total passenger figures had fallen by 50,000, and by 10,000 on the Portland service alone.

Although income from the works department had remained steady, 1908 had been a very disappointing year for salvage. The tugs had gone out on numerous occasions and taken many risks but had generated very little income. On 19th March, the steamer *Sandal* had put into Portland Harbour with her cargo on fire and with her decks so hot that the crew could barely touch her wheel or enter

Capt Pearce on the bridge of *VICTORIA*, circa 1908. Below him stand a group of Cosens' directors and local worthies. To the right of the group, wearing a straw boater, is Mark Frowde. He joined the company in 1890, was appointed Works Manager in 1903 and, after several years as Joint Manager, was promoted to Managing Director in 1925. Frowde was a founder member of the Weymouth Football Club, a Chairman of the Council of the Football Association and is remembered to this day as the donor of the Mark Frowde Memorial Cup.
AUTHOR'S COLLECTION

Capt H.J. Hardy (centre) pictured with the crew of MONARCH in 1908, shortly after he had been promoted from VICTORIA. The mate, Mr Carter, stands between the captain and the stewardess. The message on the card, which was written on 28th November 1908 by a member of the crew named Will and posted to a Mr Ted Crossland at Swanage coastguard station, explains: 'Sorry not to have written before but we have been running to the fleet late every night … lost my father and buried him two weeks ago this Saturday. What with that trouble and running to the fleet I have not had much time.'
DAVID HAYSOM COLLECTION

the engine room. Since it was impossible to get below to open her seacocks, she was immediately towed into shallow water where Cosens' and Collins' tugs, together with several Admiralty vessels, poured water into her holds until the sea flowed in over her hatch covers and she settled onto the bottom. After being left to cool for three days, she was pumped dry and re-moored. Remarkably, the fire promptly broke out again and hoses had to be brought into play once more, before *Sandal* could finally be cleared of her ruined cargo and sent on her way. In the middle of the September gales, £400 was earned when *Albert Victor* and *Queen* went to the aid of the barque *Selina Stafford* and towed her to safety. Fortunately, the Fleet was present at Portland for much of the year and the liberty boat trade assumed greater proportions than ever before. Even in late November, five steamers were still in commission and shuttling regularly to and fro between Weymouth Harbour and the anchored warships.

As this season of mixed fortunes drew to a close, Cosens received the completely unexpected news that the shareholders of the Bournemouth & South Coast Steam Packets had agreed to sell out to the Southampton Company and put their company into voluntary liquidation. Secret negotiations had apparently been underway for some time and, on 29th October, Cosens discovered that *Lord Elgin*, two tugs and the shore facilities at Poole had been transferred to their rivals for the sum of £6,500. A month later, the Bournemouth Company gave six months notice of the termination of its 1901 agreement with Cosens.

The Weymouth management must have felt extremely angry that they had neither been informed of the negotiations, nor been given the chance to make a counter-offer. Those with long memories might have considered that this clandestine agreement represented the final, spiteful act of a group of directors who had always resented Cosens' success at Bournemouth and, still smarting from their 1901 humiliation, were happy to see their old rivals discomfited. Certainly, the deal had potentially serious consequences for Cosens, who had not only lost the use of the Bournemouth Company's Hamworthy Wharf at Poole but had been deprived of the important *Lord Elgin* on the Swanage service.

Whatever their true feelings, the Cosens board responded calmly that they *'had no desire to compete for the purchase'* but noted that *'when arrangements have been carried through, some diplomatic steps may judiciously be taken with the Southampton Co. as to the future working of the Swanage and other traffic.'* Behind the scenes, Mr Fowler and Edward Bicker, the long-

Promenaders mingle with passengers from EMPEROR OF INDIA on Weymouth Pile Pier during the summer of 1908.
BRIAN JACKSON COLLECTION

standing secretary of the Bournemouth Company, were in amicable correspondence and clearly shared the same opinions about the future. In a letter dated 31st October, Fowler wrote:

'I should not like our official associations thus to close without expressing, for my colleagues and myself, our deep acknowledgements for all the courtesy and consideration we have always received at your hands …

Personally, I feel that could the respective boards be brought to see wisely how to copy the G.W.R. and L.&S.W.R. in their traffic between this and the Channel Islands (whereby they work on alternate days upon mutual agreement which has resulted in public benefit and the saving of thousands of pounds to their respective companies) they could, without surrender of any principals, cover the whole of the Bournemouth business, east and west, in a manner never before attempted and without running forward into any more capital until such became an absolute necessity.

The Railway companies' combine is further evidence in favour, and I should look upon it as a gratifying climax to my life's work here, if I saw the

south coast covered by such an arrangement on a wise and profitable basis, preventing 4 steamers from doing what 2 ought to do and earning for the shareholders hundreds of pounds that otherwise are thrown into the sea. Beyond this, no third company would ever get a footing and it would be the means of stopping abnormal expenditure as it did in March 1901 when your company and ours combined.

However, those who live longest will see the most!'

In his reply Bicker expressed his complete agreement and promised to exert his unofficial influence with the Southampton Company *'to induce them to consider favourably any approach you may make to them.'* He concluded, somewhat poignantly, *'I shall have no official connection with the Soton. Co. My steamboat days are ended and indeed I am not sorry to bury them.'*

Whether Fowler and Bicker's dream could be brought to fruition would remain to be seen. In the meanwhile, with Cosens' fleet effectively reduced by one ship and their rival's increased to four by the acquisition of *Lord Elgin*, it was evident that the season ahead would prove a very stern test indeed.

During the winter of 1907-08, Monarch's *bridge was moved to a new position forward of her funnels, as seen in this E.H. Seward photograph of her departing from Weymouth.*

AUTHOR'S COLLECTION/SEWARD

CHAPTER 12
THE YEARS OF LIGHT & SHADE
1909-1913

It is a generally acknowledged fact that the decade preceding the outbreak of the First World War represented the heyday of the British pleasure steamer. With the railways carrying ever-increasing numbers of holiday-makers to the nation's burgeoning seaside resorts and steamer fleets expanding to keep pace with the demand, it is tempting to see these years as endless golden summers of smooth seas and fat profits. The reality, however, was somewhat more complex and, for Cosens at least, it was a period marked by such tremendous swings in fortune that the Chairman, J.G. Rowe, referred to it as *'a time of lights and shades.'*

In the New Year of 1909, Cosens' immediate problem was how to respond to the shift in power at Bournemouth. With *Lord Elgin* lost to the opposition and *Brodick Castle*'s patched up boiler getting crankier by the moment, it was essential that something should be done both to defend the Swanage service and improve the excursion fleet. Several measures were taken.

Firstly, consideration was given to selling *Emperor of India* and replacing her with a new ship, probably a near sister to *Majestic*. The Turkish company, which had let the ship slip through its fingers in 1907 by

failing to pay the deposit, was evidently still interested in her and had renewed contact with Mr Constant. In February, the Turks offered £20,000 with the payments spread over twelve months but Cosens' bankers, who held a mortgage on the ship, were unhappy with this arrangement. Instead, Constant was instructed to drop the price to £18,500 in return for a cash payment.

Cosens were clearly uneasy about *Emperor of India*'s open foredeck and reasoned that a profit of £5,500 would be sufficient incentive to let the ship go and replace her with a vessel custom-built to their requirements. The Turks, however, failed to respond by the deadline of 22nd February and the deal fell through. Instead, Cosens decided to accept a tender from Day, Summers & Co of Southampton to bring her up to the same standard as *Majestic* and *Bournemouth Queen*, by plating up the bow to give her a full-length promenade deck.

Day, Summers quoted £1,060 for the initial work but, when it was found that the extra weight forward had upset the ship's trim and it was necessary to move her boiler some feet aft to correct the problem, the bill rose to £1,650. Her steel paddle floats were also replaced by timber ones with the intention of

With her open foredeck plated up and her promenade deck extended to the bows, EMPEROR OF INDIA is seen arriving at Weymouth circa 1909.
AUTHOR'S COLLECTION/
SEWARD

EMPEROR OF INDIA in Weymouth Bay.
AUTHOR'S COLLECTION/
SEWARD

Letter from David Sydenham to Mr S.J. Fowler detailing his concerns over the winter service in light of the Southampton Co's threat to commence a similar operation.
AUTHOR'S COLLECTION

The Bournemouth, Boscombe, Swanage & Weymouth
Steam Packet Company (Cosens & Co., Limited).

D. SYDENHAM, BOURNEMOUTH LOCAL MANAGER,
ROYAL MARINE LIBRARY, PIER APPROACH.

Telephone
No. 130.   Bournemouth Jan 5th   190

S. J. Fowler Esq.
    Weymouth.
Dear Mr Fowler,

        "Mate's Book," Following the comments of yours of the
2nd inst, I have arranged for a Joint Trade, and Steamer advertisement
in this book, which no doubt will meet the case.

Winter Service:- We have thought over this Service, and we think it
suicidal for the "Victoria," as well as the "Lord Elgin," during
the months of February and March, to run against each other, but
if we decide, and announce we do not intend running, it will open
the door for the "Lord Elgin," to make what little there is out of
the concern, which we have done hitherto, and as we should not give
them the Traffic without some arrangements, it seems that the
Southampton Co., should be approached, and if they agree that the
Traffic in these months is not worth the speculation, for this year
and years to come, I should say throw it up altogether, but better
still if your suggestions re the Joint Steamer Service could be
brought about for these months, and continue on *terms throughout the Season* ~~the Swanage Traffic.~~

        Yours truly,

        D. Sydenham

reducing weight, allowing her engines to run at a higher number of revolutions and increasing her speed. In the event, the increased weight of the hull cancelled out the savings from the paddle floats and her draught remained unaltered. One definite gain, however, was the increase in her passenger capacity, which now rose to 481 on cross-channel trips, 833 between Brighton and Dartmouth, 970 inside the Isle of Wight and between Weymouth and Portland, and 1,650 in smooth waters. The work was completed by the beginning of April.

Secondly, there was the matter of *Brodick Castle* and the Swanage service. Without new boilers, her days were clearly numbered and Mr Constant had already offered £1,500 to take her off the company's hands. However, with the loss of *Lord Elgin*, the company was now short of vessels and it was decided that there was no option but to patch her up again, apply for a limited passenger certificate and keep her on the Swanage service for a further season. The option of fitting new boilers was rejected and it was decided to place her on the market at the end of the year.

The winter service was also causing the management some concern. It had always been operated more for prestige than profit and one ship, crewed by men taken from the larger steamers laid up for the winter in the Wareham Channel, had just about managed to cover her fuel costs. Now, the Southampton Company, anxious to shadow every goodwill gesture that Cosens might make, was threatening to operate *Lord Elgin* on an identical winter service. To operate two ships where one could scarcely pay would obviously be suicidal but neither company seemed willing to allow the other to run unopposed. Cosens therefore prepared *Victoria* for sea but deferred the start of the season until the opposition made a move. Since the Southampton Company had adopted identical tactics a stalemate ensued and, for the first time since 1902, no winter service was operated between Bournemouth and Swanage.

As soon as the main season got under way, the Southampton Company placed both *Lord Elgin* and *Stirling Castle* on the Swanage service and adopted the former's red and black funnel colouring for both steamers. This was a clear attempt to maintain an association in the public's mind with the old 'local company' and to benefit from long-standing loyalties. Sailing bills were brazenly headed *'the 33rd season of the Bournemouth & South Coast Steam Packet's Red Funnel Boats, the newly-equipped and favourite saloon steamers* Lord Elgin, Bournemouth Queen *and Stirling Castle'* and Cosens' irritation must have been unbounded. *Bournemouth Queen* did not actually adopt the red funnel colours but retained the same all-white livery of the other more glamorous long-distance excursion steamers *Balmoral* and *Lorna Doone*. In subsequent years, the Southampton Company's fleet underwent numerous changes of livery but it is interesting to note that this seemingly small event in 1909 led eventually to the adoption of the old Bournemouth Company's colours for the entire fleet and the adoption of the trading name 'Red Funnel Steamers' which endures to this day.

Cosens were forced to respond by withdrawing *Monarch* from most of her day sailings and placing her on the Swanage service to partner *Brodick Castle*. She was only taken off this route to undertake her regular trips to Lyme Regis and Alderney or the occasional special event, at which times her place would be taken by either *Empress* or *Victoria*. Two steamers from each company were now engaged in a trade which could quite sensibly have been covered by one. Because any degree of co-operation seemed out of the question, both companies adopted almost identical departure times and the residents of Bournemouth and Swanage were deprived of the more frequent service which could have resulted had common sense prevailed.

With *Monarch* removed from the day-trip timetable, Cosens were forced to spread their other steamers more thinly. While *Majestic* remained wholly at Bournemouth, *Emperor of India* was forced to dash to and from Weymouth and Bournemouth providing long sailings from both ports, while *Victoria* and *Empress* had to be used more flexibly. Fortunately, the Southampton Company had withdrawn *Lorna Doone* to Southampton, leaving *Bournemouth Queen* to cover the day trips to the Isle of Wight and occasional long-distance sailings to Torquay, Dartmouth and Brighton. With a service speed of only 15 knots, however, she was not really suited to the longest trips and often struggled to keep to time. The westward trips to Dartmouth required that the steamer arrived just before high water, in order to connect with the onward trip up the Dart, and this meant battling against adverse tides in both directions. A fast steamer was required and *Majestic* must have benefited from her rival's inadequacies, until *Balmoral* took over once again during July.

To add to Cosens' woes, the Southampton Company chose 1909 to introduce Sunday sailings. Because neither Swanage nor Bournemouth piers would accept steamers on Sundays, these trips operated direct from Poole Quay to the Isle of Wight and proved extremely popular. Cosens' directors, while recognising that large profits could be made by accepting '*a bank holiday every week*', remained resolutely opposed to Sabbath-breaking and refused to countenance following suit. It remains a matter of conjecture whether the moral approval they won locally outweighed the loss of income until, when the local councils finally gave way and opened their piers on Sundays, a limited Bournemouth to Swanage service was introduced in 1929.

The Southampton Company also sought to invade Cosens' most sacred territory by advertising trips to Lulworth Cove by both *Lord Elgin* and *Stirling Castle*. Since these steamers were not adapted for beaching and no landing rights had been negotiated, it must be assumed that the intention was to anchor in the Cove and land passengers in small boats. As it happened, bad weather intervened and none of the sailings took place, although the idea was not abandoned and further attempts were made in subsequent years.

The increasing number of steamers using Bournemouth Pier had, for some time, led to severe congestion at the landing stages and work had been underway on constructing additional berths. On 5th June 1909, the official opening of the landing stage extension was performed by the Lord Mayor of London, Alderman Sir George Wyatt Truscott, whose father, Sir Francis Wyatt Truscott, had opened the pier itself back in 1880. *Majestic* was

STIRLING CASTLE pictured after 1909, when the Southampton Company adopted red and black funnels for both their Swanage service steamers.
JOHN PAGE COLLECTION

A splendid selection of bizarre headwear is on display as the Lord Mayor of London prepares to perform the official opening of the Bournemouth Pier landing stage extension, from MAJESTIC's *bridge, on 5th June 1909.*
AUTHOR'S COLLECTION

moored at the new stage while the splendidly-attired official party gathered on her spacious bridge to carry out the ceremony. Special trips were advertised from Weymouth and Swanage to witness the spectacle.

On 7th July, *Emperor of India* and the Southampton Company's *Prince of Wales* came into collision while leaving Ryde Pier and the former suffered damage to her paddle box. Fortunately, she was able to continue with her cruise and an Admiralty Court later found in Cosens' favour, allotting damages and costs against the Southampton Company.

In late July, warships began to gather in Spithead for a Review of the Fleet by King Edward VII on Saturday 31st July. From 29th July onwards, Cosens,

along with all the other local companies and a number of steamers from further afield, began to concentrate all of their efforts on cruises to view the Fleet. During the run-up period, *Emperor of India* and *Monarch* ran numerous double-return trips from Bournemouth to Clarence Pier, Southsea, offering passengers from both places the opportunity to sail through the lines of warships *en route*. On Review day, they were joined by *Majestic* on sailings from Bournemouth, whilst *Brodick Castle* was withdrawn from the Swanage service to offer three short cruises from Ryde and two from Cowes, together with a longer trip to witness the Review itself. On 2nd August, she offered another cruise to watch the arrival of the Czar of Russia and seven more short cruises through the lines of warships.

The year of 1909 was also the first in which catering to the company's steamers was wholly in the hands of the Catering Manager, Mr Harford. Since his appointment in 1905, Harford had made a great success of the catering on board all of the larger steamers and had contributed significantly to the company's income. Mr Lankester had tendered annually for *Empress* and *Victoria* but this arrangement was brought to a close at the end of 1908. Mr Harford had set up a stewarding depot at Swanage and, by acting as wholesale provision merchant on behalf of the company, had generated a healthy profit in addition to that made on board the steamers themselves. A subsidiary store to supply the Weymouth steamers was set up beneath the Head Office at Custom House Quay. Harford was paid a retainer through the winter months and both he and his chief stewards were paid a bonus at the end of each successful season.

Although the early season weather had been delightful, during the high-earning months of August and September rain and fog alternated with such unceasing monotony that the season was declared the worst in twenty years. Indeed, on one day during August, the weather was so bad that while *Victoria* was going astern out of Lulworth Cove, one of her seamen had been washed overboard and drowned. Admittedly the Bournemouth profits, despite the worst efforts of the weather and the Southampton Company, exceeded the previous year's by £2,000 and the engineering department had done well but everything else seemed doom-laden. The Weymouth passenger figures were down, the decline in the number of sailing ships using Weymouth Harbour had led to a fall in demand for towage, salvage work had been exceptionally barren and the Fleet had been missing from Portland for most of the summer. For the first time since the company was incorporated, no dividend was declared.

The only salvage job of note had taken place on 27th January 1909, when the steam yacht *Ilona* went ashore beneath St. Alban's Head. Five of the yacht's crew took to their boat, leaving the captain on board, and after several hours lost in the fog were rescued by the Swanage lifeboat. Meanwhile, *Queen* and *Albert*

Victor had arrived from Weymouth at low water, to discover *Ilona* well up on the rocks and heeling so alarmingly that there were fears she might slip off and fill with water before she could right herself. As high tide approached, *Albert Victor* got a rope onto the yacht, which suddenly toppled over broadside to the sea and shipped a large amount of water before gradually righting herself. *Queen* immediately went alongside and used her salvage pump to clear the casualty of water, while *Albert Victor*, towing ahead, guided her slowly towards Swanage. Once alongside Swanage coaling pier, it was discovered her hull was badly strained and that she would have to be placed on a slipway as a matter of urgency. As soon as steam was raised in *Ilona*'s boilers, in order to power a large portable salvage pump which Cosens put on board, *Queen* towed her to Southampton for permanent repairs. The only other recorded salvage award was for £80 against the barque *Selina Stafford*.

Up until about 1908, the command structure of the Channel and Home Fleets had meant that individual Admirals were free to make direct agreements with Cosens regarding the provision of steamers to act as liberty boats. Thereafter, it would appear that bureaucracy became more centralised and all contracts had to be approved by the Admiralty at Whitehall. Despite severe doubts, Cosens had entered into a new contract for 1909, whereby they guaranteed to provide a certain number of boats each day but made their profit by charging an individual fare for each officer or man carried.

Unfortunately, the Fleet was then absent from the anchorage for much of the summer and when it did return a new arrangement of 'weekend leave' was introduced for the sailors. This meant that, instead of spending their free time shuttling to and fro on the steamers and spending their wages in Weymouth, the men came ashore only once and then departed by the first train to spend their free time with their families. The steamers quickly began to run at a loss and Cosens attempted to get the Admiralty to guarantee a minimum level of income by chartering the steamers on a more formal basis. Due to the unsettled state of Parliament at the time, nobody seemed capable of making a decision and, as the date for the expiry of the 1909 agreement approached, Cosens threatened to withdraw the service completely except for a single 11am daily goods boat. Meetings were held with the Captain-in-Charge at Portland and a deputation was sent to the Admiralty in London, as a result of which a new agreement was reached for 1910.

Under this new contract, the old system of charging a fare for each man carried was replaced by a formal charter arrangement which guaranteed Cosens a set income. At the end of January, it was reported to be working well but then, on 2nd February 1910, Admiral May suddenly suspended the contract. The Fleet remained at Portland, so Cosens were faced with a choice of either reverting to charging

set advertised fares as previously or suspending the service altogether. The board decided that the best tactic would be to stick as closely as possible to the terms of the suspended contract and continue to generate income while attempting to negotiate with the Admiralty.

The MP for South Dorset became involved on the Company's behalf and, after questions were asked in Parliament during April, the Admiralty agreed to pay £3,166 in compensation for non-fulfilment of contract. While the steamers continued to operate on their old, fare-charging basis, negotiations dragged on and, during June, Cosens were invited to submit a new tender. This offered the Admiralty the alternative of either chartering the steamers outright for £10,000 per year or providing a subsidy of £7,500, while Cosens continued to charge a reduced fare for each man carried.

Any decision on this tender was delayed by the absence of the Fleet on manoeuvres throughout June and July but Cosens were meanwhile left with the dilemma of how to provide for the anticipated demand when the warships returned at the end of the month. The old *Brodick Castle*, which had been

TOP: QUEEN and ALBERT VICTOR rest at the old Swanage Pier, after salvaging the steam yacht ILONA from St. Alban's Head on 27th January 1909.
AUTHOR'S COLLECTION

ABOVE: The three-masted barque SELINA STAFFORD at anchor in Portland Harbour, after her rescue by Cosens' tugs during September 1908. The gale damage to her masts and rigging is clearly visible.
WEYMOUTH MUSEUM

replaced on the Swanage service by *Empress* from the beginning of the 1910 season, had been retained at Weymouth on a limited No.4 passenger certificate and used exclusively on the Fleet traffic. However, on 9th July, it was reported that '*she was of no further use without a new boiler*' and had been returned to her moorings in Poole Harbour, never to sail for the company again. A replacement ship had to be found but to purchase one in the face of the uncertainty surrounding the future of the contract seemed rash.

Mr Constant, the shipbroker, was able to offer the small GWR paddle steamer *Helper* for sale or charter at low cost and negotiations were immediately opened. The steamer, 131 feet 1 inch long, 20 feet 1 inch in the beam and with 10 feet draught, had been built in 1873 as *Sir Francis Drake*, for use on the railway company's excursion sailings and ocean liner tendering duties from Millbay Docks at Plymouth. Replaced by a larger vessel of the same name in 1908, she had been renamed and left lying in reserve ever since. Built of iron by W. Allsup & Co of Preston, fitted with an 80nhp simple diagonal engine with a stroke of 48 inches and cylinder diameter of 30 inches, she was a relatively small 173 ton ship, whose tendering pedigree made her ideally suited to the Fleet trade at Weymouth.

Helper was initially chartered for the month of August for £150, while further negotiations took place with the Admiralty. By the middle of the month, a draft of a new Fleet Contract had been submitted and agreed, and Cosens felt confident enough to proceed with her outright purchase. A price of £650 was negotiated but Constant then suggested that he exchange her for *Brodick Castle*.

The board agreed on the proviso that, should Constant re-boiler and refit the old steamer, they should be given first refusal for charter or re-purchase. On 14th September 1910, *Helper* formally passed into Cosens' ownership and the old *Brodick Castle*, without any fuss or comment from the community she had served for the last twenty-three years, slipped quietly away from her moorings in the Wareham Channel and departed for Holland, where Constant had a buyer for her.

The new Fleet Contract, which was formally signed on 8th October and came into force eight days later, finally put an end to the uncertainty between Cosens and the Admiralty, and remained in force until the outbreak of the Great War. Cosens agreed to supply five steamers for an initial period of twelve months, with three months notice to quit by either party and to operate the following timetable:

Weekdays: From Weymouth at 7am, 11am, 4pm and 6.30pm, returning from HM ships at 8.30am, 1.30pm, 4.30pm and 7.00pm.
Sundays: From Weymouth at 7.00am, 12.30pm and 6.30pm, returning from HM ships at 8.00am, 1.30pm and 7.00pm.

For this service, the Admiralty would pay £7,500 per annum and Cosens would additionally charge fares of 3d single and 5d return for officers, and 2d single and 3d return for men.

It was estimated that one steamer could normally serve three warships but that for the 6.30pm trip between November and January, only two steamers would be employed. On the 11.00am trip each day,

Packed with sailors returning from leave, PREMIER departs from Weymouth Harbour. In the background is MONARCH, moored to the old Ammunition Jetty beneath the Nothe Fort, where she is being prepared for the excursion season ahead. MONARCH's canvas dodgers have not yet been fitted to her rails but steam is being raised and her lifebelts are being repainted in the forward well-deck.
AUTHOR'S COLLECTION/
SEWARD

SAILORS RETURNING FROM LEAVE.

In a photograph which graphically illustrates the importance of the Navy's business to Cosens, QUEEN leads ALBERT VICTOR out of Weymouth Harbour on a liberty boat run, whilst behind the latter's mast, PREMIER is seen returning from the Fleet.
AUTHOR'S COLLECTION/SEWARD

SAILORS RETURNING FROM LEAVE.

With her paddle boxes stripped of their decorative facings to avoid damage when berthing alongside warships, the elderly BRODICK CASTLE *is seen during her last few weeks in service during the summer of 1910.* AUTHOR'S COLLECTION/SEWARD

S.S. HELPER.

HELPER, *an ex-GWR tender from Plymouth, arrived at Weymouth in August 1910 and passed into Cosens' ownership a month later in exchange for* BRODICK CASTLE. *Note her heavily-fendered paddle boxes.* AUTHOR'S COLLECTION/SEWARD

BELOW: On a warm summer's evening, sailors flood through the pier gates and along the promenade to enjoy time ashore in Weymouth. HELPER is at the landing stage, MONARCH is under the Nothe and QUEEN can just be glimpsed approaching the pier to the left of the Ritz Theatre, which was completed in 1908.
G. CARTER COLLECTION

Cosens were permitted to carry traders and wholesale goods to and from the Fleet but excursionists would never be carried on any steamer conveying officers and men. The numbers carried by each steamer would be governed by special passenger certificates issued by the Board of Trade expressly for that purpose and the Navy would supervise both embarkation and behaviour on board. No alcohol was to be sold or consumed.

A clause was built in allowing *Queen* and *Albert Victor* to be released from their duties to render urgent service to ships in distress, in return for which tugs would undertake reasonable towage duties for the Admiralty during the hours of the contract. Provision was also made for additional sailings to be requested in exceptional circumstances, or for the timings of the main timetable to be varied by mutual consent. At long last it appeared that an

THE HARBOUR. WEYMOUTH.

Packed to overflowing with sailors and listing heavily, HELPER comes astern down Weymouth Harbour on a liberty boat run, while QUEEN loads at the landing stage. Further up harbour are a number of GWR Channel Islands steamers, with either REINDEER or ROEBUCK moored outside IBEX, while in the distance MELMORE can be seen at the cargo stage. AUTHOR'S COLLECTION/SEWARD

Monarch arriving at Lyme Regis on one of her regular excursions from Bournemouth.
H.A. ALLEN COLLECTION

equitable settlement had been reached and that Cosens would be in a position to plan more rationally for the future size and disposition of its Weymouth fleet. Incidentally, a visit to Portland during November by a large fleet of American warships generated a substantial amount of additional income, all of which fell outside the terms of the new agreement.

In comparison with these crises, the issues of the excursion season seemed to pale into relative insignificance. Once again, the Southampton Company had threatened to commence its own winter service on 1st March 1910 and *Victoria* had been prepared to enter service on the same day. However, following the usual game of bluff and counter-bluff, neither steamer appeared and the winter service was never offered again. The main season, which opened on 21st March, saw *Empress* partnering *Monarch* on the Swanage service, while *Brodick Castle* was used on liberty-boat duties at Weymouth but otherwise the timetable and deployment of steamers remained largely unaltered from 1909. Both the Easter and August Bank Holiday periods were exceptionally busy but the weather for the remainder of the season was generally disappointing and discouraged potential passengers from embarking on sea excursions.

A tragic accident occurred on the night of 27th

August, while *Emperor of India* was berthed at Hamworthy Wharf at the end of her day's sailings. A small boat had come across from Poole Quay to collect six of the ship's firemen, all of whom were Poole residents, and take them home for the night. As they climbed on board from the sponson, the boat lurched and capsized, throwing them all into the harbour. Despite the best efforts of Capt Tilsed, his Chief Engineer and various local boatmen to render assistance, two of the men, Tom Jacobs and William Holmes, were drowned. Collections were subsequently held on board all of the local steamers and subscription lists opened ashore for the men's widows, who also received compensation through the Company's employees insurance scheme.

The only salvage job of note during 1910 took place in the early hours of 27th February, when the master of a Lowestoft steam drifter put into Weymouth to report that a large ship had broken down 15 miles south of Portland and required the services of a tug. *Albert Victor*'s crew were immediately assembled and, by 4am, she was alongside the 2,400 ton *Taormina*, which had broken her propeller shaft. In rising seas and wind, the tug struggled to steer the ship between the Bill and the Portland Race and succeeded in bringing her safely into Portland, where a £350 salvage award was made.

Following her quiet departure from Poole in September, *Brodick Castle* had been taken to Holland, where she had been stripped of her accommodation, machinery, paddle boxes and sponsons, and converted into a cattle lighter for use on the River Plate in South America. Her fo'c'sle head was left intact but an additional light deck and an awning were constructed above her original promenade deck level.

Re-named *Paca Nova*, she sailed from Helvoet on 25th October in tow of the Dutch tug *Maria Hendrika III* and apparently touched at Brightlingsea before commencing her trans-Atlantic tow. The two ships had made good progress down-channel and were somewhere between Portland Bill and Start Point on the night of 31st October when they were caught in a severe south-westerly gale and began to ship heavy seas. The tug's fo'c'sle and engine room began to flood and, when the tow rope parted, it was found

The old BRODICK CASTLE as the barge PACA NOVA, shortly before her departure for South America. The spelling of her new name varies between sources and is often given as 'PECA'; the version adopted by Lloyd's List has been used in this account.
AUTHOR'S COLLECTION

S.S. OKAHANDJA on the rocks Portland.

to be impossible to pick up the *Paca Nova* again. Her two-man passage crew decided to abandon ship and, wearing lifebelts, leaped overboard before being hauled on board the tug. The tug stood by the lighter all night until, during the early hours, she lost sight of her and assumed she had foundered. The tug put into Dartmouth on the afternoon of 1st November to report her loss and the position of the wreck was subsequently recorded as 50 degrees 30 minutes N, 02 degrees 20 minutes W.

If this is the case, then the wreck of the former *Brodick Castle* lies in 21metres of water, just under one mile due south of the East Shambles Buoy. After breaking free from her tug, she must have been carried by wind and tide back through the Portland Race, whose breaking seas would finally have overwhelmed her. Local divers are currently investigating the wreck but it seems somehow appropriate that the old ship's remains should lie within easy sight of her former home port.

On 8th June 1910, the German cargo steamer OKAHANDJA, loaded with oil, ran ashore in fog on Tor Rock, off Blacknor Point, Portland. Her bows were badly holed but, after a large part of her cargo had been jettisoned or unloaded, she was successfully refloated the next day. Although Cosens were involved in the rescue operations and subsequent repair of the ship, the bulk of the salvage award went to the large German tug E.M. SVITZER. In this photograph, ALBERT VICTOR is seen manoeuvring alongside the casualty.
WEYMOUTH MUSEUM

A rare photograph of MAJESTIC's engine and boiler room crew, taken in 1910. The chief engineer, Mr Rowlands, is seated in the centre, with the second engineer to his right. The rest of the 'black gang' – stokers, greasers and coal trimmers – toiled down below and were rarely seen by the passengers.
D. HAYSOM COLLECTION

The short, disappointing 1910 season, together with the costs incurred in re-tubing *Majestic*'s boiler during the previous winter and re-decking and re-boilering *Premier* during June, meant that, once again, no dividend could be declared on ordinary shares. Shareholders and directors alike prayed for better luck in 1911 but went ahead during the winter with major repairs to *Queen* and a thorough overhaul of *Helper*'s engines.

When the 1911 season opened on 3rd April, one familiar part of the Bournemouth scene was missing. *Lord Elgin*, the last link with the old Bournemouth Company, had been transferred to Southampton, stripped of her passenger accommodation and converted into a cargo vessel. In this guise, she operated between the mainland and Cowes until finally broken up in 1955, at which time she held the honour of being the last cargo paddle steamer in the British Isles.

Lord Elgin's place on the Swanage service was taken by *Princess Helena*, which ran in partnership with *Stirling Castle* until the outbreak of war in 1914. *Monarch* and *Empress* continued to maintain the service for Cosens and the other steamers in the fleet were deployed as in previous years.

The main excitement of the season was provided by the announcement that King George V's Coronation Royal Naval Review would be held in Spithead on 24th June. Planning for the great event began early in the year and *Monarch* was quickly chartered to Hickie, Borman & Co for £350, while the GWR at Bristol offered £200 for *Victoria*. Charters were also sought for the other small steamers, while it was decided to advertise *Majestic* on a pre-booked 1½ guinea public trip from Bournemouth and *Emperor of India* on a cheap public excursion from Weymouth. Insurance was taken out to cover the three largest steamers against loss of income should bad weather prevent them from sailing or the Review be postponed, as had happened back in 1902.

During April 1911, serious problems were experienced with the vital water supply on the Swanage coaling pier and as a result it was decided that the steamers would only take on water at Bournemouth, Poole and Weymouth. It is also apparent that soon after the loss of *Lord Elgin* and the use of the Bournemouth Company's Poole Harbour wharf back in 1908, Cosens had been able to obtain a lease on an alternative wharf at Hamworthy and that some of their steamers, notably *Emperor of India*, berthed there each night. Although others continued to lay overnight and

Coronation Naval Review
At SPITHEAD.
GRAND ASSEMBLAGE OF ABOUT 200 BRITISH AND FOREIGN SHIPS OF WAR.

Special Trips from RYDE (Pier Head).
(Weather and circumstances permitting)
By COSENS & Co.'s Saloon Steamship
'EMPRESS'

THURSDAY, June 22nd.   **Coronation Day.**
FLEET OF 200 SHIPS FULLY DRESSED.   Royal Salute to be fired at 12 noon.

Through the Lines of the Fleet
Leaving Ryde Pier Head at 10.45, 1.15 3.45 & 6.15.
FARE 1/4

Grand Evening Cruise Round the Fleet and to view Illuminations
Leaving Ryde Pier Head at 8.15.   FARE 2/-

FRIDAY, June 23.

Through the Lines of the Fleet
Leaving Ryde Pier Head at 10.45, 1.15, 3.45 & 6.15.
FARE 1/4

Grand Evening Cruise Round the Fleet.
Leaving Ryde Pier Head at 8.15.   FARE 1/-

SATURDAY, June 24.

Morning Cruise ROUND THE FLEET
Leaving Ryde Pier Head at 10.15, back at 11.30,   FARE 1 6

To the REVIEW
Leaving Ryde Pier Head at 1.15   FARE 3/6

TICKETS FOR ALL TRIPS ON BOARD THE STEAMER.
Tickets will not be issued in excess of the number the vessel is allowed to carry under the regulations of the Board of Trade.   *Children under 12 years of age Half Fare (except Trip to the Review).*
The great advantage of the s.s. EMPRESS is that she is under the command of CAPTAIN SHIPPICK, accustomed to the Navigation of the Solent.

THE CATERING DEPARTMENT IS UNSURPASSED.   **E. HARFORD, Manager.**
Head Office—Custom House Quay, Weymouth.   By order, COSENS & Co., Ltd.

Sydenham, Printer, Bournemouth.

Sailing bill advertising trips to the Coronation Naval Review of 1911. Note the 1s 6d fares, hand altered to 1s.   H.A. ALLEN COLLECTION

Grand Marine Trips
From SHANKLIN
(Weather and circumstances permitting).
COSENS & Co.'s CROSS CHANNEL STEAMER

"MAJESTIC"
(Second to none on the South Coast)

Monday, May 29th, to
SANDOWN

Leaving Shanklin at 1.20, returning from Sandown at 3 p.m.   **Fare 1/-** including Pier Tolls.

Single trip to Bournemouth.   Leaving Shanklin 3.10. Fare 2/- including Shanklin Pier Tolls.

Thursday, June 1st,

Single trip to Southsea and Ryde.   Leaving Shanklin at 1   Fare 2/- including Pier Tolls.

By Order,   D SYDENHAM, Local Manager,
Office—Royal Marine Library, Bournemouth.

Sydenham, Printer, Bournemouth.

Hand bill, early summer 1911. H.A. ALLEN COLLECTION

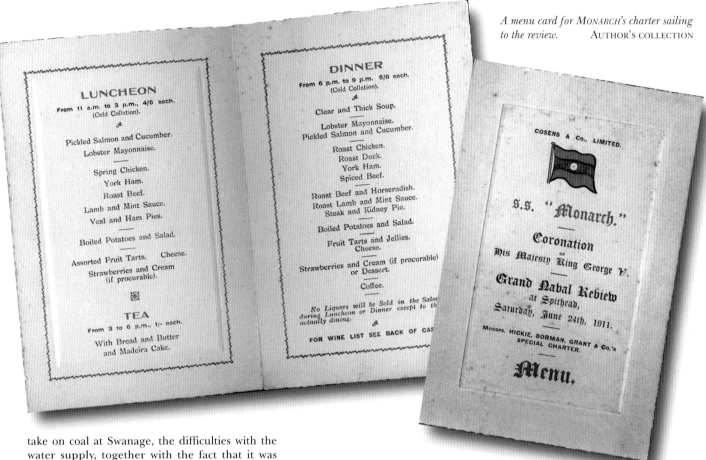

A menu card for MONARCH's *charter sailing to the review.* AUTHOR'S COLLECTION

LUNCHEON
From 11 a.m. to 3 p.m., 4/6 each.
(Cold Collation).

Pickled Salmon and Cucumber.
Lobster Mayonnaise.

Spring Chicken.
York Ham.
Roast Beef.
Lamb and Mint Sauce.
Veal and Ham Pies.

Boiled Potatoes and Salad.

Assorted Fruit Tarts.   Cheese.
Strawberries and Cream
(if procurable).

TEA
From 3 to 6 p.m., 1/- each.

With Bread and Butter
and Madeira Cake.

DINNER
From 6 p.m. to 9 p.m. 5/6 each.
(Cold Collation).

Clear and Thick Soup.

Lobster Mayonnaise.
Pickled Salmon and Cucumber.

Roast Chicken.
Roast Duck.
York Ham.
Spiced Beef.

Roast Beef and Horseradish.
Roast Lamb and Mint Sauce.
Steak and Kidney Pie.

Boiled Potatoes and Salad.

Fruit Tarts and Jellies.
Cheese.

Strawberries and Cream (if procurable)
or Dessert.

Coffee.

No Liquors will be Sold in the Saloon
during Luncheon or Dinner except to th[...]
actually dining.

FOR WINE LIST SEE BACK OF CA[...]

COSENS & Co., LIMITED.

S.S. "Monarch."
Coronation
OF
His Majesty King George V.
Grand Naval Review
at Spithead,
Saturday, June 24th, 1911.

Messrs. HICKIE, BORMAN, GRANT & Co.'s
SPECIAL CHARTER.

Menu.

take on coal at Swanage, the difficulties with the water supply, together with the fact that it was marginally cheaper to have coal delivered direct to the Hamworthy Wharf, seems to have tipped the balance and caused a gradual migration of the fleet into Poole Harbour. The decision as to where to berth each ship may have also been influenced by the make up of her crew. Significantly, Capt Tilsed and a large number of the crew of *Emperor of India* were Poole residents and liked to be able to return to their homes overnight.

The Coronation Review proved to be a magnificent affair and crowned with perfect weather. Some 167 British and 18 foreign warships were anchored in Spithead, when the new King, embarked in *Victoria & Albert* and accompanied by the steam yachts *Irene*, *Alexandra*, *Enchantress* and *Firequeen*, made his stately progress up and down the lines. Between 21st and 27th June, the local fleets were fully occupied running endless trips to

The Great Coronation Review at Spithead June 24th 1911.
The Royal Yacht with The King and Queen on board steaming through the lines

This souvenir postcard, showing Spithead with the Isle of Wight to the left, gives some impression of the vast array of warships which proved such an attraction to the steamer passengers. AUTHOR'S COLLECTION

a pleasure steamer passing H.M.S. Neptune on Review day.

3 COZENS SOUTHSEA

MAJESTIC passes across the stern of the battleship HMS NEPTUNE at the Coronation Review in Spithead on 24th June 1911. The 19,900 ton NEPTUNE had only been completed six months earlier and, with her ten 12 inch and sixteen 4 inch guns, must have made a tremendous impression on MAJESTIC's passengers. This spectacular shot was taken by another Cozens, albeit with a 'z' instead of an 's', a photographer from Southsea.
DAVID HAYSOM COLLECTION

view the Fleet and on Review day itself it appears that Cosens were certainly represented by *Majestic*, *Monarch*, *Emperor of India*, *Empress*, *Victoria* and most probably by *Queen* and *Albert Victor* as well. Cosens applied for a bar licence for *Helper*, in order that she might replace *Empress* on the Swanage service but it is not recorded whether she actually did so. Trade to the Review generated £2,332 in fares and £350 in stewarding.

As a wonderful contrast to the dismal summers of 1909 and 1910, 1911 produced a 'never-to-be-forgotten six months' of superb weather. Passengers flocked up the gangways in unprecedented numbers and, assisted by the extra trade generated by the Review and the fact that Bournemouth's population had now reached 78,674, all previous records were broken. It was noted that sailings from Clarence Pier, Southsea, had proved particularly profitable.

The season proved reasonably free of incidents although *Majestic*, while being assisted away from Victoria Pier at Cowes by the tug *Irishman*, was run into and damaged by the steam yacht *Kathleen*. *Emperor of India*, which was also at the pier, received minor damage and Cosens were awarded £359 in compensation. E.C.B. Thornton also reports that, at about this time, *Majestic* lost her mast at sea during a return crossing from Cherbourg. It seems that the weather had deteriorated and, in order to reduce rolling, Capt Rawle had ordered a steadying sail to be set on the forestay. A sudden gust then

struck the ship, the mast broke and her engines had to be stopped while the crew laboured to prevent the wreckage becoming entangled in the paddle wheels.

Helper had her normal routine interrupted by two minor rescue jobs. On 4th June, she refloated the motor yacht *Betty*, which had gone ashore on the Kimmeridge Ledges in thick fog, and brought her to Weymouth where Cosens' divers examined her hull. One of their tugs subsequently towed the yacht to Dartmouth for repairs. Fog was evidently a recurring problem for, on 19th July, the GWR Channel Islands steamer *Roebuck* had gone spectacularly aground on the coast of Jersey. It was not surprising, therefore, that general alarm was felt in Weymouth when news was received that another GWR steamer, *Ibex*, had come to a sudden halt off Portland and was flying signals of distress. *Helper* was immediately dispatched and discovered that an explosion had seriously damaged the ship's starboard engine. Since *Ibex* was still able to use her port engine, *Helper* stood by while she limped slowly back into port. *Ibex* seems to have been a rather ill-fated ship and had struck rocks and sunk on two previous occasion in 1897 and 1900. It is interesting to note that, on both occasions, the little *Helper*, in her previous incarnation as *Sir Francis Drake*, had been closely involved in the salvage work.

The new Admiralty Contract worked extremely smoothly during 1911 and, as luck would have it,

Majestic in Weymouth Harbour during the winter of 1911, having her mast replaced after it had snapped on a return crossing from Cherbourg, as detailed in the text. Queen *is moored on the opposite side of the harbour.*
AUTHOR'S COLLECTION/SEWARD

AUDREY, seen here departing from Swanage, proved a useful addition to the fleet during the summer of 1911.
AUTHOR'S COLLECTION/
SEWARD

the Fleet was in the anchorage even more frequently than normal. With every steamer stretched to the limit in coping with the extraordinary demand for regular excursion sailings, it quickly became apparent that sailings from Weymouth would have to be curtailed during the high season unless extra ships could be obtained for use as liberty boats. During June, two possible candidates were inspected, *Lord Roberts* at Great Yarmouth and *Audrey* at Cork.

Lord Roberts proved the more suitable of the two. A fee of £630 for two months charter was agreed and, on 10th June, she was delivered to Weymouth where she was taken over by a Cosens' crew. Owned by the Great Yarmouth Steam Tug Co, she was a 235 ton ship, measuring 135 feet by 21 feet 4 inches by 9 feet 7 inches and had been built by W. Allsup of Preston in 1900. She proved well-suited to both liberty boat and short-distance excursion work and fitted well with the rest of the Weymouth fleet.

At the beginning of July, a request was received from the Major commanding a brigade of territorial troops for the transport of his men, who would be spending the summer encamped at Lulworth, between Lulworth Cove and the Fleet at Portland.

Without additional capacity the request could not be considered and so the Cosens board decided to charter *Audrey* as well. The 203-ton *Audrey*, owned by the Cork, Blackrock & Passage Railway Co and with dimensions of 126 feet by 21 feet 1 inch by 8 feet, was in the hands of a Liverpool shipbroker and was immediately taken on a four week charter, with an option to extend. As soon as she entered service at the beginning of August, Cosens were able to finalise arrangements with the Major and, on Sunday 13th August, 1,066 troops were conveyed from Lulworth to the Fleet and back at a fare of 2s per head. The sight of columns of uniformed men, marching from their hill-top camp down through the narrow streets of Lulworth village to embark on one of the queue of steamers which was waiting to collect them from the beach, must have been truly remarkable.

Audrey was also kept busy on the Admiralty Contract work until the first week in September, when she was returned to her owners. *Lord Roberts'* charter expired on 15th October, when her owners, anticipating that Cosens might require her again in 1912, decided to lay her up for the winter at Poole. During the charter her boiler had been causing some concern and so, before she left Weymouth, Cosens were employed to carry out a complete re-tubing.

Blessed with wonderful weather, the Coronation Review, increased trade to the Fleet, unusually brisk sales of ice and a busy year in the works department, 1911 had proved to be one of the most remarkable seasons in the company's history. Income from passengers had increased by £10,242 and the company was once again able to declare a 5 per cent dividend. Sadly, however, two long-standing and key members of the management team were unable to share fully in the comfortable glow of satisfaction.

Early in August, Cosens' Bournemouth Manager, Mr David Sydenham, had died at the age of 89, bringing to an end a remarkable era in the history of Bournemouth. As will be recalled, Mr Sydenham had been closely involved in the very first steamer services from Bournemouth back in the 1860s and had been Cosens' manager at the growing resort since they first based a steamer there in 1881. Operating from his 'Marine Library & Bazaar' close to the pier entrance, Sydenham had built up a unique understanding of the town and its requirements and must take the major share of the credit for the growth and success of the company's operations

there. For several years he had been too unwell to come to the pier or take an active part in Cosens' affairs but his wisdom and advice had been valued up until the last. He was succeeded as Bournemouth Manager by his nephew, Mr Reginald 'Rex' Sydenham, who had worked beside his uncle for many years and was in a unique position to ensure the continuity of Cosens' operation in the town. Rex Sydenham was appointed for an initial period of ten years, and was paid 5 per cent of the gross earnings on the Bournemouth and Swanage stations, plus a £50 office allowance.

The second person prevented from enjoying the company's good fortune was Mr S.J. Fowler, Cosens' Managing Director. Suffering from a serious heart condition, he had very nearly died in the early spring and had been forced to take extended sick leave. After a period of convalescence in Hampshire and Devon, he had returned to Weymouth in the hope of resuming his duties but declined again to such an extent that he was forced to resign from his post on 16th November. Having been appointed Company Clerk in 1863, Secretary in 1874 and Manager from 1883, Fowler had been involved in the company's development since the early days of Capt Cosens

Mr David Sydenham in his later years.
BRIAN JACKSON COLLECTION

Although it was never a regular calling-place, Cosens did very occasionally land passengers by invitation at Church Ope Cove, on the east side of Portland. During 1911 and again during 1912, fund-raising fetes were held at Pennsylvania Castle on the cliffs above the cove and the steamers provided the most convenient means of access from Weymouth. Here, PREMIER *is seen preparing to embark a crowd for the return journey on 26th July 1911.*
AUTHOR'S COLLECTION/SEWARD

and Dr Drew, and his knowledge and guiding hand were sorely missed. He was voted a £200 annual pension and replaced by Mark Frowde as Joint Manager and Secretary, Frederick Jones as Joint Manager and Marine Superintendent, and Mr C.H. 'Charlie' Kaile as Cashier and Assistant Secretary.

Sadly, Mr Fowler did not enjoy his retirement for long, passing away on 2nd February 1912. The length and detail of the obituaries in the local press are a testament to his importance in many different aspects of local life. He was a much-respected magistrate, had served on the Town Council and many of its committees for eighteen years, was Chairman of the South Dorset Liberal Association and was well-known for his philanthropic work. Closely associated with the Weymouth Lifeboat, he was also an avid supporter of the local hospital, and a pillar of various sailors' and fishermens' charities, together with the local Sailors' Reading Room and the Seamans' Bethel on Custom House Quay. Most of all, however, he was remembered as a pious nonconformist Christian, who devoted thirty-seven years of his life to the Bank Buildings Baptist Church in Weymouth. He served as deacon and church secretary but was perhaps best remembered for his work to establish a mission chapel in the village of Putton where, for over twenty-five years, he superintended a flourishing Sunday School. He was sadly missed by the town and company alike.

The winter of 1911-12 saw Cosens' engineering works busy on the repair of two War Department vessels, *Russell* and *Sir Frederick Walker*, along with the Portland coal hulk *Haytian* and the tug *Verne*. In addition, a contract was obtained to build a series of large gunnery targets for the Admiralty. Known as Fisher Long Range or Battle Targets, these consisted of stout timber pontoons, surmounted by five tall poles, between which a high-visibility mesh was stretched. Towed out to sea by a tug, the targets would then be shot at by the warships of the Fleet. Cosens presumably prayed for accurate gunnery, for the more targets which were destroyed, the more

Mr. S.J. Fowler, Cosens' Managing Director 1883-1911, photographed towards the end of his life.
BRIAN JACKSON COLLECTION

One of the first long-range gunnery targets constructed by Cosens is seen on their No. 2 Slipway at Weymouth.
AUTHOR'S COLLECTION

work would come their way! In addition to the normal work on the steamers, twelve new plates were also fitted to *Premier*'s hull and a new boiler ordered for *Victoria*. A quote of £737 from Samuel Hodge & Sons of London was accepted but several serious delays occurred and the boiler was not finally fitted until January 1913.

The salvage tugs were kept reasonably busy through the winter months, although keen competition from Collins & Co's Portland tugs *Verne* and *Petrel* meant that many salvage awards now had to be shared, or could be lost altogether. Back in January 1911, great frustration had been experienced when *Albert Victor*, *Empress* and *Premier* had rushed to the aid of the Hamburg-Amerika liner *Pisa*, which was ashore near Langton Herring, only to discover that contract had already been given to Collins, who were the ship's local agents. On 13th March 1911, Cosens had again been first on the scene when the steamer *Jason* had gone aground on the Sheep Rock near Portland Bill but *Verne*, *Petrel* and the Dutch tug *Poolzee* were engaged to tow her off and Cosens had to be content with a small slice of the salvage award. Companies whose ships regularly called to take in bunkers from Collins' Portland coal hulks often appointed Collins as their agents as well and thus preferred to call on them first if a ship got into difficulties.

On 10th December 1911, a severe easterly gale swept the Dorset coast, causing serious damage ashore and afloat. The tugs were kept busy attending to various ships and *Albert Victor* damaged her stem. On the morning of 12th December, the Austrian steamer *Gros Tisza Itsvan* and the Norwegian *Condor* collided in the northern entrance to Portland Harbour and were both severely damaged. *Queen* got a hawser on board the former but it parted at the vital moment and, once again, Collins' tugs slipped in to tow her into shallow water and claim the larger part of the salvage fee. *Queen* was awarded £300 for her part in the rescue, on top of which Cosens received some income from services to the *Condor*, together with diving and repair work on both ships. *Queen* and *Helper* were also awarded £350 for services to the *Albert Clements* and £400 for the rescue of the *Pondo*, both of which jobs were shared with Collins' tugs.

As if in respect for the wishes that S.J. Fowler had expressed privately to Edward Bicker back in 1908, Cosens and the Southampton Company finally held a conference in January 1912 to agree a number of co-operative measures for the season ahead. The opening and closing dates were agreed, together with an arrangement for only one steamer from each company to run on the Swanage service in early and late season. Furthermore, it was decided that instead of competing on identical timetables, the two companies would alternate their departure times between Bournemouth and Swanage and would ensure that they did not run long-distance excursions to the same places on the same days. In case of bad weather, decisions to cancel sailing would

be applied equally by both parties. Significantly, Cosens agreed to allow the Southampton Company to use their beach landing stage and moorings at Lulworth Cove for a payment of £25 per annum, upon the strict condition that visits could only take place on days when no Cosens' vessels were calling there. This raises the intriguing question of whether *Princess Helena* or *Stirling Castle* had their bows adapted to take the ground or whether, in view of the infrequency of their calls and the relatively sheltered nature of the Cove, it was felt sufficient either to make no alterations at all or simply to fit a sacrificial iron shoe to their keels.

Unrest in the coal industry led the managers to anticipate that a miners' strike might interrupt coal supplies during the season, so Cosens purchased 1,400 tons during February and stock-piled it at Hamworthy on a piece of land taken on a seven year lease expressly for the purpose. A decision was also made to charter *Lord Roberts* for a second season on similar terms to 1911.

QUEEN stands by the stranded JASON on 13th March 1911, with the tug POOLZEE in the background.
AUTHOR'S COLLECTION

EMPEROR OF INDIA at Victoria Pier, Cowes.
DORCHESTER MUSEUM

Predictably perhaps, the lead proved too heavy for the wicker coffin and a wooden box with a hinged end had to be substituted. It took ten men to lift this contraption into the glass-sided hearse which conveyed the body from Hickman's residence at Greenhill, past the large crowds gathered on Weymouth seafront, to the waiting *Empress*. Getting the heavy coffin on board the steamer *'was a work of time but eventually accomplished'*. With the mourners on board, *Empress*, escorted by *Lord Roberts*, *Queen* and *Albert Victor*, put to sea and headed for a spot just to the east of the Shambles Bank. Here she hove to for the burial at sea service to be read.

Unfortunately it was a rough and windy day, and *Empress* had rolled and pitched heavily throughout the voyage, causing many of those on board to succumb to seasickness. As the committal was being read, she was turned broadside on to the seas and

ABOVE: While the mourners on the quay doff their hats in respect, preparations are made to transfer Spence Hickman's flag-draped coffin on board EMPRESS, *prior to his burial at sea.*
AUTHOR'S COLLECTION
RIGHT: With the coffin on board, EMPRESS *puts to sea.*
B. JACKSON COLLECTION

On the morning of 13th March 1912, a particularly eccentric event in Weymouth's history took place when Mr Spence Hickman was buried at sea. Mr Hickman was a wealthy gentleman from Chipping Norton in Oxfordshire, who had retired to live in Weymouth after visiting the port in his steam yacht during 1894. He left instructions that, upon his death, his body was to be embalmed, wrapped in 9 cwts of lead and sewn up in canvas taken from one of the sails of his yacht. It was then to be placed in a wicker coffin, which would fill and sink when tipped into the sea.

The chartered LORD ROBERTS *steaming out of Weymouth. The flag at half-mast suggests that the photograph was taken on the occasion of Mr Spence Hickman's burial at sea, when the vessel was part of the convoy of ships escorting the coffin.*
AUTHOR'S COLLECTION/SEWARD

On an excursion from Bournemouth, MAJESTIC, having made a circuit of the anchored warships in Portland Harbour, heads for Weymouth to give her passengers time ashore.
AUTHOR'S COLLECTION/ SEAWARD

the flap on the wooden coffin raised. At this moment she gave a particularly heavy lurch to port. The lead-lapped body shot out of the box and plunged into the depths of the Channel, bringing to a premature close one of Weymouth's most memorable funerals of all time!

Due to the new agreement with the Southampton Company, the opening of the excursion season on Good Friday, 5th April, was a far more sensible and economical arrangement than hitherto. Cosens were represented at Bournemouth by *Majestic* on the longer trips and *Victoria* on the Swanage service,

A well-laden MAJESTIC arriving at Weymouth.
AUTHOR'S COLLECTION/ SEAWARD

and the opposition by *Bournemouth Queen* and *Stirling Castle*. The new Swanage timetable for the Cosens' steamers was as follows:

Friday 5th April, Tuesday 9th, Thursday 11th, Saturday 13th

Bournemouth to Swanage 11.00	3.00	4.30	6.15	
Boscombe to Swanage 10.30	2.30	–	6.25	
Swanage to Bournemouth 9.00	12.10*	3.45	5.30	

Saturday 6th April, Wednesday 10th, Friday 12th

Bournemouth to Swanage 10.30	12.20	2.30	4.15	6.00
Boscombe to Swanage 10.00	–	2.00	–	6.10
Swanage to Bournemouth 9.20	11.15	1.10*	3.15	5.10*

* proceeds to Boscombe

The Southampton Company took the alternate sailings each day and the two companies rotated each week. The result was that local residents enjoyed a greatly enhanced service and both companies sailed with fuller ships. On Easter Monday, the service was even more frequent, with steamers leaving each pier at between half and three-quarter of an hour intervals.

On Good Friday and Easter Monday, *Majestic* went to Weymouth and around the Fleet in Portland Harbour, on the Saturday to the Isle of Wight, Southsea and Portsmouth Harbour, and on the Tuesday around the Isle of Wight, calling at Ventnor, Shanklin, Southsea and Ryde. On Wednesday 10th April, a special trip was made to Yarmouth, Cowes

Capt Read uses his customary skill to take Queen in close to the stranded MYRTLEDENE, from which he successfully rescued the passengers and crew on 25th March 1912.
AUTHOR'S COLLECTION

and Southampton to view the departure of the new White Star liner *Titanic* on her maiden voyage and, on the following day, another unusual trip was offered to Portland Bill and Chesil Beach to view the wreck of the steamer *Myrtledene* in Mutton Cove, before enjoying an hour ashore at Weymouth. *Myrtledene* had gone ashore on 25th March but, despite the best efforts of the salvage tugs and the fact that Capt Read in *Queen* had managed to rescue her passengers and crew, refused to float again and quickly became a total loss.

Less than a week after the Easter festivities, the whole nation was stunned by the appalling news that *Titanic* had struck an iceberg and gone down with a heavy loss of life. The fact that the majority of her crew had come from the Southampton area cast a particularly heavy pall of tragedy over the south coast and, unsurprisingly, the public felt less inclined than usual to go afloat. As it became clear that *Titanic* had carried only sufficient lifeboats for 1,176 of her 3,295 compliment and that inadequate Board of Trade regulations had contributed directly to the heavy death-toll, difficult questions began to be asked about the adequacy of life saving equipment on board the rest of the UK's passenger fleet. When Lord Mersey's inquiry announced its findings on 30th July, it came as no surprise that one of the key recommendations was that all passenger ships should henceforth have sufficient lifeboat capacity for all on board. Cosens very wisely waited for a definitive ruling from the Board of Trade before

11 - CHERBOURG - L'Avant Port et la Montagne du Roule

Very occasionally, as captured on this French postcard view, MAJESTIC and EMPEROR OF INDIA would cross the Channel to Cherbourg on the same day.
BERNARD COX COLLECTION

undertaking this expensive work and meanwhile, collections were made on board the steamers to contribute to the fund set up for the families of those lost in the sinking.

As if to add to the gloom caused by the loss of *Titanic*, the fine early-season weather gave way to poorer conditions during July, and an almost unbroken two months of wind and rain during August and September. No less than ten consecutive westward coasting trips from Weymouth had to be cancelled due to the heavy surf on the beaches, and numerous cross-channel and long distance

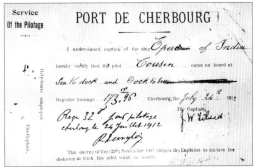

EMPEROR OF INDIA's Cherbourg pilotage certificate for 24th July 1912, signed by Capt Tilsed.
WEYMOUTH MUSEUM

The officers and deck crew of MAJESTIC, August 1912. Seated with three stripes is Capt Lewis St. Barbe Rawle. To his right is chief engineer Rowlands and to his left the mate, Mr Miles. In the middle row, right, is James Halford, who was purser of MAJESTIC and EMPEROR OF INDIA until 1925, when he became Cosens' Bournemouth agent. On the left of the same row is Mr Reckets, the ticket collector.
DAVID HAYSOM COLLECTION

Capt Rawle with MAJESTIC's 1912 catering staff. Seated in the left foreground is a youthful Ernest Cornick, who had recently joined the ship as an apprentice engineer.
DAVID HAYSOM COLLECTION

excursions westwards from Bournemouth were lost. Trips to the Solent faired little better and the steamers frequently put to sea with scarcely enough passengers to cover their running expenses. The numbers of passengers landing at Swanage Pier fell from 142,003 in 1911 to 128,039 and other routes were even more seriously affected. August was the wettest on record, with only two completely fine days and the managers searched their memories in vain for a more stormy, sunless, wintry summer. Passenger receipts for the year fell by £4,400 at Bournemouth and £1,507 at Weymouth and the annual dividend to ordinary shareholders was reduced to 4 per cent.

The miserable season drew to a close on 12th

October and *Lord Roberts* was once again laid up for the winter at Poole. Her owners let it be known that they were considering selling both her and her sister ship *Lord Nelson* and would be keen to offer Cosens first refusal. Enquiries were again received as to whether *Emperor of India* might be for sale and it was decided to give the matter serious consideration if £17,000 or more was offered. Clearly this was more than the buyer was willing to pay, for nothing more was heard of the matter.

On 4th November, the salvage tugs went to the assistance of a Russian barque *Kensington*, which had been in collision off Portland and was being towed towards Weymouth by the steamer *Lestris*. The tugs assisted with berthing and Cosens afterwards undertook repairs to the value of £200. An Army & Navy Co-operative Society motor boat which was trading to the warships in Portland Harbour was also rescued after suffering an engine failure. A £400 service was recorded to a steam ship named *Devonia* and, in late December, *Queen* brought in a French ketch named *Amis Reunis*.

Victoria's long-awaited new boiler was finally completed during November and despatched on board the cargo steamer *Gem* from London to Portland, where it was lifted on board in January 1913 using a dockyard crane. The delays in its completion may have been due to the unusual design of the boiler which, like the one it replaced, was rectangular and designed to fit the cross-section of the ship's hull. Corners were made of angle iron and internally the boiler stays were little more than a foot apart. In order to allow descaling of each of the 435 2 inch salt-encrusted boiler tubes at the

VICTORIA's unusual, rectangular, 1912 boiler was an almost exact copy of her original. Each of the four cast iron furnace fronts at the bottom of the photograph measured 2ft 6ins wide by 2ft 9ins high. Above them are the smokebox doors which, when opened, gave access to the boiler tubes. The boiler worked at a very low pressure of 30psi, and the steam and water gauges can be seen behind the top of the ladder. Two of the long slices used for raking the fires are stored overhead, together with a hanging acetylene lamp, which provided the only lighting in the stokehold.
WEYMOUTH LIBRARY

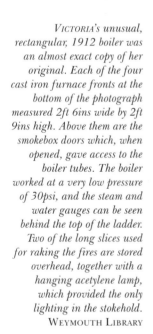
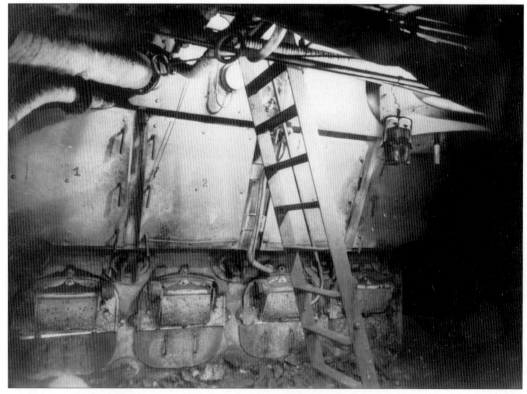

S.S. MONARCH

MONARCH *with her additional, post-*Titanic *lifeboats fitted forward of the bridge.*
H.A. ALLEN COLLECTION

end of every season, the boiler was fitted with five 12 inch by 10 inch manholes, through which workmen would crawl to carry out their filthy and claustrophobic work by the light of acetylene lamps. One Cosens apprentice, Ernest Cornick, is known to have lost a finger through getting it jammed inside the boiler during winter descaling.

The post-*Titanic* alterations demanded by the Board of Trade were also carried out during the winter months. Cork life jackets were provided for all passengers and the steamers were fitted with additional rafts, buoyant seats and, in the case of *Monarch, Emperor of India* and *Majestic*, extra lifeboats forward of the paddle boxes. *Monarch*'s dainty proportions made the positioning of the boats something of a challenge and two small side decks, supported by stanchions and projecting over the forward well-deck, had to be constructed to accommodate them.

During February, a French trawler named *Turenne* had gone ashore on Tor Rocks on the West side of Portland but had defied all attempts to refloat her. Salvage attempts were eventually abandoned

and the wreck, which was lying in a very exposed position and full of water, was sold to Mr F.J. Barnes, a well-known Portland stone merchant and haulage contractor. Barnes had intended breaking her up where she lay but, noting her ability to survive the worst that the weather could throw at her, began to wonder whether it might be possible to refloat her. Cosens were engaged on a 'no cure, no pay' basis and Capt Read was sent to supervise the attempt. A portable boiler and two large salvage pumps were placed on board and a diver set to work driving wooden wedges into each leaking seam he could locate. After two days of pumping the ship began to lift and, on the high tide of 17th May 1913, one of Cosens' tugs succeeded in pulling her off the rocks. The passage round the Bill was extremely hazardous, as one of the salvage pumps failed completely and the other became clogged with waste from the trawler's bilges. With the water rising fast, it was a race against time to clear the suction hose and continue pumping while *Turenne* was towed into Portland Harbour and grounded beside Castletown Jetty. Two days later, one of Mr Barnes'

On an official company card, EMPEROR OF INDIA *displays the additional boats which she carried from 1913 onwards.*
H.A. ALLEN COLLECTION

The stranded trawler TURENNE, which was salvaged by Cosens in May 1913. AUTHOR'S COLLECTION

traction engines succeeded in dragging the trawler up the beach where she was subsequently repaired. Both Barnes and Cosens made a handsome profit from the operation.

In view of the success of *Lord Roberts* on the Admiralty Contract work from Weymouth over the previous two seasons, it is a little surprising that Cosens decided not to purchase her in the spring of 1913. Perhaps the asking price was too great or she was in poor condition but, whatever the case, her owners declined to charter her for a further year and withdrew her from Poole to Great Yarmouth during May. Knowing that the Fleet would be at Portland from July onwards and that an additional steamer was essential to meet the terms of the contract, Cosens immediately attempted to charter an alternative ship. As nothing suitable was available, they then turned their attention to the shipbrokers' lists and located *Lune*, which was lying for sale at Fleetwood. This 253 ton steel paddle steamer, 129 feet by 24 feet 1 inch by 9 feet 5 inches, had been built in 1892 by T.B. Seath of Rutherglen for the Lancashire & Yorkshire and London & North Western railway companies' joint service between Fleetwood, Heysham and Blackpool. Her size, strong construction, relatively large beam in comparison to her length and spacious but basic accommodation all made her ideally suited to liberty boat work and Cosens purchased her immediately for £1,900. She was steamed from Fleetwood to Southampton for docking and then to Weymouth where, re-named *Melcombe Regis*, she entered service in early July. She was officially registered at the port on 17th July 1913. Incidentally, 1913 also saw Cosens introduce a new 'Carrier & Storage Department' in connection with the Fleet Contract.

The co-operative running agreement with the Southampton Company was repeated in 1913, although relationships were evidently somewhat strained. A dispute broke out in June when Cosens accused their rivals of breaching the agreement by running additional intermediate boats on the Swanage service. When Swanage Urban District Council complained about steamers dumping ashes in the bay, Cosens were also quick to insist that their captains had been forbidden from doing so and that *'the blame may be found due to some other steamers.'* In an attempt to gain a more intimate knowledge of their rival's affairs, Cosens instructed their stockbroker to purchase a block of Southampton Company shares in the name of Mr Frowde, the company secretary. However, when his identity was realised, the Southampton Company refused to accept him as a shareholder.

In March 1913, Capt Shippick resigned from the company in order to run his own small steamer on a service between Bournemouth, Boscombe and Studland Bay, and cruises in Poole Harbour. The vessel concerned was a tiny, clinker-built wooden paddle steamer named *Advance*, which measured only 72 feet long and had been purchased from Dundee owners. Shippick had personally skippered her down the North Sea during November 1912, facing several gales *en route* and spending many hours either hove to or sheltering in Ramsgate Harbour. As there was no pier at Studland Bay, he purchased a floating pontoon and a number of wheeled, sectional landing stages which he positioned on the beach just to the north of Redend Point. The pontoon, which was attached by an endless rope to a mooring laid well off-shore, would be winched out into deeper water where the little steamer, which Shippick had re-named *Studland Belle*, would come carefully alongside and disembark

Melcombe Regis arriving at Weymouth, with an array of battleships and cruisers anchored in the Bay.

A Bournemouth sailing bill for 1913.
AUTHOR'S COLLECTION

NO. 22

Pleasure Sailings by COSENS & Co.'s FLEET OF BUFF FUNNEL STEAMERS

MAJESTIC, EMPEROR OF INDIA, MONARCH,

The ONLY STEAMERS with CROSS CHANNEL CERTIFICATES running DAILY from Bournemouth (Second to none on the South Coast)

Also the Saloon Steamers VICTORIA, EMPRESS, &c., &c.

STARTING FROM THE LEFT-HAND SIDE OF BOURNEMOUTH PIER, will (weather and circumstances permitting) carry out Excursions as below:

The Company will not be responsible for any accidents, or injury to, or loss of life, or loss or damage to property of the passenger, of whatever nature, and whether caused by perils of the sea, accidents incidental to navigation or defects latent or otherwise in Hull tackle machinery or staging piers gangways or other property of the Company, or by any act neglect, or default of the Company, Pilots, Master, Engineers, Officers or Mariner or any other person in the Company's employ, or otherwise howsoever. The Return trips advertised are based upon the supposition that the Steamer performs the day trip contemplated, and that the Company will not be responsible to any passengers for any loss or expense in case they are unable to complete such return trip

NOTICE.—Any passenger booking from Bournemouth to Southampton or Portsmouth desirous of returning by rail, may do so (on day of issue only) upon surrender of the return half of the 3/6 Day Trip boat ticket and payment at the Booking Office of 1/- extra third class (including Fratton Station).

WEYMOUTH.—Circular tickets returnable by Rail or Steamer are issued from Weymouth, Dorchester, Wool or Wareham, to Bournemouth or Swanage, Fare 4/3 and 4/-. Rail tickets not available by the 12.55 p.m. train from Weymouth.

VENTNOR, SHANKLIN & SANDOWN.—Passengers landing at Ventnor, Shanklin & Sandown Piers and desiring to return by rail to Ryde, and there join the boat for Bournemouth, &c., can obtain, on production of Steamer ticket at Railway Booking Office, tickets to Ryde Pier Head. Fares: From Ventnor 2/3 first class, 1/6 second, Shanklin & Sandown 1/9 first class, 1/2 second

DAILY SERVICE between BOURNEMOUTH, BOSCOMBE & SWANAGE, week ending August 23

BY THE BUFF FUNNEL STEAMERS MAJESTIC, EMPEROR OF INDIA, MONARCH, EMPRESS and MELCOMBE REGIS.

STARTING FROM THE LEFT-HAND SIDE OF BOURNEMOUTH PIER. FIRST TRIP BOURNEMOUTH TO SWANAGE DIRECT at 10 a.m. (Boscombe 9.35 a.m.)

Bournemouth to Swanage at **10, *10.25, 11.45, 2.30, 3. 4, 5.30, 6.15 & 8** For additional & later trips see below.
Swanage to Bournemouth direct **9.20, 10.50, 12, 1.5, 3.15, 5.30, & 715** For additional & later trips see below
Boscombe to Swanage at **9.35, 10.40. 12, 2.25, 4.15 & 6.25** * Sat. Aug. 16, & for week commencing Aug. 25, 10.35 a.m.

The Steamers leaving Swanage 9.20, 10.50, 12.0, 3.15 & 5.30 proceed to Boscombe.

Note Saturday, August 16th, Wednesday & Thursday, August 20th & 21st, Additional Trip BOURNEMOUTH to SWANAGE at 2 o'clock

Return Fare 1/- any part of Steamer. Single 9d. Children under twelve years of age 6d. Deck Chairs Free. Bicycles and Dogs 6d. each Single Journey.

Early Trips (weather permitting) Swanage to Bournemouth—Saturday, Aug 16th 8.50, Tuesday 8.10, Saturday 8.50 a.m.

LATE TRIPS (weather permitting) Swanage to Bournemouth—DAILY at 7.15, also Mon. 5.40 & 9.30, Tues. 4.40, Wed. 4.30 & 8, Thurs. 5.45 & 9.15, Fri. 4.30, Sat. 4.30 & 5.45 p.m. Bournemouth to Swanage—DAILY at 8, also Mon. 10, Tues. 9.30 Wed. 10, Thurs. 10, Sat. 9.20 p.m.

Day / Steamer	Sailings
SATURDAY, August 16 Majestic	**Over 6 hours at SOUTHSEA, for Portsmouth Dockyard, Portchester Castle, &c.** Leaving Swanage **8.50**, Boscombe **9.35** (by Empress), Bournemouth **10**, returning from Southsea (Clar. Pier) 6.30 Rtn. Fare **3/6** including Southsea Pier Tolls. From Swanage 6d. extra
Majestic	PICTURESQUE MORNING CRUISE UP THE SOLENT to **Southsea.** Probably viewing the Aeroplane Flight from Netley this day. Leaving Swanage **8.50**, Boscombe **9.35** (by Empress), Bournemouth **10**, back about 2.30 Fare **2/-** From Swanage 6d. extra. Swanage passengers return by the 4.0 Steamer from Bournemouth
Majestic	**Grand Afternoon Trip to RYDE** (nearly 2 hours ashore), or **SOUTHSEA, 1 hour ashore.** Leaving Swanage **1.5** (by Empress), Bournemouth **3**, Boscombe **3.10**, returning from Southsea (Clarence Pier) at 6.30, Ryde 6.50 Return Fare **2/-** including Ryde and Southsea Pier Tolls. From Swanage 6d. extra
Emperor of India	**To SWANAGE & WEYMOUTH (1½ or 3 hours ashore), with a Cruise Round the Imposing Fleet of Warships in Portland Roads** & by kind permission of Commanding Officer, **1 hour on board one of Britain's latest Dreadnought Battleships.** Leaving Boscombe **10.20**, Bournemouth **10.50**, Swanage **11.25**. Leaving Weymouth for the Ship 2.30 Returning from Weymouth at 4, to Swanage, Bournemouth & Boscombe. Return Fare to Weymouth only **3/-** From Swanage **2/6** To Weymouth and Ship **3/6** From Swanage **3/-**
Melcombe Regis	SPECIAL TRIP to **Swanage** and Up the PICTURESQUE HARBOUR of POOLE. Leaving Bournemouth at **2**, return from Poole Quay at 3.40, Swanage 4.40, back at 5.40. Fare to Swanage **1/-**, to Poole **1/6** From Swanage **1/-**
Emperor of India	**Grand Evening trip to TOTLAND BAY (Isle of Wight)** About 1 hour ashore. Leaving Bournemouth **6.30**, Boscombe **6.40** returning from Totland Bay at 8.30. Rtn Fare **1/-** Accompanied by the BOSCOMBE TEMPERANCE PRIZE BAND of over 20 performers.
	Monarch. To SWANAGE. Leaving Bournemouth 10.35, 2.30, 4, 6.15 & 8. Boscombe 10.45, 4.15 & 6.25. Return times as above up to 7.15 also 4.30
Empress	AFTERNOON TRIP to SWANAGE, AND UP THE PICTURESQUE HARBOUR OF POOLE. Leaving Boscombe at **2.25**. Bournemouth **3**, Swanage **3.50**, arriving back B'mouth and Boscombe 5.30, Swanage 6.30. Return Fare to Swanage **1/-**, Up Poole Harbour **1/6**. From Swanage **1/-**
For SWANAGE DAILY SERVICE see above	Single Trips to WEYMOUTH Leaving Bournemouth 6.15 & 8. Swanage 7.15 & 8.45 Fare 2/- From Swanage 1/6
	SINGLE TRIP to POOLE via SWANAGE by "Empress," Leaving Bournemouth 5.30, Boscombe 5.40 Fare 6d. Landing at Poole Quay about 7.30
MONDAY, August 18 Emperor of India	**3½ hours at VENTNOR, 3 hours at SHANKLIN,** or nearly **1 hour at SOUTHSEA.** Leaving Swanage at **9.20**, (by Majestic), Bournemouth **10.15**, Boscombe **10.25**, Ventnor 12.30, Shanklin 12.50, returning from Southsea (Clarence Pier) at 3, Shanklin 4, Ventnor 4.25, back about 6.15 Return Fare **3/6** including Ventnor, Shanklin and Southsea Pier Tolls. From Swanage 6d. extra.
Majestic	**To SWANAGE & WEYMOUTH (1½ or 3 hours ashore) with a Cruise Round the Imposing Fleet of Warships in Portland Roads,** and by kind permission of Commanding Officer, **1 hour on board one of Britain's latest Dreadnought Battleships.** Leaving Bournemouth **10.25**, Boscombe **10.40**, Swanage **11.20**. Leaving Weymouth for the Ship 2.30. Returning from Weymouth at 4.0, to Swanage, Bournemouth & Boscombe. Return Fare to Weymouth **3/-** From Swanage **2/6** To Weymouth & Ship **3/6** From Swanage **3/-**
Monarch	To SWANAGE. Leaving Bournemouth 10.25 (by Majestic), 2.30, 4, 6.15 & 8. Boscombe 10.40, 4.15 & 6 25 Return times as above up to 7.15, also 5.40 & 9.30
Empress	AFTERNOON TRIP to SWANAGE, & UP THE PICTURESQUE HARBOUR OF POOLE. Leaving Boscombe **2.25**, Bournemouth **3**, Swanage **3.50**, arriving back to B'mouth & Boscombe 5.30, Swanage 6.30. Return Fare to Swanage 1/- Poole Harbour 1/6. From Swanage 1/-
	SINGLE TRIP to POOLE via SWANAGE by "Empress." Leaving Bournemouth 5.30 Boscombe 5.40. Fare 6d. Landing at Poole Quay about 7.30
Majestic	MOONLIGHT TRIP to **Swanage** (Half-hour ashore). Leaving Bournemouth **8**, Boscombe 8.10, returning from Swanage at 9 30. Return Fare **1/-** ACCOMPANIED BY THE BOSCOMBE TEMPERANCE PRIZE BAND OF OVER 20 PERFORMERS.
For SWANAGE DAILY SERVICE see above	SINGLE TRIP to WEYMOUTH by Monarch. Leaving Bournemouth 6.15, Boscombe 6.25, Swanage 7.15 Fare 2/- From Swanage 1/6
TUESDAY, Aug. 19 Majestic	**To CHERBOURG** THE FRENCH PORT & ARSENAL. Allowing over **2** hours ashore. Leaving Swanage **8.10**, Boscombe **8.50** (by Empress), Bournemouth **9.10** returning from Cherbourg at 4.15 p.m. (English time) to Bournemouth, thence Swanage Return Fare **6/6** including French Landing Tax. Season and Fortnightly Ticket Holders **2/-** each
Emperor of India (Giving passengers time at Cowes to visit Osborne House. Public admission to State Apartments, Museum, &c.)	**To YARMOUTH, COWES (for Osborne House), RYDE and SOUTHSEA.** Leaving Swanage **9.20** (by Monarch), Bournemouth **10.30**, Boscombe **10.40**, Yarmouth **11.40**, returning from Southsea (Clarence Pier) at 3.15, Ryde 3.35, Cowes 4, Yarmouth 4.45, back about 6. Return Fare to Yarmouth **2/-**, To Cowes **3/-** To Ryde or Southsea **3/6** including Ryde & Southsea Pier Tolls. From Swanage 6d. extra. Yarmouth to Cowes 1/- To Ryde or Southsea 2/-
Empress	**To SWANAGE & LULWORTH COVE,** for DURDLE DOOR, &c. About **2** hours ashore. Landing by Stage Free at Lulworth and not by open boats. Leaving Bournemouth at **10.25**, Boscombe **10.40**, Swanage **11.40**, returning from Lulworth 3, Swanage 12, 1.5, 3.15, 4.40, 5.30 or 7.15 Return Fare to Swanage **1/-** To Lulworth **2/6** From Swanage **2/-**
Monarch	TO SWANAGE. Leaving Bournemouth 10, 11.45, 2.30, 4, 6.15 & 9 Boscombe 9.35, 12, 4.15 & 6.25 Return times as above up to 7.15, also at 4.40 Fare 1/-
Melcombe Regis	AFTERNOON TRIP TO **SWANAGE**, & UP THE PICTURESQUE HARBOUR OF POOLE Leaving Boscombe at **2.25**, Bournemouth **3**, Swanage **3.50**, arriving back at B'mouth & Boscombe 5.30, Swanage 6.30. Return Fare to Swanage 1/-, Poole Harbour 1/6, From Swanage 1/-
For SWANAGE DAILY SERVICE see above	SINGLE TRIP to POOLE via SWANAGE by "Empress," Leaving Bournemouth 5.30, Boscombe 5.40. Fare 6d. Landing at Poole Quay about 7.30
	SINGLE TRIP to WEYMOUTH by "Melcombe Regis." Leaving Bournemouth 6.10, Swanage 7.0. Fare **2/-** From Swanage **1/6**
WEDNESDAY, August 20	WEYMOUTH REGATTA. WEYMOUTH EN FETE.
Majestic	**Over 6 hours at WEYMOUTH (The Naples of England), for Portland, Upwey, &c.** Leaving Boscombe **9.35**, Bournemouth **10**, Swanage **10.35**, returning from Weymouth at 6.30 Return Fare **3/-** From Swanage **2/6**
Majestic	MORNING CRUISE to **WEYMOUTH.** Magnificent Coast Scenery. Leaving Boscombe **9.35**, Bournemouth **10**, Swanage **10.35**, back to Bournemouth and Boscombe at 3, Swanage 3.50. Fare **2/-** From Swanage **1/6**
Majestic	**Grand Afternoon Cruise Round the FLEET OF WARSHIPS in Portland Roads,** & about 1 hour ashore at **WEYMOUTH** Leaving Bournemouth **3**, Boscombe **3.10**, Swanage **3.50**, returning from Weymouth at 6.30. Return Fare **2/-** From Swanage **1/6**
Emperor of India	**ROUND THE ISLE OF WIGHT, VENTNOR, SHANKLIN, SOUTHSEA and RYDE** Leaving Swanage **9.20** (by Monarch), Bournemouth **10.30**, Boscombe **10.40**, calling at Ventnor 12.35, Shanklin 1.0, returning from Southsea (Clarence Pier) at 3.30, Ryde 4 (on arrival of train leaving Ventnor 3.15, Shanklin 3.27, conveying passengers landing at Ventnor or Shanklin, see Railway arrangements) back about 6.15. Return Fare **3/6** including Ventnor, Shanklin, Southsea & Ryde Pier Tolls. From Swanage 6d. extra
Monarch	To SWANAGE Leave Bournemouth 10.25, 2.30, 4, 6.15 & 8 Boscombe 10.40, 4.15 & 6.25. Return times as above up to 7.15, also 4.30 & 8 Return Fare 1/-
Empress	**To LULWORTH** (1½ hour ashore), calling at **SWANAGE.** Landing by stage Free at Lulworth & not by open boats. Leaving Boscombe **2.25**, Bournemouth **3**, Swanage **3.45**, returning from Lulworth 6.40, Swanage 5.30, 7.15 or 8. Rtn Fare **2/-** From Swanage 1/6
Melcombe Regis	AFTERNOON TRIP to SWANAGE, & UP THE PICTURESQUE HARBOUR of POOLE. Leaving Bournemouth **2**, Swanage **2.45**, arriving back at Swanage 4.30, B'mouth & Boscombe 5.30, or return from Swanage 3.15, 4.30, 5.30 or 7.15, Fare to Swanage **1/-** Poole Harbour **1/6** From Swanage **1/-**
	ADDITIONAL TRIP to SWANAGE by s.s. Melcombe Regis, at **2**, returning at 3.15, 4.30, 5.30, 7.15 or 8 Return Fare **1/-**
	Single Trip to WEYMOUTH by Majestic. Leaving Swanage 8, Bournemouth 8.40, Boscombe 8.50. Fare **2/-**
For SWANAGE DAILY SERVICE see above.	EVENING TRIP to **Swanage** by Emp. of India Leaving Bournemouth **6.15**, Boscombe **6.25**, returning from Swanage 7.15 or 8. Return Fare **1/-**
	SINGLE TRIPS to POOLE via Swanage by "Emperor of India" & "Melcombe Regis." Leaving Bournemouth 5.30 & 8, Boscombe 5.40. Fare 6d.
THURSDAY, August 21 Emperor of India	**To SWANAGE & WEYMOUTH (1½ or 3 hours ashore), with a Cruise Round the Imposing Fleet of Warships in Portland Roads,** and by kind permission of Commanding Officer, **one hour on board one of Britian's latest Dreadnought Battleships** Leaving Bournemouth **10.25**, Boscombe **10.40**, Swanage **11.25**. Leaving Weymouth for the Ship 2.30. Returning from Weymouth at 4, to Swanage, Bournemouth & Boscombe. Return Fare to Weymouth **3/-** From Swanage **2/6**. To Weymouth & Ship **3/6** From Swanage **3/-**
Majestic	**Grand Afternoon Cruise Round the ISLE of WIGHT,** probably **viewing the departure** of Germany's Huge Liner IMPERATOR (the largest Steamer in the World, 50,000 tons), for Cherbourg and New York, via the Solent and Spithead, also giving nearly **1** hour ashore at **SOUTHSEA, or a Cruise Through Portsmouth Harbour to view H.M.S. VICTORY, &c.,** calling at YARMOUTH on the return. Leaving Bournemouth at **12.10**, returning from Southsea (Clarence Pier) at 4.10, Yarmouth 5.10. 85 miles Picturesque Scenery. Return Fare **2/6** Trip from SWANAGE to BOURNEMOUTH at **1/-** Return, at **10.50** a.m., to connect with s.s. MAJESTIC
SWANAGE REGATTA THIS DAY. NOTE INCREASED SERVICE.	
Monarch	MORNING CRUISE to SWANAGE, & UP THE PICTURESQUE HARBOUR OF POOLE. Leaving Boscombe **10.20**, Bournemouth **10.50**, Swanage **11.30**, back to Bournemouth and Boscombe at 1, Swanage 2.30. Return Fare to Swanage **1/-** Up Poole Harbour **1/6** From Swanage **1/-**
	ADDITIONAL TRIPS to SWANAGE by s.s. MELCOMBE REGIS, at **2 & 3.40**, returning at 2.45, 3.15, 4.30, 5.30, 5.45, 7.15 or 9.15 Return Fare **1/-**
Monarch	TO SWANAGE. Leaving Bournemouth 10.25 (by Emperor of India), 10.50, 2.30, 4, 6.15 & 8. Boscombe 10.20, 10.40 (by Emperor of India), 4.15 & 6.25 Return times as above up to 7.15, also at 4.30, 5.45 & 9.15 Return Fare **1/-**
Majestic	AFTERNOON TRIP YARMOUTH to BOURNEMOUTH. Over **1** hour ashore. Leaving Yarmouth **5.10**, returning at 7.30 by Emp. of India. Rtn Fare **1/-**
Emperor of India	**Evening Cruise to YARMOUTH (Isle of Wight)** Leaving Bournemouth at **7.30**, Boscombe **7.40**, back at 10 Return Fare **1/-** ACCOMPANIED BY THE BOSCOMBE TEMPERANCE PRIZE BAND of over 20 performers.
MONARCH, MAJESTIC, MELCOMBE REGIS	**EVENING TRIPS to SWANAGE, for Fireworks Display and Illumination of Bay.** Leaving Bournemouth at **5.30, 6.15, 6.30, 6.45** and **8**. Returning from Swanage at 9.15. Return Fare **1/-**
For SWANAGE DAILY SERVICE see above	SINGLE TRIPS to WEYMOUTH. Leaving Bournemouth 6.30, Swanage 7.10 and 7.45. Fare **2/-** From Swanage **1/6**
	SINGLE TRIP to POOLE via Swanage by "Empress," Leaving Bournemouth 5.30 Fare 6d. Landing Poole Quay about 7.30.
FRIDAY, Aug 22 Emp of India (Giving passengers time at Cowes to visit Osborne House, Public admission to State Apartments, Museum, &c.)	**To TOTLAND, COWES (for Osborne House), and SOUTHAMPTON,** for **Docks, Atlantic Liners, &c.** Leaving Swanage **9.20** (by Empress) Bournemouth **10.15** Boscombe **10.25**, Totland **11.30**, returning from Southampton at 3, Cowes 3.45, Totland 4.40, back at 6.15 Return Fare to Totland **2/-**, to Cowes **3/-**, to Southampton **3/6**. From Swanage 6d. extra. Totland to Cowes **1/-** To Southampton **2/-**
Empress	**To SWANAGE & LULWORTH COVE, for Durdle Door, &c.** 2 HOURS ON SHORE. LANDING BY STAGE FREE at LULWORTH & NOT BY OPEN BOATS. Leaving Bournemouth **10.25**, Boscombe **10.40**. Swanage **11.40**, returning from Lulworth 3.0, Swanage 12, 1.5, 3.15, 4.30, 5.30 or 7.15 Rtn. Fare to Swanage **1/-** To Lulworth **2/6** From Swanage **2/-**
	Monarch. To SWANAGE. Leaving Bournemouth 10, 11.45, 3, 6.15 & 8. Boscombe 9.35, 12, 2.25 & 6.25. Return times as above up to 7.15, also at 4.30
Monarch	AFTERNOON TRIP to SWANAGE, AND UP THE PICTURESQUE HARBOUR OF POOLE. Leaving Boscombe at **2.25** p.m., Bournemouth **3**, Swanage **3.50**, arriving back to Swanage 5.30, B'mouth & Boscombe 6.15. Return Fare to Swanage **1/-**, Up Poole Harbour **1/6**. From Swanage **1/-**
For SWANAGE DAILY SERVICE see above	SINGLE TRIP to WEYMOUTH by VICTORIA. Leaving Bournemouth 4, Boscombe 4.15, Swanage 5.0. Fare **2/-** From Swanage **1/6**
	SINGLE TRIP to POOLE via SWANAGE by "Empress." Leaving Bournemouth 5.30, Boscombe 5.40. Fare 6d. Landing at Poole Quay about 7.30
Saturday, August 23 Majestic	**Over 6 hours at VENTNOR (for Famous Undercliff) or SHANKLIN, for the Celebrated Chine, Sandown, &c.** Leaving Swanage at **8.50** (by Monarch), Boscombe **9.35** (by Empress), Bournemouth **10**, returning from Shanklin at 6.30, Ventnor 6.50 Return Fare **3/6** including Ventnor and Shanklin Pier Tolls. From Swanage 6d. extra.
Majestic	Morning Cruise to VENTNOR & SHANKLIN. Leaving Swanage **8.50** (by Monarch), Boscombe 9.35 (by Empress), B'mouth **10**, back about 3. Fare 2/- (From Swanage 6d. extra
Majestic	**Afternoon Trip Round the ISLE OF WIGHT** calling at **VENTNOR & SHANKLIN.** Leaving Swanage **1.5** (by Empress), Bournemouth **3.0**, Boscombe **3.10**, returning from Shanklin 6.30, Ventnor 6.50 85 miles Picturesque Scenery Fare **2/6** From Swanage **3/-**
Majestic	Ventnor & Shanklin to BOURNEMOUTH & Round the Isle of Wight. Leave Ventnor 12.5, Shanklin 12.25. Fare **2/6** including Ventnor & S'klin Pier tolls
Emperor of India	**To SWANAGE & WEYMOUTH (1½ or 3 hours ashore), with a Cruise Round the Imposing FLEET of WARSHIPS in Portland Roads** and by kind permission of Commanding Officer, 1 HOUR ON BOARD ONE OF BRITAIN'S LATEST DREADNOUGHT BATTLESHIPS. Leaving Boscombe **10.20** Bournemouth **10.50**, Swanage **11.25**. Leaving Weymouth for the Ship 2.30. Return from Weymouth 4, to Swanage, B'mth & Boscombe Return Fare to Weymouth 3/-. From Swanage 2/6 Weymouth & Ship 3/6 From Swanage 3/-
Emperor of India	**Evening Trip to ALUM BAY (ISLE OF WIGHT).** About **1** hour ashore. Leaving Bournemouth **6.35**, Boscombe **6.45**, returning from Alum Bay 8.45 Return Fare **1/-** ACCOMPANIED BY THE POOLE TOWN BAND of over 20 Performers.
Monarch	TO SWANAGE. Leaving Bournemouth 10.25, 2.30, 4, 6.15 & 8 Boscombe 10.40, 4.15 & 6.25. Return times as above up to 7.15, also at 4.30 & 5.45 Fare 1/-
Empress	AFTERNOON TRIP to SWANAGE, DURLSTON HEAD, TILLY WHIM CAVES, &c. Leaving Boscombe **2.25**, Bournemouth **3**, Swanage **3.50**, arriving back to Swanage **4.45**, Bournemouth and Boscombe 5.30. Return Fare to Swanage **1/-** To Durlston Head **1/6** From Swanage **1/-**
For SWANAGE DAILY SERVICE see above	SINGLE TRIP to POOLE via SWANAGE by Empress. Leaving Bournemouth 5.30, Boscombe 5.40. Fare 6d. Landing at Poole Quay about 7.30.

Monday, Aug. 25. s.s. Majestic. To BRIGHTON. For times of Sailings, &c., see later Bills.

The CATERING DEPARTMENT undertaken by the Owners is fully up to date combined with moderate charges. Deck Chairs (except Swanage Traffic) 1d. each. Bicycles and Dogs 1/- each.

PART SEASON TICKETS—available from July 31, to end of Season—First ticket **25/-**; Second & subsequent ticket in same family **21/-** each. Tickets for use only on Wednesdays and Saturdays (whole day & afternoon excursions) **15/-**, & from Swanage (Thursdays only) 10/6 each. FORTNIGHTLY TICKETS allowing 12 Excursions within 14 days of date of issue **15/-**

BOOKS OF COUPON TICKETS (available from Bournemouth, Boscombe & Swanage only), containing 20 6d. tickets, are now sold at 7/6 per book; or containing 20 1/- tickets at 15/-. These Coupon tickets must be produced to the Purser on board the Steamer & exchanged for an Ordinary ticket.

DAY TICKETS, SEASON TICKETS, BOOKS OF COUPONS & all information can be obtained from **SYDENHAM'S LIBRARY, opposite Bournemouth Pier.** (Tel. Bournemouth 130); **J. E. BEALE, Ltd. Central Office & Agency** (Tel. Bournemouth ONE); Messrs. M. C. FROWDE & F. M. JONES, Joint Managers, Cosens & Co. Limited, Custom House Quay, Weymouth (Tel. Weymouth **9 & 123**); Mr. A. J. WARD, Steam Packet Office, Swanage (Tel. Swanage **9**); Mr. HELLIER, Estate Agent, Boscombe (Tel. Bournemouth **945**).

Office—SYDENHAM'S LIBRARY, Opposite Bournemouth Pier.
August 15th, 1913.

R F. SYDENHAM, Local Manager,
Telephone—Bournemouth **130.**

Sydenham, Printer, Pier Approach & Oxford Road, Bournemouth.

Starting from the Left-hand side of Bournemouth Pier.

her passengers. Once the steamer had departed again, the pontoon with its human load would be hauled carefully towards the beach where the passengers would teeter ashore by way of the wheeled gangways. Although *Studland Belle* was to be seen regularly at Bournemouth and Boscombe, she did not call often at Swanage and her unusual service posed little direct threat to Cosens. A surviving sailing bill dated Sunday 3rd August 1913, for a trip from Poole to Swanage, suggests that Shippick did not share Cosens' scruples about Sabbath-breaking although, with Swanage Pier closed to Sunday traffic, it remains unclear where or whether his passengers were actually put ashore. Sadly, *Studland Belle* had a very short life on the Dorset coast as she caught fire and was burned out on the night of 2nd December 1913, while laid up for the winter above Poole Bridge.

Early in the season, Cosens were approached by the proprietors of the South Parade Pier at Southsea and invited to run a regular service to and from the pier. Although this would have given them another toe-hold in their enemy's camp, Cosens declined the offer and decided to maintain their loyalty to Clarence Pier. Their stated philosophy of not basing a ship in the Southampton Company's home waters aside, Cosens had no suitable steamer to base in the Solent and South Parade Pier was also notoriously difficult to use at low water. Even when its owners offered to dredge and maintain an all-tide access channel, Cosens refused to reconsider and nothing more was heard of the matter.

Difficulties were also experienced with lack of water at Boscombe Pier. On 16th June, *Majestic* went aground there and Cosens began to lobby the local council to undertake satisfactory dredging works. The matter was not resolved and the large steamers continued to experience increasing difficulties due to silting.

In an effort to improve their standing with the public following the *Titanic* disaster, the Board of Trade began to enforce a variety of existing regulations more rigorously than ever before. In particular, they chose to prosecute several masters, including Capt Tilsed of *Emperor of India* and Capt Goldsmith of *Balmoral*, for carrying too many passengers after dark. Arguments that the Board of Trade was unfair to enforce a regulation which it had ignored for the last thirty years fell on deaf ears. The captains were fined £10 and £20 respectively and it was made clear that passenger certificate conditions would be strictly enforced thereafter. As many long-distance excursions returned well after dark, especially as the evenings drew in from August onwards, the ruling placed Cosens in a difficult position. It was decided to fit yet more lifesaving gear to *Majestic*, *Emperor of India* and *Monarch* in order to retain their No. 2 certificates, which would allow them to run after dark, and to give careful consideration of the impact on *Victoria*'s westward coasting trips.

Overall, the 1913 season was described as being

STUDLAND BELLE backs away from the Studland pontoon.   JOHN PATRICK COLLECTION

EMPEROR OF INDIA at Clarence Pier, Southsea, which Cosens used regularly before the First World War. Having come from Bournemouth in the morning and landed her passengers for time ashore, the steamer would offer Southsea visitors a return trip to Bournemouth, before collecting her original complement for the homeward sailing during the late afternoon. The entrance to Portsmouth Harbour is directly above the ship's bow. DORCHESTER LIBRARY

Capt H.J. Hardy on the bridge of MONARCH at Bournemouth Pier, 9th July 1913.
DAVID HAYSOM COLLECTION

MAJESTIC prepares to leave Bournemouth Pier for Weymouth on 16th September 1913. Capt Rawle is on the bridge, while purser James Halford can be seen at the gangway.
DAVID HAYSOM COLLECTION

MONARCH arriving at Boscombe Pier sometime prior to the First World War. Judging by the lack of leaves on the trees the picture must have been taken very early in the season.
CRAWFORD ALEXANDER COLLECTION

like the proverbial curate's egg – *'good in parts'*. Although both the Easter and Whitsun holiday periods had been spoiled by wind and rain, the weather settled down during June and for the rest of the season the turnstiles had clicked merrily and a record 3,100,000 passengers had passed over the steamers' gangways. Although the timetable was basically unaltered from 1912, the agreement with the Southampton Company allowed one of the larger steamers to be released to operate two long trips from Weymouth each week. This innovation proved a great success, accounted for most of the

upturn in the earnings at the home station and was incorporated into the advance planning for 1914. The more sensible timings on the Swanage service saw passenger numbers increase significantly. August Bank Holiday was the busiest on record at both Bournemouth and Weymouth, and for much of the high season the steamers were filled to capacity, leaving crowds of potential passengers behind at the piers. By the end of the season income from fares had increased by £3,595 and Cosens' dividend to ordinary shareholders had returned to its accustomed, healthy 5 per cent.

THE PIER BOSCOMBE. 23.

CHAPTER 13

THE GREAT WAR

1914-1918

The opening months of 1914 found the company in buoyant mood. At the Annual General Meeting on 24th February, the directors looked back over the 1913 season with considerable satisfaction and found much upon which to congratulate themselves. In addition to the excellent passenger figures, the engineering and trading departments were doing well, loans were reduced and £9,368 had been carried forward to the revenue account. The new Admiralty Contract had been expanded during April by the addition of a 6.30am and 10.00pm boat, and an associated Carriers & Storage Department had been established. The salvage business alone had been relatively quiet during 1913, with '*only two or three small jobs*' being completed, and Mr J.D. Williams, in seconding the adoption of the annual report, was moved to express a hope that '*when the winds of Heaven are blowing ships in distress towards these shores, they blow near us rather than elsewhere.*' The addition of *Melcombe Regis* in place of the chartered *Lord Roberts* had swollen the fleet to a total of ten paddle steamers, three steam launches, and assorted pinnaces and workboats, which had proved just sufficient to meet the demands of the Admiralty Contract and the seasonal excursion trade during August. All-in-all, managers and shareholders alike had every reason to look forward to the coming season with great optimism.

As winter turned to early spring, preparations for the coming season progressed smoothly. A tender was accepted from local coal merchant G. Bryer Ash, for the supply of Best Griffin Nantyglo Large Steam Coal to Weymouth at 22s 6d per ton; the annual agreement with the Southampton Company was signed for a further year; and, three rather than the usual two berths were secured at Swanage Pier. Dissatisfaction with aspects of the previous three years stewarding accounts led the board to terminate its long-standing agreement with its catering manager, Mr Harford, who was subsequently re-engaged on a trial basis at the reduced fee of £2 per month, plus an end of season bonus of 10 per cent of the net profits. A strict set of conditions was attached, including the board's right to approve all potential catering staff before appointment. Sadly, Mr Harford died during May and was replaced by Mr G. Hunt, the chief steward of *Majestic*, at 45s per week plus 5 per cent of net profits. A lively correspondence took place between Cosens and various other excursion steamer owners, including the Liverpool & North Wales Steamship Co, regarding the implications of the Board of Trade's strict enforcement of clauses in the ships' passenger certificates forbidding trading after dark. Plans were made to form a deputation to discuss the situation with the BoT.

Victoria and *Monarch* were prevented from leaving Weymouth to open the Bournemouth season on 6th

During the depths of winter, a rust-streaked MAJESTIC, *having made the short passage from her lay-up mooring in the Wareham Channel at Poole, berths at Weymouth to begin her annual refit. The ship has been stripped of her deck seats and canvas dodgers and the master on the bridge is wearing a heavy greatcoat. The traditional wreath hoisted on the forestay suggests that the picture was taken just before Christmas.* H.A. ALLEN COLLECTION

MAJESTIC *was already fitted with a third lifeboat on her stern and for that reason she does not appear to have received extra boats forward of the paddles until a year after her fleet-mates. Now freshly-painted at the end of her refit, she is seen here leaving Weymouth to begin her 1914 season at Bournemouth.* AUTHOR'S COLLECTION/SEWARD

April 1914 by heavy gales but were able to proceed when the weather moderated on the following day. The season soon settled into a pattern of operation very similar to 1913 and, blessed with good weather, promised to be extremely profitable.

Capt Shippick, having lost his little *Studland Belle* to fire during the winter, replaced her with *Audrey* which, during 1911, had been chartered by Cosens to meet the demands of the Admiralty Contract at

MAJESTIC at Worthing Pier, on one of her regular long day trips eastwards from Bournemouth.
VICTOR GRAY COLLECTION

13 WORTHING. — The Beach and Pier. — LL.

Portland. *Audrey*, although only 126 feet in length, was a substantially larger ship than her predecessor and the previous Boscombe-Bournemouth-Studland Bay itinerary was extended to include Swanage and cruises up Poole Harbour. This brought her into direct competition with Cosens and the Southampton Company and insult was added to injury when it was discovered that the Poole Harbour Commissioners were charging the newcomer substantially lower mooring fees than the established companies. *Audrey*, more frequently marketed as *New Studland Belle*, operated successfully from Easter until the end of the season, after which she and her captain decamped to the River Medway to take up wartime ferry work for the Admiralty.

By the middle of June, under clear blue skies, the passenger figures for both Weymouth and Bournemouth were showing promise of yet another record season. The regular programme was enlivened by a number of special charters. At the request of the Admiralty, the company provided a steamer to act as tender to the French fleet which was due to arrive on 13th June and three days later, *Monarch* was chartered to the Bournemouth branch of the Navy League for an excursion to view the warships in Portsmouth Dockyard. The public interest in naval power was hardly surprising, since the growing naval rivalry between Germany and Great Britain had led, since the turn of the century, to a massive expansion of the rival fleets. Any opportunity to view these awesome assemblies was seized with open arms, as a source of national pride to the public and ready income to the steamer operators.

With the spectacle, however, came the risks. The powerful fleets and the growing armies ashore may have represented peaceful deterrents in the eyes of their own nations, accumulated to provide security and preserve the peace but to other countries they posed a threat. By 1914, Europe was divided into a series of defensive alliances and rival camps, whose complex inter-relationships meant that the slightest spark might start a chain reaction which could ignite the continent.

At Portland, naval activity became intense. With the growing threat of war, it had been decided in the spring that a test mobilization would be held in place of the usual summer Fleet manoeuvres. Reservists were called up and, by 10th July, Portland Harbour was filled with warships of the Home and Reserve Fleets. The demands upon Cosens' fleet tenders were tremendous and all available steamers were kept busy day and night, shuttling between Weymouth and the anchored Fleet. So great was the pressure that a number of advertised public sailings had to be cancelled over the Whitsuntide Bank Holiday period, and the directors became increasingly concerned about the company's ability to cope during the August peak season without further curtailment of public sailings.

On 28th June, the Austrian Archduke Franz Ferdinand and his wife were assassinated at Sarajevo. Austria-Hungary, with the backing of Germany, was determined to implicate the Serbian government in the outrage; Russia, the self-appointed protector of the Balkan Slav states would not permit Serbia to be humiliated. Tension rose.

Pressure on the excursion steamers was particularly intense between 16th and 20th July, when warships from Portland, Chatham, Devonport, Portsmouth and elsewhere assembled at Spithead for a Royal Fleet Review and 'Grand Naval Pageant'. Steamers from all along the south coast converged on the event each day, offering a staggering array of public sailings, and many strangers from further afield appeared on special charters. For Cosens, *Majestic* ran daily from Bournemouth, supported by *Monarch*, *Victoria* and *Emperor of India* on their way to and from Weymouth. *Empress* and *Queen*, in direct competition with Shippick's little *Audrey*, were based at Victoria Pier, Cowes, whilst the smaller units of the fleet appeared from both Weymouth and Bournemouth as required.

On 23rd July, with the review over and the trial mobilization successfully completed, the Grand Fleet was due to disperse from Portland but, on that very day, Austria-Hungary delivered an ultimatum to Serbia, followed three days later by a declaration of war. Orders were issued that the fleet should not disperse, and Cosens' directors called an emergency

Sailing bill for the Grand Naval Pageant on 18th July 1914. H.A. ALLEN COLLECTION

Two weeks before the declaration of war, a photographer from the Bournemouth View Co Ltd captured this happy crowd of trippers aboard MAJESTIC, *waiting to depart Bournemouth Pier on 13th July 1914.* AUTHOR'S COLLECTION

meeting to consider the urgent aquisition of another steamer to cope with the demand. Charter and purchase were both discussed but, as luck would have it, a suitable steamer was located lying for sale at Southampton.

The ship in question was *Alexandra*, of 235 gross tons, which had been built in 1879 by Messrs Scott of Greenock, for the Portsmouth & Ryde United Steam Packet Company's ferry service between Portsmouth and the Isle of Wight. In March 1880, the London & South Western and London, Brighton & South Coast railway companies had jointly purchased the Ryde company, so *Alexandra* became a railway vessel. In 1911, she was relegated to the status of spare steamer by the appearance of the new *Duchess of Norfolk*, later to appear in this story as Cosens' *Embassy*. In February 1913, she was sold to shipbrokers Fraser & White of Portsmouth, who immediately resold her to the Bembridge & Seaview Steam Packet Company, in whose ownership she remained for just over a year. Cosens were initially offered the ship through a broker at £2,500 but, by approaching her owners direct, were able to reduce the asking price to an exceptionally favourable £1,350.

The ship having been inspected and approved by Frederick Jones, the board met on the morning of 29th July to formally approve the purchase. It was a savage irony that, even as they met, the Grand Fleet, having received sailing orders on the previous evening, was weighing anchor and steaming out of Portland Harbour bound for its war station at Scapa Flow. Only the battleship *Agamemnon* remained in the deserted anchorage, to await the arrival of a second fleet later in the month. Their job done for the moment, the tenders drowsed at their moorings in Weymouth Harbour. By the time they were needed again, Britain would be at war and the reduction of the excursion programme would result in Cosens having steamers to spare. Thus, the reason for adding *Alexandra* to the fleet disappeared on the very day of her purchase and she was little, if ever, used in the role for which she was intended. Her arrival did, however, swell the company's fleet and business to its all time maximum. *Majestic*, *Monarch* and *Empress* were based at Bournemouth; *Emperor of India* and *Victoria* were at Weymouth, although regularly running trips out of Bournemouth; whilst *Premier*, *Albert Victor*, *Queen*, *Helper*, *Melcombe Regis* and *Alexandra* were on tender, salvage and excursion duties at Weymouth. In addition to these eleven paddle steamers, three

Thursday, Aug. 6th,
ALTERATION OF TRAFFIC
by Cosens & Co.'s Steamers (BUFF FUNNELS with BLACK TOPS).

Owing to the Needles Passage and Spithead being closed, the Trips to Totland, Cowes and Southsea are abandoned.

GRAND CRUISE
By Cosens & Co.'s Cross-Channel Buff Funnel Steamer

MAJESTIC
(Second to none on the South Coast).

(Weather and circumstances permitting) to

PORTLAND ROADS (in a state of Siege), & possibly viewing the 5th Battle Squadron of

Warships cleared for Action
ETC., AND

Nearly 3 hours at WEYMOUTH,
calling at SWANAGE.

Leaving Bournemouth at 10.25, Boscombe 10.40, Swanage 11.25, returning from Weymouth at 3.30, back about 6. **Return Fare 3/-** From Swanage 2/6

EVENING TRIP to Alum and Totland Bays
(NOT LANDING)
And to View the Searchlight Display at the Needles Passage.
Special Reserved Trip limited to 400.
Leaving Bournemouth 7.30, Boscombe 7.40, back about 9.45. Return Fare 1/6 Season & Fortnightly tickets not available. Accompanied by the **Boscombe Temperance Prize Band** of over Twenty performers.

Trips between Bournemouth & Swanage as advertised

For Alteration of Programme if Needles passage is still closed to Passenger Traffic on Friday, see Special Bills and Advertisement in "Bournemouth Echo."

These Trips are liable to be altered at the direction of the Naval or Military Authorities.

The Trip advertised to Torquay on Friday, August 7th, is abandoned.

Office— Royal Marine Library, Bournemouth. Tel. Bournemouth 130. R. F. SYDENHAM, Local Manager.

Sydenham, Printer, Bournemouth.

A sailing bill advertising a grand cruise by MAJESTIC *to see warships cleared for action in the lead up to the First World War.* 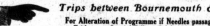 H.A. ALLEN COLLECTION

In the halcyon days before the First World War, passengers stream ashore from QUEEN *at Weymouth, whilst in the background, one of the GWR's Channel Islands steamers, either* ROEBUCK *or* REINDEER, *enters the harbour. The Southampton Company's steamer* LORNA DOONE *can be seen moored at the Pile Pier.*

AUTHOR'S COLLECTION/SEWARD

Victoria *entering the narrow harbour mouth at West Bay (Bridport) during one of her westward coasting trips. The harbour was always a difficult place to enter, because a large and unpleasant swell, as can be seen here, tended to build up between the pier heads. Strong nerves and smart seamanship were required to avoid the steamer being thrown heavily alongside and damaged. In this view, the bow rope is just being hauled ashore, while the master rings down astern on the engines. A seaman beside the paddle box waits to put the vital spring rope ashore, to prevent the vessel surging to and fro while embarking passengers.*
BRIAN STIDWELL, BRIDPORT

A fleet of battleships and cruisers assembled in Portland Harbour shortly before the outbreak of war. In the foreground is the shoreward end of the breakwater and the torpedo pier at Bincleaves.
G. CARTER COLLECTION

steam launches, *Prince George*, *Prince Edward* and *Princess*, together with several smaller pinnaces, were on War Office duties at Weymouth.

Meanwhile, international events were moving quickly. On 30th July, Russia mobilised and two days later Germany declared war on Russia. On 3rd August, Germany declared war on France and, in accordance with the Schlieffen Plan, demanded free passage for her armies through Belgium. Belgium refused and, on 4th August, Britain entered the

war in her defence. The Great War had begun.

The board met again on 7th August to consider what steps should be taken with regard to the company's business during the '*present national crisis*' and decided to appoint a committee consisting of the chairman and managers with '*powers to lay up what ships and close other portions of the company's business which they might deem advisable.*' The wave of public alarm which followed the declaration of war was compounded by the withdrawal of railway

o 22.

DAILY PLEASURE SAILINGS from Bournemouth, Boscombe & Swanage, by Cosens & Co.'s Steamers, Buff Funnels with black tops.

MAJESTIC,  MONARCH

(Second to none on the South Coast)

The ONLY STEAMERS with CROSS CHANNEL CERTIFICATES running from Bournemouth, or the Saloon Steamers VICTORIA, EMPRESS, &c.

BUFF FUNNELS WITH BLACK TOPS, will (weather and circumstances permitting) carry out Excursions as below:

The Company will not be responsible for any accidents, or injury to, or loss of life, or loss or damage to property of the passenger, of whatever nature, and whether caused by perils of the sea, accidents incidental to navigation or defects latent or otherwise in Hull tackle machinery or staging piers gangways or other property of the Company, or by any act neglect, or default of the Company, Pilots, Master, Engineers, Officers or Mariner or any other person in the Company's employ, or otherwise howsoever. The Return trips advertised are based upon the supposition that the Steamer performs the day trip contemplated, and that the Company will not be responsible to any passengers for any loss or expense in case they are unable to complete such return trip

Starting from the Left-hand Side of Bournemouth Pier.

Day / Steamer	Excursion
SATURDAY, August 29	**Day and Afternoon Trips to WEYMOUTH.** For Times and Fares see SATURDAY, SEPTEMBER 5th (below). Note Day Trip leaving Bournemouth at **10.35** a.m., Boscombe **10.45**, Swanage **11.35**, back to Swanage & Bournemouth only at 6.
	To SWANAGE, for Corfe Castle, Tilly Whim Caves, Great Globe, &c. Times and Fares as SATURDAY, SEPTEMBER 5th (see below)
	Evening Trip towards the Isle of Wight, to view the Searchlight Display at the Needles Passage. Times & Fare as Sept. 5 (see below)
	Owing to unforeseen circumstances the anticipated Excursion to WEST BAY and LYME REGIS is abandoned.
Monday, August 31 MAJESTIC	Nearly 3 hours at VENTNOR, or 2½ at SHANKLIN (Isle of Wight). **Giving Passengers a close view of the large assemblage of Merchant & other Vessels** anchored in Sandown Bay. Leaving Swanage at **9.20**, Bournemouth **10.30** a.m., Boscombe **10.40**, returning from Shanklin at 3.20, Ventnor 3.40, back about 6.15. Return Fare **3/6**, including Ventnor and Shanklin Pier Tolls. From Swanage 6d. extra.
Empress	AFTERNOON TRIP to **Swanage** AND UP THE PICTURESQUE HARBOUR OF POOLE. Leaving Boscombe at **2.30**, Bournemouth **3**, Swanage **3.45**, arriving back at B'mouth & Boscombe 5.30, Swanage 6.30, or returning from Swanage at 5.30 or 7.15 Rtn. Fare to Swanage **1/-** Up Poole Harbour **1/6** From Swanage **1/-**
Monarch / Empress	To SWANAGE **for Corfe Castle, Tilly Whim Caves, Great Globe, &c. Leaving Bournemouth** at **10**, **10.25** (by Monarch), **11.45**, **2**, **2.30** (by Monarch), **3**, **3.40**, **4**, **5.30**, **6.15** & **8** p.m. Boscombe to Swanage at **10.40** a.m., **12** (noon), **2.30**, **4.15**, **5.40** and **6.25** p.m. Swanage to Bournemouth at **9.20**, *__10.50__ a.m., **12** (noon), ***1.5**, ***3.15**, ***5.30** and **7.15** p.m. * proceeds to Boscombe. Return Fare **1/-** Single **9d.** Children under twelve years of age **6d.** Bicycles and Dogs 6d. each single journey.
Empress	**Evening Trip to POOLE** via Swanage. Leaving Bournemouth **5.30**, Boscombe **5.40**. Fare **6d.** Landing at Poole Quay about 7.30. Enabling Passengers to reach Bournemouth by rail or tram.
Monarch	**Evening Trip to SWANAGE.** Leaving Bournemouth at **6.15**, Boscombe **6.25**, back to Bournemouth only at 8.0 Return Fare **1/-** SINGLE TRIP to WEYMOUTH Leaving Bournemouth at 3.40 p.m., Swanage 4.25 Fare **2/-** From Swanage **1/6**
TUESDAY, Sept. 1 MAJESTIC	To TORQUAY about 2 hours ashore. Leaving Boscombe at **9.0**, Bournemouth **9.20** a.m., Swanage **10.0**, returning from Torquay at 4.0 p.m., back about 8.40. Return Fare **5/6** Season and Fortnightly ticket holders **1/-** Free Passes not available Arrangements have been made with the Tramways Manager for Special Cars to be at the Pier Gates to take Majestic's passengers for a Circular Tour of 12 miles through Torquay, Wellswood Babbacombe, S. Marychurch and Torre, thus affording a view of the most Picturesque and Charming Scenery of Torquay. Fare 1/-
Empress	To LULWORTH COVE (over 2 hours ashore) calling at Swanage. Landing by Stage Free at Lulworth and not by open boats. Leaving Bournemouth **10.25** a.m., Boscombe **10.40**, Swanage **11.25**, returning from Lulworth at 3.15, Swanage 12, 1.5, 3.15, 4.40, 5.30 or 7.15. Return Fare to Swanage **1/-** To Lulworth **2/6** Swanage to Lulworth **2/-**
Monarch	AFTERNOON TRIP to **Swanage** AND UP THE PICTURESQUE HARBOUR OF POOLE. Leaving Boscombe at **2.30**, Bournemouth **3**, Swanage **3.45**, arriving back at Swanage 5.30, Bournemouth & Boscombe 6.15, or returning from Swanage 4.40, 5.30 or 7.15 Return Fare to Swanage **1/-** Up Poole Harbour **1/6**. From Swanage **1/-**
Monarch / Empress	To SWANAGE **for Corfe Castle, Tilly Whim Caves, Great Globe, &c. Leaving Bournemouth** at **10.25**, **11.45** a.m. (by Monarch). **2.30**, **3** (by Monarch). **4**. **5.30**, **6.15** and **8** p.m. Boscombe to Swanage at **10.40** a.m., **12** (noon), **2.30**, **5.40** and **6.25** p.m. Swanage to Bournemouth at **9.20**, ***10.50** a.m., **12** (noon), ***1.5**, **3.15**, ***4.40**, **5.30** and **7.15** p.m. proceeds to Boscombe. Return Fare 1/- Single 9d. Children under twelve years of age 6d. Bicycles and Dogs 6d. each Single journey
Empress	**Evening Trip to POOLE** via Swanage. Leaving Bournemouth **5.30**, Boscombe **5.40**. Fare **6d.** Landing at Poole Quay about 7.30. Enabling Passengers to reach Bournemouth by rail or tram.
Monarch	**Evening Trip to SWANAGE.** Leaving Bournemouth at **6.15**, Boscombe **6.25**, back to Bournemouth only at 8.0 Return Fare **1/-** SINGLE TRIP to WEYMOUTH. Leaving Bournemouth 4, Swanage **4.45** Fare **2/-** From Swanage **1/6.**
WEDNESDAY, Sept. 2 Monarch	To SWANAGE & WEYMOUTH (2 hours ashore), **giving an opportunity of seeing the Thousands of TROOPS** including **Infantry, Artillery & Cavalry billeted** in the **Town. Likewise the captured Austrian & German Merchant Ships now lying in the Roadsteads.** Leaving Bournemouth **10.25** a.m., Boscombe **10.40**, Swanage **11.25**, returning from Swanage at 12, 1.5, 2.45, 4.30, 5.30, 7 & 7.30, from Weymouth at 3.30 p.m., back about 6 to Swanage and Bournemouth only. Return Fare to Swanage **1/-** To Weymouth **3/-** Swanage to Weymouth **2/6**
MAJESTIC	Afternoon trip to WEYMOUTH (over 1 hour ashore) calling at Swanage. Leaving Bournemouth **2.30**, Boscombe **2.40**, Swanage **3.20**, returning from Weymouth at 6, Swanage 4.30, 5.30, 7 and 7.30 Return Fare to Swanage **1/-** To Weymouth **2/-** Swanage to Weymouth **1/6**
Majestic / Monarch / Empress	To SWANAGE **for Corfe Castle, Tilly Whim Caves, Great Globe, &c. Leaving Bournemouth** at **10**, **10.25** (by Monarch), **11.45**, **2**. **2.30** (by Majestic), **3**. **3.40**. **5.30**. **6.15** & **8.10** p.m. Boscombe to Swanage at **10.40** a.m., **12** (noon), **2.30**, **2.40** (by Majestic) and **5.45** p.m. Swanage to Bournemouth at **9.20**, ***10.50** a.m., **12** (noon), ***1.5**, **2.45**, ***4.30**, **5.30**, **7** and **7.30** p.m. * proceed to Boscombe. Return Fare **1/-** Single **9d.** Children under twelve years of age 6d. Bicycles and Dogs 6d. each single journey
Monarch — Note Starting Times and Fare	Evening trip towards the ISLE OF WIGHT, **and to view the Searchlight display at the Needles Passage.** Leaving Bournemouth **7.45**, Boscombe **7.55**, back to Boscombe at 9.30, Bournemouth 9.45 Fare **1/-** BAND ON BOARD.
Empress	**Evening Trip to POOLE** via SWANAGE. Leaving Bournemouth 5.30 p.m., Boscombe 5.45. Fare 6d. Landing at Poole Quay about 7.30 Enabling passengers to reach Bournemouth by rail or tram
Monarch	**Evening Trip to SWANAGE.** Leaving Bournemouth at **6.15**, returning from Swanage at 7 or 7.30. Return Fare **1/-** SINGLE TRIP to WEYMOUTH Leaving Bournemouth at 3.40 p.m. Swanage 4.25 Fare 2/- From Swanage 1/6
THURSDAY, Sept. 3 MAJESTIC	Nearly 3 hours at VENTNOR, or 2½ at SHANKLIN (Isle of Wight). **Giving passengers a close view of the large assemblage of Merchant & other Vessels** anchored in Sandown Bay. Leaving Swanage **9.20**, Bournemouth **10.30** a.m., Boscombe **10.40**, returning from Shanklin at 3.20, Ventnor 3.40, back about 6.15. Return Fare **3/6** including Ventnor and Shanklin Pier Tolls From Swanage 6d. extra
Empress	Afternoon trip to LULWORTH (1 hour ashore) calling at Swanage. Landing by stage Free at Lulworth & not by open boats. Leaving Boscombe at **2.30**, Bournemouth **3**, Swanage **3.45**, returning from Lulworth 6.15, Swanage 5.30 or 7.30 Return Fare to Swanage **1/-** To Lulworth **2/-** From Swanage **1/6**
Monarch / Empress	To SWANAGE **for Corfe Castle, Tilly Whim Caves, Great Globe, &c. Leaving Bournemouth** at **10**. **10.25** (by Monarch). **11.45**, **2**. **2.30** (by Majestic), **3**. **3.40**, **4**, **6.15** & **8.15** p.m. Boscombe to Swanage **10.40**, **12** (noon), **2.30**, **4.15** and **6.25** p.m. Swanage to Bournemouth **9.20**, ***10.50** a.m., **12** (noon), ***1.5**, **2.45**. ***3.15**, ***4.40**. ***5.30** and **7.30** p.m. proceed to Boscombe. Return Fare 1/- Single 9d. Children under twelve years of age 6d. Bicycles and Dogs 6d. each Single journey.
Majestic — Note Starting Times and Fare	Evening trip towards the ISLE OF WIGHT, **and to view the Searchlight display at the Needles Passage.** Leaving Bournemouth **7.20**, Boscombe **7.30**, back to Boscombe at 9.20, Bournemouth 9.30 Fare **1/-** **Accompanied by the BOSCOMBE SILVER PRIZE BAND of over Twenty performers.**
Monarch	**Evening Trip to SWANAGE.** Leaving Bournemouth at **6.15**, Boscombe **6.25**, back to Bournemouth & Boscombe at 8.15. Return Fare **1/-** SINGLE TRIP to WEYMOUTH. Leaving Bournemouth at 3.40 p.m. Swanage 4.25 Fare **2/-** From Swanage 1/6
FRIDAY, Sept. 4 Empress	To LULWORTH COVE (over 2 hours ashore) calling at Swanage. Landing by Stage Free at Lulworth and not by open boats. Leaving Bournemouth at **10.25** a.m., Boscombe **10.40**, Swanage **11.25**, returning from Lulworth 3.15, Swanage 12, 1.5, 3.15, 4.40, 5.30 or 7.15 Return Fare to Swanage **1/-** To Lulworth **2/6**. From Swanage **2/-**
Monarch	AFTERNOON TRIP to **Swanage.** AND UP THE PICTURESQUE HARBOUR OF POOLE. Leaving Boscombe at **2.30**, Bournemouth at **3**, Swanage at **3.50**, arriving back to Swanage 5.30, Bournemouth and Boscombe 6.15, or returning from Swanage at 4.40, 5.30 or 7.15 Return Fare to Swanage **1/-** Up Poole Harbour **1/6**. From Swanage **1/-**
Monarch / Empress	To SWANAGE, **for Corfe Castle, Tilly Whim Caves, Great Globe, &c. Leaving Bournemouth** at **10.25**, **11.45**, a.m. (by Monarch). **2.30**, **3** (by Monarch), **4**, **5.30**, **6.15**, and **8** p.m. Boscombe to Swanage at **10.40** a.m., **12** (noon), **2.30**, **5.40** and **6.25** p.m. Swanage to Bournemouth at **9.20**, ***10.50** a.m., **12** (noon). ***1.5**, **3.15**, ***4.40**, ***5.30** and **7.15** p.m. *Proceed to Boscombe. Return Fare **1/-** Single **9d.** Children under twelve years of age **6d.** Bicycles and Dogs **6d.** each single journey.
Empress	**Evening Trip to POOLE** via SWANAGE. Leaving Bournemouth **5.30**, Boscombe **5.40**. Fare **6d.** Landing at Poole Quay about 7.30 Enabling Passengers to reach Bournemouth by rail or tram.
Monarch	**Evening Trip to SWANAGE.** Leaving Bournemouth at **6.15**. Boscombe **6.25** back to Bournomouth only at 8. Return Fare **1/-** SINGLE TRIP to WEYMOUTH. Leaving Bournemouth at 4, Swanage **4.45**. Fare **2/-** From Swanage **1/6**
SATURDAY, Sept. 5 Monarch	To SWANAGE & WEYMOUTH (2 hours ashore) **giving an opportunity of seeing the Thousands of TROOPS** including **Infantry, Artillery & Cavalry, billeted** in the **Town. Likewise the captured Austrian and German Merchant Ships now lying in the Roadstead.** Leaving Bournemouth at **10.25** a.m., Boscombe **10.40**. Swanage **11.25**, returning from Swanage at 12, 1.5, 2.45 4.30, 5.30, 7 and 7.30 p.m. From Weymouth at 3.30 p.m., back about 6 to Swanage and Bournemouth only Return Fare to Swanage **1/-** To Weymouth **3/-** Swanage to Weymouth **2/6**
MAJESTIC	Afternoon trip to WEYMOUTH (over 1 hour ashore) calling at Swanage. Leaving Bournemouth at **2.30**, Boscombe **2.40**. Swanage **3.20**, returning from Weymouth at 6, Swanage 4.30, 5.30, 7 and 7.30 Return Fare to Swanage **1/-** To Weymouth **2/-** Swanage to Weymouth **1/6**
Majestic / Monarch / Empress	To SWANAGE, **for Corfe Castle, Tilly Whim Caves, Great Globe, &c. Leaving Bournemouth** at **10**, **10.25** (by Monarch). **11.45**, **2**, **2.30** (by Majestic), **3**. **3.40** **5.30**, **6.15** & **8.10** p.m. Boscombe to Swanage at **10.40** and **12** (noon), **2.30**, **2.40** (by Majestic), and **5.45** p.m. Swanage to Bournemouth at **9.20**. ***10.50** a.m., **12** (noon), ***1.5**, **2.45**, ***4.30**, **5.30**, **7** and **7.30** p.m. *Proceed to Boscombe. Return Fare **1/-** Single **9d.** Children under twelve years of age **6d.** Bicycles and Dogs **6d.** each single journey.
Monarch — Note Starting Times and Fare	Evening trip towards the ISLE OF WIGHT, **and to view the Searchlight display at the Needles Passage** Leaving Bournemouth at **7.45**, Boscombe **7.55**, back to Boscombe 9.30, Bournemouth at 9.45. Fare **1/-** BAND ON BOARD.
Empress	**Evening trip to POOLE** via SWANAGE. Leaving Bournemouth at **5.30**. Boscombe **5 40**. Fare **6d.** Landing at Poole Quay about 7.30 Enabling passengers to reach Bournemouth by rail or tram
Monarch	**Evening Trip to SWANAGE.** Leaving Bournemouth at **6.15**, returning from Swanage at 7 or 7.30. Return Fare **1/-** SINGLE TRIP to WEYMOUTH. Leaving Bournemouth 3.40, Swanage 4.25 Fare 2/- From Swanage 1/6.

Only Britishers allowed on Board the Steamers.

The **CATERING DEPARTMENT** is fully up to date combined with moderate charges. Children under 12, Half-Fare. Deck Chairs (except Swanage Traffic) 1d. each. Bicycles & Dogs **1/-** each

SEASON Tickets available between **BOURNEMOUTH, BOSCOMBE, SWANAGE & POOLE, 21/-** Second and Subsequent Tickets **15/-** Children **10/6**

[illegible] TICKETS available on Wednesdays and Saturdays only **15/-** FORTNIGHTLY TICKETS available for twelve trips from date of issue **15/-**

[illegible]TS, available from Bournemouth, Boscombe and Swanage only, containing 20 6d. tickets, are now being issued at 7/6 per book; or containing 20 1/- tickets at [illegible] must be produced to the Purser on board the Steamer & exchanged for an Ordinary ticket.

[illegible]TS, BOOKS OF COUPON TICKETS and all information can be obtained from **SYDENHAM'S LIBRARY, Opposite Bournemouth Pier** [illegible] **BEALE, Ltd. Central Office & Agency** (Tel. Bournemouth ONE); Messrs. M. C. FROWDE & F. M. JONES, Joint Managers, Cosens & Co., Ltd (Tel. Weymouth **9** & **123**); Mr. A. J. WARD, Steam Packet Office, Swanage (Tel. Swanage **9**); or following Agents:—Mr. **HELLIER**, Estate Agent [illegible] Mr. A. IVES, Estate Agent, Fisherman's Walk (Tel. Southbourne **14y**).

DA[illegible] (Tel. [illegible] CustomHou[illegible] Boscombe [illegible] Office—SYDEN[illegible] August 28th, [illegible]

[illegible]posite Bournemouth Pier

Sydenham, Printer, Pier Approach & Oxford Road, Bournemouth

R. F. SYDENHAM, Local Manager Telephone—Bournemouth 130.

Sailing bill for the week beginning 29th August 1914, with a full range of trips still on offer. Note, however, the line at the bottom, 'Only Britishers allowed on Board the Steamers'! H.A. ALLEN COLLECTION

facilities during the initial mobilization. With all vestiges of holiday spirit destroyed, most holiday-makers quickly deserted the seaside resorts to return to their homes. The August traffic returns, which had hitherto shown a healthy upward trend, revealed a catastrophic fall of £6,467 in comparison with August 1913. It was widely assumed that all the passenger steamers would be forced to lay up but

the company made a decision to try to carry on.

At Weymouth, the bread and butter ferry run between Weymouth and Castletown Pier, Portland, had ceased on 3rd August when the Admiralty designated Portland Harbour a 'War anchorage and Trawler station' and closed it to excursion traffic. *Emperor of India* was paid off immediately and returned to her winter mooring in Poole Harbour,

Alexandra was laid up and, at Bournemouth, the crew of *Monarch* were given notice that the ship would operate on a day-to-day basis while demand remained sufficient. Due to the strategic importance of both ports, excursions to and from Southampton and Portsmouth ceased immediately but the management was able to obtain some '*rather unexpected facilities*' and was consequently able to run a restricted service to other destinations with comparatively good results. Blessed with continuing superb weather, the local residents of Bournemouth, Swanage and Weymouth turned out in abnormally large numbers to support the steamers. *Majestic* resumed her sailings to the Isle of Wight on 11th August, when she landed a large party from Bournemouth at Ventnor Pier. Passengers on this and all subsequent sailings were required to declare their nationality before embarking and considerable local excitement was caused by the billing of the ship as the 'All British *Majestic*.' On a sailing to the Island towards the end of the month, *Majestic* caused another stir when she ventured into a restricted area and had a warning shot fired across her bows by a naval vessel. At about the same time, Capt Rawle was giving his mate some practice at berthing at Swanage old pier when the ship failed to stop and struck the pier between the angled pierhead and the shore, severing a water main and tearing up a considerable amount of decking. A few days later, *Victoria* suffered £70 worth of damage when she collided with *Monarch* at Bournemouth Pier.

During September, more restrictions were introduced and, by the end of the season, the company was reduced to running a limited service between Bournemouth and Swanage.

After the outbreak of war, the Admiralty Contract remained in force and, with the 5th and 6th Battle Squadrons using the harbour together with other warships, the fleet tenders were kept reasonably busy. In addition to their usual liberty boat role, they were occasionally called upon to act as patrol vessels or as transports in connection with army route marches ashore. By the middle of August, *Queen*, *Albert Victor* and the steam launch *Prince George* had been hired by the Admiralty for service as examination vessels at Portland. Neutral ships bound for European ports were diverted into British Examination Anchorages, of which Weymouth Bay was one, and directed to anchor by the examination vessel, which then put an Examination Officer on board to check the cargo. Any cargo suspected of being bound for or of use to the enemy was confiscated before the ship was allowed to proceed. This policy was controversial, since neutral countries resented having their essential supplies intercepted and the Americans protested against the interference with the principal of 'freedom of the seas'. However, this system of blockade imposed at a distance proved very effective and ultimately proved to be a powerful element in Germany's defeat.

Always anxious to maximise their income, Cosens entered into a lengthy correspondence with the Admiralty concerning the rates and terms of hire for the examination vessels and, during October,

After war broke out, QUEEN, along with ALBERT VICTOR and PRINCE GEORGE, were hired by the Admiralty to act as examination vessels in Weymouth Bay, still in civilian colours. QUEEN is seen here whilst on liberty boat duties.

MELCOMBE REGIS *proved to be a versatile and useful addition to the fleet. Her size and basic accommodation made her ideally suited to both the Portland service and liberty boat work. Although she had a small and cosy deck-saloon forward, the after end – with the three portholes – was a simple steel shelter, open at the stern and fitted with basic wooden seats. The ship was also well-suited to towing and is seen here acting as steering tug to the large cargo steamer* TREWIDDEN, *which is being towed stern first down Weymouth Harbour by another tug, out of the picture to the left.*
CRAWFORD ALEXANDER COLLECTION

they offered *Majestic*, *Monarch* and *Emperor of India* on charter as minesweepers. The offer was declined, although the Admiralty Transport Office did write during November requesting details of all ships which might be available for hire if required. Excursion steamer companies throughout the country were busily trying to find gainful employment for their idle ships at this period, and were continually attempting to discover the rates and conditions of hire offered to rival companies. During December, the Devon Dock, Pier & Steamship Co were in optimistic contact, offering their paddlers *Duke* and *Duchess of Devonshire* to Cosens in the event of any extra boats being needed at Weymouth. At about the same time, Cosens entered into an agreement with the Admiralty to undertake various ship repair work for the duration of the war, a trade which was to prove extremely lucrative.

The threat from German submarines was somewhat difficult to predict at the beginning of the war but it was considered important to make Portland Harbour safe from torpedo attack. In November 1914, the old turret battleship *Hood* was scuttled across the southern entrance, where she remains to this day. The northern and eastern entrances were protected by booms and it was these which led to a dispute between Cosens and the Admiralty. On several occasions during the autumn and winter gales, steamers engaged on the Admiralty Contract or examination work had been interned

in Portland Harbour due to the booms being closed and had been forced to anchor off Bincleaves, in the north west corner of the harbour. Due to the poor holding ground, anchors had dragged and the ships had sustained various amounts of damage, *Premier* and *Queen* being particularly badly effected. Cosens and their underwriters wished to claim against the Admiralty, who in turn staunchly maintained that a generous allowance for both insurance and repairs had been built into the hire fee!

By the end of October, when the excursion season would normally have finished, the combined Bournemouth and Weymouth passenger returns showed a decrease of £8,756 in comparison with 1913. These depressing, if predictable, figures might have caused the Board far more alarm had it not been for the fact that J.D. Williams' wish, voiced at the last Annual General Meeting, concerning salvage work had been answered in full.

The first call had come on 7th January 1914, when, in light winds but a heavy swell, the French three-masted auxilliary schooner *Cara* went ashore on Chesil Beach near Langton Herring. *Helper* was dispatched and had little difficulty in towing her off and bringing her safely into Weymouth. It is interesting to note that once *Queen* and *Albert Victor* were taken up for examination duties, *Helper* became the chief salvage tug, frequently supported by *Melcombe Regis*.

A month later, at about ten o'clock at night on 14th

February, with an exceptionally violent gale raging in the Channel, the villagers of Abbotsbury and Langton Herring became aware of the continuous sounding of a steamer's syren. Hurrying to the beach, they discovered the 3,500 ton Dutch steamer *Dorothea* stranded broadside on to the beach where, as the tide fell away, she was left high and dry. The crew were able to scramble down the ship's side to the safety of the beach and were given temporary shelter at the Elm Tree Inn, Langton. Cosens were immediately informed of the stranding and Frederick Jones, who also served as the local representative of the Shipwrecked Mariners Society, set off immediately to arrange their transfer to Weymouth. At the same time, Capt Read took *Helper* to sea but only got as far as Portland Bill before the ferocity of the gale began to inflict damage on the tug and forced him to return to Weymouth. Writing in his journal some years later, Capt Read recalled:

'It was blowing a hurricane and the seas in West Bay and at the Bill of Portland were tremendous … Arriving off the Bill all we could see was what looked like a huge wall of broken water and the next thing we were buried right up to our foremast in a huge wave. As this washed along our decks there were cries from the engine room and stokehold. The water was pouring down below and there was imminent danger of the fires being put out. It was impossible to proceed and the only thing to do was to try and get my ship's head round and back under the shelter of the high cliffs. To get round is a very risky operation since while you are broadside on there is great danger. Well, I watched my chance and when I saw the next sea approaching was not as heavy as the two previous ones I gave the order "hard a starboard" and the ship came round to my great relief without being swept and we ran for shelter. I then thought I would go into Portland Harbour and make enquiries of the coastguards as to what had happened to the steamer. To do this I had to go to the coastguard station [where] they informed me that the steamer had been thrown broadside right up to the high water mark of the beach. When I tell you that the vessel was loaded with iron ore and drew 24 feet of water it will give you some idea of the sea that was running. I went back on board and found the crew had been examining with lanterns the damage we had received. Some of our*

A dramatic photograph of *DOROTHEA*, stranded on Chesil Beach in February 1914. After another company had failed, Cosens successfully refloated her during October.
AUTHOR'S COLLECTION

This postcard view of the German liner BULOW aground on Portland was annotated by a member of Cosens' staff, identifying just some of the vessels which attempted to earn a part of the salvage award. Here, from left to right, are the salvage steamer STITZER, and the tugs JOHN BULL and SWARTZEE with, alongside the casualty, a Government barge, the tug HERCULES and Cosens' QUEEN and diving boat.
AUTHOR'S COLLECTION

bulwarks had gone and our foredeck which previous to this had a very nice camber was now flattened out with the weight of water falling on board.'

It was not until the middle of February that the contract for *Dorothea*'s salvage was finally let to the National Salvage Association and their powerful salvage vessel *Lyons* arrived on the scene to commence operations. *Dorothea*'s cargo of iron ore was jettisoned onto the beach and powerful suction pumps were used to remove shingle from around her hull but all attempts to refloat her failed. By July, the salvage company had been dismissed. During September, she was sold by public auction and her new owner, having used local labour to construct a slipway under her keel, engaged Cosens to make another attempt to restore the ship to her rightful element. During an exceptionally high tide on 19th October, their efforts were crowned with success and *Dorothea* was towed off by two tugs and brought safely round to Weymouth. To have survived a record ten months of buffeting on the notorious Chesil Beach, *Dorothea* must have been a remarkably strong or lucky vessel.

On 22nd April, *Helper* and *Albert Victor* were dispatched to the aid of the SS *Envermeu*, which had stranded in fog on the rocks between Kimmeridge and St. Alban's Head. So thick was the fog that the Swanage lifeboat and the two paddlers searched for nearly six hours before locating the casualty in the early hours of the next morning. *Envermeu*, with a

full cargo of coal on board, was so badly holed that there seemed little prospect of getting her off the rocks but the tugs and lifeboat stood by until high water in case the crew needed to be taken off. In the event, they elected to remain on board and did not finally abandon their ship until the following weekend, when Cosens landed them at Weymouth. Two larger salvage tugs were engaged by Lloyds and, some time later, after major pumping operations, the ship was successfully refloated. At about the same time, a steamer named *Herbert* was sighted flying a signal requesting the assistance of a tug but when *Helper* arrived, her help was refused.

A quiet period followed until, on 18th June, during another dense fog, the syrens of a large vessel were heard sounding close to the western shore of Portland. During the course of the morning, the vessel could be heard feeling her way to the south but, at 11.30am, the continuous blowing of her syren indicated that she had come ashore. Hurrying to the spot, the coastguard discovered that a large steamer had grounded on the rocks in Mutton Cove, halfway between Blacknore Point and the Bill, the same spot where *Patroclus* and *Myrtledene* had come to grief some years before. She proved to be the large Norddeutscher Lloyd liner *Bulow*, on passage from Yokohama to Southampton with passengers and cargo. Finding himself embayed, her master had tried to make for the open Channel again but, mistaking Blacknore Point for the Bill, had turned east too soon and put his ship ashore at a spot known as Flew's Gangway. To the delight of local sightseers and photographers, this was one of the only points on the west coast of Portland where it was possible to descend the cliffs by a well defined path to get a close view of the wreck and salvage operations, so large crowds soon gathered.

As soon as news of the stranding reached Weymouth, Collins' *Verne* and *Petrel*, and Cosens' *Queen*, *Empress* and *Melcombe Regis* raced to the scene, closely followed by the Dockyard tugs *Pilot* and *Eggerton*. Immediate attempts to refloat *Bulow* having failed, it was decided to await the high tide early the following morning and to concentrate instead on landing the liner's passengers. Capt Hemmings, the local Lloyds' agent, and Mark Frowde, Cosens' secretary and joint manager, went out in *Queen* to supervise the transfer and a large, excited crowd gathered at Weymouth Pier gates to await the arrival of the shipwrecked passengers. Fortunately, the sea was a glassy calm and Capt Hollyoak had no difficulty in taking *Empress* alongside the casualty at about 5pm. The transfer of the 240 passengers took about an hour, after which the steamer proceeded to Weymouth, followed by *Queen* with the heavy baggage. Post Office officials were waiting on the pier with batches of telegrams to enable the rescued passengers to transmit messages to anxious friends and relatives as quickly as possible. *Bulow* had grounded so gently that there had been no injuries or alarm and many of the onlookers were a little disappointed at the calmness of the passengers, many of whom seemed more interested in enthusing about their 'pleasure cruise' ashore in *Empress* and their impressions of the French and British Fleets at anchor in the Bay, than about their experiences on board the German liner! A few spent the night in the Victoria Hotel before proceeding to Plymouth next day but the majority left for London just after midnight in a special GWR train.

Bulow failed to float on the next tide so, while the other tugs danced attendance, *Pilot* and *Eggerton* returned to Portland to collect a number of Admiralty lighters, which were used to relieve the liner of a good deal of her cargo during the next few days. Blessed with continuing settled weather, this operation was successful and, a few days later, *Bulow* was towed off having sustained remarkably little damage.

Also during June, *Empress* went to the assistance of *Cariad*, one of the large sailing yachts owned by the Earl of Dunraven, while *Monarch* and *Albert Victor* brought in *Utowana*, a large auxilliary steam yacht owned by the Armour family of Chicago.

Claims for services rendered to each of these vessels were filed in the usual manner through Messrs Kingscombe, the company's salvage solicitors. The vessels' owners would inevitably respond with a lower offer and a period of haggling would follow. If no agreement could be reached, the solicitors, who would already have prepared pleadings and possibly applied for a bail payment to allow the salvaged ship to proceed on its voyage, would refer the matter to the salvage court, where a final ruling

on a settlement and costs would be made. The case of *Utowana* is a typical example. The solicitors proposed to ask for bail in the sum of £1,250 and the owners offered £400 plus taxed costs in settlement. Cosens replied that if £600 was offered it would be considered and the owners responded with an improved offer of £500 plus costs, which was eventually accepted during October.

The salvage trial on the German-owned *Bulow* case had to be postponed, due to the outbreak of war, since alien witnesses were unlikely to attend and court the possibility of being made prisoners of war! The other cases were eventually settled for the following amounts, plus costs:

Cara	£200
Envermeu	£110
Utowana	£500
Cariad	£175
Dorothea	£150

On 30th July, *Melcombe Regis* was involved in another unusual but ultimately unsuccessful salvage attempt. Early in the evening, the suspicions of Portlanders were aroused when a ketch under full sail was seen making directly for the beach in Chesil Cove. Some even suspected that she might have ulterior designs on the oil storage tanks on the other side of the beach but quickly revised their opinion when smoke was seen rising from the after part of the ketch. A number of local fishermen put off in their boats to offer advice but, the fire having taken a firm hold, her master saw no option but to sail her ashore and abandon ship. The ketch was *Lucinda* of Jersey, with a cargo of iron turnings which had become overheated. She struck the beach as twilight was turning to darkness and made a memorable sight as first her mizzen and then her main sails and masts blazed up and fell in a shower of red-hot sparks.

Appraised of the situation, Cosens dispatched *Melcombe Regis* to the scene and, by 11.15pm, her fire and salvage pumps had got the blaze under control. Capt Gardiner of *Melcombe Regis* took up the story in a statement to the *Southern Times*:

'A tow rope was passed to the ketch which was towed slowly to Portland Bill. There was no sign of her leaking, but she lay low in the water and her decks and bulwarks were burnt out from aft to amidships. The sea was calm with a slight swell. The Lucinda *rolled heavily and at 12.40 the tow parted. We got another rope on board and soon afterwards flames broke out in the after hold. The ketch was being towed at half speed all the time and, when rounding the Bill, she was blazing furiously. At half-past one the boat took a plunge and sank. Her crew of three, including the captain, landed at Portland in their own boat and the* Melcombe Regis *returned to Weymouth.'*

The year came to a stormy end with a series of dramatic and lucrative services. On 30th November,

HELPER preparing to tow the French schooner ARDENTE off Weymouth Sands.
WEYMOUTH LIBRARY

during a south-westerly gale of exceptional violence, the Norwegian steamer *Noreg* got into difficulties in West Bay and was in imminent danger of driving ashore on the Chesil Beach near Fleet. *Helper* and *Melcombe Regis* set out from Weymouth but were only able to proceed at half speed due to the heavy seas which were running. Despite the fact that visibility was reduced practically to zero due to the blinding rainstorms, the tugs eventually located *Noreg* lying to one anchor about half a mile off the beach at Chickerell. Due to the appalling sea conditions, *Helper* required several attempts before she got her tow rope on board the Norwegian and suffered serious damage to her bulwarks and paddlebox in the process. *Melcombe Regis* then passed a rope to *Helper* and, very slowly, the two tugs succeeded in easing the casualty away from the deadly surf. Some hours later, when the little convoy had reached a position about three miles

east of the Bill, a heavy squall parted *Helper*'s tow rope and forced *Melcombe Regis* to slip her's for her own safety. *Noreg*, her propeller shaft disabled, drove rapidly towards the Shambles Bank with *Helper* in hot pursuit, whilst *Melcombe Regis* struggled to free herself from her own tangled tow rope. *Helper* eventually succeeded in passing another tow and *Noreg* was finally brought to anchor in Weymouth Bay, nine hours after the tugs had set out to her aid. The *Southern Times* felt moved to compliment Capt Leddy of *Helper* and Capt Garnett of *Melcombe Regis* for rendering services which *'were arduous and not a little hazardous … under conditions which could not have been very well worse.'* Two days later, in another severe squall, *Noreg* began to drag her anchors towards other steamers in the examination anchorage and the tugs had to render assistance for a second time, moving her through the anti-submarine boom into the safety of Portland Harbour. On 5th December, the French ketch *Rene*, laden with onions, was picked up dismasted in West Bay, and saved from driving ashore near Langton Herring.

Finally, during the afternoon of 11th December, the French schooner *Ardente*, which had anchored for shelter in Weymouth Bay, began to drag her anchors in a heavy south-easterly gale. One of the Cosens' tugs put out to offer assistance but *Ardente*'s master did not consider that his vessel was in sufficient danger, so refused the terms offered and the tug returned to harbour. The storm did not abate and the schooner continued to drag steadily towards Weymouth Esplanade, where a large crowd had gathered to watch. At 1pm, *Ardente* was seen to hoist distress signals and Mark Frowde was informed in his dual capacity as Cosens' joint manager and honorary secretary of the local RNLI. The Weymouth lifeboat, *Friern Watch*, was launched at 2.30pm, with *Queen* and *Helper* lying in readiness at the pierhead

A close-up of the Dutch ketch ZWAATZE CORNELIA on Preston Beach, Weymouth, with work underway removing her cargo in wicker baskets, in order to lighten her for towing off.
AUTHOR'S COLLECTION

to tow her to the distressed vessel. Some difficulty was experienced in passing a tow-rope, so Coxswain Spranklin decided to proceed under oars, whilst *Helper* attempted to take the Frenchman in tow. By this time, however, she was in amongst the breakers off the gently-shelving Weymouth Sands and the water was too shallow to allow the tug to approach. *Helper* was forced to stand out to sea and leave the work of rescue to the lifeboat, which finally managed to manoeuvre alongside and take off the crew of five. Attempts to tow *Ardente* off during the following day failed but the weather subsequently moderated and, with her ballast removed, she was pulled off by *Melcombe Regis* on 13th December and brought safely into Weymouth, where a claim for 50 per cent of her insured value was lodged.

On New Year's Day 1915, two more vessels, the Russian brigantine *Otto* and the Dutch ketch *Zwaatze Cornelia*, suffered almost identical accidents when they were driven ashore, side-by-side, on Preston Beach. The seas in the bay were violent and confused and, in an attempt to veer alongside the Russian to take off her crew, the Weymouth lifeboat smashed ten of her oars, before parting her anchor cable and being driven ashore herself. Coxswain Spranklin was seriously injured in the accident and the lifeboat remained on the beach for some days. Cosens towed both of the casualties off the beach towards the end of the month and actually purchased *Otto* and her cargo of flint for the sum of £175, presumably for immediate resale. They benefited twice over from the Dutchman's misfortune, as they were paid £105 for salvaging, slipping and surveying *Zwaatze Cornelia* and were then awarded the contract for carrying out repairs to the value of £385.

Other salvage services during 1915 included the Admiralty lighter *YC46*, which was picked up off the Bill by *Melcombe Regis* in January, having broken away from her tug; the schooner *Elizabeth Hampton* brought in by *Helper* during February; the disabled steamer *Strathard* towed by *Melcombe Regis* from Bournemouth during April; and *SS Martin*, rescued by *Melcombe Regis* in June. The latter service earned the company £600 in salvage and repair work, and brought to an end a very lucrative run which had done much to offset the losses suffered in the excursion trade.

While these dramas were being enacted in the Channel and the armies in Europe were becoming bogged down in the misery of trench warfare, the employment of the rest of the fleet at Weymouth settled into a routine.

The spring of 1915 found *Queen*, *Albert Victor* and *Prince George* still busy on Examination Patrol work, earning the company a useful income of between £500 and £800 per month. The Admiralty, however, was less enthusiastic about what it regarded as over-generous hire terms and gave notice to terminate the contract from 28th February, commandeering the ships instead. Cosens responded by offering to sell *Albert Victor* for £3,600, *Queen* for £5,000 and *Prince George* for £1,200, or to hire them at £20, £20 and £8 per day respectively but the offer was declined. On 1st April, *Helper*, too, was commandeered for examination work, although this only lasted until early June when she was relieved by two Admiralty drifters.

Unable to find employment with the Admiralty, *Majestic* and *Emperor of India* remained idly at their moorings in Poole Harbour. During February, they

A panoramic view taken on the same day, showing ZWAATZE CORNELIA *still stranded on the shingle beach with waves breaking against her, whilst on the right, with her masts and rigging in disarray, the Russian brigantine has been refloated. Both vessels were marooned here for nearly four weeks before Cosens were able to tow them off.*
AUTHOR'S COLLECTION

MELCOMBE REGIS steaming up Weymouth Harbour.
AUTHOR'S COLLECTION/
SEWARD

were temporarily disabled by their engineers at the request of the Mayor of Poole, who was apparently concerned they might fall into the hands of enemy agents! During June, both ships were reactivated and steamed together to Southampton for dry-docking, their hulls having received no attention for well over a year.

The remainder of the steamers found intermittent employment on the Fleet Contract although, during July, the Admiralty gave three month's notice that the contract would be terminated on 16th September and sought to negotiate alternative daily hire rates for liberty boats. *Melcombe Regis* and *Helper* were offered at £16 and £14 per day respectively, while Cosens made it clear that the redundant vessels would need to be laid up and that the Admiralty should not assume that tugs would be as readily available as hitherto. *Monarch*, *Victoria*, *Empress* and *Premier* were all offered for the purpose of taking the wounded off disabled ships should the need arise but no record exists of this actually occurring. Correspondence flowed steadily between the company and the Admiralty concerning payment for the commandeered ships, the overtime rates for their crews and regarding the liability for damage sustained by *Helper* and *Queen* whilst on examination duties.

During June, *Helper* had collided with the trawler *Fane* in the northern entrance to Portland Harbour. The Admiralty made it clear that they held her master, J.J. Marshallsay, responsible for the accident, since not only had he entered the harbour in breach of a local Port Order which gave right of way to vessels passing outwards but had made matters worse by porting his helm and increasing speed when he sighted *Fane* on his starboard bow. Marshallsay escaped with a caution on the grounds that, technically, he had never officially been informed of the Port Order. The court, however, made it very

clear that, as a master who regularly took examination boats in and out of the harbour, he was perfectly well aware of the order and must be more careful in the future.

At the beginning of 1915, there had still been some hope that the excursion trade might be able to resume by the summer and, in March, the Swanage Pier Company was optimistically enquiring how many berths Cosens might require for the coming season. By May, however, the Admiralty had announced that excursion traffic would be more or less prohibited and made subject to the final decision of the naval officer commanding each district. Applications were made to run in the immediate neighbourhoods of Bournemouth and Weymouth but both were refused by early June.

The only 'public' excursions which did operate were a series of complimentary afternoon cruises in Weymouth Bay for convalescent and wounded soldiers from local hospitals. The military authorities agreed to allow *Melcombe Regis* to sail from Weymouth Pier each Tuesday afternoon at 2.30pm, on condition that she carried a large Red Cross on each paddle box and flew an enormous Red Cross flag from her masthead, to give herself the appearance of a hospital ship. About 200 soldiers, together with their orderlies and nurses, embarked for the first trip on 27th July when, unfortunately, *'there was a fresh breeze blowing and the sea was not as placid as could have been desired.'* A somewhat tongue-in-cheek *Southern Times* takes up the story:

'On the stroke of the half hour the steamer cast off, and Capt. Garnett put her straight across the Bay for Preston, and then skirted the cliffs past Redcliffe Point and Ringstead Bay to the Durdle Door. It had been hoped to continue the cruise to Lulworth, but the weather did not permit of the longer trip and the

Melcombe Regis took a short sweep round for home again ... There was a good deal of seasickness and the nurses fell victims in a body, with the result that positions were reversed, for the wounded Tommies had to look after the sick nurses ... On the way home a shower of spray occasionally caught the unwary, but even that was better than poison gas they said. Even the horrors of mal de mer were not allowed to spoil the enjoyment of the trip ... A piano and two fiddles added to the gaiety and it was a jolly party which was set ashore again at half-past four. So successful was it and so beneficial its effects on the convalescent soldiers and the overworked nurses, that it is to be repeated.'

The trips continued on a weekly basis until late September when, just before they would have ceased for the winter, a letter arrived from the commander of the local military hospitals proffering his thanks for the company's generosity and regretting that further trips would be impossible. The reason for this was not, as one might imagine, the danger from enemy submarines but a piece of red tape in the form of Portsmouth Garrison Order No. 758, which forbad hospital patients from accepting hospitality or entertainment of any kind!

Realising that the war would almost certainly lead to the disruption or cessation of the import of block ice from the Baltic, the company turned its attention to the storage of manufactured ice. In February 1915, it purchased its rented premises on Custom House Quay from Mrs Dyer for £1,300 and immediately spent £1,676 on modifications and new refrigeration machinery. The ice wells were relined, the vacant spaces beneath the company's first-floor offices were converted for cold-storage and, by the end of the year, the new business was turning in a small profit. New 21 year leases had been signed with Mr Ayles and the Wilton Estates for the No. 1 and 2 slipways respectively; a lease had been taken on the quay outside the George Inn; and, further east, both the Swanage coal shed and the Hamworthy steamer wharf had been let to the military.

In September 1915, *Alexandra*, which had been lying more or less unused since her purchase, was chartered to the company's former master Capt Shippick, who was now well established on the River Medway, where he was contracted to run an Admiralty

ferry service between Gillingham and Sheerness. Cosens had fitted *Alexandra* with new capstans fore and aft and a new flying bridge, as part of a major refit shortly after she arrived at Weymouth, and she was obviously well-suited to her new role, as she remained on the Medway ferry service until early in 1920. Each time her charter was renewed the terms became less favourable to Cosens and in March 1916, the ship was requisitioned by the Admiralty but continued to be managed by Shippick.

The autumn of 1915 brought a minor bombshell in the form of an auditor's report, which expressed the firm view that, for a number of years, the amount written off annually for depreciation of assets had been woefully inadequate and that the steamers and plant therefore appeared in the books at a price which far exceeded their true value. Repairs and renewals to the steamers had been added to their cost price rather than being paid for out of revenue and the directors were advised that they could be held guilty of the serious offense of paying dividends out of capital. The auditor advised the board that the only course was to seek the shareholders' permission for a reduction in share capital. As part of the deliberations which followed, the Marine Superintendent, Frederick Jones, drew up a table of costs and values for all of its ships (*below*), which gives a fascinating insight into contemporary ship-building costs as well as to the scale of the company's overvaluation.

A poor condition mystery photograph, which is included because it is believed to show ALEXANDRA whilst on Admiralty ferry duties on the River Medway. The deck awnings would be better suited to tropical duties but, since the steamer never left the UK during the war, it must be assumed that they were fitted to protect deck-passengers from the British rain!
DORCHESTER LIBRARY

NAME OF SHIP	ORIGINAL COST	VALUE IN COMPANY'S BOOKS	MR JONES' VALUATION
MAJESTIC	£24,525.15.0d	£24,525.15.0d	£12,000
EMPEROR OF INDIA	£14,000. 0.0d	£15,532.14.3d	£14,000
MONARCH	£14,939. 0.6d	£15,593.16.6d	£ 5,000
VICTORIA	£10,555. 7.1d	£11,273.10.5d	£ 2,000
EMPRESS	£ 8,949.14.0d	£ 9,345.13.5d	£ 1,500
MELCOMBE REGIS	£ 1,985.14.4d	£ 1,985.14.4d	£ 2,000
ALEXANDRA	£ 1,357.12.2d	£ 1,357.12.2d	£ 1,500
PREMIER	£ 3,500. 0.0d	£ 7,040. 6.7d	£ 1,000
HELPER	£ 825. 0.0d	£ 825. 0.0d	£ 1,000
QUEEN	£ 6,168.10.0d	£ 6,168.10.0d	£ 1,000
ALBERT VICTOR	£ 3,350.19.9d	£ 3,350.19.9d	£ 1,000

The matter was raised with the shareholders at the AGM in February 1916 and a special resolution was subsequently passed and confirmed at two EGMs held on 19th May and 5th June to the effect:

'That the Capital of the company be reduced from £72,800, divided into 4,000 Preference Shares of £5 each and 10,560 Ordinary Shares of £5 each, to £29,120, divided into 4,000 preference shares of £2 each and 10,560 ordinary shares of £2 each, and that such reduction be effected by cancelling capital which has been lost or is unrepresented by available assets to the extent of £3 per share upon each of the 2,781 preference shares and 9,739 ordinary shares which have been issued and are now outstanding, and by reducing the nominal amount of all shares in the Company's Capital from £5 to £2 per share.'

Although, due to its diverse activities, the company continued to turn a respectable profit throughout the war years, this massive reduction in capital was another symbol that the fat years were drawing to a close and that things at Weymouth would never be quite the same again.

The year of 1916 also saw a significant change in pace for the steamers themselves. The first sixteen months of the war had seen the fleet based in or around its home port but now the ships began to disperse far more widely.

First to go, in early January, was *Helper*, which was taken on charter by the War Department for Examination Service at Newhaven. *Empress* sailed to join her a few weeks later and the two ships, with *Melcombe Regis* acting as relief, settled into a highly successful partnership at the Sussex port, which was to last for the next two years. The new service was, however, clouded by tragedy when, on the morning of 8th May, Capt Lewis St. Barbe Rawle, the company's senior master, was discovered drowned in Newhaven Harbour. It was assumed that Capt Rawle had slipped whilst boarding *Empress* during the night and had fallen between the ship and the quay, knocking himself unconscious.

Empress returned to Weymouth for repairs in October and was relieved by *Melcombe Regis*, which remained at Newhaven until January 1917, when she was badly damaged by heavy seas and was again replaced by *Empress*. During the same week, *Helper* was hit by *SS Duchess* in the examination anchorage but her damage was less serious and she was able to remain on station. In May, it was the turn of *Empress* to be damaged, when she was run into by *SS Koolga*, whose owners accepted full liability and eventually settled the bill of £350, whilst in September *Helper* suffered further damage in collision with *SS Sheldon*. In January 1918, the War Department handed the control of the Newhaven Examination Service to the Admiralty, *Empress* was transferred to other duties at Portsmouth and *Melcombe Regis* sailed from Weymouth to rejoin *Helper* for a final few weeks at Newhaven, before they were transferred elsewhere.

In the summer of 1916, things began to move very quickly indeed. Firstly, in June, the steam launch *Princess* was requisitioned and departed for the long trip to the River Tyne. The War Department then approached the company to request a price for the possible purchase of *Monarch*, *Victoria* and *Premier*. The Department was seeking shallow draft paddle steamers for use by the Inland Water Transport Department on the rivers of the Middle and Far East, and Cosens immediately offered the three ships for £15,000, £11,000 and £7,000 respectively. Bearing in mind the recent revaluation of assets, a sale at this price would have represented an exceedingly shrewd piece of business but, unfortunately for the company, the ships were eventually turned down as unsuitable for the particular job in mind!

Emperor of India and *Majestic* ended their long period of idleness at Poole early in June, when they were requisitioned as minesweepers and sailed immediately for Portsmouth to fit out. They were joined there by the Devon Dock, Pier & SS Co's *Duke of Devonshire*, which had been requisitioned at

An 'In Memoriam' card for Capt L. St. Barbe Rawle, who drowned in Newhaven Harbour during May 1916.
G. St. Barbe Rawle

Sunset and evening star,
And one clear call for me,
And may there be no moaning of the bar,
When I put out to sea.

Twilight and evening bell,
And after that the dark,
And may there be no sadness of farewell,
When I embark.

For though from out our bourne of time and place,
The flood may bear me far,
I hope to see my pilot face to face,
When I have crossed the bar.

*To the Beloved Memory
of*
LEWIS St. BARBE RAWLE.
*late Capt. S.S. "Majestic."
Who was Accidentally Drowned, at Newhaven,
on Saturday, May 6th, 1916,
while on War Service.
Aged 53 Years.*

*Interred at Holy Trinity Cemetery, Weymouth.
May 11th, 1916.*

the same time and had sailed from lay up in Exmouth on 3rd June. On 9th July, the three steamers, now renamed *HMS Emperor of India II* (Pennant No. 0106), *Majestic II* (0108) and *Duke II* (0107), sailed for Falmouth, where they coaled and provisioned before departing again on 18th July, escorted by the armed yacht *Rovenska* and bound for Gibraltar. After a brief stop at Lisbon, Gibraltar was reached safely and *Rovenska* handed her charges over to another armed yacht, *Safa-El-Bahr*, for the next stage of the journey to Malta.

Heavily laden with coal, the little convoy sailed from Gibraltar on the evening of 27th July and next morning, 28th July, somewhere off Oran, *Majestic II* foundered. The precise reasons for her loss remain a mystery, since no reference can be found amongst the normally meticulous records of warship losses housed in the Public Records Office but one eye-witness account does survive. Writing in 1963, *Duke II*'s chief engineer of the time, Mr James Hall, recalled 'One of the ports had not been fastened properly and the water got in. The pumps were clogged with small coal in the bilge and down she went.' Fortunately, the weather was calm and there were no casualties. *Safa-El-Bahr* took off all of the crew and returned them to Gibraltar, whilst *Duke II* and *Emperor of India II* put into Oran. The loss of their newest and finest ship in such an ignominious manner must have been a major blow to the company who, having absorbed the news, immediately requested the Board of Trade to reserve the name *Majestic* for a replacement steamer and approached A. & J. Inglis regarding the probable cost of such a vessel.

Safa-El-Bahr, having landing *Majestic II*'s survivors

at Gibraltar, returned with another armed yacht, *Eileen*, and escorted the two remaining paddlers to Malta. They left Malta again on 4th August, arriving at Suda Bay two days later to take on coal and sailed again on 10th August for Alexandria. James Hall recalled:

'The weather then became pretty foul and the Duke took a roll which stove in the purser's cabin, and every time we rolled from then on we took in a great column of water which shot from the damaged part into the air! For some two days we sheltered under some islands and then set sail for Ras-el-Tin in Alexandria to be fitted as a minesweeper. Whilst we were there some natives came round selling a dog. It was always the same dog – they had trained it to swim back every time they sold it! I kept it until it jumped ship in Port Said. When the Duke arrived at Port Said she and the Emperor of India were joined by the Cleethorpes, a river Humber ferry steamer. The Duke was a good ship and the only trouble we had was when she broke a paddle in a storm.'

The fitting out at Alexandria to which Mr Hall alluded involved the cutting back of the aft saloon of each vessel to about half its original length, in order to provide a large and uncluttered sweep deck right aft. On this deck was fitted an enormous and powerful steam winch, on the drums of which were stored the flexible steel wire ropes that formed the sweeps themselves. A large steel gallows was fitted over the stern to assist with handling and lifting the heavy sweep gear.

HMS Emperor of India II minesweeping in the Mediterranean. The large steel gallows, steam winch and sweeping gear are all clearly visible on the stern, as are the guns fitted fore and aft.
IMPERIAL WAR MUSEUM

The method of minesweeping used by the paddle steamers during the Great War was known as the A-Sweep or Paired Sweeping. The sweep wire was paid out by one ship of a pair, picked up by the second ship, brought in through her stern fairleads and made fast to a quick release device. As the two ships steamed ahead on parallel courses, the bight of the sweep wire curving astern of them would snag and break the mooring wires of enemy mines, causing them to float to the surface, where they would be sunk by gunfire. In order to cut the mine's

mooring as effectively as possible, explosive cutters were often attached to the bight of the sweep wire near its point of deepest immersion. These cutters had sharp teeth and small explosive charges which went off as the mooring wire made contact. It was theoretically possible for an entire flotilla of paddle minesweepers to operate in line abreast with a sweep between each pair of ships but, since this seriously limited their manoeuvrability in dangerous, unswept waters, it became the norm for the ships to operate in pairs.

HMS Duke II, which made the voyage out to the Mediterranean in convoy with Majestic and Emperor of India. In 1938, the vessel joined Cosens' fleet as Consul.
AUTHOR'S COLLECTION

Their conversion complete, *Emperor of India II* and *Duke II* joined the paddlers *Cleethorpes*, *Marchioness of Lorne* and *Minerva* in sweeping out of Port Said. The maintenance of clear approaches to the Suez Canal was a mundane but dangerous and vitally important task, and kept the flotilla fully occupied until well after the Armistice in November 1918.

Emperor of India II was renamed *Mahratta* in June 1918 and *Duke II* was detached from the flotilla for some months to act as a transport during the allied army's advance northward into Palestine and Syria. It appears that during this period, she acted as senior ship for a group of smaller vessels consisting of *ML 248*, the trawlers *Veresis*, *Lizzie*, *King Arthur*, *King Eric* and *Corisin*, and the drifters *Lord Wenlock*, *Ploughboy*, *Liberty II* and *Blackthorne*. Commander George Gregory, commanding officer of *Duke II*, was awarded the DSO in recognition of his '*splendid organising work in connection with the landing of stores on the exposed coasts of Palestine and Syria, thus assisting the advance of the army which was dependent upon this source of supply*.' He was congratulated on obtaining '*magnificent results from native labour*'. His first lieutenant was awarded the DSC and the officers of all the attached ships were mentioned in despatches.

Mines have no respect for human agreements and so, well after the Armistice was signed on 11th November 1918, the grim and dangerous business of mine clearance continued. Early December found *Mahratta* and *Minerva* clearing the approaches to Mersina, where a channel 1,200 yards wide was swept, an area of 15 square miles to the south of the anchorage cleared, and 15 mines destroyed. By 8th December, their work was completed and the two ships had returned to Port Said.

On 15th July 1919, the five Port Said paddlers were officially transferred to the Mine Clearance Flotilla, Black Sea & Aegean, and moved north to begin work on clearing the northern approaches to the Bosphorous. Here, they joined the paddlers *Queen IV*, *Princess Mary II*, and *Duchess of Norfolk*, a further vessel, *Duchess of Richmond*, having been

sunk by a mine on 28th June. *Mahratta* and *Duchess of Norfolk* were immediately selected as Kite Balloon Carriers. A surviving report takes up the story:

'*Operations in the eastern area commenced with a reconnaissance with seaplanes from* HMS Empress. *On 26 September the first Kite Balloon from Haidar Pasha kite balloon station was ready for work. This balloon was flown from the paddler* Duchess of Norfolk *and was followed by a second on 27 Sept from* Mahratta. *These balloons, replaced as necessary, made a thorough reconnaissance of the eastern half of the minefield, no mines were reported, but dummy mines were seen with ease ... By then, more sweepers had arrived and the paddlers and balloons confined themselves to inshore work. The Black Sea is now clear except for the Bosphorous.*'

The kite balloons referred to in this report were a new and experimental means of spotting mines in areas such as the Mediterranean, which had very clear water. The paddlers' large, clear decks and powerful steam winches proved ideal for handling the balloons, and their unique combination of shallow draft and substantial size enabled them to provide a steady working platform in conditions which forced the smaller motor launches to suspend operations.

The basic idea was for the paddler to tow the balloon, from which an observer in a basket was suspended, at a height of between 350 and 400 feet. She would approach the suspected position of the mines with the sun behind her and, in calm conditions, it was found that a good observer could spot mines at a depth of up to 30 feet beneath the surface, and as far as 300 yards away. Once the mines had been spotted, the paddler would sheer away and drop a line of dan buoys as markers for the sweepers which followed behind. The experiment was regarded as a qualified success, although a wonderfully straight-faced official report of the period, 'Remarks on Kite Balloon Work',

EMPEROR OF INDIA II was renamed HMS MAHRATTA in June 1918, in which guise she is seen here, left, in company with a Naval 'Racecourse' Class paddle minesweeper.
VICTOR GRAY COLLECTION

EMPRESS's war service plate.

revealed an unexpected problem:

> 'It is important that the observers should have a rifle in the balloon basket, with which they can fire at any single object observed in the water; it is only after the shot strikes the water that the observer can tell whether the object is a mine or a turtle. At the commencement of balloon operations several buoys were dropped near believed mines, which mines subsequently disappeared; as the observers were positive in each case that the object was a mine, it was thought that the mines must have broken away soon after the mark buoys were laid, until on one occasion the mine was seen to be swimming away.'

The mines had turned out to be turtles!

Their work completed, the ships of the mine clearance flotilla were due to leave the Bosphorous from the end of October 1919 onwards, with *Duke II* due to sail on 25th October, followed by *Duchess of Norfolk* and *Mahratta* on 14th November. In the event, by December, *Duke II* had only got as far as Gibraltar, from where the Senior Naval Officer advised by telegram that:

> 'H.M.S. Duke II *can be made structurally seaworthy for coastal passage, but it is considered that there would be considerable risk in sending her to England even by the coastal route. The ship carries 35 tons of coal stowed before the paddle boxes in position not designed for bunkers. This increases draft forward by about 32 inches and reduces freeboard of the upper deck to about 26 inches. Recommend she remains in Gibraltar for the winter.'*

It was suggested that, in order to minimise the inconvenience and loss of earnings caused to her owners by the delay, the work of reconditioning the ship should be carried out during her lay up at Gibraltar but the DDP&SSCo declined the offer and it was not until July 1920 that the little steamer finally arrived back in Plymouth.

Mahratta also remained at Gibraltar throughout the winter, during which time Cosens were approached by two potential purchasers. In March 1920, a local company inspected her with a view to

putting her to work at Gibraltar but eventually decided that she was too large for their purposes. During the following month, an Italian firm also showed considerable interest. Neither sale having come to fruition, *Mahratta* sailed in convoy with *Duke of Devonshire* and *Duchess of Norfolk*, and arrived safely at Pembroke Dockyard during July.

Back in Weymouth, the winter of 1916-17 saw *Queen* involved in two collisions. On the first occasion, 18th November 1916, she was damaged whilst attempting to assist the barque *Celticburn* and then, two months later, she was struck by the Admiralty examination drifter *Ocean Pioneer*. It is clear from the repeated reports of structural damage to the examination steamers at Weymouth and Newhaven that the business of maintaining the patrol, day and night in all weathers and laying alongside ships to put examination officers or pilots on board, was a skilled and hazardous task. It also took its toll mechanically. By the end of 1916, *Queen*'s boiler was worn out and a replacement had to be ordered from Messrs Hodge & Sons of London at a cost of £725. Owing to the scarcity of rail freightage and the risk of transporting the boiler by sea, it was decided to send *Queen* round to London under her own steam during August 1917, to have the new boiler fitted. In October, *Prince George* suffered a total boiler failure but the company was fortunate enough to obtain a second hand replacement from Willoughbys of Plymouth. The boiler, which came complete with mountings, smokebox, funnel and fittings had been removed from the War Department steamer *Joule* at the end of 1916 and cost £62 10s 0d inclusive of rail transport from Plymouth. In June 1917, it was the turn of the little *Prince Edward*'s boiler to fail and be replaced.

In March 1917, *Victoria* and the steam launch *Prince Edward* were both requisitioned, together with the company's coal wharf and sheds at Hamworthy. The Admiralty enquired whether *Melcombe Regis* was available but Cosens declined on the grounds that she was already committed as spare examination vessel. *Victoria* was quickly made ready for sea and departed for Plymouth, where she spent the rest of the war as a liberty boat and Admiralty ferry under the name *Victoria IV*. Capt Shippick wrote enquiring whether *Monarch* was available to join *Alexandra* on his Medway Admiralty ferry service but was told that her boilers would require re-tubing before she could be hired for any purpose.

Monarch's respite did not last for long, however, for, at the beginning of May, she was requisitioned and re-tubed at Weymouth before sailing for Camper & Nicholson's shipyard at Gosport, where she was fitted out as a minesweeper. Renamed *HMS Monarchy*, she joined the hired paddlers *Harlequin*, *Way* (P. & A. Campbell's *Waverley*) and *Glen Rosa*, based at Swansea. As lead ship, both she and the flotilla were commanded by Lieut G.R. Janman RNR and spent the remainder of the war minesweeping in the Bristol Channel and southern Irish Sea. During August 1917, the flotilla crossed the Irish

Sea and, using Arklow, Wicklow and Kingstown as their bases, set to work sweeping inside the banks which lie offshore between the Blackwater and Kish light vessels. While they were in the area, it appears that they took part in deception tactics which led to the sinking of at least one mine-laying U-boat. The deception involved pretending to sweep an area while not actually doing so. The U-boat, presumably informed by local spies, then returned to sow more mines, only to be blown up by its own previous cargo.

By mid August, the paddlers were back in the Bristol Channel, where they were joined by a fifth sweeper in the form of the Clyde steamer *Glen Rosa*, renamed *Glencross* to avoid confusion with her Campbell namesake. The little ships continued to carry out their arduous task in all weathers and, when the Admiralty called for a report on their suitability, the Senior Naval Officer at Swansea stated that he was '... *very favourably impressed with the five light paddlers and their seagoing qualities. Two were out lately in very severe weather and stood the strain very well.*' As winter approached, it was agreed the ships should all be fitted with additional comforts in the form of wheelhouses on their open bridges, slow combustion stoves to heat their accommodation and a number of 'luxury' items such as carpets in the officers' cabins, and an easy chair and writing desk for each commanding officer.

On the night of 15th-16th December 1917,

Monarchy, *Harlequin* and *Way*, together with several smaller vessels, were caught by a severe north-easterly gale whilst moored in Ilfracombe Harbour. The harbour is dangerously open from that quarter and as the spring tide rose, heavy seas began to break over the stone jetty at the entrance, causing the moored ships to surge heavily at their moorings. Fortunately, *Monarchy* and *Harlequin* were almost stern on to the seas and survived the ordeal until the wind backed slightly and conditions moderated.

HMS Monarchy, with HMS Harlequin alongside, lays at Ilfracombe Pier during her period as lead ship of the Bristol Channel Minesweeping Flotilla, frequently referred to as 'the Swansea paddlers'.
AUTHOR'S COLLECTION

The Bristol Channel Minesweeping Flotilla laid up at Ilfracombe after the Armistice. From left to right, the ships are HMS Glencross, HMS Monarchy, HMS Harlequin, HMS Glen Rosa and HMS Way.
CHRIS COLLARD COLLECTION

The following year, 1918, saw a steady increase in minelaying in the Bristol Channel, especially off major headlands, and *Monarchy* and the other Swansea paddlers were kept extremely busy throughout the year. On the morning of 19th August, *Monarchy*, *Harlequin* and *Glencross* had left Ilfracombe at 5.00am to sweep the area to the westward, when they came across the drifting wreck of the steamer *Charity*, which had been mined off Hartland Point a few hours earlier. The paddlers succeeded in putting a rope on board the casualty and took her first to Clovelly and eventually to Ilfracombe, where they arrived at 5.00pm. Their arduous work in the Bristol Channel was to continue until May 1919, when the flotilla was finally disbanded.

The beginning of 1918 saw the dispersal of the Weymouth fleet completed. In January, *Helper* and *Melcombe Regis* were removed from their examination work at Newhaven, fitted out as minesweepers and despatched to their new base at Belfast. Two months later, *Queen* and *Albert Victor* were sent to Portsmouth and Southampton to be converted into minelayers. Each ship was able to carry eight mines and they were employed in the Dover Straits. The gap left in the Weymouth examination service by their departure was filled by *Premier*, on temporary charter until she could be replaced during May by a more suitable vessel. In August, the Admiralty gave notice of their intention to requisition her again but Cosens were now so short of staff that no crew could be assembled and it was not until two months later that she finally left Weymouth for duty at Harwich, where she arrived on 13th October. Thus, with

Empress still busy transporting ratings and stores to warships in Portsmouth Harbour, there was not a single Cosens' paddler left at Weymouth, the company's presence being represented only by the steam launches *Prince George* and *Prince Edward*.

Financially and operationally, the final months of the war must have been a quite extraordinary period for the company and its employees. Income was being generated very largely by the monthly hire fees for the steamers, which in mid-1918 were as follows: *Emperor of India* £250, *Monarch* £195, *Victoria* £180, *Melcombe Regis* £135, *Helper* £100, *Queen* £112, *Albert Victor* £108, *Empress* £350 and *Princess* £12. Precise figures for *Prince George* and *Prince Edward* have not been located but can be assumed to approximate to those of *Princess*. This gave an overall monthly income from hire fees of approximately £1,500, a sum considerably lower than that generated by the Weymouth examination steamers alone during 1915.

Following the loss of *Majestic* in July 1916, the Admiralty made an immediate compensation offer of £13,500 which Cosens rejected out-of hand, suggesting instead that they would be willing to accept a replacement vessel of equivalent size and quality. Over the next eighteen months, the Cosens board entered into lengthy correspondence with P. & A. Campbell Ltd of Bristol, as a result of which both companies were able to bid up the sums offered by the Admiralty. The amount offered for *Majestic* rose to £17,250, then £19,000 and was finally agreed at £20,500 in October 1917, the income being promptly invested in War Bonds. This sum

On her way back to
Weymouth from Harwich at
the end of her war service,
PREMIER was chartered by the
Ministry of War Transport to
act as a tug at the launch of
a large concrete barge from
the Hamworthy Shipyard at
Poole during December
1918.
IAN ANDREWS COLLECTION

makes an interesting comparison to the £22,500 and
£29,500 paid to P. & A. Campbell for their *Brighton
Queen* and brand new *Lady Ismay* respectively, and
the £11,500 to the Southampton Company for their
smaller and older *Stirling Castle*.

With most of their seagoing staff away from their
home port and working exceptionally long hours,
the strain inevitably began to tell. At Portsmouth,
where *Empress* operated around the clock for many
months before formal conditions of hire were finally
agreed in September, the crew were reported to be
suffering from exhaustion and Capt J.J. Marshallsay
collapsed and was rushed to hospital, with an illness
'*caused by the overwork which has been thrown upon the
Empress*'. Back at Weymouth, Capt Hardy asked to
be relieved from his duties during the winter months
'*due to his nerves giving way*' and Capt Hollyoak of
Premier was injured in an accident on board. The
company's ship repairing business was kept extremely
busy with routine work and a wide range of War
Department and Admiralty contracts, including one
for the refitting of a large number of naval 'motor
scout boats' but this too ran into severe difficulties
when, by June 1918, the last of the engineering
apprentices were called up to serve in the armed
forces. So few skilled men were left that the company
had extreme difficulty keeping any work going and
was forced to decline a contract to repair the War
Department vessel *Fusee*, '*pending other arrangements*'.
Realising the strength of their position, the
workforce, acting through the National Union of
General Workers, added to the company's difficulties
by demanding a pay rise, which was reluctantly
granted in August. Despite all of these problems, it
is interesting to note that, in both 1917 and 1918,
the company managed to add substantially to its

reserves and declare a healthy dividend on all shares.

At sea, the final months of the war offered no
obvious respite to the hard-pressed crews. A
surviving log book from *Helper* has provided a rare
glimpse into the daily routine of a small excursion
steamer pressed into service as a minesweeper.

On 28th January 1918, following a brief refit at
White's Shipyard, Southampton, *Helper* ran speed
trials. The following day her Weymouth mate and
crew of eleven ratings joined in time to see the ship
commissioned into the Royal Navy, before spending
an intensive six days storing and coaling the ship,
splicing sweep wires and rigging the kites.

At 05.15am on 6th February, she sailed from
Southampton, swung her compasses off Gurnard,
dropped her pilot and compass adjuster at
Yarmouth and departed for Kingstown, Northern
Ireland. The voyage took twenty-one storm-tossed
days, with calls at Portland, Brixham (where she
was stormbound for four days), Plymouth, Penzance,
Newquay and Milford for coal, water and stores,
before an alarming passage across the mouth of the
Bristol Channel in a severe SW gale.

Helper arrived at Kingstown on 27th February
but had no sooner anchored than she began to drag
and was forced to go alongside a salvage steamer.
The next morning, a severe NW gale set in and
the log reads '*Carried away bollards aft, tore up deck,
broke moorings. With tug assistance made fast to a buoy.*'
From 2nd-23rd March, she was repaired and fitted
out at Larne Dockyard, where she received two 7
foot kites in place of her smaller Southampton ones,
sixty fathoms of sweep wire and four depth charges.

On 23rd March, she sailed for her new base at
Belfast, where she joined her fleet mate *Melcombe
Regis* and the other requisitioned paddlers *Her*

Majesty, *St. Trillo*, *Lady Evelyn*, *Princess Beatrice*, *Belle* and *Lady Clare*. For the next nine months, the seven ships were engaged in keeping the Belfast Lough clear of mines and quickly settled into a routine. On any particular day, it was normal for five vessels to be in use. Four would be sweeping in two pairs, whilst the fifth acted as guard ship and lay in readiness to sink any swept mines with gunfire. The remaining two ships would be coaling, boiler cleaning or carrying out repairs at either Belfast or Larne, with some of their crew enjoying a brief spell of leave. This arrangement worked on a rota, so *Helper* found herself paired with all the other ships at different times. The sweepers normally sailed from Belfast in order to commence work at the first light of dawn but occasionally their routine was enlivened by some unusual event, such as on 16th April when *St. Trillo*, paired with *Helper*, managed to get her sweep wire tangled round one of her paddlewheels, or on 13th May, when the flotilla was sent to dispose of a wreck by dropping depth charges and picking up the resulting debris.

During October, the crew were decimated by a severe outbreak of influenza and, on 4th November, *Helper* was in collision with *Her Majesty* whilst sweeping and suffered damage to her bulwarks. Three days later, on 7th November, she returned from sweeping and anchored off Larne at 10.23am but a severe SW gale blew up and she began to drag her anchors very rapidly. The engines were put full ahead but she continued to drag and lost her port anchor. At 11.15am, with the engines still running full ahead, *Helper* carried away her starboard lifeboat by fouling an anchored trawler. She continued to manoeuvre until 1pm, when she took the ground aft and simultaneously collided with the trawler *Elf King*. Considerable damage was done to the starboard bulwarks and sponson, the foredeck and deckhouse and the ship remained aground until midday on 8th November, when she was hauled off and proceeded to Belfast, where the crew set about clearing the wreckage.

The final, poignant entries to *Helper*'s log read:

'Monday November 11th. Peace proclaimed 11.15 (news received). Dressed ship. Chief Engineer Shepherd died in hospital. Coaled and watered ship.
Tuesday November 12th. 09.20 Under orders – proceeded to Larne, landed anchors and cables, docked in Larne Shipyard, blew down boilers.'

With her wartime duties at Portsmouth at an end, EMPRESS returned to Weymouth in January 1919 and was laid up at Trinity Quay. Still in wartime grey but with her funnel restored to its peacetime buff and black, she is seen here awaiting a refit before opening Cosens' post-war passenger service on 9th June 1919.
THE LATE D.B. HOPPINS

AFTERWORD

Following the Armistice in November 1918, the surviving Cosens' steamers were gradually released from Government service and began making their way back to Weymouth. Reconditioning of the war-weary ships took some considerable period and although *Empress* made the first post-war public sailing from Weymouth on Monday 9th June 1919, it was not until 1921 that the entire fleet was once again ready for passenger service.

The trauma of the Great War had, however, transformed the economic and social landscape in which the steamers now operated. The lucrative Fleet Contract had not been renewed and, deprived of this major source of regular income, the company was forced to dispose of several smaller steamers. A brief boom in 1919, accompanied by rapid inflation and a steep rise in fuel and wage bills, was followed by an inexorable drift towards the depression of the 1920s. The healthy state of Cosens' reserve fund and investments, combined with the diverse nature of their engineering activities and the ability to maintain their elderly but economical steamers themselves, allowed the company to survive these difficult years. Tight financial control was accompanied by further diversification into ice manufacturing and cold-

p.s. EMBASSY

storage, the introduction of a fleet of economical motor launches to operate between Weymouth and Portland, and a return to Torquay as a base for one steamer.

The 1930s were marked by a return to relative prosperity and two new vessels were added to the fleet, before the steamers were once again called away to serve their country in the Second World War. Rebuilt and refurbished, the steamers enjoyed a brief post-war boom in trade before changing public tastes, increased car ownership and the rise of foreign holidays, combined with increasing fuel and maintenance costs to drive them steadily out of business. One by one they were disposed of, until on Thursday 22nd September 1966, Cosens' last steamer, *Embassy*, made her final excursion sailing from Totland Bay to Bournemouth. She languished in Weymouth Backwater until 25th May 1967, when she was towed away to a Belgian shipbreaker's yard, bringing to an end the company's distinguished 119-year history as an excursion steamer operator. Cosens' marine and general engineering activities continued until 1996, when the loss of a number of key contracts combined with a general recession in the engineering industry forced the company into receivership.

The detailed story of these turbulent but fascinating years is told in the companion volume to this book, *Cosens of Weymouth, 1918-1996*, published by Twelveheads Press in 2001 (ISBN 0 906294 48 7).

EMBASSY, the very last of Cosens' famous 'Buff Funnel' paddle steamers, approaching Swanage Pier during 1966, her final season in operation. AUTHOR'S COLLECTION

The Last Boat from Swanage.

This humorous postcard provides a vivid reminder of the immense popularity of the steamer services in the days before the First World War. DAVID HAYSOM COLLECTION

APPENDIX ONE
FLEET LIST

(Note: In the light of much new information, this list has been updated and corrected since the publication of the previous volume.)

Name	Off. No.	Acquired / Built / Sold / Scrapped	Tonnage (grt: Gross Registered Tonnage)	Length / Breadth / Depth	Engines: Type	Cylinders Dia.	Stroke	Nom. HP	Builder / Hull Type / Engine Builder	Notes
HIGHLAND MAID (on charter)	9072	1848 / 1846 / 1848 / 1874		66ft 2ins / 13ft / 8ft				22	P. Legg / Wood / J. Harrison	1846 Tug. Registered Newcastle. 1847 Registered London 1847
PRINCESS	21528	1848 / 1847? / 1853 / 1882	60.9 burthen	112ft 5ins / 13ft 5ins / 7ft 7ins	Oscillating 2 cylinders			2 x 20 / 1849 / 2 x 16	Ditchburn & Mare / Iron / John Penn	1847-49 Owned by John Penn. 1849 New engines. 1853 Sold J.T. Leather. 1857 Sold Plymouth
WAVE QUEEN (on charter)		1852 / 1852 / 1852		220ft / 18ft				80	Robinson, Russell & Co, Millwall	
PRINCE	21519	1852 / 1852 / 1888 / 1897	60.8 burthen	120ft 5ins / 13ft 3ins / 7ft 6ins					John Scott Russell / Iron / John Penn	1878-79 Bow and rig altered. 1888 Sold to Ellett & Matthew, Exmouth
CONTRACTOR	13941	1858 / 1847 / 1863		84ft 4ins / 15ft 8ins / 8ft 9ins					J. Jackson / Wood	1852 Tug/passenger. Bought by P. Dodson. 1858 To Cosens. 1863 To Plymouth
OCEAN BRIDE	6228	1858 / 1844 / 1865 / 1867?	29.2 grt/18.4 rt	72ft / 12ft 6ins / 5ft 8ins				18	East / Wood	Tug at Newcastle. 1856 to Dodson. 1858 to Cosens. 1865 Sold to J.T. Leather. 1867 Sold to Crown
BANNOCKBURN	2102	1860 / 1847 / 1865 / 1865	53.2 grt	69ft 6ins / 16ft / 8ft 4ins				28	E. Oliver / Wood	T. Brewis, Newcastle. 1859 Sold to J. Tizard, Weymouth. 1860 To Cosens. 1865 Converted to barge
PREMIER	6387	1860 / 1846 / 1938 / 1938	98.4 grt/62 rt FROM 1878: 115.2 grt/72.6 rt	240.2x17x6.5ft FROM 1878: 148.5x17.3x6.7ft	Steeple FROM 1878: Oscillating 2 cylinders	25ins & 29ins	33ins	65 / 50	Denny / Iron / Tullock & Denny / From 1878 Penn	1846 Dumbarton Steamboat Co. 1859 To Tizard, Weymouth. 1860 To Cosens. 1878 Rebuilt, new engines

Name	Official No.	Dates	Tonnage	Dimensions	Engine	Cyl.	Cyl.	HP	Builder / Material / Engine	Notes
COMMODORE	28012	1863 1863 1890 1894	96.3 grt/26.2 rt	93ft 18ft 6ins 9ft 6ins	Side lever			60	A. Woodhouse	1890 to J. Campbell, Holyhead
EMPRESS	63915	1879 1879 1958 1958	163.5 grt/98 rt	160ft 1ins 18ft 5ins 8ft 3ins	Oscillating 2 cylinders	30ins	33ins	52	Samuda Iron Penn	1884 & 1904 Reboilered. 1904 Deck saloon fitted. 1906 Mainmast removed
QUEEN	88126	1883 1883 1920 1923	146.1 grt/77 rt	110ft 2ins 19ft 7ins 8ft 9ins	2 Side lever	26ins	48ins	70	Smit & Zoon Iron Vulcan Ironworks	1920 To Ardrossan Harbour Board
VICTORIA	82355	1884 1884 1953 1953	191.7 grt/99.8 rt	166ft 19ft 2ins 8ft 7ins	Oscillating 2 cylinders	35ins	36ins	75	S. & K. Smit Steel Penn	1888 Lengthened. 1895 Reboilered & bulkhead fitted to fore end of deck house. 1907/8 Mainmast removed
MONARCH (1)	82358	1888 1888 1950 1950	309 grt/92.7 rt	210ft 22ft 2ins 9ft	Diagonal, direct acting, condensing, 2 cylinders	41ins	48ins	130 850 IHP	R. & H. Green Steel Penn	1889 Foc's'le lengthen'd. 1906 Mainmast remov'd 1908 Bridge moved forward of funnel. 1912 For'ard lifeboats fitted. 1929-30 Reboilered and larger wheelhouse fitted
ALBERT VICTOR (ex-LASS O'GOWRIE)	86379	1889 1883 1928 1928	128.4 grt/32.7 rt	106ft 19ft 8ins 9ft 7ins	Side lever, 2 cylinders	37ins	54ins	70	Eltringham & Co Iron Reynolds & Sons	1889 From Dundee owners. 1897 Reboilered and surface condenser fitted. 192? Wheelhouse fitted
INDIA (on charter)		1895 1876 1895 1904	218 grt	138ft 9ins 30ft 6ins 11ft 5ins	Side lever	30ins	54ins	90	Westwood & Baille Iron J. Stewart & Sons	1876 Watkins. 1894 Constants. 1895 J.W. Spicer, Peckham. 1895 Tees Tug & Lighter Co. 1899 Marine, Dunkirk. 1904 Hulked
PRINCE GEORGE	104425	1898 1898 1928 1928	27.2 grt/8.5 rt	67ft 7ins 10ft 5ins 6ft 9ins	Screw, comp. inv'rt'd surface cond, 2 cylinders	7.75ins 14.25ins	12ins	9 7.5 IHP	Cosens Steel Cosens	
CYTHNIA (on charter)		1899 1892 1899 1933	235 grt	153ft 4ins 21ft 4ins 7ft 7ins	Compound diagonal	23ins & 46ins	30ins	98	J.T. Eltringham Iron J. Stewart & Sons	1892 Watkins at Margate. 1896 to Tyne. 1905 Hastings, St Leonards & Eastbourne SB Co. 1907 to Ireland. Wrecked 1933
FORTH (on charter) (ex-FLYING OWL)		1899 1893 1899 1936	129 grt	108ft 7ins 18ft 6ins 9ft 7ins	Side lever	30ins	54ins	80	J.T. Eltringham Iron J.P. Reynoldson	1883 Clyde Shipping Co. 1892 Forth Towing Co. 1895 Grangemouth & Forth Towing Co

FLEET LIST
(continued)

Name	Off. No.	Acquired / Built / Sold / Scrapped	Tonnage	Length / Breadth / Depth	Engines Type	Cylinders Dia.	Cylinders Stroke	Nom. HP	Builder / Hull Type / Engine Builder	Notes
Majestic	104427	1901 / 1901 / 1916 / 1916	408.4 grt/93 rt	215ft 5ins / 27ft 1ins / 8ft 9ins	Triple expansion, diagonal, 3 cylinders	21ins 35ins 54ins	60ins	200 / 1300 IHP	A. & J. Inglis / Steel / A. & J. Inglis	1916 Foundered off Oran
Brodick Castle	78614	1901 / 1878 / 1910 / 1910	283 grt/134 rt	207ft 6ins / 21ft 7ins / 7ft 5ins	Simple diagonal, surface condensing, 2 cylinders	38.25ins	66ins	96	McIntyre & Co / Iron / King & Co	1901 From Bournemouth and SCSP Co. 1906 Mainmast removed. 1910 Converted to barge and foundered off Portland
Emperor of India (ex-Princess Royal)	119739	1908 / 1906 / 1957 / 1957	487 grt/191 rt; From 1948: 533 grt/210 rt	From 1907: 217ft 2ins / 25ft 1ins / 8ft 4ins	Comp. diagonal, surface condensing, 2 cylinders	30ins 57ins	60ins	138 / 1450 IHP	Thornycroft / Steel / Thornycroft	1907 Lengthened by 2ft 8ins. 1909 Plated up to bow. 1948 Rebuilt
Lord Roberts (on charter)		1911 / 1900 / 1912 / 1934	235 grt	135ft / 21ft 4ins / 9ft 7ins	Simple diagonal, 2 cylinders	30ins	48ins	80	W. Allsup / Steel / W. Allsup	From Great Yarmouth Steam Tug Co. 1920 To Furness Shipbuilding Co. 1925 To Crosswaite SS Co and renamed Bilsdale for service from Scarborough.
Audrey (on charter)		1911 / 1879 / 1911 / 1929	203 grt	126ft / 21ft 4ins / 8ft	Compound diagonal, 2 cylinders	17ins 34ins	42ins	60	Armstrong Whitw'th / Steel	1897 Tyne General Ferry Co. 1910 Cork, Blackrock & Passage Co. 1914 To Capt S.J. Shippick. 1922 To New Medway SP Co
Helper (ex-Sir Francis Drake)	68324	1910 / 1873 / 1920 / 1929	172.5 grt/58.8 rt	131ft 3ins / 20ft 1ins / 8ft 4ins	Simple diagonal, 2 cylinders	30ins	48ins	80	W. Allsup / Iron / W. Allsup	1910 From Great Western Railway (Plymouth). 1920 Sold to Guernsey
Melcombe Regis (ex-Lune)	89706	1913 / 1892 / 1923 / 1923	252.9 grt/55.8 rt	129ft / 24ft 1ins / 9ft 5ins	Compound diagonal, 2 cylinders	24ins 48ins	54ins	96	Thomas Seath / Steel / Thomas Seath	Built for London & North Western Railway for service from Blackpool and Fleetwood
Alexandra	81004	1915 / 1879 / 1931 / 1934	234.7 grt/98 rt	171ft / 20ft 2ins / 8ft 5ins	Comp. diagonal surface condensing, 2 cylinders	25ins 50ins	54ins	120	Scott & Co / Iron / Scott & Co	1915 From Portsmouth. 1931 Sold to breakers (resold as 'Showboat'). 1934 Scrapped

EMBASSY (ex-Princess of Norfolk)	131994	1937 1911 1967 1967	380.7 grt/154.2 rt FROM 1948: 446.1 grt/184.4 rt	190ft 26ft 1ins 8ft 7ins	Compound diagonal, 2 cylinders	27ins 51ins	54ins	180 1000 IHP	D.&W. Henderson Steel D.&W. Henderson	1937 From Portsmouth. 1947 Rebuilt
CONSUL (ex Duke of Devonshire)	194431	1937 1896 1963 1968	256.5 grt/106.6 rt	175ft 20ft 6ins 8ft 2ins	Compound diagonal, 2 cylinders	23ins 46ins	36ins	100 500 IHP	R.&H. Green Steel Penn	1937 From Torquay. 1938 New funnel. 1949 Rebuilt
MONARCH (II) (Ex-Shanklon)	147994	1951 1961 1961	399 grt/181.2 rt 1924	190ft 26ft 1ins 8ft 7ins	Compound diagonal, 2 cylinders	27ins 51ins	54ins	187 1100 IHP	D.&W. Henderson Steel D.&W. Henderson	1951 From Portsmouth

BRODICK CASTLE, looking very spruce and bedecked with flags for some special occasion, steaming out of Weymouth Bay sometime between 1907 and 1909. AUTHOR'S COLLECTION/SEWARD

	Highland Maid	Princess	Wave Queen	Prince	Contractor	Ocean Bride	Bannockburn	Premier	Commodore	Empress
1848	J. Cosens	J. Cosens								
1849		J. Cosens								
1850		J. Cosens								
1851		J. Cosens								
1852		W. Cosens	J. Cosens	J. Cosens						
1853		W. Cosens		J. Cosens						
1854				J. Cosens						
1855				J. Cosens						
1856				J. Cosens						
1857				J. Cosens						
1858				J. Cosens	W. Cosens	J. Gibbs?				
1859				J. Cosens	WC/JG	J. Gibbs?	R. Fowler	J. Reynolds		
1860				J. Cosens	W. Cosens	J. Gibbs?	E. Mace?	J. Reynolds		
1861				J. Cosens	W. Cosens	J. Gibbs?	E. Mace?	J. Reynolds		
1862				J. Cosens	W. Cosens	J. Gibbs?	E. Mace?	J. Reynolds		
1863				J. Cosens	W. Cosens	J. Gibbs	E. Mace	J. Reynolds	W. Cosens	
1864				J. Cosens		J. Gibbs	E. Mace	J. Reynolds	WC/EM	
1865				J. Cosens		LU/JG/	E. Mace	J. Reynolds	E. Mace	
1866				J. Cosens				J. Reynolds	E. Mace	
1867				J. Cosens				J. Reynolds	E. Mace	
1868				J. Cosens				J. Reynolds	E. Mace	
1869				G. Haill				W. Cosens	E. Mace	
1870				G. Haill				W. Cosens	E. Mace	
1871				G. Haill				W. Cosens	E. Mace	
1872				G. Haill				W. Cosens	G. Ayles	
1873				G. Haill				W. Cosens	G. Ayles	
1874				G. Haill				W. Cosens	G. Ayles	
1875				EM/WB				W. Cosens	G. Ayles	
1876				W. Bowering				W. Cosens	GA/EM	
1877				W. Bowering				W. Cosens	G. Ayles	
1878				W. Bowering				W. Cosens	G. Ayles	
1879				WB/RF				WC/WB	G. Ayles	W. Cosens
1880				W. Masters				W. Bowering	H. Parsons	W. Cosens
1881				W. Masters				W. Bowering	J. Fowler	W. Cosens
1882				W. Masters				W. Bowering	G. Haill	W. Cosens
1883				W. Masters				W. Bowering	GH/HP	W. Cosens
1884				W. Masters				G. Haill	H. Parsons	W. Bowering
1885				W. Masters				G. Haill	H. Parsons	W. Bowering
1886				W. Masters				G. Hurdle	J. Fowler	W. Bowering
1887				W. Masters				G. Hurdle	J. Fowler	W. Bowering
1888				J.Cox				W. Masters	J. Fowler	WB/GHu
1889				J.Cox				W. Masters	J. Fowler	G.Hurdle
1890								W. Masters	G. Ayles	G. Hurdle
1891								W. Masters		G. Hurdle
1892								W. Masters		G. Hurdle
1893								W. Masters		G. Hurdle
1894								W. Masters		W. Stone
1895								W. Masters		W. Stone
1896								W. Masters		W. Stone
1897								W. Masters		LSBR/AM
1898								AC/JC		AM/FSC
1899								J. Cox		A.E. Pearce
1900								J. Cox		A.E. Pearce
1901								J. Cox		A.E. Pearce
1902								J. Cox		A.E. Pearce
1903								J. Cox		A.E. Pearce
1904								J. Cox		A.E. Pearce
1905								J. Cox		A.E. Pearce
1906								J. Cox		A.E. Pearce
1907								J. Cox		A.E. Pearce
1908								Painter		J. Cox
1909								P/H		J. Cox
1910								Hollyoak		J. Cox
1911								Hollyoak		J. Cox
1912								Hollyoak?		J. Cox
1913								Hollyoak?		J. Cox
1914								Hollyoak?		J. Cox
1915										
1916										L.St.B. Rawle
1917								Hollyoak		J.J.Marshallsay
1918										

Queen	Victoria	Albert Victor	Monarch	Majestic	Brodick Castle	Emperor of India	Helper	Melcombe Regis	Alexandra

APPENDIX TWO
SHIPS' MASTERS 1848-1918

LIST OF ABBREVIATIONS USED

GA .... G. AYLES	JG .... J. GIBBS	AM .... A. MASTERS
WB .... W. BOWERING	GH .... G. HAILL	WM .... W. MASTERS
FSC .... F.S. COLBORNE	HJH .... H.J. HARDY	P .... ? PAINTER
WC .... W. COSENS	H .... ? HOLLYOAK	HP .... H. PARSONS
AC .... A. COX	GHU .... G. HURDLE	LSBR .... L.ST.B. RAWLE
JC .... J. COX	WCK .... W.C. KING	WCR .... W.C. READ
F .... ? FOWLER	L .... ? LEDDY	S .... ? SYMES
G .... ? GARDINER	EM .... E. MACE	T .... ? TUCKER
ACG .... A.C. GARNETT	JJM .... J.J. MARSHALLSAY	
LU .... LAID UP		RN .... ROYAL NAVY

NB: During the war years, 1914-18 (coloured pale grey), masters were changed frequently between ships, making precise allocation impossible.

Queen	Victoria	Albert Victor	Monarch	Majestic	Brodick Castle	Emperor of India	Helper	Melcombe Regis	Alexandra
G. Haill									
J. Beale	W. Cosens								
J. Beale	W. Cosens								
J. Beale	W. Cosens								
J. Beale	W. Cosens								
J. Beale	WC/WB		W. Cosens						
A. Cox	J. Beale	G. Haill	W. Bowering						
GH/HP	J. Beale	HP/GH	W. Bowering						
H. Parsons	J. Beale	G. Haill	W. Bowering						
G. Haill	J. Cox	H. Parsons	W. Bowering						
G. Haill	J. Cox	H.J. Hardy	W. Bowering						
G. Haill	J. Cox	H.J. Hardy	W. Bowering						
G. Haill	J. Cox	H.J. Hardy	W. Bowering						
L.St.B. Rawle	J. Cox	H.J. Hardy	W. Bowering						
AM/LSBR	J. Cox	H.J. Hardy	W. Bowering						
AC/WM	LSBR/WM	H.J. Hardy	L.St.B. Rawle						
F.S. Colborne	W. Masters	H.J. Hardy	L.St.B. Rawle						
W.C. Read	W. Masters	H.J. Hardy	L.St.B. Rawle						
W.C. Read	W. Masters	HJH/S	A.F.Masters	L.St.B. Rawle	J.W. Tilsed				
W.C. Read	JC/HJH	W.C. King	AFM/HJH	L.St.B. Rawle	J.W. Tilsed				
W.C. Read	H.J. Hardy	W.C. King	A.F. Masters	L.St.B. Rawle	J.W. Tilsed				
W.C. Read	H.J. Hardy	W.C. King	A.F. Masters	L.St.B. Rawle	J.W. Tilsed				
W.C. Read	H.J. Hardy	WCK/T	A.F. Masters	L.St.B. Rawle	J.W. Tilsed				
W.C. Read	H.J. Hardy	W.C. King	A.F. Masters	L.St.B. Rawle	J.W. Tilsed				
W.C. Read	A.E. Pearce	W.C. King	H.J. Hardy	L.St.B. Rawle	S.J. Shippick	J.W. Tilsed			
W.C. Read	A.E. Pearce	W.C. King	H.J. Hardy	L.St.B. Rawle	S.J. Shippick	J.W. Tilsed			
W.C. Read	A.E. Pearce	W.C. King	H.J. Hardy	L.St.B. Rawle	S.J. Shippick	J.W. Tilsed			
WCR/WCK	A.E. Pearce	W.C. King	H.J. Hardy	L.St.B. Rawle		J.W. Tilsed	W.C. Read		
W.C.King	A.E. Pearce	H.C. Garnett	H.J. Hardy	L.St.B. Rawle		J.W. Tilsed	W.C. Read		
W.C.King	A.E. Pearce	H.C. Garnett	H.J. Hardy	L.St.B. Rawle		J.W. Tilsed	W.C. Read	Gardiner	
W.C.King	A.E. Pearce	H.C. Garnett	H.J. Hardy	L.St.B. Rawle		J.W. Tilsed	WCR/L	G/HCG	
	A.E. Pearce	H.C. Garnett	Laid up	Laid up		Laid up	WCR/JJM		W.C. Read
		H.C. Garnett	Laid up	Sank 28/7/16			A.E. Pearce		
A.C. Garnett			G.R. Janman				A.E. Pearce		
			G.R. Janman				RN crew	RN crew	

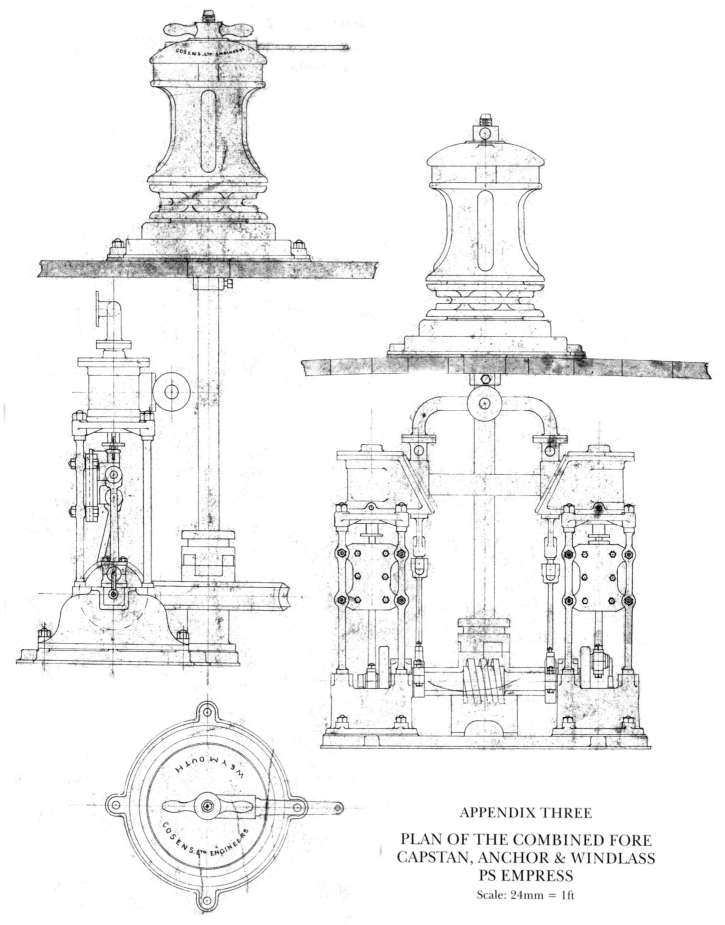

APPENDIX THREE

PLAN OF THE COMBINED FORE
CAPSTAN, ANCHOR & WINDLASS
PS EMPRESS

Scale: 24mm = 1ft

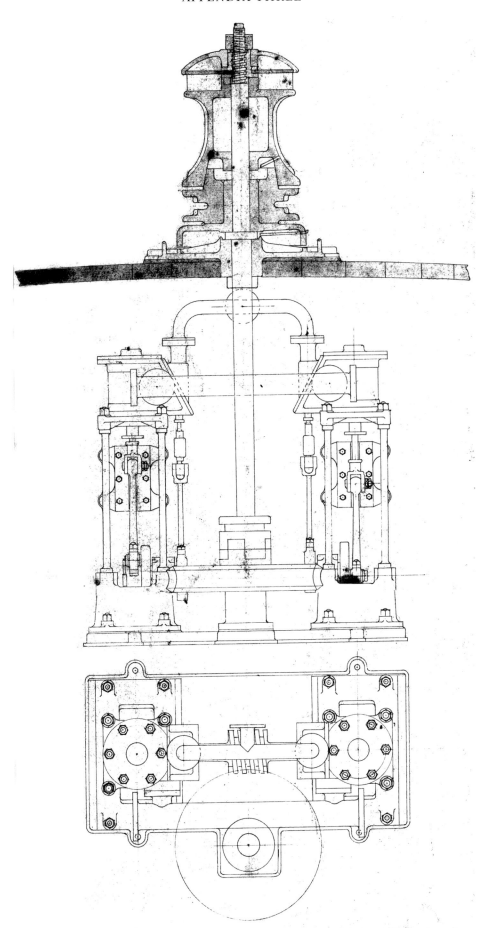

A feature shared by many of the Cosens' steamers was the neat and compact design of their capstans. The steam engine driving each capstan was housed beneath the main deck and exhausted through the ship's side, which explains why so many photographs of the paddlers berthing show clouds of steam rising from near their waterlines. A removable metal rod was inserted into a socket in the deck to control the capstan, leaving the deck uncluttered whilst at sea and preventing any possibility of interference by passengers.
AUTHOR'S COLLECTION

ACKNOWLEDGEMENTS

The publication of this second volume of the history of Cosens of Weymouth represents the culmination of almost thirty years of research. During that period the author has benefited from the unstinting generosity and encouragement of a large number of friends, correspondents and institutions, who have given freely of their time and knowledge, as well as allowing access to their photographic collections and archives. Without them the book could not have been completed.

Brian Jackson, well-known Weymouth transport historian, author and ex-Cosens apprentice, has been a tower of strength and friendship, sharing his extensive knowledge and enthusiasm for the subject at every step along the way and spending untold hours following up references in the local archives. Victor Gray, acknowledged expert on Cosens' Bournemouth activities, has shared his remarkable knowledge of both the company and the history of Bournemouth, while David Haysom, author and local historian, has given much valuable guidance concerning the company's links with Swanage. I am grateful to all three of them, together with Mike Tedstone, for their meticulous reading of the draft manuscript.

I am grateful to the following friends, former Cosens employees, collectors and historians for their assistance with this work: Keith Adams, Rodney Alcock, Crawford Alexander, Ian Andrews, Robin Ansell, Maureen Attwool, Rev Norman Bird, R.B. 'Bob' Bruce-Grice, David Chalk, Chris Collard, Nigel Coombes, Bernard Cox, Terry Cresswell, the late Reginald Fry, Michael Hughes, Sophie Hunt, Andrew Gladwell, Alan Kittridge, Martin Langley, Bill Macey, John Megoran, Margaret Morris, Stewart Morris, the late George Owen and Eric Payne, John Page, John Patrick, Alf Pover (Cosens' last chief engineer), Geoffrey Pritchard, Trevor Primett, Richard Samways, Ken Saunders, Brian Stidwell, Mike Tedstone, the late George Thomas, Jack West, Barry Wiggins, David Willshire and John Willows. Special mentions are due to A.M.C. 'Tony' Mc.Ginnity, managing owner of the ex-Cosens' steamer *Consul* during the 1960s, and my life-long friend John Megoran (master of the paddle steamer *Kingswear Castle*), both of whom have offered great encouragement over the years and have been keen advocates of the publication of this history.

I am also indebted to the following organisations and institutions: Bournemouth Library, Bridport Museum, Dorset Library Service (in particular to the local studies staff at Dorchester and Weymouth libraries), Dorset County Museum, Dorset County Records Office, Imperial War Museum, National Maritime Museum, Poole Museums Service (Local Studies Centre), Public Records Office, Swanage Museum and Weymouth Museum.

Finally, I thank my wife Carol for her boundless patience, good humour, encouragement and advice during this project and to Tom and Beth for putting up with their father's obsession for maritime history.

A NOTE ON THE ILLUSTRATIONS
The author and publishers have made every effort to establish the provenance of each illustration used in the book and apologise if any copyright has been inadvertently infringed.

Many of the photographs have been drawn from a small number of key collections. Crawford Alexander, Terry Cresswell, Brian Jackson, Victor Gray, David Haysom, John Page, John Patrick and Ken Saunders have all allowed me access to their personal collections, while Keith Adams has made available the Cosens albums and sailing bills from the H.A. Allen collection, of which he is a trustee. The late Eric Payne of Ryde always supplied copies, accompanied by meticulous historical notes, of any treasures he unearthed, while the late George Thomas could be relied upon to identify any photograph from the top six inches of a steamer's mast. Bernard Cox, the well-known Bournemouth steamer historian, has loaned his collection of copy negatives and his former collection of historical photographs is now available to the public in Dorchester Library. The local studies collection at Weymouth Library contains many unique shots, including the King Collection, recently returned to the town by a former Cosens draughtsman, who rescued a great deal of valuable material during his years with the company. Weymouth Museum holds the bulk of the Seward Collection of nautical glass plates, together with an extensive collection of local prints, engravings and items of printed ephemera, all of which have been made freely available. Bournemouth Library and the Dorset County Museum both have large collections which include many unique, early photographs. Finally, the extensive archives of the Paddle Steamer Preservation Society have been made available through the kindness of the society's archivist, Andrew Gladwell.

The author's own collection of photos, plans and ephemera have been built up over the years partly through chance finds and purchases but largely as a result of the kindness of others who have been happy to contribute to this project. I am indebted to Mrs M. Prowse, who passed on a large amount of material accumulated by her late husband Micky Prowse during his long career with the company. Whenever possible, I have acknowledged the original owner. A number of photographs credited 'Author's collection/Seward' were taken by the famous Weymouth postcard photographer E.N. Seward. Upon his death, his unique collection of glass plates passed to local collector Eric Latcham, who in turn left the Cosens plates to the author.

SOURCES

COMPANY ARCHIVES AND PUBLICATIONS:
For many years, the author had been led to understand that the Cosens' official records had been destroyed during the war but in 1990, when the company was sold by the Red Funnel Group, a truly amazing collection of documents emerged from the parent company's archive room in Southampton. Their discovery led to a complete re-appraisal of the research which had previously taken place. Thanks to the generosity of Michael Hughes, Cosens' Managing Director at the time, and David Willshire, the author was allowed free access to the archive, which has provided the backbone around which this history has been written. Following the closure of the company during 1996 the entire archive passed into the author's ownership and is due to be deposited at the Dorset County Record Office, where it will be available for inspection by the public. The archive is extensive and includes:
Minute Books 1868-1966
Share transfer, dividend and mortgage records
Accounting records 1876-1996, including ledgers, journals, day books and assorted accounts
Articles of Association
Correspondence files and assorted ephemera

Reference has also been made to:
Cosens & Co. Ltd. Official guide to Places of Interest Visited by the Company's Fleet of Pleasure Steamers, undated but c1911.

NEWSPAPERS AND MAGAZINES

Bridport News
Bournemouth Daily Echo
Bournemouth Observer
Dorset, The County Magazine
Dorset County Chronicle
Dorset Daily Echo
Dorset Evening Echo
Illustrated London News
Paddle Wheels, Quarterly Journal of the Paddle Steamer Preservation Society
Poole Herald
Portsmouth Evening News
Sea Breezes
Ship Ahoy, Journal of the South Wales Branch of the World Ship Society
Southern Times
Torquay Times & South Devon Advertiser
Wareham & Isle of Purbeck Advertiser
Abstracts relating to the steamer services compiled by the late Eric Payne of Ryde from:
      Isle of Wight Observer
      Isle of Wight County Press
      Isle of Wight Mercury

ARTICLES

Bird, N. & Abrahams, K. 'The Cosens Story', *Ship Ahoy*, Vol. 14, No. 4, 1967
Boddy, M. 'Dorset Shipwrecks', *Dorset*, No. 48-50, 1975-76
Grice, R.B. 'Cosens of Weymouth', *Ships Monthly*, Vol. 5. Nos. 2-7, April-July 1970
Hall, J. 'Memories of World War One', recounted in *Paddle Wheels*, No. 13, May 1963

PUBLIC RECORD OFFICE

ADM 53/44141-44. Ships Log HMS HELPER
ADM 137/872. Egypt, report of proceedings, 1917-18
ADM 137/757. Auxiliary Patrol Report, Malta, 1916
ADM 137/1221. Mediterranean west and general, various subjects
ADM 137/1230. Egypt, Various Subjects.
ADM 137/1573. Weekly reports of the Gibraltar Auxiliary Patrol, 1915-16
ASDM 137/1920. Grand Fleet Secret Packs, Vol LXXI, The Auxiliary Patrols
ADM 137/2153-54. Minesweeping operations, Aegean, 1915-19.
ADM 137/2284. Mediterranean post armistice records, mine clearance, etc
ADM 137/3055. Bristol Channel minesweeping records.
ADM 144. Various papers relating to the Channel Squadron/Fleet.
ADM 7153. Promiscuous Papers relating to Channel Fleet at Portland, 1893.
BT 336. Registrar General of Shipping and Seamen: Registers of Changes of Master.
MT 23/380. Hire of Vessels required for examination purposes at Weymouth & Portland

MISCELLANEOUS DOCUMENTS

Masters' Certificates of Service held in the National Maritime Museum
Weymouth Shipping registers, held at the Dorset County Record Office, Dorchester
Accounts of Voyages and Crews for Weymouth-registered ships, 1863-1913, held at the Dorset County Record Office, Dorchester.
Weymouth Town Council Minute Books, Rate Books and Council Terrier, all held by Weymouth Museum.
Company Records for Cosens & Co Ltd and The Devon Dock, Pier & Steamship Co Ltd held at Companies House, Cardiff.

BIBLIOGRAPHY

Anon. 'The Story of Cosens & Co. Ltd.', pamphlet reprinted from *The Weymouth Red Book, 1905.*
Adams, R.B. *Red Funnel and Before*, Kingfisher Publications, 1986
Beaver, P. *The Big Ship – Brunel's Great Eastern a Pictorial History*, Bibliophile Books, 1987
Boddy, M. & West, J. *Weymouth, An Illustrated History*, Dovecote Press, 1993
Burtt, F. *Steamers of the Thames and Medway*, Richard Tilling, 1949
Burtt, F. *Cross Channel and Coastal Paddle Steamers*, Richard Tilling, 1934
Carter, G. *The Royal Navy at Portland Since 1845*, Maritime Books, 1987
Collard, C. *A Dangerous Occupation – A Story of Paddle Minesweepers in the First World War*, Wheelhouse Books, 1999
Coombes, N. *Passenger Steamers of the Bristol Channel*, Twelveheads Press, 1990
Coombes, N. *White Funnel Magic*, Twelveheads Press, 1995
Cox, B. *Paddling Across the Bay*, Paddle Steamer Preservation Society, 1981
Cox, B. *The Development and Decline of Cross Channel Excursions from Bournemouth*, Unpublished historical study, King Alfed's College Winchester, 1972
Dalton, T. *British Royal Yachts*, Halsgrove, 2002
Dugan, J. *The Great Iron Ship*, Harper & Brothers, 1953
Farr, G. *Wreck and Rescue on the Dorset Coast*, D. Bradford Barton Ltd, 1971
Haysom, D. & Bragg, D. *Swanage & Purbeck in Old Photographs*, Alan Sutton, 1991
Haysom, D. & Patrick, J. *Swanage in Old Picture Postcards*, European Library, 1992

Jackson, B.L. *Isle of Portland Railways, Vols. 1-3*, Oakwood Press, 1999-2000
Jackson, B.L. *Weymouth to the Channel Islands, A Great Western Railway Shipping History*, Oakwood Press, 2002
Lane, M. *Piers of the Isle of Wight*, Isle of Wight Council, 1996
Langley, M. *A Pageantry of Steam & Paddle*, unpublished manuscript courtesy of the author.
Lewer, D. & Smale, D. *Swanage Past*, Phillimore, 1994
Lucking, J.H. *The Great Western at Weymouth*, David & Charles, 1971
Lyon, D.J. *The Denny List*, National Maritime Museum, 1975
Morris, S. *Portland, An Illustrated History*, Dovecote Press, 1985
O'Brien, F.T. *Early Solent Steamers*, David & Charles, 1973
O'Connor, G.W. *The First Hundred Years*, Red Funnel Steamers Ltd, 1961
Patterson, A.J.S. *The Victorian Summer of the Clyde Steamers*, David & Charles, 1972
Patterson, A.J.S. *The Golden Years of the Clyde Steamers*, David & Charles, 1969
Payne, D. *Dorset Harbours*, Christopher Johnson, 1953
Read, W.C. *The Journal of Capt. William Carey Read*, unpublished manuscript, Weymouth Library, ref. L921.REA.1
Shovelar, S. *Dorset Shipwrecks*, Freestyle Publications, 1996
Thornton, E.C.B. *South Coast Pleasure Steamers*, T. Stephenson & Sons, 1962.
Thornton, E.C.B. *Thames Coast Pleasure Steamers*, T. Stephenson & Sons, 1972.
Young, D.S. *The Story of Bournemouth*, Robert Hale, 1957

GENERAL INDEX
VESSELS, PEOPLE, PLACES & EVENTS
(NOTE: **Heavy Type** indicates an illustration: *Italics* indicate a ship's name)

INDEX OF SALVAGE & RESCUE JOBS CARRIED OUT BY COSENS' STEAMERS
1848-1918
(**Heavy type** indicates an illustration)